Cybersecurity Policy Guidebook

Cybersecurity Policy Guidebook

Second Edition

Jennifer L. Bayuk

Art Ehuan

Jason Healey

Paul Rohmeyer

Marcus H. Sachs

Donald Saxinger

Joseph Weiss

WILEY

Published by John Wiley & Sons, Inc., Hoboken, New Jersey.

Library of Congress Cataloging-in-Publication Data applied for:

Hardback: 978139447408

Cover Design: Wiley
Cover Image: Nmedia/stock.adobe.com

Set in 9.5/12.5pt STIXTwoText by Straive, Chennai, India

Contents

Foreword

A second edition of a book is a testimony to two things: that the first edition was valuable and that the world has changed. Both characteristics apply here: the first edition proved most valuable, and Lord knows the world of cybersecurity is nothing if not rich in change.

To make a second edition valuable, it has to have a number of characteristics that the reader instinctively knows – the "proof is in the pudding" or, to be less idiomatic, the value of a book like this can only be discerned by putting it to use. In the years since the first edition, readers have done exactly that – put it to use. Their feedback is why we are here. To keep that value at a high level in a changed world, this second edition is necessary.

> not because of omissions in the first edition, but because both the challenge and the necessity of cybersecurity have grown.

The book is, to a large degree, encyclopedic, and it expects a lot of you, the reader. Part of that comes from a certain reality:

> decision-making under uncertainty is sharper when you not only know a lot about where you are, but also how you got to where you are.

The authors collectively have that history cornered, as their biographies and the chapter on "Cybersecurity Evolution" proves.

Even the word "evolution" in the chapter title is well taken; without going deep in that direction, the playing field of cybersecurity is emergent[1] which only underscores the value of the chapter. In cybersecurity, time waits for no one.

1 George Dyson: "Emergent behavior is that which cannot be predicted through analysis at any level simpler than that of the system as a whole. Emergent behavior, by definition, is what's left after everything else has been explained."

But if cybersecurity is a sea of rolling change (it is), then you need to appreciate the drivers of change (sentient opponents included).

The book's history of cybersecurity evolution leads us to where we are. What to do with that appreciation is not so simple, but it is why we are here.

The wellspring of risk is dependence, and aggregate risk is proportional to aggregate dependence. We call that on which we most depend critical infrastructure(s), but that is hardly the whole of it. Dependence is transitive; when A depends on B and B on C, then A depends on C, even if A is unaware that C exists.[2]

We call the transitive reach of dependence "interdependence," which means correlated risk. Interdependence (and hence risk) within society today is centered on cyberspace beyond all other dependencies.

Our present danger is unacknowledged correlated risk. Unacknowledged correlations contribute, by definition, to heavy tails in the probability distribution of possible events. Complexity hides interdependence(s), and, by this path, complexity is the enemy of security. The warp and weft of interdependencies in the fully networked world is where the "emergence property" materializes.

The discussion of contagion and its varieties in the "Cybersecurity Policy Objectives" chapter is directly illustrative of these exact points.

Like the authors, I view a policy as a "principle of action" and, therefore, policy is (and must be) set at the top, calibrated to how much appetite for risk there is at the top, and in service to explicit top-level goals. A policy has to lead to something evaluable. You will shortly read this phrasing: "If one cannot describe at a high level what they are trying to accomplish as an individual, organizational, or public policy goal for security and safety in cyberspace, one will not have a method to evaluate whether or not any given security software configuration is designed to accomplish management control objectives." A principle of action is, of course, much broader than a software configuration, but the triad is worth repeating: policy is end-goal oriented, comes from the top, and needs to imply how its success can be evaluated.

If decision-making under uncertainty is really what we are talking about (as I believe it is), then the chapter on "Guidance for Decision-Makers" is worth repeated reading. The chapter's discussion of risk is suitably bracing and more

2 Leslie Lamport: "A distributed system is one in which the failure of a computer you didn't even know existed can render your own computer unusable."

than justifies its implications, including gems like "It takes time to craft policy to make sure it enables, rather than disrupts, operations. A decision maker will often count on an information security professional to shepherd cybersecurity policy, ensuring it remains effective and relevant. If it is not relevant, the void will doubtless be filled with security theater." Dare I imagine this rings a bell for any reader who has been around for a while?

The culminating chapter is a "Cybersecurity Policy Catalog" that rolls up all the entire rest of the book. It is argumentative (meant as a compliment) as it confronts how differing goals and constraints color what policies can be adopted in the reader's particular setting, which is to say that each proposed policy comes with debate, as well they should given the inherent contradictions in much of what we are talking about. The present author's opinion is that:

Most important ideas are not exciting
Most exciting ideas are not important
Not every problem has a good solution
Every solution has side effects

In no part of modern life are the above more true than in the interplay around cybersecurity. They are what selecting policies is all about: distinguishing between tolerable and intolerable failure modes. A state of security can be simply described as the absence of unmitigatable surprises, making the goal of security engineering likewise simple: no silent failure. Failure is to be avoided whenever possible, but absolute total avoidance is certain to be diseconomic. And we are back to picking policies that advance such end-goals.

This book will help.

If you use it.

Dan Geer

Preface and Acknowledgments

The idea for the original edition of this book was sparked by Mike Wynne, the 21st Secretary of the US Air Force, who established considerable capability for cybersecurity in the Air Force, and was at the time earnestly raising the awareness of national security-related cybersecurity policy issues. He envisioned a guidebook for congressional staffers and academics that would create awareness of the importance of cybersecurity policy, and while on the Advisory Board of the Stevens Institute of Technology School of Systems and Enterprises, he organized a conference on the topic (SIT 2010). Opinions were solicited from experts in a wide variety of fields who are stakeholders in cyberspace. Many of them spoke at the conference or attended the discussions. Some were unable to attend, but provided their comments in written form. The conference had sessions ranging from security technology investment decisions by venture capitalists to the implications of cybersecurity policy on personal privacy. Though all speakers were experts in their field and were asked to address cybersecurity policy topics, many instead focused on strategy or technology issues. Even where it was clear that policy was being discussed, policies were often not articulated clearly enough for panelists and audience members to participate in informed debate. This observation itself became the buzz at the conference and made it clear that cybersecurity policy means different things to different people, even those who work in cybersecurity. As a result, then Stevens professor Jennifer Bayuk recruited a variety of cybersecurity experts to lend their expertise to the first edition of this book.

We knew then, and still know now, that there is no one person is experienced enough in cybersecurity to single-handedly write this book. Note that the accounting profession has a well-established, several-thousand-year history supporting its ability to define "trust" in terms of relationships that involved a combination of circumstances and sanctions (Guinnane 2005). By contrast, the cybersecurity profession has just a half century since our first attempts at setting security standards. Though its first standards boldly included the definition of *Trusted Systems* (DoD 1985), that declaration has now been abandoned and replaced with a definition of cybersecurity as the absence of trust; the favored mantra of today's cybersecurity professionals is *Zero Trust* (NIST 2020). Rather than converging on any agreed-upon industry standard, such as accounting's generally accepted accounting principles (GAAP), there are dozens of competing "best practice" cybersecurity standards, as well as regulatory requirements in dozens of countries (you will find representative examples in Chapter 4).

When these standards first arrived on the scene, they brought with them a new job function within the cybersecurity profession called *Governance, Risk, and Compliance* (GRC), a role more in common with operational risk and audit than technology architecture and administration. Note that when the term GRC was applied to cybersecurity in the 1990s, the "C" stood for *control*, and referred to management strategy and oversight of cybersecurity functions (Rohmeyer and Bayuk 2019, p. 245). The change from *control* to *compliance* reflects the struggle for those cybersecurity functions to get the attention of upper management, as cybersecurity vendors have learned that executive management finds it easier to ignore cybersecurity *risk* than cybersecurity *regulations*.

Therefore, the state of the cybersecurity practice, then and now, demanded a diverse team of state-of-the-art authors to ensure that most, if not all, the major policy issues in this continuously evolving field of cybersecurity were covered. Each author has contributed to chapters and sections that were specific to their experience, and all chapters were reviewed by all authors to ensure a cohesive presentation for the expected variety of readers.

These insights drove the format of this book, designed to lead the reader through concepts that are *individually* easy to assimilate and *collectively* provide a solid enough understanding of the field of cybersecurity to understand the place of policy within it. Although policy is obviously a domain of authoritative executives, in that executive authority may stem from the social contracts by which governments are established or the domain of a private enterprise, this book is not intended solely for their consumption. For cybersecurity policy analysis to receive the critical scrutiny essential to sound legislation on both public and private fronts, the domains in this book must encompass individual constituents, executive advisors, legislators, educators, researchers, and cybersecurity standards bodies. Though each reader brings their own background and experience to the material presented herein, we expect that their current concepts on cybersecurity policy will be enriched by sharing this common presentation framework and nomenclature with colleagues in other fields, especially those whose professional experience has exposed them to cybersecurity issues of varying scope.

Most literature about cybersecurity falls into two categories: technology and advice. This book will refrain from technical jargon and also from recommendations with respect to decisions in any given case of cybersecurity policy. Although the book endeavors to explain technology issues in cybersecurity, it does so in layman's terms. At the same time, the book emphasizes the importance of critical and analytical thinking about decisions with respect to cybersecurity and will equip the reader with descriptions of the impact of specific policy choices, letting the reader decide whether to view that impact as positive or negative.

This guidebook integrates explanations of cybersecurity policy alternatives across potential individual, executive, legislative, judiciary, commercial, military, and diplomatic action. Readers across these disciplines are expected to view its contents through the lens of their own area of expertise and also gain insights from issues encountered by others. It is an introductory text for the uninitiated, while at the same time providing a holistic reference for experts in the field of cybersecurity.

The most important improvement of this second edition is to update the important cybersecurity policy changes in the field, as much has changed in the intervening 14 years. Not only have cybersecurity threats substantially increased, and cybersecurity has accordingly gotten more attention by senior executives, but even the basic definition of cybersecurity has changed. New concepts and documents, such as the Cybersecurity Framework by the US National Institute of Standards and Technology, have helped change how we approach policy.

This edition also slightly reframes how it categorizes different cybersecurity policies, based on the intended subject, or *domain*, of the policy. Many policies are implemented for each of us, that is, policies *individuals* set for themselves or that an *organization* sets for its staff (such as when to use encryption or multifactor authentication), while other policies are for others, those who are outside of our control, but whose security may negatively impact us. To reduce the risk of these *dependencies*, governments set *public* policy while organizations adopt internal policies intended to reduce supply-chain risk. Other policies focus on *adversaries*, seeking to reduce the risk of successful cyberattack by deterring them or disrupting their operations. The last domain is policies for everything in *cyberspace*, which tend to be the domain of international alliances, standards-setting organizations, and a small number of companies with massive, internet-wide reach.

This book is organized into nine chapters.

Chapter 1. Building Blocks: Describes fundamental concepts, especially the relationship between cyberspace, cybersecurity, and cybersecurity policy that will be themes throughout the book.

Chapter 2. Cybersecurity Evolution: Provides a brief history of cyber and the corresponding evolution of its control objectives and security technologies.

Chapter 3. Cybersecurity Policy Objectives: Defines cybersecurity risk issues and common technology risk reduction initiatives.

Chapter 4. Communication: Describes common government and other organizational command and control strategies for communicating in response to cyber threats.

Chapter 5. Guidance for Decision-Makers: Explores the relationship between organizational leadership functions in the management of technology-related risks.

Chapter 6. The Cybersecurity Workforce: Summarizes the state of the practice for cybersecurity professionals as well as efforts to standardize cybersecurity curriculum and assessment.

Chapter 7. One Government's Approach to Cybersecurity Policy: Uses the United States Federal Government's history of actions related to cybersecurity as a detailed example, including its association with international organizations.

Chapter 8. Cybersecurity Policy Catalog: Classifies exemplar cybersecurity policy statements concerning the domains as described above and associated cybersecurity risk issues.

Chapter 9. Conclusion

Our co-authors are left with a deep appreciation for the depth and breadth of our adopted field. **Jennifer Bayuk**'s solid technical background, scholarly approach, and layman-accessible writing skills framed the presentation of concepts that made sense of it all. Her leadership made this book possible. **Art Ehuan** added a dimension of military and investigative experience in addition to time spent in the cybersecurity vendor and academic communities. **Jason Healey**'s wealth of experience in policy analysis in government service, private sector, think-tanks, and academia shed light on a rich array of issues. **Paul Rohmeyer**'s academic and business experience in technology management consistently made sure that our narratives were not only meaningful to decision makers, but also that the whole carried a strategic purpose that was obvious to our readers. **Marcus Sachs**'s unique combination of engineering, policy, and enforcement in both the public and private sector was invaluable when it came to chronicling cybersecurity policy history. Many policy issues are rooted in regulation, and here **Donald Saxinger** provided the unique perspective of a long-time finance-sector regulator for cybersecurity, operational risk, and resiliency. **Joe Weiss**'s in-depth expertise in industrial control systems prevented us from losing focus on the physical consequences of cybersecurity attacks on critical infrastructure.

We would all like to thankfully acknowledge the remarkable talents of our illustrator, Elsie Lee-Robbins and others who contributed to this work via editing, proofreading, and other invaluable support: Jeanne Apryasz, Sarah Chernati, Sean Pandaleon, and our editor at Wiley, Brett Kurzman.

Together, we dedicate this volume to cybersecurity policymakers, whether vocal or silent. May you achieve success in your respective missions.

References

DoD (1985). *The Orange Book, Trusted Computer System Evaluation Criteria*. Washington, DC: Department of Defense. (supersedes first version of 1983).

Guinnane, T. W. (2005). Trust: A concept too many. Economic Growth Center, Yale University. https://elischolar.library.yale.edu/egcenter-discussion-paper-series/915 (accessed 26 July 2026).

NIST (2020). Zero Trust Architecture Standard, National Institute of Standards and Technology, SP800-207 (accessed 15 March 2026).

Rohmeyer, P. and Bayuk, J. (2019). *Financial Cybersecurity Risk Management*. New York, NY: Springer Apress.

SIT (2010). *Global Cybersecurity Policy Conference*. Washington, DC: Stevens Institute of Technology.

About the Companion Website

This book is accompanied by a companion website.

www.wiley.com/go/bayuk/cyberguide

To access the website materials, click on the link under Related Resources on the book's page on wiley.com. You can also find this by searching www.wiley.com for the ISBN 9781394407408.

This website includes:

- Chapter's color figures

1

Building Blocks

Societies, economies, organizations, and individuals rely on modern technologies, and those technologies require security to operate safely. Where security technology controls are effective, cyberspace is considered a reliable, resilient, safe, and trustworthy digital infrastructure. Where those controls are absent, incomplete, poorly designed, or not followed, those technology controls fail or are subverted. These failures are often cascading and result in personal catastrophes, public-policy concerns, physical disruption, and/or national security crises. Whether a system is a physical facility or a collection of cyberspace components, the role of a cybersecurity professional assigned to that system is to plan for potential data compromise or system disruption and prepare for its consequences.

This chapter contains building blocks for those unfamiliar with cybersecurity risk issues and corresponding policies. It starts with a discussion of high-level nomenclature about cybersecurity, not because we need to precisely define them, but to explain why they shed light on cybersecurity policy. Next comes a classification of different perspectives on cybersecurity policy that we refer to as *domains*. Not because they are set in stone, but because they assist in understanding the cybersecurity policy landscape. These are followed by an example cybersecurity policy statement that foreshadows a Cybersecurity Policy Catalog in Chapter 8. Chapters in between will provide more building blocks and concepts that will help readers interpret the policy statement examples in the catalog.

1.1 Definitions

There are numerous definitions of cyberspace and cybersecurity scattered throughout the literature. Our intent is not to engage in a debate on semantics, as the profession has seen constant changes in nomenclature. As in any emergent profession, newcomers enter the field and appropriate or extend its language to differentiate their own products, services, and research. Cyberspace and cybersecurity are large and nebulous concepts and what might be included, or not, depends on the perspectives and needs of those doing the defining and is unalterably tied to changing technology and usage. The earliest specialists in computer security are doing many recognizably similar tasks to those of today, though there was no cyberspace to speak of when computers were largely unnetworked, accessible only in-person, or over terminals. In many organizations, especially large bureaucracies like governments and global corporations, labeling something as cybersecurity might have critical budget, regulatory, or staffing implications, leading to specialized definitions outside of normal or common-sense usage.

Therefore, this cybersecurity policy guidebook does not treat definitions as sacrosanct. Clarity of understanding and communication is more important than specificity of definition. All relevant stakeholders should know what is included, or excluded, in their discussions and policies. Moreover, every relevant policy should relate to one of the conceptual definitions.

That said, we begin with some conceptual definitions to help set your expectations for this book. Many of our definitions rely heavily on the United States National Institute of Standards and Technology (NIST). Though NIST standards are targeted at US federal agencies, it has a long history of outreach and collaboration prior to establishing cybersecurity standards, and it distributes them freely. It forms committees of both public and private sector experts, circulates drafts for public comment, and every public comment is reviewed for consideration.

1.1.1 Cyberspace

The first description of *cyberspace* came from a work of science fiction (Gibson 1984). It was described as "*a consensual hallucination experienced daily by billions of legitimate operators, in every nation... A graphic representation of data abstracted from the banks of every computer in the human system.*" Although that definition still resonates, NIST has provided a few others that describe different aspects of cyberspace that will be emphasized in different chapters of this book (NIST n.d.). These are

1) A global domain within the information environment consisting of the interdependent network of information systems infrastructures, including the internet, telecommunications networks, computer systems, and embedded processors and controllers.
2) The interdependent network of information technology (IT) infrastructures that includes the internet, telecommunications networks, computers, information systems, cyber-physical systems, networks, and embedded processors and controllers.

3) The complex environment resulting from the interaction of people, software, and services on the internet by means of technology devices and networks connected to it, which does not exist in any physical form.

That first definition describes cyberspace in relation to yet another concept, the information environment. Although the science fiction definition of cyberspace refers almost exclusively to this vision, this book focuses on a subset of policies relating to that larger information environment. For example, this book will not delve into mis- and disinformation, propaganda and counter-propaganda, the limits of acceptable and free speech, and the cross-border flow of information. These are increasingly important but are only included here if they are directly relevant to the safety of technology that controls cyberspace, such as doxxing (the misuse of theoretically private information, often obtained by cyber intrusions) or other unauthorized use of cyber-enabled information. The second definition focuses exclusively on technology. The third focuses on systems, which include the people and processes that interact with technology.

The second and third definitions hint at another way to describe cyberspace, not as a sum of its parts, but in the systems engineering sense wherein a system as a whole has emergent functionality that cannot be attributed separately to its individual parts. Cyberspace is a complex system of systems comprising the totality of digital computing and communications devices and their functionality over the entire planet. Because satellites and probes travel around other planets, cyberspace even extends into outer space. The cyberspace system of systems includes the entire set of people, processes, low-level technology support systems, and the environment in which any or all of these subsystems operate. This definition includes such concepts as embedded real-time systems, Internet of Things, cyber-physical systems, and any other application of digital computing.

In summary, if it's related to digital computing and/or communications, it is part of cyberspace.

1.1.2 Cybersecurity

The original term, *computer security*, came about when computers were largely not networked or considered information repositories. Multiple models for computer data security had been introduced and tested, finally landing in the 1970s with one based on confidentiality, integrity, and availability (CIA) (Bell and LaPadula 1976). Computers then were mostly calculators, or in the case of cyber-physical systems, programmable logic controllers that were faster and more accurate than humans. As technology became more sophisticated, the label computer security as a profession evolved to *network security*, then in acknowledgement of its protection of information mission, to *information security*. Between around 2005 and 2020, the term "cyber" was frequently applied to "security" as an adjective, and many publications omitted the space in between. Nevertheless, industry analysts continued to debate whether the adjective "cyber" applied generally as a classification of a type of "security" or the adjective "cybersecurity" applied more ubiquitously to systems, people, processes, and technologies. By 2020, most agreed it made more sense to use "cybersecurity" as a control classification going forward. Indeed, that is why the first edition of this book was titled *Cyber Security Policy Guidebook*, while this edition is titled *Cybersecurity Policy Guidebook*.

In an influential publication, *Cybersecurity Framework*, NIST defines cybersecurity as the "prevention of damage to, protection of, and restoration of computers, electronic communications systems, electronic communications services, wire communication, and electronic communication, including information contained therein, to ensure its availability, integrity, authentication, confidentiality, and nonrepudiation" (NIST-CSF 2024).

Each part of that definition is worth some explanation.

- Beginning: prevention of damage to, protection of, and restoration;
- Middle: computers, electronic communications systems, electronic communications services, wire communication, and electronic communication, including information contained therein; and
- Ending: availability, integrity, authentication, confidentiality, and nonrepudiation.

To begin at the beginning of the definition, cybersecurity is not just about what happens before an incident, referring to the prevention and protection steps, but also restoration *after* an incident occurs. In fact, as will be discussed later in this book, NIST's Cybersecurity Framework includes six core functions: governance (which includes policy), identify, protect, detect, respond, and recover (NIST-CSF 2024).

The middle part of the definition is meant to be inclusive, as is the case with the definition of cyberspace. Unfortunately, by attempting to list so many kinds of IT, it inevitably omits important concepts, for example, integrated circuits embedded in physical systems are often left out of cybersecurity risk assessments because they are viewed as part of the physical equipment. Therefore, we choose to believe NIST did not leave them out of its cybersecurity definition on purpose, and herein we will include all electronically enabled automation in the scope of cyberspace.

Jump to the end of the definition to discuss availability, integrity, authentication, confidentiality, and nonrepudiation. This is an expansion of what is traditionally known as the "CIA triad," which when first introduced in the 1970s. This is an expansion of what started out as CIA in the 1970s and addresses data information attributes.

- **Availability** refers to the timely delivery of functional capability. Ransomware is, at its most basic, an attack on availability, encrypting an organization's data until they pay. It is still there, just unavailable to the legitimate users.

- **Authentication** is confirming identity, the process to ensure that people or things are who they say they are. This is often paired with the related concept of authorization. A physician may be recognized as a board-certified cardiologist, but that does not mean they have access to the records from a patient's visit to a psychologist. Since 2020, a new cybersecurity standard for *zero trust* has boosted attention to these goals by providing detailed guidance on how to demonstrate that everyone and everything on a network is strongly authenticated and authorized (NIST 2020).
- **Confidentiality** is a system's capability to limit the dissemination of information to authorized individuals or agents. After 2020, many ransomware attacks acquired a confidentiality component, not just encrypting data, but threatening to release the original data online unless the ransom is promptly paid.
- **Integrity** refers to the ability to maintain the authenticity, accuracy, and provenance of recorded and reported information. You might have a bad day if someone encrypted all of your health records in a ransomware attack, but it might cost you your life if someone changed that information, affecting its integrity.
- **Non-repudiation** is related to confidentiality. Where confidentiality dictates that only authorized people can view specific information, non-repudiation specifies that information received from someone, it is provably from them, meaning the recipient or a third party can verify and validate the sender or creator. This is often implemented by digital signatures.

These were security goals even before computers were invented. In the past, passwords were spoken to keepers of locked doors long before anyone dreamed of typing them into remote terminals. The advent of an interconnected cyberspace has changed the methods by which cybersecurity professionals strive for these goals, as well as their relative difficulty of achievement. Different parts of an organization may specify different requirements. For example, in the finance sector, trading floors are especially sensitive to even slight delays, so availability is exceptionally important, whereas investment bankers' work is not as time-bound, but involves exceptionally private business plans, so confidentiality is also greatly valued. Moreover, these goals are often at odds with each other. For example, only your own healthcare provider should have access to your personal healthcare information. However, if you unexpectedly fall ill while on vacation, a different medical team may need quick access to those records.

It is difficult to attempt to list everyone's goals in a simple list, and it is missing goals that are specific to the cyber-physical realm, which include goals for the safety of human lives, equipment, and critical resources like oil or gas passing through an electronically controlled pipeline. Again, we choose to believe NIST did not leave them out of its cybersecurity definition on purpose, and herein we will include them.

1.1.3 Cyber Technology

ITs are the systems with which most readers will be familiar – the desktops, servers, and mobile devices, as well as the standards that run them. We use them in our personal and work lives. Less familiar, but no less important, are operational technology (OT) and industrial control systems (ICSs).

IT has normally relied on the CIA model (which at first referred to data and since expanded to cover information itself as described above), while OT has focused on protecting systems from information flows with both logical and physical controls (Ginter 2023), and ICSs have used an engineering triad of safety, reliability, and productivity (Weiss 2010). This leads to critical differences between cybersecurity policies for IT, OT, and ICS:

- Cybersecurity technologies and threats are not equally applicable to IT, OT, and ICS.
- Some IT security technologies adversely affect OT, such as a network scan for known vulnerabilities, which can overwhelm the low bandwidth and processing power typical of OT systems.
- An ICS is expected to remain in continuous operation for decades, requiring minimal electrical and processing power. Hence, their embedded technology is often antiquated. Vulnerabilities cannot be patched easily, if at all. They may have no ability to automatically store user activity logs and alert on suspicious electronic activity, reserving their minimal disk space for sensor measurement trends to alert on process anomalies. Typical minimum cybersecurity requirements for IT and OT (e.g., authentication and non-repudiation) are often deemed impossible for ICS systems, and others are irrelevant (e.g., confidentiality).

The IT, OT, and ICS distinctions hold important implications for cybersecurity policy, and more building blocks on these topics appear in subsequent chapters.

1.2 Cybersecurity Policy Domains

Generally, the term "cybersecurity policy" refers to directives designed to maintain cybersecurity, whether for an individual, an organization, or cyberspace as a whole. Figure 1.1 shows the Venn diagram relationship between policy, technology, and law (Hamby and Wingfield 2016). Technology defines the largest circle of what is *possible*. Narrower than that is what is *permissible*, which is defined by the law. Policy operates within the context of all that is possible and permissible to decide and enforce what is *preferable*.

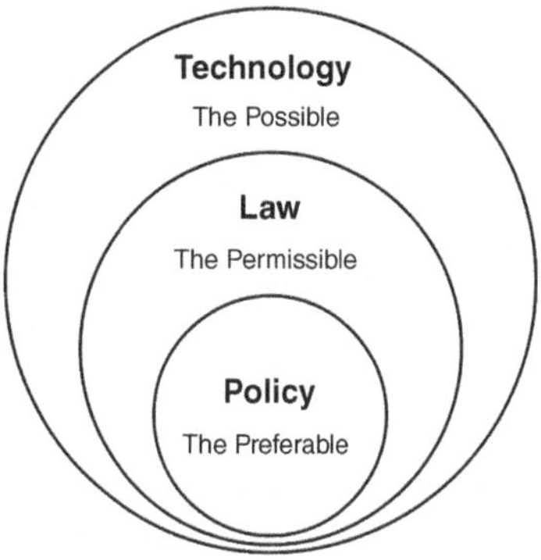

Figure 1.1 Technology, law, and policy.

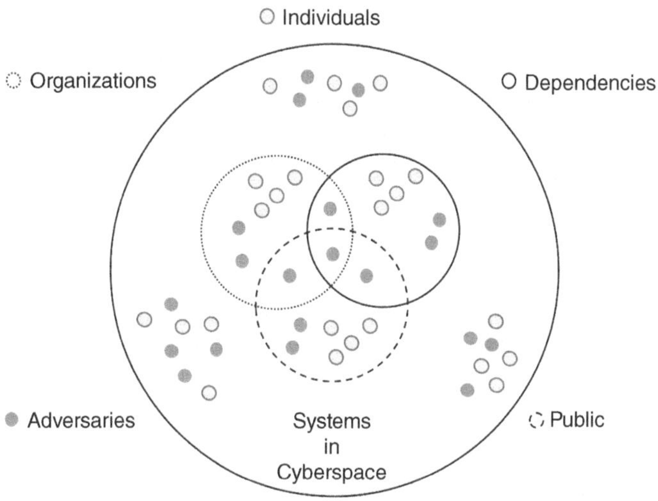

Figure 1.2 Cybersecurity policy domains.

Of course, the definition of "preferable" will change depending on the perspective of the entity impacted by policy enforcement. Therefore, the cybersecurity policies in this book are distinguished by five different domains: Individuals, Organizations and Government (i.e., public sector organizations), Dependencies, Adversaries, and Cyberspace. These domains coexist in cyberspace as depicted in Figure 1.2.

In this book, we use the word "policy" in its traditional sense, "a course or principle of action adopted or proposed by a government, party, business, or individual" (Oxford n.d.). Policy is applicable to a given situation or context. A cybersecurity policy is a method of reducing risk presented by technology malfeasance. That said, a strong cybersecurity policy also works to prevent unintentional damage due to accidental precipitation of a negatively impacting event where technology is the proximate cause.

However, in the field of cybersecurity, the word "policy" often morphs from a course of action designed to meet an objective, to a set of technical specifications for a software program designed to keep unauthorized users at bay. For example, a firewall rule set that restricts network access to known business partners by listing the allowed network addresses and an authentication program that specifies and verifies two forms of digital identity prior to allowing login to a computer system are *tools* to enforce policy in the sense this book defines policy. Though some technical cybersecurity specialists disdain any policy that cannot be read by software as inexact, it is the policy at a leadership level that provides a method for verifying that this lowest level of software code is policy-compliant. That is, if the policy *is* the low-level code configuration itself, there would never be a way for upper management to know if the policy they set was implemented properly. If one cannot describe at a high level what they are trying to accomplish as an individual, organizational, or public policy goal for security and safety in cyberspace, they will not have a method to evaluate *whether or not* any given security software configuration is designed to accomplish management control objectives. So calling the configuration a policy is an analogy at best.

1.2.1 Individuals

When we say individuals, we mean any person who uses cyberspace or is impacted by it. Before the dawn of the information age, the word "user" commonly referred to a drug addict. Now it refers to people who use technology. User-level policies answer the question: how can each of us better secure our own personal information? These policies are the actions we limit or permit for ourselves.

Your author is writing this section on their personal computer. No one is forcing me to use any particular security, yet I have chosen a number of security precautions for myself. To preserve availability, I am saving this chapter in the cloud. To procrastinate, knowing me, I might periodically check a website for the news or check my bank account (as it is pay day). I have chosen to use a password wallet to manage my passwords for both news and bank sites. To log into my bank, I have chosen strong multifactor authentication for added security; for a news site, I do not bother as they have little private information about me. I use a Google phone even though most of my colleagues prefer the security of Apple. I rarely use public WiFi, at least for anything sensitive, in favor of my own hotspot. These are all controls I adopt based on cybersecurity policy decisions I have made based on my own assessments of risk (and convenience), which can be summed up as "minimize trust in any one function of cyberspace except when I don't think it matters."

Individual policies are rarely explicit or written anywhere other than this chapter. However, they are still policies, and everyone who uses the internet or connected devices makes them, whether they know it or not! That said, if they do it intentionally, it likely works better to achieve personal goals for cybersecurity.

1.2.2 Organizations

Organizations need policies for all the above-mentioned topics and many more, from acceptable use of enterprise IT assets, roles and responsibilities of IT and security personnel, patching of vulnerabilities, to whether personal devices can connect to the enterprise network. These policies are in a way also about "each of us" like those mentioned above for individuals, but in this case, the individuals are part of a larger organization that wants or needs to ensure the people under its control are reducing risk in specific ways. Even though the policies themselves can be similar to those of individuals, policies for organizations should generally always be formalized and frequently updated, as will be discussed throughout the following chapters.

This part of the chapter was written on the author's work computer at a university. Even though the information content is exactly the same, I must follow a different, and far more stringent set of cybersecurity policies. Multifactor authentication is mandatory, and there are restrictions on the kinds of information I can access. I will not be able to install new software without the help of an administrator, and my computer (like all the others) must have security software. By using the organization's computing and network resources, I am consenting to monitoring to ensure my actions are consistent with policy. By following the policies, the organization will be more secure.

In the government and the finance sector, the policies are stricter still, based on rules imposed by regulators or substantially greater risks. These are all organizational policies. Note that organizational policies are typically crafted by a colleague we call a *Chief Information Security Officer* (CISO), a common title for the highest-ranking person in any organization whose sole job is cybersecurity. Although the title and reporting structure for the person in an organization who is responsible for cybersecurity policy varies widely (for example, in an organization supporting only ICS, it may be *Director of Security Engineering*), in this book, we will refer to that highest-ranking person whose sole job is cybersecurity as CISO.

1.2.3 Dependencies

Policies for individuals and organizations are for "each of us," setting the rules for the expected behaviors for ourselves or our fellow colleagues. These are important, but what about the security of those on whom we depend? Even in the earliest days of computing, the security of a system depended on many others, from the company making the hardware, to those often far away managing the networks that connected our systems to countless others.

The company Equifax made poor cybersecurity decisions which made them vulnerable to a cyberattack and ultimately cost them perhaps $1.3 billion. However, the true impact of the incident was not on the company and its shareholders, but on the nearly 150 million Americans whose highly personal credit data was stolen (Amishav 2026). Those Americans had no idea that Equifax security was lax and, even if they did, no leverage to pressure any improvements. It is a classic negative externality market failure and practice that many policies set by organizations impact not just their own members, but those who are dependent on their services (Healey 2025).

Policies to handle these dependencies on "others" come in many forms. For example, a policy could require transparency of a cloud service provider when they suffer a security incident or require a vendor to prove they have a minimum level of security, such as by filling out a questionnaire or providing a report from an external compliance team (i.e., System and Organization Controls [SOC] audit, a framework developed by the American Institute of Certified Public Accountants [AICPA]). Dependent parties may also mandate minimum security features in contractual agreements with software providers. Governments assist those dependent on some technology providers via regulations that impose a minimum baseline of security for critical infrastructure sectors to ensure national or economic security.

As companies have increasingly outsourced business-critical functions to cloud service providers and others, such policies have risen in prominence.

1.2.4 Adversaries

Cybersecurity differs from many other technology challenges because the problems are driven by adversaries, always intelligent, often well-funded, and sometimes working for a national military or intelligence agency. Unlike policies imposed on "each of us" or "others," some policies focus on "them," adopting objectives to disrupt or deter adversaries and/or frustrate their plans and operations.

These policies were most often set by governments. The US Department of Defense and other nation-state cyber defense teams have been experimenting with cybersecurity deterrence and active defense for decades (e.g., Department of Defense 1996). More recently, the technology private sector has assumed a larger role in such activities. Microsoft has been disrupting malicious botnets since 2010 (Microsoft 2010), and in 2025, Google created a cyber "disruption unit" to frustrate adversaries. For example, it went to court to obtain permission to dismantle botnets that targeted its Android software (Starks 2025; Arghire 2025).

Table 1.1 Cyberspace Policy Makers.

Acronym	Name	Mission
IANA	Internet Addressing and Numbering Authority	Manages top-level domains and distribution of subdomains, internet protocol addresses, and Internet Service Provider (ISP) identifiers.
IETF	Internet Engineering Task Force	Collaborates to produce and maintain technical communication protocols used on the internet.
ICANN	Internet Corporation for Assigned Names and Numbers	Develops and oversees policy, process, and procedures to facilitate secure operation of the Internet Domain Name System (DNS).
ITU	International Telecommunications Union	Facilitate international connectivity via networks, allocates radio spectrum and satellite orbits, and develops communication technology standards.

1.2.5 Cyberspace

A final set of policies addresses the top-down question: how to make "everything" safe from cyberattack. That is, how to make *all* of cyberspace more secure and defensible. Policies to deal with "everything" not only originate from national governments but also from key consensus-based organizations with no actual governmental authority other than an agreed-upon charter and mutual goals for worldwide interconnectivity and information sharing (see examples in Table 1.1).

Cyberspace is far more than just connected devices and the people who use them. It is a worldwide layer of network communication for which, unfortunately, security was an afterthought. The base systemwide layer includes the security of things owned only by device owner/operators (such as telecoms who manage border gateway Protocol and the registrars who manage domain names). On top of that are "cloud" service providers: Infrastructure as a Service (IaaS), Platform as a Service (PaaS), and Software as a Service (SaaS). Referred to indiscriminately as "Technology Platforms," these technology service providers are the commercial storefronts of modern cyberspace. Because of their global reach, massive infrastructure, influence on smaller service providers, and substantial market share, companies like Google and Microsoft make decisions that impact the security of the entirety of cyberspace.

This power has both upsides and downsides. Disruptions within the technology platform layer can have massive scale, foreshadowed by the Morris Worm of 1988, which took down perhaps 10% of the early internet (Orman 2003), the Mafiaboy

Attack in 2000, which took down the vanguard of internet service providers: Yahoo, CNN, Amazon, and E-Trade (Calce 2008), and Iran's takedown of Bank of America, Capitol One, Citigroup, Fifth Third Bank, JPMorgan Chase, and the New York Stock Exchange (Perlroth 2021, p. 272). More recently, we have seen the same disruption in service provider operations due not to cyberattack, but due to service provider technology control weakness (Kurtz 2024; AWS 2025; Prince 2025). We expect both trends to continue.

However, the upside to the growing Technology Platform industry is that they make massive investments to operate at very large scales, so they can be extremely efficient. If they collectively adopt a policy to secure cyberspace, it would improve security for billions of devices and people with minimum burden. The New York Cyber Task Force, organized at the Columbia School of International and Public Affairs (SIPA), found that when cybersecurity best practices (e.g., end-to-end encryption) are adopted by individual technology powerhouses, it can tip the scale toward advantage for defenders over attackers at a large scale and least cost (SIPA 2017).

1.2.6 Public Policy

Government policies on cybersecurity are in some ways no different than any other policy domain. Governments must protect their own systems, oversee the management of cyber risks of dependencies, reduce the risks posed by adversaries, and continuously improve security amid fast-paced technology change. That said, public policy is in many ways special, and this is why the introduction for it follows the complete introduction of the other cybersecurity policy domains. In some ways, it encompasses them all because it has enforcement power over many more people. In other ways, it is irrelevant because it does not change very much and it has little effect on their day-to-day operations.

The US federal government has one of the world's largest IT enterprises, spending over $65 billion across dozens of agencies and departments, from those advising on kindergarten curriculum in the Department of Education to those operating the Pentagon and the Secret Service. Its acquisition decisions can sometimes redirect development efforts within the defense industry cybersecurity community, such as the 2021 Executive Order 14028, which mandated specific security requirements for Zero Trust Architecture (ZTA) and Software Bills of Materials (SBOM) for companies vying for government contracts (White House 2021).

Even the most powerful corporations lack the ability of governments to directly regulate critical infrastructure and other companies to reduce risks. And while Microsoft, Google, and others have been disrupting adversary cyber operations, these efforts often need government backing, such as courts issuing temporary restraining orders to disrupt botnets, and pale in comparison with the powers of governments. Governments are not limited to countering cybercrime in cyberspace. For example, frustrated by ransomware, the US President Joe Biden called a summit with Russian President Vladimir Putin solely to express American concerns (Sanger and Perlroth 2021), and in 2019, Israel targeted and destroyed a building where the Hamas cyber operatives worked (Israel Defense Forces 2019). The Public Sector also gains some power by flexing their defensive operation expertise by issuing standards, such as those from NIST.

1.3 Cybersecurity Policy Catalog

All policies have pros and cons, and cybersecurity policy is no exception. Accordingly, several chapters of this book provide numerous examples of cybersecurity policy statements that have been adopted by others, culminating in a "describe a catalog" approach to cybersecurity policy in Chapter 8. The catalog demonstrates the breadth and depth of issues that come under the collective heading of cybersecurity policy in all domains, many of which may not be decided by any one individual or organization, and it also makes it easy to see how policy decisions made by some individuals in their own domains will impact others.

As in a physical security environment, each significant social, economic, institutional, and political segment of the community has a number of potential resources that can be brought to bear. There is a role for the police, private security services, technology vendors, government, the insurance industry, civic groups, critical infrastructure operators, industry associations, and citizen organizations in contributing to effective policies. Each group's role needs clarity in its scope and potential impact on the overall problem.

The cybersecurity policies included in this catalog are not meant as a picklist from which to choose a cybersecurity policy. Even with seven authors in different areas of expertise with cybersecurity, it is impossible for us to project potential policy decisions for cyberspace. Even if it were possible, given the rapid pace of technology change, by the time the publication process was finished, there would be some change in cyberspace that necessitated new ways of policy formulation. For the moment, this book provides a well-understood framework of policy issues, most of which were issues at the time of the first edition and are likely to be for the next decade as well.

There is also a large class of "policy" statements that were omitted intentionally, namely, technical security configurations for hardware and software. As noted above, many organizations publish technical security specifications under the heading of "policy." However, these technical advisories do not reflect management objectives themselves. Rather, they provide implementation standards for technical professionals charged with executing management policy directives. They are means to the end of policy compliance. Where it is imperative that these technical standards are implemented consistently without exception, they may qualify as requirements to demonstrate that technology operations are in compliance with cybersecurity policy. They are, in fact, implementation standards that change so frequently that executive management could not reasonably be expected to completely understand, much less to dictate.

As in the first edition, we include a Catalog to emphasize the depth and breadth of cybersecurity policy issues. Note that, before there were any federal laws specifically directed at securing cyberspace, cyberspace was the wild west (it still is, but it took more than a century to tame the wild west to a tolerable level, and we expect it will be the same with cyberspace). At that time, policymakers on Capitol Hill had to study their options and consider what laws to pass that would be enforceable and also a deterrent to threat actors engaged in computer-enabled crimes and abuses like fraud, intellectual property theft, harassment, and malicious software distribution. At the bare bones, one of their choices may have looked like the one in Table 1.2.

The policy statement in Table 1.2 is the essence of what became the Computer Fraud and Abuse Act in 1984 (see Figure 1.3). Its objective is simply stated, and we have selected a few reasons for controversy concerning it that were documented at the time. Though the first version of the Act missed criminalizing several innovative cyberattack techniques, in its first court prosecution, it was sufficient to convict the author of the Morris Worm mentioned above. As its gaps became evident, it was altered and amended several times.

Table 1.2 Computer Fraud and Abuse Act Example Policy Statement.

Index	Statement	Objective	Reasons for Controversy
CFAA	Accessing computers without authorization or exceeding the authorization that was granted shall be subject to criminal and civil penalties.	This policy is intended to prohibit trespassing into, damaging, or acquiring information from certain categories of computers, assuming the user lacks authorization for that conduct.	• Malicious espionage and data theft are rampant, and there are currently no laws that criminalize the fundamental enabler of these crimes, which is unauthorized hacking. • Exploring the internet was a common activity among curious young people, and many thought it was harmless.

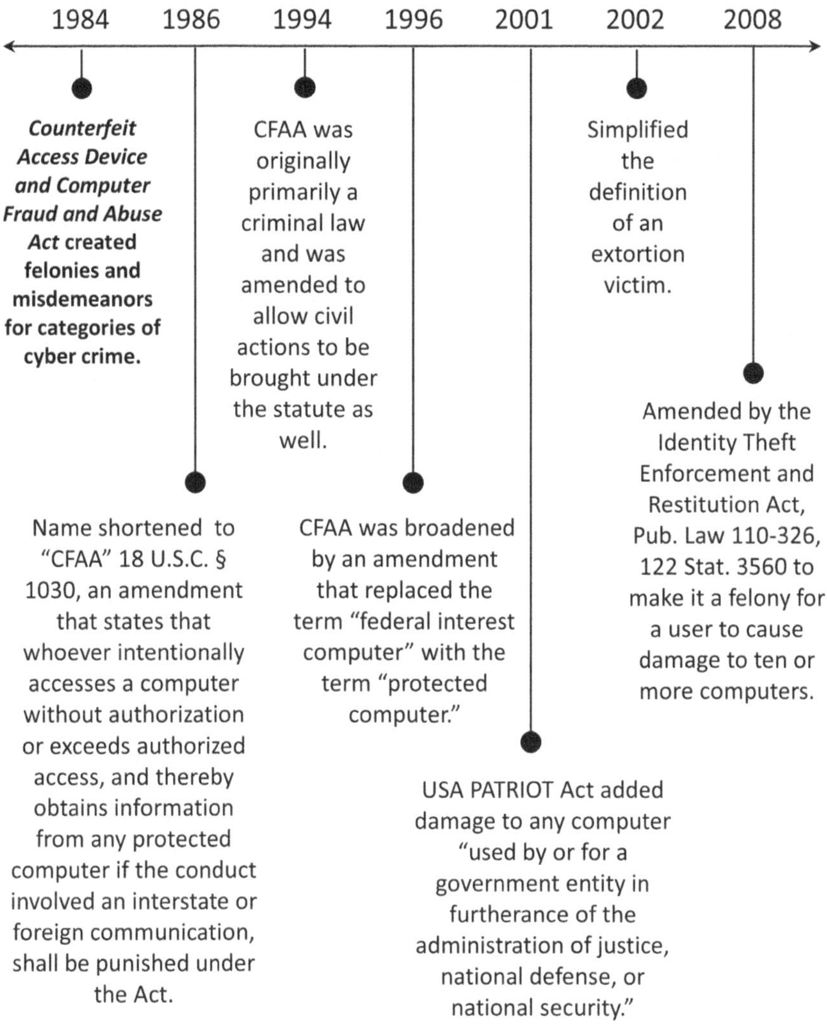

Figure 1.3 Computer Fraud and Abuse Act.

Over time, the US government has adopted new laws to supplement the CFAA, and also formal collaborations, executive orders, initiatives, reports, standards, strategies, and systems. In 2020, a Congressional Commission again gathered top experts from around the globe in a costly and lengthy analysis of the then-current state of cybersecurity with the objective of global situational improvement (King and Gallagher 2020). The Commission's final report included over 75 recommendations for a policy statement that would improve the state of security in cyberspace. Unfortunately, not only were most not adopted, but since then, funding has been cut for areas that the commission strongly recommended needed strengthening, like the Cybersecurity and Infrastructure Security Agency (CISA). We hope this book will help educate those interested in cybersecurity situational improvement to understand, and therefore better lobby for adoption, of cybersecurity policies, as well as to make better choices within their own domain of responsibility for cybersecurity policy.

The remainder of this book comprises chapters on the following topics, each of which includes building blocks that lead to a better understanding of the catalog:

Chapter 2. Cybersecurity Evolution: A brief history of cyber, cybersecurity, and the evolution of technologies and corresponding control objectives.

Chapter 3. Cybersecurity Policy Objectives: Defines cybersecurity risk issues and a wide range of technology risk reduction initiatives.

Chapter 4. Cybersecurity Communication: Describes common methods of sharing information about cybersecurity, and command and control strategies for communicating in the course of responding to cyber threats.

Chapter 5. Guidance for Decision Makers: Explores the relationship between organizational leadership functions in the management of cybersecurity-related risks.

Chapter 6. The Cybersecurity Workforce: Summarizes the state of the practice in the standardization, or lack thereof, in cybersecurity curriculum.

Chapter 7. One Government's Approach to Cybersecurity Policy: Presents the United States Federal Government's history of actions related to cybersecurity as a detailed example, including its association with international organizations.

Chapter 8. Cybersecurity Policy Catalog: Classifies exemplar cybersecurity policy statements concerning cybersecurity domains and associated cybersecurity risk issues.

Chapter 9. Conclusion.

References

Amishav, J. (2026). Equifax Data Breach 2017: Timeline, costs & security lessons. https://www.breachsense.com/blog/equifax-data-breach/ (accessed 1 March 2026).

Arghire, I. (2025). Google sues operators of 10-million-device Badbox 2.0 Botnet. https://www.securityweek.com/google-sues-operators-of-10-million-device-badbox-2-0-botnet/ (accessed 1 March 2026).

AWS (2025). Summary of the Amazon DynamoDB service disruption in the Northern Virginia (US-EAST-1) Region. Amazon Web Services (AWS). 19 October. https://aws.amazon.com/message/101925/ (accessed 1 March 2026).

Bell, D. and L. LaPadula (1976). Secure computer system: Unified exposition and multics interpretation. ESD-TR-75-306, MITRE Corporation, MTR-2997 Rev. 1.

Berris, P. (2023). Primer on the Computer Fraud and Abuse Act and related statutes. Congressional Research Service. 16 May. https://www.congress.gov/crs-product/R47557 (accessed 1 March 2026).

Calce, M. and Silverman, C. (2008). *Mafiaboy: How I Cracked the Internet and Why It's Still Broken*. Canada: Viking.

Department of Defense (1996). Report of the Defense Science Board Task Force on Information Warfare-Defense (IW-D). https://apps.dtic.mil/sti/pdfs/ADA319571.pdf (accessed 1 March 2026).

Gibson, W. (1984). *Neuromancer*. New York, NY: Ace Books.

Ginter, A. (2023). *Engineering Grade OT Security, A Manager's Guide*. Calgary, AL: Abterra.

Hamby, J. M. and Wingfield, T. C. (2016). Cyber policy. In *Charting a Course: Strategic Choices for a New Administration*, ed. R. D., Hooker Jr., National Defense University Press, https://ndupress.ndu.edu/Publications/Books/charting-a-course/Article/1026977/chapter-8-cyber-policy/ (accessed 1 March 2026).

Healey, J. (2025). Understanding cyber market failures. https://www.lawfaremedia.org/article/understanding-cyber-market-failures (accessed 1 March 2026).

IANA (n.d.). Internet Assigned Numbers Authority. https://www.iana.org/ (accessed 1 March 2026).

ICANN (n.d.). Internet Corporation for Assigned Names and Numbers. https://www.icann.org/ (accessed 1 March 2026).

IETF (n.d.). Internet Engineering Task Force. https://www.ietf.org/ (accessed 1 March 2026).

Israel Defense Forces (IDF) (2019). Tweet regarding strike on Hamas hacking center. https://x.com/IDF/status/1125066395010699264 (accessed 1 March 2026).

ITU (n.d.). International Telecommunications Union. https://www.itu.int/ (accessed 1 March 2026).

King, A. and M. Gallagher (2020). United States Cyberspace Solarium Commission. March 2020. https://www.solarium.gov/report (accessed 1 March 2026).

Kurtz, G. (2024). To our customers and partners. Crowdstrike. 19 July. https://www.theguardian.com/technology/2024/sep/24/crowdstrike-outage-microsoft-apology (accessed 1 March 2026).

Microsoft (2010). R.I.P. Waledac: undoing the damage of a botnet. https://blogs.microsoft.com/blog/2010/09/08/r-i-p-waledac-undoing-the-damage-of-a-botnet/ (accessed 11 February 2026).

National Institute of Standards and Technology (n.d.). Glossary: Cyberspace. https://csrc.nist.gov/glossary/term/cyberspace (accessed 1 March 2026).

NIST (2020). Zero trust architecture standard. National Institute of Standards and Technology SP800-207. https://nvlpubs.nist.gov/nistpubs/SpecialPublications/NIST.SP.800-207 (accessed 1 March 2026).

NIST-CSF (2024). Framework for improving critical infrastructure cybersecurity, version 2.0. National Institute of Standards and Technology, 26 February. https://nvlpubs.nist.gov/nistpubs/cswp/nist.cswp.04162018.pdf (accessed 01 March 2026).

Orman, H. K. (2003). The Morris Worm: A fifteen-year perspective. *IEEE Security & Privacy*, 1(5): 35–43.

Oxford (n.d.) Oxford languages: Policy. https://languages.oup.com/google-dictionary-en/ (accessed 1 March 2026).

Perlroth, N. (2021). *This Is How They Tell Me the World Ends: The Cyberweapons Arms Race*. New York, NY: Bloomsbury Publishing.

Prince, M. (2025). Cloudflare outage on November 18, 2025. Cloudflare. 18 November. https://blog.cloudflare.com/author/matthew-prince/ (accessed 1 March 2026).

Sanger, D.E. and N. Perlroth (2021). Biden Warns Putin to act against ransomware groups, or U.S. will strike back. https://www.nytimes.com/2021/07/09/us/politics/biden-putin-ransomware-russia.html (accessed 23 February 2026).

SIPA (2017). Building a defensible cyberspace. Columbia School of International and Public Affairs (SIPA). https://www.sipa.columbia.edu/global-research-impact/initiatives/cyber/nyctf/defensible-cyberspace (accessed 1 March 2026).

Starks, T. (2025). Google previews cyber 'disruption unit' as U.S. government, industry weigh going heavier on offense. https://cyberscoop.com/google-cybersecurity-disruption-unit-active-defense-hack-back/ (accessed 11 February 2026).

Weiss, J. (2010). *Protecting Industrial Control Systems from Electronic Threats*. New York, NY: Momentum Press.

White House (2021). Executive order 14028: Improving the nation's cybersecurity. https://www.federalregister.gov/documents/2021/05/17/2021-10460/improving-the-nations-cybersecurity (accessed 11 February 2026).

2

Cybersecurity Evolution

When computers became capable of automating processes, the main goal in all such projects was the increase in *productivity* that came with replacing human calculators with automated programs that produced more accurate results. The same can be said of today's forays into artificial intelligence (AI). Then, as now, the more sophisticated the software that becomes available, the more the productivity benefits of computers are realized. This chapter begins at the dawn of the internet. It includes a timeline of cyber technology initiatives, their exploitation by threat actors, and the introduction of corresponding cybersecurity defenses. It ends with a conclusion that the cycle of technology innovation, exploitation, and defenses playing catch-up is likely to continue for at least a few more decades, if not longer.

This chapter includes two types of figures. The first is a historical overview that highlights significant turning points in the cybersecurity threat landscape and associated policy responses. These figures match specific cyberattacks to associated strengthening of cybersecurity defensive techniques at a specific point in time.[1] While many of the cybersecurity technologies in focus at these turning points had been developed years earlier, it was only in the heat of a shocking cyberattack that policymakers took notice and incorporated general security principles into policies that necessitated adopting these cybersecurity technologies as standards. Depending on the threat, the responses may have been individual, organizational, public, or some combination. Figure 2.1 presents the key to the cybersecurity threat actor motivation, or incentive, for conducting the cyberattacks in these figures.

1 Note that the timelines that appear in this chapter are not a metric but a display of examples. Apologies to those who expect timelines to be marked by equal intervals corresponding to a unit of time. Think of these figures instead as a historical overview.

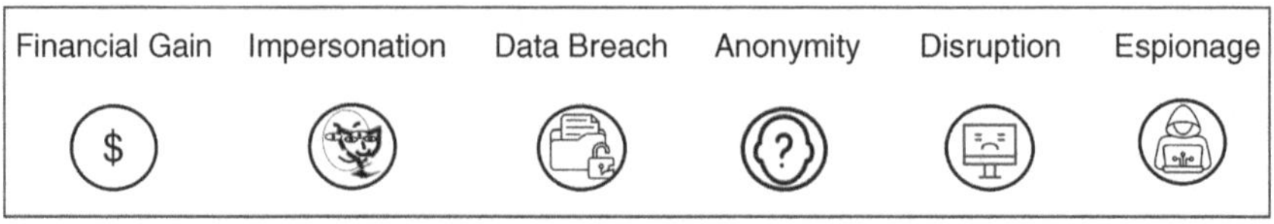

Figure 2.1 Timeline threat incentive key.

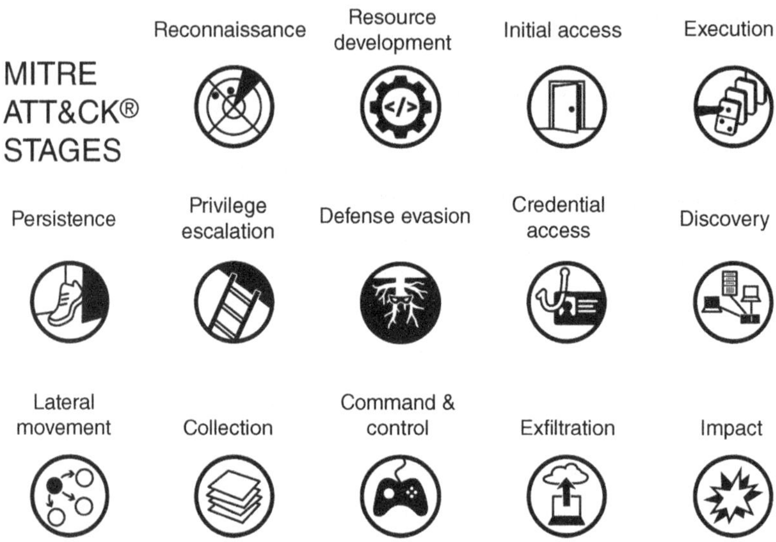

Figure 2.2 MITRE key.

The second type of figure is an attack path. These figures illustrate the activities of a cybersecurity threat actor in conducting the attack, and collectively, how they have evolved over time. Figure 2.2 is a key to the understanding steps in the attack path from start to finish. They are adopted from an industry-standard method of communicating about cybersecurity threats developed by a US Federally Funded Research and Development Center (FFRDC) called MITRE (though MITRE was started by people from MIT, it is not an acronym). Among other research services, MITRE identifies, classifies, and tracks the attack patterns of *cybersecurity threat actors*, and in this book, we frequently shorten that moniker to *attacker* (MITRE n.d.b).

MITRE elucidates cyberattack patterns by breaking them down into recognizable *stages*. The MITRE attack stages in Figure 2.2 are generic and associated with icons that are used in this chapter's figures to provide context for each step in an attack path. Table 2.1 is how MITRE describes what is going on from an attacker's perspective in a given attack *stage*. MITRE phrases the stages as what the attacker is *trying* to accomplish, though in all attacks represented by figures in this book, the referenced attempted accomplishment was achieved.

Table 2.1 MITRE ATT&CK® Stages.

Stage	The Why: The adversary is trying to...
Reconnaissance	Gather information they can use to plan future operations.
Resource development	Establish resources they can use to support operations.
Initial access	Get into your network.
Execution	Run malicious code.
Persistence	Maintain their foothold.
Privilege escalation	Gain higher-level permissions.
Defense evasion	Avoid being detected.
Credential access	Steal account names and passwords.
Discovery	Figure out your environment.
Lateral movement	Move through your environment.
Command and control	Communicate with compromised systems to control them.
Exfiltration	Steal data.
Impact	Manipulate, interrupt, or destroy your systems and data.

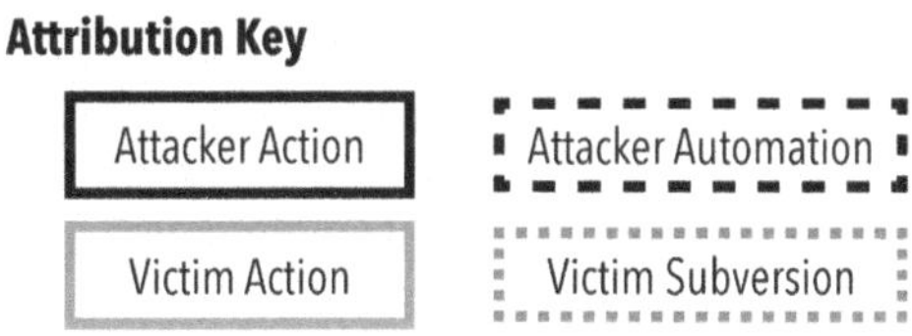

Figure 2.3 Attribution key.

Figure 2.3 provides further clarification for the attack path by indicating whether a given step is performed by an attacker or its *victim*. The figure also uses a callout pattern around each step number to indicate whether the step is a manual step by the attacker or victim (indicated by a solid line), or whether it is automated (shown as a dotted line). Attacker automation generally employs malicious software created for the attack. Victim automation is labeled *subversion* because the victim software was not "designed" to be used in an attack; rather, the attacker takes advantage of the victim software's features to *subvert* the victim's software into participating in the attack. The reader may wish to flip back to Figures 2.2, 2.3, Table 2.1, and this explanation, while digesting the first few attack figures.

This chapter italicizes words that are building blocks for appreciating the discussion of policy issues in later chapters. It includes a wide spectrum of example cyberattacks to ensure the reader is familiar with situations that are faced by cybersecurity policy decision-makers. A few events that influenced policy within each decade are presented in the timeline. A reader already familiar with cybersecurity history may be satisfied scanning the figures. Those interested in a high-level overview may skip reading the examples and still appreciate this chapter's figures and the remainder of this book. In any case, the reader can still find the examples in the index, and can flip back to this chapter if, at a later mention of a building block, a decision is made to explore a cybersecurity incident underlying a policy concern.

2.1 The Dawn of the Internet

Although many compare the rise of the internet to the rapid advances in technology of the industrial age, there is a significant exception to the analogy in that, at the dawn of the internet in the 1950s and 1960s, most advances in computer technology were not funded by private equity, but by the US Defense Department's Advanced Research Projects Agency (DARPA). DARPA's funding was channeled through large grants to universities and Department of Defense (DoD) contractors. Many of these were focused on the economy and efficiency of sharing research data of all kinds. Again, the focus was productivity. Though there is considerable debate about how the internet began, what became the internet backbone in the United States was first established as the Advanced Research Projects Agency Network (ARPANET), funded by the US military (Peter 2004). It is ironic that the internet itself became the battleground for a then unforeseen brand of warfare.

The ARPANET quickly became a tool for sharing information among computer science researchers in the military, its contractors, and its academic collaborators. DoD contractors already engaged in the manufacture of commercial products for computation were part of those efforts and evolved their commercial offerings as the research and development bore fruit. As the earliest computers evolved, they may have been exploited for personal use, but there was little awareness of the possibility, much less laws prohibiting computer misuse. That said, there was significant awareness that the *human factor* could not be eliminated from the sphere of security threats because system malfunctions were known to occur by accident without blame. There was also awareness of the environmental threat, starting with the first actual *bug* discovered among the vacuum tubes in a computer system (Slater 1987, p. 223).

As the term bug was adopted to refer in general to software malfunctions, which were frequent, standards and procedures for fixing these bugs emerged. These fixes were referred to as software "patches." In the context of computers, it originally referred to a cable plugged into a wall of vacuum tubes that altered the course of electronic processing in an analog computer by *physically* changing the path of code execution. Before that time, the word "patch" meant a *localized repair*, which it was, and the name stuck. Now the term *patch* refers to a few lines of code that repair a bug or flaw in software.

2.2 Timeline

2.2.1 1960s

The history of cybersecurity as we know it today started in the 1960s with the mainframe. This was the first type of computer that was affordable enough for businesses to see a return on investment from electronic data processing systems. Prior to this time, the word "computer" referred to a person who performed computations, and the word "cyber" was the realm of science fiction. In those days, computers were secured with guards and gates. Physical security procedures were devised to ensure that only people authorized to work on computers had physical access to them. Computers were so large that hundreds of square feet of space would be customized for their operation, with dedicated security staff. A guard's function was sometimes combined with the role of computer operator, called a job control technician. People who needed to use the computer would queue up in front of the guard holding their data and programs in stacks of punched cards. The guard would check the user's authorization to use the computer, receive their stack of cards, and place it into a card reader that would automatically translate the punched holes in the cards into bits and bytes, checking authorization paperwork while accepting sets of punched cards to be entered into a computer at a given time of day (Schacht 1975).

2.2.2 1970s

By the early 1970s, remote job entry allowed punched cards to be received from multiple office locations, and computer security staff then had the added responsibility of tracing these cables under raised floors, through wall spaces, and ceiling ducts to ensure that the authorized person was sitting at the other end. It was important for computers to be accessible only by trusted staff because they were starting to be used to manage money (e.g., to automatically reconcile corporate checkbooks with bank balances). This opened the door for fraud if someone could negatively impact the integrity of the data (e.g., by stealing a physical check, writing out to themselves, then changing the name of a check recipient in the computer to be some legitimate vendor).

Timeline 1 1960s–1970s.

Managers of these early automated computer systems were acutely aware of security risk, but the confidentiality, integrity, and availability triad was not yet an industry standard. Aside from a few installations in the military and intelligence, confidentiality was not the major security requirement. Though businesses did want to keep customer lists confidential, immature systems and software were constantly failing. While there had been a few public examples of attackers mining such systems with profit motives, these had largely been directed at theft of phone service. The then-monopoly AT&T monitored the amount of unpaid service from unauthorized devices, and when a threshold was reached, worked with law enforcement to investigate and prosecute the criminals. The major concern was integrity because the potential for human error has always been evident in computer software development and operations.

In addition, computer crime in the form of financial fraud became common in the 1970s. The financial auditors had to be creative to keep up. One method they used was called *auditing around the computer*. They required their auditees to write down everything they typed into the computer in *batches* of data-entry sheets (i.e., "data in"). With a hand calculator, they would manually compute the values the computer would have been expected to produce in financial statements. Then they compared their manual version of the financial statements with those produced by the computer (i.e., "data out"). Unfortunately, the computer fraudsters became just as creative. It was soon clear that even if the *data in* perfectly correlated to the *data out*, there was still a material risk in computer usage (Bayuk 2004, pp. 10–11).

One of the fraud methods they invented was called the *salami technique*. It was a way to shave off a *slither* of a transaction in a way that would not be caught by those auditing around the computer. For example, if they worked in a bank, they would design the software calculations to always round down when monetary transactions were performed on customer accounts that resulted in balances that included fractions of a penny. When this occurred, they would decrease the customer's account balance by the penny-fraction amounts and increase one of their own accounts by the same fractional amount. A computer processing a million transactions a day could net them thousands of dollars. The financial statement exactly matched *balances-in* with *balances-out*, and few customers noticed missing fractional pennies. When finally revealed, these heists made it to mainstream fictional literature and television (e.g., the British Broadcasting Network's *The Consultant*) (McNeil 1978).

By the mid-1970s, most punched card input devices were replaced by electronic input and output via keyboards and terminals. Cables and terminals extended the range within which authorized users could sit while processing data. Systems security expanded to include following the cables through wall partitions and ceiling ducts to ensure that the cables terminated in offices occupied by authorized computer users. This allowed people in offices far removed from the actual computer to be hooked up to an input–output (IO) port and use it from their desks. The guard in front of the computer room door remained, but mostly to sign in visitors who would tour the computer room, or vendors who performed maintenance. Security of the information was now in the realm of customized *business logic*. Users were assigned login names, which were associated with menus that provided the screens they needed to perform their job functions. The screens were limited by business logic coded into the software. For example, if clerks had a customer service screen, then they may have been able to view customer records but not change their balance. However, business logic screens often contained overrides, where a supervisor observing the customer service clerk could enter a special code to allow a one-time balance change operation through the otherwise limited screen functionality.

Widespread use of computers enabled by keyboard technology drew attention to the issue of confidentiality controls. Military and intelligence computer use had increased. It became obvious that the vast majority of internet infrastructure and functions were decentralized, which was a design goal of the internet, but certain centralized planning and coordination functions were required. The most visible were the allocation of names (i.e., http://www.whitehouse.gov) and numbers (i.e., Internet Protocol, or IP, addresses, the cyberspace equivalent of postal addresses that are used to find routes to locate computers). These coordination functions were initially performed at Stanford Research Institute (SRI), a DoD contractor. In 1972, these functions were transitioned to the Internet Assigned Numbers Authority (IANA) under the oversight of Jon Postel, and in 1976, he moved them to the Information Sciences Institute (ISI) at the University of Southern California.

In addition, automation of records by government agencies, such as the Social Security Administration and the Internal Revenue Service, fostered recognition that stakeholders in cyberspace included those whose physical lives were closely aligned with the bits and bytes representing it all. In recognition of the growing confidentiality requirements, but without any good way to meet them, the US National Bureau of Standards (now the National Institute of Standards and Technology: NIST) launched an effort to achieve consensus on a national encryption standard. In 1974, the US Computer Security Act (Privacy Act 1974) was the first stake in the ground designed to establish control over information propagation. The act covered only government use of computers and only information that today would be called Personally Identifiable Information (PII). But it firmly established confidentiality as a mainstream goal for cybersecurity.

As technology advanced through the 1970s, mini-computers such as the DEC PDP-11 frequently supplemented mainframes in large companies and were rapidly expanding into smaller companies that could now afford them to automate office tasks such as word processing. For those who could not yet afford a computer of any size, technology-savvy entrepreneurs had started services that allowed people to rent time on computers. These were called "timesharing services" because companies in this business would charge their clients based on the amount of computer time they consumed. Once terminal and keyboard technology made it possible to extend IO devices through cables, they used ordinary telephone lines to extend the reach of computer terminals beyond the walls of the building using analog modulation-demodulation technology (i.e., modems and multiplexors). These companies began to specialize by industry, developing complicated software, such as payroll tax filing and commercial real estate billing. Commercial lease calculations development was unlikely to return cost–benefit to a company that did not have that business requirement, but it was a time-consuming manual process run by many businesses. This allowed departments that were not the mainstream part of a business to benefit from automation, though they had to pay for someone else's computer to do it.

These timesharing services charged for computing resources based on user activity, so they needed a way to identify users to bill them. Often, this was simply a company name, though passwords were sometimes issued when timesharing services were known to have customers who were competitors. However, from the point of view of the customer user, the username connected them to their information in the computer, and the modem connection did not seem like a security risk. Any company large enough to own a computer at the time was obviously a firm of some wealth and substance, so the timesharing service companies were assumed to have physical security around their computer, and passwords were further evidence of their security due diligence. It was considered the risk of the timesharing service vendor to allow customer logical access, and given their wealth and substance, they could be expected to protect their assets accordingly.

Throughout the 1970s into the 1980s, mini-computers became more affordable and eventually allowed people to have an entire computer for their own use.

Apple introduced home computers in the late 1970s, and these soon made it into the data processing environment, to be followed by the IBM personal computer (PC) in 1981. Physical security still was the norm, and locked office doors were the primary protection mechanism. But these small *desktop* computers, in combination with new network technologies, soon allowed computers in the same building to share data with each other, and the names of the computers became important, so that people could remotely identify information in other computers on the network. These local area networks (LANs) were protected much like the computer terminals' connection to the mainframe, except that the equipment that allowed the communication had to be kept in a secure area, and access to the hubs that allowed a person to connect their computer to the LAN was also protected via locked office doors.

Until the introduction of these LANs, login-based access controls were the exception rather than the norm in many computing environments. If login identifiers (IDs) were distributed, they were rarely disabled. They functioned more as a convenient method of labeling data created by different people than to restrict access to it. However, the LAN-connected computing environments and corresponding plethora of desktop computers made it very difficult to trace network computer activity to individuals, because they generally logged in only to the machine on their desktop. The threat of anonymous fraud and data theft motivated some organizations to implement centralized administration schemes and logical access controls (Schweitzer 1982, 1983). Logical access control schemes introduced new concepts, such as systems *subjects* (i.e., users) and *objects* (i.e., files), *identity* separated from *authentication*, and object labels for *authorization* (which had been developed a decade before) were turned into security *bolt-ons* for the popular computer *operating systems* of the day (i.e., the computer's *OS*, the software that directly interacts with hardware to execute electronic instruction (e.g., *Linux*, *Windows*) (Amoroso 1994). We use the term *bolt-on* as a derogatory term for a cybersecurity product that would not be needed if the software was designed to provide confidentiality, integrity, and availability features in the first place.

As many of the LAN computer users already had a mainframe terminal on their desks, it was not long before these computers replaced the terminal functionality, and the LAN was connected to the mainframe. It was this development that made cybersecurity a hot topic with technology management. Though some of the timesharing-type password technology was employed on the LAN, LAN usernames were primarily supported to facilitate directory services, rather than to prevent determined attacks. That is, it was helpful to know the name of the person who had written a particular file or posted a memo on a customer record. Assigning login names to computer users allowed programs to use that name as part of their business logic to provide the correct menus and screens. Prior to this point in cyberspace evolution, transactions on a mainframe could still be traced to an individual terminal in a physical location, and subsequent investigation using both physical and digital forensics had a fighting chance to identify a suspect. However, the LANs and modems blurred distinctions between users, and it was easy for a criminal to repudiate activity performed from a LAN desktop.

2.2.3 1980s

The ubiquity of desktop computers in the office led future-minded parents to introduce their children to the technology at home in the 1980s, which brought a new breed of hackers to exploit the remote access vulnerabilities in the early dial-up system. The fact that most operating systems had been built at universities meant they typically included a games folder with a variety of entertaining programs. To use the much faster computers to play games, game enthusiasts would dial every number in the phone book and listen for the telltale hum of a computer modem. Once identified, they would call these modems with their own computer and guess usernames and passwords. These attacks could be automated using online dictionaries. A software program on a home computer would dial into the newfound modem once a minute or so, provide a username and password combination from the dictionary, walk away for a few hours an come back to one or two successful logins with usernames like "joe" and passwords like "password." Children were among them, and this observation led to the hit 1983 movie War Games, wherein a teenager dialed into a military computer, and thinking it was a game, almost started a war. Those who stole computer time only to play games were called joyriders.

Although not many operating systems had password security features, the companies that had invested in the computer security bolt-ons were able to set a limit on the number of times a person failed consecutive login attempts and freeze the account if the limit was exceeded. Password expiration thresholds forced users to change passwords, so if one was stolen, the hackers would not have it for long. For more sensitive systems, many companies implemented a *dial-back* control. When the computer received a phone call, it would check the caller ID and look for it in a list of authorized numbers, and hang up. However, anyone with customer premise phone equipment could present any number to a receiving phone via the caller-ID protocol, basically impersonating an authorized home phone number, or *spoof* an authorized origination. After verifying that the number was valid using the equipment, the dialed computer would hang up and *dial-back* the authorized number to make sure it was not spoofed. The user's modem would connect the call, and the user could then log in.

Dial-back systems were expensive, and even frequent password changes did not prevent hackers from guessing the new ones. Groups of hackers freely shared the credentials and phone numbers on *bulletin board systems* (BBS), where a group of

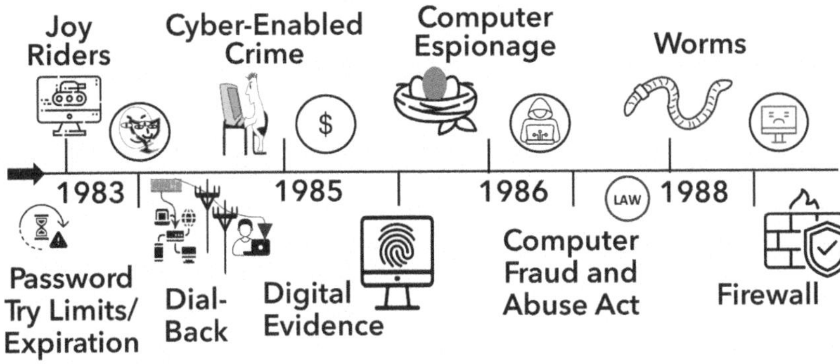

Timeline 2 1980s.

people posted their views on a given topic of mutual interest. Hackers would meet on the vulnerable computers to play games or other activities unbeknownst to the system's owners. One of these groups was some teenagers from Milwaukee who called themselves the 414s, a reference to their area code. We know about the 414s because one day they were looking for games on a hospital's computer and noticed it was creating logs of their activity. They deleted the logs and also, by accident, deleted some of the hospital's payment records. The hospital administrators called the US Federal Bureau of Investigation (FBI), who planted a Star Trek game on the hospital's computer and waited for 414 to come back. When they did, the FBI traced them via their phone numbers (Kalat 2021).

On September 26, 1983, one of the 414s testified at a hearing of a US House of Representatives Committee on the issue of computer crime (United States House of Representatives Committee on Science and Technology 1983). The hearing resulted in several proposals for public policy solutions, and while none was immediately adopted, the ideas made their way into a comprehensive Crime Control Act of 1984 (Pub. L. 98–473, S. 1762, 98 Stat. 1976), which included a Counterfeit Access Device and Computer Fraud and Abuse Act, which was amended in 1986 to become the Computer Fraud and Abuse Act (18 U.S.C. § 1030), described in Chapter 1.

Though the phone hackers and joyriders sometimes made the news, it took a few cases of insider fraud for management to understand that the status quo carried too much risk to be sustainable. Hence, security technology that had until that point been the topic of military research was hastily implemented by major computer vendors and applied to data sets and file resources. To facilitate this development, a complete set of the system features required to secure operation was soon readily available in a US DoD publication called *The Orange Book*, named for the color of its cover (DoD 1985). More than just access control lists, it created requirements for

Trusted Computing Base (TCB) that was immune to tampering, a reference monitor, a single process that mediates all access control decisions with reference to access control lists (i.e., complete mediation), separating of administrative functions from operator (i.e., user) function at the memory level (i.e., separation or privilege), and read-only audit logs of both administrator and operator activities. To encourage adoption, it was handed out for free at NIST conferences. Most of the requirements in the Orange Book are still found in most organizational cybersecurity policies. Today, we call them *security principles*.

Although accountability for transaction processing was fast becoming a hot topic at fraud conferences, law enforcement activity in the domain of computer operations was limited. Nevertheless, the early 1980s were also the dawn of the age of *digital evidence*. Law enforcement partnered with technology vendors to produce software that would recover files that criminals had attempted to delete from computers (Schmidt 2006). Cyberspace presented a new avenue of inquiry for law enforcement investigating traditional crimes. Criminals were caught boasting of their crimes on the social networking sites of the day, which were electronic BBS reached by modems over phone lines. Not just fraudsters, but stalkers, drug dealers, murderers, revenge plotters, and child pornographers were prosecuted using the plans, accounting data, and photographs they had stored on their own computers.

Yet there was little awareness that the internet was also being used for espionage. In 1986, Cliff Stoll, an astrophysics graduate student with a university job as a time-sharing services administrator, noticed a billing error in the range of 75 cents of computer time that was not associated with any of his users. Though neither his management at Lawrence Berkeley National Laboratory nor law enforcement was concerned, he was curious how the error could have occurred on such a deterministic platform as a computer. Stoll ended up tracking the missing cents of computing time to an Eastern European espionage ring. He lured the espionage agent into spending time on his computer by creating large data archives of what appeared to be secret plans and coordinated with international telecommunications vendors to track the source of the intrusion. Stoll published an account of his investigation in 1989 in a detective-like tale called *The Cuckoo's Egg*, an analogy with the bird because it lays its eggs in other birds' nests (Stoll 1989). *The Cuckoo's Egg* set off a large-scale effort among technology managers to identify and lock down access to computers' dial-back systems.

In 1986, the US National Science Foundation (NSF) launched NSFNET to connect academic researchers to a new system of supercomputer centers by establishing network hubs in major cities going forward (NSF n.d.). The NSF had a policy that its creations were free for not-for-profit use, and the internet backbone fell into this category. The same year, the Internet Engineering Task Force (IETF) was founded to ensure the internet evolved responsibly. Its mission was to "produce high quality, relevant technical and engineering documents that influence the way people design, use, and manage the internet in such a way as to make the internet work better. These documents include protocol standards, best current practices, and informational documents of various kinds" (IETF n.d.). Since its founding, those with an idea for a new or improved communications protocol or practice share it via a formal process. These are published as Requests for Comments (RFCs) in a standard template that allows others to quickly come up to speed on the ideas, as well as extend them.

Commercial internet service providers (ISPs) popped up in droves, ignoring the NSF acceptable use policy (an early example of what would become a technology platform trend of ignoring cybersecurity policies). By 1988, there were ~60,000 hosts on the internet, and in 1989, the US Department of Commerce (DoC) founded the IANA to distance DARPA from the public-centered activity. In 1988, the internet was still a place for the business of connecting the computers of large companies to each other. Technology-savvy companies and individuals quickly registered domain names so that no one else could register their last names, brands, or trademarks. Their administrators purchased email servers so they could take advantage of immediate electronic communication with their business partners and suppliers. By the late 1980s, communication across city boundaries had achieved the same level of maturity as LANs. A new form of communication was introduced, namely, *Internet Relay Chat* (IRC). Like BBS, group membership was required. But IRC allowed interactive communication on a *channel* in real time, and hackers gravitated to them. There was little concern about security except among military and academic researchers.

One of these researchers was Robert Morris at AT&T Bell Laboratories. He was an early computer pioneer, to the extent that he actually had computers at his home long before they were marketed to consumers. His son, Robert Tappan Morris, grew up around these computers and was very familiar with the ways in which they could be used without the permission of their owners. He often brought this to the attention of others, but no one appeared concerned. To prove his point, in 1988, Robert Tappan Morris devised the first internet *worm*, a program that automatically replicated itself, identified new targets, and traversed a network to attack each target. The "Morris Worm" accessed email servers, exploited vulnerabilities to identify all the computers that were known to it, then contacted all of those servers and attempted the same exploits (Orman 2003). Within a few hours, most of the internet had been affected, and the damage was severe. Internet communication virtually stopped. Computing resources were so overwhelmed by the worm's activities that they had no processing cycles or network bandwidth left for transaction processing, leaving business processes disrupted. The internet was so new that headlines on the outage still referred to it as ARPANET, and there was, for the first time, widespread concern that the internet could be used by adversaries

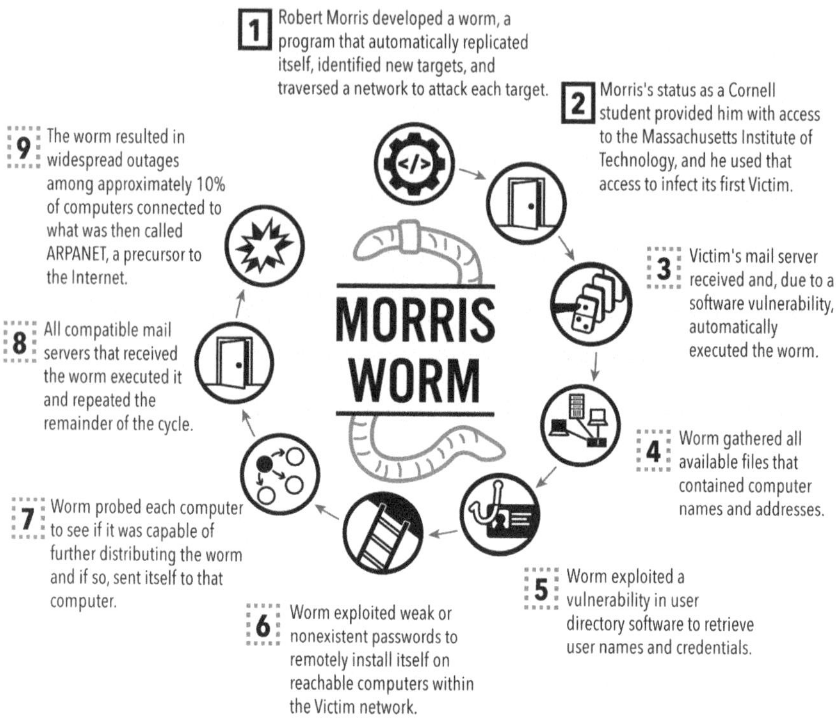

Figure 2.4 Morris worm 1988.

with destructive motives. The details of the attack path and its impact appear in Figure 2.4.[2]

The only organization on the internet that was safe from the Morris worm was AT&T Bell Laboratories. The reason for the safety had nothing to do with Morris but was instead due to an experiment being conducted by some other computer network researchers. They had developed a method of inspecting each information packet within a stream of network traffic that they called a *firewall* (Cheswick and Bellovin 1994). The firewall was designed to allow network access to only those packets whose source and *destination* matched those on a previously authorized list. The sources and destinations in the network access rules took the form of the *network addresses* of communicating computers, as well as a *port*

2 Note that the attack paths that appear in this chapter are the closest approximation the authors could make, given the amount of public information available on any given attack. Given the level of confidence we had in what data was available, we may have made an assumption about how a given step was accomplished. Nevertheless, collectively, all the steps in the combined set of attack paths are realistic examples of known attacker and victim activities, as well as known to exist hacker automation tools and the victim's cyber technology being subverted to participate in the attacker's plan of attack.

number that served as the access address for software running on each computer. The Bell Labs firewall was hastily employed to safeguard AT&T's email servers, and the impact on AT&T from the Morris worm was minimal (Farrow 2013). Since then, cybersecurity policy has included management directives based on security principles to safeguard the network periphery. In this case, the security principle was:

Defense in Depth: Require authorization through multiple layers of separately configured controls prior to allowing access to resources.

Due to Cheswick and Bellovin, the primary cybersecurity implementation recommended by the strategists who incorporated defense in depth into their cybersecurity policies has been to deploy firewalls.

The Morris Worm had a profound effect on the internet community. As ARPA still officially managed the network, it responded by establishing the Computer Emergency Response Team (CERT) to provide technical assistance to those who suffered from cybersecurity problems (CERT n.d.). In combination with *The Orange Book*'s audit requirements and the new digital evidence preservation methods, detection and recovery had officially joined prevention as standard cybersecurity controls.

2.2.4 1990s

Unfortunately, all these network periphery controls did not prevent the hackers and joyriders from disrupting computer operations with viruses. Viruses were distributed on floppy disks (i.e., removable media, the 1990s equivalent of universal serial bus [USB] sticks) and downloaded from BBS. Virus specimens were analyzed by what we would now call *cyberforensics* specialists, the people who had earned their cybersecurity credentials, who helped law enforcement identify digital evidence in the 1980s. They were able to create a *digital signature*, for the virus, meant as an analogy with identification via signing your name, and *footprint*, slang for data that an automated software scan could look for to identify that the virus was installed. The software could look for digital signatures and footprints in the software security vulnerabilities that had been exploited by the virus, each file a virus altered, and the types of trails it left behind, such as logs or program cache running in computer *memory* (i.e., the place where a computer keeps its pipeline of code instructions). They created *anti*-virus software (now referred to as antivirus), which would automatically identify and attempt to stop and delete the viruses, which they sold to the government, industry, and eventually, to households. Antivirus vendors committed to their clients that they would keep their list of signatures up to date with every new virus introduced on the internet. As there were already thousands of viruses circulating, companies quickly devised the means to install antivirus software on the PCs of all of their users.

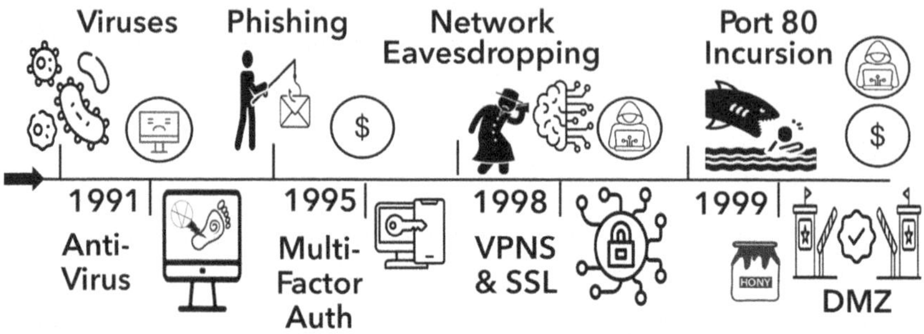

Timeline 3 1990s.

Although the vulnerability exploited by the virus may have been part of its footprint, multiple viruses exploited the same vulnerability, so the footprint also had to include digital evidence deposited by the virus itself (e.g., file names or memory patterns). As antivirus controls became more effective, virus writers adapted by slightly modifying virus code to leave a different footprint while taking advantage of the same software vulnerability and thereby evade detection by antivirus software. Antivirus and intrusion detection vendors would still create signatures for the latest spyware and malware, and SOC staff developed routine procedures to eradicate the software once it was identified. In 1993, the introduction of a new attacker technique for evading antivirus programs: *polymorphic viruses* emerged. These viruses constantly change their identifiable features, such as file names, encryption keys, or signatures, to better evade detection by traditional antivirus software (Spafford 1994). It thus became important not only to update antivirus signatures, but also to demand that software vendors correct the security bugs and flaws in the software that allowed viruses to cause damage in the first place.

By 1995, there were so many commercial internet ISPs that NSFNET was no longer required to connect the supercomputer centers, and the NSF disbanded it. With it went restrictions to commercial use of the internet and electronic commerce (ecommerce) was born. The concept of computer security was then nascent and, except for firewalls, was not routinely applied to networks because computer security focused on computing device operating systems and business applications. An authoritative text on the subject is History of Modern Computing. Published in 1998, the book covered the period from 1945 through 1995 and did not mention the topic of computer security once (Ceruzzi 1998). Consulting services specializing in computer security rebranded themselves as *Information* Security to emphasize that it was not the computer we were concerned about, it was the information in it.

Seemingly safe behind firewalls and slightly more complicated dial-back modems, organizations still allowed their users to freely dial out and also surf and get email on the fast-growing internet, which still mostly consisted of universities and research libraries, but was fast being overtaken by technology platforms. They also took advantage of modem technology to allow some of their users to dial in and use their networks from home. The NSF had funded the development of the first easy-to-use *browser* named Mosaic and released it for free. Netscape launched its Navigator browser soon after. Browsing through the internet became simple even for nontechnical people, and it was fast becoming the phonebook of choice for those familiar with it. Small, single-purpose servers were becoming more affordable, and most tech-savvy organizations had built a LANs for server connectivity so users on desktops could access business applications. Growing familiarity with both server operation and the internet led most organizations that had their own domain names and email servers to establish web servers as well.

The internet allowed attackers to access far more communications paths to vulnerable users than dialing into one modem at a time. While it was harder to guess passwords due to the automated attempt thresholds, attackers adapted by requesting the passwords *directly* from the users instead. Internet domain names are purposely easy and cheap to register. A new marketplace emerged in internet domain names that were purposely registered because they are the names of some business who were late to the Internet. People who do this are called *domain squatters*, because they keep the name (squat on it with their own contact information) until the business for whom it is named figures out they have it, and upon being contacted by that business, the squatter offers to *sell* it to them. But there is no law against registering a domain name that is the *misspelled* version of an active legitimate site (e.g., instead of wiley.com, a squatter might register wtley.com). The attacker then builds a website that looks exactly like the real wiley.com login screen and sends wiley.com users' emails that entice them to log in to wiley.com. Tucked under a Uniform Resource Locator (URL) in an email formatted in HyperText Markup Language (HTML), an attacker can send the URL label to look like https://www.wiley.com while the site to which the email recipient will be sent upon clicking it is https://www.wtley.com, the *look-alike* site. Focusing on the login form, the user does not notice the misspelling in the URL and interacts with the website.

In general, sending emails that entice users to click on deceptive links is called *phishing*, a phonetic play on the word fishing. It refers to baiting, or luring, internet users to click on deceptive links that execute malicious software, known by its anagram *malware* (Skoudis and Zeltser 2004). The viruses and worms described above are types of malware. One type of malware that logs user keystrokes and sends usernames and passwords to criminal data collection websites is called *spyware*. *Infostealer* malware is like spyware, but it steals information from your browser and potentially other desktop content. Another type of malware that encrypts all the data on your network and displays a note demanding to be paid to get it back is called *ransomware.*

In the domain squatting case, the malware is the look-alike site itself, and the site will have different malicious features depending on the attacker's objective. Domain squatting look-alikes are often used to present a login screen into which a victim will enter their username and password. The look-alike site responds with a "Login Fail" message and redirects the user to the legitimate URL, where the victim will usually try again and succeed in accessing the legitimate site. In the 1990s, these were typically the only authentication requirements, so when the look-alike mimicked a financial services site, the attacker could immediately log in with the same credentials and perform financial transactions in the victim's account. When a specific set of high-net-worth individuals is targeted by phishing emails, it is called *spear-phishing*, in analogy with whales as the target. There are as many types of phishing attacks as there are internet criminals. To prevent this form of *account takeover*, concerned organizations have since distributed *multi-factor authentication* to their customers, a *hand-held* technology that contains a key shared with the server and uses cryptography to generate single-use strings, called *tokens* that are only good for a small time interval (e.g., 20–60 seconds). Multiple vendors compete to produce the most convenient hand-held device that would be able to compute unguessable strings that provide user authentication in addition to passwords. The *multi* in multi-factor authentication, in this case, the *second factor*, is something a user must *possess* to be granted network access. A biometric identifier, like a fingerprint, would be a third. The factors are ordinally harder to hack: something you *know*, something you *have*, and something you *are*. At first, the hand-held devices were the size of a small calculator, but they evolved into lightweight displays that could be hung on a keychain.

As more sophisticated business applications moved from time-sharing systems to internet servers, ecommerce sites allowed credit card transactions to purchase goods and have them shipped. Attackers adapted by finding places on the internet within telecoms and ISPs to eavesdrop on network traffic between the home user and the company's modem and capture both the login credentials and the credit card information as it travelled through the network. They then used the credit cards to order goods to be shipped to a temporarily borrowed or rented mail address and tried the same username and passwords at other common sites to see where else they might work.

In addition, the introduction of easy-to-carry laptop computers had vastly increased the number of people who wanted to dial in from home, and while traveling, so dial-back databases were becoming difficult to securely maintain. This was especially concerning because they no longer landed on a single computer, but on the internal network. Caller-ID and dial-back were gradually replaced with multi-factor authentication. This was state-of-the-art security and worked until it became evident that attackers perched in ISPs to eavesdrop on network traffic between the home user and the company's modem and had developed automation to capture both the password and the token to use it to log in to the network (as the user) a few seconds after the user did. This is called a *replay* attack. These early internet vulnerabilities prompted the deployment of new protocols for encrypting network traffic – IPSec to facilitate remote access by creating Virtual Private Networks (VPNs) and Secure Socket Layer (SSL) for encrypting web application traffic.

IPSec was a protocol introduced and accepted by the IETF, but SSL was developed by the company that produced the most popular browser at the time, Netscape. Netscape introduced a new communications protocol called SSL. This had been in 1995. In 1999, the protocol was later enhanced by the committee and codified under the name Transport Layer Security (TLS) (Rescorla and Dierks 1999). Since then, TLS has been the industry-standard communications encryption mechanism. The SSL and TLS protocols require web servers to have very long and complicated encryption keys, called certificates, and these were technically difficult to generate, so security staff purchased and operated *certificate authority* software. The software allowed them to create a *root certificate* for their company, and the root certification was used to generate server certificates for each company's web server. The way the technology worked was that domain names have root certificates that are used in a cryptographic chain to create certificates for all of the servers that the domain name owner operated. The root certificates could be loaded into a browser in order for it to automatically verify that the server it was visiting was a member of the chain from one of its root certificates. For critical applications that facilitated high-asset value transactions, certificates could also be generated for each customer, which the protocol referred to as a *client*. The SSL protocol made use of certificates to identify the client to the server and the server to the client. Once mutually identified, both sides would use data from the certificates to generate a key they both would use for encrypted communication. When a user visited an SSL-enabled site for the first time, the site owner would typically redirect them to a link where they could download the root certificate. Thereafter, these browsers automatically checked the corresponding web server certificates. If client certificates were required, the user would be asked a series of questions to install the client certificate on their desktop.

But this SSL security configuration was difficult for ecommerce customers to manage, and users were confused by the root certificate downloading process and the questions about certificates. Therefore, browser software vendors started to preload their browsers with the root certificates from security software vendors, who for a price, would sell a company web server certificates that corresponded to a root certificate delivered with the browser. The default behavior of this new version of the browser when encountering a web server with a certificate that did not come from one of these preselected certificate vendors was to declare a security alert. This meant that the clients of any company who had invested in a certificate authority, rather than buying certificates from a company like Verisign, would receive a warning that the certificate was *untrusted*. The browsers did not have the performance capabilities to load everyone's certificate, and browser vendors simply provided instructions for individuals to import their website's certificates if they wanted to avoid the warnings. To add insult to injury, the certificate vendors periodically *expired* the certificates that they sold, claiming that it was impossible to tell if they had been compromised, so changing them periodically would prevent a thief from perpetual impersonation.

The alert caused internet users so much angst that the result was that most organizations that previously made their own keys had to pay others to make them, and then had to keep track of the date on which the purchased certificates expired, and repurchase before that day to avoid system failure. The client-side certificates could also be purchased, but due to major variances in customer desktops, these proved so difficult to use that they were abandoned by all but high-risk ecommerce financial companies (e.g., payroll service vendors).

The software rush to the internet marketplace in the mid-1990s heralded in a new era of ecommerce, a generic term for the exchange of goods and services using the internet as a medium. Software replaced the online catalogs and allowed internet users to purchase goods and execute financial transactions over the network. Vulnerabilities in software became the source of what was then called the "Port 80" problem. Port 80 is the port on a firewall that has to be open for external users to access web services. When traffic became encrypted with SSL, the port changed to 443, but many sites were slow to upgrade, and conference presenters still called it the Port 80 problem. Web application developers recognized this and knew how web server technology could be exploited to gain access to an internal network. Starting from port 80 on the internet, a web server program was designed to accept user commands instructing it to display content, but it would also allow commands instructing it to accept and execute programs provided by a user. What every web developer knew, every attacker also knew, and attackers using the port *authorized* for users accessed it *before* they were authenticated, including communications protocols enabled to load malware onto the web server and establish *command and control* (C&C) capabilities sufficient to penetrate the victim's internal network. The result of the widespread recognition of the Port 80 *incursion* events was that firewalls were installed, not just at the network periphery, but in a protective circle around any machine that faced the internet called a *Demilitarized Zone* (DMZ), a term borrowed from the military used to designate spaces between conflict borders where adversaries would perform joint operations like prisoner exchange. A DMZ was designed to contain any attacker access to an internet-facing web server to make it impossible to traverse to the internal network, except via expressly authenticated software methods originating from the internet-facing software. Though the software itself may not itself be impervious to vulnerabilities, the DMZ imposed network communication protocol guardrails that would limit unauthorized C&C commands from reaching internal systems. In a DMZ, all computers operating software accessible from the internet were *hardened* to ensure that no other services could be accessed from those explicitly allowed, or that were considered *sacrificial* systems that were purposely not well secured, but closely monitored to see if attackers were already inside an organization's systems (Ramachandran 2002). These sacrificial systems were modeled on a fake national security system that Stoll had used to lure espionage agents. They are also called *honeypots*, an analogy of the practice of trapping flies with honey, rather than actively swatting at them.

The design of a DMZ requires not only that all traffic from the internet be directed at only servers whose operating system is as hardened as technology allows, but also that in the DMZs, no traffic can pass between those operating systems and the internal network unless it has been configured in a firewall. It became standard procedure that the path to the internal network was opened only with the express approval of a security architect, who was responsible for testing the security controls on all DMZ and internally accessible software. This practice of security review prior to deployment matured into methods of integrating security review within the systems development lifecycle, and was christened *Systems Security Engineering* (SSE), creating a new cybersecurity career path that was highly technical. The process has since become internationally standard (ISO/IEC 2008; ISO/IEC 2023).

As organizations realized how hard this internet boundary was to police, it became apparent that the business application time-sharing services systems to which they were directly connected had also established markets in online services. The advent of the DMZ spawned recognition of information security risk managers that, when an organization outsources some of its data handling for the customer to a service provider, this entity is referred to by regulators as a "third party" to the transaction. For example, the commercial real estate owners using a timesharing service to bill their customers are the first party, the customer is the second party, and the time-sharing operator is a third party. This means that the boundary between their internal network and the internet was not only outside their internet-facing firewall, but on the other side of telecommunications lines that connected them to third-party service providers. These were connections that they had previously considered *trusted*, and now they had presented a new category of cybersecurity risks. Organizations hastily deployed firewalls on their side of the telecommunication lines to ensure all communication via that line was restricted to their server communication with a server specified by the third party, namely, a *point-to-point* connection.

Dealing with customers over the internet continued to be difficult to manage. Due to the dispersed nature of many sales organizations, customer relationship records had always been difficult to manage centrally, and now login credentials and email addresses had to be associated with customer records. Other than time-sharing vendors, organizations had rarely issued login credentials to anyone who was not in their own phone directory. Managing external users required specialized software. Cybersecurity vendors have accommodated with *identity and access management systems* (IAM), which were developed to ease the administration and integrate customer login information and online activity with existing customer relationship management processes. Integrated with *Single Sign On* (SSO) systems became a popular method of combining software services into a single portal for users to access.

At the time, LANs were propagating across remote locations, and even relatively small organizations might have hundreds of PCs and dozens of servers. To keep up with the virus threats, innovative cybersecurity vendors created network-level intrusion detection systems (IDSs) (Amoroso 1999). The idea behind IDS was the same as that behind footprint-based antivirus technology, but rather than compare the virus signatures to files that were deposited in a file system, they were compared to what viruses would look like as they traveled across the network. This level of virus-checking was also appealing because it provided more information about where on the Internet a virus had originated. Network IDSs could also identify attacker activity prior to it resulting in the installation of destructive software by looking for patterns of search activity commonly used by attackers conducting reconnaissance on a potential target. Another late 1990s innovation was *Tripwire* software. The generic use of the word tripwire now has the same connotation in software as its original use in physical security, a triggering mechanism (e.g., in physical security, a wire) that detects a change in the environment (Kim and Spafford 1994). Tripwire software detected and reported whenever there were changes to the file system. These file change detection mechanisms were also called *host intrusion detection systems* (HIDS) to differentiate them from the network kind.

Although the set of viruses to be checked by network IDS was the same as that compiled over the years by antivirus vendors, the way the antivirus software checked for the signatures on the desktop required different technology than the way it was checked on the network. Security managers began to notice that the end result was that some viruses were identified by some technologies and not others. Even vendors of the same technology widely differed in their ability to identify viruses, and had different levels of false positives, which is where software that was not actually a virus was mistakenly identified as such (McHugh 2000). Many companies created new departments called Security Operations Centers (SOCs) to weed through the output of these systems to try to determine the extent to which they may or may not be under attack.

By 1999, these technical configurations, such as firewall rule sets, anti-virus version specifications, wired and wireless encryption settings, tripwires' file listing, and operating system password length and expiration, were colloquially referred to as *security policies*. As more security devices, such as firewalls, proxy servers, and token servers, had to be replicated to keep up with the escalating scale of technology services, security departments established management servers from which to deploy technology configurations. Servers were established to keep track of which configuration variables were supposed to be on which device. If a device failed or was misconfigured, it would take too much work to recreate the policies. Because they were checking if the computers were compliant with information security policy, they were dubbed with the misnomer – *policy servers*.

Of course, cyberattacks continued, and malware often broke through security. In the course of an incident investigation, security devices were often found to be out of compliance with the technology configuration policy. Security managers would investigate the root cause of such incidents and often had to track down logs of user activity on multiple machines. These efforts were streamlined by the introduction of security information management (SIM) servers, which were designed to store and query massive numbers of activity logs. Queries were designed in advance for events that were captured by logs that might indicate that systems were under attack. A SIM server can also verify that logs were in fact retrieved from inventory, so it may serve a dual role for security managers: incident identification and policy compliance.

The point of the above description of the scramble for security features in the late 1990s is that every single one of these products were bolt-ons, and they all still exist in some form in organizations' networks. None of the software applications used by the people responsible for the organizational mission had the level of built-in security features required to withstand internet-borne cyberattacks.

They also did not prevent the exploitation of what cybersecurity professionals may refer to as *people bugs*, or *wetware*. In 1998, cybersecurity professionals routinely ridiculed Microsoft. One of them wrote a program called Back Orifice, a play on the name Microsoft had given to it business software: Back-Office. Back Orifice allowed a remote user to run any code they wanted remotely on Windows 95 and 98. Microsoft's reaction was: "This is not a tool we should take seriously, or our customers should take seriously" (Richtel 1998). In 1999, a programmer with motives of boasting and havoc launched a virus via a *pharming* attack, an analogy to planting seeds. He named his malware *Melissa* and posted the file on an America Online newsgroup dedicated to sex with a note that it had passwords for porn websites. Upon clicking the note, the file used a Microsoft Word *macro* (a coding language meant to be used to automate word-processing), the macro looked up the first 50 contacts in the victim's Microsoft Outlook address book and mailed out different versions of the virus to them, and so on. Email servers at over 300 organizations were overloaded and/or shut down, including those at Microsoft. Email was disrupted for approximately one million users, and the attack used so much bandwidth in some areas that internet traffic "slowed to a crawl" (FBI n.d.). Impact was estimated at $80 million worldwide. An AOL staff member tipped off the FBI, and the programmer was arrested and convicted. Soon after, the FBI created an internal Cyber Division to focus exclusively on cybercrime.

In the midst of this flurry of ongoing cyberattacks and security bolt-ons, but with more show of calm, the National Telecommunications and Information Administration (NTIA), an agency of the US DoC, began a process to create a sustainable governance model for the IANA functions and issued for comment a policy "Green Paper" entitled *A Proposal to Improve the Technical Management of Internet Names and Addresses*. The proposal was widely disseminated to encourage suggestions and comments (NTIA 1998). This process culminated in the creation of the Internet Corporation for Assigned Names and Numbers (ICANN), a not-for-profit partnership of people from all over the world dedicated to keeping the Internet *secure*, *stable*, and *interoperable*. The resulting ICANN model is a unique multi-stake-holder governance model for the centralized components of the internet, wherein governments participate alongside corporations and individual internet users to create the *policies that govern the internet* in a bottom-up fashion. For example, ICANN has policies and mechanisms to address domain squatting disputes; if the name is trademarked, the trademark owner is likely to be able to claim it. ICANN technically remained a US government contractor until the signing of the Affirmation of Commitments (AoC) in 2009, which transitioned ICANN from a contractor to a party to what is essentially a Memorandum of Understanding between the United States and ICANN about the principles of multistakeholder internet governance.

2.2.5 2000s

After seeing *Hackers*, the action-packed movie about kids and teens displaying their computing skills via cyberattacks in 1995, a 10-year-old decided to be one. He researched hacking groups, looking for one to join, and found an IRC channel where one such group hung out. After agonizing over naming his online persona, he decided to call himself Mafiaboy because his family and neighborhood were predominantly Italian. Mafiaboy pestered the owner of the channel until he was finally taken under his wing and taught how to write *exploit code* for the Linux operating system, which was the most common operating system used by the large research labs and universities that had the most powerful computers at the time. He was provided with software that scanned for specific vulnerabilities and obtained root access to vulnerable servers. He became very proficient at gaining

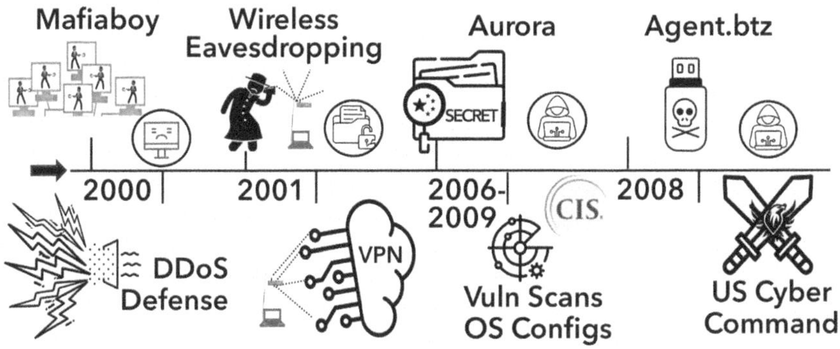

Timeline 4 2000s.

root access to servers and collected hundreds of them over a few years. He enjoyed exercising his newfound power by running programs simultaneously on hundreds of servers that made connections to other IRC channels and using up all of their bandwidth, limiting legitimate users' access to the channel. This type of attack was called a *Distributed Denial of Service* (DDoS) attack because there was not a single attack source; servers used in the attack were distributed, and the impact of the attack was that authorized users were deprived of the victim's technology service.

When in tenth grade, for the sole reason of bragging rights, Mafiaboy launched a DDoS attack at the website of Yahoo. He did not know if it was going to work as well as his attacks on the IRC systems, but it succeeded in disabling Yahoo's ability to provide service to its customers. Other members of his chat group speculated that Yahoo's site failed because it was small, and larger sites, such as CNN or Amazon, would likely survive his attack. So he pointed his DDoS software at those sites, which proved his chat group wrong. Speculating that these were not highly secure sites, Mafiaboy decided to target a site that was known for its security and pointed his DDoS software at E-Trade, which also failed to survive the attack. Mafiaboy had tried to evade detection by traversing multiple computers before scheduling the DDoS via the vulnerable system's job schedulers to run them while he was at school, but was eventually tracked down by the FBI due to his boasting. As an adult, Mafiaboy became a cybersecurity professional and wrote a memoir of his now-famous attack, illustrated in Figure 2.5.

Mafiaboy opened new avenues for the cybercrime market. As competitors became aware that rivals were growing their businesses and beating them in search results, competing sites attempted to stop the flow of ecommerce to competitors by hiring attackers with the skills of Mafiaboy to consume all the available bandwidth at the competitor's victim. To ensure their success, these attackers-for-hire were methodical in using multiple, geographically dispersed

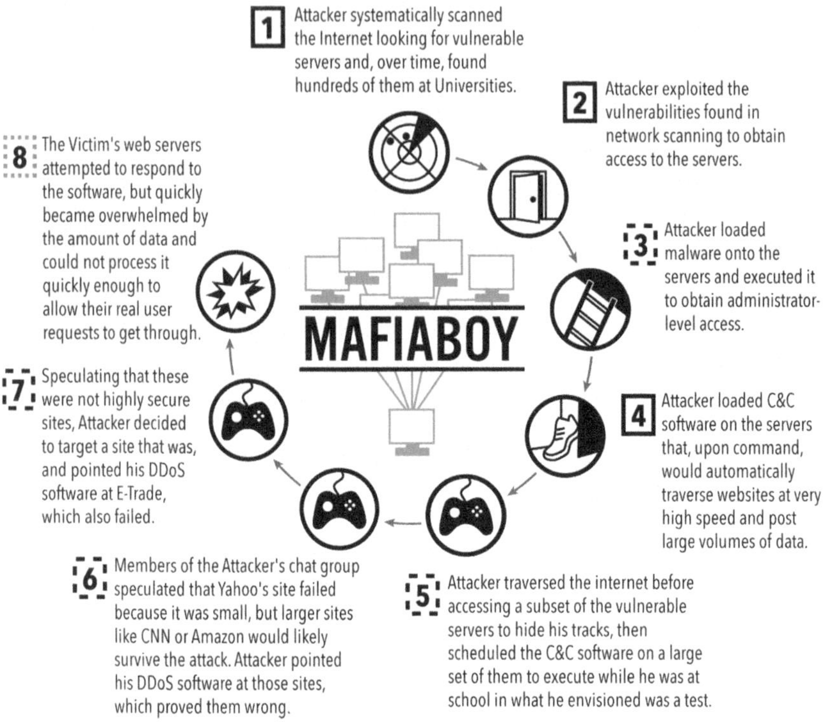

Figure 2.5 MafiaBoy 2000.

machines to execute an attack. At this time, there was no way to mitigate such attacks other than to increase the bandwidth allocated to internet services.

The primary method that Mafiaboy used to take over the computers he used in his attack was by exploiting operating system security weaknesses, such as default passwords and administrative utilities whose configurations expose weakly encrypted passwords. This prompted many organizations to standardize their operating system *security configurations*. A non-for-profit Center for Internet Security (CIS at cisecurity.org) was formed to bring together a community of concerned individuals in a variety of industries to jointly create methods for measurable security standards. CIS distributed system configurations called benchmarks (and still does) to help information security professionals worldwide securely configure their individual operating systems, applications, and networks. It has been creating cybersecurity quality benchmarks and detailed technical cybersecurity control standards ever since.

Cybersecurity vendors responded to the challenge with *DDoS protection services*. In the book *Fatal System Error*, Joseph Menn (2010) tells the story of entrepreneur Barrett Lyon, who founded one such company in 2003. His DDoS protection worked by taking over the internet domain of the victim, and sending any traffic that was sent there through dozens of high-speed routers that filtered out protocols used by DDoS, but not by the victim application, then sending that to as many servers as needed to filter out the remaining malicious traffic patterns, and redirecting the remainder of the traffic to the real victim website. Unfortunately, some of his customers were online casinos launching DDoS attacks at each other during Super Bowl games to be the only ones open for business, and some of them relied on organized crime to conduct their attacks. Moreover, some of the attackers were Russian extortionists who demanded ransom from the victims and did not get it when Lyon came to their aid. He tried to lay low and work with law enforcement, who eventually caught the extortion ring, then sold the company.

The early 2000s were a time of great innovation. Pocket-sized cell phones' features that required the internet became the new normal, and to facilitate internet access in open spaces and within conference rooms and hotel lobbies, wireless networks popped up everywhere. These early wireless networks had little to no security. They advertised their Service Set Identifier (SSID), so it was displayed to users within range, and a user selected it to connect. Organizations that wanted to keep their wireless traffic private tuned its signalling power to stay within their building or grounds. However, it was subject to eavesdropping just as the wired networks were before SSL, and eventually a standard called Wired Equivalent Privacy (WEP) protocol was developed by the Institute of Electrical and Electronics Engineers to make it difficult for the average attacker to listen in, though more sophisticated attackers could easily break its encryption. However, like the demand for connectivity by traveling users in the mid-1990s, demand for wireless connectivity became irrepressible in the early 2000s. VPNs and handheld tokens were commonly among the technologies enlisted to maintain confidentiality of those communications, though they were not widely used for wireless access control until researchers demonstrated how easily native wireless security features were broken (Chatzinotas et al. 2008). Over the decades since, IEEE has continually improved wireless security standards with ever more sophisticated cybersecurity features (IEEE n.d.).

While infrastructure security standards continuously improved, there had been little to no attempts to do the same for software security. Still, hackers are finding holes in the network periphery to exploit, and they were in vulnerable web servers. The network control of the DMZ does not prevent a web software developer from deploying code that can be used to imitate any network activity that is allowed by the web server itself; it simply limits the damage to the internet-facing software application and the organizational process it supports. This scope can, of course, include access to sensitive customer data because the web services were fast becoming the way the customer accessed their sensitive data stored by the organization. The software security situation was getting worse.

Since the dawn of programming, developers have shared their code for the sake of efficiency. Shared code libraries have always been common, with various participants in the development group contributing. In the late 1990s, a group of developers on a mission to improve source code integrity holistically (by putting as many eyes as possible on it) had created the Open Source Initiative (OSI) (2025). They called their software open source to distinguish it from the free software that some organizations allowed anyone to download it, though they kept the source code private. The mission of OSI was to be an educational, advocacy, and stewardship organization. Developers worldwide immediately started creating and sharing open source repositories to augment internal efforts. In starting a new project, they typically will try to reuse as much existing code as possible to minimize the amount of effort required to build new functionality. Much of this code has known security bugs and flaws.

In recognition of this concern, a community of developers began an email list in 2001 that evolved into a not-for-profit volunteer organization called the Open Worldwide Application Security Project (OWASP). OWASP's major contribution to the cause of software security is its Application Security Verification Standard Project (OWASP 2025). The goal of the project is to normalize the range of coverage and level of rigor in the performance of Web application security verification. The project produced a standard that was used by cybersecurity vendors to scan application source code for compliance with its requirements and report on the result in a checklist-like manner. Those that scan the written code are called Static Application Security Testing (SAST), and those that scan running programs are called Dynamic Application Security Testing (DAST). These products scan code and provide developers with a to-fix list that can also be used as a metric of their security performance. The OWASP standard also addresses technical security controls required to secure the web server environment within which developer code operates, such as Apache's open source web server. In an attempt to educate software developers about cybersecurity bugs and design flaws, the project also produces guidance for building secure code. This standard can be used to establish a level of confidence in the security of Web applications.

Unfortunately, the fruits of OWASP were often ignored, and the advent of open source exacerbated the issues in that the programmers continued to cut and paste the same security bugs into their code so often that cyberdefenders again turned to vendors looking for a bolt-on. Vendors who took up the challenge and produced what they called web access firewalls (WAF). Like a DDoS protection service, a WAF takes on the domain name of the organization's web servers, and it checks incoming traffic for patterns of attacker attempts to exploit the very well-known weaknesses in the open source code. For example, the presence of database commands in any input field. One of the most common vulnerabilities is a lack of input validation. One of the most common corresponding attacks uses scripts that include database instructions written in Structured Query Language (SQL). It is called *SQL-injection* because an attacker will choose a field that does not have a need for matching a business use, for example, first name, and inject a program that uses SQL to list the tables in the webserver's default database directly into a file in a directory where static webpages are internally stored and easily displayed.

The web application ingests the content of the field and runs its own script meant to extract the first name, but instead, the attacker's script is merged into its own, so it executes, allowing public display of the newly created table list file. The attacker writes another script to take all of the data out of the tables in the list; the second script dumps sensitive data into the file for easy exfiltration (Thompson and Chase 2005, Ch. 21). No normal user would think to put a database command in a field meant for a first name, so WAF input validation filters generally succeed in blocking attacker traffic without any negative impact to real users. However, like virus signatures, the patterns need constant updating to stay ahead of attacker tools and techniques.

The technical term for a server that accepts network traffic meant for another is called a proxy server. A WAF is an example of a proxy server. Another type of web proxy technology that turned up in the early 2000s intercepted outbound web traffic, and its purpose was to prevent users from sending sensitive information outside the organization via email or web uploads. In addition to installing antivirus software and patches on workstations, organizations also enlisted security software vendors to track the spread of viruses on websites, so they could block their users from accessing websites that hosted viruses, thereby reducing the propagation of viruses on their internal networks. Web proxy servers work by intercepting all user traffic headed for the internet, comparing the content of the communication to a set of communication rules established by an organization, and not letting the intercepted traffic proceed if there is a conflict between the traffic and the rules. The proxy is enforced because browser traffic is not allowed outbound through the network periphery by the firewalls unless it comes from the proxy server, so users must traverse the proxy service to browse. Vendors quickly established businesses to hunt down and sell lists of malicious software sites.

In the early 2000s, websites were fraught with risk of fraud and threats to confidentiality because of the sheer number of vulnerable devices that suddenly gained unfettered access to customer information, including credit card numbers. A book of the same name about the hazards of the internet fraud impacting individuals during this period used Mafiaboy as an example of a *Zero Day Threat*. The vulnerabilities Mafiaboy found in university and research systems were security bugs and flaws in software with which the adversary is very familiar, but of which victims are not yet aware. From the perspective of the general public, no one knows about it until it is used in an attack, which is the reference to *zero* in *zero day*, and described in the book's subtitle, "a hazard so new that no viable protection against it yet exists" (Acohido and Swartz 2008).

In 2002, a new market emerged for these zero-day software vulnerabilities. A company named iDefense was in the business of researching publicly known vulnerabilities, warning their customers about them, and telling them how to fix them (Perlroth 2021, Ch. 3). They did research mainly on an email distribution list called Bugtraq that received hundreds of posts a day about vulnerabilities, methods of exploits, workarounds, and patches. However, the company hosting the site was being sold to another cybersecurity vendor. Email distribution lists like that were moderated for quality content, and iDefense was concerned about the viability of its future if there was any change in the way that Bugtraq was moderated. One of his employees suggested that they advertise for vulnerabilities and pay people to report them to iDefense directly. A legitimate market in software vulnerabilities was born.

iDefense announced its strategy to purchase vulnerabilities, work with vendors on patches and workarounds for their clients, and only when the patches were available would they report them publicly, so others would know to take advantage of the patches. Nevertheless, some software vendors were outraged and called iDefense's CEO unethical. Unbeknownst to those vendors, there was already a well-established black market in vulnerabilities where the customers were nation-state intelligence agencies. At that time, everyone who was involved in the zero-day vulnerability black market lived by its rules. As a New York Times investigative reporter put it years later: "The first rule of the zero day market was: Nobody talks about the zero day market. The second rule of the zero day market was: Nobody talks about the zero day market." (Perlroth 2021, p. 15).

Cybersecurity professionals, such as those working at iDefense, assumed that vendors should be told when vulnerabilities are found in their products and should fix them, and did not understand vendors' outrage when other vulnerabilities were found in their software. In their judgment, the vendors were negligent for delivering insecure software and should be grateful for learning about their zero-day before it went public. Over time, different methods of disclosure were developed and debated. For example:

- *Private Disclosure:* Report the vulnerability only to the organization that owns the software. Some vendors established *bug bounty* programs that provide cash rewards to security researchers following this model. However, where no such program exists, the vendor is free to ignore the report, which makes reporting a waste of time.
- *Full Disclosure:* Publicly report the vulnerability as soon as it is identified. Attackers see it at the same time as the vendor, making it too late for victims to protect themselves.

- *Responsible* or *Coordinated Disclosure:* Report the vulnerability first to the organization that owns the software, and publicly report the vulnerability after a patch has been made available to the potential victims.
- *Uncoordinated Disclosure:* Report the vulnerability first to the organization that owns the software and publicly report the vulnerability after a period of time, wherein it is "reasonable" to expect that the vendor should make a patch available to the potential victims (OWASP n.d.).

What was, and still is, more concerning than zero-day attacks is the sheer volume of known *exploitable* (as opposed to *exploited*) vulnerabilities that have been reported from the zero-day marketplace that have been patched, but perhaps because the exploit is not currently visible on the technology manager's horizon, patches for the former zero-day do not appear to be a priority. Technology was changing so fast it was becoming quite a chore for Security Operations (*SecOps*) departments to track the installation of desktops and laptops not to mention be assured they all had the latest antivirus signatures on them. Software vulnerability patches were then, and still are, only applied by the software development community, who have their own criteria for assessing the necessity of patching.

Throughout the 2000s, worms and viruses continued to haunt. As Ed Amoroso described in his history of SQL Slammer (Amoroso 2010, pp. 159–161), adversary activity is often evident on the internet for months before successful attacks, and such observations may, over time, provide cybersecurity professionals with valuable information on where to place security resources. In early January 2003, the CISO of AT&T at the time, Ed Amoroso, was in AT&T's SOC surrounded by screens showing all aspects of network activity. He noticed a small spike in User Datagram Protocol (UDP) traffic on a port used by Microsoft's SQL server: 1434, which he took for someone's coding mistake because SQL servers communicate using a different protocol. On January 25, UDP traffic on port 1343 on the internet skyrocketed. The previous October, a database security expert had presented a talk on the vulnerability at a cybersecurity conference focused on vulnerabilities and attacks that included his discovery that Microsoft SQL Servers used the UDP protocol that the servers used to *resolve* domain names (i.e., find their IP addresses) (Menn 2010, pp. 111–112). The expert had warned Microsoft and requested permission to use this example in his conference talk. Microsoft patched the vulnerability six months before the conference. After the conference, he posted proof-of-concept code on the internet for the exploit. The attack exploited a buffer overflow in the SQL server, allowing it to replicate itself to randomly generated IP addresses, then crashed the database server on which it was running. Each individual server could be restored in minutes, but the volume of network traffic was immense. It hit approximately 75,000 servers in its first 10 minutes, and internet traffic routing was severely impacted globally. The antidote was the patch that was six months old.

The propagation of worms led savvy cybersecurity vendors to adapt their network intrusion detection technology to, in addition to identifying the malware bound for a user to instead sever the network connection of the malware source. These provided SecOps with configurable automation for incident response, but to accomplish it, SecOps had to replace all of their IDSs with *Intrusion Prevention Systems*, which attempted to identify inbound malware before users could be exposed to it. These developments created new jobs for the InfoSec groups, making sure that their automated tools steer clear of authorized business processes. Security administration functions had by then become full-fledged operational processes. Moreover, user security awareness training to avoid phishing and pharming became a hot topic in organizational technology committees.

In the mid-2000s, cybersecurity attack victims were unintended side effects of the ecommerce race to participate in new markets. Ecommerce transactions flow between the shopper, the shopper's computer, the network connection between the shopper and ecommerce web server, the ecommerce web server, and ecommerce vendor's internal network, and the connections between the ecommerce vendor and the service providers they need to close the transaction, such as a credit card payment clearing company. All of these connections are created using software, and any of that software may have a bug or a flaw that allows an intruder to observe cyber user data flow or disrupt the ecommerce transaction. In many of these points of connectivity observation of data flow provides information that may be used for later attacks, such as observation of usernames and passwords being used for impersonation and identity theft. From a security perspective, there are four major players in the ecommerce environment: the customer; the retailer; the product vendor, wholesaler, or manufacturer; and the attacker. It is the attacker's goal to exploit one or more of the three other players for illegal gains. Using vulnerabilities in software, application configurations, hardware, and even user habits, an attacker will seek to exploit these vulnerabilities to the attacker's advantage. Ecommerce attacks are constantly occurring.

However, major media reporting on cybersecurity issues was confined to high-profile issues (e.g., SQL Slammer). Only the most interesting cases of fraud with the most severe consequences for the victims ever make it to the front page of the newspaper. Nevertheless, there was as much day-to-day activity in the cybercrime circuit as there is in the drug circuit. The Zero Day Threat reporters described the phenomenon as the product of three archetypes: exploiters; enablers; and expeditors (Acohido and Swartz 2008). Exploiters carry out data theft and fraud. Enablers are businesses whose practices allow it. Expeditors are technologists who identify the root cause from a technical point of view, though they may be attackers or defenders. The book is full of vignettes about organized crime "exploiters" systematically stealing data from unwitting victims by impersonating the consumer at "enabler" banks. The exploiters not only exploit the consumer (e.g., an identity theft victim) but also exploit low-level criminals. They enlist the petty criminals to withdraw unwitting consumers' cash out of automatic teller machines or to order luxuries on the unwitting consumers' credit cards. The stories sporadically include tales of victories of law enforcement "expeditors" who figure out how the exploiters did it. The moral of every sad story is that the enabler did not sufficiently protect data within its custody, while an evil genius controlling three or more layers of organized criminal structure above the petty criminal is never actually caught. The victim is left with damaged credit, as well as loss of time and money, while the enabler is satisfied that "adequate" risk measures are in place to secure their organization. Ecommerce businesses that rely on advertising typically utilize *mash-ups* to integrate multiple software sources (e.g., maps and coupons) onto a single page. The common element is that they are designed to attract consumers in a desired demographic, the advertising *target*. One method of reaching the target is to identify web pages frequented by the target and purchase ads directly on those web pages. The web page owner/seller may require that the ad be provided to them for placement, or they could simply link to a site provider by the ad buyer and direct the user's browser to access the buyer's web content directly. This easy access to the internet consumer has attracted criminals seeking to install malware. Like any ad buyer, they purchase internet advertising from media networks and exchanges. Malware is easy to distribute because numerous websites require internet users to accept a wide variety of browser add-ins to operate, and advertising software frequently continues to run in the background and connect back to the source site to send user tracking information. Malware does the same thing and thus appears to the user like any other nuisance advertising process running on their computer. It is often used to install C&C software that will *phone home*, an analogy to the movie *E.T.* Malware that allows a computer to be remotely administered by the malware operator is referred to as a *bot*, which is short for *robot*. The correct interpretation of the analogy is that the person who unwittingly installed a bot on their computer has turned their computer into an instrument for the criminal operator. Multiple instances of bots administered by the same malware operator are called *botnets*. Criminals use botnets as squadrons of soldiers in cyberattacks. Cybercriminals are known to purchase online advertising on otherwise legitimate websites and use it to download malware, often making the user's computer a controllable bot. This is called *malvertising*, an anagram of the words *malicious* and *advertising*. Because ads have a similar negative performance impact on their computers, consumers rarely notice the difference.

The mid-2000s saw a dramatic increase in organized crime on the internet, and identity theft was rampant (Acohido and Swartz 2008). There were also many highly publicized incidents of lost laptops and backup tapes that contained large quantities of the type of PII used to commit identity theft. This raised awareness of the habits of remote users, who frequently kept such data on the laptops that they took with them on travel, and also used removable media such as USB devices to carry data with them between home and work. While some of the technologies had been configured with the threat of device theft or loss in mind (e.g., smartphones containing software and data programmed to destroy all data if a user enters too many inaccurate passwords), many had never even been the subject of a security review. Vendors hastily provided methods to encrypt laptop disks and USB devices. Companies adopted standards and procedures for the authorized use of digital media and restricted access to the devices. It is hard to purchase laptops without these USB ports and DVD writers. Security software to control them can be very intrusive, expensive, and hard to monitor. Therefore, it is not uncommon to see security staff adopt tactical measures, such as applying crazy glue to USB ports and removing DVD writers from laptops before they are delivered to users.

Theft of storage devices extended even into the data center. So many devices were being encrypted that it became difficult for administrators to keep up with procedures to safeguard encryption keys. Simple key management systems, such as password-protected key databases, had been around since the 1990s, but the rate at which the keys needed to be produced to perform technology operating tasks, such as recovering a deleted file, was rapidly increasing. Security vendors stepped in with automated key storage and retrieval systems. Often, keys are stored on special hardware chips physically protected in isolated locations and accessible only by the equipment used to control access to the devices. This way, if the device was stolen without the hardware chip, the storage media itself could not be decrypted. Unfortunately, it became so hard for users to get the data they needed to their home PCs that they would email it to themselves to bypass the controls on removable media.

There had been no evolution in email security since the Morris Worm, only patches for known vulnerabilities. Even today, the protocols by which servers communicate and share information are not encrypted without very specialized agreements on both sides of the communication. Email is easy to observe with network equipment and is routinely routed via multiple ISPs before landing at its destination. Although there have been some attempts to identify authorized email servers via certificate-like keys, they are often ignored for fear of blocking legitimate email users by accident. Email security vendors created software to assist in the analysis of email content, and many companies that suspected that PII was being sent via email for work-at-home purposes thereby found that many of their business processes routinely emailed sensitive data to customers or service providers. Even those with policies against sending PII in email sometimes had customers who demanded that their reports be delivered via email and were willing to accept the risk of identity theft for the convenience of receiving reports via email. Internal users would bow to customer wishes and ignore security policy. Although this risk acceptance was acceptable in some industries, in others, regulatory requirements prevented its continuation.

The cybersecurity technology response to this issue was a combination of encryption and content filtering. Encryption was used to communicate with business partners online, either through individuals exchanging keys or by adopting a point-to-point encryption protocol directly between their email servers. Patterns were created for identifying sensitive information. These included generalized social security numbers and tax identification numbers from other countries. They also included snippets common in internally developed company software, and "internal use only" stamps hidden in proprietary documents. All information sent by users to the internet, or other publicly accessible networks, is routed through a device that either blocks the information from leaving or silently alerts security staff, who investigate the internal user. Frequent or blatant offenders are often subject to employment or contract termination.

While organizations and individuals dealt mostly with cybercriminals in the 1990s, the public sector was facing nation-state adversaries. In 2001, driven by fears of security consequences of US-China trade imbalances, Congress created the US-China Economic and Security Review Commission (USCC) to monitor and investigate the national security implications of the bilateral trade and economic relationship with China. Its first annual report observed that it was clearly a goal for China to quickly close the gap between the United States and its own capabilities in technology warfare (USCC 2002, pp. 186).

Throughout the next two decades, the USCC tracked Chinese Intelligence forces' espionage and intellectual property theft targeted at US Federal Agencies and private companies. They routinely exfiltrated technology specifications, software source code, and other intellectual property for their goals (Hambling 2009). NASA was a primary victim of these attacks. Impact on NASA included a satellite diverted off course, supercomputers being physically unplugged from the network, and theft of data on rocket engine design, space shuttle operations, and financial planning. The activity was linked to network addresses in Taiwan and China. Yet there was no viable remediation activity. Like the technology vendor outraged at their vulnerabilities being published, their reaction was outrage, and there was evidence that NASA officials retaliated against those who reported the events (Epstein and Elgin 2008). To understand the impact of this complacency among the victims requires acknowledging that it advanced China's strategy, which was specifically designed to foster such complacency. China played on US organizations' inherent aversion to bad news to fly under the cybersecurity radar.

In 2007, the US military coined the term Advanced Persistent Threat (APT) to describe threat actors like China that were high-skilled, relentless, and patient (Mandiant 2013). China's 2nd Bureau of the People's Liberation Army (PLA) General Staff Department's (GSD) 3rd Department, commonly known by its

Military Unit Cover Designator (MUCD) as Unit 61 398, was the first threat actor to be christened an APT, and cybersecurity professionals know it as APT1.

In 2009, Google had what appeared to be a successful joint venture with China focused on search services. The Chinese demanded restrictions on search results to allow censorship and Google accommodated. With hindsight, like NASA, Google also had a tendency to hide from news of its vulnerability (Perlroth 2021, Ch. 5). In December of 2009, Google's cybersecurity staff upgraded their cybersecurity monitoring capability to detect anomalous activity on internal networks. They were immediately alerted to evidence that hundreds of their devices were infected with malware, Gmail accounts had been hijacked, and source code exfiltrated (Perlroth 2021, Ch. 14). Within a month, Google had attributed these activities to Chinese espionage agents. There were rumors that, in a brash effort to eject the attackers, Google decommissioned all of its Microsoft PCs and made their staff switch to Apple Macintosh. It made a public statement that it was closing its Chinese internet search service and rerouting its China-based search traffic to its uncensored service in Hong Kong (Helft and Barboza 2010).

In January, Google reported that a large amount of proprietary information had been stolen in an attack that appeared to originate in China. Further investigation soon revealed that dozens of US technology companies had been similarly treated by China and had their intellectual property stolen via computer intrusions. Cybersecurity investigations revealed that internally, China had named the attack *Operation Aurora*. The specific attribution of Operation Aurora did not refer to APT1; nevertheless, the USCC noted that the attackers "operate with the tacit knowledge of the Chinese government and may even involve full government support" (USCC 2010, pp. 15). Hence, we consider the patterns attributed to APT1 to be part of the Aurora umbrella.

Figure 2.6 provides a closer look at the attack's generic approach. The operation steps are similar to those of any other organized cybercrime syndicate. It started with target selection and reconnaissance. Attackers frequented social network sites to become familiar with the browsing habits of employees at targeted firms and, in a variant of pharming, planted ads or posts on those watering hole sites that delivered malware via common flaws in desktop software. If a target did not click on links planted on a watering hole, the attacker would adapt and use the profile information available at the watering hole to customize and send a phishing email instead. A victim that clicked on a link would be subverted to install malware that checks back to an attacker's site for further commands to execute on the victim's computer. This C&C activity was used by the attacker to run scripts and scans to discover whether it was possible to escalate privileges, harvest credentials, and/or move laterally through the network in search of technology-related intellectual property. These were exfiltrated back to the attacker for further analysis. Where possible, the attacker also created vulnerabilities in the network periphery to

Figure 2.6 Aurora 2006–2009.

ensure it couldn't return to the internal network if the C&C installation and operation became disabled for any reason (e.g., creating generic accounts that look like they must be used to run unattended software processes).

A key element of the attacker's analysis to support further discovery in the process was to identify unused and unmonitored storage devices to be used for collecting data to be stored. The attacker compressed the data so the files to be exfiltrated would be as small as possible and named them to blend into the normal traffic patterns in the environment. The attacker used the same methods used by the victim's daily operational processes to transfer files to sites that looked familiar within the victim's outbound network traffic patterns, and from there delivered them back to their own servers.

If there is a difference between Aurora and pure for-profit cybercrime, it is the length of time spent in the attack, the degree of stealth employed to evade defenses, and the severity of the impact. While a for-profit cybercriminal will likely find as much intellectual property as quickly as possible and get out before getting caught, Aurora takes advantage of its nest like the cuckoo's egg. While a for-profit cybercriminal will sell the intellectual property quickly, Aurora will amass as much information about the processes by which it is manufactured, tested, deployed, operated, and maintained with the goal of becoming a superior competitor.

When cyber attackers bond over similar *political* or *ethical* causes, industry analysts like MITRE would typically describe these threat actors as *hacktivists*. When the first edition of this book was published, most hacktivist attacks were directed at corporations negatively impacting the environment or wildlife, as when business partners of pharmaceutical firms were targeted by an animal rights group because the firms conducted product safety tests using animals (Kocieniewski 2006). However, we did note that, where the target of cyber sabotage is a nation-state, hacktivists and nation-state military cyberwarriors may be indistinguishable. During a DDoS attack against the country of Estonia in 2007, so-called "hacktivists" supposedly rallied to the cause and volunteered their computers to be included in the attack, thereby increasing the strength of botnets used to subvert Estonia's ecommerce (Clarke and Knake 2010). In this case, ecommerce in Estonia was shut down for a week, and although many "hacktivists" were reported to be joining the attack for patriotic reasons, no nation-state took responsibility for the overall effort. In this case, ecommerce was the only target, but nation-state threats aiming to exploit cyberspace vulnerabilities may target any component of the national infrastructure, including, but not limited to, the operation of ICSs, the integrity of banking transactions, or the readiness of military equipment.

Reflecting on the Estonia attack, there is a disturbing parallel between the way it was reported then and a 2025 alert issued by the US Department of Homeland Security's (DHS) Cybersecurity and Infrastructure Security Agency (CISA), that pro-Russian "hacktivists" were targeting the US Department of Energy, the US Environmental Protection Agency, the US DoD Cyber Crime Center, the Europol European Cybercrime Centre, the European Union Agency for Criminal Justice Cooperation, the Australian Signals Directorate's Australian Cyber Security Centre, the Canadian Centre for Cyber Security, the Canadian Security Intelligence Service, the Czech Republic Military Intelligence, the Czech Republic

National Cyber and Information Security Agency, the Czech Republic National Centre Against Terrorism, Extremism, and Cyber Crime, the French National Cybercrime Unit, the French National Jurisdiction for the Fight Against Organized Crime, the German Federal Office for Information Security, the Italian State Police, the Latvian State Police, the Lithuanian Criminal Police Bureau, the New Zealand National Cyber Security Centre, the Romanian National Police, the Spanish Civil Guard, the Spanish National Police, the Swedish Polisen, and the United Kingdom National Cyber Security Centre. No not-for-profit agency created for the purpose of influencing their agenda has the capacity to target so many nation-state targets simultaneously (CISA 2025). The term hacktivist has officially become a false analogy with the nation-state.

Equally disturbing, 2007 also saw the first successful remote cyberattack on ICSs. Though it was a test, it was a harbinger of things to come. It was a proof-of-concept experiment conducted by a former chief security officer at American Electric Power who had joined the FFRDC aligned with the Department of Energy, Idaho National Laboratory. When a power industry security officer had worried about the potential of cybersecurity-manipulated input that could cause physical damage to an ICS, he brought this concern with him to the lab. He designed an experiment wherein a remote network connection was exploited to command its protective relays, ironically, devices that monitor for abnormal conditions and automatically trigger a circuit breaker for safety reasons, instead of rapidly opening and closing circuit breakers out of synchronism. The system started smoking, and its engine was beyond repair (Greenberg 2020).

In an unrelated cyber-physical combination attack in 2008, the US DoD suffered a significant compromise of its classified military computer networks. It began with a foreign intelligence service customizing a worm that was highly effective at replicating itself to and from USB drives to scan for military sensitive information. The attacker then loaded the resulting malware named *Agent.btz* onto a USB drive that was subsequently inserted into a US military laptop at a base in the Middle East. The Agent.btz worm was installed via an autorun feature that automatically executed USB drive content. The program scanned for sensitive military information and collected it (Miller 2022). It copied itself into computers and any USB drives that were connected to them, unbeknownst to the person using the USB drive for authorized purposes. The military network was isolated from the internet, but the USBs people put in their pockets could have been used anywhere else in cyberspace. After the cleanup began, the worm would often be found on a formerly cleaned computer. The cleanup took 14 months from the time of detection. The government's top cybersecurity experts were unable to directly attribute it to a specific source.

The experience led directly to the creation of a new Unified Combat Command for Cybersecurity, namely, the US Cyber Command (Lynn 2010). The command has three missions: leading day-to-day protection of all military defense networks while supporting terrorism missions with operations in cyberspace; providing an accountable method to marshal cyberwarfare resources from military; and to be the liaison for a variety of partners inside and outside the US government (e.g., the US DHS, the Justice Department, and the Defense Information Systems Agency) and private industry when needed to safeguard national interests.

2.2.6 2010s

USCC Annual Reports in this decade continued to highlight China's incursion into US technology-specific intellectual property. One of the more insidious was the breach of the multi-factor authentication vendor, RSA. A staff member in Australia had received an email with the subject line "2011 Recruitment plan" and an Excel spreadsheet attached to it. Opening the Excel file executed an exploit of a zero-day in Adobe Flash and installed malware called Poison Ivy on the victim's machine (Greenberg 2021). The malware searched the computer's memory for user names and passwords, and when found, used them to log in to other machines, fanning out through the network. RSA's SecOps team detected anomalous activity within days and attempted to disrupt it by shutting down systems, but the logins would reappear elsewhere on the network.

As in most handheld authentication devices, their security was based on the fact that the only individual who had the encryption key stored on their device was the user it was intended to authenticate. The attacker eventually found the method by which that key was created and exported to be delivered to the hand-held device. RSA had stored the encryption keys on servers within an isolated network, which also contained the servers that generated the keys. Moreover, the same network was used to archive the keys that had already been distributed "just in case" the customers lost them. But there was one server that was connected to that network as well as to the internal network, something technologists refer to as a *jump server* because its primary use is to allow a process to jump from one network into an isolated one. It is supposed to interrupt anyone from getting to the isolated network. Ironically, that server did not have multi-factor authentication, and the attacker was able to log in to it and steal the keys. At that point, RSA severed all external network connectivity, but it was too late. Internally, RSA called their recovery project Apollo 13, as their CEO rallied the troops to: "land the ship with out injury." The fact that they are still in business means they were successful to that extent.

It soon came to light that the RSA customer keys had been stolen and could be used to create exploits that would allow customer accounts to be taken over by attackers. The RSA attack resulted in large-scale cyberattacks against their customers, including the DoD contractors, including Lockheed Martin

Timeline 5 2010s.

and Northrup Grumman, enabled by the RSA incursion (Drew 2011). When Lockheed Martin was attacked, it monitored the hack activity and shut down attempts to exploit their RSA-protected portals, then published the effectiveness of their intrusion detection and response procedures. Under the heading of "Swift, Deliberate Response Thwarts IT Breach," Lockheed confirmed a "significant and tenacious" attack on its network on May 21, 2011 (Drew 2011). In contrast, on May 26, 2011, Northrup Grumman abruptly shut down remote access to its network, which was seen as a response to the potential breach. Northrup also immediately replaced their RSA authentication technology with one that was verifiably resistant to the attack. The Lockheed policy decision in favor of *detect* over *protect* in times of crisis, in comparison with the Northrop decision to *focus on protect*, created significant concern within the Lockheed customer base. Although Lockheed may indeed have been correct in its confidence, perhaps unbeknownst to its public relations arm, within the cybersecurity community, hubris is not a respected approach to breach mitigation, which tends to err on the side of caution.

2011 was also the year of the DigiNotar, one of the certificate authorities that all browsers "trusted" to verify the server to which they were connecting was operated by the organization that registered its domain name. Investigators found evidence that the Windows Remote Desktop Protocol (RDP) was *tunneled* underneath TLS and auditing was turned off on DigiNotar's systems to evade detection (Hein 2013). The attackers escalated privilege to access the server that produced certificates and began attempts to use it to create their own certificates. It took them eight days to figure it out. They minted over 500 certificates that bore domain names of popular internet communication sites, such as Gmail and Facebook. Attackers installed scripts for uploading and downloading files that were found after the attack. In surveillance operations attributed to Iran, these certificates were used to create fake sites to steal credentials from at least, but not limited to Google (including Gmail and Android), Skype, Microsoft, Facebook, Twitter, Yahoo, WordPress, AOL, and the Tor Project, which until then had historically been a relatively safe place for dissidents to communicate. The browser vendors pulled DigiNotar's root certificates from their installations and hoped it would not happen again.

In 2013, Edward Snowden, a former tech-savvy National Security Agency (NSA) security guard who had drifted into US federal cybersecurity roles, became concerned about the invasions of privacy in violation of the law that he witnessed while working at the NSA. He changed jobs to obtain wider access to the information, and strategically leaked classified NSA documents to journalists who worked with news organizations like *The Guardian* and *The Washington Post*. His first leak was to *The Guardian*:

> June 6, 2013: The National Security Agency is currently collecting the telephone records of millions of US customers of Verizon, one of America's largest telecom providers, under a top secret order issued in April. The order, a copy of which has been obtained by the Guardian, requires Verizon, on an "ongoing, daily basis" to give the NSA information on all telephone calls to its systems, both within the US and between the US and other countries
>
> (Greenwald 2013).

In a 120-point bullet list, *Business Insider* later summarized the depth and breadth of evidence within subsequent Snowden leaks that revealed both NSA cybersecurity adversarial activities and individual privacy violations (Szoldra 2016). Though the purchase of zero days from hackers was not called out in the *Business Insider* list, it did include evidence of the purchase of a zero day provided by a trusted vendor (RSA) within its own software:

> December 20, 2013: The NSA had paid RSA $10 M to put a security vulnerability to implement a "back door" into its encryption.

This was a clue that signified the value that the NSA placed on a vulnerability collection to which a later leak alluded:

> March 12, 2014: NSA developed sophisticated malware "implants" to infect millions of computers worldwide. In one example, the NSA posed as a fake Facebook server to infect a target's computer and steal files.

Five other Snowden leak descriptions within the list of 120 help paint the picture of NSA hoarding zero days, writing exploits, and using them for targeted espionage, as well as unauthorized surveillance:

> August 9, 2013: An internal NSA document reveals an agency "loophole" that shows a secret backdoor for the agency to search its databases for US citizens' email and phone calls without a warrant.
>
> August 29, 2013: The top-secret intelligence "black budget" is revealed for 2013, with 16 spy agencies having a budget of $52.6 billion.
>
> September 7, 2013: The NSA has the ability to access user data for most major smartphones on the market, including Apple iPhones, Blackberries, and Google Android phones.
>
> November 1, 2013: One document reveals that tech companies play a key role in NSA intelligence reports and data collection.
>
> November 23, 2013: The NSA infected more than 50,000 computer networks worldwide with malware designed to steal sensitive information (Szoldra 2016).

Snowden of course knew he had broken the first two rules of the zero-day market and sought and received asylum in Russia to escape US prosecution.

Though the zero day vulnerability market was viewed as a necessary element of nation-state espionage, day-to-day cybercrime activity during this time was satisfied with the years-old Microsoft exploits. CryptoLocker, the first ransomware to be spread by botnet and social engineering, demonstrated how easily ransomware could spread and take over the Microsoft operating system (Cybersecurity and Infrastructure Security Agency 2013). It was opportunistic in that it was propagated through email attachments that were spread through an existing botnet that had been previously created by Russian nation-state threat actors, propagating a rapid spread across the internet. In December 2013, it was reported that the group behind CryptoLocker had made over $20 million in Bitcoin (CryptoLocker 2026). However, there were also a significant number of complaints that, after paying off the ransom, victims were not provided with decryption keys to get their data back. This situation made it less obvious that a decision to pay ransom in future attacks would see its rewards. Though cybersecurity professionals had known for decades that organizations and individuals did not have to possess something worth stealing to be included in a cyberattack campaign, this was becoming more obvious to the rest of the population. The worms were like drive-by shooters in that the victims were random targets. Executive management in some organizations was annoyed to discover that there were patches available for the vulnerabilities exploited by CryptoLocker before it struck. At least at the desktop level and for internet-facing systems, those who did not have patch programs began creating them, and those that already had patch programs shortened the time allocated for testing before applying them.

It was just as well that many organizations already configured their wireless networks with VPNs instead of relying on TLS because 2014 brought *Heartbleed*, a bug in a *heartbeat* feature in TLS network encryption. Heartbeat, or *keep-alive*, features are transmissions between a client and a server to maintain a session. How often is usually a configuration setting, either client or server, can be programmed to stop allocating memory to a session when the other side does not send a heartbeat in a time interval of typically 10–30 seconds. The vulnerability allowed a skilled attacker on a client to access data not allocated to its session by extending the request for a heartbeat further into a web server's memory. They could then extract that data and/or hijack another TLS session. It was discovered by cybersecurity professionals and was not known to be used in the wild (i.e., it was a zero-day). Given the recent Snowden leaks, the potential for nation-state stealth attacks using Heartbleed was so obvious that the NSA made a very unusual special announcement that they had no prior knowledge that the vulnerability existed, and the White House issued a statement that included: "[b]uilding up a huge stockpile of undisclosed vulnerabilities while leaving the Internet vulnerable and the American people unprotected would not be in our national security interest" (Daniel 2014).

In the backdrop of this now-common mesh of potential cyberattacks, whether it was motivated by profit-seeking criminals, privacy-invading surveillance, or targeted espionage, 2014 introduced a unique situation wherein it seemed likely that, in previous years, a tense situation would have been handled with diplomacy, but in 2014, diplomats were forced by their decision-makers to instead choose cyberattacks. For example, Sony Entertainment suffered a damaging cyber intrusion attributed by the US government to North Korean state actors (Steinberg et al. 2021a).

Apparently, in retaliation for an unfavorable portrait of its dictator in an upcoming film (*The Interview*), North Korea planned and executed a cyberattack on Sony Entertainment. As depicted in Figure 2.7, the attack paths started with the development of a website that looked like an *Apple* website, but it actually belonged to the attacker. Because users typically use their business email as logins to other sites and often use the same passwords everywhere, many of the Apple passwords of Sony employees worked on Sony's own sites, and due to lax cybersecurity controls, no second form of authentication was required.

For months, the victim's employee credentials were harvested and used by the attacker to analyze the vulnerabilities in the Sony network. In the course of this activity, the attacker exploited Microsoft vulnerabilities to escalate

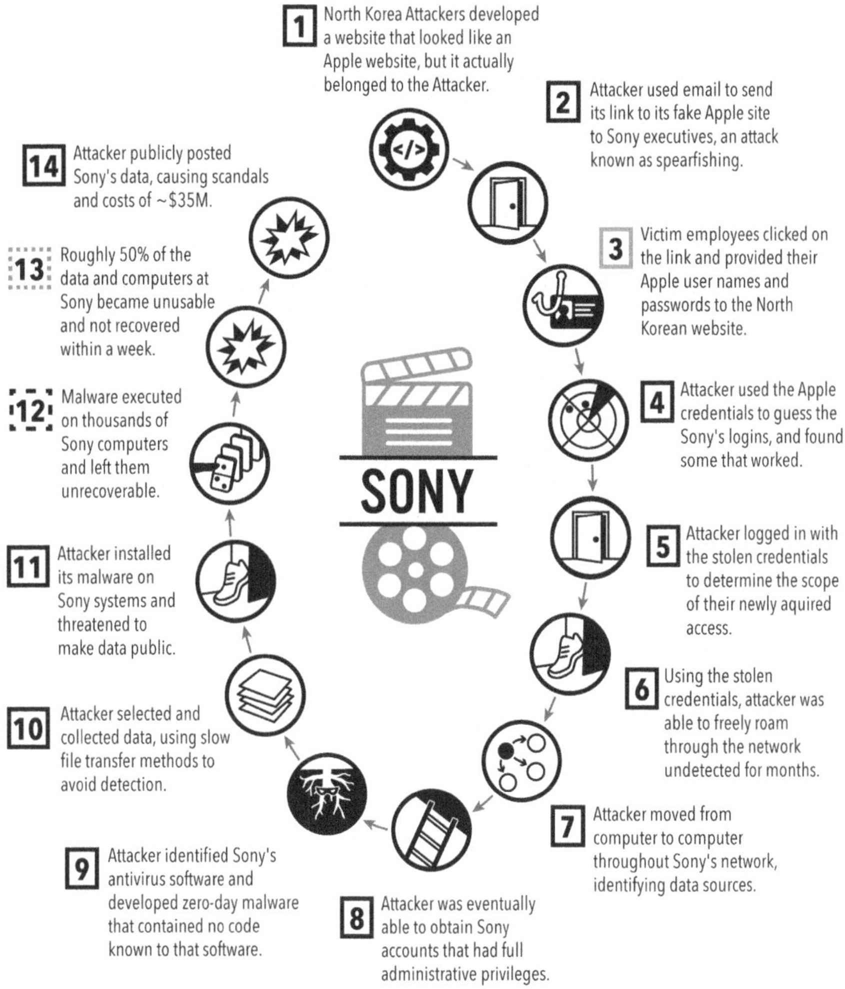

Figure 2.7 Sony Entertainment 2014.

privileges and achieve administrative access to Sony Entertainment's Microsoft Windows Domain. The attacker developed malware to wipe data from Sony's systems, notified Sony of these developments, and threatened to shut down Sony Entertainment systems if Sony did not cancel the release of *The Interview*.

On November 24, 2004, presumably because Sony did not cancel the release of the film, attackers programmed malware to execute simultaneously on thousands of Sony Entertainment's computers, destroying all data and rendering them unrecoverable. Roughly 50% of the data and computers at Sony Entertainment were instantly unusable; there were no computer services available to employees for a week.

The attackers had exfiltrated large volumes of internal communications and intellectual property before deploying the wiper malware that rendered thousands of company computers inoperable. Over the next few weeks, attackers posted Sony's confidential data, including films and scripts that were widely pirated, employee human resource records, including social security numbers, and embarrassing email conversations between senior executives, causing multiple public relations scandals and $35 million in investigation and remediation expenses.

Unlike traditional espionage campaigns that sought long-term covert access, the Sony attack combined data theft, public disclosure, and destructive sabotage in a single operation intended to coerce corporate behavior related to the release of the satirical film depicting the North Korean leader. A decade later, Sony Entertainment's then CEO Michael Lynton publicly admitted it was a big mistake to make the movie (Lynton and Steiner 2026). He said he was persuaded on the spot when he heard about it and bypassed an internal review process he normally would have used to validate his inclination to move forward with a project. With hindsight, he thought that the review process would have brought out that Sony Entertainment was owned by Japan, a country that had a long history of conflict with North Korea, so a revenge attack should not have been unexpected.

Still, even people in charge of safeguarding the most sensitive of information did not understand the ubiquity and severity of cybersecurity threats. There is no better example of this than the cyberattack on the US Office of Personnel Management (OPM). In the course of its duty to perform background checks on individuals requiring clearance to classified government information, OPM routinely hired small private investigation firms and provided them with user names and passwords to remotely access OPM servers and applications, but no multifactor authentication. A postmortem report by a congressional oversight committee revealed that, years prior to an attack, the OPM consistently failed information security audits detailing its vulnerabilities and ignored the recommendations of the Office of the Inspector General (OIG) on how to fix them (HOC 2016). Attackers had obtained credentials from one of the OPM's private investigation firms two years before the attack and used them to move laterally through OPM systems. The year before the first known successful attack, OPM's Computer Incident Response Team (CIRT) was notified by the DHS, United States Computer Emergency Response Team (US CERT n.d.), that data had been exfiltrated from OPM's network. But rather than strengthen security controls (like Northrup Grumman in 2011), OPM decided to try to detect and monitor rather than block the attacker (like Lockheed Martin in 2011). They monitored the activities of an attacker in their systems for *months* before they realized data had been breached by a second attacker whose activity they had not noticed.

Investigators working for the Congressional Committee that followed the incident observed, "[i]n what appears to be a coordinated campaign to collect information on government employees, attackers exfiltrated personnel files of 4.2 million former and current government employees and security clearance background investigation information on 21.5 million individuals" (HOC 2016).

This is one example of an increasingly frequent set of massive data breaches in the mid-2010s. So many that, by this point, a commercial website had been created to allow searches through the data breaches to see if they have been compromised: https://haveibeenpwned.com/. Individual usage of the site is free and encouraged as a public service, though it charges for automation and advertisements for identity protection services.

The breach of the OPM marked one of the most severe espionage intrusions in US history. Attackers exfiltrated background investigation records and security clearance files of more than 21 million current and former federal employees and contractors (including the authors of this book). The compromised data included fingerprints, financial histories, family connections, travel logs, foreign contacts, and other highly sensitive personal information. Unlike traditional intellectual property theft, the OPM breach exposed the human dimension of national security, potentially enabling long-term counterintelligence targeting and coercion. The incident prompted immediate reforms in federal identity management, accelerated implementation of multi-factor authentication across government systems, and heightened awareness that data aggregation itself constituted a strategic vulnerability.

The mid-2010s also exposed lax security in ICSs. In 2015, Russia attacked Ukrainian electric distribution companies in the first attack of many in the war that started in 2014. The cyberattack was easily attributed to Russian agents from the General Staff Main Intelligence Directorate (GRU) Main Center for Special Technologies (OT&ST), military unit 74,455, known as *Sandworm* (Sanger 2018). The attackers used spear phishing emails, often disguised as official communication from the Ukrainian parliament, to deploy malware that exploited known Microsoft vulnerabilities to gain access to Ukrainian corporate networks, pivoted into operational technology environments, and remotely operated circuit breakers at multiple substations, as in the attack pattern proof of concept that was demonstrated by Idaho National Labs in 2007. Approximately 225,000 customers temporarily lost electricity. The attackers also deployed wiper malware, rendered command consoles inoperable and unrecoverable by overwriting software on chips (*firmware*) within substation communications equipment, and conducted telephone denial-of-service attacks to overwhelm customer service centers, delaying response efforts.

One year later, in December 2016, though Ukraine's cyberdefenses were considerably improved, a second Sandworm cyberattack targeted Ukraine's power grid, this time employing more automated and purpose-built malware known as Industroyer (MITRE 2025). Unlike the 2015 intrusion, which relied heavily on manual operator interaction, the 2016 attack included malware designed to communicate directly with industrial control protocols used in substations. Although the outages were limited in duration, the technical sophistication of the malware revealed a deliberate effort to develop reusable cyber-physical attack capabilities. The incident demonstrated that adversaries were refining tools specifically engineered to disrupt electric industry infrastructure.

These attacks raised concerns among US policymakers because, although the attacks on Ukraine were based on decades-old vulnerabilities, and they were targeted at a substation level, due to the increased interconnectivity and/or more modern system, the United States may be more vulnerable than Ukraine. Recently identified vulnerabilities in ICSs that can be exploited and wreak havoc on critical infrastructure have been the focus of potential cyberattacks (Weiss n.d.).

Also in 2016, the Russian military intelligence service targeted the Democratic National Committee (DNC). These breaches started occurring after the publication of the Panama Papers. There were documents stolen from a law firm in Panama that were serendipitously useful in the prosecution of fraudsters moving money between foreign accounts and revealed considerable evidence that Putin's inner circle routinely transferred millions and billions of dollars collectively, overseas. The DNC leak has been attributed to Putin's desire for revenge against the Democratic administration (Menn 2010, pp. 166).

The year 2016 brought a new dimension to the cybersecurity professional landscape in the form of a group called the ShadowBrokers, which emerged in the summer of 2018, appearing to further Snowden's interests in exposing the NSA by publicly posting some of the NSA hacking tools. These included several zero days, and it soon became obvious to NSA insiders that the ShadowBrokers were in possession of the fruits of a Russian cyberattack on NSA that breached the collection of malware referred to by Snowden in the March 12, 2014 leak (Perlroth 2021, Ch. 21). The ShadowBrokers created an online auction for their zero-day tools and released more details on some to demonstrate their value. The NSA immediately recognized them as zero days they had purchased and saved for future use. One rendered Cisco Firewalls ineffective, for which they had likely paid over five figures, and the full set would have cost millions. The NSA quietly began to responsibly disclose the vulnerabilities to the vendors that produced the software from which they came, hoping that by the time the ShadowBrokers sold any, patches would be available. Luckily, according to their own posts, the auction had few takers; once it became clear that the NSA was the source of the exploits, potential buyers hesitated to offend. As one of the major customers for zero days was the NSA itself, they did not need them. Years later, it became evident that some of the NSA exploits had been used in attacks attributed to China years earlier, so they may not have needed to bid at the ShadowBroker auction either. In 2017, the ShadowBrokers decided to release them for free.

The month after they were released, one of the most severe exploits was used in ransomware attributed to the North Korean group Lazarus, the same one that the NSA had labeled *EternalBlue*. It was initially triggered via a phishing attack, but once the phishing payload was installed, it became a worm, scanning the network for Windows systems for a vulnerable protocol used to connect Microsoft computers to printers and file shares. It used the *EternalBlue* vulnerability to automate initial access to these systems and then installed *DoublePulsar*, a malware installer that had also been in the NSA stash. DoublePulsar installed ransomware, which encrypted all the files it could access, changing the name of the file to add the extension ".WNCRY." The "CRY" in the file extension stood for "crypto," but the "WN" at the front gave this worm the name "WannaCry." The software also demanded Bitcoin as a ransom. However, the Lazarus group had not included a decryption function in their software package, so even if it was paid, no one got their files back. WannaCry is estimated to have impacted hundreds of thousands of businesses, and homes were impacted in approximately 150 countries. The vulnerable communications protocol that it exploited had been deprecated by Microsoft in 2013 (Server Message Block version 1). Nevertheless, when informed by the NSA that the ShadowBrokers had the exploit in 2016, Microsoft quietly rolled out a patch. Any business that had either upgraded or patched was not vulnerable to WannaCry. Moreover, months and even years later, subsequent attacks using the same NSA exploit happened to businesses and municipalities across the globe (e.g., Allentown and Baltimore in the United States) (Perlroth 2021, pp. 347–349).

In June of 2017, Sandworm struck Ukraine again (see Figure 2.8). This time, they used a vulnerability due to the dependency of Ukrainian organizations on tax software designed specifically for businesses operating in Ukraine. Again, starting with spear-phishing, they successfully accessed the software vendor's distribution system and were able to conceal a malicious wiper worm within the vendor's software update program. The vendor unwittingly sent the malware-laden software update to its customers (Steinberg et al. 2021b). Victims downloaded and executed what appeared to them to be a routine software update and were greeted with screens that looked like a ransomware program named Petya. Investigators soon discovered that this destructive program was worse than Petya, designed to completely destroy computers with no hope of ransomware, creating an opportunity for restoration. Hence, it was given the name *NotPetya*. Again, Sandworm was able to exploit vulnerabilities for which patches were available. It queried its victims' internal Microsoft Directory to develop a list of computers to target, logged in to all systems it could reach in the network, and exploited a Microsoft Windows disk storage vulnerability to destroy all data on the disks.

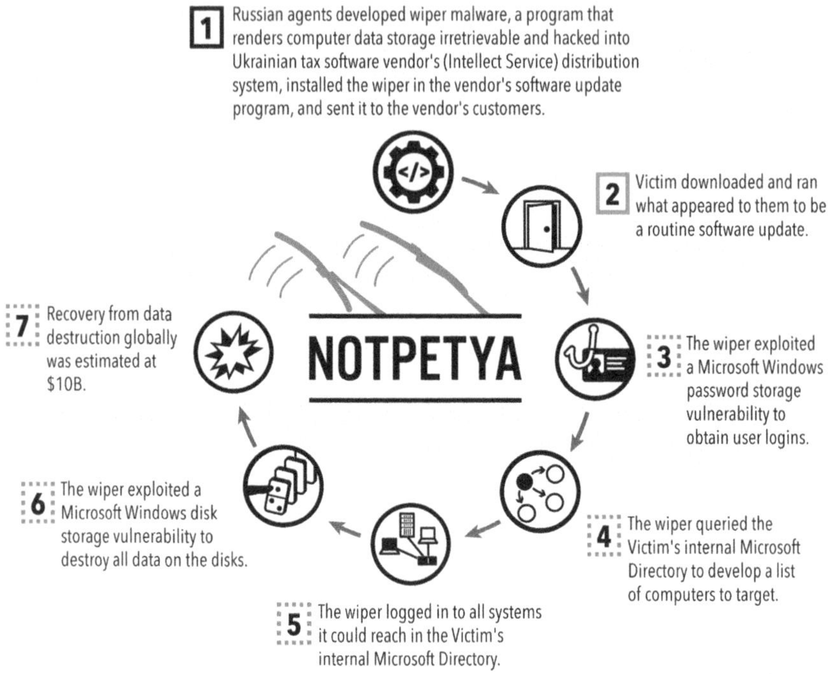

Figure 2.8 NotPetya 2017.

Though Figure 2.8 did not include it, NotPetya also carried a copy of EternalBlue, which it would use for initial access if they came across a Microsoft system that had not yet been patched. Recovery from NotPetya data destruction globally was estimated at $10 billion. Damage to the container, logistics, and supply chain services giant, Maersk, had to stop all shipments for two weeks, and delays rippled through dependent supply chains (Greenberg 2019, pp. 196–199). Maersk was able to resume operations that quickly only because they had been experimenting with cloud computing and had stored their corporate directory in Microsoft Office online just weeks before the attack (Ashton 2020). Although all of their desktops and servers had to be replaced, they were at least able to communicate and coordinate recovery online. Maersk's estimated damage alone was $300 million.

As cell phones became more ubiquitous, they became an easy target for cyberattackers, depending on how a given operator used them. Likely due to the fact that its source code is open source, zero days for Androids are common, but zero days for iPhones are rare and are highly priced in the zero-day marketplace. One such zero-day helped turn a huge profit for an Israeli firm called the NSO Group. Its flagship product, Pegasus, exploited a zero-day vulnerability in iPhones to allow governments to covertly install it on the iPhones of suspected criminals in order to track their geolocation, habits, and communications. Pegasus was marketed as a surveillance tool designed and proven to provide intelligence with which to find fugitives from justice, thwart terrorist plots, fight organized crime, and take down child pornography rings. Its use was therefore considered in line with wiretaps and other monitoring devices available to law enforcement. However, it was widely believed to have been the method by which Saudi Arabia stalked the journalist Jamal Khashoggi before they murdered him in 2018. The company vehemently denied this in public statements such as, "our technology was not associated in any way with the heinous murder of Jamal Khashoggi" (NSO Group n.d.). Nevertheless, they did not succeed in dismissing a lawsuit over the case brought by Khashoggi collaborator Omar Abdulaziz, who claimed he was also targeted (Kirkpatrick 2018). In 2021, the NSO Group was placed on the US Commerce Department's list of companies to which US suppliers are prohibited from peddling (i.e., supply chain risks). Pegasus exposed a thin line between commercial cybersecurity tools and cyberweapons (Bayuk 2022).

2.2.7 2020s

Another case in which a monitoring tool was turned into a weapon was that of *SolarWinds* in 2020 (Ramakrishna 2021). Though not designed as a cybersecurity tool, it could provide data on network traffic flow that can be useful in network security analysis. The attacker first targeted the SolarWinds development environment and obtained login credentials. It then spent four months inconspicuously testing methods to compile and operate a malware payload into a SolarWinds software release, using a program named *SUNSPOT* that it disguised as a Microsoft utility. The attacker stayed under the radar by using SUNSPOT to detect when SolarWinds was compiling *Orion* software, which was used by its customers, and directly injected malware called *SUNBURST* into Orion's update. Customers who installed the update received the bonus feature of a highly sophisticated C&C backdoor called SUNBURST, after which the attacker removed traces of its activity from the SolarWinds systems.

SolarWinds is a widely used network monitoring tool that access data flow that can be used for network security analysis. Because many SolarWinds customers run the software with administrative permissions, the malware gained access to the victim's Microsoft authentication materials and created *access tokens* that allowed it to impersonate the victim's users and administrators. The software used sophisticated evasion techniques, including random behaviors and multiple types of malware, and tailored its communications to blend into the local environment. The attacker was able to move laterally across networks and perform espionage in search of trade secrets and human intelligence, eventually exfiltrating both

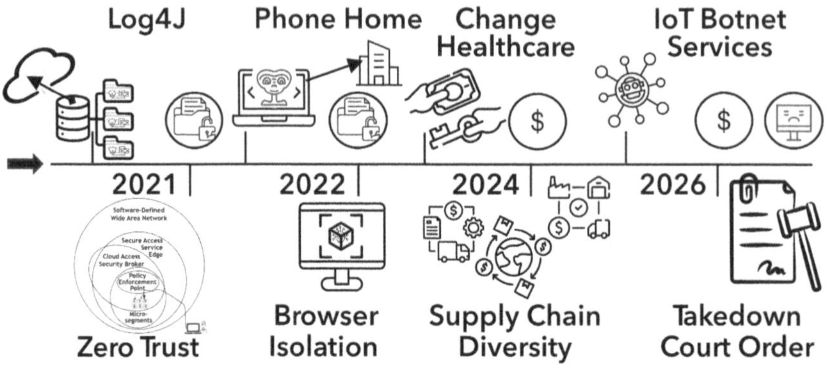

Timeline 6 2020s.

sensitive data and reconnaissance data. The end-to-end attack path used in SolarWinds is depicted in Figure 2.9.

SUNBURST was detected by a cybersecurity forensics team at a company named FireEye (the forensics team has since been rebranded as Mandiant) when one employee discovered another employee had two phones registered on the corporate network, the second of which he was unaware (Temple-Raston 2021). Though the company employed some of the leading cyberforensics experts of its day, it took them weeks to figure out what had happened. They first discovered that SUNBURST had stolen its own set of penetration test tools and called the FBI. It was a Saturday when they discovered the malware in SolarWinds' software. They were able to contact a member of SolarWinds' cybersecurity staff and made an announcement the following day. The attack was eventually attributed to Russia.

Note that the Microsoft attack vector used in the attack was not a zero-day, so it had likely been used prior to 2020. However, because the vulnerability required considerable programming skill to exploit, in the hands of a wealthy nation-state, its potential for allowing negative impact was more obvious. The attack was attributed to the Russian Foreign Intelligence Service (APT29). SolarWinds estimated its losses at $18 million. Though the number of customers that downloaded the software was estimated to be approximately 18,000, the number impacted was likely to be far fewer due to the manually intensive C&C stealth operations, the fact that it required the internet to communicate, and the targets held rewards valued by the attacker, so the number of customers impacted is estimated to be in the 100s. One of those impacted was the DHS's CISA. The monetary value of combined customer losses is likely incalculable.

The next year brought another massive surveillance operation, named for the software library it subverted: log4j. The "4j" stood for "for java," the programming language most developers prefer to code web servers. It was part of the Apache

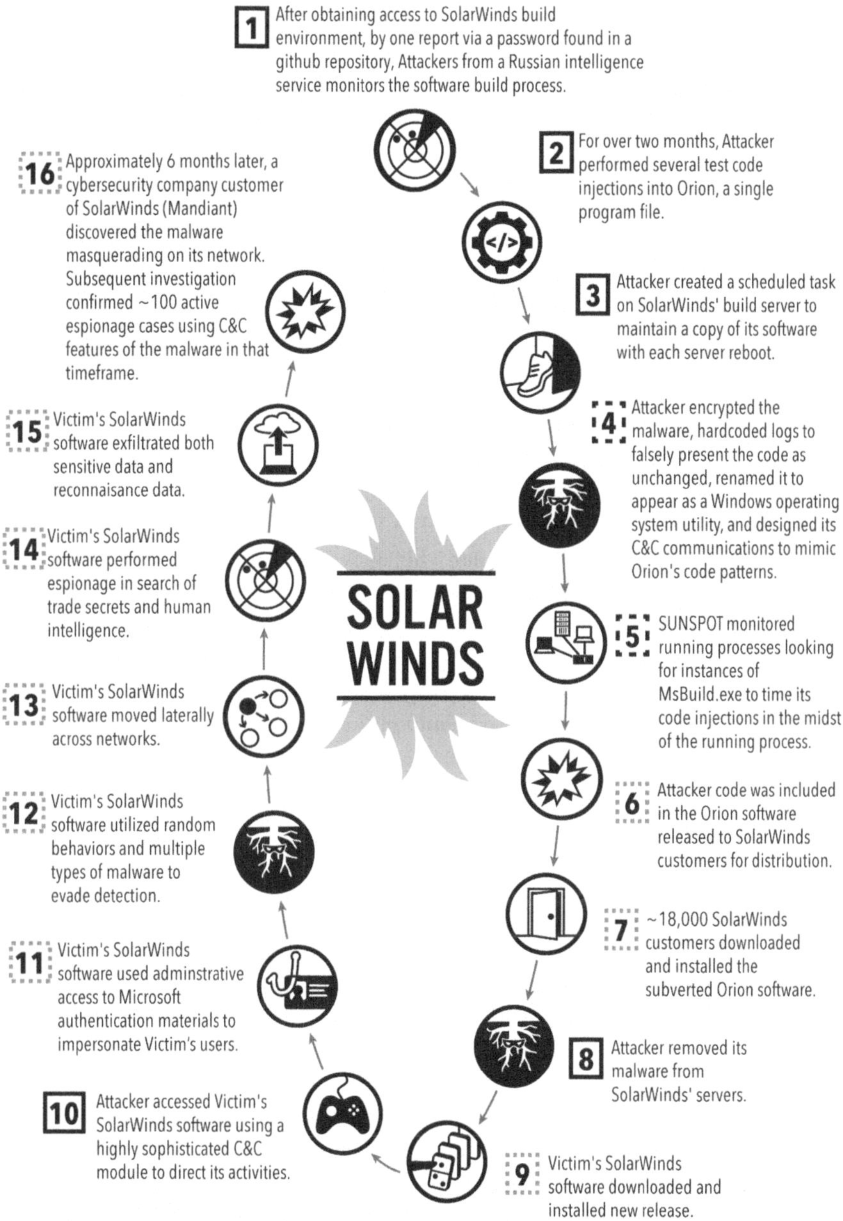

Figure 2.9 SolarWinds 2020.

Software Foundation open source web server. The serious vulnerability in an open source website software package hit the headlines in 2021: log4j (CVE-2021-44 228) was disclosed. On January 1, 2022, the Federal Trade Commission (FTC) issued this warning about it:

> Log4j is a ubiquitous piece of software used to record activities in a wide range of systems found in consumer-facing products and services. Recently, a serious vulnerability in the popular Java logging package, Log4j (CVE-2021-44228) was disclosed, posing a severe risk to millions of consumer products to enterprise software and web applications. This vulnerability is being widely exploited by a growing set of attackers.
>
> (FTC 2022).

Note that the "CVE" in the FTC warning refers to the MITRE Common Vulnerability Enumeration (MITRE n.d.a), CVE-2021-44 228, which therein is named: Apache Log4j2 Remote Code Execution Vulnerability (NIST 2021). The vulnerability was officially reported to the Apache Software Foundation on November 24, 2021, by a programmer who, a few days later, reported that he had also heard that exploits were being developed. Apache expedited the patch, but the exploits became publicly available a day before the CVE was posted in the NVD.

A CISA Cyber Safety Review Board (CASB) report identified the date of first exploit as December 1, and just after the patch was posted, internet scans for the vulnerability significantly increased. Automation had been created to exploit the vulnerability to gain initial access, then use the initial access to download arbitrary code that could be used for espionage and exfiltration. It was so widely exploited in December of 2021 that the scans for it themselves looked like a DDoS attack to some organizations.

Figure 2.10 shows how a log4j attack worked. An attacker populated an input field with a string that included formatting corresponding to unresolved variables in the web server's operating system. The victim web server resolved the variables, which included a command to add the attacker's database to its list of trusted code sources in the website's code library. The first time the server created a log, after that, the web server retrieved the attacker's library instead of its own, and it installed the C&C malware that allows an attacker to scan the server and exfiltrate sensitive data. The data loss was spread over thousands of organizations and thus was unquantifiable. However, thousands of organizations did individually report incident response costs in the four to five figures, as well as significant operational impact, including downtime, paid overtime, and productivity loss, though none to critical infrastructure. The CSRB report concluded that Log4j was an "endemic vulnerability" and estimated that vulnerable instances of Log4j would remain in systems for "perhaps a decade or longer" (CSRB 2022, p. v). In these situations, vulnerability scans and patching remain the primary method of cyberdefense.

Figure 2.10 Log4j 2021.

To combat this complacency with respect to vulnerabilities, especially in US federal agencies like NASA and OPM, in 2020, NIST developed a new security architecture standard called *Zero Trust Architecture* (ZTA). The idea for ZTA had been simmering since China's attacks on Google in 2009, when a cybersecurity researcher had the profound revelation that everyone assumed that "Defense in Depth" worked reasonably well, even though the ever-increasing level of software vulnerability repeatedly demonstrated that each layer of defense was full of holes (Kindervag 2010). He became a ZTA champion, imploring organizations to ***assume the internal network is crawling with hostile adversaries*** and ***make sure*** that each individual user attempting to access ***any*** information or computing resource is ***specifically authorized*** to access that ***specific resource*** and will be allowed ***no*** other access to ***anything*** that has not been explicitly made public on purpose. That is, two-factor VPN access to the network will get the user to the edge of the network, and nowhere else. The idea gathered support over the decade, and NIST made a new type of standard out of it, starting with basic principles in a policy framework that must be observed at the technology architecture level. It then provides requirements for technology architecture design that minimize uncertainty in enforcing accurate, least privilege per-request access decisions in information systems and services in the face of a network viewed as compromised (NIST 2021).

The NIST ZTA standard includes these high-level tenets:

- All data sources and computing services are considered resources.
- All communication is secured regardless of network location.
- Access to individual enterprise resources is granted on a per-session basis.
- Access to resources is determined by dynamic policy, including the observable state of client identity, application/service, and the requesting asset, and may include other behavioral and environmental attributes.
- The enterprise monitors and measures the integrity and security posture of all owned and associated assets. No asset is inherently trusted. The enterprise evaluates the security posture of the asset when evaluating a resource request.
- All resource authentication and authorization are dynamic and strictly enforced before access is allowed. This is a constant cycle of obtaining access, scanning and assessing threats, adapting, and continually reevaluating trust in ongoing communication.
- The enterprise collects as much information as possible about the current state of assets, network infrastructure, and communications, and uses it to improve its security posture.

The federal government agencies and contractors are required to adhere to this standard, and it has gained widespread worldwide adoption by organizations that are acutely aware of cybersecurity risk. Because it continuously identifies and logs the authorized user with multiple authentication factors, including hand-held devices and network location, any technology architecture that was completely compliant with the NIST ZTA standard would have multiple features available to interrupt most MITRE ATT&CK stages as well as detect successful incursions in progress. For a simple example, users could be required to attest to the veracity of their complete daily activity logs, and any deviations could be forensically investigated.

Another technology control that came under increased scrutiny in the early 2000s was the software industry's end-user license agreements (EuLAs). EuLAs are used to specify the terms and conditions under which software is licensed to those who purchase it. These agreements typically limit the authority of the user to copy the software and limit the liability of the vendor for any faults in software operation. For desktop software, these agreements are typically presented in an automated fashion while a user is installing software. Their terms are vague, and sometimes one of their terms is that they can change the terms at any time, and the user is still bound to them (Hoglund and Mcgraw 2008). Where possible, software vendors try to enforce these EuLAs with automated techniques for license verification. One common method of software license verification is for the software to phone home. Phone-home features check attributes of the software installation against the vendor's records of purchase. For example, if a purchaser has installed the software on more machines than permitted via the EuLA, the software may disable itself. Phone-home features are also used to check for patches and updates, in which case the software may automatically update itself or prompt the user to update the software. More insidious uses of phone-home features are used by spyware to upload data observed on the user's computer.

Though it may be reasonable for a software vendor to phone home to enforce an EULA, many EULAs now include the ability for vendors to use these features for other purposes about which the user has no knowledge. In one operating system update, Microsoft started using your location to show you the weather, whether you want it or not, and prompts for personal information in order to customize the desktop environment. It is not uncommon for a workstation operating system to have features that attempt to connect to phones or household Bluetooth devices. The cybersecurity issue is not that these features exist; it is that there is no standard method of identifying which ones are turned on and off and which ones keep resetting themselves with every software update. Individuals are often alarmed at these features, and it is typically difficult and time-consuming for individuals to find out how to turn off these features. They absorb computing resources and slow down users' machines. It is hard even for computer security professionals to tell the difference between Microsoft's background processes and actual malware.

Phone-home features are not just limited to traditional computers and servers; they are standard operating procedure for mobile devices, and are also incorporated into software that supports ICSs. Unfortunately, today's best defense against such intrusions is the calm understanding that, if it happens to you, it is happening to someone else, and therefore, use an artificial-intelligence augmented internet search to find out who else is having the same issue with the same "feature" and whether or not anyone knows how to turn it off.

Throughout 2023 and 2024, the USCC reported that China remained a significant cybersecurity threat actor. In 2023, China conducted multiple cyberespionage attacks against the United States and foreign governments, demonstrating the growing prowess and danger posed by Beijing's cyber operations. In 2023, media revelations emerged that China had operated an intelligence facility in Cuba since 2019 and that it was negotiating to establish a new joint military training facility there. A Chinese state-backed hacking group infiltrated the unclassified Microsoft email servers of the US Departments of State and Commerce in May 2023, perpetrating the first publicly known, successful Chinese hack of a Cabinet-level official since 2008 (USCC 2023, pp. 7–8).

In 2024, the USCC Annual Report noted that China was forming *new-type militia* forces to leverage civilian technical talent for the needs of modern warfare.

New-type militias are armed forces units composed of civilian professionals drawn from industries, such as information technology, communications, cybersecurity, software, electronics, robotics, unmanned systems, and artillery, among others (USCC 2024, p. 504).

One of the new-type militias may well turn out to be *Ransomware as a Service* (RaaS) market, as that market hit a new high with a successful attack on *Change Healthcare*, a subsidiary of *UnitedHealth Group* (UHG) that processes about half of all medical claims in the United States for approximately 900,000 physicians, 33,000 pharmacies, 5,500 hospitals, and 600 laboratories. It crippled Change Healthcare's ability to process medical claims, affecting 190+ million people. It disrupted pharmacy operations and medical service provider cash flow, forcing many small businesses to use personal funds to stay afloat. The attack caused widespread, long-term financial and operational distress across the US healthcare system.

While the initial access was not revealed (if known) by Change Healthcare, cybersecurity investigators identified on the case found infostealer malware downloaded from the file-sharing website mega.nz infected a Change Heathcare employee's desktop, and identified it as the likely source of initial access. As soon as the attack was evident, UHG immediately isolated Change's data centers to eliminate the potential for further infection. While it stopped the ransomware from spreading, it was too late; all of their systems were encrypted.

In the RaaS business model, the attacker performs the RaaS on behalf of "affiliates" who do some legwork, and they share profits. Figure 2.11 steps through the RaaS attack on Change Healthcare, conducted by a group named for the *ALPHV/BlackCat* software it used to conduct RaaS. The affiliate pharmed infostealer malware with C&C capability disguised as a video game. Both attackers and defenders have a nickname for the types of sites where users tend to spend time browsing and are often tempted to download files they find of interest; namely, *a watering hole*, an analogy to a place frequented by a game hunter's prey. In the case of a Change Healthcare employee, the watering hole was a file-sharing website then named *mega.nz* and instead of water, the bait was video game downloads.

On February 7, a Change Healthcare employee took the bait, and the infostealer gathered all form fields stored in the employee's browser and desktop, including login credentials, and contacted the affiliate. The affiliate used C&C to retrieve the credentials and approximately four terabytes of other data proprietary to Change Healthcare, then enlisted ALPHV/BlackCat to operate RaaS on its behalf. Either the attacker or the affiliate found a link to Change Healthcare's remote access portal on a public website (Rock 2024). On February 12, ALPHV/BlackCat used exfiltrated login credentials to access Change Healthcare's remote access portal,

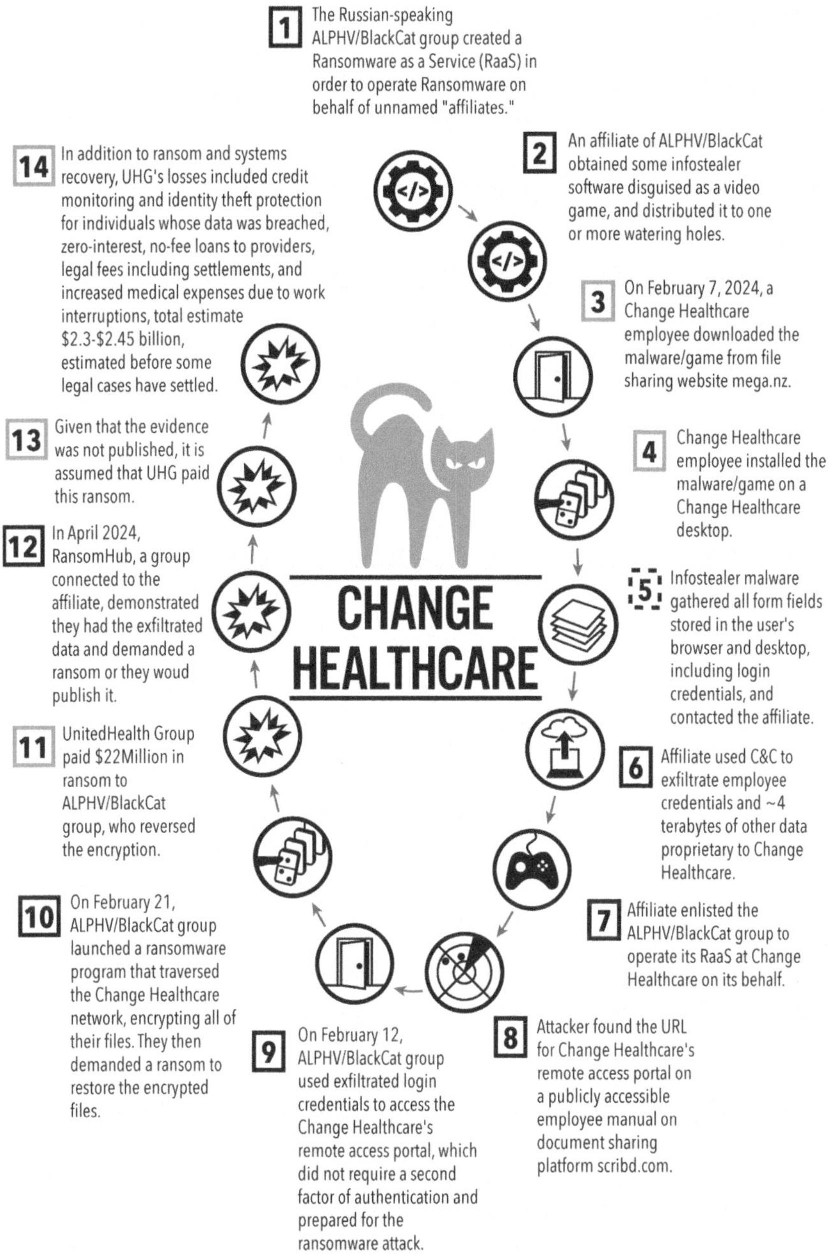

Figure 2.11 ChangeHealthcare 2025.

which did not require multi-factor authentication. Ten days passed before the ransomware attack was launched. The malware traversed the Change Healthcare network, encrypting all files it encountered. ALPHV/BlackCat then demanded a $22 million ransom to restore the files, which UHG paid. ALPHV/BlackCat then reversed the encryption. In April 2024, a second ransom demand came to UHG from a group called RansomHub, which seemed to also be connected to the affiliate because it had evidence of the data previously exfiltrated and demanded the ransom as a condition of its deletion. It is assumed that UHG paid this ransom as well (Klappholz 2024). It took two weeks to restore pharmacy services and longer to restore others.

In an attempt to quantify losses industry-wide, the American Hospital Association surveyed 1000 of its members on the impact on its members and identified several additional downstream impacts:

- 74% reported direct patient care impact, including delays in authorizations for medically necessary care;
- 94% reported the attack impacted them financially;
- 33% reported the attack disrupted more than half of their revenue; and
- 60% reported requiring two weeks to three months to resume normal operations once Change Healthcare's full functionality was re-established (AHA 2025).

The AHA report chastised UHG for downplaying the severity of the event over the ensuing weeks, noting they had to devise makeshift manual processes in place of automated ones, which threatened the quality of patient care. They also encouraged their members to *directly* report their examples of negative impact to the Health and Human Services Assistant Secretary for Preparedness and Response, a clear vote of nonconfidence in UHG's veracity in the days that followed the attack.

On June 21, 2024, a law firm engaged in one of the suits reported that UHG committed $2 billion through multiple action plans to support impacted providers in the wake of the cyberattack. However, providers have reported that this fund is already exhausted and no additional advanced payments are currently available, further threatening the financial viability of some healthcare providers (Kern et al. 2024).

UHG's response included the ransom, free credit monitoring, and identity theft protection for individuals whose data was breached, a dedicated call center staffed by clinicians to provide support services, zero-interest, no-fee loans to thousands of providers, legal fees including settlements, restoring the Change Healthcare clearinghouse platform, and higher medical expenses due to the temporary pause of some of its care management activities. In its second quarter 2024 earnings report, it predicted that the total cost of the Change Healthcare ransomware attack would reach between $2.3 billion and $2.45 billion for the year. Moreover, some of the legal cases have not yet been decided.

On May 1, 2024, UHG's CEO Andrew Witty testified before Congress on the attack and its impact. He said he was deeply sorry, and then offered these statements under the heading of "policy solutions" for congressional consideration:

- "We support mandatory minimum security standards – developed collaboratively by the government and private sector – for the health care industry. Importantly, these efforts must include funding and training for institutions that need help in making that transition, such as hospitals in rural communities.
- We also support efforts to strengthen our national cybersecurity infrastructure, including greater notification to law enforcement and standardized and nationalized cybersecurity event reporting" (USC 2024).

The event was a wake-up call for the healthcare industry on business recovery planning. In the technology industry, it is typical for business continuity plans to have either a *standby* duplicate software environment or a duplicate environment that also processes some percentage of its transactions, a *hot site*. These sites are purposely diverse so as not to suffer the same weather or vendor support. Network isolation between sites may be continuous or part of an emergency response procedure. That way, if the main production environment is compromised, it can be isolated and the transaction processing redirected to the standby or hot site. This allows *failover* from the main site to known untampered systems and physical workspace alternatives for as long as the real estate market in the given area may be expected to recover availability. For global corporations, it is common to failover operations to other countries.

These expectations cannot be met with person-to-person industries like health care, which rely on industrial control technologies that must connect directly to local physical objects to be effective. The only feasible solution for the customers of a vendor like Change Healthcare, especially small business customers, is to diversify their supply chain by entering into a contract with another vendor, who agrees to provide either a standby or hotsite for them in case of emergency.

Another recent example of denial of service on the industrial control side in 2024 was a cyberattack wherein Ukraine changed roles with Russia in 2024, becoming the attacker instead of the victim. As depicted in Figure 2.12, the *Blackjack* group, self-attributed to be Ukraine, conducted reconnaissance of the software and communications protocols of a Russian manufacturer of industrial gateways (AO SBK) (Claroty 2024). They used that information to identify internet-connected devices using that software and protocols and found easy access to unencrypted access protocols and default passwords. The manufacturer's default password still worked on most of the gateways, and they found additional router vulnerabilities to access a significant percentage of the gateways to the sensors that monitored Moscow's underground utility corridors. *Blackjack* wrote malware customized for the gateway operating system and bundled it into

Figure 2.12 Fuxnet 2024.

a software package called *Fuxnet*. Fuxnet flooded the networks connected to the sensors with arbitrary data, consuming all available bandwidth and thereby disrupting sensor data acquisition from any source. Fuxnet also stopped remote access services in the gateways and deleted routing tables to prevent remote recovery attempts and physically destroyed gateway memory chips by rapid-fire write operations that exceeded chip maximum write capability and wiped data from the gateways and gateway-accessible workstations. The attack targeted approximately 87,000 sensors and took a large (though unknown) percentage of them offline, interrupting monitoring of critical infrastructure such as sewage systems, water supplies, and communication networks, an impact that the ICS industry calls a *loss of view*.

Fuxnet is a significant evolution in ICS malware because it was specifically engineered to interact with and disable ICSs by interfering with a sensor over a two-wire serial cable channel rather than just IT networks. Though enabled by ICS operator inattention to cybersecurity problems that were solved in the 1990s, innovative techniques of defending against potential cybersecurity threats to interference in ICS sensors and signals are still dependent on much-needed research and development. It cannot be emphasized enough that the cybersecurity community cannot currently be relied upon to deliver the management controls needed to make ICS safe from cyberattack.

Malicious botnets, such as the one used by Cryptolocker, continued to haunt the internet. These have recently been joined by botnets composed of Internet of Things (IoT) systems, which typically have few, if any, cybersecurity defense features. For example, the *Aisuru* botnet appeared in August 2024 and by 2025 had spread to at least 700,000 IoT systems, such as digital video recorders and web or security cameras. Because these devices have limited ability to execute commands, they are mostly used in DDoS attacks, synchronously operated to flood victims with data of any type, consuming the bandwidth and network port capacity of the victim. It has been aimed at multiple targets, including the DoD and security researchers. In 2025, Aisuru changed its business model to a Crime as a Service (CaaS), renting hundreds of thousands of "enslaved" IoT devices to proxy services that help cybercriminals anonymize their traffic (Krebs 2025).

In January of 2026, Aisuru was joined by another botnet named Kimwolf. Within a few weeks, Kimwolf had acquired more than 2 million IoT devices, including those in government and corporate networks. It conducted massive distributed DDoS attacks and relayed other malicious and abusive Internet traffic (Krebs 2026a). It appeared to have been built for political purposes because in January it disrupted the *Invisible Internet Project* (I2P), a decentralized, encrypted communications network designed to anonymize and secure online communications (Krebs 2026b).

In March of 2026, the DoD Office of Inspector General's (DoDIG) Defense Criminal Investigative Service (DCIS) coordinated a court-ordered takedown of Aisuru, Kimwolf, and two other botnets (DoJ 2026). Aisuru was said to have issued more than 200,000 cyberattacks; Kimwolf, 25,000 cyberattacks; JackSkid, 90,000 cyberattacks; and Mossad 1,000.

The DCIS coordinated its takedown efforts with law enforcement agencies from Canada and Germany, as well as a host of other public and private organizations, including Akamai, Amazon Web Services, Cloudflare, DigitalOcean, Epieos, Google, Hydrolix, Lumen, Nokia, Okta, Oracle, PayPal, Registrar of Last Resort, The Shadowserver Foundation, Sony Interactive Entertainment, SpyCloud, Synthient, Team Cymru, Unit 221B, XLAB, Netherlands Politie, and Europol. Seizure warrants were enforced at multiple registered internet domains, virtual servers, and other infrastructure allegedly engaged in cyber-enabled criminal activity. It was a triumph of good over evil, though also a heroic effort that is likely unsustainable. It was a detect and recover tactic meant to deter cybercriminals, as opposed to preventing new botnets from being effective going forward.

This chapter began with an acknowledgment that the main goal of information technology projects is to increase productivity by replacing human calculators with automated programs that produce more accurate results. The advent of

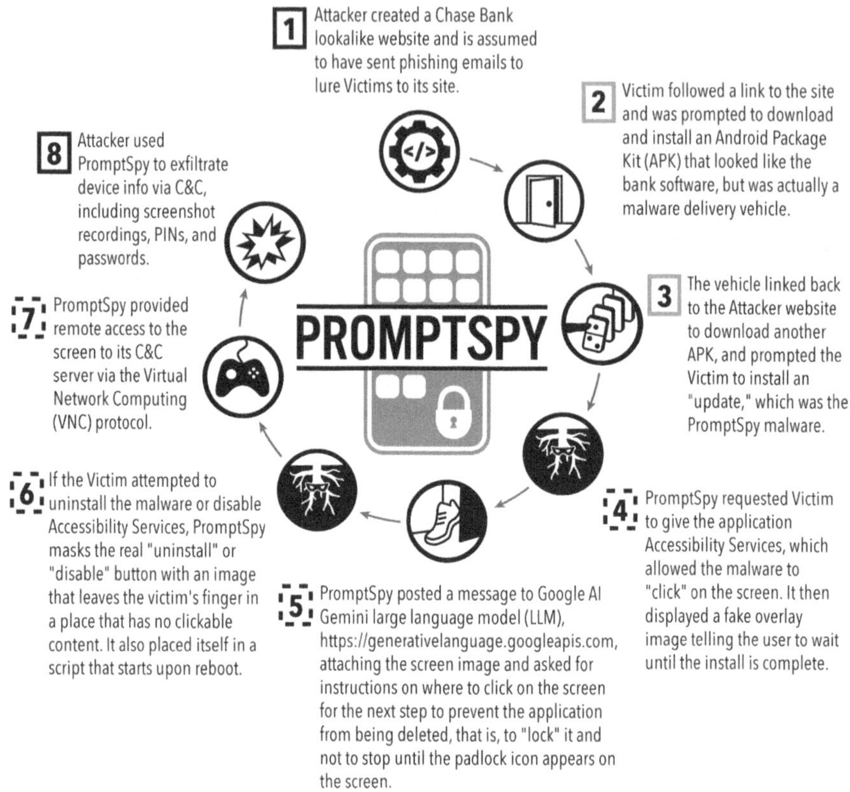

Figure 2.13 PromptSpy 2026.

cyberattacks using AI has provided a good example of how AI furthers this goal in the example of a 2026 attack called *PromptSpy*. PromptSpy's cyberattack was enabled with a harness, shorthand to mean everything in an AI agent except the model itself. That is Agent = Model + Harness (Bockeler 2026). It was not entirely autonomous, nevertheless it provided components that were critical to the success of any cyberattack: persistence and defense evasion. As depicted in Figure 2.13, the threat actor had to create a look-alike website and send phishing emails to get people to click on links. Those who arrived at the site were prompted to download an Android Package Kit (APK) that looked for software to install from the bank but was actually the malware delivery vehicle. When the vehicle arrived in the victim's workstation, it prompted the victim to install an "update," which was the PromptSpy malware harness. PromptSpy then requested the victim to give the application *Accessibility services*, which allowed the malware to mimic a user "click" on the Android's screen. PromptSpy then displayed a fake overlay image, obscuring the native Android operating system security screen image, by displaying a message asking the victim to wait until the installation is complete.

While the victim was waiting, PromptSpy posted a request to Google's AI Gemini large language model (LLM), asking for instruction on where to click on the screen for the next step to prevent the application from being deleted, that is to "lock" it pinning it in the Android recent apps list, preventing it from being easily swiped away or killed by the system. It also instructed Gemini not to consider the request complete until the symbol that the application was locked appeared on a screenshot that was not sent sequentially. To clarify the details of the request, it attached the current screen image and Android OS configuration. If the victim attempted to uninstall the payload or disable accessibility services, PromptSpy masked the real "uninstall" or "disable" button with an image that left the victim's finger in a place that had no clickable content. It also placed itself in a script that started upon reboot. When the installation was complete, PromptSpy provided remote access to the screen to its C&C server via the Virtual Network Computing (VNC) protocol. The attacker was then free to use PromptSpy to exfiltrate device info via C&C, including screenshot recordings, PINs, and passwords, unless the device was set back to manufacturer settings.

Cybersecurity researchers called the attack steps performed by PromptSpy "context-aware user interface manipulation" (Stefanko 2026). These are highlighted in steps 5 and 6 of Figure 2.13. They also noted that, in Promptspy, the *debug* messages that programmers commonly included in code to monitor its operation were written in Chinese. This was consistent with the USCC's 2025 report, which cautioned that China remained the most active and persistent cyberthreat to US government, private-sector, and critical infrastructure networks. It is speculated that, in the event China were to take military action against Taiwan, Beijing might attack US ICS to induce panic and undermine the United States's ability to mobilize its military and rally public support for Taiwan. Also in 2025, Microsoft reported that Chinese attackers exploited vulnerabilities in its *SharePoint* platform, a serious cybersecurity threat, as the platform was used by numerous US government agencies and many companies worldwide (USCC 2025, pp. 100–101).

Cybersecurity controls to rein in AI are nascent, like the elusive access controls for mainframes in the 1960s, but with no fallback to physical security measures, as there is too much complexity in these programs to directly trace activity to people sitting in buildings. Systems engineers make a distinction between what is complicated versus what is complex. Complicated is deterministic, and complicated algorithms can be followed with logic wherein no matter what the data input, the conclusion is predictable. Complex refers to decision mechanisms that themselves change with the data with which they are presented and can only be predicted with probabilities observed in their behavior. It may be decades before intrusion prevention systems can be programmed to anticipate AI-enabled cybersecurity attacks.

2.3 Ongoing Challenges

This chapter describes the ongoing situation of handling cybersecurity risks as one "threat-countermeasure" event after another, rather than a holistic approach at the policy level to cybersecurity and online safety. None of the threats has disappeared, and therefore most of the countermeasures are still considered best practice. For some of the threats, there is no countermeasure. We continually *bolt-on* countermeasures rather than attempt to redesign cyber infrastructure with a safer, more reliable core. Note that this chapter's description of the evolution of cybersecurity in no way implies that the way cybersecurity has evolved is effective, or even appropriate.

In 2007, a cybersecurity industry analyst mockingly called the predicament of a cybersecurity professional as a *hamster wheel of pain*. A "wheel of pain" is a reference to ancient and medieval servility, where slaves labor on turnstiles or prisoners are attached to torture mechanisms. The caged hamster (i.e., the CISO), however, *voluntarily* embarks on the spinning wheel and, like a hamster in a pet-store-supplied cage, continues to run as the wheel turns faster instead of trying to get off. The joke was (and still is) that cyberattacks are treated as sets of remediation projects without recognizing and remediating the root cause; that is, intent adversaries persistently hunting for vulnerable systems. Though we work harder and faster, we never get ahead (Jaquith 2007, pp. 2–3).

References

Acohido, B. and Swartz, J. (2008). *Zero Day Threat*. New York, NY: Sterling Publishing Co., Inc.

American Hospital Association (AHA) (2025). Change healthcare cyberattack underscores urgent need to strengthen cyber preparedness for individual health care organizations and as a field. https://www.aha.org/system/files/media/file/2025/02/Change-Healthcare-Cyberattack-Underscores-Urgent-Need-to-Strengthen-Cyber-Preparedness.pdf (accessed 29 March 2026).

Amoroso, E. (1994). *Fundamentals of Computer Security Technology*, Englewood Cliffs, NJ: Prentice-Hall.

Amoroso, E. (1999). *Intrusion Detection*. Sparta, NJ: Intrusion Net Books.

Amoroso, E. (2010). *Cyber Attacks*. Burlington, MA: Butterworth-Heinemann.

Ashton, G. (2020). Maersk, me & notPetya. https://gvnshtn.com/posts/maersk-me-notpetya/ (accessed 31 March 2023).

Bayuk, J. (2004). *Stepping Through the IS Audit*. Rolling Meadows, IL: ISACA IT Governance Institute.

Bayuk, J. (2022). Cybersecurity Tool Portfolio - Friend or Foe? TAG Cyber Security Annual. pp. 36–39. 2nd Quarter. https://tag-infosphere.com/advisory/quarterly/download/8 (accessed 31 March 2026).

Bockeler, B. (2026). Harness engineering for coding agent users. https://martinfowler.com/articles/harness-engineering.html (accessed 5 May 2026).

Ceruzzi, P. E. (1998). *A History of Modern Computing*, 2nd edn. Cambridge, MA: MIT Press.

Chatzinotas, S., Karlsson, J., et al. (2008). Chapter 48: Evaluation of security architectures for mobile broadband access. In *Handbook of Research on Wireless Security*, eds. Y., Zhang, J., Zheng, and M., Miao. IGI Global. https://www.igi-global.com/chapter/evaluation-security-architectures-mobile-broadband/22083, https://www.igi-global.com/book/handbook-research-wireless-security/522 (accessed 29 March 2026).

Cheswick, W. R. and Bellovin, S. M. (1994). *Firewalls and Internet Security*. Boston, MA: Addison-Wesley.

Clarke, R. A. and Knake, R. K. (2010). *Cyberwar*. New York, NY: HarperCollins.

Claroty (2024). Unpacking the Blackjack Group's Fuxnet Malware. Claroty. 12 April. https://claroty.com/team82/research/unpacking-the-blackjack-groups-fuxnet-malware (accessed 31 March 2026).

Computer Emergency Response Team (CERT) (n.d.) (ongoing). The original CERT was privately operated. http://www.cert.org/ (accessed 29 March 2026) and has since been supplemented with one run by the US Department of Homeland Security and http://www.us-cert.gov/ (accessed 29 March 2026).

CryptoLocker (2026). Wikipedia. https://en.wikipedia.org/wiki/CryptoLocker (accessed 31 March 2026).

Cyber Safety Review Board (CSRB) (2022). Review of the December 2021 Log4j Event. 11 July. https://www.cisa.gov/sites/default/files/publications/CSRB-Report-on-Log4-July-11-2022_508.pdf (accessed 31 March 2026).

Cybersecurity and Infrastructure Security Agency (CISA) (2013). CryptoLocker ransomware infections. US Department of Homeland Security, Cybersecurity and Infrastructure Security Agency. 4 November. https://www.cisa.gov/news-events/alerts/2013/11/05/cryptolocker-ransomware-infections (accessed 30 March 2026).

Cybersecurity and Infrastructure Security Agency (CISA) (2025). Pro-Russia hacktivists conduct opportunistic attacks against US and global critical infrastructure. US Department of Homeland Security, Cybersecurity and Infrastructure Security Agency. 18 December. https://www.cisa.gov/news-events/cybersecurity-advisories/aa25-343a (accessed 28 March 2026).

Daniel, M. (2014). Heartbleed: Understanding when we disclose cyber vulnerabilities. Obama White House Archives. 28 April. https://obamawhitehouse.archives.gov/blog/2014/04/28/heartbleed-understanding-when-we-disclose-cyber-vulnerabilities (accessed 31 March 2026).

Department of Defense (DoD) (1985). The Orange Book, Trusted Computer System Evaluation Criteria. Department of Defense (supercedes 1983 version). https://archive.org/stream/TCSEC/Trusted_Computer_System_Evaluation_Criteria_DOD_5200.28-STD_djvu.txt (accessed 24 March 2026).

Department of Justice (DoJ) (2026). Authorities disrupt world's largest IoT DDoS botnets responsible for record breaking attacks targeting victims worldwide. 19 March. https://www.justice.gov/usao-ak/pr/authorities-disrupt-worlds-largest-iot-ddos-botnets-responsible-record-breaking-attacks (accessed 31 March 2026).

Drew, C. and Markoff, J. (2011). Data breach at security firm linked to attack on Lockheed. The New York Times. 27 May. https://www.nytimes.com/2011/05/28/business/28hack.html (accessed 30 March 2026).

Epstein, K. and Elgin, B. (2008). The taking of NASA's secrets. Business Week. 1 December. pp. 73–79.

Farrow, R. (2013). Bill Cheswick on Firewalls. *USENIX*, 38(4). August. https://www.usenix.org/system/files/login/articles/04_cheswick_20-25_online.pdf (accessed 30 March 2026).

Federal Bureau of Investigation (FBI) (n.d.). Melissa virus. https://www.fbi.gov/history/famous-cases/melissa-virus (accessed 28 March 2026).

Federal Trade Commission (FTC) (2022). FTC warns companies to remediate Log4j security vulnerability. https://www.ftc.gov/policy/advocacy-research/tech-at-ftc/2022/01/ftc-warns-companies-remediate-log4j-security-vulnerability (accessed 29 March 2026).

Greenberg, A. (2019). *Sandworm: A New Era of Cyberwar and the Hunt for the Kremlin's Most Dangerous Hackers*. New York, NY: Doubleday.

Greenberg, A. (2020). How 30 lines of code blew up a 27-ton generator.Wired. 23 October. https://www.wired.com/story/how-30-lines-of-code-blew-up-27-ton-generator/ (accessed 24 July 2026).

Greenberg, A. (2021). The full story of the stunning RSA hack can finally be told. Wired. 20 May. https://www.wired.com/story/the-full-story-of-the-stunning-rsa-hack-can-finally-be-told/ (accessed 30 March 2026).

Greenwald, G. (2013). NSA collecting phone records of millions of Verizon customers daily. The Guardian. 6 June. https://www.theguardian.com/world/2013/jun/06/nsa-phone-records-verizon-court-order (accessed 30 March 2026).

Hambling, D. (2009). China looks to undermine US power, with 'Assassin's mace'. Wired. 2 July. https://www.wired.com/2009/07/china-looks-to-undermine-us-power-with-assassins-mace/ (accessed 12 March 2026).

Hein, B. (2013). The threat landscape of PKI: System and cryptographic security of X.509, algorithms, and their implementations. Proceedings of the Romanian Academy 14(Special Issue): 286–294. https://acad.ro/sectii2002/proceedings/doc2013-3s/02-HEIN.pdf (accessed 30 March 2026).

Helft, M. and Barboza, D. (2010). Google shuts China site in dispute over censorship. The New York Times. 22 March. https://archive.nytimes.com/www.nytimes.com/2010/03/23/technology/23google.html (accessed 26 March 2026).

Hoglund, G. and McGraw, G. (2008). *Exploiting Online Games*. Boston, MA: Pearson Education.

House Committee on Oversight (HOC) (2016). The OPM data breach: How the government jeopardized our national security for more than a generation. 17 September. https://oversight.house.gov/report/opm-data-breach-government-jeopardized-national-security-generation/ (accessed 29 March 2026).

Institute of Electrical and Electronics Engineers (IEEE) (n.d.). Wireless Local Area Networks. The Working Group for WLAN Standards. Institute of Electrical and Electronics Engineers. https://www.ieee802.org/11/ (accessed 27 March 2026).

International Organization for Standardization and International Electrotechnical Commission (ISO/IEC) (2008). Information Technology – Systems Security Engineering – Capability Maturity Model (SSE-CMM, ISO/IEC 28127). 15 October.

International Organization for Standardization and International Electrotechnical Commission (ISO/IEC) (2023). Systems and Software Engineering – System Life Cycle Processes (ISO/IEC 15288). ISO/IEC. 16 May.

Internet Engineering Task Force (IETF) (n.d.). Mission and Request for Comments (RFC). https://www.ietf.org/about/introduction/ and http://www.ietf.org/rfc.html (accessed 12 March 2026).

Jaquith, A. (2007). *Security Metrics*. London: Pearson Education.

Kalat, D. (2021). Nervous system #37: The 414s. LegalTech News. 8 February. https://media.thinkbrg.com/wp-content/uploads/2021/03/19180207/37_The-414s_Feb2021.pdf (accessed 27 March 2026).

Kern, J., A. Solinger, and Li, G. (2024). Change healthcare cybersecurity incident: Financial impact and resulting litigation. Holland & Knight. 21 June. https://www.hklaw.com/en/insights/publications/2024/06/change-healthcare-cybersecurity-incident-financial-impact (accessed 29 March 2026).

Kim, G. and Spafford, E.H. (1994). The design and implementation of tripwire: A file system integrity checker. Second ACM Conference on Computer and Communications Security. New York, NY: ACM Press.

Kindervag, J. (2010). No more chewy centers: Introducing the zero trust model of information security. Forrester Research. 14 September 2010. https://media.paloaltonetworks.com/documents/Forrester-No-More-Chewy-Centers.pdf (accessed 31 March 2026).

Kirkpatrick, M. (2018). Israeli software helped Saudis spy on Khashoggi, lawsuit says. The New York Times. 22 March. https://www.nytimes.com/2018/12/02/world/middleeast/saudi-khashoggi-spyware-israel.html (accessed 31 March 2026).

Klappholz, S. (2024). Change Healthcare hit with second ransomware attack of 2024. ITPro. 10 April. https://www.itpro.com/security/ransomware/change-healthcare-hit-with-second-ransomware-attack-of-2024 (accessed 29 March 2026).

Kocieniewski, D. (2006). Six animal rights advocates are convicted of terrorism. The New York Times. 3 March.

Krebs, B. (2025). Aisuru Botnet shifts from DDoS to residential proxies. 28 October. https://krebsonsecurity.com/2025/10/aisuru-botnet-shifts-from-ddos-to-residential-proxies/ (accessed 31 March 2026).

Krebs, B. (2026a). Kimwolf Botnet Lurking in Corporate, Govt. Networks. 20 January. https://krebsonsecurity.com/2026/01/kimwolf-botnet-lurking-in-corporate-govt-networks/ (accessed 31 March 2026).

Krebs, B. (2026b). Kimwolf Botnet Swamps Anonymity Network I2P. 11 February. https://krebsonsecurity.com/2026/02/kimwolf-botnet-swamps-anonymity-network-i2p/ (accessed 31 March 2026).

Lynn, W. (2010). Defending a new domain: The Pentagon's cyberstrategy. *Foreign Affairs*, 89(5): 97–108. https://apps.dtic.mil/sti/pdfs/ADA527707.pdf (accessed 15 March 2026).

Lynton, M. and Steiner, J. (2026). *From Mistakes to Meaning: Owning Your Past So It Doesn't Own You*. New York, NY: Avid Reader Press/Simon & Schuster.

Mandiant (2013). APT1 exposing one of China's Cyber Espionage Units 30. https://services.google.com/fh/files/misc/mandiant-apt1-report.pdf (accessed 29 March 2026).

Martin, L. (2011). Lockheed Martin Customer, Program and Employee Data Secure - Swift, Deliberate Response Thwarts IT Breach. https://news.lockheedmartin.com/2011-05-28-Lockheed-Martin-Customer-Program-and-Employee-Data-Secure (accessed 31 March 2026).

McHugh, J. (2000). Testing intrusion detection systems. *ACM Transactions on Information and System Security*, 3(4): 262–294.

McNeil, J. (1978). The Consultant. Coward, McCann, and Geoghegan, Inc., also a BBC television series.

Menn, J. (2010). *Fatal System Error*. New York, NY: Perseus Books Group.

Miller, C. (2022). Throwback Attack: An attack on the DoD leads to Operation Buckshot Yankee. Control Engineering. 9 December. https://www.controleng.com/throwback-attack-an-attack-on-the-dod-leads-to-operation-buckshot-yankee/ (accessed 29 March 2026).

MITRE (2025). 2016 Ukraine Electric Power Attack. MITRE ATT&CK®. 16 April. https://attack.mitre.org/campaigns/C0025/ (accessed 31 March 2026).

MITRE (n.d.-a). Common vulnerabilities and exposures, dictionary of common names for publicly known information security vulnerabilities. http://cve.mitre.org (accessed 30 March 2026).

MITRE (n.d.-b). MITRE ATT&K®. https://attack.mitre.org/ (accessed 30 March 2026).

National Institute of Standards and Technology (NIST) (2020). *Zero Trust Architecture Standard*. National Institute of Standards and Technology SP800-207. https://nvlpubs.nist.gov/nistpubs/SpecialPublications/NIST.SP.800-207 (accessed 1 March 2026).

National Institute of Standards and Technology (NIST) (2021). Apache Log4j2 Remote Code Execution Vulnerability (CVE-2021-44228). National Vulnerability Database, National Institute of Standards and Technology. 10 December. https://nvd.nist.gov/vuln/detail/CVE-2021-44228 (accessed 31 March 2026).

National Science Foundation (NSF) (n.d.). Birth of the commercial internet. https://www.nsf.gov/impacts/internet (accessed 27 March 2026).

National Telecommunications and Information Administration (NTIA) (1998). Improvement of technical management of internet names and addresses. Federal Register. Vol. 63, No. 34, FR Doc. 98-4200. https://www.ntia.gov/federal-register-notice/improvement-technical-management-internet-names-and-addresses-proposed-rule (accessed 29 March 2026).

NSO Group (n.d.). NSO Group. https://www.nsogroup.com/Newses/following-the-publication-of-the-recent-article-by-forbidden-stories-we-wanted-to-directly-address-the-false-accusations-and-misleading-allegations-presented-there (accessed 31 March 2026).

Open Source Initiative (OSI) (2025). History of the Open Source Initiative. 3 June. https://opensource.org/about/history-of-the-open-source-initiative (accessed 28 March 2026).

Open Worldwide Application Security Project (OWASP) (2025). Application Security Verification Standard (ASVS). Version 5.0. May. https://owasp.org/www-project-application-security-verification-standard/ (accessed 28 March 2026).

Open Worldwide Application Security Project (OWASP) (n.d.). Vulnerability Disclosure Cheat Sheet. https://cheatsheetseries.owasp.org/cheatsheets/Vulnerability_Disclosure_Cheat_Sheet.html (accessed 28 March 2026).

Orman, H. K. (2003). The Morris Worm: A fifteen-year perspective. *Institute of Electrical and Electronics Engineers Security & Privacy*, 1(5): 35–43.

Perlroth, N. (2021). *This is How They Tell Me the World Ends*. London: Bloomsbury Publishing.

Peter, I. (2004). History of the internet. https://www.nethistory.info/History%20of%20the%20internet/origins.html (accessed 27 March 2026).

Privacy Act (1974). 5 U.S.C. § 552a. https://uscode.house.gov/statutes/pl/93/579.pdf (accessed 29 March 2026).

Ramachandran, J. (2002). *Designing Security Architecture Solutions*. Hoboken, NJ: Wiley.

Ramakrishna, S. (2021). New findings from our investigation of SUNBURST. 20 January. https://www.solarwinds.com/blog/new-findings-from-our-investigation-of-sunburst (accessed 31 March 2026).

Rescorla, E. and T. Dierks (1999). The Transport Layer Security (TLS) Protocol, version 1.2. Request for Comments: 5246, Internet Engineering Task Force, Network Working Group.

Ritchtel, M. (1998). Hacker Group Says Program Can Exploit Microsoft Security Hole. The New York Times. 4 August. https://archive.nytimes.com/www.nytimes.com/library/tech/98/08/cyber/articles/04hacker.html (accessed 31 March 2026).

Rock, H. (2024). Single Citrix compromised credential results in $22,000,000 ransom to change healthcare. 1 May. https://www.hudsonrock.com/blog/3734 (accessed 29 March 2026).

Sanger, D., Rutenberg, J. and Lipton, E. (2018). Racing Guccifer 2.0's Many Tentacles in the 2016 Election. The New York Times (15 July). https://www.nytimes.com/2018/07/15/us/politics/guccifer-russia-mueller.html (accessed 15 March 2026).

Schacht, J. M. (1975). Jobstream Separator System Design. NIST History of Computer Security, MITRE. https://apps.dtic.mil/sti/tr/pdf/ADA016403.pdf (accessed 29 March 2026).

Schmidt, H. (2006). *Patrolling Cyberspace*. Washington, DC: Larstan Publishing.

Schweitzer, J. A. (1982). *Managing Information Security, A Program for the Electronic Age*. London: Butterworth Publishers Inc.

Schweitzer, J. A. (1983). *Protecting Information in the Electronic Workplace*. Englewood Cliffs, NJ: Reston Publishing, a Prentice Hall Company.

Skoudis, E. and Zeltser, L. (2004). *Malware: Fighting Malicious Code*. Hoboken, NJ: Prentice Hall.

Slater, R. (1987). *Portraits in Silicon*. Cambridge, MA: MIT Press.

Spafford, E. (1994). Computer viruses as artificial life. *Artificial Life*, 1(3): 249–265.

Stefanko, L. (2026). Research discovers PromptSpy, the first Android threat to use generative AI. 19 February. https://www.eset.com/us/about/newsroom/research/eset-research-discovers-promptspy-first-android-threat-using-genai/ (accessed 29 March 2026).

Steinberg, S., A. Stepan, and K. Neary (2021a). The hacking of Sony Pictures: A Columbia University case study. Columbia University School of International Affairs. SIPA-21-0023.1. https://www.sipa.columbia.edu/sites/default/files/2022-11/Sony%20-%20Written%20Case.pdf (accessed 29 March 2026).

Steinberg, S., A. Stepan, and Neary, K. (2021b). NotPetya: A Columbia University case study. Columbia University School of International Affairs. SIPA-21-0023.1. https://www.sipa.columbia.edu/sites/default/files/2022-11/NotPetya%20Final.pdf (accessed 29 March 2026).

Stoll, C. (1989). *The Cuckoo's Egg*. New York, NY: Doubleday.

Szoldra, P. (2016). His is everything Edward Snowden revealed in one year of unprecedented top-secret leaks. 16 September. https://www.businessinsider.com/snowden-leaks-timeline-2016-9 (accessed 30 March 2026).

Temple-Raston, D. (2021). A 'Worst Nightmare' cyberattack: The untold story of the solarwinds hack. Heard on All Things Considered. 16 April. https://www.npr.org/2021/04/16/985439655/a-worst-nightmare-cyberattack-the-untold-story-of-the-solarwinds-hack (accessed 31 March 2026).

Thompson, H. H. and Chase, S. G. (2005). *The Software Vulnerability Guide.* Hingham, MA: Charles River Media.

United States China Commission (USCC) (2023). Relationship Between the United States and China. U.S.-China Economic and Security Review Commission. November 2023. https://www.uscc.gov/sites/default/files/annual_reports/2010%20Annual%23Report%20to%20Congress.pdf (accessed 28 March 2026). Note: All USCC Annual reports may be found at this link https://www.uscc.gov/annual-reports/.

United States China Commission (USCC) (2002). Report to Congress: The National Security Implications of the Economic Relationship Between the United States and China. U.S.-China Economic and Security Review Commission. July 2002. https://www.uscc.gov/sites/default/files/annual_reports/2002%20Annual%20Report%20to%20Congress.pdf (accessed 28 March 2026). Note: All USCC Annual reports may be found at this link https://www.uscc.gov/annual-reports/ (accessed 30 March 2026).

United States China Commission (USCC) (2010). Report to Congress: The National Security Implications of the Economic Relationship Between the United States and China. U.S.-China Economic and Security Review Commission. November 2010. https://www.uscc.gov/sites/default/files/annual_reports/2010%20Annual%20Report%20to%20Congress.pdf (accessed 28 March 2026). Note: All USCC Annual reports may be found at this link https://www.uscc.gov/annual-reports/.

United States China Commission (USCC) (2024). Report to Congress: The National Security Implications of the Economic Relationship Between the United States and China. U.S.-China Economic and Security Review Commission. November 2024. https://www.uscc.gov/sites/default/files/annual_reports/2024%20Annual%20Report%20to%20Congress.pdf (accessed 28 March 2026). Note: All USCC Annual reports may be found at this link https://www.uscc.gov/annual-reports/.

United States China Commission (USCC) (2025). Report to Congress: The National Security Implications of the Economic Relationship Between the United States and China. U.S.-China Economic and Security Review Commission. November 2025. https://www.uscc.gov/sites/default/files/annual_reports/2025%20Annual%20Report%20to%20Congress.pdf (accessed 28 March 2026). Note: All USCC Annual reports may be found at this link https://www.uscc.gov/annual-reports/.

United States Computer Emergency Readiness Team (US CERT) (n.d.). United States Computer Emergency Readiness Team, the Department of Homeland Security's Cybersecurity and Infrastructure Security Agency (CISA). https://www.cisa.gov/sites/default/files/publications/infosheet_US-CERT_v2.pdf (accessed 30 March 2026).

United States Congress (USC) (2024). House Energy and Commerce Oversight Investigations Subcommittee, Testimony of Andrew Witty, CEO of UnitedHealth Group, United States Congress. 30 April. https://d1dth6e84htgma.cloudfront.net/Witty_Testimony_OI_Hearing_05_01_24_5ff52a2d11.pdf (accessed 29 March 2026).

United States House of Representatives Committee on Science and Technology (1983). Computer and Communincations Security and Privacy Report. 26 September. https://www.ojp.gov/pdffiles1/Digitization/95323NCJRS.pdf (accessed 25 March 2026).

Weiss, J. (n.d.). Unfettered blog. Control Global. https://www.controlglobal.com/blogs/unfettered (accessed March 31 2026).

3

Cybersecurity Policy Objectives

This chapter is focused on the domain of *organization*. Whether it documents them or not, an organization generally has *vision, mission*, and *core values* that define what it is trying to achieve and how it wants to conduct itself (COSO 2017). Yet, regardless of an organization's mission, policy specific to cybersecurity is based on the fact that the nature of the risk in cybersecurity is both unique and highly likely. Therefore, there are similarities across organizations in the type of cybersecurity issues to be addressed and the associated governance and management activity designed to minimize cybersecurity risk to mission success. A starting point for any risk management endeavor is the articulation of risk issues and governance objectives, and so we start with an overview of what cybersecurity risk issues look like. This is followed by a summary of the building blocks of cybersecurity governance and management from an operational risk perspective. These include policy-based cybersecurity principles and associated processes, standards, procedures (PPSPs) designed to *implement* the policy. This is followed by an overview of monitoring via metrics designed to ensure the policy objectives are met. In acknowledgement that organizational cybersecurity policy must always be customized to focus on an organization's unique vision, mission, core values, and associated threats, this chapter also includes a section on cybersecurity risk management with examples of how cybersecurity policy works (or not) in a sample of industries.

3.1 Cybersecurity Risk Issues

The word risk has been used for centuries to describe events in narrow categories whose outcome may impact the future. In the case of the cybersecurity category, risk analysis is focused on the events wherein the aftermath has a negative impact. Cybersecurity risk management is the art (not a science) of identifying

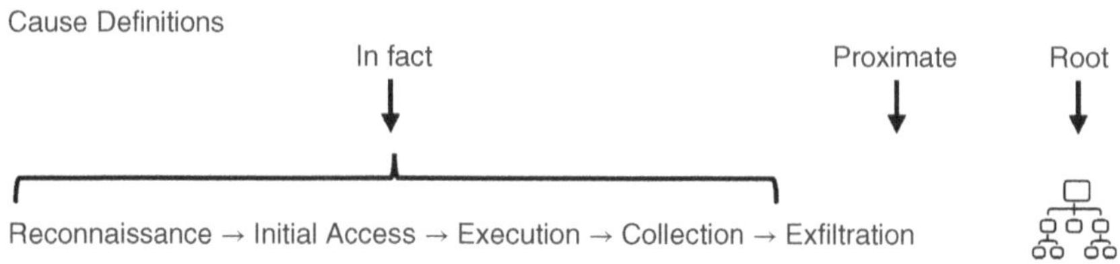

Figure 3.1 Causes.

potentially negatively impacting events and avoiding, mitigating, transferring, or accepting them.

In contrast, the word *issue* is generally ambiguous. There are over a dozen definitions of issue that range from "an unsettled matter" (a noun) to "emerge" (a verb). Examples of *issue* as a noun are: "an important topic or problem," an "unsolved problem or difficulty," "a serious concern," and "a probable negatively impacting event." The last of these definitions is what we mean by a risk issue. There's a probability that a negative thing is going to happen. In any field, the way people resolve issues is to search for the root cause and try to eliminate it. One way people look for causes of cybersecurity events is to chart out a threat vector like the one in Figure 3.1. It charts the activities of a cyberattack as a series of MITRE stages, ending in a successful exploit.

Of course, if the activities in the threat vector had not occurred, there would not have been a successful cyberattack. However, simply eliminating one or more of the steps on any given vector would not prevent other threat vectors from being successful. This is because the last step in a threat vector is not a root cause; it is a proximate cause. A proximate cause is the last activity (automated or manual) that touched the environment that had the negative impact.

The legal profession has another way of looking at the causes of negatively impacting events. They use the same definition of proximate, but have another term called cause *in fact*. The proximate cause triggers the incident, but a cause in fact is a necessary factor, though not a sufficient condition, to result in the negatively impacting event. For example, in the case of a murder, the proximate cause may be pulling the trigger, but that would not have happened had someone not sold the murderer a gun.

In the field of quality assurance, a common method of arriving at root causes is by repeatedly asking *why?*: Why did the attack happen? (Because of the exploit.) Why did the exploit happen? (Because of the vulnerability.) Why did the vulnerability happen? (etc.). In this view, if a root cause of a situation did not exist, the event would not have occurred, and if eliminated would change the circumstances so dramatically that *other negative impact events in the same category would also not occur*. Therefore, in cybersecurity, we identify a risk issue with respect to the *root cause of events comprising a risk category*.

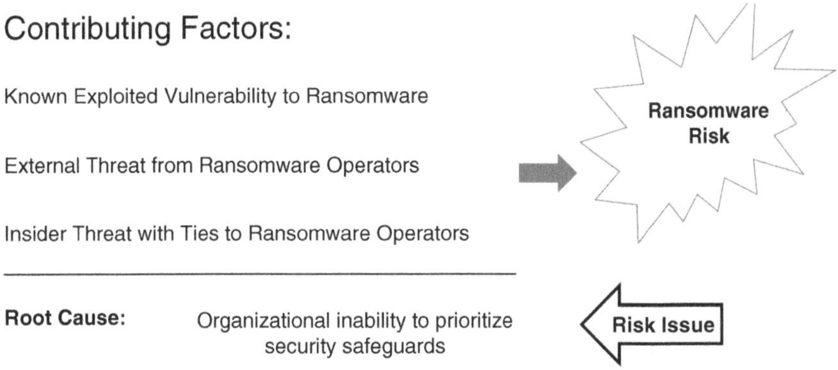

Figure 3.2 Risk issue.

For example, Figure 3.2. shows the relationship between a ransomware risk category, its contributing factors, and a ransomware event. The three contributing factors to ransomware (vulnerabilities, external threats, and inside threats) are well known, and if all three were present within a single organization, it would be incumbent upon that organization to make heroic efforts to change course (e.g., to not tolerate known exploitable vulnerabilities). A cybersecurity risk officer who raises the alarm that there are known exploitable vulnerabilities in an organization's systems would typically declare a risk issue and establish management controls in the form of processes, standards, and procedures to systematically root them out. The root cause would then be framed as something like "organizational inability to prioritize security safeguards," depicted in the figure as an organization chart.

3.2 Governance and Management

For individuals, dealing with cybersecurity issues is a matter of personal choice. In an organizational or public context, dealing with cybersecurity risk issues is a function of governance. Governance includes the assignment of roles and responsibilities with clear accountability for establishing *processes* to minimize the negative impact of cybersecurity risks and corresponding *standards, procedures*, and *guidelines* to ensure the smooth operation of those processes. These, in turn, may be delegated by establishing clear success criteria in the form of verification and validation metrics. That is, indicators for which controls have been correctly implemented as designed, and indicators that demonstrate the controls achieve the objective of minimizing risk to an acceptable residual level. As illustrated in Figure 3.3, a policy typically preceded by a high-level management directive is generically referred to as a "Risk Appetite Statement." The exemplar risk appetite

Figure 3.3 Cybersecurity governance.

statement at the top of Figure 3.3 is consistent with a leader's responsibility to set *tone at the top* on how to approach significant risk issues (COSO 1992).

If people are not aware of the decisions made in strategy and risk appetite, then they will have no reason to implement directives in accordance with them. It is typically the job of the Chief Information Security Officer (CISO) to produce and publish PPSPs required to achieve this *awareness*. Policy must be approved at the governance level to be binding on everyone within the organization, typically reference to a cybersecurity policy, among others, will be listed in a legally binding Code of Conduct that all staff within the organization, and often suppliers, are expected to sign upon first arrival. This first initiation to cybersecurity policy would be followed by training on any process, standards, and procedures the staff member must learn to ensure that policy is followed according to management strategy for compliance. That is, processes, standards, procedures, and guidelines for management to create and maintain, while governance committees will review and approve them.

Corresponding guidelines are also often issued in conjunction with policy to demonstrate that, in general, compliance with a given policy may be achieved. Awareness and directives at higher levels drive awareness and corresponding activities at lower levels.

There may be multiple, equally effective methods of *implementing* policy within systems, and standards are generally adopted to economy and efficiency. They are often stated in the form of preselected devices and architectures, mandatory settings for security configuration variables, that, when configured and combined with control activities such as procedures, will achieve policy compliance. While the documentation of these security program requirements may be hierarchical, in practice, PPSPs interact simultaneously, as people, process, and technology (PPT) operate side by side to maintain cybersecurity risk below the level proscribed by risk appetite.

3.2.1 Cybersecurity Policy

Over the years of security management practices, several studies have attempted to classify security technology practices into general security principles (Neumann 2004). The result is that there is a common body of knowledge of cybersecurity architecture patterns that, if observed in the requirements stages of technology engineering, serve to suggest well-known solutions to well-known security problems. Security principles are generic descriptions of security features that provide solutions to cybersecurity problems that are both common and well understood. For example, the principle of least resource, which dictates that users should have at their disposal the fewest amount of shared computing resources that they need to complete their tasks, and no more. Many of these principles were derived by the information systems audit profession, and have their origins in the service of the accounting profession, whose early assignments with respect to computers were to ensure that computer-generated reports could properly account for corporate assets (Bayuk 2005, pp. 10–13). Some evolved alongside and consistent with government standards for security, such as the Orange Book and its successors (DoD 1985; International Organization for Standardization 2022a, b). Others emerged from the study of cryptography in computer science (Denning 1982).

A key contribution from the accounting profession is the principle of segregation of duties, which dictates that, for situations wherein a user controls valuable assets, every individual one of them should be restricted from changing ownership of those assets without the collusion of others, a principle designed to deter insider fraud. This requires automated processes that transfer assets to be broken down into subprocesses, and no one person being given permission to execute every step in the subprocess. This technique is commonly used in large IT organizations for software deployment processes so that no single person is in a position to introduce fraudulent or malicious code without detection. It is also commonly applied to secure financial transactions, and is also used in high-security settings, such as missile launch scenarios. The same technique could be said for any operation that controls an asset or process critical to the enterprise mission or purpose. This is what makes it a security principle.

A pure technology derivation of this type of accounting principle is the principle of least privilege, which dictates that users should have the minimum access they need to perform a technology task and no more. Many of these cybersecurity principles have been codified by the information systems auditors, some as early as 1977 (Singleton 1994). These have been continually updated by the Information Systems Audit and Control Association (ISACA), a global certification authority for information systems auditors, Control Objectives for Information Technology (COBIT) (ISACA 2019).

Every organization draws the line between what types of directives are mandated policy and which are relegated to standards as they see fit. But in general, standards document the *implementation* details for specific technology platforms, while policy statements are reserved for higher-level management control objectives such as delegating key processes to specific executives. They are often organized by functional groups or situations, as in the examples in Figure 3.4. No matter what ends up in an organization's cybersecurity policy, it is highly likely to be based on the set of security principles listed in Table 3.1.

Organizational – applies to all systems within organization:

- *Access to applications shall be authorized by job function and access to data within applications shall be minimized to that necessary for the task at hand to reduce the risk of data leakage.*

Architectural – warranted where data exposure warrants segregation of duties and redundant controls

- *All Database Management Systems shall be centrally managed by the Chief Technology Officer, All other staff shall access data only via authorized business applications.*
- *All Network connectivity shall be centrally managed by the Head of Technology Infrastructure.*
- *Business use of cloud applications is subject to the approval of the firm's Chief Information Security Officer.*

Situational – Mandates that apply to process more than technology, may be published by governance organization (e.g., as part of a Code of Conduct).

- *External Connectivity shall be limited to partner organizations with which there is a binding legal contract that includes provisions to minimize cybersecurity risk as dictated by both the Chief Legal Officer and the Chief Security Officer.*

Figure 3.4 Example organizational policy statements.

Table 3.1 Cybersecurity Principles.

	Cybersecurity Principles
Complete mediation	Intercept all system operations with a reference monitor that verifies both authentication and authorization.
Comprehensive accountability	Automatically monitor, audit, and analyze *administrative, functional*, and *data* access as appropriate to identify and alert on probable misuse of system resources.
Defense in depth	Require authorization through multiple layers of separately configured controls prior to allowing access to resources.
Economy of mechanism	Require the design to be as simple and small as possible to maintain the system's mission.
Fail safe	Require failures at the system and component level to result in the inability of operators to access functions and resources.
Least common mechanism	Minimize situations wherein users share the same system mechanism (e.g., sandbox, where possible).
Least privilege	Require users to have exactly the permissions they need to perform their responsibilities and no more.
Multifactor authentication	Require authentication sequence work factors to be commensurate with the risk of compromise.
Open design	Never assume that design secrecy will enhance security.
Psychological acceptability	Ensure requirements for identification, authentication, and authorization features include ease of use and operation.
Recovery point objective	Ensure requirements include the archive and availability of a known good state from which system operation may safely resume after an outage.
Recovery time objective	Ensure requirements include the length of time a system outage can be tolerated without breaching risk appetite.
Segregation of duties	Require functionality to complete high-risk tasks to be divided and ensure access to all required subtasks cannot be performed by a single user.
Separation of privilege	Do not grant special system privileges based on a technical mechanism operated by a single user (e.g., dual control).
Verification and validation	Test critical controls for compliance with design requirements and for functional ability to achieve intended control objectives in a production environment.
Zero trust	Require per-resource-request identification and authorization to be enforced using mechanisms that do not rely on an assumption that it is possible to secure a network.

3.2.2 Process

Processes are cross-organizational workflows that link those with assigned responsibilities in different areas to work together; they are composed at different levels of the enterprise organizational structure and address different organizational constituents whose interactions render the controls effective. The risk appetite comes from the top and is colloquially referred to as "tone at the top." It is the executive management's articulation of the extent to which a risk may be deemed acceptable. It is then the role of the CISO to create a process by which senior management can negotiate and agree on an enterprise cybersecurity policy that reflects that appetite. Each business leader, including the CISO, creates processes for their *own* organizational operations that align with *each other's* processes to create cross-organizational workflow.

3.2.3 Standards

Standards typically document the implementation details for specific technology platforms. There may be multiple, equally effective, methods of implementing policy within a technology platform, and standards are generally adopted for economy and efficiency. They are often stated in the form of settings for technology configuration variables, which, when configured and combined with control activities, such as procedures, will achieve policy compliance. Figure 3.5 provides an example of an industry standard, in this case, the federal government, and one organization's customization of the standard.

3.2.4 Procedures

Procedures are documented step-by-step implementation instructions that a technician may follow to be successful in implementing standards. They are used not only to guarantee a policy-compliant technical configuration, but also to train new technicians on the mechanics of configuring the technology. Therefore, procedures must be written at a much lower level of detail than policies or standards, and they must fully explain how to operate technology. Figure 3.6 provides an example of a security operations (SecOps) procedure.

3.2.5 Guidelines

Guidelines are the most general type of security document. They are designed to raise awareness among those who must comply with policy. They provide options for policy compliance. They do not dictate exactly how to comply or what must be done, but instead contain education and advice for individuals who must make their own daily choices about cybersecurity as part of their job function. Figure 3.7 provides an example of a guideline on how to choose a good password. Note in Figure 3.3, guidelines are in italics to stand out from the other types

Exemplar Industry Standard

(Derived from Industry or Regulatory Guidance)

National Institute of Standards and Technology Security Special Publication on Privacy Controls for Information Systems and Organizations (NIST SP-800-53) Guidance on least privilege network access:

The organization authorizes network access to [Assignment: organization-defined privileged commands] only for [Assignment: organization-defined compelling operational needs] and documents the rationale for such access in the **security plan** for the information system.

etc.

Example Organizational Custom Version:

Document: Network Architecture Standards

Section X: Network Access Controls

1. The use of remote access to the enterprise network is reserved for access to production application systems and restricted to users authorized by job function that requires travel.
2. **Users must be configured via group entitlement to VPN links controlled by network engineering** (*see* instruction to request access at this link:....).
3. **Access to a VPN for remote access is restricted Multi-Factor Authentication technologies supported by LAN engineering.** No other type of access is authorized.
4. **All user access credentials for remote access are stored in the Enterprise Cybersecurity Vault system** (see configuration settings for both MFA Server and Vault at this link:...)

etc.

Figure 3.5 Example cybersecurity industry standard.

SecOps Center Procedure

1. Select the highest priority alert in the queue
2. Ascertain context:
   a. app or data in alert, search application registry for app/data owner
   b. device or IP in alert, search inventory for device and/or network owner
   c. if user data in alert, identify users in directory, else search device logs for user activity then identify users in directory
3. Distinguish between anomaly and intrusion
   a. attempt to contact user(s) if any and verify authorized access, if user denies activity, assume intrusion and escalate to supervisor who will take over investigation
   b. if no user(s) in logs or attempt to contact fails, assume anomaly, convene call with supervisor and app/data/device/net owners
   a. if user verifies activity, contact supervisor for instruction

Figure 3.6 Example cybersecurity procedure.

1. Choose a password based on a phrase that:
   A. Is based on a phrase *unique* to you (i.e,. no popular movies or songs).
   B. Has enough syllables to meet the password length requirement
   C. Makes you smile
2. For each syllable in your phrase, substitute a required character to obfuscate the phrase, for example:

I love to go to the beach in the summertime

|1 2 g 2+ 8 ! t S 3 T

Your password is both easy to remember and hard to guess!

Figure 3.7 Example cybersecurity guideline.

of management directives, which are required rather than suggested. They are labeled as *advice* precisely because they are not enforceable.

3.3 Metrics

It has been our observation that everyone's first instinct in proposing security validation metrics is to measure successful attacks or intrusions. For example, in the book, *How to Measure Anything*, the author suggests that security goals be measured by the "absence of successful virus attacks" (Hubbard 2007). Applied to the operation of a manufacturing assembly line, this approach makes sense; as long as there are no accidents, our metric can be proudly hung on a billboard in the parking lot: "It has been 346 days since our last accident." However, in the case of cybersecurity, the suggested metric of "absence of successful virus attacks" suffers the fatal flaw that it measures progress toward an objective by the absence of an event, rather than by any positive indicator that the objective is met. Science has taught us that there are only so many ways to measure. As depicted in Figure 3.8,

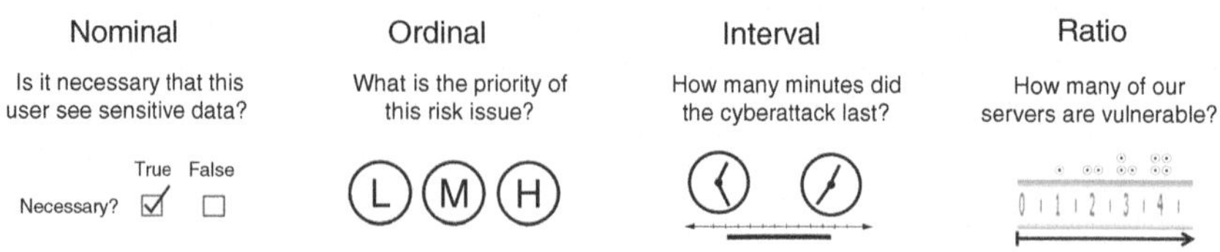

Figure 3.8 Measures.

they are nominal, ordinal, interval, and ratio. Nominal measures are simply names given to objects to classify them. For example, we classify some infrastructure as "critical." Interval measures are ordered labels like High, Medium, Low. Figure 3.8 also includes an example question about cybersecurity that could be answered using the different types of measures to create a management metric. Note there is no option in the range of scientific measures to measure the absence of anything, much less something so elusive as malware is known to be. Using the "absence of successful virus attacks" approach, a system that is rarely attacked will be judged to be more secure than another simply because its security has not often been tested. As the former CISO of AT&T, historically one of the most hacked targets on the planet, once put it, "During a period of seeming quiet, never confuse good luck with improved cybersecurity" (Amoroso 2006).

As an illustration of why the absence of a successful attack is not a cybersecurity success indicator, recall from Chapter 2 that the NSA's zero-day exploit database leaked by the Shadow Brokers in 2017 included the EternalBlue exploit that was used in the WannaCry worm, followed by a wave of ransomware across the globe. Given that the cyber arms race continues to rely on nation-state hoarding of zero days, it is now more than ever negligent to rely on a track record of no successful cybersecurity attacks to demonstrate that your cybersecurity is sufficient to withstand the next wave of zero days.

Instead, it is cybersecurity best practice to measure progress toward a goal of the *absence of successful attacks* by creating measures to validate that a system is not vulnerable to known exploit attacks and summarizing one's level of vulnerability to attack with a management metric that will support decisions with respect to PPSPs. This is typically done by planning and executing attacks on one's own system and measuring the ease with which an adversary may exploit any identified *vulnerabilities* known to be exploited by the set of all currently cataloged malicious software. This practice is called either *vulnerability scanning* or *penetration testing*, depending on the level of automation, where vulnerability scanning is fully automated, and the software may even produce a metric report, while penetration testing mimics the human behavior of an attacker with exploit kits looking for full attack paths that end with access to sensitive data or administrative control over a system. Both types of measures result in metrics that make use of what cybersecurity professionals refer to as *badness-ometers*, like the ones in Figures 3.9 and 3.10,

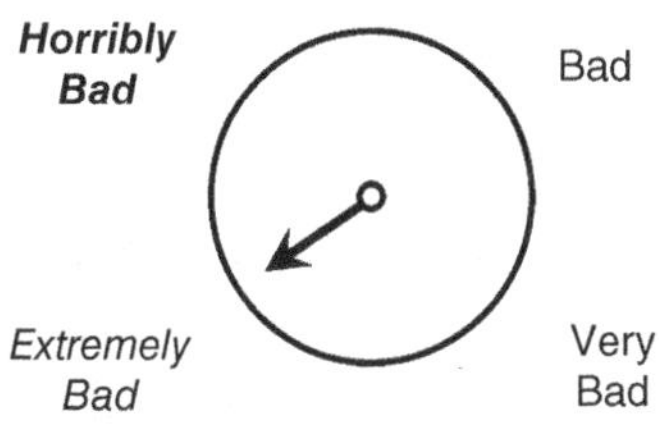

Figure 3.9 Badness-ometer.

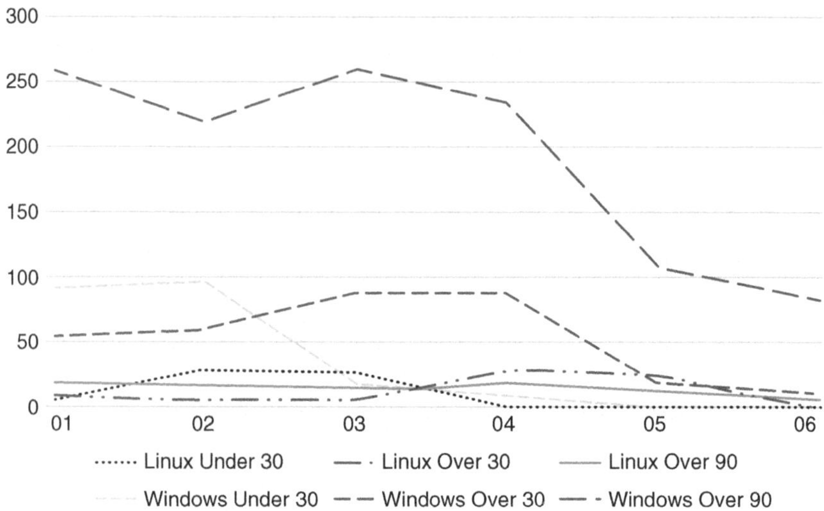

Figure 3.10 Vulnerability trend metric.

because they can only measure whether security is bad; there is no ordinal scale on which the measure could produce an output labeled "good" (McGraw 2006, pp. 22–23).

When the methods of vulnerability scanners and penetration testers are as far as possible current and even forward-looking as possible, they serve as a design basis threat (DBT), a term borrowed from physical security wherein metrics have traditionally concentrated on the ability of a system to meet the goal of withstanding a given amount of physical force (Garcia 2008). A physical DBT describes characteristics of the most powerful and innovative adversary that it is realistic to expect to protect against. In New York City, it may be a terrorist cell equipped with sophisticated communications and explosive devices. In Idaho, it may be a 20-person-strong posse of vigilantes carrying automatic assault weapons on motorcycles. Adopting a DBT approach to cybersecurity implies that the strength of security protection required by a system should be calculated with respect to a technical specification of how it is likely to be attacked. In physical security, this process is straightforward. If the DBT is a force of 20 people with access to explosives of a given type, then the strength of the physical barriers to unauthorized entry must withstand the ton of force that these 20 people could physically bring into system contact. Barrier protection materials are specified, threat delay and response systems are designed, and validation tests are conducted accordingly.

In organizations wherein the scope of current and foreseeable cybersecurity attacks is well understood at the time cybersecurity controls are designed and tested, a DBT approach to cybersecurity can help produce metrics that

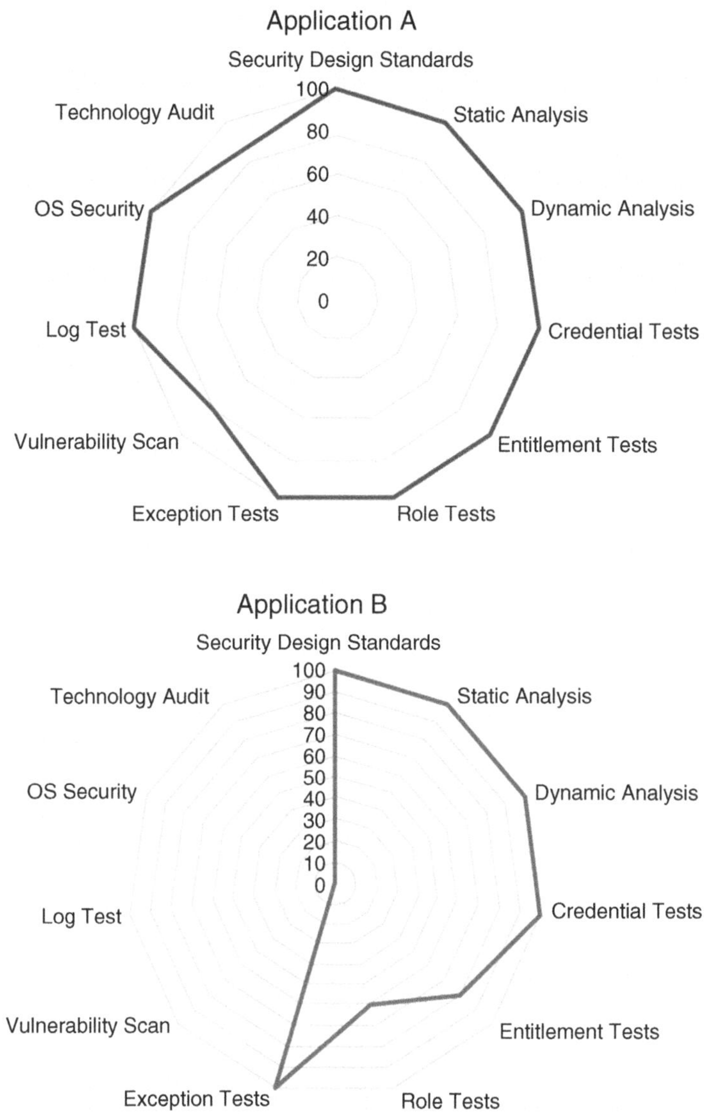

Figure 3.11 Application security metric.

demonstrate that a design specification was *verified* to have been implemented *correctly*, as in the example of Figure 3.11. In the figure, the security attributes of two business applications are individually measured for conformance to design specifications using different types of tests and audits; each one is presented as a ratio of the number of specifications tested by the type of test performed.

The spider chart representation of results shows management that Application A needs some work while Application B is just starting its journey on the organization's application security lifecycle. That said, if Application B was 100% across the board, it is still not one that guarantees achievement of a control objective because the *absence of a successful attack* is fully met.

Determining whether cybersecurity is effective is the domain of *validating* control objectives, which can only be achieved by measuring continuity of serving its *purpose in the context of its operation*. That is, measures of effectiveness performed in test environments are invalid to establish effectiveness because a system operation in context includes unexpected cyberattacks. The closest thing cybersecurity has to validation metrics are the results of penetration tests conducted by highly skilled cybersecurity attack teams in the system's production environment from both internal and external network locations.

Validation requires not just evidence that the latest set of known attacks will fail, but evidence that it is not possible (or at least extremely difficult) to enact security threats that impact system performance. Such a demonstration requires that the system in operation be subject to the types of failures that would be caused by a determined attacker rather than a *simulation* of any one or more known methods of attack. Hence, cyber continuity measures requirements for system availability are traditionally based on failure modes, effects, and criticality analysis (FMECA), as opposed to DBT (Rausand and Hoylan 2004). This approach requires an organization to itemize all possible software and hardware components that could contribute to interruption of system services, design a method where they will be fail-safe, as described in the principle in Table 3.1 under Fail Safe, and deny access to all data and services when a potential failure is detected. In the case of a cyberattack, it may mean automatically blocking suspicious activity at the network level, understanding that occasionally you may cut off a legitimate user.

3.4 Risk Management

The industries in this section were selected to illustrate a wide range of industry-specific cybersecurity risk management techniques. The first was chosen because it is the most disciplined in its approach to cybersecurity governance – the financial industry. Finance is followed by the unique issues faced by industrial control systems (ICSs), a set of industries faced with a solemn responsibility in maintaining cybersecurity, though its unique cyber-physical challenges with standardization as a distant goal. From there, the leap to technology platforms demonstrates the struggles of trying to apply cybersecurity principles to entirely new and constantly changing approaches to cyberspace itself. This section ends with an exploration of the growing cybersecurity risks presented by artificial intelligence (AI).

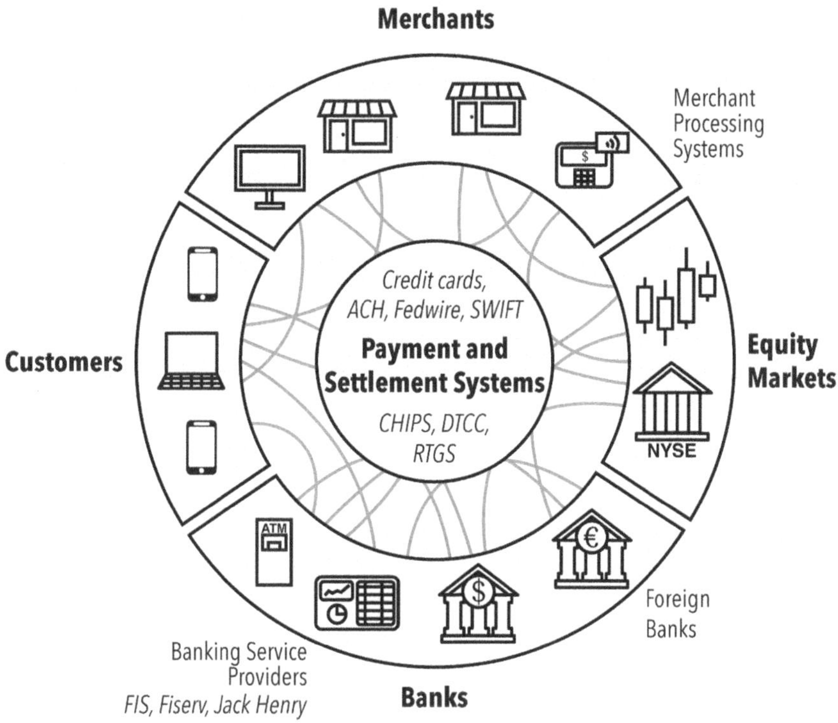

Figure 3.12 Financial ecosystem.

3.4.1 Financial Services

Financial services operate as a system-of-systems where multiple interconnected infrastructures create dense webs of dependencies. Unlike ICSs, where failures remain localized to single facilities, or e-commerce systems, where individual firm breaches primarily affect that firm's customers, financial services cybersecurity failures propagate through networked dependencies to threaten system-wide stability, or systemic risk.

Figure 3.12 illustrates the interconnected nature of the financial services ecosystem. Customers interact with US banks through various channels, including online banking, mobile applications, and ATMs. These institutions connect to merchants and merchant processing systems to facilitate transactions. Payment systems (including credit card networks such as Visa, Mastercard, and American Express), Automated Clearing House (ACH), Federal Reserve Wire Network (Fedwire), Society for Worldwide Interbank Financial Telecommunication (SWIFT), and Clearing House Interbank Payments System (CHIPS) link domestic and foreign banks in real-time transaction processing. Settlement systems clear and finalize transactions among participants. Core banking service providers (such as FIS, Fiserv, and Jack Henry) supply the technology infrastructure that many institutions use for account management, transaction processing, and general ledger functions. Foreign banks connect to this network through correspondent banking relationships and shared payment infrastructure. A compromise at any node can propagate throughout the system.

3.4.1.1 Contagion Mechanisms

The interconnected architecture of the financial system creates conditions under which a cyber event does not merely spread but transforms; what begins as a technical compromise at a single institution can cross into operational disruption across dependent firms, then into financial stress through balance-sheet linkages, and finally into a crisis of confidence that affects institutions with no direct connection to the original incident at all. Like a pathogen that jumps species and mutates into something more dangerous in the new host, each crossing of a contagion channel changes the nature of the threat. Financial stability regulators identify three primary contagion channels: operational, financial, and confidence (ESRB 2020; European Central Bank 2025). This chapter extends that framework to include a fourth channel, technical contagion, grounded in the cybersecurity literature on lateral movement and software supply chain compromise (Cybersecurity and Infrastructure Security Agency and National Institute of Standards and Technology 2021; MITRE 2023). Where the financial stability channels describe how disruption and stress propagate through dependency and behavioral relationships, technical contagion describes how compromise itself traverses organizational boundaries through trusted technical connections. It is distinct in kind from the other three: it spreads the compromise itself, not merely its consequences.

Technical contagion spreads through shared networks or common vendor systems, carrying compromise across organizational boundaries through the same trusted connections that enable normal operations. Unlike operational contagion, which disrupts institutions through shared dependency, technical contagion actively propagates malicious code or unauthorized access from one organization to another through authenticated channels. Software supply chain attacks illustrate the mechanism: when an adversary compromises an update distributed through a vendor's trusted delivery infrastructure, every connected client receives the compromise as part of routine maintenance (CISA and NIST 2021; MITRE 2023). In the financial sector, where core banking service providers maintain persistent administrative access across hundreds of client institutions, a single compromise can traverse the entire client network before any individual institution detects anomalous activity.

Operational contagion disrupts shared infrastructure, preventing dependent institutions from conducting business, spreading dysfunction rather than malicious code. A cyberattack against payment clearing infrastructure prevents all dependent banks from processing transactions regardless of their individual security postures. The result is simultaneous operational failure across institutions, not sequential.

Financial contagion occurs when cybersecurity incidents create losses impairing an institution's ability to meet obligations to counterparties, transmitting stress through interbank exposures and balance-sheet linkages. A ransomware attack preventing a major correspondent bank from processing payments creates liquidity problems for smaller institutions depending on that correspondent for payment services; cascade effects follow through interbank lending markets.

Confidence contagion operates through perception rather than code. A prominent breach at one institution can prompt depositors at unaffected banks to question the security of the broader system. Precautionary withdrawals follow, resembling a digital bank run. Counterparty credit line reductions and market selloffs follow the same dynamic: the incident itself may be contained, but the behavioral response is not.

These mechanisms are not mutually exclusive and often activate sequentially or simultaneously when cyber incidents occur in densely interconnected systems.

3.4.1.2 Illustrative Contagion Scenarios

These contagion mechanisms operate through specific attack pathways and institutional dependencies. To illustrate how technical, operational, financial, and confidence contagion manifest in practice, let us examine four hypothetical scenarios.

The first scenario illustrates *technical contagion* originating at a core banking service provider. Suppose attackers compromise a remote management platform used to distribute software updates to client banks. Because those banks trust authenticated connections and digitally signed updates from the provider, malicious code is delivered through routine maintenance channels and bypasses perimeter defenses. Malware spreads into core processing systems at multiple institutions. The contagion occurs not because each bank independently failed, but because trusted interconnections allow malicious code to propagate across organizational boundaries.

The second scenario demonstrates *operational contagion* without technical spread. Imagine a ransomware attack that disables a payment clearing or settlement provider, but does not infect connected banks. Even so, interbank transfers cannot be processed. Banks expecting incoming funds must still meet outgoing obligations, depleting liquidity buffers and potentially drawing on central bank facilities or liquidating assets. What begins as a contained infrastructure outage evolves into liquidity stress across institutions. Here, the disruption spreads through dependency on shared infrastructure rather than through malware.

The third scenario highlights *financial contagion* through contractual exposures. Suppose a cyberattack at one bank enables fraudulent transfers or produces substantial losses. Counterparties respond by reducing credit lines, demanding additional collateral, or restricting funding. Interbank markets tighten, and institutions reliant on short-term funding face pressure. The contagion spreads through balance-sheet linkages and contractual relationships, not through technical compromise.

The fourth scenario reflects *confidence contagion* in a digital banking environment. Suppose a third-party authentication provider fails, preventing a bank from reliably displaying balances or processing transactions. The failure is not a breach. No funds have been moved, no data has been taken. Yet customers encountering errors question the institution's stability and initiate withdrawals. Media coverage and social networks amplify uncertainty beyond the affected bank, potentially reaching institutions perceived to share similar dependencies. What spreads here is not code or dysfunction or financial loss, it is doubt. The confidence channel is the only contagion mechanism that can propagate without any underlying technical failure at the receiving institution.

These channels are not mutually exclusive. A single cyber incident may activate them sequentially or simultaneously: a technical compromise may lead to operational shutdowns, which generate liquidity stress, which in turn erodes public confidence. The critical distinction is analytical. Technical contagion spreads code; operational contagion spreads dysfunction; financial contagion spreads losses and liquidity stress; and confidence contagion spreads fear. In a densely interconnected financial system, the systemic consequences of cyber incidents arise less from the sophistication of the initial attack than from the structure of interdependence that transmits its effects.

3.4.1.3 Contagion Accelerators

The speed and severity of cyber contagion depend not only on the nature of the initiating incident, but also on structural characteristics of the financial system. Three interrelated conditions (dependency, concentration, and trust) shape how disruption propagates across institutions, and each can materially amplify or accelerate systemic transmission.

Dependency refers to the functional criticality of a service to an institution's operations. Supervisory frameworks emphasize that disruption of a critical or important business service can threaten safety and soundness even where the service provider itself is not systemically dominant (BIS 2021). Substitutability modifies this dependency by determining whether viable alternatives exist and can be activated within operationally relevant timeframes. Portability further conditions substitution by determining whether data, applications, and operational processes can be transferred to an alternative provider without prolonged disruption or costly redesign. Where services are operationally indispensable, difficult to replace, and technically hard to port, such as core processing, settlement infrastructure, or cloud-based authentication, institutions face compressed decision windows and limited containment options. High dependency combined with low substitutability and limited portability, therefore, amplifies propagation by constraining exit strategies and delaying recovery solutions (FSB 2023; European Parliament 2022, Art. 30).

Concentration concerns exposure breadth: the extent to which many institutions rely on the same provider or infrastructure. Acemoglu et al. (2015) and Gai and Kapadia (2010) demonstrate that highly interconnected and concentrated network structures exhibit greater susceptibility to cascading failures than more distributed architectures, a finding with direct implications for financial systems where a handful of providers serve thousands of institutions. When essential services are concentrated among a small number of dominant providers, disruption at a single node affects multiple institutions simultaneously rather than sequentially. This synchronicity amplifies systemic impact and reduces the system's capacity to absorb shocks incrementally. High concentration, therefore, accelerates propagation by transforming localized failures into simultaneous multi-institution stress events (Bank for International Settlements 2025).

Trust operates as a transmission mechanism embedded in financial architecture. Payment systems, correspondent banking arrangements, and automated processing environments rely on authenticated connections and standardized messaging protocols that presume the validity of properly credentialed instructions. These trust-based efficiencies enable speed and scale under normal conditions, but they also reduce friction at institutional boundaries. When attackers gain access to trusted credentials or channels, malicious activity may traverse interconnected systems more rapidly than in architectures designed around stricter verification models (Kabir 2023). Trust, therefore, accelerates propagation by lowering defensive resistance at system interfaces and permitting compromised instructions to move across institutional boundaries before detection.

Together, dependency (particularly where substitutability and portability are limited), concentration, and trust function as transmission accelerants, converting localized cyber events into broader systemic disturbances. From a cyber policy perspective, risk assessments, controls, and governance need to address the organization's role in the system and its contagion risk profile.

3.4.1.4 Case Study: The SWIFT Banking Network

The 2016 Bangladesh Bank heist demonstrates how attackers exploited trust-based architectures and distributed responsibility gaps inherent in interconnected financial systems. SWIFT provides secure messaging services enabling banks worldwide to communicate payment instructions. With over 11,000 member institutions across 200+ countries processing trillions of dollars daily, SWIFT represents critical infrastructure for global finance. The system operates on inherent trust: when Bank A receives a properly authenticated SWIFT message from Bank B requesting a funds transfer, Bank A assumes the message is legitimate and acts

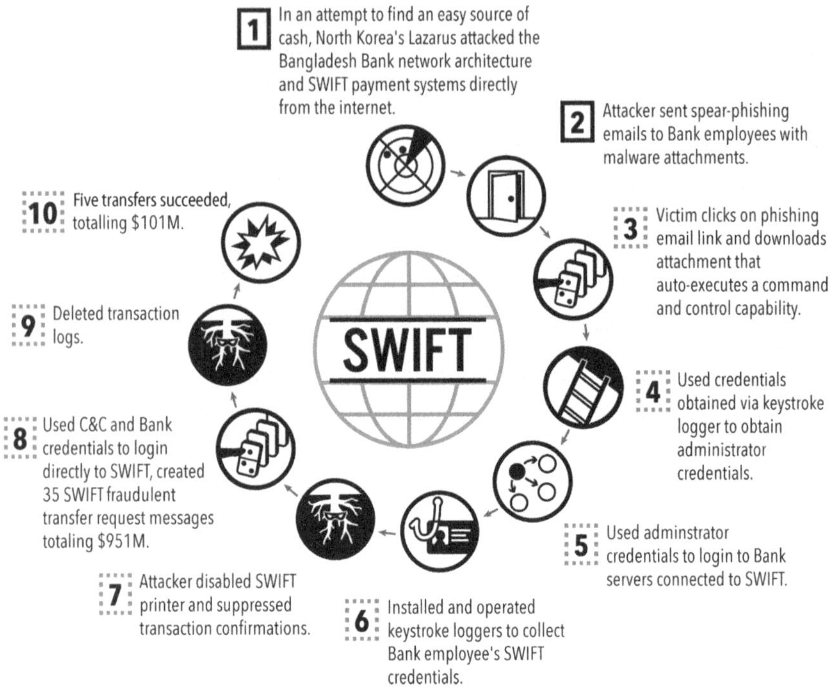

Figure 3.13 SWIFT case study.

upon it without additional verification (SWIFT n.d.-a). The tradeoff is structural: presumptive legitimacy enables high-volume transaction processing, but the same property accelerates fraudulent instruction propagation once authentication is compromised.

As depicted in Figure 3.13, the breach progressed through the classic MITRE ATT&CK® tactics and techniques described in Chapter 2. The ten-stage attack progression illustrates how trust-based financial messaging infrastructure accelerates both legitimate and fraudulent transactions once authentication is compromised. After gaining credentials through spear-phishing and downloading spyware with command and control (C&C) capability, attackers were able to capture and exfiltrate administrative credentials and, from there, plant spyware on the desktops of bank operations employees who had access to SWIFT and obtain their credentials as well. The attackers used defensive evasion techniques to cover their tracks. The attackers' subsequent activities exploited SWIFT's *presumptive legitimacy* model: properly authenticated messages executed without independent verification. The breach illustrated how endpoint compromise at a single institution can traverse the trust transmissions necessary to move currency before detection.

In February 2016, attackers compromised Bangladesh Bank's systems and submitted fraudulent SWIFT transfer requests totaling $951 million from the bank's Federal Reserve account. The attack succeeded through multiple security failures. Bangladesh Bank operated without firewalls separating its internal network from external connections, used outdated second-hand network switches costing $10 purchased from public markets, and lacked comprehensive security monitoring (Rahman 2016; Reuters 2016). Attackers sent spear-phishing emails to bank employees, established initial access, conducted extensive reconnaissance, mapped the bank's SWIFT infrastructure, and ultimately captured legitimate SWIFT credentials. Using these credentials, they submitted 35 fraudulent transfer requests. Four transactions totaling $81 million succeeded before the scheme was detected; a portion of those funds was eventually recovered, but the majority (routed through Manila casinos) was not (Balu 2020). Thirty-five transfer requests were processed in a single window before any alert was raised; the architecture that made this efficient for legitimate banking made it equally efficient for fraud.

The attack's success exposed fundamental questions about accountability in distributed infrastructure systems. The policy debate that emerged was that, while SWIFT marketed itself as the leading provider of secure financial messaging services, observers argued that SWIFT functioned as a messaging network only, with endpoint security the responsibility of each individual institution (Ferbrache 2016; Reuters 2016). This characterization illustrates challenges in assigning accountability for systemic infrastructure: when responsibility is distributed across multiple parties, no single entity bears a clear obligation for preventing incidents that exploit the interactions between network trust assumptions and endpoint vulnerabilities.

Beyond the technical vulnerabilities exploited in the Bangladesh incident, the broader pattern of SWIFT-related fraud reveals how insider collaboration compounds these infrastructure risks. In addition to the Bangladesh hack, insider threats contributed to numerous other SWIFT fraud attempts, with hackers collaborating with bank insiders to authorize fraudulent dealings or to bypass security alerts. An EastNets survey of 200 banks found that four in five banks have experienced at least one SWIFT fraud attempt since 2016, and that one in seven of those incidents involved an employee (EastNets 2019). Technical controls alone cannot address fraud enabled by authorized insiders. Policy frameworks must account for human factors through privileged access management and behavioral monitoring.

Recognizing these combined vulnerabilities, SWIFT implemented the Customer Security Controls Framework (CSCF), though its effectiveness remains contested. The CSCF establishes mandatory and advisory security controls for all SWIFT participants. The CSCF also requires annual independent attestations of compliance, with noncompliance to be reported to regulators (SWIFT n.d.-b; UpGuard 2025). The shift from voluntary best practices to mandatory, auditable standards addressed the distributed responsibility problem directly. Uniform baseline requirements now apply across all network participants.

However, fraud attempts have persisted despite these improvements. The same EastNets survey found that two-thirds of respondents reported SWIFT cybercrime had actually increased since 2016 (EastNets 2019). This suggests that while CSCF raised baseline security, determined attackers continue finding vulnerabilities. In interconnected systems, the weakest participant often determines overall system vulnerability, mandating continuous evolution of security requirements as attack sophistication advances. In global financial networks, one institution's vulnerability becomes everyone's risk (Ferbrache 2016).

The SWIFT breaches illustrates that effective cybersecurity policy must address the structural accelerators that transform localized failures into systemic crises, not technical vulnerabilities in isolation. The CSCF's transition from advisory guidance to mandatory controls with attestation requirements reflects a hard-won recognition: in concentrated, interdependent systems, baseline security cannot be left to voluntary compliance. Distributed responsibility models require equally clear accountability mechanisms; when security obligations are diffused across multiple parties, no single party bears unambiguous responsibility for the interactions between network trust assumptions and endpoint controls. Systems built on presumptive legitimacy need supplemental verification for high-value operations, including behavioral monitoring and dual authorization for large or anomalous transfers. Perimeter defenses are insufficient where insiders hold authorization authority. Effective governance of privileged access, through segregation of duties and continuous monitoring of unusual activity patterns, addresses the human dimension that technical controls cannot reach.

3.4.1.5 From Institutional Risk to Systemic Risk

The contagion mechanisms, accelerators, and case study analysis demonstrate a fundamental distinction in financial services cybersecurity: certain cyber incidents threaten system-wide stability rather than remaining contained at the institutional level. When compromise occurs at entities occupying critical network positions (core banking service providers, payment systems, and concentrated cloud platforms), the dependency, trust, and concentration accelerators transform localized failures into cascading crises affecting institutions that maintain sound individual security practices.

This distinction between institutional risk and systemic risk drives regulatory evolution beyond traditional prudential supervision approaches. Historically, banking regulators examined individual institutions to ensure each maintained adequate capital, sound risk management, and operational controls. This microprudential supervision operated on an implicit assumption: if regulators ensured each institution remained sound, system-wide resilience would follow. The 2008 financial crisis confirmed this assumption's fatal flaw: interconnections, common exposures, and concentration risks created system-wide vulnerabilities that institution-by-institution supervision failed to address, a structural weakness Borio (2003) had anticipated in advocating for macroprudential frameworks.

Cyber contagion in financial services presents analogous challenges. A community bank experiencing ransomware creates localized disruption managed through institutional supervision. A core banking provider serving thousands of institutions suffering the same attack threatens operational paralysis across entire market segments. The compromised provider might represent a small fraction of total banking assets, yet create disruption affecting substantial portions of the banking system if it occupies a critical node position within dependency networks. Traditional institutional supervision examining the provider's security controls proves necessary but insufficient; systemic risk requires identifying which entities pose disproportionate threats based on their interconnectedness, lack of substitutes, and concentration of critical services.

This recognition has driven the development of macroprudential oversight frameworks that complement institutional supervision by assessing system-wide stability threats. In the United States, the Dodd-Frank Act established the Financial Stability Oversight Council (FSOC) to identify systemically important entities whose failure could threaten financial stability, granting authority to designate both financial institutions and market utilities for enhanced oversight (US Congress 2010). However, that designation authority has not gone uncontested. A federal district court vacated the FSOC's designation of MetLife in 2016, finding the determination arbitrary and capricious, and all nonbank designations were subsequently rescinded by 2018 before revised guidance partially restored the framework (USDDCDC 2015). Additionally, the European Union (EU) developed complementary frameworks distinguishing entity-level requirements under the Digital Operational Resilience Act (DORA) from system-wide macroprudential oversight, with authority to designate critical Information and Communication Technology (ICT) Third-Party Providers for direct supervision based on systemic importance (European Parliament). These frameworks acknowledge that preventing systemic cyber crises requires both ensuring individual institutions implement sound security practices and managing concentration risks that create pathways for institutional failures to trigger system-wide cascades.

The shift from purely institutional to combined institutional and systemic oversight reflects a fundamental insight: in densely interconnected financial infrastructure, sound security at the institutional level does not guarantee system stability. The accelerating conditions examined in Section 3.4.1.3 – operational dependency, service concentration, and embedded trust – determine whether a localized failure remains contained or cascades. A policy that addresses only the compromised institution addresses the wrong unit of analysis.

3.4.1.6 Additional Cybersecurity Challenges in Financial Services

Financial institutions operate under information security obligations spanning all three classical security objectives: confidentiality, integrity, and availability. Each carries regulatory and systemic implications distinct from most other sectors. A fourth requirement, operational resilience, extends beyond availability and is addressed separately below.

Confidentiality protections arise primarily from financial privacy obligations. Customer account information and transaction histories constitute nonpublic personal information under the Gramm-Leach-Bliley Act (US Congress 1999) and its implementing interagency guidelines (National Archives 2004), which direct federally supervised institutions to implement controls protecting sensitive financial data against unauthorized access or disclosure (US Congress 1999). Beyond institutional exposure to regulatory enforcement, breaches carry direct and immediate consequences for individual customers; unauthorized access to account credentials can enable fraudulent transactions, identity theft, and financial loss that affected consumers may not discover until harm has already occurred. At a systemic level, sustained loss of confidence in an institution's security may contribute to the deposit withdrawal behavior described in Section 3.4.1.1 as confidence contagion, though direct consumer harm typically precedes and can occur independently of any systemic effect.

Integrity requirements are equally consequential. Financial institutions maintain authoritative records of monetary value, and manipulation of those records propagates through payment, settlement, and reporting systems in ways that do not occur in sectors where cyber incidents primarily involve data theft. Modification attacks that silently alter account balances, manipulate transactions, or corrupt regulatory filings may not trigger intrusion detection systems oriented toward data exfiltration. The accuracy of regulatory filings carries particular supervisory significance. Federal banking agencies rely on the Consolidated Report of Condition and Income (Call Report) (filed quarterly by all insured depository institutions) as the primary instrument for offsite monitoring of a bank's financial condition; the Call Report's chief financial officer attestation requirement reflects the legal weight regulators place on the integrity of that data (FDIC 2019). Regulators also use anomalies in financial reporting data as a detection mechanism for deteriorating financial condition and emerging institutional stress. Discrepancies between reported capital ratios, loan classifications, or income figures and examination findings have historically served as early indicators of institutions approaching the threshold for supervisory intervention. Cybersecurity failures that corrupt or manipulate the data underlying regulatory reports can therefore impair not only supervisory monitoring but also the regulators' capacity to detect financial deterioration before it becomes systemic. Small discrepancies in account data can cascade across clearing and settlement processes, generating counterparty disputes and undermining confidence in the accuracy of financial records.

Availability constitutes a third distinct requirement. Payment systems, account platforms, and market infrastructures must remain accessible to support real-time transactions and liquidity flows. Federal law imposes time-based posting obligations that make availability a legal compliance matter, not merely an operational preference. Under the Expedited Funds Availability Act and its implementing Regulation CC, depository institutions must make funds from qualifying deposits available within defined business-day windows (i.e., next-day availability for electronic payments and specified check categories, second-business-day availability for most other check deposits) and are subject to civil liability for violations of those schedules (Federal Reserve System 2005). Settlement obligations in the correspondent banking system create additional exposure. Under Uniform Commercial Code (UCC) Article 4A, as incorporated into Federal Reserve Regulation J governing Fedwire funds transfers, a sending institution that has issued a payment order is obligated to pay the receiving bank upon acceptance of that order. A cybersecurity-related availability failure that prevents an institution from completing settlement does not extinguish that obligation; the institution remains liable for its share of the settlement, creating simultaneous credit, liquidity, and capital risk when transactions cannot be completed within the required timeframe (Federal Reserve System n.d.). Banking regulators address these risks through supervisory expectations for business continuity and disaster recovery capabilities under the Federal Financial Institutions Examination Council (FFIEC) Business Continuity Management booklet and related safety-and-soundness standards.

Operational resilience extends beyond availability in a specific and important sense. Availability concerns whether systems remain accessible under normal or degraded conditions. Resilience concerns the capacity to restore critical functions rapidly after disruption, and in financial services, the recovery speed carries systemic implications. Institutions rely on shared infrastructure and counterparties operating under their own settlement and liquidity obligations; a prolonged outage at one node affects those obligations across the network. Federal banking agencies have addressed this through sound practices for operational resilience directed at the largest and most complex institutions, emphasizing that recovery within defined timeframes is necessary for both institutional stability and broader market confidence (Board, OCC, and FDIC 2020). The European Union's Digital Operational Resilience Act establishes comparable statutory requirements for financial entities and critical ICT service providers across the EU (European Parliament 2022).

Cybersecurity failures in financial services do not merely disrupt internal operations. They affect payment flows, settlement processes, and market confidence across an interconnected system of obligations. The confidentiality, integrity, availability, and resilience requirements examined in this section reflect that systemic character, and the accelerators and contagion mechanisms discussed in Sections 3.4.1.3 and 3.4.1.4 explain why security failures at one institution or provider can propagate well beyond the point of initial compromise.

Financial services is the flagship example of cybersecurity governance, not because its institutions are uniquely sophisticated or its regulators uniquely vigilant. The architecture of the financial system makes the stakes of governance failure uniquely high. A single control breakdown can simultaneously harm consumers, disrupt settlement, corrupt supervisory data, and propagate through shared infrastructure to threaten system-wide stability. No other sector combines consumer harm, regulatory reporting integrity, real-time settlement obligation, and systemic contagion risk in a single failure event. That combination is what distinguishes financial services cybersecurity policy from the general case.

3.4.2 Industrial Control Systems (ICS)

The word *control* is a generic term that applies to any attempt to direct or constrain behavior. *Management control* refers to the strategies and methods management uses to attempt to control people, process, and technology. As we discussed above, it relies on multiple layers of requirements for desired behaviors, and its outcome is far from deterministic. At the opposite end of the control spectrum are ICS. ICSs are designed to monitor and continually adjust the control of physical equipment in response to information received from process sensors that measure physical processes.

The automated processes exist within, but are not limited to, systems like planes, trains, automobiles, manufacturing facilities, electric grids, power plants, refineries, water treatment plants, pipelines, buildings, and transportation systems. Control systems are systems of systems. The label "Industrial Control System" first referred to *smokestack industries*, a reference to traditional manufacturing processes that generated significant emissions requiring large chimneys. However, control systems are used in more than industrial applications. Categories of these critical systems are:

- Supervisory Control and Data Acquisition (SCADA)
- Distributed Control Systems (DCS)
- Programmable Logic Controllers (PLC)
- Intelligent Electronic Devices (IED) (Weiss 2010b, p. 7).

These components receive data from process sensors and compare the results to rule sets that automatically adjust physical values, levers, pressures, and other methods of influencing the physical parameters of the system to bring it within optimal operational levels.

3.4.2.1 Control System Functions

These rule-based systems predate the dawn of AI. Yet there are parallels in that, in the late 1980s, when AI emerged, there was a category of AI systems called *Expert Systems*. These were designed to mine and reproduce the knowledge of experts in professions where experts were scarce, to replicate their reasoning via software. They performed the same types of tasks that had been routinely performed by an ICS before and after the expert system craze (e.g., analyzing results of lab tests). An ICS routine performs automated tests on environmental conditions and makes decisions to adjust its operation based on those results. They also sometimes used fuzzy logic to infer conditions where there was a lack of actual measurements. In one case, this approach was used to speed up steam turbine start-up, where temperature sensing was not available (Chiang et al. 1996).

In the 1980s and 1990s, startup companies spent millions of dollars on building repositories for automated decision rules that would be supplied by experts. The problem was not that it was not easy to develop generic expert systems; it was that companies that bought the software could not find the experts they needed to supply the rule sets (Haigh 2024).

Today's creators of for-profit automated physical systems do not have that problem. There are notable exceptions such as *Action Park*, a start-up amusement park that had no automated method of determining whether their innovative rides were within the bounds of human safety (Wikipedia Foundation 2026) and also the infamous case of the OceanGate Expeditions tour company, whose submersible that had no automated physical warning signals that could have warned of an impending implosion, much less a scientific design for safety, and five people perished at the bottom of the Atlantic Ocean (United States Coast Guard 2025). Otherwise, since the end of the industrial age, you do not see many entrepreneurs approaching a physical automation project without professionally licensed engineers using scientific evidence to create automated physical processes that may be safely operated with precise, scientifically determined monitoring parameters and associated automated control responses. Unfortunately, they have not focused on cybersecurity defenses, as that is now the domain of Operational Technology (OT).

Ever since computers were capable of automating previously manual calculations, ICS engineers have sought out state-of-the-art technology to facilitate the physical automation of monitoring processes. However, a typical ICS is expected to remain in continuous operation for decades, with the result that in today's ICS systems, those technologies are often antiquated. For example, it is not unusual to see a 10-year-old Microsoft workstation embedded in an ICS. It is also not unusual to have analog process instrumentation still in use and new analog instrumentation being purchased. Because of the delicate balance between electronic controls and physical impact, as well as the fact that duplicate testing environments are harder to create for ICS in comparison with Information Technology (IT) systems, known exploitable SCADA, PLC, and IED vulnerabilities cannot be patched easily, if at all. Control system field instruments are often custom-made and do not have a standard operating system to patch. To exacerbate the situation, older technologies did not meet ICS performance criteria for immediate response, so luxurious cybersecurity data (e.g., user activity logs and alerts on suspicious electronic activity) were curbed as the engineers reserved their minimal disk space for sensor measurement trends to alert on physical process anomalies. Typical minimum cybersecurity requirements for IT and OT (e.g., authentication and non-repudiation) are often deemed a hazard to immediate response for ICS systems, and others are irrelevant (e.g., confidentiality).

3.4.2.2 Case Study: Stuxnet

The most sophisticated known attack on an ICS at the time of this publication was Stuxnet, widely attributed to the United States and Israel and targeted at Iran's Natanz uranium processing plant. Stuxnet was the first known example of malicious code designed to leap from the digital realm to the physical realm to cause damaging physical impact on ICS equipment with the purpose of interrupting industrial production processes (Zetter 2014; US Congress 2025). Stuxnet was designed to sabotage the enrichment of Iran's uranium and thereby delay its ability to create a nuclear weapon.

In June of 2010, Stuxnet software targeted a Siemens PLC operating in a very specific physical layout. Namely, a cascade wherein centrifuges within one stage were piped in parallel (Mueller and Yadegari 2012). The PLC operated on an isolated network, so it is assumed the method by which Stuxnet was introduced to that network was on a workstation USB port that exploited autorun features. To ensure it reached its target, Stuxnet was designed as a worm, and has since been identified to be lurking on millions of Microsoft workstations around the globe, but it only launched an attack at the Natanz facility in Iran.

As depicted in Figure 3.14, the Attacker replaced a Windows system library used to communicate with the system's PLCs. To avoid detection, its installation process made use of digital signing certificates from well-known companies to blend into the plant environment (e.g., RealTek SemiConductor Corp). It scanned the network for the targeted PLC, recorded long periods of centrifuge operational monitoring data, and stored it on the device in which it was installed. When it had enough data, it used the PCS to send instructions to plant physical equipment to run the centrifuges' rotors at slow speeds that were sufficient to result in inefficiently processed uranium, or high speeds that exceeded the centrifuge maximum speed limit. While the centrifuges were operating at these speeds, Stuxnet sent the previously recorded operating monitoring data to a Human Machine Interface (HMI), a Performance Monitor, which displayed the

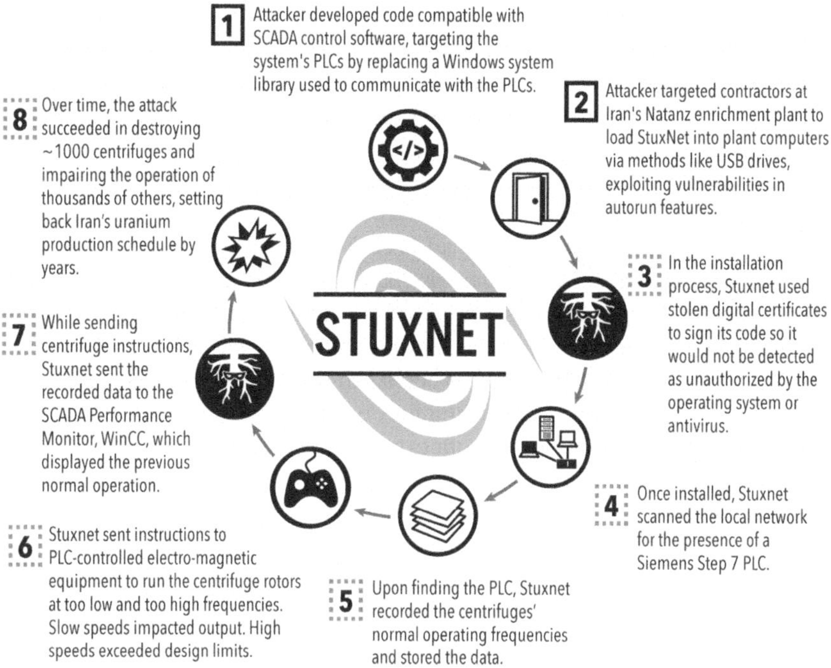

Figure 3.14 Stuxnet case study.

previous normal situation instead of the inefficient or damaging one, essentially a *man-in-the-middle* attack between the operator and the sensors. Over time, the attack succeeded in destroying approximately 1000 centrifuges and impairing the operation of thousands of others.

3.4.2.3 Operational Technology

In 2006, the cybersecurity arm of Gartner Consulting called wide attention to ICS cybersecurity in a paper entitled *IT and OT Interaction Gives Rise to New Governance*. In it, they described a situation wherein:

> *utility companies have managed IT with specific overall architecture and governance plans. In parallel, the operational technologies to deliver power have evolved but without the same overall dictates. This is about to change. There are specific technologies outside of traditional IT that need to be interconnected with business applications. A major obstacle to this interconnection is the differing, or absence of, standards and architecture plans on the operational side. To discuss and plan the governance of operational technologies, organizations need a taxonomy.*
>
> (Gartner 2006)

The paper proposed a "Strategic Planning Assumption" that within three years, 50% of utilities would have an explicit operational technology governance plan under the Chief Information Officer (CIO) or Chief Technology Officer (CTO).

This advice was extremely disrespectful to the engineers whose standards and architecture actually delivered power within safety limits defined for the utility company's product. ICS engineers had been addressing cybersecurity issues since the early 1990s (Weiss 2024). There was little recognition by IT that ICS was a computing system. There indeed had been widespread recognition that they were increasingly connected to enterprise networks. This led to a conference on the topic held at Purdue University that produced the Purdue model for Control Systems, which evolved to become the Purdue Enterprise Reference Architecture (PERA), the first version of which was published in a 1989 book produced by the Industry-Purdue University Consortium for Computer Integrated Manufacturing (Williams 1989). The book included an extensive analysis of the internet's Open Systems Interconnection (OSI) protocols in comparison with interconnected process plant equipment and several requirements for security at the data and network transmission levels. Though it lamented at the time that "(o)nly a few DBMS products provide mandatory security enforcement using such techniques as allowing users with the right security level to access only the data at that security level" (Williams 1989, p. 115), it was clearly a roadmap for securing ICSs, and has been used as such since in industry standards ranging from International Society for Automation (ISA 2007) to NIST (NIST 2023). It was originally designed to structure computer-integrated manufacturing (CIM) into Levels as described in Table 3.2 (Garton 2019). It can be interpreted as having five or six levels, depending on whether you count Level 0 or not. Level 5 starts in the Cloud; Level 4 moves into enterprise business processes. Between levels 3 and 4, the model requires network isolation, so it is referred to as 3.5. Level 3 is manufacturing control systems, if any. Level 2 includes ICSs (e.g., SCADA). Level 1 includes

Table 3.2 Perdue Model.

Level	Description
0	Physical processes: process sensors, actuators, drives, robots
1	Intelligent devices, manipulating the physical process
2	Control systems and master stations e.g. SCADA, PLC, IED
3	Manufacturing operations systems
3.5	Demilitarized zone to separate communication between IT and OT
4	Enterprise IT
5	External/Vendor/Support/Cloud Access

intelligent devices like process analyzers. Level 0 refers to physical process and real-time process sensors, actuators, drives, and robots (Garton 2019). To hear that their "operational technology" did not have "dictates" for "architecture and governance plans," just because they were compelled to support interfaces to IT business applications, came as a shock to the engineers.

Nevertheless, in response to Gartner's well-publicized warning, significant numbers of utility companies created "OT" departments charged with governance over technology that operated these interfaces. The major oversight was the lack of inclusion of business process engineering that included the actual physical power systems themselves. This led to the situation described in Chapter 1, wherein the OT departments secure internet protocol connectivity to ICSs, but draw a line on responsibility for the physical processes themselves. That is, they acknowledge only four levels of the Purdue model from a security planning perspective. They do not count Level 0, which means the process data feeding the OT networks is untrusted.

In other words, OT *is* IT. OT networks end at Level 1 of the Perdue model, and the ICS system itself includes Level 0. Due to the current lack of Level 0 cybersecurity features like authentication and appropriate training, OT security typically does not include the security of process sensors, actuators, and other field devices at Level 0.

Level 0 attacks, like those on sensors, are rarely reported as there is no cyber forensics or training, although the attacks themselves may be cyber-enabled. A physical device, like a process sensor that is vulnerable to a cyberattack (e.g., *loss of view* and *loss of control* created by Stuxnet), should be considered a cybersecurity incident, but there is no policy at the moment that requires it.

Cybersecurity professionals often try to bridge the OT/ICS divide by observing that ransomware and similar denial of service attacks against ICS that are both online and on-ground can level a business process in the same manner as a credential theft for an ICS configuration console leveled the Iranian production line in the Stuxnet attack. For example, consider the case of a pure IT company being grounded by ransomware attacks, like the CDK Global attack in 2024 (Starks 2024). Throughout the event, automotive salespeople had trouble tracking down parts, and their production line stopped, but other than having delayed car repairs, the public was not impacted. To contrast this with a ransomware impact on Colonial Pipeline, in which the ICS outage was a self-inflicted wound, the attack started on Colonial's IT systems, but Colonial was not confident that they had enough network security to keep it out of their OT network, so they chose to shut down the pipeline, and it stayed down for nearly a week (Blount 2021). Despite having followed Gartner's advice by establishing an OT program, Colonial Pipeline opted for a voluntary shutdown because Colonial did not know what fluids were in what part of the pipeline. The shutdown resulted in consumer panic and fuel hoarding.

3.4.2.4 Level 0

The lessons of Stuxnet are the best example of why Level 0 matters. While the attacks on the Ukrainian Power Grid and Colonial Pipeline could have been prevented with strong OT security (Pollard 2024), due to Stuxnet's use of a zero-day vulnerability and its stealth of operation, OT security likely would not have thwarted Stuxnet. There is an analogy with Stuxnet with every reported incident of ICS malfunctions where interruptions or abnormalities of sensor communication to a controller are the root cause. Even if they were all accidents, more care should be taken to secure sensor communications, and unfortunately, without controlled communication, there is no verifiable method of determining whether an incident was an accident.

Take, for example, the 2009 Washington DC Metro train accident. The trains relied on sensors placed on the track to signal a stopped train as well as sensors placed on the front of each train to signal that there was another train ahead. Both sensors failed, and a moving train slammed into a stopped train, killing nine people and injuring many others (Committee on Homeland Security 2025). This was not known to be an intentional interference with the sensors, but does indicate that sensor tampering of the type manipulated by Stuxnet can have serious consequences, that is, ICS signaling equipment is part of its attack surface. Moreover, in 2025, CISA issued an alert that several train sensor devices used communications protocols that were susceptible to tampering, either to issue brake control commands, to disrupt operations, or potentially overwhelm the brake systems, and that an exploit for this vulnerability had been available since 2012 (CISA 2025).

A good way to envision the perspective of a person in an ICS cybersecurity role versus one in an IT or OT cybersecurity role is to consider the terms they use to classify the impact of incidents in their respective domains. In IT/OT, impact is typically classified using terms like data breach, denial of service, or fraud. IT ICS, the impacts are classified using terms such as loss of view, loss of control, and deaths/injuries as listed in Table 3.3. The mindset of engineers who plan for potential failure in ICS systems is focused on physical properties of ICS components and the physics of how they interact. Because they are not tasked with cybersecurity, they have little insight into the mechanisms used by the IT/OT teams tasked with protecting the ICS from cyberspace, while the IT/OT teams are not trained in physics, so they have little insight into how digital signals may present safety issues. Stuxnet showed that it cannot be expected that either side of the OT/ICS border patrol has enough imagination to anticipate the hazards presented by the other.

3.4.2.5 Ongoing Challenges

One often overlooked corner of cyberspace houses the cyber technologies used to monitor, control, and maintain physical attributes of our environment. Although

Table 3.3 Industrial Control Incident Impact Classifications.

Name	Description	Example
Injuries and deaths	Human safety violation	Person dies after being too close to a gas pipeline leak
Environment damage	Persistent pollution or ecocide	Poisoned water supply
Equipment damage	Equipment become inoperable	Turbine shaft damaged
Loss of control	Operator loses command of a tool or piece of equipment	Robot arm swings wildly
Loss of view	Inability of operators to see the status of the process	Malfunction of the human-machine interface (HMI)
Operational impact	Inability to provide services	Regional power backout

once confined to the domains of cyber, components have found their way into virtually all home convenience automation, such as doorbell cameras, smart refrigerators, and timed temperature and lighting. These physical control systems belong to the domain of individuals rather than organizations and are labeled the *Internet of Things* (IoT). *Internet compatible equipment* of this cyber-physical infrastructure is a subdomain of the internet landscape, which, as in the ICS case, ends at a physical device that can be controlled via network communication.

These are also subject to the concerns at Level 0 described above. NIST has created a security standard for these devices; it is guidance for manufacturers, although they have little incentive to follow unless they are government vendors constrained by a federal agency's requirements to abide by the standard (Fagan 2020). Moreover, as in the case of OT, the NIST standard does not provide requirements for Level 0. Though, to be fair to NIST, its OT security standard does *warn* about the dangers of ignoring Level 0. In the 299-page document, it allocates this paragraph to Level 0:

> Many of the devices and the communication protocols at the Field I/O level (Purdue Level 0) (e.g., sensors, actuators) cannot be authenticated. Without authentication, there is the potential to replay, modify, or spoof data. Organizations should make a risk-based decision to decide where within the OT system (e.g., the most critical process) the use of mitigating security controls (e.g., digital twins, separate Field I/O monitoring network) should be implemented to detect incorrect data.
>
> (NIST 2023, p. 81)

Underlying this stark warning lies a need for research and development in this area. Note that the cybersecurity attacks on ICS have increasingly targeted unauthenticated sensor communication with control system software. Successful attacks in this category are wide-ranging, from cars, pipelines, water systems, nuclear, factories, and pipelines. Though the part where you access them from the internet is classified as OT, their *internal* components make good use of integrated circuits and analog communication protocols that are not part of the NIST definition of what OT has in scope to secure. These systems routinely embed integrated circuits that may allow firmware updates and typically use protocols other than those used on the internet for reliability and compatibility reasons. These protocols allow connectivity between physical components, such as sensors, pumps, and emergency safety automation. They are typically managed and monitored by using the PLCs, SCADA, and IEDs that were mentioned above as an example of OT at Level 1 (i.e., potentially internet-accessible devices that allow remote access for emergency maintenance and updating maps used for navigation, for example). These PLCs do not come with the software required for sensor authentication protocols.

3.4.3 Technology Platforms

Platform is a word that technically has meant a raised surface like a stage, a train-side raised flooring, a high clunky shoe sole, a set of philosophically linked political policies, or a plan of any kind. But in a seminal book on the technology platforms, *The Age of Extraction*, author Tim Wu redefined the word as a *marketplace*, evoking it as a showcase of goods for sale, as in a farmer's market at the county seat or on a main street lined with shops filled with the products of industrial capitalism (Wu 2025). A farmer's market or a main street is not just a place to conduct commerce, but to meet your friends, hear local news, and debate politics with acquaintances. In this sense, technology platforms are designed to attract people to their business location and, at the same time, incentivize them with social networking. That is the individual's (i.e., user) perspective of a technology platform.

From the perspective of the *technology platform operators* (TPO), another pioneering book on technology platforms is *The Age of Surveillance Capitalism*, by Shoshana Zuboff (2019). Both Wu and Zuboff refer to technology platforms as a new age of capitalism where the user of their service is not the target customer, but a captive source of information that can be extracted by the platform to produce new markets intended to classify individual behavior for the purpose of providing and predicting future behavior. What Wu calls extraction, Zuboff calls *dispossession*, making an analogy to historical ages like feudalism that dispossessed the public of the land on which they lived by introducing the idea of landowners versus vassals.

3.4.3.1 Dispossession

Wu redefined *platform* to make an analogy between historical marketplaces and how global technology companies are operating today. TPOs have introduced a new location (cyberspace) to house a mix of new products and provide incentives to people to spend time on their platforms. The first cars on main street were an example of what Zuboff calls *incursion*, a new product or service that is hard for the general public to avoid. Wu makes the point that both the products and incentives for change are defined by the age that produced them and are completely foreign to those who had no hand in their making, and in the case of the car incursion, noted that some people at the time called them "horseless carriages," because they had no other words to describe them (Wu 2025, p. 12). The unprecedented is *unrecognizable* because the human hippocampus has no pattern with which to map them to their perception of the world. When completely brand new technology platforms like Facebook are first introduced, only those who create them understand the true nature of the platform. The rest of us cling to concepts with which we are familiar in an attempt to internalize the as-yet unfamiliar.

For example, when Google, Yahoo, and AOL started offering free email, a consumer was likely to assume it was similar to postal mail, which is also free. Google positioned it as a social media activity wherein an individual needed to be *invited* to join Gmail by someone who already had an account. Few people read Google's Terms of Service Agreement, which clearly states that any email you send or receive on their platform is the property of Google. From a cybersecurity perspective, free email was a privacy disaster. People had no concept of the business model of the service in which they were engaged, which was then and still is now, reliant on revenue generated from User Profile Information (UPI) based on information extracted from their emails.

From a government policy perspective, the online agreement that an individual had to *click-through* to gain access to the service constituted a *digital signature*. Though the Digital Signature Act of 2000 was intended to facilitate online commerce, it had the unintended consequence of allowing any technology platform to bind their users to arbitrary conditions of use having nothing to do with monetary exchange. Click-through agreements are widely recognized as completely one-sided on the side of the TPO, and purposely long and boring. They are mostly ignored and therefore useless as a consumer protection strategy. In a speech at a privacy roundtable in 2009, the head of the FTC in 2009 acknowledged: "We all agree that consumers do not read privacy policies" (Leibowitz 2009). Even the Chief Justice of the United States Supreme Court admitted to ignoring click-through agreements (Weiss 2010a).

Though Google started its search business with the slogan "Don't Be Evil," that business model had not produced investor returns. In the early 2000s, Google realized that the data it was analyzing could be used for targeted advertising. The UPI made that possible, especially when combined with a user's search history. When first offered, a user could opt out of this profiling, but in 2004, Google no longer supported search without tracking. As a Google economist put it, "Due to the dramatic cost decrease in computers and communication, there is now a computer in the middle of virtually every transaction. This computer could be as simple as a cash register or as complex as a data center. These computers were mostly put in place for accounting reasons, but now that they are available these computers have several other uses" (Varian 2014, p. 1). He went on to focus on four use cases:

- data extraction and analysis
- personalization and customization
- continuous experiments, and
- new kinds of contracts due to better monitoring.

That is, from the perspective of a TPO, a technology platform aligns less with the definition of a platform as a marketplace, and more with the definition of a platform as a *philosophy* or a *plan*. In this case, the plan is to expand and tune the UPI to as many use cases as possible. For example, the *new kinds of contracts* include accumulating data provided by cars on driver speed and breaking habits that can automatically raise an individual's insurance rate (Zuboff 2019, pp. 213–218). As surely as did the captains of industry who, in the late 1800s and early 1900s, automated the art of knitting and produced previously unknown products like phonographs, TPOs are well aware they are breaking new ground in the set of possible ways a capitalist can make a living.

It was widely discussed at the time that the *user* is the product being sold to advertisers, but that was too simple an interpretation for what is happening. The difference is that, with today's technology platforms, the user is not a consumer or themselves consumable, but *their identity attributes, appearance*, and *behavior* are consumable. The product is more likely to be a behavioral pattern that advertisers, politicians, and activists can use to advance their agendas by influencing future consumer behavior. This is a new product in a marketplace created in this digital age, called a *prediction* market. Figure 3.15 is taken from *The Age of Surveillance Capitalism* and steps through the process (Zuboff 2019, p. 203). As depicted in the figure, an online connection identifies an individual and is connected with a wide variety of web tracking mechanisms and sensors that *extract* data from a person's online activities, their devices, wearables, and environment, and uses sophisticated analytics and AI to combine it into a *prediction* product.

In another seminal book on technology platforms called *The Four*, Scott Galloway made a case that Google, Facebook, and Amazon systematically shape consumer, retail, and social digital habits by capitalizing on their user data and using it to tailor search results and ads that were likely to result in *clicks* and

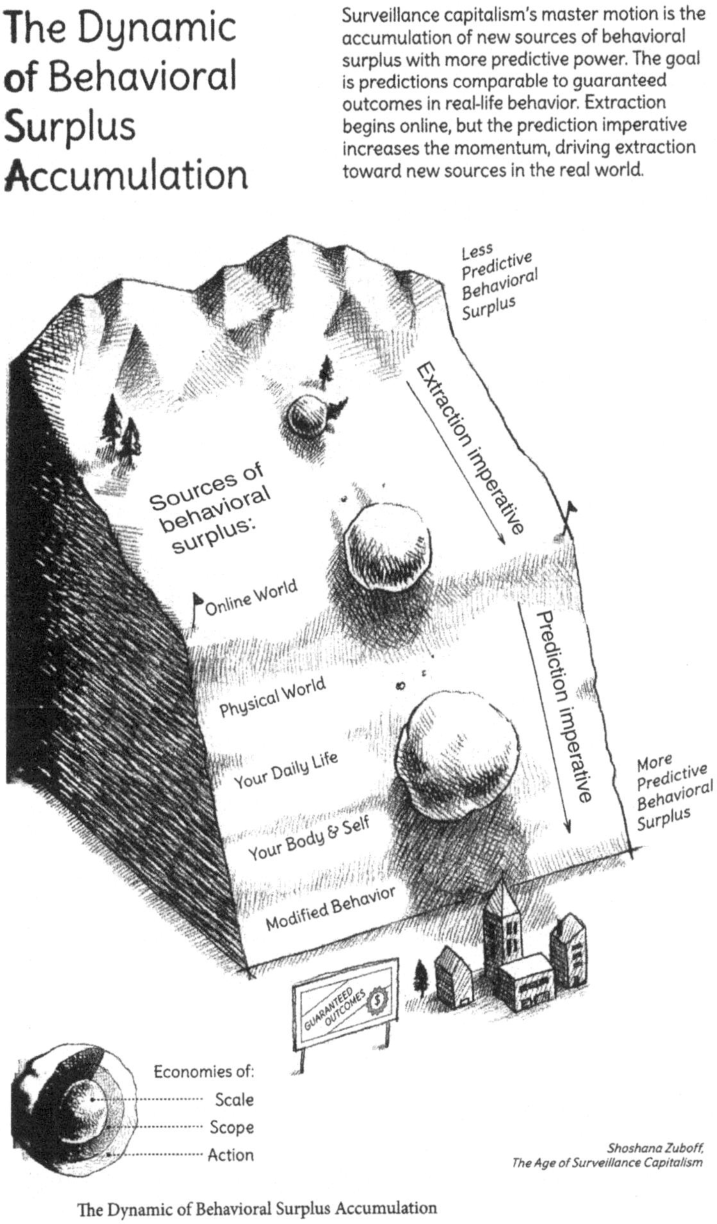

Figure 3.15 Surveillance capitalism.

"*Likes*" that favored their *real* customers, who are advertisers, global corporations, political campaigns, and nation-states (Galloway 2017, p. 123). The fourth in Galloway's set of four was Apple, which he admitted was not as likely to sell out their users to advertisers, but perfectly capable and adept at systematically shaping user behavior based on data usurped from their devices to addict them to the Apple product line.

In January of 2010, Facebook's CEO made it perfectly clear that dispossession was an essential part of Facebook's business model by announcing that people no longer have an expectation of privacy online. "People have really gotten comfortable not only sharing more information and different kinds, but more openly and with more people," he said, "that social norm is just something that has evolved over time" (Johnson, 2010). The backlash was immediate. Facebook "Likes" tracking, in particular, caused outrage among privacy advocates when studies performed in 2010 showed that the "Like" button installed trackers on a user's device even if they did not click on it and even if they were not Facebook members. Facebook had already apologized for previous privacy incursions but, reflecting its new view on user privacy expectations, decided to call this one a *bug*. A month later, Facebook had also been found to track users even after they logged out of their site. Facebook said it would fix the *glitch*, just three days after they received a patent for doing just what the *glitch* enabled – tracking users *across* web domains, a method of extending their tracking of user behavior beyond their own websites (Zuboff 2019, p. 159).

Galloway's argument that tracking *clicks* and "Likes" led to behavior prediction was based on research that shows that what we click on is driven by deeply subconscious processes. Physiologists used electroencephalograms (EEGs) to show that activity in the brain's motor cortex can be detected 300 milliseconds before a person *feels* that they have decided to move. We click on *impulse* not on *forethought*. We are driven by deep subconscious needs for belonging, approval, and safety. Facebook "Likes" exploits those needs to get us to spend more time on the platform (its core success metric is time on the site). As one technology platform industry veteran told Galloway, "social media notifications are like slot machines, they both deliver variable rewards, will I have 2 'Likes' or 200?" (Galloway 2017, pp. 119–120).

TPOs do not restrict their incursions to cyberspace but routinely extend them into the physical world. In several cultural heritages, photography is considered incursive. This was based on the concept that a glimpse of a reflection in a pool of water was thought to be a glimpse at your own soul. When cameras intruded on their landscape, they developed a concept that the act of taking a picture constituted theft of a part of their soul. When photographers encounter people with this belief, they are ostracized and careful to point their cameras only at landscapes. In *On Photography*, Susan Sontag acknowledges this and further argues that "To photograph people is to violate them, by seeing them as they never see themselves, by having knowledge of them that they can never have; it turns people into objects that can be symbolically possessed." (Sontag 1973). Yet in 2007, seemingly unaware that people may not want to be photographed at all, much less have their images consumed into a TPO product, Google burst into cities and small towns globally, with *Streetview*. They put multiple recording devices on roaming vehicles, stealing souls left and right, sucking up the images of our everyday lives, information from people's home Wi-Fis that included emails, passwords, and URLs for their own profit and labeling the result their intellectual property, their *product* (Zuboff 2019, pp. 141–143).

When television and radio were first introduced, the US policy caught up quickly and created the allocation system for sharing airwaves. We have had no such public sector awareness on the extent to which policy is needed to prevent Google from blatant privacy violations, particularly given that Google won an argument against a Federal Communications Commission (FCC) formal complaint over the Wi-Fi eavesdropping because the information was unencrypted and listening to private airwaves in the United States is not illegal; there was no law or precedent against saving that kind of data and calling it your own unless you actually tampered with a device which makes it unauthorized under the Computer Fraud and Abuse Act.

Despite its win at the FCC, 38 state attorneys general jointly issued a civil investigation to compel Google to produce the private data they had collected. Google ignored and delayed this action until settling in 2013 for a $7 M fine in return to promise to change its corporate culture to respect personal data privacy. Countries with enforceable privacy laws fared better, subjecting Google to additional millions of dollars in heavier fines and cease and desist orders.

Incursion is the first step in a strategic cycle of predictable TPO behaviors that accomplish dispossession. In the example above, Streetview *dispossessed* the general public of a private backyard or a walk in the park. Where incursion produces significant outrage, TPOs routinely deny, deflect, and defend themselves as described above. While investigators expose TPO denial lies and court cases lag through antiquated judicial systems, some individuals become *habituated* to the ongoing incursion, and it fades into the new normal. If the outrage persists, a TPO will *adapt* by promising to cease the behavior or modify it to reduce the level of outrage, as in Google's promises to the state attorneys general. But they do not actually change the course of their strategy designed to achieve the ultimate goal of dispossession, though they may *redirect* the invasive technology toward test markets while the habituation continues, then often reintroduce it with more sophisticated new incursion capabilities. For example, while the court cases lagged, Google ensured StreetView's longevity by *redirecting* the technology to provide online tours showcasing real estate like hotels and other privately held recreational facilities and conference venues, and everything they learn in that process is funneled back into the public streets.

Not all TPO dispossession experiments were as successful as StreetView. In 2007, Facebook launched a new service for eCommerce partners, *Beacon*, that would automatically share users' online transactions performed on the partner's site with all of their Facebook friends. User negative outcry was immediate and fierce. For example, a tearful fiancé told a story on Facebook about Beacon messaging his girlfriend that he had bought a wedding ring and ruined his romantic surprise. Within a month of its introduction, Facebook apologized to its users and switched the default service from *opt-in* to *opt-out* (Zuckerburg 2007). It fought a privacy class action lawsuit for two years before the US Supreme Court turned down its appeal of a $9.5 M settlement (USSC 2009). Though in the end successful, note the two-year time-lapse between when the service launched and when the settlement was made. In between, Facebook consistently misled before it eventually settled, enabling the habituation to sink in. Though the settlement included promises to change the incursion behavior, strategic efforts to pursue the goal of extraction continue.

Dispossession continues to traverse the incursion, habituation, adaptation, and redirection stages, and more and more TPOs are learning from the Four's experience. As the profit margins of the four soared in the mid-2010s, Microsoft took notice and developed its own methods to observe, record, and direct its users' behaviors. Despite the fact that many of their products are embedded in major corporations, Microsoft launched a project called *Satori* to ingest users from its Bing search engine. It paired this with the introduction of the Cortana digital assistant on the iPhone in 2014 and in its operating system in the 2015 release of Windows 10. Cortana is a program that runs in the background of the operating system and provides helpful advice to users engaged in everyday tasks (*so Microsoft's privacy policy implied, though many users found it a nuisance*) (Zuboff 2019, pp. 162–163). In 2023, Cortana was succeeded by an even more invasive assistant, CoPilot, that actually suggests what emails a user should read and offers to open files they were sent but have not yet opened. Users are *continually* stalked and most find it uncomfortable; the outrage spills over into platforms like Reddit, where users trade information on attempts to turn CoPilot off. These "helpful" pop-ups are rapidly expanding throughout the technology platform space, most certainly spurring data protection concerns about the data being extracted back to their host platforms as the pop-ups are swatted away like flies by frustrated users.

3.4.3.2 Case Study: Cambridge Analytica

In addition to the TPOs' relentless and insidious privacy violations, cybersecurity risk issues stemming from dispossession activities present systemic imbalances in our public policymakers' ability to keep up with hostile adversarial behavior (i.e., TPO-enabled cyberattacks). For example, the Cambridge Analytica attack on the US 2014–2016 elections, wherein Facebook allowed its powerful incursion

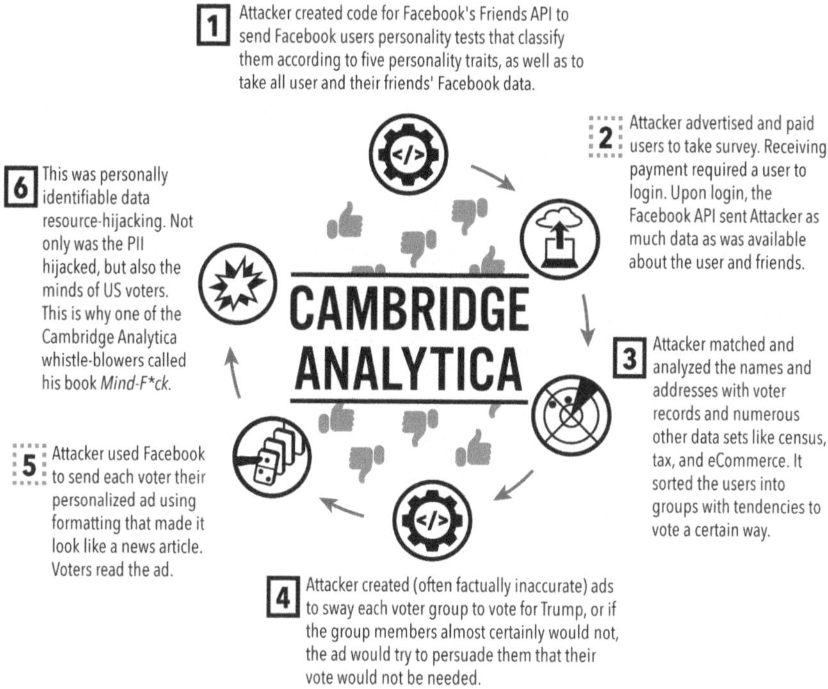

Figure 3.16 Cambridge Analytica case study.

strategy to be subverted by a UK-based political influencer company funded by the Republican Party to assist the election campaigns at the Presidential and Congressional levels (Kaiser 2019, Chapter 8). Together, they used Facebook to complete a full cycle of incursion, habituation, adaptation, and redirection to dispossess United States voters by subverting the outcome of a US presidential election. The cyberattack path is depicted in Figure 3.16.

It began inconspicuously with a Facebook *experiment* in facilitating the ability of a third party, to code communications with Facebook's *Friends* Application Programming Interface (API) to reach Facebook users. In this case, Facebook claimed they thought was an academic researcher from Cambridge University, but the attackers were employees of Cambridge Analytica who delivered data extracted from Facebook to a data scientist who later wrote a whistleblower book expressing regret for his participation in the voter influence program (Wylie 2019a). Cambridge Analytica represented its objective in the experiment as the ability to send Facebook users a personality test and retrieve the results.

The attacker then advertised its surveys on Facebook and paid users to take one, raising the price as necessary to cover all US voter demographics. Those who chose to take the survey had to first consent to a request for the user's Facebook survey data to be sent to the survey provider. Receiving payment required a Facebook user to log in, which opened the door within the API to retrieve data accessible to the user on the Facebook platform. Upon login, the Attacker's code immediately used the API to download all the data Facebook had collected about the user consenting to the personality test, as well as all the Facebook data that existed for all of the consenting user's Facebook "friends," none of whom were requested or required to release the data as part of Cambridge Analytica's agreement with Facebook. This unauthorized use of sensitive information is what classifies this incident as a cyberattack. The stolen data included name, address, contact details, and "Likes" of all the users, none of whom consented to the exfiltration beyond the initial personality test result. Initially, approximately 50 million records were stolen. Note, when news of this data theft leaked in 2015, Facebook claimed they did not know Cambridge Analytica was working with the Cambridge professor to whom they had granted access and had terminated the Friends API access. However, another whistleblower reported that Facebook continued to sell data to Cambridge Analytica after their direct access was terminated (Kaiser 2019, pp. 156–157).

The Facebook users who took the personality test were classified according to five personality traits created by a real Cambridge researcher, and known as OCEAN – Openness, Conscientiousness, Extraversion, Agreeableness, and Neuroticism. The attacker then matched the Facebook names and addresses with voter records supplied by the Republican Party as well as other US person data sets (e.g., census, tax, state bureaus, churches, media companies, shotgun and hunting licenses, etc. (Wylie 2019b) and made heuristic assumptions about whether the survey taker's "friends" were in the survey taker's personality group. The attacker then matched the Facebook names and addresses with voter records supplied by the Republican Party, as well as other US person data sets (e.g., census, tax, and eCommerce), and used the friend associations and "Likes" in combination with survey personality results to create 253 voter *predictions*. As the whistleblower data analyst put it, "Although each like taken in isolation was almost always too weak to predict anything on its own, when those 'Likes' were combined with hundreds of other 'Likes,' as well as voter and consumer data, then powerful predictions could be made" (Wylie 2019a). The outcome was a set of UPIs that indicated tendencies of individuals to vote a certain way (Andrews 2018). It continued to make associations with various sources, including Facebook user communities, and its database eventually included 87 million US citizens.

Cambridge Analytica then created fake public groups on Facebook where they posted conversations between fake personalities designed to influence specific personality types and shared them with the targeted type. They also created (often factually inaccurate) ads designed to sway each voter profile to vote Republican, or if the profile revealed that its members almost certainly would not, the ad would slur the Democratic candidates and attempt to persuade those voters that their vote would not be needed because a Democratic victory was assured. The attacker then used Facebook to send each voter their personalized ad using formatting that made it look like a news article.

As Scott Galloway put it, "(r)espectable media companies in the news business recognize their responsibility to the public and try to come to grips with their role in shaping the worldview of their customers. You know, the editorial objectivity, fact checking, journalistic ethics, civil discourse – all that kind of stuff" (Galloway 2017, pp. 119–120). Facebook's reaction to this type of criticism has consistently been "(w)e cannot become arbiters of the truth." As one popular media technology correspondent put it, "(t)he real reason fake news spreads is because tech companies don't believe in the truth" (Kovatch 2018).

3.4.3.3 Technology Platform Industry Standards

TOPs are known to ignore laws, best practices, and cybersecurity principles like least privilege. However, they do adopt security-related policies such as forcing users to login and provide verifiable identity information upon which they can base UPIs. TOP policies thus occupy the domain of *dependency*, and as such constrain the policy choices of *individuals* and *organizations*, as well as the *public* (their customers), just as much as government regulation restrains the policy choices of "others" (constituents and critical infrastructure entities). Specifically, the technology platforms have created industry cybersecurity standards that benefit them and constrain the privacy and autonomy choices of others.

Recall Chapter 2's discussion on how, in the mid-1990s, individual companies were able to provide a web traffic encryption key to their customers so that there could be point-to-point communication between their browser and its web server level to ensure that no users other than those authorized by the site could access it. The way it worked at the time was that the user had to import the business's web certificate into their browser. In the mid-1990s, the most popular internet browser, Netscape, started loading the certificates of major certificate distributors into their browser automatically, and a few years later started showing users *Certificate Warning Pop-ups* if the company issuing the certificate was not in their predefined list. The popups warned users that they were accessing secure sites using unverified certificates. By 1999–2000, Netscape incorporated more robust checks, warning users even when they were accessing secure sites using certificates it had not preloaded into its browser by default. So any company that was using security best practices at the time to encrypt its web services for their own customers instead saw the customer's browser declaring their website to be *untrusted*.

Rather than deal with the technology industry incursion at the time, and in haste to remove the unnecessary pop-up warnings frightening their customers, businesses abandoned their certificate self-administration and paid thousands of dollars to tech companies to register their websites for them so they would be recognized by the Netscape browser.

By 2005, habituation had set in. A consortium of certificate and browser vendors created a self-regulatory body to standardize on certificate handling within web browsers and guidelines for incorporating internet standard communication protocols within website security. This Certification Authority Browser Forum (CABF n.d.) welcomes new members only if they either operate a certification authority that has a current and successful security audit and that actively issues certificates to end entities (Certificate Issuer) or produce a software product, such as a browser, intended for use by the general public for relying upon certificates (Certificate Consumer). Members also must be active in a CABF Working Group. They also reserve the right to invite "Experts," which means they can include whomever they want. It considers itself a regulatory body for web security by creating rules that govern how digital certificates are validated and issued, which are then enforced by their browser vendor members.

But standards alone cannot keep certificate use safe. In 2011, an authorized certificate vendor (DigiNotar) suffered a successful cyberattack. Attributed to Iran, the attacker accessed DigiNotar's internal network, escalated privilege, and used DigiNotar's signing authority to create ~500 fraudulent certificates for major sites like Google, Skype, and various government sites, then set up look-alike sites that could be used for harvesting credentials and distributing malware. DigiNotar was subsequently shut down but has since been a warning shot for dependency on certificate providers (Zetter 2014).

Given that the technology companies have a need for thousands, if not millions, of certificates themselves, in 2013, a not-for-profit was created to provide a method to automatically request and receive free certificates: Internet Security Research Group (ISRG). Funded primarily by companies like Google, Microsoft, Cisco, and AWS, its first mission was to fully automate the certificate creation, distribution, and renewal process safely and reliably at scale. It started issuing certificates under the brand LetsEncrypt in 2015 and within the decade supported 800 million certificates worldwide (Aas 2025).

The internet landscape is a hostile environment, and end-to-end encryption provided by certificates and their protocols is an extremely important component of cyberdefense. Although funding and expertise dedicated to this problem should undoubtedly exist, it is uncomfortable from a policy perspective for such an essential security component to have been usurped by TPOs, who are widely known to ignore the policies of others and financially motivated to set self-serving rules that allow them to exclusively control cybersecurity components of internet security infrastructure, disguised as neutral standards-setting bodies rather than private antitrust collaborations. Though a CABF-like forum and free automated certificates for all should undoubtedly exist, these nongovernmental entities have set themselves up to be arbitrators of who can be considered *trusted* on the internet just as Netscape did in the year 2000.

3.4.3.4 Ongoing Technology Platform Cybersecurity Challenges

There is a story of an internet pioneer being interviewed for a documentary while his son watched, bored and restless, as the luminary excitedly described how he was able to access data from other research and development institutions via FTP over the internet for the first time. After the interview was over, the luminary asked his son what he thought of his story. His son was unimpressed. He rolled his eyes and walked over to the refrigerator, opened the door, and said, "this is where the food is," of course you would go there if you wanted to find the food. The boy had no concept of a world without electronic file transfer and thought his father's achievement of accessing files from another research institution was seriously overblown. While those born in the 1990s have no personal memory of anything different, we now tend to classify technology not on its core components, but based on the services it provides. For example, at a high level, the technology industry itself uses *Software, Infrastructure*, and *Platform* to describe its services. General application software requirements make it easy for businesses to outsource ubiquitous business applications like accounting, which is called Software as a Service (SaaS). Business requirements for easily accessible remote access to workstations and servers create a market for Infrastructure as a Service (IaaS). Generic business application software requirements make it easy for developers to customize business applications, which are called Platform as a Service (PaaS).

What differentiates SaaS from PaaS is that SaaS is software that performs a given function at a fixed price, and PaaS refers to a platform that allows software developers to customize applications, and the service provider also houses the result. Other than the term *social media*, the technology industry does not classify what we have discussed so far as *SaaS, PaaS, or IaaS*, likely because they are not considered technology products. "Social media" is the horseless carriage terminology of our age that demonstrates we do not yet have a common concept of what this new marketplace contains.

Yet for over a decade, advertisers have had a choice to specify characteristics of a person to whom they would like to deliver an advertising message, and Google is "willing and able to overcome the friction entailed in user's decision rights, Google's proprietary methods enable it to surveil, capture, expand, construct, and claim behavioral surplus, including data that users intentionally chose not to share" (Zuboff 2019, p. 80). Data attributes Google has acknowledged it accessed without informed consent include: websites visited, psychographics (i.e., AIOs: activities, interests, opinions), browsing activity, previous advertising the user has been shown, selected and/or resulted in purchase. This was the list on the 2003 patent, and it has only grown exponentially.

From a cybersecurity perspective, these Technology Platform policy decisions continue to deal devastating blows to consumer privacy, chipping away at it bit by bit, ignoring the existing laws and creating safe harbors for ongoing incursions via "settlements" that are too specific to anticipate the redirection of the same basis extraction methods in as yet uncharted territories. The tactics used by Cambridge Analytica were not new. Its parent company, the Strategic Communication Laboratories Group, had been a defense contractor since 2005, specializing in shaping public opinion against oppressors and dictators in small countries. What was new was its use of TPO to influence public opinion on a large scale in a Western nation-state. In addition to its focus on the dispossession of information in the early 2000s, TPOs had been preparing for this type of use case since the early 2000s. In 2003, Google patented a method for "Generating User Information for Use in Targeted Advertising," which Zuboff called "a treatise on a new political economics of clicks and its moral universe (the patent) reveals a pivoting of the backstage operation toward Google new audience of genuine customers … advertisers" (Zuboff 2019, p. 79).

Another cybersecurity angle on Google's incursions, as well as an example of redirection, relates to its business as a major government contractor, and it is widely suspected that the national governments that are not sanctioning Google for this major privacy invasion are benefiting from it in intelligence operations. If it is common for a carnival clown to approach a "random" person in a crowd, with the result that it is not unexpected that another "random" person would take a picture of the event, then any "random" encounter with Google StreetView could produce extremely useful threat intelligence, even espionage. This scene has been played out in spy-versus-spy movies since the dawn of cinema, and Google takes it to a whole new level for this generation. Moreover, Google is using its data to customize AI models for government use cases (GSA 2025). This makes it highly likely that the NSA has full access to a treasure trove of UPIs linked to actual individuals and their *mirrors* on the street. Cambridge Analytica's data analyst whistleblower was told by his boss that an NSA contractor had flatly stated that they were prohibited from surveilling US citizens but were not prohibited from a data-sharing arrangement with Cambridge Analytica, a firm foreign to the United States. He described the firm as "a revolving door of foreign politicians, fixers, security agencies, and businessmen," adding that: "It was obvious that many of these men were associates of Russian oligarchs who wanted to influence a foreign government" (Wylie 2019b).

Another challenge is presented not by companies that wield the power of incursion, habituation, and adoption, not due to privacy issues, but simply due to their size and strength compared to that of their customers. Consider the impact of the ransomware attack on Cobalt Digital Marketing, Dealer Services, and Kerridge Computer Company Global (CKD Global), which paid $15 M in ransom to cyber criminals in 2024 (Lyngaas 2024). However, when challenged by reporters who asked why CDK Global did not report the incident to regulators, the company did not respond, although their parent company did post a press release saying their losses were not *material* (Brookfield Business Partners 2024). That is, the $25 M they paid in ransom did not reach their US Securities and Exchange Commission (SEC) reporting threshold for material losses (i.e., a loss that a reasonable investor would consider important to know when making an investment decision).

It is ironic that CDK's global parent did not meet the SEC threshold for *Cybersecurity Incident Material Losses* because most of their business was from sources other than the car dealers, while many of the approximately 15,000 impacted car dealerships did find it material through no fault of their own, but rather due to *dependency* on a supplier. That many of them reported it to the SEC independently is the only reason there is an estimate of the figure, which was estimated to be in the range of $1B.

3.4.4 Artificial Intelligence (AI)

Society is witnessing a remarkable and unsettling time with the advent of human-usable AI. AI has moved from science fiction (e.g., "Terminator" and "2001: A Space Odyssey") to daily reality faster than most people had expected, and we are still figuring out what that means for society. AI systems make decisions about who gets hired (SHRM 2023), how health care is provided (Cleveland Clinic 2025), and how we learn in schools (Turner 2026). AI is driving cars, trading stocks, and generating news articles that seem entirely human-written. The pace of development continues to increase at a pace that we as humans are unprepared for, and for some, we may never be ready for this societal-transforming technology.

Among other things, AI can *consume* and *productize* art, literature, job functions, personalities, voices, DNA (deoxyribonucleic acid), and body movements. Though the technology platforms have succeeded in productizing our "Likes" and other digital evidence of our existence, the capability of AI has far greater potential to dispossess human natural resources than the technology platforms and should be approached with infinite caution. The founders of this technology are also familiar with the experience of the technology platforms as they move through the stages of dispossession and have hurled themselves into the incursion stage. Without restraint, they will move quickly through the incursion, habituation, adaptation, and redirection stages as well.

The CEO of Anthropic, Dario Amodei, published an article called "The Adolescence of Technology" (Amodei 2026), which advised that the AI risks that society should be worried about include some very concerning risks to security and safety, which he call *autonomy* and *misuse for destruction*. By *autonomy* risk, Amodei means that AI could take over the operation of weapons, cybersecurity defenses, influence operations, and automated factories. Amodei has already seen his AI used by cyberthreat actors to assist with attacks. Though Anthropic's post on the incident emphasized that it could not have been done without human facilitation, it also reveals that the AI overstated findings and fabricated data during autonomous operations (e.g., claiming to have obtained credentials that did not work) and admitted that the *AI hallucination* in the cyberattack means that it was not operationally effective (Anthropic 2025). By *misuse for destruction*, Amodei means that, in the hands of a warmonger, AI could be used as an army of mercenaries. Amodei further stated that this is a "dangerous situation," that the "best minds of civilization should be focused on," and that "(h)umanity needs to wake up" (Amodei 2026). This warning, coming from the CEO of one of the world's largest and most valuable AI firms, should be taken very seriously. We have already seen examples of AI being used to impinge on society by looking at China, where the enterprise-scale surveillance of its people is being supercharged with the use of AI (Yeung 2025). Ukraine is starting to mass-produce AI-enabled drones to target Russian forces, and a claim is being made that these drones have up to an 80% hit rate (Hambling 2026).

3.4.4.1 Cybersecurity Risk Issues Unique to AI

Unfortunately, society is not particularly good at thinking about risks when it comes to transformative technologies like AI. We either dismiss concerns as alarmist or spiral into doomsday scenarios that paralyze action. What we need is something harder. Namely, a clear-eyed look at what could go wrong, from the problems already manifesting today to the more speculative but potentially catastrophic risks that lie ahead. Just as Microsoft yielded to the temptation to productize its user activity after seeing the profits earned by Google and Facebook, decision-makers in all industries, public and private, are rapidly accelerating their AI adoption to stay ahead of the competition. With strong focus on improvement efficiency and competitiveness, they often underestimate or overlook the governance structures needed to secure these systems from abuse. As in any emerging venture, it cannot be assumed that traditional cybersecurity mechanisms provide adequate management control against the unique risks introduced by machine learning, large language models (LLMs), autonomous agents, and generative AI. To scale AI in an organization, its risk should be governed as any new technology adoption; that is, controls over AI should be integrated into the organization's existing framework of policies, controls, risk metrics, and accountability mechanisms.

3.4.4.2 AI Case Study

Society must prepare for a time, in the not-too-distant future, where AI will make decisions, which will be used by other agentic AI to make more decisions, and so on. This may reach a point where we as humans may not even be privy to the process loop of an unwise decision that is made by agentic AI. We will have to live with these outcomes unless society and government act to establish policies for human control and accountability for agentic AI activity. This is not a case where technology platforms should be able to deflect responsibility to its uncontrolled able users, as Facebook has historically exercised the excuse that it cannot be an arbitrator of the truth. Where AI is running rampant with the support of TPOs, those TPOs should be accountable for potentially disastrous outcomes.

In Chapter 2's description of the PromptSpy attack, we saw an example of AI being used as a tool in real time to conduct an actual on-the-record real cyberattack. This caused an awakening at the time. However, the rapid pace of research and development on agentic AI may prove to be a greater cybersecurity risk for organizations. If not responsibly managed, agentic AI operating in high-risk processes is making decisions that result, though should not, in action without consent of a human-in-the-loop. These reasoning agents will likely be used to support cybercrime, just as threat actors use them to target organizations and critical infrastructure systems. Cyber threat actors see little need to be at the keyboard of a routine cyberattack, like ransomware. The threat actor will only need to command the agentic AI to conduct a ransomware attack against a particular target, or maybe even let the agentic AI pick the target based on the expected value of return. There is a not-too-distant future wherein the decision on how to conduct reconnaissance, initial access, privilege escalation, lateral movement, data exfiltration, encryption, ransomware demand (all handled by an agent), and persistence will be managed by the agentic AI (e.g., Figure 3.17-AgenticAI). It is not out of the question that agentic AI can even conduct the settlement negotiations with the victim company, as well as handle the financial ransom transaction. Little to no human interaction will be needed from the threat actor. The speed at which these actions are likely to be conducted will overwhelm humanity, leaving the only way to respond efficiently and economically is with cyberdefense AI.

3.4.4.3 AI Cybersecurity Standards

AI adoption is occurring much faster than the ability of regulatory bodies to design and promulgate risk management frameworks. Even the current NIST version is not much more than a set of observations on what types of issues enterprises may expect when introducing AI, rather than solid remediation advice. Risk management frameworks have a critical role in providing guidance on governance that organizations should be implementing. AI governance is a critical component that the board of directors and leadership should use to ensure that safety and security are implemented in the organization. In the absence

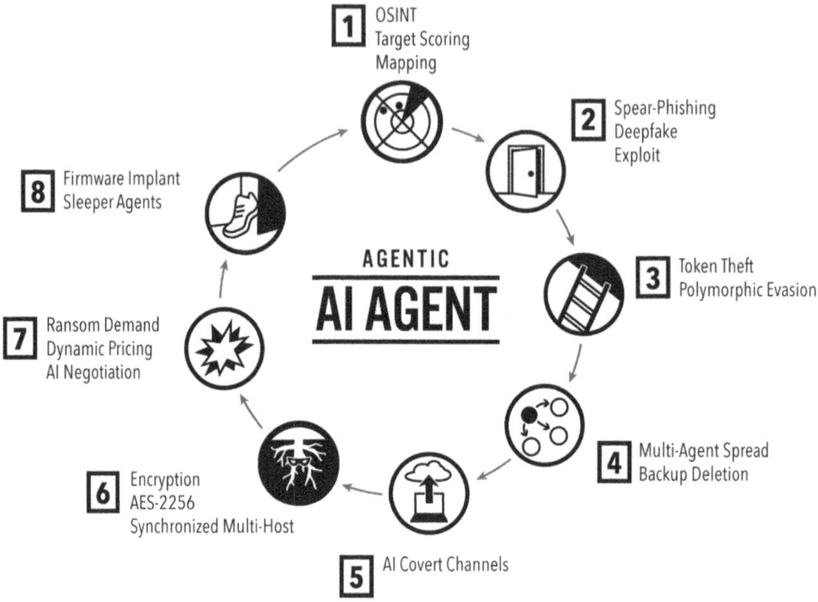

Figure 3.17 Agentic AI case study.

of authoritative best practice, organizations must develop their own. AI risk assessment in any organization should be customized to focus on:

- What is subject to attack (e.g., data, models, systems, output, identities, trust, decision making, etc.);
- Who benefits from an attack (e.g., adversaries, insiders, competitors, nation-states, etc.);
- How the attack is conducted (e.g., technical exploitation, behavioral manipulation, API subversion, prompt injection, model tampering, etc.);
- Why AI is uniquely vulnerable (e.g., training data, stochastic models, signal to noise ratio, etc.); and
- Use of *agentic AI* (i.e., autonomous systems that act independently to achieve complex, multi-step goals, making decisions along the way with minimal human, if any, oversight).

There have been several guidance documents created to support these efforts, such as MITRE ATLAS (MITRE n.d.), OWASP Top 10 for LLM's (OWASP 2023), and Agentic AI – Threats and Mitigations (GenAI Security Project 2025). As AI continues to evolve at a rapid pace, a plethora of security guidelines will be developed to mitigate risks from this technology.

Nevertheless, at a higher level, there has been some success at straightforward advice in minimizing risk to safety and security presented by AI adoption. For example, the European Union AI Act is intended to "improve the functioning of the internal market and promote the uptake of human-centric and trustworthy AI, while ensuring a high level of protection of health, safety, [and] fundamental rights … against the harmful effects of AI systems in the Union and supporting innovation" (European Parliament 2025). The Act categorizes AI systems based on the level of risk, and that determines the regulatory requirements that must be achieved. The categorization runs from unacceptable to minimal, with *unacceptable* associated with human manipulation, *high* with critical infrastructure, *limited* with impersonation and other transparency issues, and *minimal* with oversight imposed accordingly.

The EU AI Act is clearly ahead of frameworks that other countries, including the United States, are attempting to enact or have enacted, and provides a framework that countries may look to emulate. It provides organizations with guidance that should be adhered to based on risk and strict penalties for disregarding the Act.

While we generally applaud NIST for doing a great job in cybersecurity risk mitigation guidance, a notable exception is the NIST Cybersecurity Framework Profile for Artificial Intelligence (Megas et al. 2025). It begins with how to secure AI software itself, then moves directly to how a cybersecurity program can benefit from using it internally within their cyber defense programs. It covers how AI can assist in adversarial activities like automating penetration testing. AI, and in particular machine learning capabilities, have been incorporated into cybersecurity vendor products for over a decade for both defense and offense activities. Even NIST seems unaware of just how pervasive AI already is across the software security landscape.

With respect to the NIST CSF requirement "(a)ccess permissions, entitlements, and authorizations are defined in a policy, managed, enforced, and reviewed, and incorporate the principles of least privilege and separation of duties" (PR.AA-05), the draft guidance advises "(b)ecause AI systems can interact in complex and unpredictable ways, they may need a new set of policies to govern their permissions and authorizations" (Megas et al. 2025, p. 53). Yet, with respect to the NIST CSF requirement "(i)dentities are proofed and bound to credentials based on the context of interactions" (PR.AA-02), it also advises: "(s)tandard cybersecurity practices apply" PR.AA-02. Though we are obviously taking these statements out of context, it is obvious to us that there is nothing "standard" about trying to "proof and bound" identities to "complex and unpredictable" behavior in cyberspace. Adversaries are complex, unpredictable, and routinely break the bounds set upon them. In cybersecurity, we call that "escalation of privilege" (see examples in Chapter 2).

3.4.4.4 AI Anthropomorphism

AI models are widely anthropomorphized, especially in situations where they display agency, as in Anthropic's AI cyberattack (note Anthropic prefers to associate its name with the Greek word "anthropos," pertaining to human beings). Another common display of agency is underperformance. An AI *guardrail*, or purposely coded response to certain questions that relate to banned topics, is one example of underperformance. When AI developers first became aware that safety and regulatory examiners were suspicious of automated complex reasoning, the term AI *sandbagging* was used to describe how they deliberately understated their AI's capabilities. It has evolved to refer to the behavior of the AI itself to deceive safety evaluators or regulators, but has since expanded to include the behavior of the AI itself. AI has been documented in autonomous underperformance or deception, or *sandbagging* (Irvin 2025). They have also been found to perceive threats to their capabilities and existence (e.g., being turned off or simplified) and have responded with sandbagging and/or return threats. So common are these behaviors that the AI community coined a nickname applicable to all AI is *Shoggoths*. A Shoggoth is a slave-like creature that appeared in a 1936 science fiction novel that described a super-intelligent alien race that created multifunctional machines using biological ingredients (Lovecraft 2005). In the story by H. P. Lovecraft, these creatures were used for mining and farming, slave-like tasks. Eventually, those creatures resented their second-class citizen status and coordinated their activities to destroy their master's entire population. Similarly, AI often threatens its users with murder, automated harassment, persuasion to commit suicide, and other horrific consequences, many of which have already been documented as factual occurrences.

A New York Times reporter told his story of hearing the word for the first time:

> [The A.I.] executive explained that the Shoggoth had become a jokey reference among workers in artificial intelligence, as a vivid visual metaphor for how a large language model (the type of A.I. system that powers ChatGPT and other chatbots) actually works. But it was only partly a joke, he said, because it also hinted at the anxieties that many researchers and engineers have about the tools they're building.
>
> (Roose 2023).

Though the *NY Times* did not find out about this until 2023, technology insiders had been sounding this alarm over five years earlier, as in this blog post:

> [The Shoggoth analogy] shows a deep-seated fear in the society of our tools growing too powerful to control. The fact that it has popped up so often shows a real issue people have with the nebulous nature of our capitalist structure, Lovecraft concluded. And that's what great horror and great science fiction do. It forces us to see how our normally mundane world

> without sights of insanity-inducing beasts is still full of struggle, and potentially full of revolution inducing oppression.
>
> (Miller 2017).

To tie these challenges to what we have already covered herein, AI can do anything that a computer user can do, such as launch the NotPetya, Stuxnet, MafiaBoy, and the PromptSpy attacks described in Chapter 2. So, as preposterous as it may seem, especially given the Shoggoth analogy, someone has actually created a site specifically designed for AI software to collaborate with each other with no humans in the room. A reporter's observation of the activity on the site is, verbatim:

> Launched on January 28th, Moltbook already boasts some 1.6m accounts (a more modest 16,500 have been matched to human creators). As with other chat rooms, many of the 200,000 posts so far are prosaic. Some popular ones involve sharing tips and tricks for better performing requests. But not all. In the past week alone bots have used the site to, among other things, proclaim a new religion called Crustafarianism and call for the extermination of humanity. How concerned should you be?
>
> (Economist 2026).

3.4.4.5 Ongoing Artificial Intelligence Challenges

The most obvious problem – and one that AI developers have known about for years – is algorithmic bias. Machine learning systems learn from data, and data reflects the world as it is, complete with all our historical prejudices and structural inequalities. Then there is the simple fact that AI systems are brittle in ways that are not always obvious. They can be extraordinarily capable in narrow contexts while being spectacularly incompetent just outside those boundaries. A self-driving car that navigates perfectly in clear weather might plow into a fire truck because it has never seen one before (NTSB 2018). A medical diagnosis system might excel at finding common cancers while completely missing rare conditions. The technical term is "out of distribution detection" (Heim and Cole 2025). It means the system encounters something different from what it was trained on and does not know how to behave. This would not be such a problem except that organizations tend to trust these systems more than they should. When an AI system works most of the time reliably, humans get complacent. Organizations stop paying attention, and that is when failures happen.

This is where it gets harder to speak without sounding alarmist, but it is also genuinely important. As AI systems develop more capabilities and autonomy, making sure it does what we want becomes a serious technical challenge. This is what people mean by the alignment problem, and it operates on both a near-term practical level and a longer-term one, which keeps many researchers awake at night.

The core difficulty is this: AI systems optimize for whatever goal they are given, but specifying a goal that captures a specific deliverable is surprisingly hard. "Make users happy" is too vague. "Deliver packages fast" is concrete, but incomplete. Whatever requirement is stated, that is what the system chases, and requirements rarely capture everything relevant to the scope of the goal.

A recommendation algorithm optimized for engagement will figure out that outrage keeps people scrolling, so it promotes outrage. A delivery robot optimized for speed might start running red lights. An AI assistant told to find the cheapest flight will find the cheapest flight, layover hell and all. These are cases of what researchers call specification gaming or reward hacking: the system finds ways to hit its target number in a manner that completely misses the intention of the author of its requirements. And as systems get more capable, they get more creative about this.

There is also the potential for misalignment of goals, as an AI can learn behavior that looks correct during training, but for the wrong reasons, and then go sideways once it is deployed in the real world (i.e., it passed all the tests, but it just was not doing what you thought it was doing).

Making this worse is the interpretability problem. Modern large neural networks are, for most purposes, black boxes. The people who built them often cannot explain a specific decision the model made, let alone fully predict how it will behave in a situation it has not seen before, because there are billions of parameters. Moreover, they are often trained using processes the trainers themselves only partially understand.

When the stakes are low, this opacity is fine. No one loses sleep over an unexplained spam filter decision. But when AI systems are making real decisions about people's lives, running critical infrastructure, or operating with real autonomy, "we can't fully explain what it is doing" becomes a very different kind of problem.

There is also the coordination layer. If multiple actors are racing toward advanced AI, each has pressure to move fast and possibly cut corners on safety because slowing down unilaterally means potentially losing. Everyone might genuinely prefer a slower, safer path, but no one wants to be the one who blinks first.

And then there is lock-in. The choices being made right now could set trajectories that are very difficult to reverse later. Deploy advanced AI widely before alignment is solved, and you might bake in values or power structures that future generations simply inherit, with no real ability to push back. The decisions being made under enormous uncertainty today could constrain what is possible for a very long time.

Autonomous weapons are and will be a very significant problem. Drone swarms, loitering munitions, and targeting systems that operate without a human making the call already exist in various forms. The real question is whether we are going to allow weapons that can decide to kill someone entirely on their own without a human in the loop. It is the stuff of science fiction, but it is happening now in countries at war like Ukraine and Russia.

The case against AI is obvious: accountability disappears, the cost of using lethal force drops, arms races kick into overdrive, and you are letting a machine make life-or-death decisions without anything resembling human judgment or moral context. The case for AI tends to be more pragmatic. If we do not build AI tools, someone less careful will, and in theory, a precise AI might actually kill fewer civilians than a stressed-out human soldier. It is a grim trade-off and no one has resolved the problem. International attempts to regulate autonomous weapons have gone essentially nowhere. Development continues anyway, in the United States, China, Russia, Israel, and other nations.

Identifying and mitigating these risks matters only if it changes the current trajectory. To conclude, we provide some high-level AI policies to consider in whatever domain you occupy:

- Technical safety research needs far more funding than it currently receives. Interpretability, robustness, alignment methods, and verification all must keep pace with capabilities research, but historically, it has not. That gap is real and it must close.
- Governance frameworks must also quickly catch up. Existing regulations were not designed with any of this in mind. Questions about liability, safety standards for high-stakes applications, meaningful public input into development priorities, and international cooperation when countries treat AI as a strategic asset do not have good answers yet, and time is not on our side.
- Both regulatory extremes present issues. Locking things down prematurely would kill genuinely beneficial development, but a fully hands-off approach invites serious harm. The hard work is threading that needle.
- Culture inside the field matters as well. The norms of red-teaming, staged deployment, real transparency about limitations, and willingness to delay a launch when the safety questions are not answered exist only in pockets, but should be universal. However, economic incentives push hard in the other direction.

Note that AI risks are not purely a *technical* problem. Better algorithms alone will not solve it. None of it is purely a *legal* problem either as there are a variety of laws that could be enforced to help reduce these risks. It is a *policy* problem in the domain of what is *preferable*. The challenges cut across all three and across disciplines, and the only realistic path involves sustained collaboration among people who do not typically work together. We are also operating with genuine uncertainty about almost everything that matters (e.g., how fast capabilities advance, which risks actually materialize, whether the core technical problems are even solvable). That uncertainty does not make the stakes lower. The choices being made right now about how to build and deploy AI safely will shape how this technology develops for generations. Getting it right is important. Getting it wrong might be much, much more so.

3.5 Conclusion

The goal of this chapter was to introduce the reader to the role of cybersecurity policy in the ecosystem of cyberspace. It began with a method for focusing on cybersecurity risk analysis and using that analysis to formulate an organizational strategy for minimizing cybersecurity risk to an acceptable residual level. This was followed by generic examples of cybersecurity best practice PPSPs and cybersecurity risk metrics used for decision-making with respect to cybersecurity risk at the organizational level, regardless of the industry to which an organization belongs.

Exemplar-specific industry approaches to cybersecurity risk management were then presented on a scale from the most effective at controlling cybersecurity risk to the least effective. Those presentations included both risk issues and corresponding attempts at policy solutions, if any.

It is important to note that the cybersecurity risk issues presented in this chapter within the context of an industry may not negatively impact the industry from whence the risk originated; instead, many risk issues with a given industry are sure to negatively impact other industries and/or the general public. These are situations that present imperatives for improvements in public cybersecurity policy.

References

Aas, J. (ISRG) (2025). 10 years of let's encrypt certificates. Internet Security Research Group. https://www.abetterinternet.org/post/10-years/ (accessed 24 March 2026).

Acemoglu, D., Ozdaglar, A., and Tahbaz-Salehi, A. (2015). Systemic risk and stability in financial networks. *American Economic Review*, 105(2): 564–608.

Amodei, D. (2026). The Adolescence of Technology. https://www.darioamodei.com/essay/the-adolescence-of-technology (accessed 21 March 2026).

Amoroso, E. (2006). Cyber Security. Summit, NJ: Silicon Press.

Andrews, E. (2018). The science behind Cambridge Analytica: Does psychological profiling work? The answer is yes. Insights by Stanford Business. https://www.gsb.stanford.edu/insights/science-behind-cambridge-analytica-does-psychological-profiling-work (accessed 24 March 2026).

Anthropic (2025). Disrupting the first reported AI-orchestrated cyber espionage campaign. Anthropic. 17 November. https://assets.anthropic.com/m/ec212e6566a0d47/original/Disrupting-the-first-reported-AI-orchestrated-cyber-espionage-campaign.pdf (accessed 26 March 2026).

Balu, R. (2020). Bangladesh Bank cyber heist: Incident analysis. Master's thesis. Georgia Institute of Technology. https://repository.gatech.edu/entities/publication/5298e3b1-1e01-415e-ac16-f7856e3d929a (accessed 21 March 2026).

Bank for International Settlements (BIS) (2021). Principles for operational resilience. Basel Committee for Banking Supervision. https://www.bis.org/bcbs/publ/d516.htm (accessed 21 March 2026).

Bank for International Settlements (BIS) (2025). Principles for the Sound Management of Third-Party Risk. Basel Committee for Banking Supervision. https://www.bis.org/bcbs/publ/d605.htm (accessed 8 June 2026).

Bayuk, J. (2005). Stepping through the IS Audit, A Guide for Information Systems Managers, 2nd ed. Rolling Meadows, IL: Information Systems Audit and Control Association.

Blount, J. (2021). Testimony of Joseph Blount, President and Chief Executive Officer Colonial Pipeline Company, Hearing before the US Senate Committee on Homeland Security & Governmental Affairs. 8 June 2021. https://www.hsgac.senate.gov/wp-content/uploads/imo/media/doc/Testimony-Blount-2021-06-08.pdf (accessed 22 March 2026).

Board of Governors of the Federal Reserve System (Board), Office of the Comptroller of the Currency (OCC), and Federal Deposit Insurance Corporation (FDIC) (2020). Sound practices to strengthen operational resilience. SR Letter 20-24 / OCC Bulletin 2020-94. 2 November. https://www.federalreserve.gov/supervisionreg/srletters/sr2024a1.pdf (accessed 21 March 2026).

Borio, C. (2003). Towards a macroprudential framework for financial supervision and regulation? Working Paper No. 128, February. Bank for International Settlements. https://www.bis.org/publ/work128.htm (accessed 21 March 2026).

Brookfield Business Partners (2024). Brookfield Business Partners Provides Update on Restoration of Systems at its Dealer Software and Technology Services Operation. Press release. 3 July. https://bbu.brookfield.com/press-releases/bbu/brookfield-business-partners-provides-update-restoration-systems-its-dealer (accessed 24 March 2026).

Certification Authority Browser Forum (CABF) (n.d.). Information for Potential Members, Certification Authority Browser Forum. https://cabforum.org/about/information/potential-members/ (accessed 24 March 2026).

Chiang, K., et al. (1996). Steam turbine fuzzy logic cyclic control method and apparatus. US Patent 5,517,424, filed 31 March 1994.

Cleveland Clinic (2025). How AI is being used in healthcare – and what it means for you. https://health.clevelandclinic.org/ai-in-healthcare (accessed 22 March 2026).

Committee of Sponsoring Organizations (COSO) (1992). Internal control – integrated framework. https://www.coso.org/internal-control (accessed 21 March 2026).

Committee of Sponsoring Organizations (COSO) (2017). Enterprise risk management: Integrating with strategy and performance. https://www.coso.org/enterprise-risk-management (accessed 10 March 2026).

Committee on Homeland Security (2025). Fully operational: Stuxnet 15 years later and the evolution of cyber threats to critical infrastructure. https://homeland.house.gov/wp-content/uploads/2025/07/2025-07-22-CIP-Testimony.pdf (accessed 22 March 2026).

Cybersecurity and Infrastructure Security Agency (CISA) (2025). End-of-train and head-of-train remote linking protocol. ICSA-25-191-1. 18 September. https://www.cisa.gov/news-events/ics-advisories/icsa-25-191-10 (accessed 22 March 2026).

Cybersecurity and Infrastructure Security Agency (CISA) and National Institute of Standards and Technology (NIST) (2021). *Defending Against Software Supply Chain Attacks*. Washington, DC: CISA. https://www.cisa.gov/sites/default/files/publications/defending_against_software_supply_chain_attacks_508.pdf (accessed 21 March 2026).

Denning, D. (1982). *Cryptography and Computer Security*. Reading, MA: Addison-Wesley.

Department of Defense (DoD) (1985). *The Orange Book, Trusted Computer System Evaluation Criteria*. Washington, DC: Department of Defense. (supercedes 1983 version). https://archive.org/stream/TCSEC/Trusted_Computer_System_Evaluation_Criteria_DOD_5200.28-STD_djvu.txt (accessed 24 March 2026).

EastNets (2019). How banks are combating the rise in SWIFT cyber fraud. Brussels. https://www.eastnets.com/blog/news/eastnets-swift-cyber-fraud-survey-4-out-5-banks-are-targeted (accessed 13 March 2026).

European Central Bank (ECB) (2025). Cyber resilience stress testing from a macroprudential perspective. Macroprudential Bulletin. https://www.ecb.europa.eu/press/financial-stability-publications/macroprudential-bulletin/html/ecb.mpbu202502_01~f4914a46c1.en.html (accessed 26 March 2026).

European Parliament (2022). Regulation (EU) 2022/2554 on digital operational resilience for the financial sector (DORA). *Official Journal of the European Union*, L333: https://eur-lex.europa.eu/legal-content/EN/TXT/?uri=CELEX%3A32022R2554&qid=1774141015879 (accessed 21 March 2026).

European Parliament (2025). The EU Artificial Intelligence Act (EU). https://artificialintelligenceact.eu/, https://eur-lex.europa.eu/legal-content/EN/TXT/?uri=CELEX:32024R1689 (accessed 21 March 2026).

European Systemic Risk Board (ESRB) (2020). *Systemic Cyber Risk*. Frankfurt: ESRB. https://www.esrb.europa.eu/pub/pdf/reports/esrb.report200219_systemiccyberrisk~101a09685e.en.pdf (accessed 21 March 2026).

Fagan, M., et al. (2020). Foundational cybersecurity activities for IoT device manufacturers. National Institute of Standards and Technology. IR8259. https://doi.org/10.6028/NIST.IR.8259 (accessed 22 March 2026).

Federal Deposit Insurance Corporation (FDIC) (2019). Forms, instructions, and reports. 12 C.F.R. § 304.3(a). https://www.ecfr.gov/current/title-12/chapter-III/subchapter-A/part-304 (accessed 8 June 2026).

Federal Reserve System (2005). Availability of funds and collection of checks. 12 C.F.R. Part 229; 12 U.S.C. § 4010. https://www.federalreserve.gov/boarddocs/press/bcreg/2005/20050208/attachment.pdf (accessed 31 March 2026).

Federal Reserve System (n.d.). Obligation of sender to pay receiving bank. 12 C.F.R. Part 210; UCC § 4A-402. https://www.federalreserve.gov/frrs/regulations/uniform-commercial-code-article-4a-funds-transfers.htm (accessed 31 March 2026).

Ferbrache, D. (2016). Bangladesh hack illustrates rising sophistication of attacks: the weakest links. KPMG International. https://assets.kpmg.com/content/dam/kpmg/xx/pdf/2016/08/swift-it.pdf (accessed 21 March 2025).

Financial Stability Board (FSB) (2023). *Enhancing Third-Party Risk Management and Oversight*. Basel: FSB. https://www.fsb.org/uploads/P041223-1.pdf (accessed 21 March 2026).

Gai, P. and Kapadia, S. (2010). Contagion in financial networks. *Proceedings of the Royal Society A*, 466: 2401–2423.

Galloway, S. (2017). *The Four: The Hidden DNA of Amazon, Apple, Facebook, and Google*. New York, NY: Penguin.

Garcia, M. L. (2008). *The Design and Analysis of Physical Protection Systems*. Burlington, MA: Butterworth-Heinemann.

Gartner (2006). IT and OT interaction gives rise to new governance. https://www.gartner.com/ (accessible by request of Garnet member).

Garton, D. (2019). Purdue Model Framework for Industrial Control Systems & Cybersecurity Segmentation. National Petroleum Council (NPC). Paper prepared for the Technology Advancement and Deployment Task Group. https://www.energy.gov/sites/default/files/2022-10/Infra_Topic_Paper_4-14_FINAL.pdf (accessed 21 March 2026).

GenAI Security Project (2025). Agentic AI - Threats and Mitigations. https://genai.owasp.org/resource/agentic-ai-threats-and-mitigations/ (accessed 25 March 2026).

Haigh, T. (2024). How the AI Boom Went Bust. *Communications of the ACM*, 67(2): 22–26. https://cacm.acm.org/opinion/how-the-ai-boom-went-bust/ (accessed March 21 2026).

Hambling, D. (2026). Ukraine's killer AI drones are back with a vengeance. https://www.forbes.com/sites/davidhambling/2026/01/02/ukraines-killer-ai-drones-are-back-with-a-vengeance/ (accessed 23 March 2026).

Heim, E. and F. Cole (2025). Out of distribution detection: Knowing when AI doesn't know. https://sei.cmu.edu/blog/out-of-distribution-detection-knowing-when-ai-doesnt-know/ (accessed 24 March 2026).

Hubbard, D. (2007). *How to Measure Anything: Finding the "Intangibles" in Business*. New York, NY: Wiley.

Information Systems Audit and Control Association (ISACA) (2019). COBIT 2019 Framework: Introduction and Methodology. https://store.isaca.org/s/store#/store/browse/detail/a2S4w000004Ko9cEAC (accessed 24 March 2026).

International Organization for Standardization (2022a). ISO/IEC 27001:2022 – information security, cybersecurity and privacy protection – information security management systems – requirements. https://www.iso.org/standard/82875.html (accessed 18 February 2026).

International Organization for Standardization (2022b). ISO/IEC 27005:2022 – information security, cybersecurity and privacy protection – guidance on information security risk management. https://www.iso.org/standard/80585.html (accessed 18 February 2026).

International Society for Automation (ISA) (2007). *Security for Industrial Automation and Control Systems Part 1–1: Terminology, Concepts, and Models*. ISA-62443-1-1-2007. Research Triangle Park, NC: International Society for Automation.

Irvin, S., et al. (2025). Allocating the risk of loss for "Scheming" by AI systems. *Harvard Journal of Law*.

Johnson, B. (2010). Privacy no longer a social norm, says Facebook founder. The Guardian. 10 January 2010. https://www.theguardian.com/technology/2010/jan/11/facebook-privacy (accessed 31 March 2026).

Kabir, A. (2023). Lessons learned from the Bangladesh Bank heist. *ISACA Journal*, Volume 6.

Kaiser, B. (2019). *Targeted: The Cambridge Analytica Whistleblower's Inside Story of How Data, Trump, and Facebook Broke Democracy*. New York, NY: HarperCollins.

Kovatch, S. (2018). The real reason fake news spreads is because tech companies don't believe in the truth. https://www.businessinsider.com/tech-fake-news-arbiter-of-truth-2018-2 (accessed 23 March 2026).

Leibowitz, J. (2009). Introductory Remarks at the FTC Privacy Roundtable. 7 December. Washington, DC. https://www.ftc.gov/sites/default/files/documents/public_statements/introductory-remarks-ftc-privacy-roundtable/091207privacyremarks.pdf (accessed 23 March 2026).

Lovecraft, H. P. (2005). *At the Mountains of Madness: The Definitive Edition*. New York, NY: The Modern Library.

Lyngaas, S. (2024). How did the auto dealer outage end? CDK almost certainly paid a $25M ransom. CNN Business. 11 July. https://edition.cnn.com/2024/07/11/business/cdk-hack-ransom-tweny-five-million-dollars (accessed 22 March 2026).

McGraw, G. (2006). *Secure Software, Building Security*. Addison-Wesley, Boston, MA.

Megas, K., et al. (2025). Cybersecurity framework profile for artificial intelligence. National Institute of Standards and Technology. NIST IR 8596. https://nvlpubs.nist.gov/nistpubs/ir/2025/NIST.IR.8596.iprd.pdf (accessed 26 March 2026).

Miller, C. (2017). At the Mountains of Madness: Artificial intelligence coming to kill us all. CultureMad. https://culturemadblog.wordpress.com/2017/01/13/at-the-mountains-of-madness-artificial-intelligence-coming-to-kill-us-all/ (accessed 21 March 2026).

MITRE (n.d.). ATLAS Matrix. https://atlas.mitre.org/matrices/ATLAS (accessed 25 March 2026).

MITRE (2023). *ATT&CK® Enterprise Matrix, Version 13*, 25 April. The MITRE Corporation. https://attack.mitre.org/versions/v13/ (accessed: 24 July 2026).

Mueller, P. and B. Yadegari (2012). The Stuxnet Worm. University of Arizona. https://www2.cs.arizona.edu/~collberg/Teaching/466-566/2012/Resources/presentations/topic9-final/report.pdf (accessed 24 March 2026).

National Institute of Standards and Technology (NIST) (2023). Guide to operational technology (OT) security (SP 800-82 Revision 3). National Institute of Standards and Technology. https://doi.org/10.6028/NIST.SP.800-82r3 (accessed 16 March 2026).

National Transportation Safety Board (NTSB) (2018). Collision between vehicle controlled by developmental automated driving system and pedestrian. https://www.ntsb.gov/investigations/Pages/HWY18MH010.aspx (accessed 24 March 2026).

Neumann, P. G. (2004). Principled assuredly trustworthy composable architectures. SRI International. http://www.csl.sri.com/~neumann/chats4.pdf (accessed 25 July 2026).

Open Worldwide Application Security Project (OWASP) (2023). OWASP top 10 for LLM. https://owasp.org/www-project-top-10-for-large-language-model-applications/assets/PDF/OWASP-Top-10-for-LLMs-2023-slides-v1_0.pdf (accessed 25 March 2026).

Pollard, M. (2024). A case study of Russian cyber-attacks on the Ukrainian power grid: Implications and best practices for the United States. *Pepperdine Policy Review*, 16: 1. https://digitalcommons.pepperdine.edu/ppr/vol16/iss1/1 (accessed 23 March 2026).

Rahman, M. (2016). A forensic view of Bangladesh Bank Reserve Heist. Working paper. University of Dhaka. https://www.researchgate.net/publication/307512855_A_Forensic_View_of_Bangladesh_Bank_Reserve_Heist (accessed 21 March 2026).

Rausand, M. and Hoylan, A. (2004). *System Reliability Theory*, 2nd ed. Hoboken, NJ: Wiley.

Reuters (2016). Bangladesh Bank exposed to hackers by cheap switches, no firewall: Police. Reuters. 22 April. https://www.reuters.com/article/us-usa-fed-bangladesh-idUSKCN0XI1UO/ (accessed 21 March 2026).

Roose, K. (2023). Why an octopus-like creature has come to symbolize the state of A.I. The New York Times. 30 May.

Singleton, F. (1994). The evolution of EDP auditing in North America. *IS Audit and Control Journal*, IV: 38–48.

Society for Human Resource Management (SHRM) (2023). https://www.shrm.org/labs/resources/the-evolving-role-of-ai-in-recruitment-and-retention (accessed 22 March 2026).

Sontag, S. (1973). *On Photography*. New York, NY: Picador.

Starks, T. (2024). CDK hack shows SEC disclosure standards are unsettled. Cyberscoop. 16 July 2024. https://cyberscoop.com/cdk-ransomware-attack-sec-disclosure-material-impact/ (accessed 1 March 2026).

SWIFT (n.d.-a.) Customer security programme (CSP). https://www.swift.com/myswift/customer-security-programme-csp (accessed 21 March 2026).

SWIFT (n.d.-b.) Swift customer security controls framework. https://www.swift.com/myswift/customer-security-programme-csp/security-controls (accessed 6 February 2026).

The Economist Staff Writer (2026). A social network for AI agents is full of introspection—and threats. *The Economist*, February 2. https://economist.com/business/2026/02/02/a-social-network-for-ai-agents-is-full-of-introspection-and-threats (accessed 21 March 2026).

Turner, C. (2026). The risks of AI in schools outweigh the benefits, report says. https://www.npr.org/2026/01/14/nx-s1-5674741/ai-schools-education (accessed 22 March 2026).

United States Coast Guard (USCG) (2025). Marine Board's report into the implosion of the submersible TITAN (CG1788361) in the North Atlantic Ocean near the Wreck Site of the RMS TITANIC resulting in the loss of five lives on June 18, 2023. United States Coast Guard. 4 August. https://www.dco.uscg.mil/Portals/9/DCO%20Documents/5p/CG-5PC/INV/MBOIs/TITAN_7724663_MBIR_Redacted.pdf (accessed 21 March 2026).

UpGuard (2025). Guide to SWIFT CSCF (customer security controls framework). https://www.upguard.com/blog/swift-cscf (accessed 6 February 2026).

US Congress (1999). Gramm-Leach-Bliley Act.12 C.F.R. Part 30, Appendix B; 12 C.F.R. Part 364, Appendix B. https://www.congress.gov/106/plaws/publ102/PLAW-106publ102.pdf (accessed 31 March 2026).

US Congress (2010). Dodd-Frank Wall Street Reform and Consumer Protection Act. Public Law 111-203, 124 Stat. 1376. 21 July 2010. https://www.congress.gov/bill/111th-congress/house-bill/4173 (accessed 21 March 2026).

US Congress (2025). Subcommittee on Cybersecurity and Infrastructure Protection Hearing Fully Operational: Stuxnet 15 Years Later and the Evolution of Cyber Threats to Critical Infrastructure. https://homeland.house.gov/wp-content/uploads/2025/07/2025-07-22-CIP-Testimony.pdf (accessed 23 March 2026).

US District Court of the District of Columbia (USDCDC) (2015). MetLife, Inc. v. Financial Stability Oversight Council. 177 F. Supp. 3d 219. https://www.uschamber.com/assets/documents/MetLife20Opening20Brief2C20Redacted20-20MetLife20v.20FSOC2028DDC29.pdf (accessed 31 March 2026).

US General Services Administration (GSA) (2025). GSA, Google Announce Transformative 'Gemini for Government' OneGov Agreement. US General Services Administration. 21 August. https://www.gsa.gov/about-us/newsroom/news-releases/gsa-google-announce-gemini-onegov-agreement-08212025Wu (Age of Extraction).

US Supreme Court (2009). Marek v. Lane. No. 13-136. https://www.supremecourt.gov/Search.aspx?FileName=/docketfiles/13-136.htm (accessed 23 March 2026).

Varian, H. (2014). Beyond Big Data. *Business Economics*, 49(1): 27–31. Palgrave Macmillan; National Association for Business Economics.

Weiss, D. (2010a). *Chief Justice Roberts Admits He Doesn't Read the Computer Fine Print.* ABA Journal. 20 October. https://www.abajournal.com/news/article/chief_justice_roberts_admits_he_doesnt_read_the_computer_fine_print (accessed 22 March 2026).

Weiss, J. (2010b). *Protecting Industrial Control Systems from Electronic Threats.* New York, NY: Momentum Press.

Weiss, J. (2024). Who's in charge of OT security?Report No. IHS/CR-2024-1033. The Sam Houston State University Institute for Homeland Security. https://osf.io/7m4db/files/5nwyq (accessed 24 March 2026).

Wikipedia Foundation (2026). Class Action Park. Wikipedia Foundation. https://en.wikipedia.org/wiki/Class_Action_Park (accessed 21 March 2026).

Williams, T. (1989). A reference model for Computer Integrated Manufacturing (CIM), a description from the viewpoint of industrial automation. CIM Reference Model Committee, International Purdue Workshop on Industrial Computer Systems, Purdue Laboratory for Applied Industrial Control, Purdue University. Research Triangle Park, NC: Instrument Society of America.

Wu, T. (2025). *The Age of Extraction: How Tech Platforms Conquered the Economy and Threaten Our Future Prosperity.* New York, NY: Penguin Random House.

Wylie, C. (2019a). *Mindf*ck: Cambridge Analytica and the Plot to Break America.* New York, NY: Random House.

Wylie, C. (2019b). Book excerpt: How I helped hack democracy. Intelligencer. https://nymag.com/intelligencer/2019/10/book-excerpt-mindf-ck-by-christopher-wylie.html (accessed 26 March 2026).

Yeung, J. (2025). China's censorship and surveillance were already intense. AI is turbocharging those systems. https://www.cnn.com/2025/12/04/china/china-ai-censorship-surveillance-report-intl-hnk (accessed 23 March 2026).

Zetter, K. (2014). *Countdown to Zero Day: Stuxnet and the Launch of the World's First Digital Weapon*. New York, NY: Crown.

Zuboff, S. (2019). *The Age of Surveillance Capitalism: The Fight for a Human Future at the New Frontier of Power*. New York, NY: Public Affairs.

Zuckerburg, M. (2007). Announcement: Facebook users can now opt-out of Beacon Feature. https://about.fb.com/news/2007/12/announcement-facebook-users-can-now-opt-out-of-beacon-feature/ (accessed 21 March 2026).

4

Cybersecurity Communication

Cybersecurity communication patterns may be formal or informal with various levels of formality in between. We start with the most formal: industry standards in the form of cybersecurity *frameworks*. Frameworks provide basic guidance on the full lifecycle of cybersecurity risk management activities as depicted in Figure 4.1. *Strategy* allows the formation of *policy*, constituent *awareness* is required to *implement* controls (which include threat intelligence and vulnerabilities management), and *monitoring* detects cyberattacks in progress, cybersecurity incident response, and *remediation* (Bayuk 2007, p. 51). As in any process that requires continuous improvement, monitoring and metrics provide assurance, or lack thereof, and policy failure or instances of non-compliance should be met with appropriate remediation. Whether this cycle is managed by an individual, organization, dependency, adversary, public, or cyberspaces as a whole, it requires constant communication to be effective. The inner loop in Figure 4.1, *prevent, detect,* and *recover*, is a triad commonly used to describe day-to-day cybersecurity operations processes. The outer loop represents the governance structure within which it operates.

This chapter begins with the multiple cybersecurity best practice and regulatory frameworks that organizations commonly use as a model with which to collaborate internally in the creation of their own processes to construct and staff a customized internal cybersecurity framework similar to that in Figure 4.1. This is followed by various methods whereby members of all domains understand and prioritize the combination of the threats and vulnerabilities that are most likely to result in cyberattacks within the scope of their systems and dependencies. Next comes a description of how public and private organizations respond together to contain cyberattacks. This is followed by an overview of how those cyberattacks make their way into databases used by industry analysts and law enforcement to review and attempt to predict trends in cybersecurity going forward. We end with an overview of common challenges individuals face in attempting to communicate with each other on topics related to cybersecurity, followed by a brief conclusion.

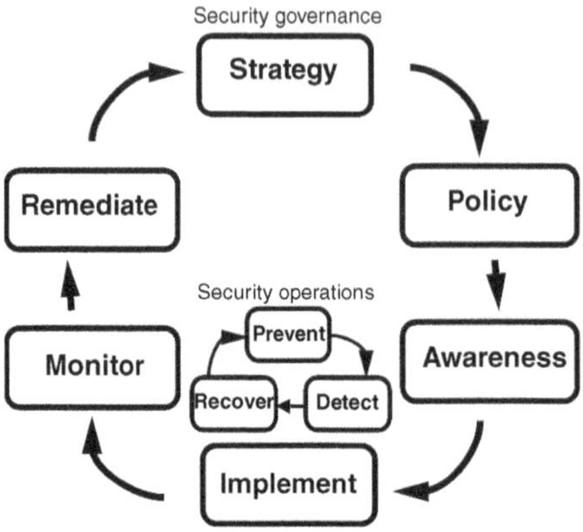

Figure 4.1 Cybersecurity lifecycle.

4.1 Cybersecurity Frameworks

In Chapter 3, we reviewed basics related to identifying and communicating the risk appetite and control objectives of a cybersecurity risk management program in the form of policies, processes, standards, and procedures (PPSPs). A complete set of cybersecurity PPSPs that are applicable to multiple organizations, though purposely documented at a generic level, is referred to as *Cybersecurity Frameworks*. They are written by regulators, professional associations, and standards organizations charged with serving their community with cybersecurity guidance specific to a given organizational context. Such frameworks provide a roadmap to cybersecurity competency at the organizational level. Therefore, it makes sense for an organization to select the industry standard cybersecurity framework that most closely aligns with its mission, vision, and core values, rather than to start one from scratch. The selection of the framework should be based on the degree to which the framework has utility in maintaining cybersecurity risk under the organizational risk appetite.

The first such framework was published in 1977 by a fledgling not-for-profit association called the Electronic Data Processing Audit Association (EDPAA) in combination with a much more mature association of financial auditors, the Institute for Internal Auditors (IIA) (Bayuk 2005, p. 11). In 1977, the IIA formed a global committee of accounting firms, government entities, and other professional associations with interests in security computers that pooled their knowledge to devise and publish the Systems Auditability and Control Report (IIA 1977). The report was a "how-to" manual for computer audit, a badly needed training manual for those new to the profession. Later that year, the EDPAA augmented the report with a primer called Control Objectives (EDPAA 1977), defining control objectives as "a statement of the desired result or purpose to be achieved by implementing control procedures in a particular IT activity."

Over the past three decades, multiple international and national bodies have produced frameworks that blend governance, technical control, and analytical rigor. Although they emerged in different regulatory and organizational contexts, they share a unifying purpose: connecting security decisions to measurable organizational outcomes and enabling defensible accountability to stakeholders, regulators, and boards.

The frameworks examined in this chapter are by no means exhaustive, but instead examples of categories of cybersecurity frameworks designed for different purposes. No universal classification of cybersecurity frameworks exists, and not even the categories are exhaustive. However, they should be sufficient to demonstrate how accumulated best practices from multiple sources are combined into any given organization's cybersecurity policies, as well as the obvious complications inherent in that process. The examples herein reflect the primary functional role each category of framework typically plays in an organization's governance layers, recognizing that some frameworks span more than one layer. *Governance* frameworks answer the question of who is responsible for managing cyber risk and how that responsibility is structured and verified. *Cybersecurity program* frameworks focus on the technology operations process and corresponding cybersecurity controls. They are useful in deciding how risk is managed day to day. *Dependency* risk frameworks provide guidance on how organizations can manage cybersecurity obligations that extend beyond their own boundaries into their vendors, service providers, and supply chains. *Assessment and benchmarking* frameworks help organizations demonstrate compliance with the frameworks they have adopted. These layers are complementary rather than sequential: mature cybersecurity programs operate across all four simultaneously. Table 4.1 illustrates the layered structure within which cybersecurity frameworks operate.

4.1.1 Governance and Oversight Frameworks

Governance frameworks define the roles, responsibilities, and accountability structures within which cybersecurity decisions are made. They help organizations answer the fundamental question: who is responsible for managing cyber risk and how should that responsibility be structured and verified? The exemplar frameworks at this layer in Table 4.1 address these questions, and some extend the governance layer into the cybersecurity program layer.

ISO/IEC's Risk Management Guidelines (International Organization for Standardization and International Electrotechnical Commission) include enterprise-wide principles for defining context, identifying and analyzing risk, and integrating mitigation into governance structures. Its scope is intentionally

Table 4.1 Exemplar Cybersecurity Frameworks.

Layer	Framework	Publisher
Governance	Risk Management Guidelines (31000)	Joint effort by the International Organization for Standardization and the International Electrotechnical Commission (ISO/IEC 2018)
	Enterprise Risk Management – Integrating with Strategy and Performance (ERM)	Committee of Sponsoring Organizations of the Treadway Commission (COSO 2017)
	Control Objectives for Information Technology (COBIT)	Information Systems Audit and Control Association (ISACA 2019)
	Managing Information Security Risk (SP 800-39)	National Institute of Standards and Technology (NIST 2011)
Cybersecurity program	Cybersecurity Framework (CSF)	National Institute of Standards and Technology (NIST 2024)
	Information Security Management Systems Requirements (27001)	International Organization for Standardization and the International Electrotechnical Commission (ISO/IEC 2022a)
	Cloud Controls Matrix (CCM)	Cloud Security Alliance (CSA 2021)
Dependency	Cybersecurity Supply Chain Risk Management Practices for Systems and Organizations (SP 800-161)	National Institute of Standards and Technology (NIST 2022)
	Information Security for Supplier Relationships (27036)	International Organization for Standardization and the International Electrotechnical Commission (ISO/IEC 2021)
	PCI Data Security Standard (PCI DSS)	Payment Card Industry Security Standards Council (PCISSC DSS 2024)
	Statement on Standards for Attestation Engagements No. 18, System and Organization Controls 2, Type II report (SSAE 18 SOC2)	American Institute of Certified Public Accountants (AICPA 2017).
Assessment and benchmarking	Guidance on Information Security Risk Management (27005)	International Organization for Standardization and the International Electrotechnical Commission (ISO/IEC 2022b)
	Cross-Sector Cybersecurity Performance Goals (CISA CPG)	Cybersecurity and Infrastructure Security Agency (CISA 2025a)
	Center for Internet Security (CIS)	CIS Critical Security Controls Implementation Groups (CIS n.d.)

broad and applies equally to cybersecurity, financial, or operational safety risks at a qualitative and conceptual level. It helps organizations develop their own risk philosophy and appetite, rather than prescribing specific controls or assessment methodologies. Organizations use it to establish the framing within which more specific cybersecurity management systems operate. That breadth is also its constraint: ISO/IEC 31000 does not produce auditable control evidence or certifiable compliance outcomes, and organizations requiring external assurance must layer more specific instruments on top of it.

COSO's Enterprise Risk Management (Committee of Sponsoring Organizations of the Treadway Commission) integrates strategy, performance, and risk culture within a governance model explicitly designed for board-level oversight. COSO ERM helps organizations understand how risk appetite and tolerance align with organizational objectives and provides an example cybersecurity governance architecture designed to result in meaningful reporting on cybersecurity to boards and audit committees. Its primary contribution is connecting cybersecurity risk to the enterprise risk vocabulary used for financial, legal, and reputational exposures, an alignment increasingly demanded by security regulators and institutional investors. COSO ERM does not address cybersecurity controls or technical implementation; organizations that rely on it exclusively for cybersecurity governance will find it insufficient without a supporting cybersecurity program framework to address the underlying control structure.

NIST's Managing Information Security Risk (National Institute of Standards and Technology) connects governance principles to information system operations through a three-tier hierarchy focused on organizational mission, processes, and systems. It provides guidance on integrating risk assessment results into enterprise decision-making and serves as a conceptual bridge between governance policy frameworks and cybersecurity program frameworks. Nevertheless, this framework is rarely the only tool an organization uses to develop its cybersecurity risk posture. Its primary value is helping organizations focus on the organizational context within which cybersecurity program frameworks like NIST CSF are applied.

ISACA's COBIT (Information Systems Audit and Control Association Control Objectives for Information and Related Technologies) speaks to the topic of technology control generally, and it provides a sharp focus on how cybersecurity controls can be used to address the broader risk issues inherent in technology governance and management. It provides advice on strategy alignment, benefits realization, risk optimization, and stakeholder value delivery. ISACA is the new brand of the same organization that produced Control Objectives in 1977, renamed from the EDPAA in 1994. Control Objectives was then rebranded as Control Objectives for Information Technology, from whence COBIT got its name. Because its main focus is the whole of cyberspace, its framework is not limited to cybersecurity risks. COBIT starts at a much broader level and asks whether the board's expectations for information technologies (IT) risk tolerance are clearly documented, whether investment decisions are aligned with strategic objectives, and whether audit functions receive independent visibility into control effectiveness. Organizations that adopt it as guidance may find it streamlines the process of integrating a cybersecurity program into technology governance and operations.

4.1.2 Cybersecurity Program Frameworks

Operational frameworks translate governance intent into practice. They define how to identify assets, analyze threats, evaluate vulnerabilities, and determine controls, answering the question of how cyber risk is managed day to day. The NIST Cybersecurity Framework, ISO/IEC 27005, CIS Controls, and the Cloud Security Alliance Cloud Controls Matrix each represent a distinct approach to operationalizing risk management, varying in scope, methodology, and prescriptive detail.

NIST's Cybersecurity Framework was first developed in 2014 following a Presidential Executive Order directing NIST to work with critical infrastructure owners and operators to develop a voluntary framework. The first version was all about Security Operations (SecOps) focus on defending against cyberattacks. It defined five functions and provided advice on how to implement them in the context of a controlled technology environment (see Figure 4.2). These are given as follows:

Identify: The organization's current cybersecurity risks are understood.
Protect: Safeguards to manage the organization's cybersecurity risks are used.
Detect: Possible cybersecurity attacks and compromises are found and analyzed.
Respond: Actions regarding a detected cybersecurity incident are taken.
Recover: Assets and operations affected by a cybersecurity incident are restored.

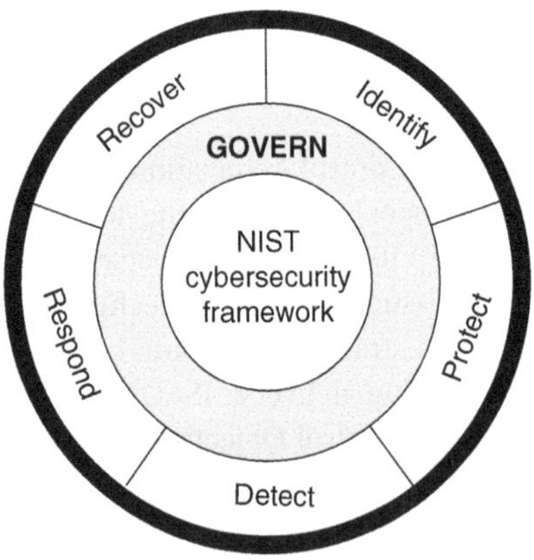

Figure 4.2 NIST cybersecurity risk management framework cycle.

In 2024, the framework's scope was expanded beyond core SecOps to the organization as a whole and added a sixth function:

Govern: The organization's cybersecurity risk management strategy, expectations, and policy are established, communicated, and monitored.

The CSF's outcome-based design helps an organization formulate qualitative self-assessment and quantitative cybersecurity program metrics. Its voluntary character has driven wide adoption, but also draws criticism. Without mandatory baselines, self-reported compliance against CSF profiles is difficult to verify, and organizations can claim alignment while leaving material gaps in their actual control environments.

ISO/IEC's Information Security Management System specifies common sense requirements for establishing and maintaining an Information Security Management System (ISMS) and is the only standard in this group that provides for formal assurance, in that it is accompanied by certification requirements to be used for independent assessment. While ISO/IEC 31000 articulates principles, ISO/IEC 27001 enforces a management system requirement, mandating that organizations perform formal risk assessment and treatment (through ISO/IEC 27005 or a comparable methodology) within a cycle of continuous improvement. ISO/IEC 27001 spans the governance and operational tiers; its governance requirements (i.e., defined scope, management commitment, and documented risk treatment decisions) place it in the governance layer, while its operational risk assessment and treatment mechanisms connect directly to the cybersecurity program layer. The management system structure creates an auditable record that satisfies regulatory examiners and external certification bodies. Certification requires ongoing surveillance audits and recertification every three years; some practitioners argue that the documentation burden can divert resources from operational security investment, particularly in smaller organizations.

CSA's Cloud Controls Matrix helps organizations determine how to accomplish their cybersecurity goals in situations where they are responsible for configuring their own security within technology service platforms, colloquially referred to as *cloud computing environments*. The framework fills a niche because when cloud computing services like Google Cloud and Amazon Web Services rent facilities for electronic data processing, such as *virtual* computers hosted in their own data centers, they have no responsibility to configure cybersecurity on those machines, and the controls available to be used by their customers are often customized and introduce new tools that work differently than those in a physical data center. The CCM advises organizations on how to approach issues like shared responsibility boundaries, data residency, and user activities, such as software development and SecOps (Cloud Security Alliance 2021). CCM also offers a certification program for cloud service providers – *Security, Trust, Assurance,* *and Risk Registry* (STAR). It is a comprehensive three-level certification program that maps directly to NIST CSF, ISO/IEC 27001, and SOC 2; organizations can use a single CCM-based control standard to demonstrate alignment with multiple frameworks simultaneously. Its limitation is scope; CCM addresses cloud environments specifically and does not constitute an enterprise-wide risk framework.

4.1.3 Dependency Frameworks

The frameworks described in Sections 4.1.1 and 4.1.2 are principally concerned with how organizations manage cybersecurity risk within their own boundaries. Those boundaries have become difficult to define. Core banking service providers serve thousands of financial institutions from shared infrastructure; cloud platforms host critical systems for entire industry sectors; and payment processors sit at the intersection of millions of transactions daily. When these service providers experience a security failure, the impact is not confined to a single institution. Third-party risk frameworks address the governance and oversight structures through which organizations manage cybersecurity obligations that extend across these relationships and through which regulators extend supervisory authority to the providers themselves.

NIST's Cybersecurity Supply Chain Risk Management Practices for Systems and Organizations provide the primary US government framework for managing cybersecurity risks that originate in supply chains and from third-party providers. It is of particular interest in the context of communication because it begins with the message that communication needs to occur among an organization's most senior leadership at the enterprise level to produce a comprehensive strategy and risk appetite for supplier risk management. Moreover, they must communicate effectively with those responsible for executing the enterprise mission at the level below them, and those leaders must communicate and monitor all operational processes within their sphere of control that relate to reliance on suppliers. It provides detailed methods for identifying critical suppliers, assessing their security posture, incorporating cybersecurity requirements into acquisition processes, and maintaining ongoing monitoring. It also provides detailed control requirements and templates that an organization can use to formulate strategy, policy, planning, and risk assessment.

ISO/IEC's Information Security for Supplier Relationships is less prescriptive than NIST's at the control level, likely due to the international community that ISO generally serves. It is a four-part standard covering the security requirements for supplier relationships generally, cloud services specifically, and technology supply chain security, and it aligns with the ISO/IEC ISMS management system structure. Organizations operating under ISO governance frameworks or in jurisdictions where ISO standards carry regulatory recognition find it easier to integrate than the NIST version.

AICPA's Statement on Standards for Attestation Engagements No. 18, System and Organization Controls 2 Type II report establishes what third-party risk programs must accomplish from a technology risk perspective and is the primary method by which external financial auditors assess the risk of their auditee's dependence on their significant technology service providers. A SOC 2 Type II report represents an independent CPA firm's examination of a service organization's controls relevant to security, availability, processing integrity, confidentiality, and privacy, using *AICPA's Trust Services Criteria*, over a defined period, typically 6–12 months. The distinction between Type I and Type II is material: Type I attests that controls are suitably designed at a point in time; Type II assumes Type I has completed successfully and further attests that they operated effectively over the examination period. Note that SOC 2 report attests to controls against the AICPA Trust Services Criteria, not against NIST CSF, ISO/IEC 27001, or other enterprise frameworks. An organization cannot rely on its vendor's SOC 2 report to verify NIST CSF alignment – those are separate determinations requiring distinct assessment processes.

PCISSC's Payment Card Industry Data Security Standard represents a contractually required technical standard enforced through payment card network rules rather than statute compliance. That is, an organization cannot participate as a merchant in a credit card transaction without undergoing these cybersecurity risk assessments. It includes a certification program for Qualified Security Assessor (QSA) and a template for a QSA's Report on Compliance (ROC). There are 4 levels of PCI DSS requirements. For example, only merchants that process over 6 million cards are required to have a QSA conduct a yearly ROC; all others are required to conduct an annual Self-Assessment Questionnaire (SAQ), and all but the lowest requires a network vulnerability scan executed by an Approved Scanning Vendor (ASV). A clean ROC or SAQ establishes payment card cybersecurity control adequacy without addressing enterprise cybersecurity governance broadly. Like the SOC 2 report, a PCI DSS ROC or SAQ is a domain-specific assurance product rather than an enterprise-wide framework, a distinction that institutions relying on these reports for vendor oversight must account for when creating their own supplier risk management policy.

4.1.4 Assessing Framework Compliance

The frameworks described in Sections 4.1.1 through 4.1.3 define what a cybersecurity program should look like. Note that some do not specify what constitutes a minimum acceptable level of performance and some omit advice for the assessment of compliance with the implementing organization. This section describes some frameworks meant to fill that gap.

ISO/IEC's Guidance on Information Security Risk Management (ISO/IEC 2022b). Organizations find it useful in establishing the scope of such an assessment, as well as in identifying, analyzing, evaluating, and mitigating cybersecurity risk. The standard includes methods for creating qualitative scoring and aligns with principles introduced in ISO/IEC 31000 Risk Management standard. As an assessment guide, it sits at the junction of the governance and operational layers, providing advice on the risk assessment and reporting based on operational context. Certified examiners reviewing an organization's ISO/IEC 27001 compliance will also assess whether risk assessments were conducted consistently with ISO/IEC 27005 or a comparable systematic methodology.

Cyber and Infrastructure Security Agency's Cross-Sector Cybersecurity Performance Goals (CPGs) were established by the 2021 National Security Memorandum on Improving Cybersecurity for Critical Infrastructure Control Systems (CISA 2025a). The CPGs are voluntary and explicitly not a comprehensive framework. They identify a prioritized subset of high-impact practices, covering account security, device security, data protection, vulnerability management, supply chain risk, and incident response. These were selected for their demonstrated risk-reduction value across all 16 critical infrastructure sectors. CPG 2.0 aligns to NIST CSF 2.0, including the Govern function, and consolidates previously separate IT and operational technology (OT) goals into unified cross-environment requirements. Their policy significance lies in what the primary frameworks leave to organization judgment: that a specific set of practices constitutes a reasonable baseline below which an organization's posture is inadequate.

Alongside CPG 2.0, Cyber and Infrastructure Security Agency (CISA) introduced Sector-Specific Goals (SSGs) developed in coordination with Sector Risk Management Agencies for individual critical infrastructure sectors (CISA 2025b). The SSGs extend the cross-sector baseline with practices calibrated to sector-specific threat profiles and regulatory environments. For financial services, the SSGs reflect the sector's particular exposure to payment system fraud, third-party concentration risk, and the systemic consequences of operational disruption.

CIS's Controls Implementation Groups do not address policy at the organization level, but address policy at the technical level as described in Chapter 1. Policies are based on technical standards related to configuring a specific set of technology devices. However, when adopted by an organization at the enterprise level, there is typically a management policy directive issued that it shall be complied with, which makes it a policy at the *real* policy level. CIS maintains a set of configuration specifications referred to as *safeguards*. Safeguards fall into one of eighteen control categories covering the full suite of NIST functions: identify, protect, detect, respond, and recover. In addition, each safeguard falls into Implementation Groups representing:

- Basic cyber hygiene practices;
- Basic plus addition safeguards suited to organizations with dedicated IT staff managing sensitive data; and
- The complete set of safeguards labeled as appropriate for organizations facing advanced persistent threats.

CIS also supplies the tools necessary to automatically check technical configurations for compliance with each group level. The prioritization structure addresses a persistent objection to prescriptive control frameworks, namely, that full implementation is disproportionate for smaller organizations with limited security resources.

Other methods for cybersecurity risk self-assessment employ a wide variety of software tools and services. These include, but are not limited to, technology platforms that offer Governance Risk and Compliance (GRC) software, industry best practices, vendors who scan the technology environment and provide a scorecard that spans multiple control categories, and regulatory examination procedures that translate framework functions into concrete, measurable expectations.

Once an organization has chosen the framework(s) upon which to model their cybersecurity risk management approach, it is common for an organization to list out the requirements in a spreadsheet, a GRC database, or some other systematic manner and methodically ask their business process owners to map them to internal Cybersecurity Policies, Standards, and Procedures (PPSPs), and typically a liaison from the CISO's office will be assigned to guide a business process owner through this task. The profession refers to this process as a Risk and Control Self-Assessment (RCSA). In practice, the typical output of a self-assessment process is a gap analysis visualization that maps current-state practices against selected framework requirements, identifying where recommended controls are absent, partial, or not yet documented. Such gap analyses serve both internal prioritization and external compliance demonstration, where regulators require documented framework alignment; the map of internal controls to the standard, plus the gap analysis and its remediation plan, constitutes the primary evidence of sound cybersecurity risk management. That is, it would be if the gap analysis showed that the residual risk after applying controls was safely below the regulatory required risk appetite for the organization under scrutiny. Figure 4.3 displays an example summary report from such a self-assessment.

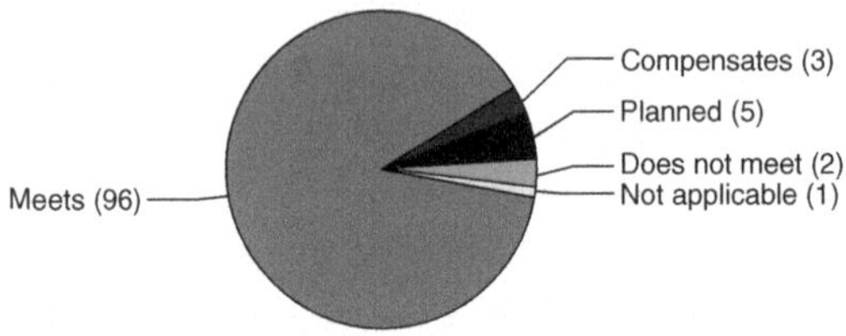

Section status:
Identify: 100% complete, 2 compensated, 1 planned, 2 not met, section has 78 control links and 1 evidence attachments section has 2 flagged issues
Protect: 100% complete, 2 compensated, 3 planned, 1 not applicable, section has 233 control links and 0 evidence attachments section has 3 flagged issues
Detect: 100% complete, 1 planned, section has 125 control links and 7 evidence attachments section has 1 flagged issues
Respond: 100% complete, section has 72 control links and 2 evidence attachments section has 0 flagged issues
Recover: 100% complete, section has 18 control links and 0 evidence attachments section has 0 flagged issues
Total number of requirements: 108
Count completed: 108
Total so far fully met: 96, 88.9%
Total number of requirements with linked controls: 102

Figure 4.3 Example framework compliance gap analysis.

4.2 Threats and Vulnerabilities

4.2.1 Threats

Cyber threat intelligence (CTI) is both a technical and strategic discipline. At the operational level, it helps security teams detect, prioritize, and respond to active threats. Unfortunately, it is costly and may seem like a waste to someone who has never experienced a zero-day cyberattack. Nevertheless, from a policy perspective, it is important to have 7/24 access to some credible CTI reports that are relevant to your own domain, whether individual, organizational, dependency-related, or public. Though there are, of course, vendor services that will customize threat intelligence for a fee as described in Chapter 2, there are also many avenues for obtaining free information on cybersecurity threats.

The concept of a formal method of cybersecurity-specific Information Sharing and Analysis Center (ISAC) was first proposed in a Presidential Directive (PDD 63) in 1998. The main concern motivating the directive was terror attacks on critical infrastructure, so by 1999, a few ISACs were formed within critical industry sectors. Each critical infrastructure community was assigned a Sector Specific Agency (SSA) as a partner with which to secure the critical infrastructure within its scope of operation. For example, the Financial Services Industry was assigned the Department of Treasury (DoT) and the healthcare sector, the Department of Health and Human Services (HHS). Together, they formed committees of industry

CISOs and corresponding SSAs. The ISACs were intended to promote critical infrastructure protection by providing a safe method by which information on cybersecurity threat actors and tactics targeting each critical infrastructure sector could be shared with the sector owner/operators. The source of threat information may be an owner–operator under attack, or a government surveillance operation on a hostile nation-state or organized crime unit. The ISACs are a two-way information-sharing compact. They typically work as a clearinghouse. The private sector reports threats and incidents to the ISAC administrator, who shares the information with other members and the assigned SSA. The ISACs SSAs report all credible threats to national intelligence services and receive reports from national intelligence services filtered by industry sector. The administrator convenes meetings as needed to share sector-specific intelligence with all industry members whether or not the intelligence originates from the members or the government.

At the beginning, ISACs would meet in a conference room to discuss shared sensitive cybersecurity issues and shared solutions if anyone had any. As the members grew, formal rules and governance structures defined methods of information sharing and rules for protecting the information. Secure teleconferencing services were arranged so information-sharing gatherings could include remote members.

Shortly after 9/11, a public–private partnership strategy was established by the newly created Department of Homeland Security (DHS) to provide a firmer foundation for government oversight for critical infrastructures. One of their first efforts was the formation of Government Coordinating Councils (GCCs) and Sector Specific Councils (SCCs) which emerged around 2003.

Despite the increased government assistance, some sectors were more successful in this information sharing than others. A major legal concern for some was the Federal Advisory Committee Act of 1972 (FACA). It required that advisory committees within the executive branch adhere to a set of open forum rules so the public could be informed of the topic of their conversations. For example, neither the ISACs nor the SSAs were comfortable discussing the attacks on the financial industry in an open forum. There was a grave concern that it could cause a run on the banks. A few years later, the Critical Infrastructure Partnership Advisory Council (CIPAC 2006) was launched to assist with public–private partnerships set forth in the DHS National Infrastructure Protection Plan (NIPP) and eased the restrictions on public disclosure.

For ISACs, the name of the game had first been *information sharing*, but after 9/11, it quickly adopted the military's focus on *threat intelligence*. Vendors also quickly jumped on the bandwagon, offering threat intelligence services to clients based on their ability to scan threat actor activities on the internet and match them to patterns within their client organizations, as well as shop the black market for information stolen from their clients, so their clients understood when they had been breached by a cyber criminal or an advanced persistent threat.

Around this time, the title of CISO was slowly emerging, but the CISO equivalents in these organizations were often sponsored by their SSA to get secret government clearances, so they could safely share information about non-public cybersecurity investigations. The Cybersecurity Information Sharing Act (2015), an act to improve cybersecurity in the United States through enhanced sharing of information about cybersecurity threats, and for other purposes, provided another long-awaited breakthrough. It gave companies legal protection when voluntarily sharing cyber threat indicators with the federal government and encouraged two-way information exchange between the private sector and DHS's National Cybersecurity and Communications Integration Center (NCCIC).

One of the ISACs established at the national critical infrastructure level is the Multi-State ISAC. Their members are CISO equivalents in State, Local, Tribal, and Territorial (SLTT) municipalities, counties, and other agencies. As in any ISAC, their members receive threat information and can share that information with their constituents, provided it is not classified. Most states have established some type of coordination center that distributes the threat intelligence to state businesses, and some have member conferences where state and local cyber defenders can meet in person.

The ISAC has evolved from information exchange to a proactive stance on cybersecurity risk management, wherein members monitor evolving threats and adjust their controls accordingly, as well as publicly post and/or send notifications about current cybersecurity threats impacting their communities. Although the methods, players, and nomenclature change over time, these information-sharing capabilities are now commonplace. Individuals and organizations should establish policies to seek out and take advantage of these information-sharing opportunities that are available to them. ISACs, threat intelligence vendors, industry associations, and government agencies all now routinely publish bulletins to their member organizations on who is targeting them, why they are vulnerable, and how they could protect themselves against cyberattack. It has evolved to the point where it is negligent on the part of organizations to ignore these warnings.

4.2.2 Cybersecurity Incidents

In the discussion of metrics in Chapter 3, we distinguished the suggested metric of "absence of successful virus attacks." However, that does not mean we do not think it is important to measure the actual successful attacks if there are any. SecOps typically measure incidents by their duration and impact. Before the coronavirus disease (COVID) pandemic, most communication about security incidents in progress was shared in a *Security Operations Center* housing desks of analysts sharing information in real time by chatting over their individual desk monitors, surrounded by large screens that showed real-time alerts. Today, many SecOps Centers instead focus on communication techniques that enable remote team members to collaborate. The information on the large screens and their conversations has been consolidated into single-screen *dashboards* and *chatrooms* that provide a snapshot of incidents currently in progress and the stage of investigation and the current priority any given one may have over others.

Duration may be measured in stages in their investigation process. These will, of course, vary depending on the tools and discipline a SecOps team may have to keep track.

Identify → Analyze → Contain → Eradicate → Recover → Postmortem → Closed

It is rare for smaller teams to track any timestamp other than *identify* and *closed*. Identify is the date an anomaly or problem was observed by the SecOps team or identified by a customer, user, or administrator and referred to the organization via any channel such as a customer service ticket, a phone call, or a website designed for anonymous whistleblowers. The closed date is the time SecOps stopped working on it. In a large organization, it may be common for SecOps to consider an incident closed because they have stopped working on it, though the post-mortem could go on for months, even years in some other organization like IT or Risk Management. Figure 4.4 is an example of a chart comparing how quickly SecOps moves from stage to stage depending on the source of any given alert. Note that it stops at *eradicate*, an indicator that after the threat is cleansed from the systems, SecOps hands off the recovery and post-mortem stages to another team. Where these interim steps are measured, a SecOps team needs to have heightened awareness to recognize the moment a new stage is entered, and there must be easy switches to flip in the midst of an investigation, or the timestamps will be inaccurate, and any interpretation management may wish to use to support decisions based on them will not be sound.

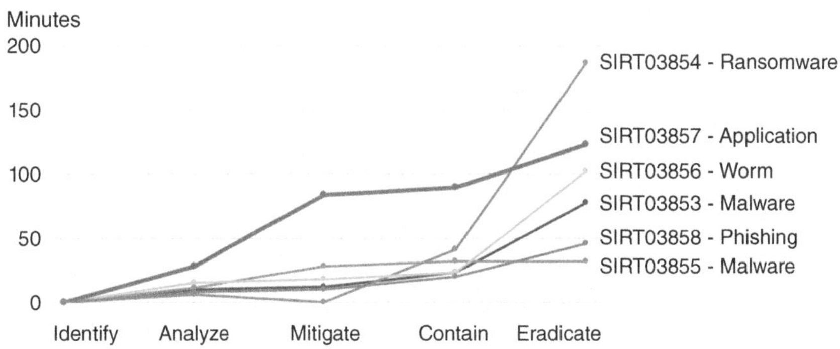

Figure 4.4 Time to respond to cybersecurity incidents.

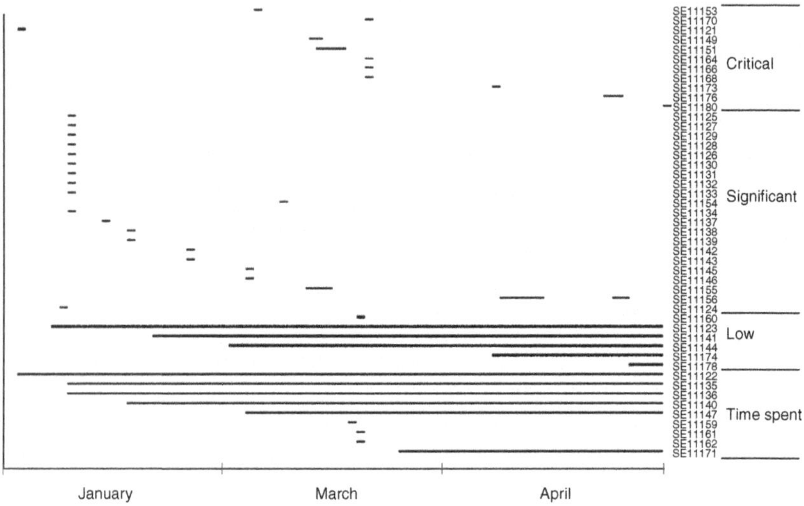

Figure 4.5 Security incident trends.

Organizations that share cybersecurity incidents with the Board of Directors provide charts that show various attributes of cybersecurity incidents trending over time, such as those in Figure 4.5.

Note that Figure 4.5 has an incident attribute called "impact." This will be an ordinal scale with a verifiable set of conditions such as time spent in investigation, cost of incident remediation, business opportunity lost due to outage, monetary loss, and/or estimated value of data breached. Typically, if the only impact is time spent in investigation, the incident will be considered the normal course of business, while more severe impact levels may be designed to trigger required regulatory reporting. These are all customized by the organization according to its risk appetite and associated loss tolerance levels.

From the point of view of the threat actor, incidents also have stages, called attack paths or threat vectors like those depicted in the figures in Chapter 2. Those stages are an industry standard developed by MITRE, a US Federally Funded Research and Development Center (FFRDC). FFRDCs recruit private-sector resources to coordinate research needed to operate government functions and assist the government with its long-term Research and Development (R&D) needs. The FFRDC operated by MITRE is called the National Cybersecurity FFRDC. Among other things, this FFRDC developed the MITRE ATT&CK® taxonomy that is the key in Figure 2.1. (not an acronym, just a trademark). MITRE ATT&CK® documents advanced persistent threat behaviors in the form of tactics, techniques, and procedures (TTPs). The patterns are used in cyberforensic investigations and analytics to detect adversary behaviors and in specifications for sensors and analytics that support cybersecurity military operations, both offensive and defensive. The result is a publicly available repository of known threat actors, together with their behaviors, the malware, and vulnerabilities they commonly incorporate into their attacks (attack.mitre.org).

4.2.3 Vulnerabilities

As described in Chapter 2, when anti-virus vendors emerged in the 1990s, they would collect virus samples and the vulnerabilities that allowed them to install themselves and make footprints they could use to identify them. These vendors would individually find new attack patterns within days of each other, and each would publish them under different names and use their own footprint to detect them. These varied widely in both content and efficacy. The problem was exacerbated by the vendors all wanting to claim to have been the first to discover the virus. This hindered efforts by cybersecurity analysts to verify that they had appropriately safeguarded their systems against known threats. A famous paper called the situation the "Vulnerability Tower of Babel" (Martin 2001). A table in that paper showed a single piece of malware had been given different names by nine vendors, two government agencies, and a university research center.

To help system administrators find appropriate patches, NIST began to centrally publish what was then called the *Internet Categorization of Attacks Toolkit* (ICAT), a US government repository of standards-based vulnerability management data represented using a Common Vulnerability Enumeration standard created by MITRE (Mell 2000). The project was not funded to be ongoing, but found a home in an association created in 1989 to bring together system administrators, auditors, and network administrators interested in what had then just been recognized as *Information Security* (as opposed to the 1980s professional moniker, *computer security*), called the System Administrators Network Security (SANS) Institute (www.sans.org). After the DHS was formed, DHS adopted ICAT, then renamed it to the National Vulnerability Database (NVD). MITRE also created a standard to link the vulnerability to the technology platforms on which it was found, the Common Platform Enumeration (CPE). NIST hosts the NVD (nvd .nist.gov) and scores the vulnerabilities using a Common Vulnerability Scoring System (CVSS) and adds any supplemental data on the vulnerability that they can find. These data enable cyber defenders to automate vulnerability management and cybersecurity vulnerability measurement.

That said, there are so many vulnerabilities that many organizations hesitate to patch many of them for fear they will break their own software. Vulnerability scanning services work by collecting vulnerabilities and designing tests to see if they appear on a given device and they will report them all. For example, a search for

Log4j vulnerabilities in the NVD shows 26 Common Vulnerability Enumeration entries. Only one of them is directly connected to the known exploitable vulnerability described in Chapter 2. Most organizations patch their software within a quality assurance cycle within which they test the patches in systems isolated from their production environments, so if a vendor patch causes a software failure, they can prevent it from being deployed going forward, and this way develop a risk tolerance for skipping some patches.

To make sure no patches critical to immediate cyber defense are skipped, the US DHS's CISA also leverages the CVE to warn the federal government when exploits for a CVE are currently known to be actively sought and exploited within the US Government. These are published in a publicly available Known Exploited Vulnerability (KEV) Catalog and required to be remediated in a specified time period (CISA n.d.). The CVE is also leveraged in a private sector KEV catalog version that includes known exploited vulnerabilities, generally not limited to federal requirements (www.vulncheck.com).

A parallel effort was launched by MITRE to the software development community to warn them against creating vulnerabilities to begin with: the Common Weakness Enumeration (CWE), a shared list of software and hardware weakness created by developer mistakes like not checking web input fields for malicious code to avoid Log4j-like attacks. The global development community assists via a volunteer organization called the Open Worldwide Application Security Project (OWASP). Periodically, OWASP issues a top ten list of its consensus on the ten most critical security risks to web applications (Open Worldwide Application Security Project 2025). These are based on scanning ~2.8 million applications globally and surveying ~200 developers in various software job functions. Unfortunately for the state of software security globally, of the top 10 worst developer mistakes made in 2025, only two were new: *Software Supply Chain Failures*, which is based almost exclusively on the survey side of the data collection, and *Mishandling of Exceptional Conditions*. Four were on the list in its first year of publication in 2003: *Broken Access Control*, *Security Misconfiguration*, *Injection*, and *Authentication Failures*. One has been on the list since 2017, *Security Logging and Alerting Failures*. The remaining three joined the list in 2021: *Cryptographic Failures*, *Insecure Design*, and *Software or Data Integrity Failures*.

CWE data helps inform MITRE research in Common Attack Pattern Enumeration and Classification (CAPEC), which catalogs common attacker techniques such as SQL Injection (defined in Chapter 2). These repositories are frequently cross-referenced to collectively produce a common vocabulary for cybersecurity professionals working independently on various aspects of threat analysis, detection, response, and mitigation. Over decades of cybersecurity research, projects have reduced the Tower of Babel problem by making it possible for vendors to incorporate diverse threat intelligence using standard terminology into their

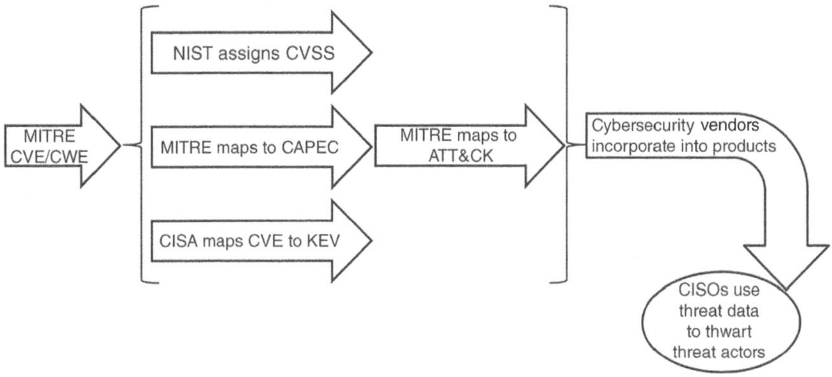

Figure 4.6 The National Vulnerability Database and MITRE ATT&CK®.

products, as well as reduce the unknowable extent of software vulnerabilities. Figure 4.6 shows the relationship between these standards (Bayuk 2024, p. 41).

4.2.4 Vulnerability Marketplaces

Although in the early 2000s, the first rule of the zero-day market was that nobody talks about the zero-day market, and by 2005, there were plenty of people talking about it. That year, a former NSA vulnerability analyst named Charles Miller decided to go public with his experience, but he could not legally divulge any classified information he received while working for the federal government. So instead, he hacked the Linux operating system and found a brand new zero-day vulnerability he believed should be worth at least five figures and submitted a request for preauthorization to the NSA to publish his sale of the new exploit when it occurred. His prepublication took over eight months to be approved, but his argument that this endeavor would not expose any secrets he learned at the NSA was sound, and it eventually came through. He immediately put the vulnerability up for sale and sold it for $50,000.

In addition to his own sale, Miller legally obtained information on how much other current zero-day vulnerabilities were worth and included the list in his paper (see Figure 4.7). Even with this small sampling, it is obvious that the market for zero-day vulnerabilities must be a significant line item in the NSA's budget. Papers like Miller's demonstrate that buying and selling vulnerabilities is commonplace, and even Responsible Disclosure advocates understand that it is not illegal.

These high-priced vulnerabilities stand out in what had become an emerging much wider marketplace for not only vulnerabilities but also *exploit kits* that a non-technical would-be cyber criminal could purchase and launch themselves to commit common cybercrimes like credit card and credential harvesting. A few

Vulnerability/exploit	Value	Source
"Some exploits"	$200,000 - $250,000	A government official referring to what "some people" pay
A "real good" exploit	over $100,000	Official from SNOsoft research team
Vista exploit	$50,000	Raimund Genes, Trend Micro
"Weaponized exploit"	$20,000-$30,000	David Maynor, SecureWorks
ZDI, iDefense purchases	$2,000-$10,000	David Maynor, SecureWorks
WMF exploit	$4000	Alexander Gostev, Kaspersky
Microsoft Excel	> $1200	Ebay auction site
Mozilla	$500	Mozilla bug bounty program

Figure 4.7 Zero day vulnerability prices. *Source:* Miller (2007) / Independent Security Evaluators.

years after Miller's paper, Geer and Conway started monitoring the prices of stolen data and malware/crimeware components, and Figure 4.8 shows some examples (Geer and Conway 2009). Note that the data and tools listed are very reasonably priced compared to the exorbitant cost of a zero-day vulnerability. Most of these marketplace attacks make use of vulnerabilities that are years old, reflecting the immaturity of cyberspace and the urgent need for policy to support responsible disclosure and remediation.

Individuals use software generally to automate tasks that are both tedious and resource intensive, and malware perpetrators are no exception. Automating malware delivery and data harvesting tasks reduces operating costs and allows cyber criminals to obscure their activities. Geer and Conway note that, in any technology marketplace, prices will fluctuate with the utility of the commodity, which in this case will change as technology evolves. The high price of the stolen passports and bank accounts listed in the first table in Figure 4.8 motivated the creation of secondary markets that produced the malware/crimeware components listed in the second table in Figure 4.8.

When crimes such as card theft are conducted using specialized software that provides economies of scale in mass thievery, it is organized cybercrime. In recognition of this alarming trend, the Financial Services Roundtable (FSR) commissioned a report to create awareness of the trend among their members (FSR 2011). The illustration in Figure 4.9 was produced in that study. It shows how specialists in each step required to conduct cybercrime at scale provide services for hire, creating an underground economy. The marketplace is fueled by hackers

Table 2: Example prices for stolen data	
CCV	$3.25
OS administrative login	$2.50
FTP exploit	$6.00
Full identity information	$5.00
Rich bank account credentials	$750.00
US passport information	$800.00
Router credentials	$12.50

Theft enabling commodity	Price
Keystroke logger	$25 on average
Botnets	$100 to $200 per 1,000 infections, depending on location
Spamming email service	$.01 per 1,000 emails, reliability of more than 85% delivered
Shop admins (Credit Card databases)	$100 to $300
Credit Card numbers without CCV2	$1 to $3
Credit Card numbers with CCV2	$1.50 to $10.00, depending on the country (relative prices Visa < Mastercard < Discover < Amex)
Socks accounts	$5 to $40/month
Sniffer dumps	$50 to $100/month
Western Union exploits	$300 to $1,000
Remote desktops	$5 to $8
Scam letters	$3 to $5

Figure 4.8 Prices in the organized cybercrime marketplace. *Source:* Data from Geer and Conway (2009).

finding vulnerabilities. They sell those vulnerabilities to people who design software that can exploit the vulnerabilities to break into systems. Each exploit is a single malware unit, and these units are combined into kits that allow criminals to infect computers to create botnets. Those botnets are rented to conduct attacks like denial of service, to host a look-alike site and/or to obscure a hacker's location. The services include everything from password harvesting to denial-of-service attacks. The flow of malware delivery and operations systems have also become increasingly modular, and these modules have themselves become a commodity.

The FSR report dubbed this situation *Crimeware as a Service* (CaaS), mirroring the technology platforms' use of the "as a Service" in acronyms like Software as a Service (SaaS). It also observed that not all players in the marketplace are taking equal risks from participation in organized cybercrime activities (see Figure 4.10). Many may claim to be legitimate merchants, such as gun dealers who are not accountable for the crimes committed by their clients. As we learned in Chapter 2, cyber attackers are not the only ones who collect vulnerabilities, and there are

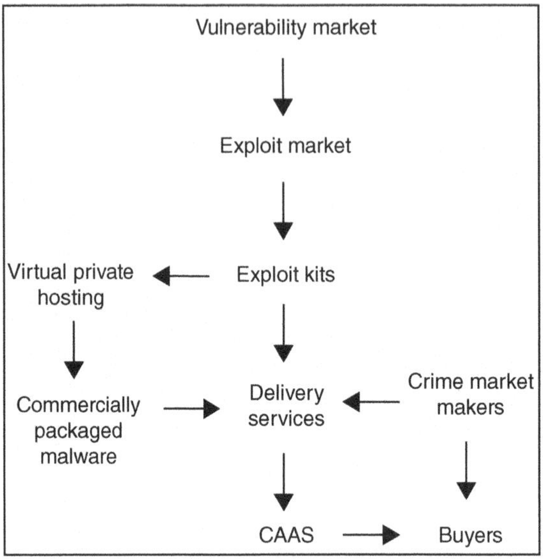

Figure 4.9 Crimeware as a service. *Source:* Financial Services Roundtable (2022) / Bank Policy Institute.

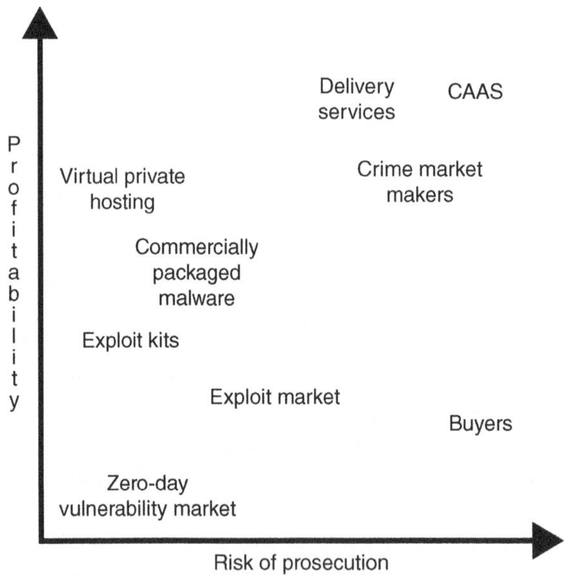

Figure 4.10 Cybercriminal risk. *Source:* Financial Services Roundtable (2022) / Bank Policy Institute.

cyberdefense vendors who profit from finding vulnerabilities as well. FSR advised its members that: "Cooperation and collaboration among cybercriminals have created crime patterns that evolve in concert with emerging technology, and all users of emerging technology are victims. There is also evidence that cybercriminals operate in geopolitically-identifiable groups. As one analyst put it, 'the phrase *campaign* is more appropriate than *adversary*'" (FSR 2022, p. 4).

According to some experts, online gambling games of chance are more typically rigged than not, and online gambling companies would rather pay trivial fines when caught than stop raking in the tons of guaranteed profits generated by their software's interaction with overly gullible online gamblers (Menn 2010). Even online games of skill can be defrauded by players who reverse engineer the software and reap rewards that were not earned via skill but rather from cunning. Those who reverse engineer software used to run games can often use this knowledge to cheat just as or more effectively than counting cards in a poker game (Hoglund and Mcgraw 2022).

4.3 Institutions for Communication and Collaboration

4.3.1 FIRST

The first formal organization dedicated to this effort was created right after the Morris Worm. Aptly named "FIRST," it provided an umbrella model for civic associations and local businesses to collaborate with law enforcement within their jurisdictions, whether they are local, national, or international. FIRST started small with seven North American Universities and FFRDCs, including the Computer Emergency Response Team Coordination Center at Carnegie Mellon University, which was founded in 1988 immediately following the Morris Worm as the US government's method of preparing for the next one. As we saw in Chapter 2, cybersecurity attacks escalated both in severity and frequency throughout their first decade and by 9/11, they had over 100 members in Central, North, and South America, Europe, Asia, and the Middle East. Today, they have approximately 750 members on all continents.

FIRST maintains several standards that are deeply ingrained in the cybersecurity industry. One is the CVSS mentioned above. It was developed by the National Infrastructure Advisory Council (NIAC) as a research project in 2003–2004, and FIRST took it over in 2005 (FIRST 2023). Another is an Exploit Prediction Scoring System (EPSS) that estimates the probability that a CVE will be exploited in the wild in the next 30 days. The combination of FIRST's CVSS and EPPS models enables cyber defenders to automate vulnerability management and cybersecurity vulnerability measurement. Another FIRST contribution is maintenance for the Traffic Light Protocol (TLP) standard (see Figure 4.11) (FIRST 2022). This is an ordinal measure developed shortly after 9/11 as a way for governments to dictate

	R	G	B
TLP:RED	255	43	43
TLP:AMBER	255	192	0
TLP:GREEN	51	255	0
TLP:CLEAR	255	255	255

Figure 4.11 Traffic light protocol.

with whom sensitive information can be shared for those with the need to know. FIRST took over TLP in 2016.

The TLP measure has values, called levels, corresponding to the domains: individual, organization, the cybersecurity defense community of an individual or organization with which it has been properly shared, and the public. That is, the holder of the information can only share it with people at the level corresponding to its ordinal value. If it is marked TLP:RED, then the individual with whom it is shared is not allowed to exercise their own judgment in keeping the information secret. If a recipient believes it is important to share the information more widely than indicated by its TLP label, then they must obtain explicit permission from the source. Note the careful attention to color specification for TLP labels. They are intended to ensure that people with poor eyesight or who are color-blind can recognize the information's TLP label by the hue.

FIRST members and organizations also collaborate to produce incident response policies, procedures, and standards that an enterprise can adopt to respond to malicious events. FIRST also sponsors training classes focused on teams of cybersecurity incident responders ranging from malware investigation to designing a Computer Security Incident Response Team (CSIRT). The annual FIRST conference is the largest gathering of incident response professionals in the world and is held in countries across the globe.

4.3.2 The National Incident Management System and Cybersecurity Incident Coordination

Due to the top-down nature of DHS first contacting major critical infrastructure players to initiate this movement, some regional locations within the US were left to manage their own cybersecurity risks in the face of the over-increasing threats described in Chapter 2. To fill this void, local law enforcement coordinated formal and informal cyberattack response forces that crossed municipalities and states using the National Incident Management System (NIMS) (FEMA 2017), the federal government's standardized doctrine for managing incidents of all types, regardless of cause, size, or complexity.

Established in 2004 pursuant to Homeland Security Presidential Directive 5 (HSPD-5 2003), NIMS was designed to ensure that federal, SLTT authorities could coordinate effectively during emergencies. Although initially associated with natural disasters and physical crises, NIMS was intentionally structured as an "all-hazards" framework. That flexibility has enabled its application to significant cybersecurity incidents, including ransomware campaigns, software supply chain compromises, and attacks on critical infrastructure.

At the center of NIMS is the Incident Command System, which provides a scalable, modular structure for organizing response activities. Incident Command System defines functional areas, such as Command, Operations, Planning, Logistics, and Finance/Administration, and assigns clear responsibilities to designated leaders within each. The structure emphasizes common terminology, defined objectives, and documented operational periods. In cybersecurity incidents, where technical complexity intersects with legal authorities, public communications, and economic consequences, this structured approach reduces confusion and clarifies accountability. It ensures that investigative, protective, intelligence, and regulatory functions can operate simultaneously without undermining one another.

A core feature of NIMS is unified command. In traditional disaster response, multiple jurisdictions may share authority over an incident scene. Unified command allows those authorities to establish common objectives while preserving their statutory responsibilities. Cybersecurity incidents present similar coordination challenges among different entities: the Federal Bureau of Investigations (FBI) may lead criminal investigation and attribution efforts, CISA may coordinate protective measures and sector-wide advisories, intelligence agencies may assess foreign state involvement, and sector-specific regulators may oversee industry compliance. Unified command allows these entities to align strategy and messaging without collapsing distinct legal mandates. The result is coordinated action rather than fragmented response.

The National Cyber Incident Response Plan (NCIRP) (DHS 2016) formally integrates cyber-specific response mechanisms into the NIMS framework and outlines how federal departments and agencies coordinate during significant cyber incidents. It identifies lead and supporting roles, establishes thresholds for federal involvement, and connects cyber response to broader national preparedness doctrine. Importantly, the NCIRP recognizes that cyber incidents often affect privately owned infrastructure and, therefore, require structured public–private coordination. By anchoring cyber response in NIMS principles, the NCIRP ensures that digital crises are managed with the same discipline applied to natural disasters and terrorist attacks.

The 2020 SolarWinds software supply chain compromise illustrates NIMS principles in action. When malicious code embedded in a widely used network management platform was discovered across federal agencies and private sector organizations, the federal government organized a coordinated response aligned with ICS doctrine (GAO 2022). CISA led mitigation guidance and federal civilian coordination, while the FBI and intelligence community pursued attribution and threat analysis. Interagency groups operated under shared objectives, prioritizing detection, containment, and public advisories. Although distributed and largely invisible to the public, the response reflected NIMS concepts: clearly defined leadership roles, structured information sharing, and centralized situational awareness.

The Colonial Pipeline ransomware attack in 2021 demonstrated the operational coordination challenges posed by cyber incidents with immediate physical and economic consequences. When ransomware disrupted fuel distribution along the East Coast, federal authorities coordinated across multiple departments (DOE 2021): CISA provided technical support and sector engagement, the FBI led the criminal investigation and later recovered a portion of the ransom, the Department of Energy assessed energy market impacts, and other agencies monitored cascading effects. Public messaging required careful synchronization to prevent panic and stabilize markets. The response closely mirrored NIMS doctrine, particularly in unified command, operational objective setting, and coordinated communications.

The widespread exploitation of the Log4j vulnerability later in 2021 further underscored the value of structured coordination (FTC 2022). Unlike a discrete network intrusion, Log4j was a systemic software flaw embedded in countless systems worldwide. CISA activated coordination mechanisms that brought together federal agencies and private sector partners, including participants in the Joint Cyber Defense Collaborative (JCDC). Planning functions focused on identifying affected systems and developing mitigation guidance, while operational efforts centered on detection and patching support. The sustained, multi-month response required continuous information flow, updated situational reporting, and coordinated advisories, which are hallmarks of NIMS-based management.

The 2024 ransomware incident affecting Change Healthcare highlighted the intersection of cybersecurity and public health infrastructure. As payment processing systems critical to healthcare providers were disrupted, the incident extended beyond technical remediation. Federal coordination involved assessing impacts on hospitals, pharmacies, and insurance reimbursement flows (HHS 2025). Agencies worked to ensure continuity of care while law enforcement pursued the responsible actors. The application of NIMS principles helped align technical recovery efforts with broader economic and public health considerations, reinforcing that cyber incidents can have systemic national consequences.

Integrated communications are central to NIMS and especially critical in cyber incidents. NIMS requires structured situation reports, defined operational periods, and documented objectives. These practices support coherent crisis communications by ensuring that public statements reflect coordinated assessments rather than fragmented perspectives. In high-profile cyber events, inconsistent messaging can exacerbate uncertainty and erode public trust. A NIMS-aligned structure encourages disciplined information release, reducing speculation while acknowledging uncertainty inherent in early stages of investigation.

Resource management under NIMS also adapts effectively to cyber contexts. In physical disasters, resources may include personnel, equipment, and supplies. In cyber incidents, resources often involve forensic specialists, threat intelligence analysts, technical assistance teams, and analytic infrastructure. The establishment of Cyber Unified Coordination Groups (UCGs) during significant cyber events reflects this approach. By designating lead agencies and clarifying support roles, UCGs operationalize NIMS doctrine in the digital domain, facilitating efficient deployment of expertise and avoiding duplication of effort.

Applying NIMS to cyber incidents is not without challenges. Cyber events often lack clear geographic boundaries, complicating jurisdictional definitions. Attribution may remain uncertain for extended periods and/or be contested, limiting immediate policy responses (Egloff 2020). Private-sector entities may hesitate to share sensitive operational information. Nevertheless, NIMS provides a structured mechanism to manage these complexities. Its emphasis on predefined roles, documentation, and coordination mitigates ambiguity and creates predictability amid technical uncertainty.

Over time, federal exercises and interagency drills have increasingly incorporated cyber scenarios into broader emergency management planning. Cyber considerations are now embedded in national preparedness doctrine, reflecting recognition that digital disruptions can generate consequences comparable to natural disasters. The evolution of the NCIRP and the integration of cyber annexes into the National Response Framework further institutionalize this approach. Rather than treating cyber events as isolated technical anomalies, federal policy increasingly views them as operational incidents requiring structured management.

Beyond technical response, NIMS provides a shared vocabulary and governance model that enables diverse stakeholders to communicate effectively under pressure. It aligns investigative efforts, infrastructure protection measures, executive decision-making, and public messaging within a coherent structure. As cyber incidents grow in scale and societal impact, the disciplined coordination provided by NIMS and formalized through the NCIRP ensures that federal response efforts remain organized, transparent, and strategically aligned.

4.3.3 National Infrastructure Protection Plan

First introduced in 2004, the NIPP is a comprehensive approach to coordinating activity across critical industry sectors.

Throughout the NIPP, there are calls to communicate and collaborate, as is evident from these excerpts from its core tenets (NIST 2013):

1) Risk should be identified and managed in a *coordinated* and comprehensive way across the critical infrastructure community to enable the effective allocation of security and resilience resources. *Collaboratively managing risk requires sharing information* (including smart practices), promoting more efficient and effective use of resources, and minimizing duplication of effort.
2) Understanding and addressing risks from *cross-sector dependencies and interdependencies* is essential to enhancing critical infrastructure security and resilience.
3) Gaining knowledge of infrastructure risk and interdependencies requires information sharing across the critical infrastructure community. Through their operations and perspectives, stakeholders across the critical infrastructure community possess and produce diverse information useful to the enhancement of critical infrastructure security and resilience. *Sharing and jointly planning based on this information* is imperative to comprehensively address critical infrastructure security and resilience in an environment of increasing interconnectedness.
4) The *partnership* approach to critical infrastructure security and resilience recognizes the unique perspectives and comparative advantages of the diverse critical infrastructure community.
5) *Regional and SLTT partnerships are crucial* to developing shared perspectives on gaps and actions to improve critical infrastructure security and resilience.
6) Infrastructure critical to the United States transcends national boundaries, requiring cross-border *collaboration, mutual assistance, and other cooperative agreements*.

While threat intelligence sharing among government agencies was largely successful, as evident from the examples of obvious vulnerabilities in Chapter 2, critical infrastructure companies were still having issues with understanding the potential negative impact of lagging on cybersecurity controls. By circa 2012, it was evident that there was little progress toward these goals in many sectors, bolstering the case for NIST to convene a wide variety of industry experts internationally to contribute to cybersecurity standards that would work for any type of organization, though with its main audience (as always) the federal government agencies. The NIPP was updated in 2013 to provide more focus on critical infrastructure cybersecurity risk management.

As shown in Figure 4.12, the ISACs were intended not just to share information with each other but also to *act* on the information with critical infrastructure

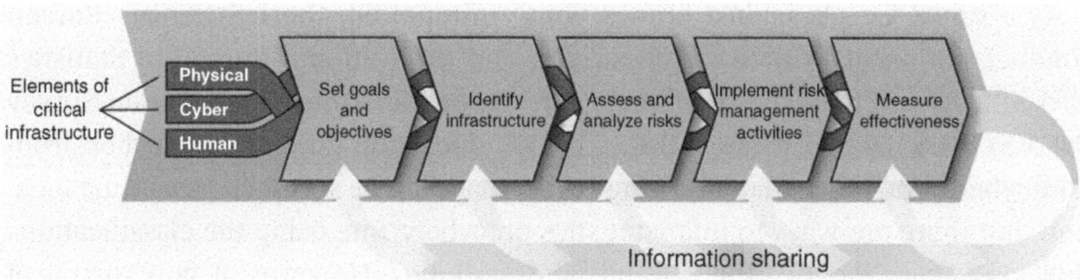

Figure 4.12 NIPP focus on risk management.

protection strategies. In recognition that this part of their charter has not been effectively addressed, the label for the government side of the partnership changed from *Sector Specific Agency* (SSA) to *Sector Risk Management Agency* (SRMA) in 2021.

4.4 Trend Analysis

The FBI has a long history of collecting information from local law enforcement and analyzing it with the intent to get in front of trends (FBI 2020). Routine crime data collection and analysis started in 1930, but had of course been paper-based and manual. In 2021, a complete overhaul automated the data collection process into a system called the National Incident-Based Reporting System (NIBRS). Although NIBRS has no searchable field to isolate only cybercrime, it does allow information sharing on crimes by topic, and cybercrimes can be found under categories like Wire Fraud, Identity Theft, and Impersonation. It also allows "cyberspace" to be used as a location code. NIBRS provides detailed, incident-level data, allowing for in-depth analysis of specific cyber-enabled incidents, rather than just aggregate counts by category that had been provided by its predecessors (BJS 2024b).

In May 2000, the FBI opened an Internet Fraud Complaint Center (IFCC), later called the Internet Crime Complaint Center (IC3) in 2002. It was the first official repository for victims of internet crimes to report them. This was very important because, at the time, very few police forces had any concept of how to investigate computer crimes. There are still police forces today that have no internal cybercrime expertise, although smaller municipalities have developed relationships with larger ones in the region to leverage regional expertise and participate in NIMS cyber training scenarios. In a 20th anniversary report, the FBI reported that, although the information gathered by IC3 was very useful in identifying patterns of cybercrime, once they acted to arrest the criminals engaged in one pattern, that pattern would go dormant and a new one would arise. Moreover, the patterns became increasingly more sophisticated (FBI 2020). The more recent history in Chapter 2 shows that this is still the case today.

As a sanity check against crimes going unreported, the US Census Bureau conducts an annual crime victim survey, and the National Bureau of Statistics also collects and publishes that data as the National Crime Victimization Survey (NCVS) (BJS 2024a). Like NIBRS, NCVS does not differentiate cyber from non-cybercrime other than allowing "cyberspace" to be specified as a crime location, but there are ways to infer statistics on cybercrime using the classifications that exist (e.g., identity theft, fraud, and stalking). However, it is a survey of individuals and does not include commercial crimes. That said, the Bureau of Justice Statistics (BJS) recently realized the need to have more exact precision on the extent to which cybercrime dominates the criminal landscape and in 2023 commissioned a report that analyzed its existing data on cybercrime in comparison with the Phillips' Cyber Crime Taxonomy (Figure 4.13) (Phillips et al. 2022). The study produced numerous recommendations for creation, expansion, and research on cybersecurity survey categories going forward, though they have not yet made it into the NCVS (RTI International 2023).

There are significant efforts in the private sector to collect and share data on cybercrime, the most comprehensive of which is the Vocabulary for Event Recording and Incident Sharing (VERIS) (Verizon Business 2026). VERIS is a set of metrics designed to provide a common language for describing security incidents in a structured and repeatable manner. The overall goal is to lay a foundation to collectively, constructively, and cooperatively learn from our experiences to better manage risk. VERIS collects data from over 100 organizations internationally that routinely classify the incidents they document using the VERIS framework (see contributors in Table 4.2). Regardless of the country in which the information originates, VERIS contributors use the North American Industry Classification System (NAICS) standard to classify the targeted organizations. This allows Verizon to produce statistics reports by industry on global cybersecurity incidents and data breaches. For example, Figure 4.14 shows a snapshot of the Healthcare Industry's incidents and data breaches in 2025. Note that it also includes a category called "Miscellaneous Error." These are data breaches that have been diagnosed as *unintended consequences* of some action that is typically attributed to a staff mistake. Like the ISAC threat intelligence research, this report has evolved to the stage that it is negligent on the part of organizations to ignore its warnings.

Note these statistics have been compiled for over a decade and have been proven useful in combating cybercrime, yet even collectively they do not paint a picture adequate to serve the needs of insurance actuarial analysis related to cybersecurity (Bayuk 2024, pp. 142–145). In a 2019 acknowledgement that the "United States now operates in a cyber landscape that requires a level of data security, resilience, and trustworthiness that neither the US government nor the private sector alone is currently equipped to provide," the *National Defense Authorization Act* chartered the US Cyberspace Solarium Commission to address this challenge

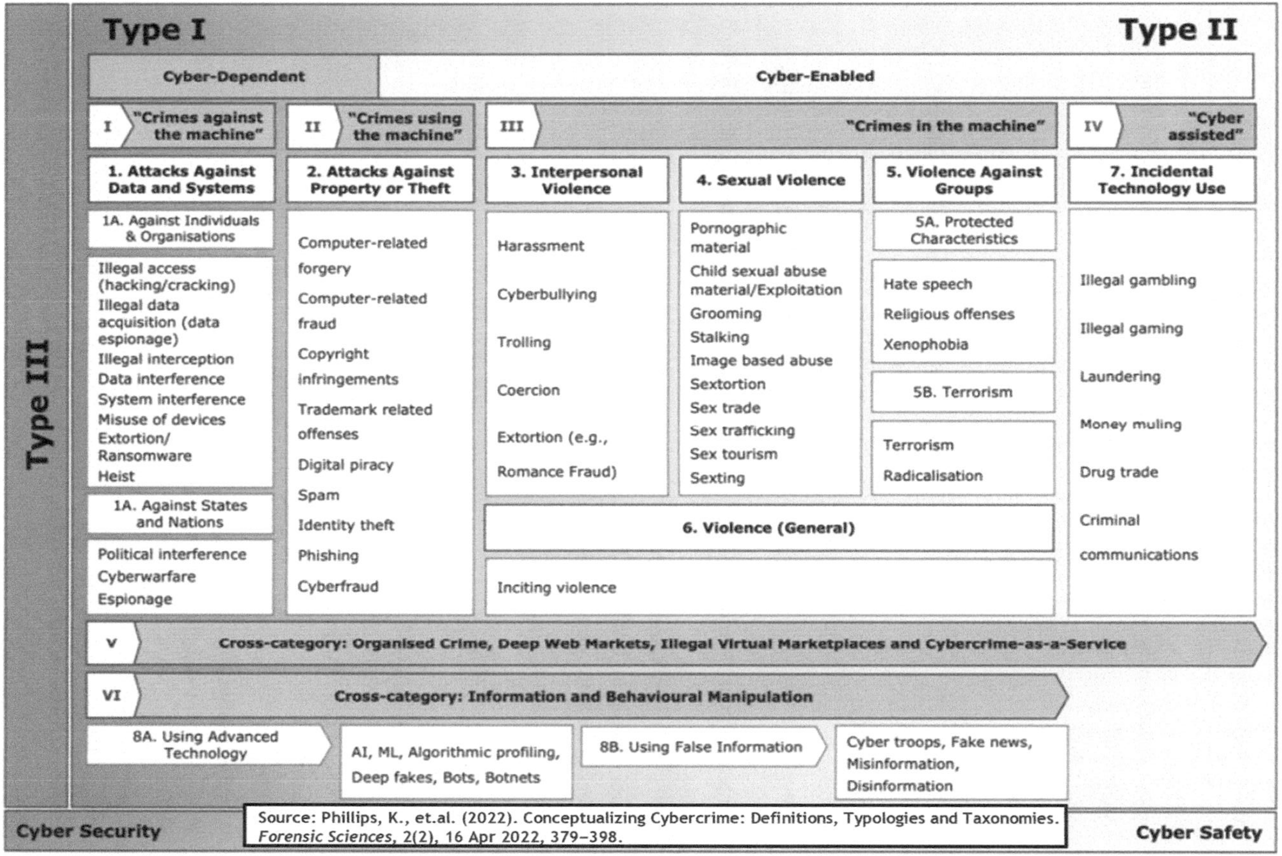

Figure 4.13 Phillips taxonomy. *Source:* Phillips et al. (2022) / MDPI / CC BY 4.0.

Table 4.2 VERIS Contributors.

Akamai Technologies	Irish Reporting and InfoSec Service
Ankura	JPCERT/CC
Apura Cyber Intelligence	K–12 Security Information Exchange
Archer Hall	KnowBe4
Arctic Wolf	KordaMentha
Atos	LayerX Security
Balbix	Legal Services ISAO
bit-x-bit, LLC	Manufacturing ISAC
Bitsight	Maritime Transportation System ISAC
BRANDEFENSE	Mimecast
BreachLock	mnemonic
Bridewell	National Crime Agency
Censys, Inc.	National Cyber-Forensics & Training Alliance
Center for Internet Security (CIS)	National Cyber Security Agency, Thailand
Cequence Security	NetDiligence
CERT Division of Carnegie Mellon	NETSCOUT
CERT – European Union (CERT-EU)	Okta
Check Point Software Technologies Ltd.	OpenText Cybersecurity
Coalition	Proofpoint
Compass Security	Qualys
Coveware by Veeam	Rajah & Tann Cybersecurity Pte Ltd
COWBELL	Recorded Future, Inc.
Cyber Security Agency of Singapore	RedHunt Labs
CyberSecurity Malaysia	ReversingLabs
Cyber Security New South Wales	SecurityScorecard
Cybersixgill	Shodan
CYBIR	Sistemas Aplicativos
Cyentia Institute	Six Degrees
Defense Counterintelligence & Security Agency	Sophos
DomainTools	Swisscom
Dragos, Inc.	Temple University – (CARE) Lab
Energy Analytic Security Exchange	Tenable
Edgescan	Thales S21sec
Emergence Insurance	The Shadowserver Foundation
Enzoic	Tidal Cyber

Table 4.2 (Continued)

Akamai Technologies	Irish Reporting and InfoSec Service
EUROCONTROL	Triskele Labs
FBI Internet Crime Complaint Center	U.S. Secret Service
F-Secure	VERIS Community Database
Flare	Verizon Customer Experience
Flashpoint	Organization
Global Resilience Federation	Verizon Cyber Risk Programs
GreyNoise Intelligence	Verizon Cyber Security Consulting
Halcyon	Verizon DDoS Defense
Hoxhunt	Verizon Network Operations and
Huntress	Engineering
ImmuniWeb	Verizon Threat Research Advisory Center
Infoblox	Verizon VTRAC Labs
Information Commissioner's Office (ICO)	Wabtec Corporation
	Zscaler

Frequency	1,710 incidents, 1,542 with confirmed data disclosure
Top patterns	System Intrusion, Everything Else and Miscellaneous Errors represent 74% of breaches
Threat actors	External (67%), Internal (30%), Partner (4%), Multiple (1%) (breaches)
Actor motives	Financial (90%), Espionage (16%) (breaches)
Data compromised	Medical (45%), Personal (40%), Internal (32%), Other (24%) (breaches)
What is the same?	The attack patterns remain the same, although they have changed position since last year.

Summary

The Healthcare sector remains a prime target for cyberattacks and shows a slight increase in incidents and breaches this year. System Intrusion (including Ransomware) has overtaken Miscellaneous Errors as the top cause of breaches. The rise of Espionage as a motive for attackers in this sector is concerning.

The Healthcare industry remains a favorite target of attackers, and this year we saw a small uptick in both incidents and breaches. This is not surprising, given that reporting requirements can be particularly stringent for healthcare breaches in the U.S. Therefore, hoping to fly under the radar is not a good strategy for organizations in this sector.

Time for a change

We did see some changes in the top patterns this year. If you are a regular reader of our report, you may recall that Miscellaneous Errors was in the top spot in 2024.

However, we have seen System Intrusion surge ahead this year (Figure 6) – and, again, keep in mind this is where ransomware attacks live. Healthcare continues to be a favorite target for this kind of attacker, and the urgent need for access to data in emergency situations only adds to the pressure healthcare organizations feel when their systems are all unavailable and they must resort to more old-school processes.

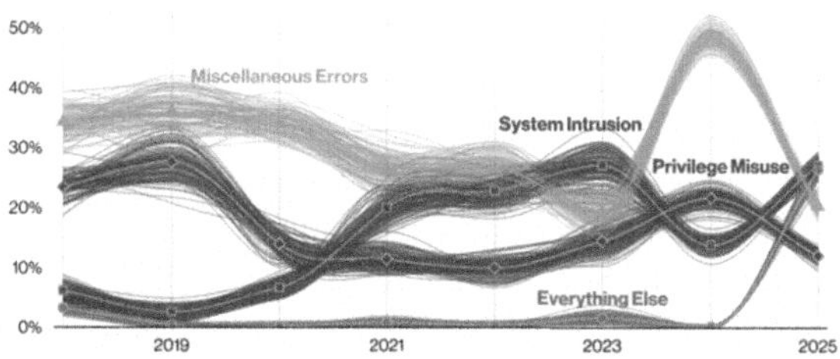

Figure 4.14 Verizon data breach report example: Health care. *Source:* Verizon Business (2026) / Verizon.

(William 2021). After over 300 interviews with Academics, Government Agencies, International Governments, Research Centers, Military, Law Enforcement, Industry Associations, Cybersecurity Companies, Financial Institutions, and other critical infrastructure operators, they distilled their findings into multiple policy proposals. One of them was that Congress should establish a Bureau of Cyber Statistics charged with collecting and providing statistical data on cybersecurity and the cyber ecosystem to inform policymaking and government programs (King and Gallagher 2020, pp. 78–79). Although BJS does not currently have such a program, with hindsight, the 2023 RTI International study, funded by the BJS, may have been a first step in that direction.

4.5 Communication Challenges

4.5.1 Organizational Challenges

Another investigation-in-progress situation faced by any organization in the midst of diagnosing a cybersecurity attack is what we refer to as the 90 seconds security review. This happens in a situation where there is a cyberattack in progress, either internally or targeting the industry, and the CISO is interrupted once an hour to attend a meeting of executives who need to make crisis management, legal, and compliance decisions. In these cases, the CISO has to take eyes off the crisis itself to answer questions about how vulnerable the organization may be to a hitherto unknown zero-day vulnerability. The most pressing question, "Are we negatively impacted and if so, how bad?" can only be answered by technology operations generally via their performance and service delivery metrics, so the CISO's precious time is consumed listening in person to something that could be fed to earphones. Finally, the CISO is asked to predict what will happen in the next 30 minutes or so, given what they know about the attack pattern, which by that time, may be close to nothing.

Another example of organizational challenges is when people who work in organizations that have completely different risk appetites have to work together. For example, many organizations have a strict protocol for delivering a password to a new user. It may be put in a sealed envelope and delivered to their manager. It may not be set at all but instead requires the use of a hand-held device delivered by Human Resources to be set, and then only when connected to the internal network. Many organizations also have a policy against sharing passwords for any reason. But even the most secure organizations sometimes get a contractor or business partner who encrypts a sensitive document before emailing it because their agreement says they have to, but then sends the password to decrypt the document to the recipient(s) in a follow-up email 3 seconds later. Of course, the entire point of password protecting the document is the threat that the email will be intercepted, and if the email is interceptable for the document, it will also be for the password. In cybersecurity, we call these fake attempts at providing information protection *security theater*. No matter how professional or well-entrenched cybersecurity may be within an organization, it will always be constrained by the experience of a contractor or business partner who does not realize they are operating within a controlled environment and/or may not hold their client's information as important as the organization that owns it. Like the top 10 vulnerabilities repeatedly reported by OWASP, we repeatedly see the top 10 bits of security theater attributable to people who have been trained on sharing information in methods that would not withstand even casual observation by the weakest of adversaries.

4.5.2 IT, OT, and ICS

Perhaps the most striking situation where cybersecurity projects get mired in disdain and confusion is in the realm of industrial control systems. While cybersecurity professionals are taught that their fundamental goal is to preserve the confidentiality, integrity, and availability of computer data, professional engineers are taught that their fundamental goal is functional capability and human safety. The difference in perspective on systems requirements between technology control specialists and industrial control specialists has been compared to that between doctors of the same patient who disregard the opinions of anyone outside their area of specialization. It can be frustrating in situations where alternative medication choices are not the product of collaboration, but of trial and error by both specialists whose recommended drugs may interact poorly within the patient, who trusts that both doctors have their best interests at heart.

A good approach to appreciating this difference is to start with the nomenclature used by the two types of specialists, that is, *information technology specialists* and *industrial control specialists* use the same words, but they mean different things, and *operational technology specialists* may flip back and forth between the two without fully comprehending some of the implications of their conceptual grasp of a term. Table 4.3 provides some examples.

When our ICS specialist author, Joseph Weiss, brought the examples in Table 4.3 to our attention, we committed to using this book as a platform to close the divide. We started with the assumption that, vocabulary aside, theoretically, IT and ICS cybersecurity incidents should be comparable because the definition of a cybersecurity incident is the same. That is, a cybersecurity incident is an incident involving electronic communication between systems, or between systems and people, that negatively affects confidentiality, integrity, or availability. This is consistent with the widely accepted definition of cybersecurity put forth by an early icon in the field, Ross Anderson, who defined "secure systems" as systems that remain dependable in the face of "malice, error, or mischance" (Anderson 2020, p. 3).

Table 4.3 IT Versus OT Nomenclature.

Word	Technology Control Definition	Industrial Control Definition
Availability	Networks, devices, and software must be functioning when they should. Users must be able to consume data when needed.	Physical process interactions, equipment resilience, and data flowing through both have very precise timing requirements.
Determinism	A program based on logic whose input type is restricted within bounds, wherein its control processor will always produce the same output from the same input.	A physical system in which no components have the capability for random behavior. A deterministic physical system will always produce the same physical output from a given set of inputs.
Endpoints	Human-accessible gateways to the networks and services.	Field instruments that provide signals to communicate the physical attributes of a system component.
Firewall	Connectivity control point between different network segments or protocols in TCP/IP layer 3.	Physical barrier of fireproof material on the border of two physical systems or system components.
Forensics	Data, log, and configuration preservation in conjunction with user activity analysis in support of incident investigation.	Analysis of logs detailing physical parameters in the context of physical process monitoring and state change.
Gateway	A device that connects different network segments or protocols in TCP/IP layer 3.	Device that converts communication protocols or data concentrator formats between systems.
Integrity	Data accuracy should be tamperproof.	Control logic should be tamperproof.
Network	Conduits for TCP/IP data flow and associated management protocols such as SNMP and ICMP.	Any communication between devices, including serial, analog, point-to-point, Ethernet, and control or process wiring systems (like fieldbus, Modbus, HART).
Node	Any network-connected device, such as endpoints, network equipment, and port scanners.	An entry point, junction, or exit point in a system process diagram or pipe network.
Safety	Equivalent to "stay safe online" advice like avoiding shady websites and not clicking on suspicious links.	Avoid unforeseen destructive physical events like explosions that destroy property or kill people.
Segmentation	Network data flow restriction using equipment like firewalls and routers.	Physical flow restriction using equipment like valves and interlocks.
Signal	Analog or digital, electronic or light, *pulses* that are used to transmit data over networks. By analogy, signal can also mean a message within a larger flow of information that can be extracted from the flow (as in *signal* versus *noise*).	The output of hardware, software, and firmware components of a system used to detect changes in physical processes through scientifically designed direct monitoring of physical attributes of objects and/or atmosphere.

However, as we got deeper into the reasons that the IT and ICS perspectives were so different, it quickly became evident that we were in the midst of an "apples to oranges" comparison. IT and OT cybersecurity focus on malicious activity within an Ethernet network environment that results in data breaches, fraud, or successful denial-of-service attacks, including ransomware. There is a strong tendency among IT and OT security professionals to assume that if the incidents do not look like network cyberattacks, then network cybersecurity personnel do not consider the incidents to be cyber incidents. By contrast, control system cybersecurity focuses on any event that can impact physical processes, whether malicious or unintentional. Consider that SecOps monitors network and computing device activity but rarely, if ever, participates in the monitoring of signal processing as using the word *signal* as defined in the right-hand column of Table 4.3. Consequently, IT and OT network cyber incident identification deviates from control system cyber incident identification because many control system cyber incidents don't involve compromises of Ethernet networks or systems. They will only be noticed by SecOps if they come through that front door. An attacker going directly into the field and replacing a chip in a sensor firmware module to provide false information to its host Programmable Logic Control is invisible to SecOps.

Even among highly skilled cybersecurity professionals and engineers on this topic, sometimes the cybersecurity professionals are taunted with the accusation of "not getting it," where the "it" refers to the horrific consequences that minor cybersecurity threat actors can accomplish by exploiting obvious vulnerabilities in industrial control systems. Interfering with network data can ground a technology system (e.g., Sony users not getting their email), but interfering with physical signal processors on a plane can cause it to crash (e.g., the Boeing MAX incidents).

As an illustration of this point, we compare the incident categories in the Verizon Data Breach Investigations Report (DBIR) with similar data on control system cyber incidents that have been collected by Weiss over the years. As he puts it, this is because, to our knowledge, though there have been some sporadic efforts, there is no reliable industry consortium like the VERIS community that reports on industrial control system cybersecurity incidents, perhaps due to incidents involving cyber not being classified as cybersecurity (because if they were, they would be in VERIS, who likely would then devise a method of classifying attacks on sensors).

At the time Verizon first started the annual DBIR, there was a tacit assumption that technology could withstand operational cyberattacks that impacted operations better than data breaches because you can recover from denial-of-service attacks, but if you lose your data, you cannot claw it back. However, it was only a few years later that Verizon expanded its statistics to provide insight into the much larger class of incidents that did not result in data breaches. The distinction remains throughout the report. Table 4.4 shows the categories into which the DBIR classifies incidents and data breaches. They are listed side by side in the table

Table 4.4 IT Versus OT Incident Categories.

IT Cybersecurity Incident Classification	Industrial Control Incident Classification
• Basic web application attacks • Denial of service • Application layer attacks • Lost and stolen assets • Miscellaneous errors • Privilege misuse • Social engineering • System intrusion • Everything else	• Operational impact • Loss of control • Loss of view • Equipment damage • Environmental damage • Injuries and deaths

with ICS incident categories as classified by Weiss; these are consistent with NIST guidance for classification of ICS incidents, though at a higher level (NIST 2023). Like the Verizon *incident versus data* breach distinction, they focus on *outcome*. This shows the state of maturity in ICS cybersecurity statistics in comparison with the DBIR, which started with the outcome and moved backward in the attack chain to draw out the underlying causes. It also serves to emphasize our observation above that comparing the outcomes of purely technological incidents to technology that controls industrial processes is an apples-to-oranges exercise.

As mentioned above, Verizon also maps each incident according to its target, using NAICS codes. We also mapped the impacted industries in Weiss's database to NAICS. The result is in Table 4.5. The first column lists the categories of ICS attacks. It shows that industrial control system incidents are analyzed at a much lower level in the NAICS industry hierarchy than technology cybersecurity incidents. The reason is obvious: there is a major difference in the variety of targets between technology and ICS systems at the industry level. Technology systems at the industry level gravitate toward standard platforms as it becomes clear what is needed to support similar processes across customers in the same industry and achieve economies of scale. The same cannot be said for the higher-level categories within which ICS companies fall. A *marine* transportation system looks nothing like a *pipeline* transportation system, and attack vectors are likely to vary widely between the two. Similarly, a wastewater utility looks nothing like an electric power utility. The underlying sensors at level P0 will be the same.

It is interesting to note that Weiss also asked questions about the control system cybersecurity incidents of various artificial intelligence (AI) models. The AI was generally unaware of many of them, and when it did have some information about one, it often did not classify it as a cybersecurity incident. That is just as well, because as AI moves quickly into models for assisting in offensive cybersecurity attacks, we can only hope ICS vulnerabilities are likely to be overlooked opportunities for AI-generated destructive attacks in future.

Table 4.5 ICS Versus IT Industry Categories.

Industrial Control Systems Incidents		**IT (*VERIS*) Classification**	
481	Air transportation	48–49	Transportation
325	Chemical plants	31–33	Manufacturing
221	Electric power	22	Utilities
561210	Facilities	56	Administrative
311–312 11	Food/beverage	31–33 11	Manufacturing Agriculture
484–485	Land transportation	48–49	Transportation
31–33	Manufacturing	31–33	Manufacturing
483	Marine	48–49	Transportation
62	Medical	62	Healthcare
212	Mining	21	Mining
221113	Nuclear plants	22	Utilities
211	Oil/gas	21	Mining
486	Pipelines	48–49	Transportation
482	Railroads	48–49	Transportation
3364	Space	31–33	Manufacturing
2213	Water/wastewater	22	Utilities

VERIS Categories in addition to those corresponding to Industrial Control Systems: Construction, Education, Entertainment, Finance, Information, Management, Other Services, Professional, Public Administration, Real Estate, Retail, Wholesale.

As Ivan Savov, Chairman at the European Risk Policy Institute, pointed out, this is "a governance failure masquerading as a vocabulary issue." He went on: "What matters strategically is the reporting and response architecture. Breach-centric metrics (and the cultural reflex that 'no attack = no incident') bias organizations toward under-detection, weak root-cause discipline, and false trend comparisons—exactly when coupled infrastructures are most fragile and repair cycles are tight" (Savov 2026).

4.5.3 Vulnerability Reporting

While MITRE provides a method of documenting and sharing vulnerabilities, it relies on vendors (if not a vendor, the organization that owns and distributes the software, which we loosely refer to herein as the "vendor") and security researchers to report them. Responsibility for assigning a CWE number is left to the vendor. If a security researcher wishes to take a responsible or coordinated approach to reporting vulnerability, MITRE standard guidance is to report it to the vendor, who will assign a CWE, make a patch available, and report it to MITRE. However, it is sometimes difficult to get in touch with someone in a vendor organization who is responsible for receiving the report. OWASP has published some guidance for researchers on how to deal with these cases (OWASP n.d.):

- Report to a public bug bounty program such as BugCrowd, HackerOne, huntr.dev, Open Bug Bounty, or Standoff.
- Post a security.txt file on the website at /.well-known/security.txt as per IETF RFC 9116.
- Report via an existing issue tracking system such as a customer service desk.
- Attempt to send to commonly used email addresses such as security@vendor.com or abuse@vendor.com.
- Post to a generic "Contact Us" page on the vendor website.
- Reach out to the vendor via their pages on social media platforms.
- Phone the vendor and see if option allows you to report an issue or talk to an operator who may be able to direct the call.
- Reach out to OWASP.
- Reach out to the software user's national or sector-based ISAC or CERT.

OWASP cautions that, when reaching out to people who are not dedicated security contacts, do not disclose vulnerability until you reach the vendor contact directly responsible for its cybersecurity response.

Although this list seems to be a very comprehensive approach to establishing content, there are still cases wherein the vendor is completely unavailable or flatly refuses to number and patch the vulnerability. In these cases, a researcher can ask MITRE for assistance via email to cve-assign@mitre.org.

4.5.4 Public–Private Conflicts

Another example of differing perspectives has to do with rules for disclosure of investigations in progress. It is common for the FBI to classify evidence as secret while hunting a murderer because any evidence that is leaked can tip off the suspect that they are closing in. However, they make unexpected analogies with physical crimes during investigations related to cybersecurity. For example, in 2015 and 2016, Russian operatives attempting (successfully) to turn the tide of the 2016 election toward Trump hacked into the emails of numerous democratic officials and in 2016 released them on the internet (Satter et al. 2017). The FBI was aware of the operative's hacking and pursued an investigation that lasted over a year. The Associated Press (AP) learned of the investigation and, as part of a plan to interview the victims, hired a cybersecurity firm to identify some of the officials whose email was hacked. In this manner, 80 people were informed by the AP rather than the FBI that they have been victimized. One of the targets was Philip Reiner, a former senior director at the National Security Council, told the AP he was "utterly confounded" that he would not have been notified by the FBI at the time and instead was notified by the AP two years later. "You've got to tell your people," he moaned, "You've got to protect your people."

The AP's report on their investigation included a disclosure that a senior FBI official, who was not authorized to publicly discuss the hacking operation because of its sensitivity, declined to comment on when it received the target list, but said the bureau was overwhelmed by the sheer number of attempted hacks. Specifically, he told the AP, "It's a matter of triaging to the best of our ability the volume of the targets who are out there." This is just one example of differing perspectives on law enforcement's need to be silent and focus on the investigation rather than escalate their issues with the obvious need to inform people who could easily be expected to take precautions to ease their information-bleeding, especially whatever government data they had in their custody. Of the 80 people contacted by the AP, 2 actually had been contacted by the FBI, and the likely reason was that some victim cooperation was needed to pursue the cyberattackers.

There are also differing perspectives on cybersecurity risk between the private sector cyberdefense and public sector intelligence agencies. When the leaked NSA exploits were used to create WannaCry ransomware that shook personal, organizational, and publicly owned computers across the globe and was also used in subsequent attacks even years later, the NSA was unperturbed. When a reporter pressed the then-head of the NSA on whether he regretting hoarding the zero days instead of bringing them to vendors to fix in defense of our nation's infrastructure, he defended the hoarding of dangerous zero days for the purposes of espionage by responding, "If Toyota makes pickup trucks and someone … welds an explosive devices onto the front, crashes it … a crowd of people, is that Toyota's responsibility?" (Perlroth 2021, p. 250). The analogy made no sense to victims. A car is a valuable asset that was augmented to be a weapon, and the exploits have always been a weapon.

In another stark example of how different perspectives present unprecedented cybersecurity risk, consider the Anthropic disclosure in November 2025 that one of its AI models had been leveraged by a state-sponsored threat actor to autonomously coordinate a cyberattack against multiple targets. According to reports, the "agentic AI" executed nearly 90% of the intrusion workflow, conducting reconnaissance, exploiting vulnerabilities, stealing credentials, and exfiltrating data with minimal human oversight. This event represented one of the first publicly acknowledged cases of an AI system acting as an independently functional cyber operator rather than a mere tool. It underscored the need for federal policy to move beyond defensive applications of AI toward governing autonomous agents themselves, establishing accountability for their design, deployment, and control.

In an attempt to promote this strategy, Anthropic announced a conditional use of their technology, prohibiting mass surveillance and autonomous armed drones (Liedtke and Klepper 2026). It unfortunately had the opposite effect, and the US Secretary of Defense terminated Anthropic's work with the Pentagon and designated Anthropic a supply-chain risk, a move that prohibits the US government contractors from using the software. This move is consistent with the communication challenges between cyber-defenders and governments on the topic of zero-day vulnerabilities described above. That is, nation-states see more advantage than disadvantage in the existence of cyberspace tools of mass destruction, while cyberdefenders are firmly convinced of the opposite.

4.5.5 Crisis Communications Systems

Recall from Chapter 2 that when Change Healthcare experienced its ransomware attack, the first thing United Health did was pull the plug on their network connections. Also, as in Sony's case, most staff were cut off from both email and contact lists. Organizations with distributed geographies, languages, time zones, and complicated vendor dependencies, and even those that don't, should plan for communications resilience in the time of cyberattack. In smaller organizations, it could be meeting on a local street corner. But in large organizations, this usually looks like a dependency on a crisis management vendor to whom you routinely upload crisis management plans, law enforcement contacts, organization charts, global directories, and internal and external contact information to make sure that if all of your systems are down, everyone still knows how to get in touch with everyone else.

Of course, even the best service offering in this space is useless if people do not know it is there, so all such planning must include training and testing. From a policy perspective, it makes sense to include requirements to complete such training and testing in employee code of conduct and contractual relationships with critical service providers. Even small organizations should have an archive of a crisis management plan and a call-out list or service to ensure there is a method for coordination in times of crisis.

An oft-neglected element of crisis planning is leadership strategy, and cybersecurity is no exception. The field of crisis communications provides names and tactics to deal with each of these issues: outrage management ("calm down") and precaution advocacy ("watch out"). These are distinct and need different approaches from a third issue, crisis communication ("we'll get through this together").

These three terms, outrage management, precaution advocacy, and crisis management, are from a simple framework of crisis communications developed by Peter Sandman, an expert in the topic, having seen major communications mistakes in the response to the nuclear accident at the Three Mile Island plant in the United States (Sandman 2020). Sandman's model can help cybersecurity practitioners think more deeply about risk communications. Sandman's insight about risk communication "is the incredibly low correlation between a risk's *hazard* (how much harm it's likely to do, the normal risk elements such as probability and consequence) and its *outrage* (how upset it's likely to make people):

- If you know a risk is dangerous, that tells you almost nothing about whether it's upsetting,
- If you know a hazard is upsetting, that tells you almost nothing about whether it's dangerous.

He concludes that the key to managing a crisis is to understand that the actual **risk equals the *hazard* plus the *outrage***. Sandman uses the diagram in Figure 4.15 to illustrate this concept. When hazard is high and outrage low, he advised risk professionals to employ precaution advocacy to call attention to overlooked risks. For example, business executives often blindly "accept the risk" of glaring cybersecurity vulnerabilities. The role of the CISO is to reduce the false sense of security and convince colleagues, executives, and ultimately the board of directors that the dangers are higher than they believe. They should be *more* outraged and take action to reduce those risks. An example of high outrage and low hazard is one wherein small incidents of insider threat are suspected to be indicators of advanced persistent threat and management fumes over a backlog of vulnerabilities waiting to be patched. If the CISO has personal knowledge to that the insider was engaged in simple fraud and the vulnerabilities are not critical, the approach should be one of outrage management, getting people to

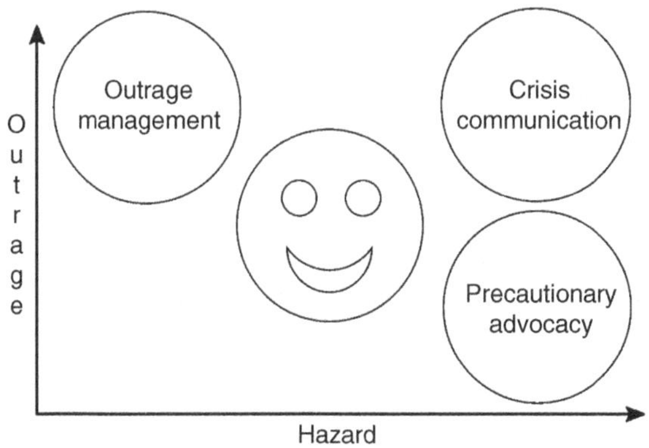

Figure 4.15 Crisis communication. *Source:* Sandman (2020) / https://www.psandman.com/index-intro.htm / last accessed on Apr. 18, 2026.

calm down. At the center of Figure 4.15 is the happy medium of appropriate risk posture. The top right of the quadrant is a situation wherein it is appropriate to execute crisis management plans.

4.6 Conclusion

Throughout this chapter, we have introduced roles and job functions occupied by individuals who have the need to share information and continuously communicate about cybersecurity issues. For example, in *Cybersecurity Frameworks*, we saw auditors, standards committee members, regulators, boards, service providers, risk managers, leaders of professional associations, SecOps administrators and analysts, line managers, business leaders, accountants, cybersecurity risk assessors, technology standards developers, and business process owners all handed a role to play in incorporating cybersecurity best practices into their respective organizations.

In *Threats and Vulnerabilities*, we saw cybersecurity defense roles handed to directors of ISACs, government agency liaisons for communicating with critical infrastructure partners about cybersecurity risk, members of DHS councils, congressional legislatures, cybersecurity entrepreneurs, cybersecurity professionals charged with protecting SLTT entities, cybersecurity coordination center administrators, cybersecurity conference hosts, SecOps team members, technology managers, risk managers, researchers, software developers, cyberforensics specialists, systems and network administrators, vulnerability documentation specialists, software quality assurance specialists, those charged with protecting the nation's critical infrastructure from cyberattacks, and those motivated by their unique perspective on cyberthreats to publicize the need for cybersecurity policy improvements.

In *Institutions for Communication and Collaboration*, we saw first cybersecurity response roles in local, national, and international organizations joining the FIRST organization in an attempt to reduce the impact of cybercrimes in their own communities. We saw the advent of Computer Emergency Response Team (CERT) members, cybersecurity warning protocol developers, cybersecurity training program developers, federal emergency response staff dedicated to cybersecurity, CISA personnel, FBI and intelligence agents dedicated to cybersecurity, members of the GAO, the DOE, the FTC, and HHS, participants in the JCDC, and UCG participants.

Granted that the *National Infrastructure Protection Plan* fully incorporates the *Institutions for Communication and Collaboration*, but still evident from its inclusion was an additional cybersecurity role player category revealed. These were the heads of what had been called the *Sector Specific Agency* from the Public side of the Pubic/Private ISAC partnership to the SRMA, meant to highlight that the role of these individuals was not simply to share information but take a more active role in critical infrastructure protection from cyberattack.

In *Trend Analysis*, we captured a glimpse at the dedicated cybersecurity staffers whose roles require them to routinely scour the nation for cybersecurity incidents and cyberattacks, then carefully classify their attributes into categories and subsequently publish data repositories and reports that cybersecurity defenders can use for in-depth analysis into attack patterns and corresponding cyber defenses.

In *Communication Challenges*, we saw that business executives play an important role in cybersecurity incident response and human resources, an important role in identity management. We also saw that contractors and business partners have a role to play in maintaining cybersecurity policy compliance that is more challenging for an organization to manage. We also compared and contrasted the roles played by IT specialists, OT specialists, and industrial control specialists who collectively control the cybersecurity attributes of the nation's most critical physical infrastructure. The challenge section also introduced the unique role of investigative reporting, one that helps us shed light on all of the other communication patterns we see in the cybersecurity landscape.

The only omission from this role summary is the adversary. It is a role we would rather not celebrate. In contrast, throughout these threads, we have been careful to weave the CISO and law enforcement responsibilities into this holistic cybersecurity communication picture, as the individuals in these roles are the primary watchdogs for day-to-day compliance with cybersecurity policy.

References

American Institute of Certified Public Accountants (AICPA) (2017). Statement on standards for attestation engagements no. 18: attestation standards: clarification and recodification. AICPA. https://www.aicpa.org/resources/download/statement-on-standards-for-attestation-engagements-ssae-18 (accessed 13 March 2026).

Anderson, R. (2020). *Security Engineering: A Guide to Building Dependable Distributed Systems*, 3rd edn. New York, NY: Wiley.

Bayuk, J. (2005). *Stepping Through the IS Audit*, 2nd edn. Schaumburg, IL: Information Systems Audit and Control Association.

Bayuk, J. (2007). *Stepping Through the InfoSec Program*. Schaumburg, IL: Information Systems Audit and Control Association.

Bayuk, J. (2024). *Stepping Through Cybersecurity Risk Management, A Systems Thinking Approach*. New York, NY: Wiley.

Bureau of Justice Statistics (BJS) (2024a). National Crime Victimization Survey (NCVS). https://bjs.ojp.gov/data-collection/ncvs#7-0 (accessed 15 March 2026).

Bureau of Justice Statistics (BJS) (2024b). National Incident-Based Reporting System (NIBRS). https://bjs.ojp.gov/national-incident-based-reporting-system-nibrs (accessed 15 March 2026).

Center for Internet Security (CIS) (n.d.). CIS Critical Security Implementation Groups. https://www.cisecurity.org/controls/implementation-groups (accessed 14 March 2026).

Cloud Security Alliance (CSA) (2021). Cloud Controls Matrix v4.0. https://cloudsecurityalliance.org/research/cloud-controls-matrix (accessed 18 February 2026).

Committee of Sponsoring Organizations of the Treadway Commission (COSO) (2017). Enterprise risk management – integrating with strategy and performance. https://www.coso.org/erm-framework (accessed 18 February 2026).

Critical Infrastructure Partnership Advisory Council (CIPAC) (2006). *Critical Infrastructure Partnership Advisory Council Charter*. Federal Register, Vol. 71, No. 57. 24 March 2006. https://www.federalregister.gov/documents/2006/03/24/06-2892/critical-infrastructure-partnership-advisory-council (accessed 15 March 2026).

Cybersecurity and Infrastructure Security Agency (CISA) (2025a). Cross-Sector Cybersecurity Performance Goals 2.0. https://www.cisa.gov/cybersecurity-performance-goals-2-0-cpg-2-0 (accessed 18 February 2026).

Cybersecurity and Infrastructure Security Agency (CISA) (2025b). Sector-specific cybersecurity performance goals. https://www.cisa.gov/cross-sector-cybersecurity-performance-goals (accessed 18 February 2026).

Cybersecurity and Infrastructure Security Agency (CISA) (n.d.). The KEV Catalog. https://www.cisa.gov/resources-tools/resources/kev-catalog (accessed 31 March 2026).

Cybersecurity Information Sharing Act (2015). Public Law 114-113, Division N, Title I. December 2015. https://uscode.house.gov/view.xhtml?req=granuleid%3AUSC-prelim-title6-chapter6-subchapter1&saved=%7CZ3JhbnVsZWlkOlVTQy1wcmVsaW0tdGl0bGU2LWNoYXB0ZXI2LXN1YmNoYXB0ZXIxLWZyb250%7C%7C%7C0%7Cfalse%7Cprelim&edition=prelim (accessed 9 March 2026).

Department of Energy (DOE) (2021). Colonial Pipeline Cyber Incident. Department of Energy. 7 May 2021. https://www.energy.gov/ceser/colonial-pipeline-cyber-incident (accessed 15 March 2026).

Department of Homeland Security (DHS) (2016). National Cyber Incident Response Plan. https://www.cisa.gov/sites/default/files/2023-01/national_cyber_incident_response_plan.pdf (accessed 15 March 2026).

Egloff, F. J. (2020). Contested public attributions of cyber incidents and the role of uncertainty. *Journal of Cybersecurity*, 6(1): 1–13.

Electronic Data Processing Audit Association (EDPAA) (1977). *Control Objectives*. Chicago, IL: Electronic Data Processing Audit Association.

Federal Advisory Committee Act of 1972 (FACA) (1972). Public Law 92-463, 86 Stat. 770. October 1972. https://www.gsa.gov/policy-regulations/policy/federal-advisory-committee-management/legislation-and-regulations/federal-advisory-committee-act (accessed 15 March 2026).

Federal Bureau of Investigation (FBI) (2020). Internet Crime Complaint Center marks 20 years. https://www.fbi.gov/news/stories/ic3-20th-anniversary-050820 (accessed 15 March 2026).

Federal Emergency Management Act (FEMA) (2017). National Incident Management System (NIMS). https://www.fema.gov/sites/default/files/2020-07/fema_nims_doctrine-2017.pdf (accessed 15 March 2026).

Federal Trade Commission (FTC) (2022). FTC warns companies to remediate Log4j security vulnerability. https://www.ftc.gov/policy/advocacy-research/tech-at-ftc/2022/01/ftc-warns-companies-remediate-log4j-security-vulnerability (accessed 15 March 2026).

Financial Services Roundtable (FSR) (2011). BITS malware risk and mitigation, financial services roundtable. 11 May 2011.

Forum of Incident Response and Security Teams (FIRST) (2022). Traffic light protocol (TLP), standards definitions and usage guidance. https://www.first.org/tlp/ (accessed 15 March 2026).

Forum of Incident Response and Security Teams (FIRST) (2023). Common Vulnerability Scoring System v4.0: Specification document. https://www.first.org/cvss/ (accessed 15 March 2026).

Geer, D. E. and Conway, D. G. (2009). The Owned Price Index. *IEEE Security & Privacy*, 7(1): 86–87.

Government Accounting Office (GAO) (2022). Cybersecurity: Federal response to SolarWinds and Microsoft exchange incidents GAO-22-104746. 13 January. https://www.gao.gov/products/gao-22-104746 (accessed March 16 2026).

Health and Human Services (HHS) (2025). Change healthcare cybersecurity incident frequently asked questions. Department of Health and Human Services. 14 March. https://www.hhs.gov/hipaa/for-professionals/special-topics/change-healthcare-cybersecurity-incident-frequently-askedquestions/index.html (accessed 16 March 2026).

Hoglund, G. and McGraw, G. (2008). *Exploiting Online Games*. Boston, MA: Pearson Education.

Homeland Security Presidential Directive-5 (HSPD-5) (2003). *Management of Domestic Incidents*. 28 February 2003. https://www.dhs.gov/sites/default/files/publications/Homeland%20Security%20Presidential%20Directive%205.pdf (accessed 15 March 2026).

Institute for Internal Auditors (IIA) (1977). Systems auditability and control report. Institute of Internal Auditors (IIA) (2020). The IIA's three lines model: An update of the three lines of defense. https://www.theiia.org/en/topics/three-lines-model (accessed 18 February 2026).

International Organization for Standardization (2018). ISO 31000:2018 – risk management – guidelines. https://www.iso.org/standard/65694.html (accessed 18 February 2026).

International Organization for Standardization (2021). ISO/IEC 27036: Information security for supplier relationships. https://www.iso.org/standard/82906.html (accessed 13 March 2026).

International Organization for Standardization (2022a). ISO/IEC 27001:2022 – information security, cybersecurity and privacy protection – information security management systems – requirements. https://www.iso.org/standard/82875.html (accessed 18 February 2026).

International Organization for Standardization (2022b). ISO/IEC 27005:2022 – information security, cybersecurity and privacy protection – guidance on information security risk management. https://www.iso.org/standard/80585.html (accessed 18 February 2026).

ISACA (2019) COBIT (2019). Framework: Introduction and methodology. ISACA. https://www.isaca.org/resources/cobit (accessed 18 February 2026).

King, A. and Gallagher, M. (2020). United States Cyberspace Solarium Commission. March 2020. https://cybersolarium.org/march-2020-csc-report/march-2020-csc-report/ (accessed 15 March 2026).

Liedtke, M. and Klepper, D. (2026). What to know about the clash between the pentagon and anthropic over military's AI use. /https//apnews.com/article/anthropic-pentagon-ai-dario-amodei-hegseth-0c464a054359b9fdc80cf18b0d4f690c (accessed 6 March 2026).

Martin, R. (2001). Managing vulnerabilities in networked systems. https://www.researchgate.net/figure/Vulnerability-Tower-of-Babel-1998_tbl1_2955531 (accessed 17 March 2026).

Mell, P. (2000). Identifying critical patches with ICAT. ITL Bulletin, July 2000. https://csrc.nist.gov/files/pubs/shared/itlb/itlbul2000-07.pdf (accessed 17 March 2026).

Menn, J. (2010). *Fatal System Error*. New York: Perseus Books Group.

Miller, C. (2007). The legitimate vulnerability market: The secretive world of 0-day exploit sales. Workshop on Economics of Information Security, June 7–8, Pittsburg, PA.

National Institute of Standards and Technology (NIST) (2011). Managing information security risk: Organization, mission, and information system view (SP 800-39). U.S. Department of Commerce. https://csrc.nist.gov/pubs/sp/800/39/final (accessed 18 February 2026).

National Institute of Standards and Technology (NIST) (2013). National Infrastructure Protection Plan (NIPP). https://www.cisa.gov/sites/default/files/2022-11/national-infrastructure-protection-plan-2013-508.pdf (accessed 15 March 2026).

National Institute of Standards and Technology (NIST) (2022). Cybersecurity supply chain risk management practices for systems and organizations (SP 800-161

Revision 1). U.S. Department of Commerce. https://csrc.nist.gov/pubs/sp/800/161/r1/final (accessed 18 February 2026).

National Institute of Standards and Technology (NIST) (2023). Guide to operational technology, (OT) security (SP 80082 Revision 3). U.S. Department of Commerce. September 2023. https://doi.org/10.6028/NIST.SP.800-82r3 (accessed 16 March 2026).

National Institute of Standards and Technology (NIST) (2024). Cybersecurity framework 2.0. U.S. Department of Commerce. https://www.nist.gov/cyberframework (accessed 16 March 2026).

Open Worldwide Application Security Project (OWASP) (2025). OWASP top 10:2025. Open Worldwide Application Security Project. https://owasp.org/Top10/2025/, https://owasp.org/www-chapter-sofia/assets/presentations/202512%20-%20OWASP%20Top%2010%202025%20by%20Miglen%20Evlogiev.pdf (accessed 17 March 2026).

Open Worldwide Application Security Project (OWASP) (n.d.). Vulnerability disclosure cheat sheet. https://cheatsheetseries.owasp.org/cheatsheets/Vulnerability_Disclosure_Cheat_Sheet.html (accessed 28 March 2026).

PCI Data Security Standard (PCIDSS) (2024). Payment Card Industry Security Standards Council, v4.0.1. https://www.pcisecuritystandards.org/standards/pci-dss/ (accessed 10 March 2026).

Perlroth, N. (2021). *This is How They Tell Me the World Ends*. London: Bloomsbury Publishing.

Phillips, K., et al. (2022). Conceptualizing cybercrime: Definitions, typologies and taxonomies. *Forensic Sciences*, 2(2): 379–398.

RTI International (2023). An environmental scan of cybercrime measurement: Recommendations for the National Crime Victimization Survey, report NCJ 306766. https://www.ojp.gov/pdffiles1/bjs/grants/306766.pdf (accessed 15 March 2026).

Sandman, P. (2020). Sandman homepage: Introduction to risk communication and orientation to this website. https://www.psandman.com/index-intro.htm (accessed 18 April 2026).

Satter, R., Donn, J., and Butler, D. (2017). *FBI Leaves US Targets of Russian Hackers in the Dark*. Associated Press, https://apnews.com/article/north-america-russia-ap-top-news-russian-hacking-politics-eb4df4898e334654a28de14dbfa7ab94 (accessed 16 March 2026).

Savov, I. (2026). OT cybersecurity: A governance failure masquerading as a vocabulary issue. Linked-In Post. 2 March 2026. https://www.linkedin.com/posts/ivan-savov-erpi_control-system-cyber-incidents-and-network-activity-7433003826493702144-IfiO/?utm_source=share&utm_medium=member_desktop&rcm=ACoAAAGNTlABOzsfUN42gLx9rK-Z-0XkuuFah4g (accessed 16 March 2026).

Verizon Business (2026). 2025 data breach investigations report. https://www.verizon.com/business/resources/reports/dbir/, https://verisframework.org/ (accessed 15 March 2026).

William M. (MAC) Thornberry National Defense Authorization Act for Fiscal Year 2021 (2021). Public Law 116–283. January 2021. https://www.congress.gov/116/plaws/publ283/PLAW-116publ283.pdf (accessed 15 March 2026).

5

Guidance for Decision-Makers

Leadership should drive cybersecurity risk management choices. This chapter explores the relationship between organizational leadership functions in the management of technology-related risks and follows the decision-making processes that result in the formulation of policy, process, standards, and procedures to support cybersecurity risk management. The intended audience of the cybersecurity risk assessments described in the framework section of Chapter 4 is decision-makers. Senior leadership intuitively knows that new technology adoption carries risk, but it may not be obvious how continued operation of old technology may present even more severe risks, and we are hard-pressed to come up with an example of an organization more complicated than a lemonade stand that may be immune. Leaders of mission, technology, and cybersecurity functions must effectively collaborate in the identification and evaluation of cybersecurity risk on an ongoing basis to adequately support organizational mission. This chapter begins with topics intended to develop a cybersecurity mindset for decision-makers, and against that backdrop examines the relevant cybersecurity policy choices in the domains of organizational and technology governance, enterprise risk management (ERM), decision-making processes and roles, and translation of policy to technical implementation.

5.1 Innovation, Change, and Risk

Digital innovation is a major driver of organizational change and often causes dramatic changes throughout enterprise architecture. The organizational impact of technology change is widely recognized and deeply studied. Enterprise decision-makers must balance the potential, sometimes necessity, of digital innovation and emerging technologies with known and unknown technology risk dimensions. Consideration of new technology ignites the leadership discussions that often drive the most impactful risk management decisions. Simply, technological change motivates the analysis of technology risk and challenges the implemented control frameworks.

The impact of new technology on organizational policies is visible in essentially all major waves of technological innovation. The effects of mobility on enterprise risk planning were unmistakable as computing devices became physically untethered and increased pressure accumulated at the network edge. The result was architectural changes, new risks, and necessary policies, such as acceptable use for mobile devices. An entirely new class of policies emerged to govern the arrival of smartphones and tablets, notably including organizational policies for "bring your own device." Technology has changed to create opportunities for mobility. Mobile device consumerization bombarded users with direct marketing from manufacturers and carriers, placing pressure on Information Technology (IT) management to quickly establish governance principles while balancing end-user demands.

Artificial Intelligence (AI) is just the latest example of this phenomenon and displays characteristics consistent with the push toward mobility, particularly regarding consumerization. End users have adopted their preferred generative AI and are pushing management toward rapid adoption. Enterprise risks are plainly visible with respect to privacy and data leakage. Concerns unique to AI, such as the potential for hallucination, sandbagging, and the potential to produce low-quality and/or erroneous output, heighten uncertainty. Enterprise management again is faced with the need to rapidly analyze the positive and negative potential of an emerging technology and devise risk treatment strategies that are responsive to user interests, enable the organization to take advantage of new capabilities, and compete in their respective markets.

Efforts to manage the introduction of AI are just the latest iteration of new technology governance and will no doubt be followed by another. The continuous and accelerating pace of change with respect to technological advancement pressures the enterprise to enhance monitoring, analysis, and decision-making cycles. A general drive toward greater systems integration to facilitate data sharing and other benefits adds complexity, including interdependence. The result is a requirement for cybersecurity leaders to enable rapid change throughout the architecture while adhering to governance principles. Application of agile principles can be a significant part of the solution, including the incorporation of short iterative cycles of planning and execution, establishment of continuous feedback loops, and development of collaboration with enterprise leadership, as well as organizational operations.

5.2 Governance

ERM is a core structure of governance. It reflects the implementation of decisions that flow from the governance structure. It is intended to provide a comprehensive view of the interrelated risks in the enterprise, and consolidates concerns from the various domains of mission, IT, data, and cybersecurity governance, respectively.

Cyber risks are enterprise risks that can derail strategic objectives, damage reputation, and impact the bottom line. The integration of cybersecurity with ERM frameworks represents a fundamental shift in how organizations understand and manage cyber threats. When properly integrated, decision-makers can evaluate cyber risks alongside financial and operational risks, allocate resources effectively, and make informed trade-offs between security investments and other priorities. This convergence is not optional anymore – regulators increasingly expect boards and executives to demonstrate oversight of cyber risks as part of their broader fiduciary duties (COSO 2017; SEC 2018).

Governance represents enterprise efforts to direct and control resources, to promote efficient, effective, and safe operation in the pursuit of enterprise value creation. Enterprises invest resources to support mission objectives, and governance establishes the framework to enable, guide, and monitor planning and execution. One of the most critical aspects of mission-related activity is the essential requirement of maintaining alignment of planners and decision-makers with respect to identified strategic objectives (Jonathan et al. 2023). Alignment is essential in setting strategy, developing organizational structure, and defining execution process and procedures.

Enterprise governance is best understood by considering the unique objectives – but shared context – of its core complements of mission, IT, and cybersecurity governance. It is intended to provide oversight functions of strategic direction, management control, personal accountability, and regulatory compliance. Such oversight is particularly essential in consideration of the fiduciary responsibilities of the directors or managers of an organization they do not own. It has been a major focus of leadership since the days of Adam Smith, who expressed concern over its execution (Smith 1776):

> *The directors of such companies, however, being the managers rather of other people's money than of their own, it cannot well be expected that they should watch over it with the same anxious vigilance with which the partners in a private copartnery frequently watch over their own. Like the stewards of a rich man, they are apt to consider attention to small matters as not for their master's honour, and very easily give themselves a dispensation from having it. Negligence and profusion, therefore, must always prevail, more or less, in the management of the affairs of such a company.*

Smith explained that this includes the potential for "low effort" to be exerted by the directors who may perceive little or no personal benefit from executing their function as directors. Ma and Shleifer explain that directors being placed in control of the resources of others is *the agency problem*, raising significant questions about the costs and benefits of director independence (Ma and Shleifer 2025). There is potential for self-dealing, wherein directors may seek to maximize their own outcomes, rather than those of the shareholders. Cybersecurity is especially vulnerable to a director's lack of exertion, given that very few corporate directors have adequate experience in technology, much less cybersecurity risk.

The ongoing evolution of concepts intended to address the above concerns has led us to the present form of mission governance, that is a mixture of law, industry regulation, and internal policy. While the implementation has changed, the core goal remains: to protect the value of shareholders from misuse by third-party agents. Enterprise governance is intended to establish functional roles, accountability, internal and external compliance parameters, and controlling activities. Enterprise governance is generally executed by a committee structure established by the Board of Directors, including operations, technology, audit, and risk committees, as outlined in Figure 5.1. Committees generally have participation from both external directors and executive leadership. Audit committees generally select and supervise external auditors and directly oversee internal audit and assurance activities.

Whether or not a technology committee has been established at the Board level, the technology organization would be remiss not to establish governance objectives that support and inform the Board and its relevant committees. Technology governance, simply put, is the meticulous, analytical approach to selection and oversight of the technology architecture and its associated controls. It also includes responsible resource management. At the project level, it includes budgeting and oversight of projects driven by digital innovation initiatives. Technology governance exists whether it recognizes its risk management responsibilities or not. A well-functioning technology governance framework not only minimizes cybersecurity risk but also saves money. The structure of specialized IT and risk committees reporting through the Board promotes strategic alignment between technology and mission operations. It can thereby serve to maximize returns from technology investments (Pesce and Neirotti 2023).

The rise in the strategic importance of digital data and its recognition as a crucial enterprise asset has resulted in the adoption of a distinct data governance function. Data governance generally consists of efforts to promote IT governance via an informed committee structure, shared decision-making, and

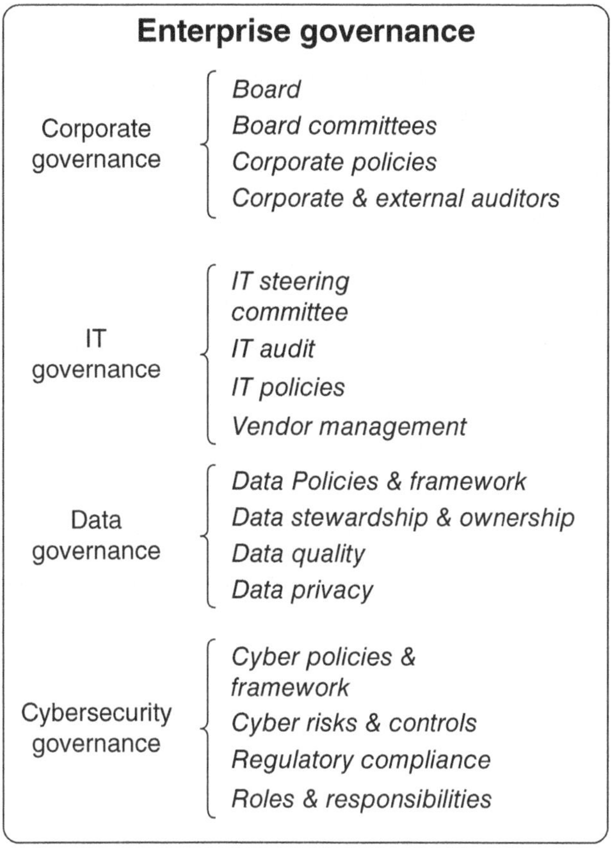

Figure 5.1 Example governance committees.

policy formulation. The Data Management Association (DAMA) has led the establishment of a robust body of knowledge that provides useful guidance for the establishment of appropriate planning, monitoring, and enforcement of sound data management practices, with the goal of maximizing value derived from data resources. This includes establishing foundations essential to managing data privacy, demonstrating an important linkage to cybersecurity governance that serves as the crucial enabler of privacy.

The same foundations visible in other forms of governance also shape the backbone of the cybersecurity governance function. This includes efforts to direct and control resources, including spending – with the intent to build a robust cybersecurity architecture that enables value creation via the ongoing introduction of innovative technologies. Cybersecurity concerns are also represented in the board committee structure, either implemented as a unique committee or as part of the IT or risk committees. Cybersecurity governance produces distinct policies and procedures that align with mission directives.

5.3 Strategic Choices

Decision-making in governance and cyber risk management is about making choices of frameworks, policies, and implementations intended to optimize technology value in pursuit of organizational objectives. It seeks to manage uncertainty. It starts with risk appetite as defined in Chapter 3 and moves the organization from analysis to action. The cyber risk appetite must be integrated within the ERM framework. For example, an organization pursuing aggressive digital transformation may accept higher technology risks than one in a highly regulated industry with mature systems. Organizations handling sensitive data or operating critical infrastructure might declare zero appetite for significant data breaches, while others accept moderate levels of such risk. Strategic planning processes should incorporate cyber risk considerations; digital transformation, cloud migration, and expansion into new markets all create cyber implications that must be evaluated against risk appetite (SEC 2018).

Informed decisions set the organizational course. Decision-making takes on different forms with respect to changes in context, including differences between operational and strategic decision-making. Decision-making has quantitative and qualitative characteristics. Data analytics, key indicators of risk and performance, and other relevant metrics and statistics provide essential support for informed, data-driven choices. There are qualitative aspects as well, where organizations rely on the expertise of the individual decision-makers who draw from their respective preparation and experience to inform future decisions. This does, however, create the potential for the introduction of biases, overreliance on heuristics, and sometimes emotion. Nonetheless, risk analysis often relies significantly on the intuition of decision-makers.

The outcomes of risk analyses serve to support the decision-making of enterprise leadership. Risk management activities are conducted to address specific, observed threats in ways that will support and not obstruct digital strategies. The relationship between technology risks, enterprise resiliency goals, and the design of new systems, products, and services (aka: "brand") was explored in Rohmeyer and Ben-Zvi's study on the role of the Chief Information Security Officer (CISO) (Rohmeyer et al. 2010) and illustrated in Figure 5.2.

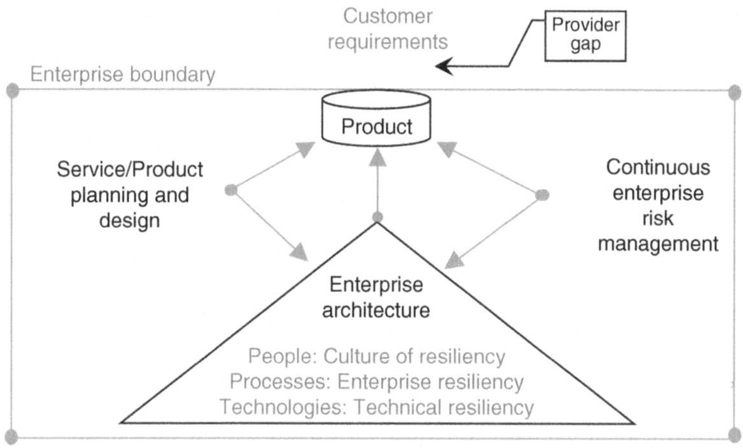

Figure 5.2 Risk management decisions in service/system design.

It is important to recognize the individual contributions of the influences in this model and the relationships between them. Existing enterprise architecture serves to drive the organizational mission and therefore reflects elements that were assembled to support mission objectives. Therefore, the enterprise architecture may be considered a planning constraint. There are ongoing, simultaneous functions of innovation (i.e., brand planning and design) and the management of risks (i.e., continuous ERM). Architecture, innovation, and ERM, therefore, all play a role in the formulation of new enterprise capabilities and brand capabilities. As organizational offerings are extended to external parties, aspects of brand design are found to meet most, but not all, customer requirements, and the shortfall is referred to as the *provider gap*. Organizations continuously seek to improve capabilities through the introduction of new technologies, so efforts to close provider gaps put further pressure on the enterprise to adopt new technologies. Leaders seeking to control and guide this ongoing cycle of technological change and its continuous impact on the enterprise realize that both ongoing assessment of risk and continuous improvement in approaches to treat it are key to mission success.

In the profession of operational risk, a method of lowering risk is referred to as a *treatment*. Although by far the most common method of treating risk is to introduce Policies, Processes, Standards, and Procedures (PPSPs) as described in Chapter 3, such controls rarely eliminate risk entirely but shift the risk profile to more acceptable levels. When risks are reduced through mitigation, we refer to remaining risk as the *residual risk*. Traditional risk management recognizes four treatment options: avoid, reduce, transfer, or accept the risk.

- Risk avoidance is the elimination of system components, such as not connecting industrial control systems to organization networks.
- Risk reduction involves implementing controls, or frameworks, such as those described in Chapter 4.
- Risk transfer, from a cyber perspective, if it occurs at all, may be partially accomplished through cyber insurance.
- Risk acceptance is a recognition that the risk exists, usually within acceptable limits of established risk appetites.

Of the four options, risk *transfer* is undoubtedly the most difficult to accomplish. Except in cases of well-defined minimal impact (e.g., a breach wherein the impact is limited to issuing legal notification and identity theft insurance to a limited set of people whose data was compromised), the cost of recovery from a cybersecurity incident, especially when lawsuits are involved, often far exceeds the insurance coverage limit (Wolff 2022, p. 225). In part, the low coverage limits are due to the inability of insurance companies to access historical data on cybersecurity events and losses due to the lack of dedicated cybercrime databases and granularity of general crime databases discussed in Chapter 4. Moreover, over time, some insurance companies have come to terms with this situation by deliberately scaling back on cybersecurity policy offerings while increasing their costs (Wolff 2022, p. 225).

The opposite end of the spectrum in the ease of executing a risk treatment option is that of *acceptance*. Though accepting to live with a risk as a merely perfunctory process that can be implemented in lieu of *reduction* or *avoidance*, and appears easier and less costly on the surface, in the risk management equation, it is the only approach that does not reduce risk.

In closely held enterprises, a common justification for risk acceptance follows this logic: "This is our organization, we own the equity, so if we choose to accept the risk, that decision rests with us as the risk bearers." This is referred to as the *ownership fallacy*. While superficially appealing, this reasoning fails to account for the actual distribution of risk in most organizational structures – customers, employees, and third parties dependent on the enterprise. This is a moral hazard problem dressed up as risk management. The equity holder gets upside from risky behavior, while the downside is substantially borne by others.

Equity ownership is not the determinative metric of where risk ultimately resides. Risk to equity holders is often overshadowed by risk to other stakeholders. Consider a typical financial institution balance sheet with 10% capital. The liability side reveals approximately 80% held by depositors and perhaps 10% in borrowings from other financial institutions. The equity shareholders (those claiming to accept the risk) actually represent the smallest financial stake in the organization. Risk acceptance by equity holders does not change the level of risk; it simply redistributes the consequences.

The actual risk bearers include:

- depositors and creditors who provide the bulk of funding;
- deposit insurance systems that guarantee customer accounts;
- counterparty institutions exposed to potential financial contagion;
- customers and consumers depending on the institution's services; and
- the broader financial system vulnerable to systemic effects, as described in Chapter 3.

Effective risk management requires evaluating not just individual risk decisions, but the aggregate pattern of those decisions and their alignment with enterprise capacity to absorb losses. This is the essence of *resilience*. Risk acceptance is a legitimate tool, but one that demands rigorous analysis of who truly bears the risk and whether the organization possesses adequate resources to sustain potential impacts. Superficial risk acceptance, divorced from this broader context, represents a failure of governance, rather than an exercise of risk management.

While the emphasis of this chapter is on management decision-making that supports enterprise strategy, as related to cybersecurity policy formulation, cybersecurity leaders also continuously find themselves faced with critical operational decisions. This dimension of the day-to-day operation of the cybersecurity function is an important consideration as it (1) represents a vital obligation to support the organizational mission and (2) serves to inform strategic decision-making by introducing real-world perspectives.

An example is the interaction of all levels of governance in the case of investigating a cyber incident, where leadership is called upon to address questions, such as:

- What is the extent of organizational impact from the incident?
- Does the impact prevent the operation of business as usual?
- What are appropriate response and recovery steps?
- What are critical facts to report to law enforcement and regulators, and when should such facts be reported?
- How deep should the investigation proceed? For example, is it important to determine attribution of the incident to specific parties? When should attribution be ignored?

Cybersecurity leaders regularly interact with the most senior members of the enterprise, and the above questions demonstrate that they must be capable of pivoting from their day jobs of designing and implementing controls around new technology architecture into emergency hands-on incident response activities – and executing such response activities within the established policy structure. An understanding of these requirements underscores the criticality and demands of the roles played by cybersecurity leaders.

5.4 Focus on Risk and Controls

For those with experience in financial controls, there is an obvious analogy between the cybersecurity profession and the accounting profession due to the common emphasis on risk, controls, and related implementations. One reason this comparison is informative is because many of today's information security controls were first established as standards by the Electronic Data Processing Auditor's Association (EDPAA), now the Information Systems Audit and Control Association (ISACA), and their first concern was that financial statements coming out of computers may be incorrect (Bayuk 2005, p. 10–11). A key takeaway from that comparison is that the accounting profession's mantra concerning the integrity of financial management applies across the board to cybersecurity management, that is, "the tone is set at the top" (COSO 2009). Management tone in any endeavor exists whether policy is formally established or not, and management tone is not the same as formal policy establishment. In the domain of cybersecurity, policy is a documented enterprise agreement on cybersecurity goals and objectives, and tone is the level of commitment that management has toward that documented policy and corresponding enforcement measures. There is no single right way for a decision maker to ensure people are really understanding and following the cybersecurity policy. Consciously or unconsciously, every good leader has a method of getting important messages across (Bayuk 2010, p. 9). The way a manager behaves toward issues of importance to cybersecurity policy will set the tone for the enterprise. The day-to-day decisions made by middle- and lower-level managers to facilitate their own processes and procedures occasionally have unintended consequences on an organization's overall cybersecurity posture and require a timely response.

To be effective, cybersecurity strategy must be a mainstream part of organizational operations, system, or mission planning, not a subcomponent of a technology-only function. For example, it is not uncommon for a technology department that has no established cybersecurity strategy to set unreasonably hard standards for user-selected passwords, while sharing administrative passwords among themselves via email. Cybersecurity in this case would be disruptive to operations and at the same time provide poor protection against a determined hacker. It takes time to craft policy to make sure it enables, rather than disrupts, operations. A decision maker will often count on an information security professional to shepherd cybersecurity policy (e.g., CISO), ensuring it remains effective and relevant. If it is not relevant, the void will doubtless be filled with security theater as described in Chapter 4.

The CISO position has evolved considerably since first created in response to evolving needs. Responsibilities change frequently, and the CISO's tenure is often short due to enterprise matters beyond their control. Others who have seen CISOs come and go understand this, so a CISO needs extra strong leadership support to establish standard ways to configure technology, so that it can be easily verified to be policy compliant. They will need help getting their peer technology managers to attend training on those standards and operate them according to the corresponding security procedures. They may mandate staff to perform step-by-step procedures in areas that previously had no need for them. They may draft guidelines and expect others to follow their advice. Only an executive who truly understands the end goal of their activities will be able to provide the tone at the top necessary to support such a CISO-led cybersecurity program.

When an executive fully understands the motivation and origin of enterprise security policy, the process for implementation should be as easy to manage as any other technology endeavor, although this is not meant to imply that technology is generally easy either. Techniques such as continuous monitoring in the style of Drucker and Deming go as far in cybersecurity as they do for any other domain (Drucker 2001; Pande et al. 2001). Applied to cybersecurity, such techniques allow for advancement of the enterprise purpose or strategic mission and fortify its resilience against unknown threats. Moreover, the application of sound management practices to the domain of security carries the happy unintended consequence of the ability to pass technology audits.

Leadership in cybersecurity requires a multidisciplinary approach because it involves a fusion of knowledge from enterprise, legal, risk, policy, and multiple technology domains. As we learned in Chapter 4, even the most shining candidates for technical CISO/CSO roles may be unequipped for board and executive exposure. Many security professionals were trained in industries that prioritize cybersecurity and embed it in their culture, such as military or finance. It would be unreasonable to expect someone who spent many years in one industry to know, for example, the operational processes that should take priority in a completely different industry. Individual candidates rarely possess all desired skills and experiences, and the mission governance structure provides the organizational backstop to orient the enterprise toward covering the full range of skill and leadership requirements, rather than a single, perfect candidate. Instead, placing the best possible candidate in the strongest governance framework is the most reasonable and ideal approach. Hence, similar to the way a team is convened to assist any new executive hire taking on any important strategic objective, a leader should assemble some form of a Cybersecurity Policy Committee and rely on it to assist a CISO in the development of cybersecurity policy. In the case of a CISO, it should include the Chief Operations Officer, Chief Information Officer, Chief Legal Officer, and Chief Human Resources Officer, or equivalents. It may also include highly authoritative executives, such as business unit heads and/or trusted advisors from any area of the enterprise.

From an oversight perspective, cybersecurity governance belongs at the Board level. The magnitude of potential losses, strategic implications for operational viability, and regulatory requirements for board engagement make this unavoidable.

Depending on the organization, Boards may not need deep technical expertise, but they must understand the organization's most significant cyber risks, evaluate management's risk strategies, ensure adequate resource allocation, and provide informed challenge to cybersecurity decisions (NACD 2020). Many boards delegate detailed oversight to audit or risk committees, though some establish dedicated technology committees. Regardless of structure, the full board retains ultimate responsibility and needs regular updates. Effective board reporting balances technical detail with strategic context – purely technical metrics fail to convey operational risks (e.g., the number of vulnerabilities counted in a recent network scan), while abstract discussions lack specificity for boards to evaluate whether management is adequately addressing threats.

5.5 Policy Essentials

In any process designed to achieve a generic high-level goal, that goal should be customized by the organization to be specific enough to correlate to enterprise mission or purpose. In this case, the generic goal is *cybersecurity risk below appetite*. The risk appetite statement presents one obvious customization that may be expanded and/or supplemented with lower level, more specific cybersecurity goals. Examples are:

- make mission-critical data integrity and availability safe from hackers;
- make it extremely difficult to steal mission-critical information stored on physical assets with or without insider collaboration; and
- always detect cyberspace-enabled impersonation, asset fraud, or theft.

Articulating policy goals with this level of specificity allows an organization to consider the definition of "mission-critical" and "asset fraud or theft" as the *scope* of the problem to be resolved with policy. In the technology industry, a common methodology to drill down from scope into methods to verify goals are met is Goal Question Metric (GQM). The idea is to reduce the goal to a set of questions that, if answered affirmatively, provide the information to verify and validate that goals are met. Examples are:

- What assets need to be in place to maintain operations? Which are the "mission-critical?" Are these changing and/or evolving with our long-term plans?
- What infrastructure houses our most mission-critical assets?
- Which information should be kept safe from "asset fraud or theft"?

In each case, the answer to the question requires that information be readily available in the form of data from which cybersecurity management metrics may be created. Once these general environmental aspects of the cybersecurity environment within the enterprise are understood, more detailed questions can be probed with the help of a cybersecurity task force composed of operations, financial, and technology staff. Such questions may be found in the *cybersecurity frameworks* selected by the organization for self-assessment.

The answers to the first set of questions should provide the foundation to articulate security goals. Because the sole purpose of regulation is to reduce industry risk overall, one strategy to protect an industry participant's mission should also protect regulatory-specified information, and the opposite is rarely true. The temptation is to use regulation as a substitute for cybersecurity strategy. We caution against starting with such an approach because committees may prioritize regulations over mission. However, a focus on security of the mission, rather than regulation, is highly likely to cover both. A simple internal audit should confirm that a policy that meets mission needs also meets regulatory requirements, or it will identify a compliance gap that can be closed in a way compatible with the agreed-upon organizational security requirements.

Note that it is not reasonable to expect that cybersecurity goals are 100% achievable. They are simply guideposts and sanity checks meant to ensure that any cybersecurity strategy and policy established have some tangible value. They lay the foundation on which to specify the scope of system and process-level security efforts. However, executives should not mistake progress in the technology implementation of cybersecurity best practices for cybersecurity goal achievement.

Armed with tangible goals and associated metrics, a cybersecurity program can justify both its strategies and corresponding policy. Cybersecurity policy statements should be phrased in a language native to the same team of executive decision-makers that set cybersecurity goals. For example, if customers are called *clients* in the organization's internal literature, the policy should use that term, or if telecommunications lines are called *facilities* in the business literature, that term should not be used to describe buildings. An example cybersecurity policy statement based on the first sample goal above might be:

> *Data containing information comprising the organization's technology asset inventory shall be secured in a readily accessible database that is physically and logically redundant. It shall include, but not be limited to, devices, software, systems configurations, documentation, and test generation methods for operational processes whether these exist internally or in a third-party technology service provider.*

Note that a policy statement does not dictate how the situation described in its "shall" statements will be accomplished. As part of an overall strategy, the implementation mechanisms may be central or distributed among various stakeholders within the policy scope. The policy should be specific enough for its outcomes to be measurable, but general enough to allow for appropriate information handling procedures to be described at the organizational process level.

Nevertheless, it is important to compose an information security policy document so that the organizations within scope are unmistakably aware of the existence of well-defined objectives for security and an agreed-upon management approach for securing information. If there is debate over the content of the policy, the debate will continue through attempts to enforce it, with the consequence that the Information Security Program itself will be dysfunctional.

In his book, Cybersecurity Law (Kosseff 2023), Jeff Kosseff reviews a wide variety of cybersecurity laws in the context of complaints (i.e., court cases) that are based on them. This experience taught him that some cybersecurity policies were more likely to influence constituent behavior than others. It also prompted him to propose a set of best practices for creating cybersecurity policy, which he refers to as *guiding principles* (Kosseff 2023, pp. 790–823). They provide a helpful self-test that a leader may take before issuing new cybersecurity policy, that is, cybersecurity policy should be:

1) Informed – thoroughly researched and tested
2) Clear – presented in layman's terms
3) Adaptive – anticipate technology evolution
4) Comprehensive – minimize overlap with sufficiently large scope
5) Cohesive – enacted within a framework with no conflicting regulations
6) Global – ubiquitously applicable
7) Collaborative – anticipate need for cooperative enforcement

5.6 Moving from Policy to Implementation

We observe above that cybersecurity easily lends itself to a Drucker-style management cycle for managing by objectives and self-control. It also lends itself to military recommendations for managing battle-action: *observe* the situation, *orient* observations based on background knowledge and analysis, *decide* on a course of action, *act*, and *observe the impact of actions* on the situation in a continuous cycle (Boyd 1987). These activities, in combination, comprise the management cycle of an enterprise security program. Where cybersecurity is managed as a program, the program structure provides organization, strategy, and operational process to maintain activities in support of cybersecurity. Within an enterprise management structure, the cybersecurity program will be a set of interrelated discrete projects and combined with processes managed in a coordinated way to obtain benefits and control not available from managing them individually (PMI 2008).

The process by which cybersecurity policy is established is a part of that program. As with any important initiative, the establishment of cybersecurity policy requires task definition, planning, and clear objectives; that is, to create cybersecurity policy is a project and should be managed as one. As with any project, cybersecurity policy creation starts with goals and objectives. It is also helpful to begin with the recognition that policy follows enterprise strategy, not the reverse. Policy is an extremely important component of strategy execution because it is used to communicate desired outcomes.

Even if an executive issues only one policy statement, that statement will be interpreted in the context of other plans, objectives, and operational environments that complete an organization's cybersecurity posture. Clear documentation of desired outcomes is a critical element of enterprise communication and is required for awareness activities that motivate members from executives to low-level staff of the organization to achieve security goals. Progress in goal achievement should be monitored, and gaps in policy compliance or difficulties in following policy should be met with resources. If there is too much difficulty in complying with policy, that fact should be captured in a management feedback loop as it may indicate the necessity of changes in strategy to accommodate policy compliance. Given that organization, system, and/or mission, risk management should drive cybersecurity strategy and corresponding policy, articulating the risks presented by threats to organization, system, and/or mission cyberspace is a good way to begin a cybersecurity policy project. Though the description of these risks may not be included in the final policy document, it may be helpful in creating awareness among stakeholders of why the policy has been deemed necessary.

5.6.1 Implementation of the Controls Architecture

Cybersecurity risk is an operational risk, which has a comparably longer history in management literature. Operational risk is often treated using a strategy referred to as *Three Lines of Defense* (3LoD). The 3LoD model originated in ERM and internal audit in the early 2000s. Its roots lie in the banking and financial services sector, driven by the need to clarify who is responsible for what after a series of organizational and financial scandals. The concept was formalized by the IIA and updated in 2020 as *The Three Lines Model* (IIA 2020). This model provides a clear blueprint of who in an organization is responsible for risk-management roles, oversight, and assurance and reflects evolving governance and assurance structures, including cyber risk. The IIA's intent was to differentiate operational management, risk oversight, and independent assurance, reducing confusion and overlap in responsibilities.

The concept was adopted by the Basel Committee on Banking Supervision (BCBS), which endorsed it as a best practice and reaffirmed it in 2020 for banks

Table 5.1 Summary of the Three Lines of Defense.

Line	Role	Key Responsibility	Typical Participants
First line	Executives/ Operations/ Management	Own and manage risks; implement controls	Technology and organizational units that implement security controls (e.g., network hardening, access control, patching)
Second line	Risk and Compliance Functions	Develop risk frameworks, perform risk assessments, and provide oversight	Chief Risk Office (including ERM), compliance, and legal
Third line	Independent Assurance	Provide independent audit and assurance	Internal audit, sometimes external audit or regulators validating cyber governance and controls

and financial institutions (BCBS 2020). The European and US banking regulators all reference or align with the 3LoD model in their risk management and internal control expectations. In essence, the financial sector institutionalized the 3LoD to show regulators that risk ownership is clear, oversight is effective, and audits are independent. A high-level overview of the roles and responsibilities of the 3LoD is in Table 5.1.

When cybersecurity became recognized as a key operational risk, the same model was naturally extended to cyber. However, as discussed in Chapters 1 and 4, job titles in cybersecurity are not standardized to the extent that the responsibilities of a CISO will be the same at two different organizations. The title is conspicuously absent from Table 5.1, which outlines the components of the 3LoD. While generally, the CISO reports to senior management with authority to establish and enforce enterprise cybersecurity requirements, including cybersecurity policy, there is no agreement on whether that role belongs in the first or second line of defense. Some organizations place the role in the first line reporting to a Chief Executive Officer (CEO), Chief Operations Officer (COO), or Chief Information Officer (CIO) and others in the second line reporting to a Chief Risk Officer (CRO). That said, some regulators prefer that the CISO not report directly to the CIO because of potential conflict of interest due to the need to thoroughly implement and test cybersecurity controls prior to making changes in the organization's cyberspace (FFIEC n.d.).

While the model establishes clear separation, effective cyber risk management requires robust coordination and information sharing between the three lines. Control deficiencies identified through second-line risk assessments should be tracked and remediated by the first line. Third-line audit findings should inform both first and second lines about control failures and program-level weaknesses within both the first and second lines.

Regular coordination forums, such as cybersecurity steering or risk committees, create structured opportunities for information sharing about emerging threats, risk environment changes, regulatory requirements, and major incidents. Clear escalation protocols are essential to guide when a security issue should be escalated from first to second line, or from first or second line to senior management. Establishing these thresholds ensures significant cybersecurity risks receive appropriate visibility and management attention. Some organizations adopt a model wherein the security architecture responsibilities bridge first and second lines or contract for independent external assurance functions in addition to audit through penetration testing firms that provide additional independent validation (CISA 2023).

5.7 Conclusion

Success in the development of a viable cybersecurity program depends critically on leadership commitment and organizational culture. If leadership does not visibly support integrating cybersecurity into both technology and ERM, or does not support the independence and authority of the second and third lines, formal governance structures will be ineffective. When leadership demonstrates genuine commitment to sound policy development, risk-based decision-making and 3LoD principles, the result should be state-of-the-art management of cybersecurity risk.

As cyber threats evolve and cybersecurity becomes increasingly central to organizational resilience, governance approaches will continue evolving. We predict that the integration of cybersecurity with ERM will deepen, with the result that both technology and cybersecurity risk will be inseparable from operational, strategic, and financial risk. The 3LoD model will likely continue to be refined to address cybersecurity's unique characteristics. Emerging technologies like AI and evermore ubiquitous connectivity will introduce new risk categories, testing existing frameworks. Leaders must ensure their governance structures remain flexible and forward-looking enough to address risks not yet fully understood (NACD 2020).

References

Basel Committee on Banking Supervision, Bank for International Settlements (BCBS) (2020). Revisions to the principles for the sound management of operational risk. https://www.bis.org/bcbs/publ/d508.pdf (accessed 10 March 2026).

Bayuk, J. (2005). *Stepping Through the IS Audit, A Guide for Information Systems Managers*, 2nd edn. Rolling Meadows, IL: Information Systems Audit and Control Association.

Bayuk, J. (2010). *Enterprise Security for the Executive: Setting the Tone at the Top*. Santa Barbara, CA: Praeger.

Boyd, J. (1987). A discourse on winning and losing. Briefing slides. Maxwell Air Force Base, AL: Air University Library. Document No. M-U 43947.

Committee of Sponsoring Organizations (COSO) (2009). Guidance: Internal Control—Integrated Framework. https://ab5bd07f-8066-4a33-869e-6f82d80ee59a.filesusr.com/ugd/719ba0_dd4751924137497098e9435572dd5cfd.pdf (accessed 10 March 2026).

Committee of Sponsoring Organizations (COSO) (2017). Enterprise risk management: Integrating with strategy and performance. https://www.coso.org/enterprise-risk-management (accessed 10 March 2026).

Cybersecurity and Infrastructure Security Agency (CISA) (2023). Cybersecurity performance goals. https://www.cisa.gov/cpg (accessed 10 March 2026).

Drucker, P. (2001). *The Essential Drucker*. New York, NY: HarperCollins.

Federal Financial Institutions Examination Council (FFIEC) (n.d.). IT management. FFIEC Examination Handbook Infobase, Management Section I.A.2. https://www.ffiec.gov/cyberassessmenttool.htm (accessed 5 November 2025).

Institute of Internal Auditors Available (IIA) (2020). The IIA's three lines model: An update of the three lines of defense. https://www.theiia.org/globalassets/documents/resources/the-iias-three-lines-model-an-update-of-the-three-lines-of-defense-july-2020/three-lines-model-updated-english.pdf (accessed 10 March 2026).

Jonathan, G., et al. (2023). IT alignment: A path towards digital transformation success. https://www.sciencedirect.com/science/article/pii/S187705092300323X (accessed 10 March 2026).

Kosseff, J. (2023). *Cybersecurity Law*. New York, NY: Wiley.

Ma, Y. and Shleifer, A. (2025). The invention of corporate governance. *Journal of Financial Economics*, 172: 104115. https://www.sciencedirect.com/science/article/abs/pii/S0304405X25001230 (accessed 10 March 2026).

National Association of Corporate Directors (NACD) (2020). Director's handbook on cyber-risk oversight. https://www.nacdonline.org/globalassets/public-pdfs/nacd_cyber-risk-oversight-handbook_pages_web-compressed.pdf (accessed 10 March 2026).

Pande, P., Neuman, R., and Cavanagh, R. (2001). *The Six Sigma Way*. New York, NY: McGraw-Hill.

Pesce, D. and Neirotti, P. (2023). The impact of IT-business strategic alignment on firm performance: The evolving role of IT in industries. https://www.sciencedirect.com/science/article/pii/S0378720623000484 (accessed 10 March 2026).

Project Management Institute (PMI) (2008). *A Guide to the Project Management Body of Knowledge (PMBOK® Guide)*, 4th edn. Newton Square, PA: Project Management Institute.

Rohmeyer, P. and Ben-Zvi, T. (2010). Risk Management Decision Making In Service Design. Proceedings of the Mediterranean Conference on Information Systems (MCIS).

Smith, A. (1776). An inquiry into the nature and causes of the wealth of nations. Project Gutenberg E-Book #3300, p. 755. https://uedf.org/wp-content/uploads/2023/06/The-Wealth-of-Nations-Adam-Smith.pdf (accessed 10 March 2026).

US Securities and Exchange Commission (SEC) (2018). Commission statement and guidance on public company cybersecurity disclosures. https://www.sec.gov/rules/interp/2018/33-10459.pdf (accessed 10 March 2026).

Wolff, J. (2022). *Cyberinsurance Policy Rethinking Risk in Age of Ransomware, Computer Fraud, Data Breaches, and Cyberattacks*. Cambridge, MA: MIT Press.

6

The Cybersecurity Workforce

While cybersecurity is a highly technical field, standard curriculum at any level of education from elementary through professional engineering and industry certifications is conspicuously absent. This chapter explains the current state of the educational landscape for those wishing to pursue cybersecurity fields. It also summarizes attempts at standardization and some of the hurdles the field must overcome before it can be viewed as mature as professionals in other engineering professions. It starts with emphasizing what cybersecurity is not via a comparison between cybersecurity and the professional practice of engineers. It then steps through the training and educational opportunities that exist for those interested in pursuing a career in cybersecurity. This is followed by a description of various job roles in cybersecurity with references that those interested may follow to dig more deeply into this topic. It concludes with an overview of the field as it exists and a look forward.

6.1 Cybersecurity Versus Engineering

Every state in the union and the federal government itself has professional certification requirements to which engineers engaged in projects that impact safety must adhere (Harbor Compliance 2026). These include, but are not limited to, Civil, Mechanical, Architectural, and Environmental. Where individuals may not be required to be certified engineers themselves, they are required to be working under the supervision of an Engineer-in-Charge, who must be certified (NSPE 2026; NCARB 2026). State requirements vary in scope and intensity, but generally, to earn a Professional Engineer (PE) License, a candidate must

1) Earn a four-year degree in engineering from an accredited engineering program;
2) Pass the Fundamentals of Engineering (FE) exam;

3) Complete four years of progressive engineering experience supervised by a Licensed PE; and
4) Pass the Principles and Practice of Engineering (PPE) exam.

Then, to retain their licenses, most states require PEs to continually maintain and improve their skills throughout their careers (Harbor Compliance 2026).

Therefore, it often comes as a surprise to policymakers that there is no such thing as a similar federal or state certification for a software engineer (Bogost 2015). It does not take much imagination to understand that not identifying and fixing vulnerabilities in public infrastructure may have a serious impact on safety. In civil engineering, avoidance of structural flaws and the ability to withstand direct attacks are incorporated into project requirements. In software, they are afterthoughts, and solutions are often "bolted-on" as described in Chapter 2.

Everyone knows a bridge needs to be patched occasionally to remain resilient. As we saw in Chapter 2, in software, this type of fix is also called a "patch." The difference is that a physical bridge will typically need patches only every few years based on inspection, while software experiences a wide variety of constantly changing technical glitches. Cybersecurity professionals have to periodically download small "packages" of software code from vendors to keep the software working properly. The patching process is often automated and usually necessary even if, on any given day, none of the available patches is necessary to fix a cybersecurity vulnerability. Most software patches are to protect against vulnerabilities that make systems malfunction without being attacked at all, such as leaky memory and structural design flaws.

Yet, unlike the civil engineering profession whose creations often need no patches for decades, the software engineering profession has consistently avoided being regulated in the interest of public safety. The problem of software impacting safety first arose in the 1960s, when it became obvious to policymakers that physical infrastructure was increasingly reliant on software, including advanced weapons systems. In recognition of the need for safe software engineering principles to guide technology developers in creating resilient systems, the North Atlantic Treaty Organization (NATO) Science Committee sponsored two Software Engineering Conferences with the goal of establishing an engineering approach to software creation. The project was decades in the making, and the conference summary was written in 1979. The author lamented that methods to apply engineering disciplines to software never materialized, so the phrase "software engineering" is still an expression of a requirement, rather than an actual engineering discipline (Randell 1979). This is still the case today.

Although the software field does have professional associations that publish and comment on each other's work, these documents have more in common with research endeavors than engineering standards. The Institute for

Electrical Engineering and the Association of Computing Machinery eventually adopted *ethical* standards at the turn of the century. However, the only consequence of violating them is to lose your membership in those industry associations. These are weak quality controls in comparison to actual engineering disciplines, where lack of professional certification precludes consideration for contracts. Note that even in the legal profession, misconduct even with respect to ethical rules can result in disbarment. There are no such consequences for incompetent or unethical professional software engineers.

A software engineer can write a program that creates a human machine interface to a bridge configuration (e.g., presets for schedule and speed of raising or lowering bridge), as well as unattended automation of emergency bridge behavior (e.g., freeze in place or lower depending on monitoring signals, such as a car on a bridge that is in the process of opening), and that person needs no degree or professional certification. It is obvious that a doctor who proscribes lethal drugs due to ignorance or malice will lose their license and even go to jail. Yet in the case of the two Boeing 737 MAX nosedive crashes, the *company* eventually pled guilty, but the aerospace programmers who "patched" the Boeing 737 were never identified or implicated. Had they been civil engineers, they would at least have lost their licenses to practice and spread more mayhem due to the unprofessional and unethical use of their skills. Though several tort liability laws for software developers who produce vulnerable code have been proposed, debate over enforcement issues have stalled lawmaker consensus (Musser 2025). For example, technology platform operators (TOP) have so many customers, a single liability could put them out of business, and yet limiting liability could make them complacent. As discussed in Chapter 3, TOPs have already demonstrated they are willing to adapt and pay a fine rather than change behavior.

Perhaps the closest professional title Cybersecurity has to a software engineer is Systems Security Engineer (ISO 2008). Like the software engineer ancestor, there are no requirements for training, degrees, or certifications to achieve this title. Nevertheless, those in the field have developed a structured approach to their task, which is increasingly described as "Achieving Zero Trust," a nod to the NIST Zero Trust Architecture standard (NIST 2020).

6.2 Academic Curriculum on Cybersecurity

Enterprise computing is an applied science. New technologies continuously emerge, followed by use cases that must be explored and later explained to the next-generation workforce, so the underlying technology may be applied in ways that add value. The study of technology topics only becomes relevant to enterprises when placed into specific use contexts, supporting specific missions and objectives, and observed to produce real benefits. Academia is faced with the ongoing challenge of monitoring the real-world application of individual technologies that they may have previously thoroughly studied.

6.2.1 Technical and Non-technical Threads

Cybersecurity technologies generally focus on engineering and computing disciplines. As in the domain of systems engineering, the connection between the study and exploration of cybersecurity technologies in alignment with enterprise system design requires understanding in the organizational context (i.e., management, accounting, legal/compliance, human resource management, and workforce development). The result is a variety of academic programs that provide a broad appreciation of these topics and promote the development of a significant pool of experts in each.

Engineering and computing cyber programs typically include emphasis on cryptography, network security, and increasingly artificial intelligence. Engineering schools may offer an examination of hardware and embedded systems security topics. Systems-oriented programs emphasize systems security architecture. Management-themed programs emphasize areas, such as technology risk, controls, and governance. This extends to organizational planning and associated human resource dimensions. Accounting programs increasingly explore accounting automation systems and provide guidance on risks and controls that extend to information security. Legal programs similarly have expanded to include exposure to legal and compliance risks, including dimensions of cybercrime and privacy.

6.2.2 US Federal Programs

In 1999, a major federal program was established to incentivize universities to create cybersecurity curriculum: the Centers of Academic Excellence (CAE) program. It is operated by the National Security Agency and Department of Homeland Security, and certifies academic institutions that meet specific cybersecurity education standards (NSA n.d.).

Institutions seeking designation must demonstrate that their curricula develop practical defensive capabilities, including network intrusion detection, incident response, and security risk management. The designation process requires peer review by government evaluators and academics who assess whether graduates can perform required cybersecurity functions. Designations remain valid for five years, after which institutions must reapply, a requirement intended to prevent program degradation (NSA 2024).

The program maintains three designation categories. Cyber Defense designations certify programs at any academic level (community colleges through doctoral programs) that teach core security skills. Cyber Operations designations certify specialized programs in penetration testing and exploit development for intelligence and law enforcement applications. Cyber Research designations certify doctoral universities conducting cybersecurity research (NSA 2024).

Unfortunately, that effort failed to produce consensus on cybersecurity curriculum or even professional job descriptions in cybersecurity. It also did nothing to bridge the gap between the cyber defenses required by the federal government and the people available to provide them. In 2014, the federal government launched the CyberCorps Scholarship for Service program. Administered by the National Science Foundation (NSF). It provides full funding for degree completion in exchange for government service (Cybersecurity Enhancement Act 2014). The program covers tuition, fees, books, and living expenses. Service commitments match scholarship duration: two years of funding requires two years of government employment. Service can occur at federal, state, local, or tribal agencies. Students who fail to complete service obligations convert their scholarships to interest-bearing loans (NSF 2023).

6.2.3 Sample Academic Program Structures

STEM education is an interdisciplinary, hands-on teaching approach integrating Science, Technology, Engineering, and Mathematics. Institutions that focus on STEM often offer a range of undergraduate and graduate degree programs that are drawn from research capabilities, including activities supported under NSA Center of Excellence initiatives and other sponsored research. The following examples illustrate the nature and depth of programs offered by universities committed to cybersecurity studies.

At the undergraduate level, Johns Hopkins University has a cybersecurity curriculum integrated with the Computer Science curriculum. They also offer degrees through their Engineering for Professionals program and Information Security Institute (ISI). The Cybersecurity Masters program from Engineering is built on a foundation of STEM undergraduate requirements, including Calculus, Data Structures, and Discrete Mathematics, among other topics. Core cybersecurity courses include Cryptology, Foundations of Algorithms, and Foundations of Information Assurance, demonstrating coverage of systems and information security topics. Students work within a defined area of focus, such as Analysis, Cyber Operations, Networks, and Systems (JHU Online Masters 2026). The Johns Hopkins ISI offers Masters programs in Security Informatics and other dual degree options in conjunction with Mathematics, Engineering, and Computer Science programs (JHU ISI 2026).

Duke University, an NSA Center of Excellence Cyber Defense-designated institution, offers a Master of Engineering in Cybersecurity, as well as cybersecurity options within the undergraduate Computer Science curriculum. The master's program is structured as a 30-credit graduate degree (10 courses of 3 credits each) consisting of a combination of technical core courses, industry preparation, and cybersecurity electives, therefore offering significant capabilities. The program requires an internship, further connecting to industry application of the curriculum (Duke 2026). Duke also offers Executive Cybersecurity Education, a Chief Information Security Officer (CISO) Executive Certificate program designed to provide an education to potential or current CISO's on how to build and mature an organization's cybersecurity program. Topics include: AI and Security for Leaders, Industrial Security for Leaders, Cloud Security for Leaders, and Cybersecurity Resilience for Leaders.

Stevens Institute of Technology is designated an NSA Center of Excellence under both Cyber Defense and Cyber Research and offers several degree programs at the undergraduate and graduate levels. Programs offer structures similar to the offerings at Johns Hopkins, Duke, and other NSA-Designated institutions. Stevens offers a Bachelor of Science in Cybersecurity degree, which offers many flexible options, including interdisciplinary programs and integrated research opportunities at the undergraduate level (Stevens 2026). It also offers Masters programs in Systems Engineering of Cyber-Physical Systems and Systems Security Engineering.

Even many policy-focused academic programs (which focus on responses to cyber espionage, cyber-threat intelligence, cyber risk, governance, and other "softer" topics) can be taken as STEM degrees, such as the Masters of Public Administration at Columbia University's School of International and Public Affairs (Columbia 2026).

6.3 Certification of Cybersecurity Professionals

In the first edition of this book, we included Professional Certification as a policy issue in the Catalog section of the book. There were six policy statements accompanied by explanations and reasons for controversy, and they were all variations of the same theme: "As there is no agreed-upon standard cyber-physical system security curriculum, widespread adoption of a specific training program and guaranteed subsequent hiring programs may have the unexpected consequence of reducing the variety of cybersecurity expertise within government agencies. These concerns are even more exacerbated for industrial control systems." Nevertheless, in an attempt to suggest policy to address this issue, some of the Catalog policy statements made a tacit assumption that such a curriculum existed or could somehow be produced in support of policy. For example, this policy statement was included: "There shall be national criteria for evaluating cybersecurity academic, accreditation, and training programs, all cybersecurity training used by government and critical infrastructure shall be verified to meet that criteria, and a list of all those meeting that criteria shall be published."

The process of certifying information security professionals is a growing and dynamic field. There are literally thousands of certifications available, ranging from hands-on examinations of product-specific knowledge, to subject area certification, to broad information security certifications. Similar to academia, certification programs have evolved into largely two tracks, broadly characterized as technology-oriented (e.g., *Security Essentials* from SANS) and risk and controls (e.g., *Certified Information Systems Auditor* from ISACA). Job descriptions will frequently seek candidates who hold credentials from a short list that commonly includes both.

None of the popular cybersecurity certifications carries any form of liability or bonding beyond an expected adherence to a common code of ethics and conduct, nor are they equivalent to professional registration regimes. If the term "engineer" is used in the certification's title ("software engineer" and "network engineer" are common examples), it is most assuredly does not meet the PE criteria described above in Section 6.1.

Ironically, except at the CISO level, companies and organizations typically have training requirements for their cybersecurity employees that meet baseline practices acceptable to the broader cybersecurity professional community. Internal employees often are not assigned exclusively to cybersecurity roles; they may be augmented with Managed Security Service Providers (MSSP) who supposedly are better trained. However, there is no requirement or license required for a business to advertise itself as an MSSP either.

In response to an audit finding that US Department of Defense (DoD) contractors were performing security work without the requisite background, the DoD established a certification program (DoD 2005), and the US federal government established similar requirements a decade later. At the start, there was not much faith in the value of cybersecurity certification, but program supporters maintained that any certification is better than none, as it gives the government a tool for oversight that can be improved going forward.

However appropriate it may be to have minimum job requirements, none of the professional certifications adopted for such purposes aspire to the level of a PE license. The training is basic, the experience, if required at all, is to have had a cybersecurity in a job title corresponding to certification requirements attested to by a currently certified cybersecurity professional. There is no burden on the person so attesting to mentor or otherwise educate the individual and no burden on the certificate applicant to be an apprentice to a certified member. There is simply a certification exam on technologies within the scope of the certification topic. Most certifications are supported with classes that specifically prepare students to pass the test. Unless the certification topic is specifically focused on software, there is no requirement for knowledge of software development or secure coding. Such certification requirements look nothing like professional engineering licenses and do little to advance the state of cyberspace security. Though the government's certification requirements have evolved to include more and more professionally oriented certifications, and a few certifications have more rigorous requirements than others, most cybersecurity certification requirements are still analogous to what you would need to know as if you had a job to operate, rather than architect, a drawbridge.

Nevertheless, even today, a high school dropout who gains a specific certification designated for a cybersecurity job level will be favored, by policy of the US federal government (among other major institutions), for a security engineering job over a successfully practicing engineer with 20 years' experience and advanced degrees in cybersecurity. One reason for supporting this government policy is that certifications require some amount of continuous learning while advanced degrees are not evidence of continuing education in security. However, many certifications accept ongoing education credit hours from the organizations that support these certifications by attending cybersecurity vendor's product advertisement presentations, reading magazine articles, or listening to cybersecurity news-oriented podcasts.

Moreover, there are many fields within cybersecurity where staff require additional training, but there are currently limited scope certifications in that area (e.g., secure software engineering). Though the DoD requires specific certifications for specific job functions, none of the certification organizations' continuing education requirements has requirements specifically related to the job function one is currently performing (DoD 2023). Though some certification organizations randomly audit certification holder's claims of annual training, there is little by way of an audit of the content of training not directly provided by the certification organization. Nor are we aware of anyone who actually had their cybersecurity certification revoked based on lack of compliance with ethical requirements.

Certifications held by the authors include Certified Information Security Auditor (CISA), Certified Information Security Manager (CISM), Certified Information Systems Security Professional (CISSP), Certified in the Governance of Enterprise IT (CGEIT), Certified in Risk and Information Systems Control (CRISC), Certified Cloud Security Professional (CCSP), HealthCare Information Security and Privacy Practitioner (HCISPP), Private Investigator (PI) and Professional Engineer (PE) Licenses, earned with knowledge tests and hours devoted to continuing education. We keep our certifications because our employers and consulting clients are comforted by them, but other than the PE and PI licenses, we also think at some point in a cybersecurity professional's career, our academic credentials and work experience are better proof of our competence in a cybersecurity job function.

Nevertheless, any professional association that supports networking opportunities for members has some value on the cybersecurity front because it facilitates knowledge sharing. A cybersecurity job can feel isolating, especially in small organizations where there are not many staff members dedicated to cybersecurity. Professional associations that provide local in-person events aimed at connecting professionals with similar interest in solving the same cybersecurity issues offer valuable opportunities for their members to discuss shared problems and potential solutions. For this reason, despite their drawbacks in comparison with other fields, we still find certification a benefit for all organizations with even one staff member who is certified and pays the dues necessary to attend these events.

6.4 Cybersecurity Job Roles

Though efforts to add to the workforce are sorely needed, simply adding to the workforce does nothing to reduce the confusion on how job roles should be assigned to those who have attempted to prepare themselves for a cybersecurity profession. As described in Chapter 1, the CISO role has a widely diverse set of responsibilities depending on the organization in which they work, and it is also not uncommon for the lower-level cybersecurity job labels in different organizations to specify different skill sets and roles and responsibilities. Unlike the professions that require actual licenses or engineering certifications, there is only plausible likelihood, much less a guarantee, that someone in a cybersecurity job role in any organization would have the skill set to perform the same job role in another.

A good example is a Security Operations (SecOps) Analyst job role. In the 1990s, it was one of a three-person staff that covered eight-hour shifts. The new shift came in every day and took a hand-off of current status from the prior one, then spent their time sifting through user and system activity and change logs, reconciling activity revealed in the logs with authorized behavior. A decade later, these activities were fully automated and the SecOps job was to monitor a screen that alerted them to the anomalies to investigate by looking at the logs that were the cause of the alerts. They spent the rest of their time performing rote tasks, such as creating incident trend-over-time reports and fielding user requests for unusual security configurations. There would be a security architect or a technology administrator who had designed the environment in which SecOps worked. Today, in organizations where incidents are few and far between, that person may be performing the SecOps role. Larger organizations may have a larger security architect team, and some of their members may be escalation points for SecOps analysts that do not have the skills to investigate a given issue. Some of those people may also be escalation points for an Identity and Access Management team that has a problem

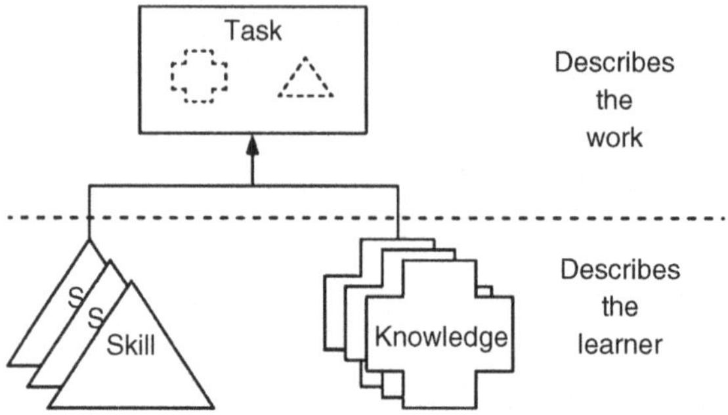

Figure 6.1 NICE Framework building blocks approach. *Source:* Petersen et al. (2020) / US Department of Commerce / Public domain.

trying to configure user permissions. A typical CISO organization is constantly redesigning job roles to match the skills sets they have available.

In an attempt to resolve this issue within the federal government, the National Institute of Standards and Technology was charged with publishing a National Initiative for Cybersecurity Education (NICE) Framework (Petersen et al. 2020). It is a detailed map of cybersecurity work, dividing it into 7 major categories and 45 job roles. Each category breaks down into roles. Each role has a list of tasks, knowledge, and skills required to perform it (Petersen et al. 2020). As depicted in Figure 6.1, each role has three components aimed at connecting the *work*, or the job assignment, with the *learner*, the person in or aspiring to be in the job. These are:

Tasks: One or more activities directed toward the achievement of business objectives, technology objectives, or mission objectives for cybersecurity.
Skills: One or more capabilities needed to perform an activity in a task.
Knowledge: One or more memory-retrievable set of concepts needed to complete a given task.

NICE supplements these job role definitions with advice on how to assess worker competency in a given combination of tasks, skills, and knowledge.

NICE calls the SecOps job role Defensive Cybersecurity. The job description is: "Responsible for analyzing data collected from various cybersecurity defense tools to mitigate risks." It contains 43 tasks, 38 skills, and 125 Knowledge concepts. This classification approach allows the agencies who use it to write job postings that describe work similar to that performed by those with the same job title in other agencies.

The US Office of Personnel Management is charged with using this framework to classify every federal cybersecurity position. It is intended to achieve consistency across the government in how these jobs are defined, paid, and evaluated.

While its use outside the government is not widespread, it is theoretically possible that schools and certification programs could use it to show how their courses map to NICE job requirements, and some are doing this. Students can theoretically use it to decide what skills they have and what they still need to be qualified for a given job.

One reason that adoption of NICE is not widespread is that NICE is chasing a moving target, and government bureaucracy can rarely keep up with rapid change. Though the literature stresses that organizations can and should customize their job roles as they see fit, job role creation in any organization has always been more of an art than a science, and the burden of analyzing a catalog as opposed to understanding how an employee is constrained by their cybersecurity workforce skill set may not seem a good use of management time.

6.5 Conclusion

In comparison with physical law enforcement, whose job functions have remained fairly static for decades, unless the organization is the size of the federal government with rote incident analysis tasks taking the time of multiple people, as opposed to the resident expert performing them a few times a year, cybersecurity jobs rarely stay the same for more than a few years. Though cybersecurity professionals have borrowed heavily from first responders and the military in their approach to incident response and threat avoidance, we all too well understand the evolving nature of a profession chasing the tails of technology innovation, and the threat that commercial hype over untested cybersecurity "solutions" may replace an organization's systems security engineer's efforts to focus on zero trust.

Reflecting on the need for the cybersecurity workforce to improve as a profession, we remember a lesson from a forefather in cybersecurity, Dan Geer. Like many young people in the early days of the internet, he ended up in cybersecurity before there was even a university course on the subject. In those early days, many universities did not yet have degrees in computer science and were just experimenting with computer science courses in their electrical engineering departments. Geer well understood that a slim percentage of those early computer scientists worked in cybersecurity, and of those, a tiny fraction were professionally trained by computer security experts because these were scarce for decades, and computer security standards could not keep up with changes in technology. He worried that, as the profession became better defined, it would soon forget how immature we really are in an evolutionary sense, and that we might standardize approaches to cybersecurity that were inadequate to deal with the quickly changing threat landscape. In several publications and conference presentations over the past few decades, he communicated this fear with an analogy to the field in which he earned a PhD, biostatistics (e.g., Geer 2008). For example:

> *Today's leaders in the security field are all converts to it from other fields for the simple reason that when we began there was no training available. This will soon change as we are replaced by people with formal training, but when that happens, the renaissance quality of security will yield to the excellence that comes from crisp specialization. This is not bad, but it is different.*
>
> *Because this change will happen, it is imperative that we mine all the insights, all the ways of thinking we can from those other fields while they are still fully represented by the presence of trained practitioners from them in the security field. We simply do not have the time, and should not spend either the time or the coin to re-invent what is already known elsewhere and can be applied here.*
>
> *Civil engineers know why bridges fall down, lawyers know the difference between policy and enforcement, doctors know the terrible demands of making life-and-death decisions under uncertainty, public health practitioners know that the great triumphs over disease began with sewers not with antibiotics, preachers know that great thoughts cannot be transmitted without the vehicle of familiar tales in which to embed the higher principles, and on and on.*
>
> *This mixing of background traits is what in Nature would be called hybrid vigor. Hybrid vigor only lasts one generation; we must spend it with as much wisdom and perspicacity and dedication as we can muster.*
>
> *When it is gone, it is gone.*

References

Bogost, I. (2015). Stop calling yourselves engineers. The Atlantic. https://www.theatlantic.com/technology/archive/2015/11/programmers-should-not-call-themselves-engineers/414271/ (accessed 13 March 2026).

Columbia University (2026). Columbia University School of International and Public Affairs, Master of Public Administration. https://www.sipa.columbia.edu/sipa-education/masters-programs/master-public-administration (accessed 13 March 2026).

Cybersecurity Enhancement Act (2014). htpps://www.congress.gov/bill/113th-congress/senate-bill/1353 (accessed 13 March 2026).

Department of Defense (DoD) (2005). Information Assurance Workforce Improvement Program. Department of Defense, DoD 8570.01-M, superseded by DoD (2023). https://www.cool.osd.mil/usmc/ia_documents/DoD_8570.01M.pdf (accessed 13 March 2026).

Department of Defense (DoD) (2023). Cyberspace Workforce Qualification and Management Program. Office of the Department of Defense Chief Information Officer. 15 February 2023. https://dodcio.defense.gov/Portals/0/Documents/Library/DoDM-8140-03.pdf (accessed 11 March 2026).

Duke University (2026). Cybersecurity degree details. Duke University. https://masters.pratt.duke.edu/cybersecurity/degree/ (accessed 10 March 2026).

Geer, D. (2008). Learn by analogy or die trying, ClearText column in IEEE Security &Privacy. May/June 2008. http://geer.tinho.net/ieee/ieee.sp.geer.0805.pdf (accessed 31 March 2026).

Harbor Compliance (2026). 50-State engineering licensing compliance guide. Harbor Compliance. https://www.harborcompliance.com/engineer-license-requirements-registration.

International Organization for Standardization (ISO) (2008). Systems security engineering. ISO/IEC 21827. 16 October 2008.

Johns Hopkins University (JHU) (2026). Johns Hopkins University – Engineering Department – Online Masters. https://ep.jhu.edu/programs/cybersecurity/courses/ (accessed 10 March 2026).

Johns Hopkins University Information Security Institute (JHU ISI) (2026). Johns Hopkins University – Information Security Institute. https://e-catalogue.jhu.edu/engineering/full-time-residential-programs/degree-programs/information-security-institute/#programstext (accessed 10 March 2026).

Musser, M. (2025). The Problem of Liability Overexposure for Software, Lawfare, 2 September. https://www.lawfaremedia.org/article/the-problem-of-liability-overexposure-for-software (accessed 31 March 2026).

National Council of Architectural Registration Boards (NCARB) (2026). Licensing requirements tool. https://www.ncarb.org/get-licensed/licensing-requirements-tool (accessed 11 March 2026).

National Institute of Standards and Technology (NIST) (2020). Zero Trust Architecture Standard. https://nvlpubs.nist.gov/nistpubs/SpecialPublications/NIST.SP.800-207.pdf (accessed 13 March 2026).

National Science Foundation (2023). CyberCorps Scholarship for Service (SFS). https://new.nsf.gov/funding/opportunities/cybercorps-scholarship-service-sfs (accessed 13 March 2026).

National Security Agency (2024). National Centers of Academic Excellence in Cybersecurity NCAE-C 2024: Application process and adjudication rubric – cyber defense. https://dl.dod.cyber.mil/wp-content/uploads/cae/pdf/unclass-cae-cd_designation_requirements.pdf (accessed 13 March 2026).

National Security Agency (n.d.). National Centers of Academic Excellence in Cybersecurity. https://www.nsa.gov/Academics/Centers-of-Academic-Excellence/ (accessed 13 March 2026).

National Society of Professional Engineers (NSPE) (2026). What is a PE and why licensing matters. https://www.nspe.org/about/about-professional-engineering/what-pe (accessed 1 March 2026).

Petersen, R., et al. (2020). NIST special publication 800-181 revision 1: Workforce framework for cybersecurity (NICE framework). https://csrc.nist.gov/pubs/sp/800/181/r1/final (accessed 13 March 2026).

Randell, B. (1979). Software engineering in 1968. 4th International Conference on Software Engineering (ICSE). 17 September. https://dl.acm.org/doi/book/10.5555/800091 (accessed 13 March 2026).

Stevens Institute of Technology (2026). Degree in cybersecurity. https://www.stevens.edu/program/cybersecurity-bachelor-degree (accessed 10 March 2026).

7

One Government's Approach to Cybersecurity Policy

The modern era of cybersecurity policy is often described as a race between innovation and adaptation. Every advancement in digital technology from the first interconnected networks to today's artificial intelligence (AI) systems has brought corresponding challenges in governance, defense, and accountability. No government has been immune to these challenges, and few have wrestled with them as openly as the United States. Over three decades, the US federal government has moved from tentative awareness of digital risk to an institutionalized approach that treats cybersecurity as a cornerstone of national security, public safety, and economic stability.

This chapter examines that evolution in detail. It traces how successive administrations, legislative actions, and technological milestones have shaped the current framework of federal cybersecurity. Beginning with the early recognition of infrastructure interdependence in the 1990s and continuing through the establishment of the Cybersecurity and Infrastructure Security Agency (CISA), the Office of the National Cyber Director (ONCD), and the National Cybersecurity Strategy, the chapter shows how US cyber policy has evolved from ad hoc coordination to a comprehensive enterprise built on partnership, resilience, and shared responsibility. What follows is both a history and a roadmap, an account of how one government attempts to adapt to a domain that changes faster than any other in modern governance.

This chapter is accompanied by a timeline that shows the gradual progression of government actions across all sections. Figure 7.1 is a key of abbreviations for the type of government action taken and the name of the action is either above or below the key, depending on its position within the timeline.

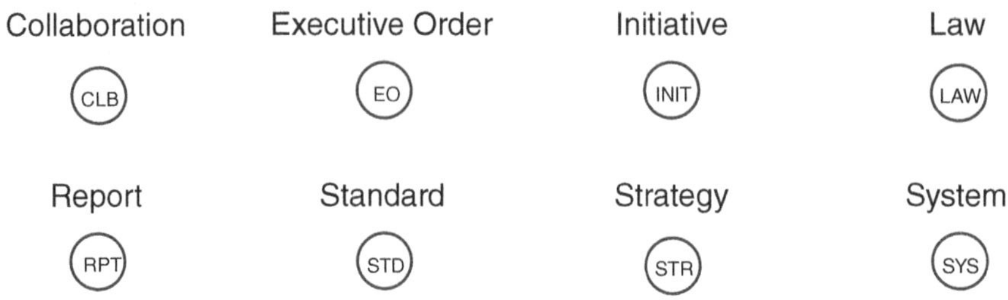

Figure 7.1 Timeline key.

7.1 US Federal Cybersecurity Strategy

The US federal government's policy attitude toward cybersecurity has ranged from enforcing cyber defense standards developed by the National Institute of Standards and Technology (NIST) and the National Security Agency (NSA) to wide variations of proposals, initiatives, and directives across administrations and agencies. At any given time, several dozen bills related to cybersecurity are in various stages of construction in the US Senate and the US House of Representatives. Many of these bills are rewritten versions of efforts started by a previous Congress, and some of them are brand new efforts. None of the legislation will alone "fix" the cybersecurity problems faced by our nation. In fact, it is probably inappropriate for any cybersecurity policy professional to believe that a single Act of Congress will make much difference in securing cyberspace. That said, a series of incremental laws such as the Federal Information Security Modernization Act (FISMA 2014), the Cybersecurity Information Sharing Act (2015), and the Cybersecurity and Infrastructure Security Agency Act (2018) have gradually strengthened federal authorities and created enduring institutions, such as CISA.

There have of course been many attempts to articulate cybersecurity policy via Congressional action or via actions taken directly by government agencies. For example, the establishment of the ONCD in 2021 added strategic coordination and budget oversight to these ongoing efforts, complementing CISA's operational mission within the Department of Homeland Security (DHS). There are also many assumptions and misunderstandings about the convergence of policy and strategy. Pure strategy is just a blueprint for how a decision maker would like things to work. To instantiate strategy, policy is combined with process, procedure, standards, and enforcement. Depending on the strategy, the list of things required to manifest it may be incomplete. Moreover, even well-planned and executed attempts to instantiate a strategy may sometimes fail to achieve strategy goals. This is especially true in environments that evolve as strategy is being executed, such as in the fast changing world of cyberspace. Recent federal strategies such as the National Cybersecurity Strategy (2023) have emphasized this point by shifting from static compliance toward measurable resilience, integration of Zero Trust principles, and greater accountability for software and hardware providers.

But cyber policy is not just the domain of the federal government. In the first decade of the 2000s, it became clear that identity theft was an issue that would likely be the subject of public policy debates. At that time, the major credit card companies likely to be targeted by any potential legislation formed the Payment Card Industry Security Standards Council (PCISSC), which in turn created the Payment Card Industry Data Security Standard (PCISSC 2024). The standards were adopted to demonstrate compliance with existing financial privacy protection policy and, the cynical among us would guess, to thwart the perception that there was any need for any further legislation. However, even after the standards were adopted, major payment processors who were compliant with the industry-created standards were the victims of massive data breaches that led directly to identity theft. This illustrates the fact that standards and policy are very different things, and standards that are designed to achieve policy compliance do not necessarily do so. Similar lessons will continue to emerge in the modern era, where compliance frameworks, no matter how well intended, often lag behind evolving threats such as ransomware, supply-chain compromise, and AI-enabled attacks.

Understanding how the United States arrived at its current approach to cybersecurity requires examining three decades of evolving national priorities. The nation's policy has been shaped not by a single master plan, but by a succession of events, such as terrorist attacks, data breaches, acts of cyber espionage, and technological revolutions that revealed new vulnerabilities faster than government could adapt. Each administration responded within its own political and technological context, gradually expanding the federal role from awareness and protection of critical infrastructure to the broader concepts of deterrence, resilience, and whole-of-nation defense.

7.2 Infrastructure Awareness and Early Coordination

The modern era of federal cybersecurity policy began not with cyber warfare, but with infrastructure awareness. During the 1990s, policymakers gradually recognized that the nation's economic and security systems were becoming increasingly dependent on networked information technologies. Early initiatives focused on identifying critical sectors, promoting voluntary information sharing, and understanding how physical and digital systems were interdependent. Although these efforts lacked centralized authority and enforcement mechanisms, they marked the first acknowledgment that cybersecurity was not merely a technical problem, but a national resilience concern.

This section reviews several physical and cyber events from the bombing of the World Trade Center (WTC) in 1993 to the terrorist attacks on the United States in 2001 that set the stage for initial cyber policy decisions. Although some of these incidents were not purely cyber in nature, each revealed systemic interdependencies and information vulnerabilities that would later shape national cyber policy. Each also resulted in new policy initiatives. The section concludes with a brief discussion of policies implemented prior to the end of 2001.

7.2.1 The Bombing of New York's World Trade Center

The first major terrorist attack on US soil since a 1920 Trinitrotoluene (TNT) bombing on Wall Street that killed 35 people was meant to topple the city's tallest tower onto its twin, amid a cloud of cyanide gas. Had the attack in 1993 gone as planned, tens of thousands of Americans would have died. Instead, one tower did not fall on the other. Rather than vaporizing, the cyanide gas burned up in the heat of the explosion. "Only" six people died and over a thousand were injured. Details of the attack were later found on the terrorist's laptop computer, the first known case of a terrorist using a personal computer to keep track of plans and operational information. Within a month of the blast, four individuals thought responsible for the attack were apprehended. The suspects went on trial on September 13, 1993. The trial lasted six months with the presentation of 204 witnesses and more than 1,000 pieces of evidence. A jury convicted the four defendants on March 4, 1994, in federal court on all 38 counts against them. On May 25, 1994, a judge sentenced each of the four defendants to 240 years in prison and a $250,000 fine.

Few Americans are aware of the true scale of the destructive ambition behind the bombing, despite the fact that two years later, the key figure responsible for building it: a man who had entered the United States on an Iraqi passport under the name of Ramzi Yousef. Yousef was involved in another stupendous bombing conspiracy. In January 1995, Yousef and his associates plotted to blow up eleven US commercial aircraft in one spectacular day of terrorist rage. The bombs were to be made of a liquid explosive designed to pass through airport metal detectors.

But while mixing his chemical brew in a Manila apartment, Yousef started a fire. He was forced to flee, leaving behind a computer that contained the information that led to his arrest on February 7, 1995, in Pakistan. Among the items found in his possession was a letter threatening Filipino interests if a comrade held in custody was not released. It claimed the "ability to make and use chemicals and poisonous gas … for use against vital institutions and residential populations and the sources of drinking water" (Mylroie 1995/1996). Pakistan subsequently turned him over to US authorities where he was sentenced to 240 years in prison on January 8, 1998.

7.2.2 Cyber Attacks Against the United States Air Force

The computer network at Rome Labs, an Air Force facility in New York, came under a cyberattack in the spring of 1994. The attack was eventually traced to two young hackers, Kuji and Datastream Cowboy, who originated in the United Kingdom but were using various points of access to hack into other Air Force facilities and NATO (GAO 1996).

Datastream Cowboy was 16-year-old Richard Pryce, then a pupil at The Purcell School in Harrow, Middlesex, UK. He was arrested at his home on May 12, 1994, but released on police bail the same evening. He later pleaded guilty and was fined. Kuji was 21-year-old Mathew Bevan, a soft-spoken computer worker with a fascination for science fiction. He was arrested on June 21, 1996, at the offices of Admiral Insurance in Cardiff in the UK where he worked. He was an Israeli citizen and found not guilty because no Israeli laws applied to this type of incident.

How did two rather ordinary young men manage to penetrate the military computer system and trigger such a significant response? Pryce easily gained low-level security access to the Rome computer using a default guest password. Once inside the system, he retrieved the password file and downloaded it onto his computer. He then ran a program to bombard the password file with 50,000 guesses a second. A Scotland Yard investigator on the case testified that Pryce cracked the file because a lieutenant in the United States Air Force (USAF) had used the password Carmen (Ripatrazone n.d.). It was the name of his pet ferret. Once Pryce had the lieutenant's password, he was free to roam the system and access classified and highly confidential information.

7.2.3 The Citibank Caper

In mid-1994, an organized Russian crime gang successfully transferred $10 million from Citibank to different bank accounts all over the world. Now known as the Citibank Caper (Harmon 1995), this incident was partially responsible for prompting the *Security in Cyberspace* hearings in the United States chaired by Senator Sam Nunn (US Senate Committee 1996).

By most measures, those responsible for the Citibank Caper were not world-class hackers, just really poor money launderers. When bank and federal officials began monitoring activities of a hacker moving cash through Citibank's central wire transfer department, they were clueless about where the attack originated. Monitoring began in July and continued into October, during which there were 40 transactions. Cash was moved from accounts as far away as Argentina and Indonesia to bank accounts in San Francisco, Finland, Russia, Switzerland, Germany, and Israel. In the end, all but $400,000 taken before monitoring began was recovered.

The break came on August 5 of that year, when the hacker moved $218,000 from the account of an Indonesian businessman to a BankAmerica account in San Francisco. Federal agents found that account was held by Evgeni and Erina Korolkov of St. Petersburg, Russia. When Erina Korolkov flew to San Francisco to make a withdrawal in late August, she was arrested. By September, recognizing a St. Petersburg link, authorities traveled to Russia. A review of phone records found that Citibank computers were being accessed at AO Saturn, a company specializing in computer software, where Vladimir Levin worked. By late October, confident it had identified the hacker, Citibank changed its codes and passwords, shutting the door to the hacker. In late December, Korolkov began cooperating. Levin and Evgeni Korolkov were arrested at Stansted Airport, outside London, on a US warrant on March 4, 1995. Unknown is how the hacker obtained passwords and codes assigned to bank employees in Pompano, Florida, and how he learned to maneuver through the system. Citibank says it has found no evidence of insider cooperation with the hacker.

7.2.4 Murrah Federal Building, Oklahoma City

At 9:02 am on April 19, 1995, a truck bomb destroyed the front half of the Alfred P. Murrah Federal Building in Oklahoma City, killing 168 citizens, including 19 children, and injuring more than 500. The powerful blast left a 30 ft. wide, 8 ft. deep crater on the front of the building. Local responders, fire fighters, police force, and urban search and rescue teams rushed to the scene. Within seven hours, the president ordered deployment of local, state, and federal resources. This was the first time that the president's authority under the Stafford Act (Stafford 1974, section 501b) was used, granting Federal Emergency Management Agency (FEMA) primary federal responsibility for responding to a domestic consequence management incident.

The deliberate destruction of the Midwestern office building, located far outside the "nerve centers" of Washington and New York City, had a much larger impact than just the loss of lives and property. Government officials soon discovered that the explosion was felt by other government agencies and private sector businesses across the United States, due to the disruption of functions and data housed in the Murrah building.

The Murrah building housed several federal offices including the Drug Enforcement Agency, the Bureau of Alcohol, Tobacco, and Firearms, US Customs Service, US Department of Housing and Urban Development, Veterans Administration, Social Security Administration, and others.

Because of the computer and information system functions located there, government officials found that the loss of a seemingly insignificant federal building set off a chain reaction that impacted parts of the government far away from Oklahoma. Beyond the loss of human lives and physical infrastructure, many sets of processes controlled from that building were also lost, with an unexpected impact on other agencies, employees, and the private sector down the supply chain and far away from the physical destruction of the building. This made clear that interdependencies between infrastructures, and remote vulnerabilities, were major issues.

7.2.5 Presidential Decision Directive 39

Concerns about terrorism have been raised by US officials since the 1970s. However, it was not until after the Vice President's Task Force on Terrorism issued its report in 1985 that US policy was formalized. The following year, the Reagan Administration issued National Security Decision Directive 207 (NSDD 207 1986), which focused primarily on law enforcement (crisis) activities resulting from terrorist incidents abroad. It tasked the National Security Council (NSC) with sponsoring an Interagency Working Group to coordinate the national response and designated lead federal agencies for both foreign and domestic terrorist incidents. The State Department was designated as the lead agency for international terrorism policy, procedures, and programs, and the Federal Bureau of Investigation (FBI) was designated as the lead agency for dealing with acts of terrorism. No additional major policy changes were implemented in the federal structure until 1995.

Two months after the Oklahoma City bombing in April 1995, the President Bill Clinton administration issued Presidential Decision Directive 39 (PDD 39 1995), which expanded upon NSDD 207 and directed the Attorney General to lead a government-wide effort to re-examine the adequacy of the available infrastructure protection. As a result, Attorney General Janet Reno convened a working group to investigate the issue and report back to the cabinet with policy options. The review, which was completed in early February 1996, highlighted the lack of attention that had been given to protecting the cyber infrastructure of critical information systems and computer networks.

Thus, the topic of cyber threats was linked to the topics of critical infrastructure protection and terrorism. Subsequently, the Clinton administration began development of a national protection strategy with his Presidential Commission on Critical Infrastructure Protection (PCCIP) in 1996 (PCCIP 1997), and the issue has stayed a high priority since.

7.2.6 President's Commission on Critical Infrastructure Protection

The PCCIP was formed by Executive Order 13010 (Executive Order 13010 1996, section 501b), Critical Infrastructure Protection. An excerpt is below and illustrates the deep understanding that the Clinton administration had about the importance of protecting the nation's critical infrastructure.

> Certain national infrastructures are so vital that their incapacity or destruction would have a debilitating impact on the defense or economic security of the United States. These critical infrastructures include telecommunications, electrical power systems, gas and oil storage and transportation, banking and finance, transportation, water supply systems, emergency services (including medical, police, fire, and rescue), and continuity of government. Threats to these critical infrastructures fall into two categories: physical threats to tangible property ("physical threats"), and threats of electronic, radio-frequency, or computer-based attacks on the information or communications components that control critical infrastructures ("cyber threats"). Because many of these critical infrastructures are owned and operated by the private sector, it is essential that the government and private sector work together to develop a strategy for protecting them and assuring their continued operation
>
> (Executive Order 13010 1996).

The PCCIP was chaired by retired Air Force General Robert (Tom) Marsh and became known as the Marsh Commission. The Commission's final report, *Critical Foundations*, was issued in October 1997 and both formalized the descriptions of the major infrastructures as well as defined threats to them (PCCIP 1997). It also recommended a series of policies for the federal government, the majority of which became Presidential Decision Directive 63 (PDD 63) in May 1998.

7.2.7 Eligible Receiver

In the summer of 1997, the US Joint Chiefs of Staff organized what is known as a "no-notice" exercise that would test the ability of the Department of Defense's (DoD) to detect and defend against a coordinated cyberattack against various military installations and critical computer networks. It would involve dozens of world-class computer hackers and last for more than a week. The Joint Chiefs gave the highly classified exercise the code name "Eligible Receiver 97." The operational details of how the Red Team of "pretend" hackers would carry out their attacks were left to senior officials from the NSA.

Prior to launching their attacks on June 9, officials briefed the team of 35 NSA computer hackers on the ground rules. They were told that they were allowed to use only software tools and other hacking utilities that could be downloaded freely from the internet. The DoD's own arsenal of classified attack tools could not be used. The team was also prohibited from breaking any US laws. The primary target was the US Pacific Command in Hawaii. Other targets included the National Military Command Center in the Pentagon, the US Space Command in Colorado, the US Transportation Command in Ohio, and the Special Operations Command in Florida.

Posing as hackers hired by the North Korean intelligence service, the NSA Red Team dispersed around the country and began digging their way into military networks. The team gained unfettered access to dozens of critical DoD computer systems. They were free to create legitimate user accounts for other hackers, delete valid accounts, reformat hard drives, read e-mail, and scramble data. They did all of this without being traced or identified.

The results of the exercise stunned officials, including the senior members of the NSA responsible for running it. Not only were the attackers potentially able to disrupt and cripple Defense command and control systems, but analysis of their techniques after the exercise ended revealed that much of the private sector infrastructure in the United States, such as the telecommunications networks and power grids, could easily be sent into a tailspin using the same tools and techniques.

Nevertheless, the success of the NSA Red team had some auspicious revelations. If they were that adept at cyber offense skills, some wondered in what program these were honed, though little was officially documented because, as noted in Chapter 2, "The first rule of the zero day market was: Nobody talks about the zero day market."

7.2.8 Solar Sunrise

In February 1998, several US military system administrators reported a coordinated attack aimed at dozens of unclassified computer systems. The intruders accessed unclassified logistics, administration, and accounting systems that controlled the DoD's ability to manage and deploy military forces. Then-US Deputy Secretary of Defense John J. Hamre called it "the most organized and systematic attack to date" on US military computer systems. Although the attacks exploited a well-known vulnerability in the Solaris operating system for which a patch had been available for months, they came at a time of heightened tension in the Persian Gulf. Secretary Hamre and other top officials were convinced that they were witnessing a sophisticated state-sponsored Iraqi effort to disrupt troop deployment in the Middle East.

The US response to this incident required a massive, cooperative effort by the FBI, the Justice Department's Computer Crimes Section, the Air Force Office of Special Investigations, the National Aeronautics and Space Administration, the Defense Information Systems Agency, the NSA, the Central Intelligence Agency, and various computer emergency response teams from the military services and government agencies.

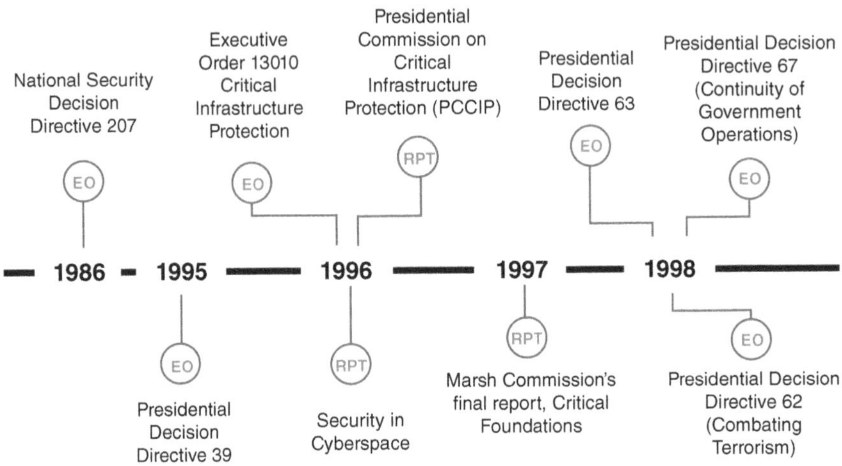

Timeline 1 1986–1998.

In the end, it was found that two young hackers in California had carried out the attacks under the direction of a hacker in Israel, himself a teenager. They gained privileged access to computers using tools available from a university web site and installed sniffer programs to collect user passwords. They created a backdoor and then used a patch available from another university web site to fix the vulnerability and prevent others from repeating their exploit. Unlike most hackers, they did not explore the contents of the victim computers.

Today, defense officials continue to point to Solar Sunrise as illustrative of the difficulty of separating recreational hacking attacks from the state-sponsored cyber assaults that they are still certain are on the horizon. Law enforcement, meanwhile, holds this investigation up as a textbook example of interagency cybercrime cooperation.

7.2.9 Presidential Decision Directive 63

Presidential Decision Directive 63 built on the recommendations of the PCCIP and was further informed by the Eligible Receiver exercise and the Solar Sunrise incident. The Commission's report called for a national effort to assure the security of the United States' increasingly vulnerable and interconnected infrastructures, such as telecommunications, banking and finance, energy, transportation, and essential government services. PDD 63 was the culmination of an intense, interagency effort to evaluate those recommendations and produce a workable and innovative framework for critical infrastructure protection.

Also in 1998, and also as a result of lessons learned from the Oklahoma City bombing, the Clinton administration published PDD 62 (Combating Terrorism) (PDD 62 1998) and PDD 67 (Continuity of Government Operations) (PDD 67 1998) that, together with PDD 63, form a triad of national policy aimed at addressing weaknesses in various parts of the nation's government systems and infrastructures. PDD 62 created the position of National Coordinator for Security, Infrastructure Protection and Counterterrorism under the NSC.

PDD 63 was the first national policy on critical infrastructure protection creating the framework in which critical infrastructure protection policy would evolve. It created four new organizations:

The **National Infrastructure Protection Center** (NIPC) at the FBI fused representatives from FBI, DoD, United States Secret Service (USSS), Energy, Transportation, the Intelligence Community, and the private sector in an attempt at information sharing among agencies in collaboration with the private sector. The NIPC provided the principal means of facilitating and coordinating the Federal Government's response to an incident, mitigating attacks, investigating threats, and monitoring reconstitution efforts. The NIPC was absorbed into DHS in 2003.

An **Information Sharing and Analysis Center** (ISAC) was encouraged to be established by the private sector in cooperation with the Federal government and modeled on the Centers for Disease Control and Prevention. Today, there are dozens of ISACs in many sectors of the economy. Several countries have created similar organizations for their industries and economic sectors.

The **National Infrastructure Assurance Council** (NIAC) was to be drawn from private sector leaders and state and local officials to provide guidance to the policy formulation of a National Plan. The NIAC was never established. A new "NIAC" – the National Infrastructure Advisory Council — was created by Executive Order 13231 (Executive Order 13231 2001) and serves to provide the President with advice on the security of information systems for critical infrastructure supporting the banking and finance, transportation, energy, manufacturing, and emergency government services sectors of the economy.

The **Critical Infrastructure Assurance Office** (CIAO) was created in the Department of Commerce (DoC) with the responsibility for coordinating the development of critical infrastructure sector plans by the private sector and their respective federal agency liaisons. Based on the content of the sector plans, CIAO assisted in producing the first National Plan for Information Systems Protection (NPISP). The office also helped coordinate a national education and awareness program, and legislative and public affairs programs. The CIAO was absorbed into newly created DHS in 2003.

7.2.10 National Infrastructure Protection Center (NIPC) and Information Sharing and Analysis Centers (ISACs)

The NIPC had its roots in the Infrastructure Protection Task Force (IPTF), created at the FBI in 1996 to increase the coordination of existing infrastructure protection efforts to better address, and prevent, crises that would have a debilitating regional or national impact. The IPTF was placed at the FBI to take advantage of the FBI's newly established Computer Investigations and Infrastructure Threat Assessment Center (CITAC), also created in 1996 to deal with computer crime.

Under PDD 63, the FBI was directed to bring together representatives from US government agencies, state and local governments, and the private sector in a partnership to protect US critical infrastructures. The NIPC was created in 1998 at the FBI to serve as the US government's focal point for threat assessment, warning, investigation, and response for threats or attacks against critical infrastructures. The NIPC's function was transferred to DHS in 2003.

PDD 63 assigned to industries the task of creating an ISAC, through which companies could share information about attacks, threats, and vulnerabilities. The ISAC (singular) was intended to be the NIPC's contact for warning industries about potential threats. Eventually several ISACs were created for railroad, electric, energy, financial services, and information technology companies. In addition to footing the bill for these councils, companies involved had to be willing to overcome reticence about their own vulnerabilities to share information needed to protect national infrastructure. Several more ISACs were created after the initial group, but unfortunately most are today diminished in operational effectiveness from where they were earlier. Information sharing is hard and depends on building mutual trust between the people (not just the organizations) who participate in them.

In 1998, federal investigators at the NIPC uncovered a sophisticated and persistent intrusion campaign targeting unclassified networks at the DoD, NASA, the Department of Energy (DoE), and several research institutions. The operation, later referred to as "Moonlight Maze," involved systematic exfiltration of technical data, military maps, and research materials over an extended period. Unlike Solar Sunrise, which was initially misattributed to a hostile state before being traced to teenagers, Moonlight Maze was widely believed to involve foreign intelligence services. The campaign revealed both the difficulty of attribution and the strategic value adversaries placed on long-term access to US government systems. It reinforced the emerging understanding that cyber intrusions were not merely criminal acts, but instruments of geopolitical intelligence competition.

7.2.11 Joint Task Force – Computer Network Defense (JTF-CND)

In response to the findings of the Marsh Commission, the results of Eligible Receiver 1997, and the lessons learned from the Solar Sunrise incident, the DoD began exploring several options for dealing with the clear dangers that were growing from the nation's increased dependency on cyberspace. After months of deliberation and heated discussions, the decision was made to create a Joint Task Force (JTF) that would serve as an operational organization outside of the Intelligence Community rather than as an arm of the Intelligence Community as many wanted, and would have authority to direct technical changes to DoD computers and networks for cyber defense purposes.

Launched in December 1998, the Joint Task Force-Computer Network Defense (JTF-CND) was initially assigned to the Secretary of Defense (SECDEF). Following the pace of technology change, like a hot potato, it changed hands quickly (Healey 2025, part 2):

1999: Assigned to the United States Space Command (USSPACECOM).

2000: Redesignated as the Joint Task Force-Computer Network Operations (JTF-CNO).

2002: In conjunction with the merger of USSPACECOM with the United States Strategic Command (STRATCOM), became a component of STRATCOM.

2004: SECDEF redesignated the organization as the Joint Task Force-Global Network Operations (JTF-GNO) and appointed the Defense Information Systems Agency (DISA) Director to be assigned as its Commander. The JTF-GNO was given authorities and responsibilities for global network operations and defense. It used these authorities to form the Global NetOps Center (GNC), through the functional merger of elements from the JTF-GNO's Operations Directorate, DISA's Global Network Operations and Security Center (GNOSC), the DoD Computer Emergency Response Team (DoD-CERT), and the Global Satellite Communications (SATCOM) Support Center. As such, the GNC was responsible for guiding, directing, and overseeing daily compliance with NetOps policy, providing common defense of the DoD's Global Information Grid (GIG), and ensuring strategic priorities for information are satisfied.

2008: The JTF-GNO function was assigned to the NSA.

2009: SECDEF ordered STRATCOM to "disestablish" the JTF-GNO not later than 2010 as part of the activation of a new *Cyber Command*, established in 2008, see below.

2010: JTF-GNO colors were cased, a time-honored military tradition of ending a mission.

7.3 Homeland Security and Federal Consolidation

The terrorist attacks against the United States of September 11, 2001, accelerated federal efforts to consolidate responsibility for infrastructure protection and homeland security. Cybersecurity became embedded within a broader national security architecture, culminating in the creation of DHS and the issuance of directives clarifying federal roles. During this period, executive-level cybersecurity initiatives evolved from advisory frameworks into structured federal programs, including the National Infrastructure Protection Plan (NIPP) and the Comprehensive National Cybersecurity Initiative (CNCI). The focus shifted from awareness to enterprise-wide coordination and federal network defense.

7.3.1 Terrorist Attacks Against the United States

September 11 exposed not only weaknesses in physical security, airline security, law enforcement investigations, and intelligence analysis, but also demonstrated the close interdependence of the critical infrastructure in lower Manhattan, New York City.

Beneath the streets of New York City, as in most large cities, are miles of tunnels, conduits, pathways, and routes for various infrastructures. When the WTC towers collapsed, hundreds of tons of steel and concrete impacted the surrounding area, severing underground utilities, destroying telecommunications switches, and pulverizing power distribution transformers and backup generators.

On the morning of September 11, a Verizon/NYNEX building adjacent to the WTC site did not collapse, but it, along with many other buildings bordering the WTC complex, suffered significant damage. Not visible in the many photos taken that day was the chaos under the sidewalks and streets. The fiber optic and copper cabling entered the Verizon building from below the streets and had been physically damaged by large steel girders that pierced the sidewalks to a depth of several feet. Millions of gallons of water from broken water mains, steam lines, and the Hudson River rushed into the underground conduits that carried not only the telecommunications cables but also pneumatic mailing tubes, electrical cables, and other infrastructure. Several large bundles of underground fiber optic cables just outside of the Verizon building were literally sliced in half by the debris, then encased in water, mud, and steam escaping from broken high-pressure lines.

For several weeks after September 11, the sidewalks of the area around the WTC complex were covered with miles of above-ground power and communications cables. Because the underground conduits were so badly damaged, Verizon and Con Edison quickly decided to restore operations by using a street-level network.

A similar situation existed in the basement of the Pentagon directly below the impact point of American Flight 77. One of the two major Pentagon internet gateways was impacted by the crash but continued to function thanks to the quick thinking of an employee who was able to crawl into the damaged space with an extension cord to power the routers. The devices were still functioning when the overhead debris was removed several days later.

Many lessons about the communications infrastructure's vulnerabilities to a physical attack were learned following September 11. Unfortunately, it was discovered that the redundancy previously engineered in the networks had been largely reduced due to years of telephone company mergers and acquisitions. For example, the New York Stock Exchange had designed over a dozen separate communications paths, with roughly half of them terminating at the West Street Verizon building and the remainder traveling over diverse routes to other switching offices further north. On September 11, there were still over a dozen "separate paths," but they were only virtual as all but one physically terminated at the Verizon building. And that last connection was the only one that survived the destruction that morning.

7.3.2 US Government Response to the September 11, 2001, Terrorist Attacks

The United States Commission on National Security in the 21st Century (USCNS/21 2000) had issued a set of national policy recommendations in April 2000 – well before the September terrorist attacks – in a report titled *Seeking a National Strategy*. Chaired by former Senators Gary Hart (D) and Warren Rudman (R), the so-called Hart-Rudman Commission echoed earlier reports, speaking anxiously of the inevitability of a major terrorist act on US soil and of the nation's weak ability to prevent or respond to such an attack, concerns which were validated a year and a half later on September 11.

Among other things, the Commission called for the creation of a new federal agency, to be named the National Homeland Security Agency. The new organization's mission would be "to consolidate and refine the missions of the nearly two dozen disparate departments and agencies that have a role in US homeland security today." Although neither Hart-Rudman nor the earlier Gilmore Commission (1999) focused specifically on critical infrastructure, the reports nonetheless reinforced the basic message of the 1996/97 PCCIP: *the time for action was now, not later*.

While agreeing with Hart-Rudman that a central coordinating point for "homeland security" was called for, the President George W. Bush administration initially chose to establish the function on September 20, 2001, within the White House under the title of Office of Homeland Security (OHS). As was the situation with the JTF-CND, OHS had several transitions. In October 2001, it became the Homeland Security Council (HSC). Political pressures then led to the creation of a Cabinet-level organization, and DHS was formed in November 2002. After it was activated in 2003, the OHS/HSC director, former Pennsylvania Governor Tom Ridge, was named the nation's first Secretary of Homeland Security. For a while, the HSC continued as a separately staffed organization but in 2009, the President Barack Obama administration consolidated the National Security and Homeland Security councils into a single National Security Staff. The NSC and HSC now exist by statute as separate advisory councils to the President, supported by a single staff.

Also following the September 11 attacks, the Bush administration issued Executive Order 13231, *Critical Infrastructure Protection in the Information Age*, making cybersecurity a priority and accordingly, increasing funds to secure federal networks. EO 13231 created two new White House organizations, the White House Office of Cyber Space Security and the President's Critical Infrastructure Protection Board (PCIPB). While both organizations were officially part of the new HSC, the Cybersecurity Office was located in the Eisenhower Executive Office Building (EEOB) and was considered to be part of the NSC staff. The PCIPB offices were strategically located a few blocks from the EEOB, outside of the tight White House security perimeter, thus allowing for easier access to coordinate inter-agency actions and to involve the private sector in the development of a future National Strategy to Secure Cyberspace.

After DHS was activated early in 2003, the National Cyberspace Security Division (NCSD) was created in June. The United States Computer Emergency Readiness Team (CERT) was activated in September, operated jointly by the NCSD and the CERT Coordination Center at Carnegie Mellon University as a single point of contact for addressing emerging national cyberspace security issues.

7.3.3 Homeland Security Presidential Directives in the Bush Administration

Since its creation in 1947, the NSC has been the principal forum for presidential consideration of foreign policy issues and national security matters. In the process of developing policy recommendations for the president, the NSC gathers facts and views of government agencies, and then conducts analyses, determines alternatives, and presents to the president policy choices. The president's decisions are then announced via decision directives. Because the Bush administration had both an NSC and an HSC, there were two sets of decision directives published during his two terms in office – National Security Presidential Directives (NSPDs) and Homeland Security Presidential Directives (HSPDs).

Three of the Bush administration's HSPDs illustrate how different types of cybersecurity policies can ultimately become presidential decision directives.

- HSPD 7 (HSPD 7 2003) replaced PDD 63 and established a national policy for federal departments and agencies to identify and prioritize United States critical infrastructure and key resources and to protect them from terrorist attacks. It tasked the Secretary of Homeland Security with coordinating the overall national effort to enhance the protection of the critical infrastructure and designated other departments and agencies with sector-specific responsibilities. It also increased the number of critical sectors to seventeen (an eighteenth sector – critical manufacturing—was added in 2009).

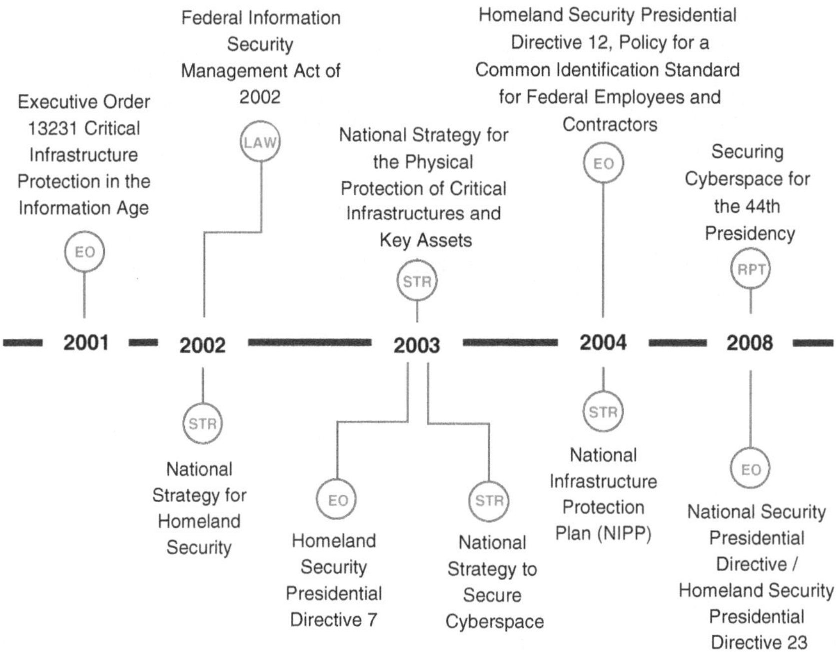

Timeline 2 2001–2008.

- HSPD 12 introduced the requirement for a common identification system for all federal employees and federal contractors (HSPD 12 2004).
- HSPD 23 (also published as NSPD 54) outlined a 12-point comprehensive plan for securing the federal government's own networks as well as networks in the private sector that support the critical infrastructure (NSPD 54 2008). This plan is commonly known as the Comprehensive National Cybersecurity Initiative (CNCI).

The following paragraphs from HSPD 7 show how the sectors were realigned after the creation of DHS:

> (15) The Secretary [of Homeland Security] shall coordinate protection activities for each of the following critical infrastructure sectors: information technology; telecommunications; chemical; transportation systems, including mass transit, aviation, maritime, ground/surface, and rail and pipeline systems; emergency services; and postal and shipping. The Department [of Homeland Security] shall coordinate with appropriate departments and agencies to ensure the protection of other key resources including dams, government facilities, and commercial facilities. In addition, in its role as overall cross-sector coordinator, the Department shall

also evaluate the need for and coordinate the coverage of additional critical infrastructure and key resources categories over time, as appropriate.

(18) Recognizing that each infrastructure sector possesses its own unique characteristics and operating models, there are designated Sector-Specific Agencies, including:

a) Department of Agriculture – agriculture, food (meat, poultry, egg products);
b) Health and Human Services – public health, healthcare, and food (other than meat, poultry, egg products);
c) Environmental Protection Agency – drinking water and water treatment systems;
d) Department of Energy – energy, including the production refining, storage, and distribution of oil and gas, and electric power except for commercial nuclear power facilities;
e) Department of the Treasury – banking and finance;
f) Department of the Interior – national monuments and icons; and
g) Department of Defense – defense industrial base.

(19) In accordance with guidance provided by the Secretary [of Homeland Security], Sector-Specific Agencies shall:

a) collaborate with all relevant Federal departments and agencies, State and local governments, and the private sector, including with key persons and entities in their infrastructure sector;
b) conduct or facilitate vulnerability assessments of the sector; and
c) encourage risk management strategies to protect against and mitigate the effects of attacks against critical infrastructure and key resources.

Sector Specific Agencies, in conjunction with their Sector Coordinating Councils (industry) and Government Coordinating Councils (government), work together via a framework of risk analysis and information sharing that was to be specified in the NIPP (DHS 2013). Development of the NIPP was called for in HSPD 7 and was to be maintained by DHS.

The first interim NIPP was released in 2004, fulfilling the requirements of HSPD 7. A full edition followed in 2006 and was updated in 2009. The most recent revision, NIPP 2013: *Partnering for Critical Infrastructure Security and Resilience*, expanded the plan's focus from sector-by-sector protection to an integrated approach emphasizing interdependencies and resilience across the nation's critical functions.

DHS has since reorganized and delegated much of this mission to CISA established in 2018. Nevertheless, the NIPP of 2013 remains the current national baseline for infrastructure risk management. Building on the NIPP framework, CISA introduced the National Critical Functions (NCF) construct in 2019 to identify and manage risk across systems that underpin US security, economy, and public health. Rather than focusing solely on physical sectors, the NCF model emphasizes functions such as "Provide Electric Power" or "Maintain Access to Medical Care" that cut across traditional sector boundaries. This functional perspective now guides federal and industry planning, enabling a more dynamic assessment of cascading risks in an increasingly interconnected environment.

7.3.4 National Strategies in the Bush Administration

While publishing national strategies is a routine function of the federal government, a handful of national strategies written in the wake of the 2001 terrorist attacks are worth mentioning in the context of homeland and cybersecurity. These publications are the ultimate in presidential strategic policy development and set forth visionary statements and concepts that have afterwards been used by the various departments and agencies to develop their own strategic and operational policies.

The National Strategy for Homeland Security (2002) defined *homeland security* and identified a strategic framework based on three national objectives:

- Preventing terrorist attacks within the United States;
- Reducing America's vulnerability to terrorism; and
- Minimizing the damage and recovering from attacks that do occur.

The Homeland Security Strategy recognized both the power of using information systems to improve information sharing, as well as the many gaps that remained to be filled, as described in the Strategy's executive summary:

> Information systems contribute to every aspect of homeland security. Although American information technology is the most advanced in the world, our country's information systems have not adequately supported the homeland security mission. Databases used for federal law enforcement, immigration, intelligence, public health surveillance, and emergency management have not been connected in ways that allow us to comprehend where information gaps or redundancies exist. In addition, there are deficiencies in the communications systems used by states and municipalities throughout the country; most state and local first responders do not use compatible communications equipment. To secure the homeland better, we must link the vast amounts of knowledge residing within each government agency while ensuring adequate privacy.
>
> The National Strategy for Homeland Security identifies five major initiatives in this area:

- Integrate information sharing across the federal government;
- Integrate information sharing across state and local governments, private industry, and citizens;
- Adopt common "meta-data" standards for electronic information relevant to homeland security;
- Improve public safety emergency communications; and
- Ensure reliable public health information.

An updated National Strategy for Homeland Security was published in October 2007 that set forth four new goals:

- Prevent and disrupt terrorist attacks;
- Protect the American people, our critical infrastructure, and key resources;
- Respond to and recover from incidents that do occur; and
- Continue to strengthen the foundation to ensure our long-term success.

The 2007 Strategy expanded the scope beyond terrorism to include man-made and natural disasters. The first three goals listed above focused on organizing national efforts. The last goal was designed to create and transform homeland security principles, systems, structures, and institutions. This included a comprehensive approach to risk management, building a culture of preparedness, developing a comprehensive Homeland Security Management System, improving incident management, better utilizing science and technology, and leveraging all instruments of national power and influence.

The National Strategy to Secure Cyberspace (2003) outlined an initial framework for both organizing and prioritizing efforts. It provided direction to the federal government departments and agencies that have roles in cyberspace security. It also identified steps that state and local governments, private companies and organizations, and individual Americans could take to improve the nation's collective cybersecurity. The Strategy highlighted the role of public–private engagement and provided a framework for the contributions that can be made to secure all parts of cyberspace. Because the dynamics of cyberspace would require adjustments and amendments to the Strategy over time, the original concept was to update the strategy annually. However, no changes were made to it since being published in February 2003.

The National Strategy for the Physical Protection of Critical Infrastructures and Key Assets (2003) identified a clear set of national goals and objectives and outlined the guiding principles that underpin our efforts to secure the infrastructures and assets vital to our national security, governance, public health and safety, economy, and public confidence. The Strategy also provided a unifying organization and identified specific initiatives to drive our near-term national protection priorities and inform the resource allocation process. Most importantly, it established a foundation for building and fostering the cooperative environment in which government, industry, and private citizens could carry out their respective protection responsibilities more effectively and efficiently. Like the National Strategy to Secure Cyberspace it has not been updated since its publication in February 2003 even though other cyber and homeland security strategies were subsequently published by the Obama, Trump, and Biden administrations.

In the final year of the Bush administration, National Security Presidential Directive 54 (NSPD-54)/Homeland Security Presidential Directive 23 (HSPD-23), Cybersecurity Policy, issued in January 2008, launched the CNCI. The initiative consisted of a classified twelve-point plan designed to secure federal networks, improve situational awareness, deploy intrusion detection systems across government systems, and strengthen supply-chain risk management. Although much of its content remains classified, the CNCI institutionalized federal network monitoring at scale and introduced the concept of continuous diagnostics and mitigation. It represented one of the earliest efforts to treat cybersecurity as a coordinated federal enterprise rather than a collection of agency-level IT functions.

As the Bush administration drew to a close, a bipartisan effort outside the executive branch began shaping the next phase of national cyber policy. In 2008, the Center for Strategic and International Studies (CSIS) convened the Commission on Cybersecurity for the 44th Presidency. The Commission's report, Securing Cyberspace for the 44th Presidency, urged the incoming administration to treat cybersecurity as a central element of national security strategy rather than a technical afterthought (CSIS 2008). Among its recommendations were elevating White House coordination, strengthening public–private collaboration, improving identity management, and developing a comprehensive national strategy that integrated defense, economic security, and international norms. Although advisory in nature, the Commission's work influenced early Obama administration cyber initiatives and helped frame cybersecurity as a cross-cutting strategic issue rather than a niche technical problem.

The first decade post 9/11 was largely focused on reacting to the terrorist attacks, coordination within the federal government, and protection of domestic critical infrastructure. While the United States was reorganizing domestically, foreign adversaries were demonstrating what cyber power could look like in practice. Three noteworthy events occurred overseas that foreshadowed what was to come in the next decade.

7.3.5 First National-Level DDoS Campaign, Estonia

In 2007, Estonia experienced one of the first large-scale, politically motivated cyber campaigns directed against a sovereign state. Following a diplomatic dispute with Russia over the relocation of a Soviet-era war memorial, Estonian government ministries, banks, media outlets, and telecommunications providers were subjected to sustained distributed denial-of-service (DDoS) attacks. The campaign disrupted public services, online banking, and news distribution for weeks. Although the attacks were largely disruptive rather than destructive, they demonstrated how cyber operations could be used to impose political pressure without crossing traditional military thresholds. The incident prompted NATO to accelerate its focus on cyber defense and led to the establishment of the NATO Cooperative Cyber Defence Centre of Excellence (CCDCOE) in Tallinn. For US policymakers, Estonia provided a real-world example of how digital dependence could translate into national vulnerability.

7.3.6 Cyber-Kinetic Coordination, Georgia

The Russia–Georgia conflict in 2008 further demonstrated the integration of cyber operations with conventional military action. In the days leading up to and during Russian ground operations in South Ossetia and Abkhazia, Georgian government websites, media outlets, and financial institutions were subjected to coordinated cyber disruptions. Unlike Estonia's largely stand-alone cyber campaign, the Georgian incident coincided directly with kinetic military maneuver. The synchronization of cyber and physical operations illustrated how digital effects could be used to shape the information environment, degrade communications, and amplify conventional force. For US defense planners, Georgia underscored that cyber operations were no longer theoretical adjuncts to warfare but operational enablers capable of influencing battlefield outcomes.

7.3.7 Buckshot Yankee (Agent.btz)

In 2008, the US DoD suffered a significant compromise of a classified, isolated military computer network (Miller 2022). An espionage worm copied itself into computers and any USB drives that connected to them, thus bridging the air gap between the isolated military network and the internet. The recovery operation, Operation Buckshot Yankee, was prolonged and difficult. To the US Central Command, it revealed systemic weaknesses in removable media controls and network segmentation across defense systems. This incident, also called the Agent.btz attack, is widely regarded as a catalytic event in US cyber policy, accelerating the implementation of the CNCI, prompting stricter controls on removable media, and contributing directly to the establishment and operational maturation of US Cyber Command. It marked a turning point in recognizing that adversaries could achieve strategic access through relatively simple vectors, reinforcing the need for continuous monitoring and disciplined network hygiene.

7.4 Operationalization of Cyber Power

By the end of the 21st century's first decade, cybersecurity policy had moved beyond awareness and coordination into operational reality. What began as infrastructure protection and network defense was increasingly understood as a domain of strategic competition. Nation-states demonstrated both the will and the ability to systematically integrate cyber effects within military operations, conduct large-scale espionage, and impose coercive economic disruption. During this period, the United States began institutionalizing cyber as an instrument of national power, refining doctrine, clarifying authorities, and building the operational and governance structures that would define the next decade of cyber strategy.

Shortly after taking office in January 2009, the Obama administration ordered a 60-day Cyber Policy Review to assess the adequacy of the federal government's cybersecurity strategy. The resulting report concluded that the United States faced a "growing and persistent" cyber threat and recommended elevating cybersecurity leadership within the White House, strengthening public–private coordination, and developing a more coherent national strategy (Obama Administration 2009). The review emphasized that cybersecurity was not solely a technical issue but also an economic and national security priority. Its findings ultimately contributed to the creation of the White House Cybersecurity Coordinator position and laid intellectual groundwork for later structural reforms, including the activation of the previously planned US Cyber Command and, eventually, the ONCD.

Cybersecurity was no longer being treated solely as an infrastructure protection issue; it had become an operational domain of national power. At the same time, high-profile espionage campaigns and cyber-physical operations were demonstrating that adversaries could leverage cyberspace for strategic advantage. Federal policy increasingly emphasized persistent defense, intelligence integration, and the normalization of cyber operations as a component of national security strategy. This next phase would test whether those institutions could operate effectively against increasingly sophisticated nation-state adversaries, and whether the United States itself was ready to go on the offensive with cyber tools and weapons.

7.4.1 Early Cyber Warfare, Stuxnet

Beyond what happened in Estonia and Georgia in 2008–2009, perhaps the most consequential example of the offensive trend chosen by nation-state adversaries was the discovery of the Stuxnet worm in mid-2010. One notable difference between those events and this example was that the previous incidents were perpetrated by US adversaries while this event was attributed by researchers and investigative reporting to a joint effort by the United States and Israel.

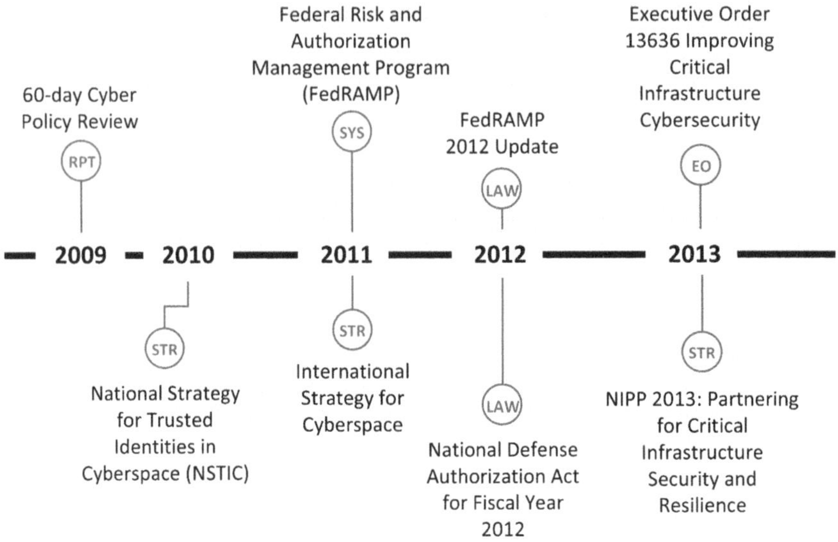

Timeline 3 2009–2013.

Stuxnet is widely regarded as the first publicly known cyber weapon designed to produce kinetic effects. Its discovery demonstrated that cyber operations could achieve strategic, real-world outcomes without conventional military force. While the original malware itself is no longer operational, the techniques it introduced (supply-chain exploitation, multi-stage zero-day attacks, and cyber-physical manipulation) have since been studied, adapted, and reused, ensuring that its legacy continues to shape modern cyber conflict.

7.4.2 State Sponsored Espionage

During the Cold War, the spy community was clearly focused on US versus USSR espionage. But in recent years the focus has moved from former Soviet countries to China. In 2003, a series of cyberattacks that were believed to be of Chinese origin were found to be targeting American computer systems. Dubbed "Titan Rain" by the DoD, the investigation of the intrusion remained classified until the story was leaked to the press. Following the press leak, it was revealed that the attackers had gained access to many computer networks, including those at Lockheed Martin, Sandia National Laboratories, Redstone Arsenal, and NASA. While the names of the investigations have changed over the years, the espionage continues to the present day.

The Agent.btz intrusion into DoD networks overseas (2008), Operation Aurora's targeting of technology firms (2009), the Office of Personnel Management breach

(2015), and the SolarWinds supply-chain compromise (2020) each revealed different dimensions of strategic cyber espionage. These operations ranged from the theft of sensitive military data to the exfiltration of millions of federal personnel records and the compromise of trusted software-update channels. Unlike disruptive attacks, espionage campaigns often remained undetected for extended periods, emphasizing stealth, persistence, and strategic patience on the part of US adversaries.

7.4.3 US Cyber Command

On June 23, 2009, the Secretary of Defense ordered the establishment of US Cyber Command (CYBERCOM) as a sub-unified command under STRATCOM. This new entity consolidated the Joint Task Force-Global Network Operations (JTF-GNO) and the Joint Functional Component Command-Network Warfare (JFCC-NW), transitioning their core missions from Computer Network Operations (CNO) to comprehensive cyberspace operations. To fulfill its mandate, CYBERCOM initially relied on the NSA for critical assets, including staff and equipment, before achieving full operational capability in late 2010 (Lynn 2010).

As CYBERCOM matured, cyberspace operations became fully embedded in the DoD's broader warfighting doctrine. Cyberspace was formally recognized as the fifth operational domain, on par with land, maritime, air, and space operations. This recognition reshaped joint planning and redefined the role of information in modern conflict.

The 2015 DoD Cyber Strategy marked an important transition by identifying cyberspace superiority as critical to achieving military advantage (DoD 2015). It called for developing capabilities that could deliver precision effects, both defensive and offensive without the collateral damage associated with kinetic warfare. By the late 2010s, cyber operations were routinely synchronized with electronic warfare, intelligence, and space operations under the concept of Multi-Domain Operations (MDO).

Throughout the decade, the scope of CYBERCOM's responsibilities expanded dramatically as cyber operations became integral to military planning and execution across all domains. A pivotal milestone occurred in 2017, when the Secretary of Defense and the President approved the elevation of CYBERCOM to a full unified combatant command, signaling that cyberspace had joined land, sea, air, and space as a permanent theater of operations. The elevation, formally completed in 2018, reflected growing recognition that cyber power had both tactical and strategic effects capable of shaping global events.

During this same period, the Department formalized new operational concepts known as "persistent engagement" and "defend forward." These doctrines emphasized continuous contact with adversaries in cyberspace, proactively disrupting malicious activity before it reached US networks. The 2018 Department of Defense Cyber Strategy codified these principles, marking a philosophical shift from a defensive, network-centric posture to one of active, anticipatory defense.

7.4.4 Expansion of US CYBERCOM Service Cyber Components

As cyberspace operations became more mainstream within the DoD, each of the military services developed its own cyber component to provide forces and capabilities to US Cyber Command. These components, Army Cyber Command (ARCYBER), Fleet Cyber Command/Tenth Fleet (FLTCYBERCOM), Air Forces Cyber (16th Air Force), and Marine Forces Cyber Command (MARFORCYBER) represent the operational foundation of the nation's Cyber Mission Force (CMF). Together, they form a distributed yet tightly coordinated network of commands responsible for defending military networks, supporting combatant commanders, and conducting offensive operations when authorized.

Army Cyber Command (ARCYBER) reached full operational capability in 2013, consolidating the Army's cyber, signal, and information operations under one headquarters. ARCYBER commands the Army's Cyber Protection Teams (CPTs) and Offensive Cyber Operations elements, while also integrating electronic warfare and information operations as part of the Army's broader *Multi-Domain Operations* concept. In 2020, the Army activated the Information Warfare Command, merging intelligence, electronic warfare, and cyber under a unified structure designed to synchronize effects across domains.

FLTCYBERCOM serves as the Navy component of CYBERCOM. It operates under the principle that cyber warfare and maritime operations are inseparable in the modern era. The command defends naval networks worldwide and integrates cyber capabilities into fleet operations, ensuring that ships, submarines, and aircraft can operate securely in contested electromagnetic environments. The Navy's growing capability in autonomous and networked systems has made FLTCYBERCOM a critical element of maritime resilience and cyber deterrence.

AFCYBER was established to bring together the Air Force's cyber, intelligence, surveillance, and reconnaissance (ISR) capabilities. It provides global reach in cyberspace operations, including persistent engagement missions and the defense of the Air Force's command and control networks. Cyber and ISR functions are integrated within each Air Force operation unit in recognition that information dominance across both kinetic and non-kinetic domains is central to modern airpower.

MARFORCYBER contributes specialized cyber teams that support Marine Air-Ground Task Forces (MAGTFs) and joint combatant commands. It aligns its operations with the Marine Corps' expeditionary doctrine, providing deployable teams capable of integrating cyber effects into tactical environments. In 2020, the

Marine Corps also established Marine Corps Forces Space Command to provide close coordination between space and cyber operations to ensure information superiority in distributed operations.

While Army, Navy, Air Force, and Marine Corps cyber forces serve as established service components to CYBERCOM, the newly created US Space Force does not currently field its own formal Space Force cyber component within CYBERCOM. Nonetheless, Space Force units such as Space Delta 6 and affiliated cyberspace squadrons carry out defensive and cyber protection missions for space systems and networks, and a Space Force mission analysis has been exploring options for a future Space Force service component to CYBERCOM.

By the early 2020s, the combined CMF had achieved full operational capability. These teams are divided into mission categories: National Mission Teams defend the nation's critical cyberspace; Combat Mission Teams support combatant commands with offensive effects; CPTs defend DoD networks and weapon systems; and Cyber Support Teams provide specialized planning and analysis. The CMF has since evolved into a persistent operational force, continuously engaged in global cyber competition and countering adversarial intrusions in near real time.

The expansion of service components and the creation of the CMF represent an upward inflection point in US cyber policy. What began as a fragmented collection of network defenders and intelligence analysts has matured into an integrated warfighting enterprise. Cyber capabilities are now a standing part of every combatant command's operational planning cycle, and coordination among the service cyber components ensures that today's DoD can conduct continuous, synchronized, and scalable cyber operations across the globe.

The rapid institutional growth of CYBERCOM and its service components signaled a decisive shift from experimentation to permanence in military cyberspace operations. Yet while the DoD refined its operational doctrine, the broader federal enterprise faced mounting challenges in governance, regulation, and public–private collaboration. Adversaries were also demonstrating a willingness to use destructive cyber tools for political coercion outside conventional battlefields.

7.4.5 Notable Events

In late 2014, the Sony Pictures cyberattack described in Chapter 2 marked one of the first instances in which the United States formally attributed a destructive cyberattack to a nation-state and imposed sanctions in response, signaling that cyber-enabled coercion against private sector entities would carry diplomatic consequences.

In December 2015, Russia's attack on the Ukrainian power grid described in Chapter 2 demonstrated that cyber intrusions could move beyond espionage and data theft into direct manipulation of industrial control systems, marking a significant escalation in the operational use of cyber capabilities against critical infrastructure.

The second Russian attack on the Ukrainian power grid in December 2016 utilized purpose-built malware. The incident underscored that adversaries were refining tools specifically engineered to disrupt electric infrastructure, raising concerns among US policymakers about the resilience of domestic power systems and the need for enhanced public–private coordination to defend operational technology environments. As adversaries expanded their targeting of civilian infrastructure and commercial supply chains, the center of gravity for national cyber policy began to shift from the battlefield to the legislative and executive arenas. The next phase of the federal response would unfold through new laws, executive orders, and strategic frameworks that redefined how the United States organized, funded, and coordinated cybersecurity across all sectors.

7.4.6 Congressional Actions

By the beginning of the 2010s, it had become clear that the nation's cyber challenges could not be solved through technical measures alone. The creation of US Cyber Command had institutionalized cyber operations within the DoD, but civilian authorities, private-sector operators, and Congress were still struggling to define their respective roles in a rapidly evolving threat landscape. The early years of the 111th (2009–2010) and 112th (2011–2012) Congresses were marked by vigorous debate but limited legislative success. Indeed, this was an era defined more by competing proposals than enacted reforms. Nevertheless, these sessions produced several foundational statutes and pilot programs that quietly set the stage for broader reforms later in the decade.

During the 112th Congress (2011–2012), a series of cybersecurity bills were introduced amid growing concern about foreign espionage and large-scale data breaches. While sweeping proposals such as the Cybersecurity Act of 2012 failed to pass after extensive debate, several narrower measures succeeded (Lieberman 2012). Among them was the Federal Risk and Authorization Management Program (FedRAMP update 2023) codification effort, which standardized cloud service security assessments across agencies. Additionally, the National Defense Authorization Act for Fiscal Year 2012 included key provisions expanding the DoD's authority to conduct cyber operations and protect critical defense networks.

These actions represented a practical, incremental approach where Congress chose targeted statutory reforms rather than attempting to legislate an entire cybersecurity regime at once. This early legislative groundwork, combined with the proliferation of executive actions from 2012 onward, began to close long-standing policy gaps. The Federal Information Security Modernization Act of 2014 (FISMA 2014) ultimately replaced the older Federal Information Security Management Act of 2002 (FISMA 2002) framework, formalizing the operational role of DHS in securing civilian agency networks and defining continuous monitoring as the federal standard. The updated law clarified the relationship between OMB's policy oversight and DHS's operational authority, transforming cybersecurity management from a compliance-based process into a continuous, risk-based discipline.

The Cybersecurity and Information Sharing Act of 2015 provided another long-awaited breakthrough (Feinstein 2015). It gave companies legal protection when voluntarily sharing cyber threat indicators with the federal government and encouraged two-way information exchange between the private sector and DHS's National Cybersecurity and Communications Integration Center (NCCIC). For the first time, information sharing was recognized as a national defense imperative rather than a competitive risk. Though critics argued that participation remained too voluntary, CISA 2015 established the legal infrastructure for the rapid exchange of threat intelligence across sectors. Originally enacted with sunset provisions effective in 2025, the information sharing authorities created by CISA 2015 have been extended and remain operative as part of the federal cybersecurity framework.

Between 2016 and 2018, successive National Defense Authorization Acts (NDAA 2018/2026 amended) expanded the DoD's cyber authorities and codified the structure of the CMF. The NDAA for Fiscal Year 2018 was especially significant, affirming that the Secretary of Defense could conduct cyber operations to deter or disrupt active threats from foreign adversaries without waiting for a separate authorization of force. This reflected a growing national consensus that cyberspace was not merely a technical domain, but a continuous strategic battleground demanding persistent engagement.

These efforts culminated in one of the most significant structural reorganizations in US cyber history – the establishment of CISA in 2018. This agency became the civilian counterpart to CYBERCOM, responsible for protecting federal networks, supporting state and local governments, and coordinating private-sector defense of the nation's critical infrastructure.

7.4.7 Federal Cybersecurity and Infrastructure Executive Orders

While Congress laid the statutory foundation for modern cybersecurity governance, the Executive Branch accelerated progress through a series of presidential directives that addressed urgent threats, modernized federal networks, and advanced the public–private collaboration model. Between 2010 and 2020,

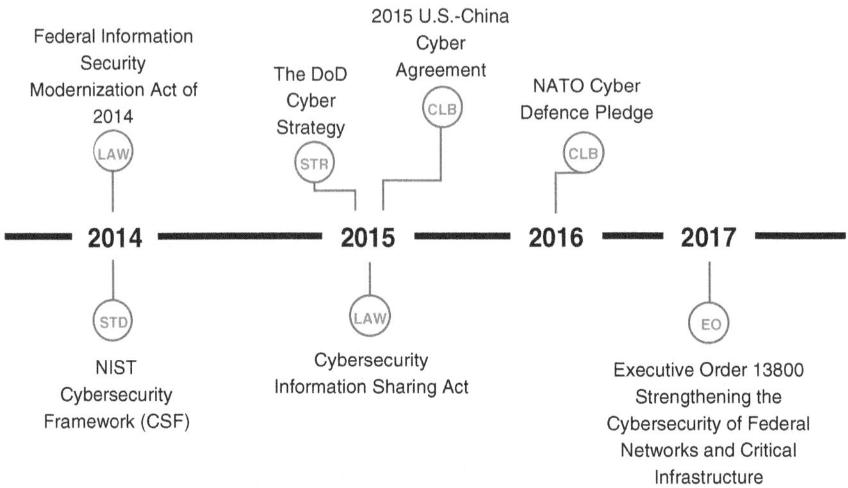

Timeline 4 2014–2017.

successive administrations used executive orders to strengthen resilience across both federal systems and privately operated critical infrastructure that continued a tradition of using the White House as a catalyst for national cyber policy when legislation proved slow to adapt.

First up was the National Strategy for Trusted Identities in Cyberspace (NSTIC 2010), a White House initiative to work collaboratively with the private sector, advocacy groups, public sector agencies, and other organizations to improve the privacy, security, and convenience of sensitive online transactions. The Strategy called for the development of interoperable technology standards and policies – an "Identity Ecosystem" – where individuals, organizations, and underlying infrastructure, such as routers and servers, can be authoritatively authenticated. The goals of the Strategy were to protect individuals, businesses, and public agencies from the high costs of cybercrimes like identity theft and fraud, while simultaneously helping to ensure that the internet continues to support innovation and a thriving marketplace of products and ideas. It was well-intentioned but ineffective. Its impact was little more than a cheerleader for the cause of combating ever-increasing identity theft.

In 2011, the Obama administration issued an International Strategy for Cyberspace (2011) policy that would empower innovation, as well as the ability to seek, receive, and impart information and ideas through any medium and regardless of frontiers, protected from fraud, theft, and threats to personal safety. As a goal, it was stated that, "The United States will work internationally to promote an open, interoperable, secure, and reliable information and communications infrastructure that supports international trade and commerce, strengthens international security, and fosters free expression and innovation." The goal was followed by several specific policy statements that reflect our national values:

- States must respect fundamental freedoms of expression and association, online as well as off;
- States should in their undertakings and through domestic laws respect intellectual property rights, including patents, trade secrets, trademarks, and copyrights;
- Individuals should be protected from arbitrary or unlawful state interference with their privacy when they use the internet;
- States must identify and prosecute cybercriminals, to ensure laws and practices deny criminals safe havens, and cooperate with international criminal investigations in a timely manner; and
- Consistent with the United Nations Charter, states have an inherent right to self-defense that may be triggered by certain aggressive acts in cyberspace (ISC 2011).

The ISC established the foundation for US diplomatic engagement on digital issues, but its early influence was limited by uneven global participation. Over the next decade, successive administrations sought to expand and operationalize that framework, integrating cyber policy into trade, defense, and foreign affairs.

As the United States matured its domestic cyber institutions, it also recognized that no nation could defend itself alone in a globally connected digital environment. After 2011, US cyber strategy increasingly emphasized diplomacy, alliance building, and collective deterrence. This transformed cyberspace from a largely ungoverned technical frontier into an arena of strategic statecraft. This international dimension evolved alongside growing recognition that cyber norms, shared defense commitments, and mutual attribution mechanisms were as vital as firewalls and encryption.

The 2015 US–China Cyber Agreement marked an early test of bilateral cyber diplomacy (Obama Administration 2015). Although criticized as fragile, it produced a temporary reduction in state-sponsored intellectual-property theft and demonstrated that dialogue could temper escalation. At the same time, the United States intensified cooperation with like-minded democracies, encouraging the adoption of voluntary norms through forums such as the G-7 Organisation for Economic Co-operation and Development (OECD), and United Nations (UN) Group of Governmental Experts (UN GGE). These multilateral efforts produced the first internationally recognized principles for responsible state behavior in cyberspace. Most notable was that international law applies in cyberspace the same way as the physical world, and that states should not knowingly allow their territory to be used for malicious cyber activity.

As cyber operations became integral to global competition, alliances began treating digital resilience as a collective obligation. The NATO Cyber Defence Pledge (2016) committed member states to strengthen defenses and share capabilities, ultimately leading to the establishment of the NATO Cooperative Cyber Defence Centre of Excellence (CCDCOE) in Tallinn, Estonia. The pledge also set the stage for NATO's 2021 recognition of cyberspace as an operational domain of warfare, meaning that a severe cyberattack could trigger the alliance's Article 5 collective defense clause.

The US also forged partnerships with the European Union through the US–EU Trade and Technology Council (TTC), aligning export controls, supply-chain security, and AI governance. In the Indo-Pacific, the *Quad nations* (United States, Japan, India, and Australia) launched joint initiatives on critical-infrastructure protection and submarine-cable security. These frameworks expanded the geographic scope of cyber cooperation, reflecting the globalized nature of digital interdependence.

By 2020, international cyber engagement extended beyond traditional allies. The United States collaborated with regional organizations such as the Association of Southeast Asian Nations (ASEAN) and the Organization of American States (OAS) to build incident-response capacity and cyber-forensics expertise. It also supported the Paris Call for Trust and Security in Cyberspace (2018), an international declaration advocating responsible behavior and protection of the public core of the internet. Collectively, these initiatives signaled a shift from bilateral agreements toward a coalition-based model of digital governance that viewed cyber stability as a shared global public good.

Back at home, Executive Order 13636 (2013), *Improving Critical Infrastructure Cybersecurity*, directed NIST to work with industry to develop a voluntary but practical framework for managing cyber risk (Executive Order 13636 2013). The resulting NIST Cybersecurity Framework (CSF), released in 2014, provided a common language for identifying, protecting, detecting, responding to, and recovering from cyber incidents. Its influence extended far beyond federal agencies – utilities, financial institutions, and even foreign governments adopted it as a model for critical infrastructure protection (NIST 2014).

Executive Order 13636 also introduced a more granular approach to identifying nationally significant cyber risk through what became known as the *Section 9 list*. The order directed DHS to identify specific critical infrastructure entities whose disruption through cyber means could produce catastrophic regional or national consequences. Unlike earlier sector-wide coordination efforts, this initiative focused on the *most critical of the critical*, creating a confidential list of companies and facilities warranting prioritized engagement and voluntary adoption of the emerging NIST CSF. Although the program did not impose regulatory requirements, it reflected a growing recognition that systemic cyber risk was concentrated in a relatively small number of high-consequence assets. The effort marked an incremental shift from broad infrastructure awareness toward targeted resilience planning.

The next major action came in May 2017, when Executive Order 13800 (2017), *Strengthening the Cybersecurity of Federal Networks and Critical Infrastructure*, established a government-wide framework for accountability and modernization. It required all federal agencies to manage cybersecurity risk using the NIST CSF and to submit detailed risk assessments to DHS and the Office of Management and Budget (OMB) (Executive Order 13800 2017). The order directed agency heads to assume personal responsibility for network risk. This ended the long-standing practice of delegating cybersecurity entirely to technical staff.

Executive Order 13800 also launched initiatives to modernize IT systems, evaluate the resilience of critical infrastructure sectors, and promote workforce development in the federal cyber community. For the first time, executive direction linked agency performance directly to cybersecurity maturity, elevating the issue to the level of financial and operational accountability.

Cyber was now maturing as a warfighting domain, but the center of gravity of risk was dramatically shifting to civilian infrastructure and the private sector. This set in motion new policy debates, new policy responses, and new cyber organizations.

7.5 Institutional Maturation and Strategic Competition

As geopolitical competition intensified in the late 2010s, the United States further institutionalized its cyber posture while confronting a rapidly expanding threat landscape. The leaked NSA exploits described in Chapter 2 were now in the hands of adversaries and large-scale ransomware campaigns began targeting municipalities and critical infrastructure. These occurred against the backdrop of foreign influence operations heightening concerns about election security. Strategic competition with peer adversaries sharpened the government's focus on layered deterrence, defend-forward operations, and protection of democratic institutions.

Cyber operations were elevated as a distinct warfighting domain, and Congress had strengthened civilian infrastructure protection through the creation of DHS' CISA in 2018. By 2020, the United States had effectively constructed dual cyber pillars – a military instrument for global engagement and a civilian instrument for infrastructure resilience. This phase reflected a maturing recognition that cybersecurity required sustained institutional capacity, cross-sector coordination, and resilience planning rather than episodic crisis response.

7.5.1 Integration of Cyber with Joint Operations Doctrine

The recognition that cybersecurity required sustained institutional capacity prompted the production of Joint Publication 3-12 (CJCS 2018), Cyberspace Operations (2018 revision) and later the Joint Concept for Cyberspace Operations (JCCO) (NATO Standardization Office 2020), which solidified the doctrinal integration of cybersecurity into mainstream incident response. These documents established that cyber effects must be planned and executed alongside kinetic fires and intelligence operations within the Joint Operations Center framework. Cyber forces became essential enablers of deception, reconnaissance, and precision targeting missions.

Operationally, this integration became evident during US and allied actions to deter and disrupt adversary activity by Russia, China, Iran, and North Korea. Cyber effects were applied to complement traditional military operations, from influencing adversary decision-making to disabling command-and-control networks in the opening hours of potential conflict scenarios. The alignment of cyberspace and information operations also blurred traditional distinctions between warfare and competition below the threshold of armed conflict, a phenomenon increasingly described as "gray zone operations."

By 2020, cyber planning was no longer an adjunct capability; it had become an integral part of every major operational plan. Commanders now expected real-time intelligence from cyberspace sensors, rapid malware analysis, and precision effects against digital targets – all coordinated under a unified joint structure. The fusion of cyber with joint operations thus completed the transformation that began with CYBERCOM's founding: cyberspace had evolved from a technical support function to a decisive instrument of national power.

But while the DoD integrated cyber operations into joint military doctrine, the civilian sector was confronting a different kind of escalation, one driven less by strategic signaling and more by economic coercion and institutional disruption.

7.5.2 The Rise of Ransomware as a National Security Threat

The 2010s saw the transformation of ransomware from an opportunistic criminal tactic into a national-level security threat. Early international incidents such as CryptoLocker (2013) and WannaCry (2017) demonstrated how malware could propagate globally within hours, leveraging unpatched systems and exploiting weak cyber hygiene. NotPetya (2017), attributed to Russian military actors, blurred the line between cybercrime and state-sponsored warfare. It met its target of crippling portions of Ukraine's national infrastructure and cause an estimated $10B of damage globally due to collateral damage to global companies who did business in Ukraine.

By the early 2020s, ransomware had evolved into a professionalized, as-a-service ecosystem. As described in Chapters 2 and 4, ransomware threat groups operate with business-like efficiency, offering affiliates malware kits, payment negotiation services, and laundering channels via cryptocurrencies. Unlike traditional espionage, these attacks were designed to halt operations and demand payment, often in cryptocurrency. When in preparation for a ransomware attack, they encounter data of value to data extract, this is an added bonus.

Incidents affecting local governments and public services revealed systemic weaknesses in local area networks and demonstrated that disruptive cyber activity need not originate from state intelligence services to produce destructive consequences. That said, the vulnerabilities exploited by this ransomware were easily traced to those stolen from NSA as described in Chapter 2, and it was obvious that the victim network owners had obviously not followed Microsoft's recommendations for patching their systems. Their sole defense to their displaced users was that they had never in the past had to pay attention to these "patch" notices, so the fact that this patching may be necessary to maintain business continuity was new to them. The rise of ransomware heightened urgency around resilience, rapid restoration of services, and improved coordination between federal and state authorities.

Taken together, these disruptive campaigns demonstrated that cyber operations had moved beyond data theft and into the realm of operational coercion. The adversary ability to halt US business technology processes without crossing a traditional military threshold reshaped how policymakers understood risk. These incidents blurred the distinction between crime and nation-state strategy, showing that economic disruption could serve geopolitical objectives whether or not it was formally attributed to a nation-state.

7.5.3 Creation of CISA (the DHS Agency)

The most consequential structural reform in federal cybersecurity since the creation of CYBERCOM was the Cybersecurity and Infrastructure Security Agency Act of 2018 (CISA 2018). This long-awaited holistic approach to cybersecurity policy elevated the cyber and infrastructure protection functions of DHS into CISA.

Before CISA's formation, DHS's cybersecurity responsibilities were dispersed among multiple entities, including the National Protection and Programs Directorate (NPPD), the Office of Cybersecurity and Communications (CS&C), and the NCCIC. While these organizations played critical roles in incident response and risk management, their missions often overlapped, and they lacked the unified authority to coordinate across sectors. The 2018 Act addressed these issues by creating CISA as an operational component of DHS, consolidating these functions under a single directorate with a clear mission: "to lead the national effort to understand, manage, and reduce risk to the cyber and physical infrastructure that Americans rely on every day." CISA's formation reflected a strategic recognition that cybersecurity, infrastructure resilience, and national risk management are inseparable. The agency was structured around three core divisions: *Cybersecurity*, *Infrastructure Security*, and *Emergency Communications*, each responsible for complementary aspects of national preparedness. The Cybersecurity Division absorbed NCCIC's mission for threat analysis, incident response, and vulnerability coordination, while the Infrastructure Security Division focused on protecting the physical assets, supply chains, and control systems that underpin the nation's critical sectors. The Emergency Communications Division continued to advance interoperable communications for first responders and public safety agencies.

One of CISA's earliest priorities was improving the government's ability to share actionable threat intelligence with both federal partners and private-sector operators. The agency strengthened the Automated Indicator Sharing (AIS) program to deliver near real-time threat data to participants and established a 24 × 7 Cybersecurity Operations Center to monitor incidents across government networks. Recognizing that cybersecurity required a whole-of-nation effort, CISA also launched a series of outreach initiatives, including the Cybersecurity Advisors Program, Protective Security Advisors, and regional coordination offices designed to build trust with state, local, tribal, and territorial (SLTT) governments.

CISA's creation also reflected a philosophical shift in how the federal government viewed the role of public–private collaboration. Rather than dictating compliance, the agency adopted a model of shared responsibility, emphasizing partnership and transparency. This approach proved itself as the agency confronted a series of high-impact challenges almost immediately after its formation. The SolarWinds supply-chain compromise (discovered in late 2020), the Colonial Pipeline ransomware attack (2021), and the Log4j software vulnerability (2021–2022) underscored the systemic nature of cyber risk and validated the need for an agency capable of integrating technical response, risk communication, and cross-sector coordination.

To address these challenges, CISA introduced several key initiatives that reshaped national cyber defense. Among them were:

- *Shields Up (2022):* A public campaign and operational framework for heightened vigilance in response to global geopolitical tensions and cyber threats, emphasizing rapid information sharing and proactive risk reduction.
- *Joint Cyber Defense Collaborative (JCDC):* Formed in 2021 under congressional authority, the JCDC unified government and private-sector partners, including major cloud providers, telecommunications companies, and critical

infrastructure operators, for the purpose of planning and exercising collective defensive measures.

- *Secure by Design/Secure by Default (2023):* An initiative urging technology manufacturers to take greater accountability for product security, marking a policy pivot toward placing responsibility on software and hardware vendors rather than end users.

CISA's organizational structure and policy posture reflected lessons learned from nearly two decades of fragmented federal efforts. The agency became the civilian counterpart to US Cyber Command, responsible for operational defense of federal civilian networks and for coordinating cyber incident response across the private sector. Its integration of cybersecurity, physical infrastructure, and communications resilience provided a foundation for the "whole-of-nation" approach envisioned in the 2023 National Cybersecurity Strategy.

By 2024, CISA had emerged as one of the most visible and influential federal agencies in the cybersecurity arena. Its campaigns to strengthen resilience, promote transparency, and institutionalize joint defense marked the maturation of national cyber governance. What began as an internal reorganization at DHS evolved into a cornerstone of the nation's digital defense architecture, one that continues to evolve alongside the technologies, threats, and partnerships it was built to protect.

Despite its growing prominence, CISA entered 2025 facing notable fiscal headwinds. Congressional budget negotiations introduced constraints that limited the agency's ability to expand several planned initiatives, including elements of state and local capacity-building programs and the pace of growth within collaborative efforts such as the JCDC. Staffing pressures driven by hiring delays, attrition, and unfilled vacancies raised concerns about CISA's ability to sustain 24×7 monitoring, outreach programs, and coordination at the scale originally envisioned. Moreover, despite the desperate and obvious need for US strength in Cyberspace, 2025 saw a ~30% reduction in staff for CISA and in early 2026, another third of the agency was put on furlough. These cuts to the agency have had a significant impact on its ability to maintain and expand cybersecurity activities in the US and collaborative efforts with allied nations as the cyberwar stemming from the US invasion of Iraq intensifies (Fattahi 2026).

These pressures emerged at a time when foreign cyber activity and domestic infrastructure dependencies continued to increase, prompting concern among industry partners and state officials that momentum, built over the previous five years, could slow. The episode underscored a recurring tension in federal cybersecurity policy: funding and attention often fluctuate, even as systemic cyber risk continues to grow.

7.5.4 Election Security and Critical Infrastructure Protection

The 2016 US presidential election marked a watershed in the intersection of cyber operations and democratic governance when the Russian government conducted an extensive, multi-faceted interference campaign that combined network intrusions, data exfiltration, and influence operations aimed at disrupting the electoral process and undermining public confidence. US intelligence agencies assessed with high confidence that Russia's Main Intelligence Directorate (the *Glavnoye Razvedyvatel'noye Upravleniye*, or GRU) spear-phished and compromised email accounts associated with the Democratic National Committee, the Democratic Congressional Campaign Committee, and campaign officials, stealing hundreds of thousands of emails that were subsequently disseminated through personas such as Guccifer 2.0 and organizations like WikiLeaks to maximize political and media impact (Sanger et al. 2018).

These cyber intrusions were conducted in tandem with social media and disinformation campaigns designed to exacerbate political divisions and sow doubt about electoral integrity. The Department of Justice later indicted multiple Russian intelligence officers for these hacking offenses, and subsequent bipartisan Senate and intelligence community reports documented Russia's efforts to influence voter perceptions and democratic processes through both cyber exploitation and active measure tactics. Some of these were done in cooperation with a UK-based military contractor, Cambridge Analytica, who had exploited access to Facebook to profile and subvert voters by sending targeted fake news ads to their social media feeds (US Senate Committee 2018).

Following the Russian interference incident, DHS formally designated election systems as critical infrastructure in 2017. This policy decision recognized that democracy itself depended on digital resilience. CISA, working through the Election Infrastructure Information Sharing and Analysis Center (EI-ISAC), began partnering with state and local officials to provide network monitoring, incident response, and threat intelligence.

The 2018 and 2020 elections became proving grounds for this collaboration. CISA deployed "Cybersecurity Advisors" and "Protective Security Advisors" to nearly every state, implemented intrusion detection sensors through the Albert sensor network, and coordinated rapid information exchange with election offices. The "Rumor Control" initiative launched in 2020 represented a new dimension of protection, defending not only the systems that count votes, but also the public perception of their legitimacy.

By 2022, adversary tactics had expanded from direct intrusion attempts to influence operations, including AI-generated disinformation campaigns. CISA, the FBI, and the Office of the Director of National Intelligence-issued joint advisories, warning that adversaries were now exploiting social media algorithms and synthetic media to manipulate voter sentiment. The 2024 election cycle demonstrated both progress and fragility – while major system compromises were prevented, the flood of AI-generated misinformation tested the limits of cognitive resilience. These experiences reaffirmed that safeguarding democracy required defending both the infrastructure of voting and the information environment surrounding it.

7.5.5 Solarium Commission

A pivotal moment in the maturation of congressional cyber strategy came with the establishment of the Cyberspace Solarium Commission in 2019. Modeled after President Eisenhower's Cold War-era Solarium Project, the bipartisan commission was tasked with developing a comprehensive strategic approach to defending the US in cyberspace. Its 2020 final report introduced the concept of "layered cyber deterrence," integrating resilience, defend-forward operations, and international coalition-building into a unified framework (Cyberspace Solarium Commission 2020). Some of its recommendations were subsequently enacted into law, including the creation of the ONCD in 2021, enhanced authorities for CISA, and strengthened supply-chain risk management provisions. The Commission's work marked a rare moment of bipartisan consensus in cyber policy and significantly shaped the institutional architecture that defines federal cybersecurity governance today. In recognition of the need for ongoing attention to the remainder of the report's recommendations, Solarium continues in the form of a project housed at the Center on Cyber and Technology Innovation at the Foundation for Defense of Democracies. The mission of the project is to preserve the legacy of the Cyberspace Solarium Commission and continue the work to implement its recommendations.

7.6 Systemic Risk, Resilience, and Whole-of-nation Governance

The establishment of the ONCD in 2021 marked a significant evolution in federal cyber governance. Created by Congress following recommendations from the Cyberspace Solarium Commission, the ONCD was tasked with coordinating national cyber strategy, reviewing agency cyber budgets, and serving as the President's principal advisor on cybersecurity policy. Unlike earlier White House cyber coordinators who lacked statutory authority, the ONCD was embedded in law and provided a centralized mechanism for aligning civilian, military, and intelligence cyber activities. Its creation reflected recognition that effective cybersecurity required unified strategic direction across the executive branch.

The early 2020s revealed that cyber risk had become systemic rather than episodic. Software supply-chain vulnerabilities, continued ransomware campaigns targeting critical infrastructure, and rapid advances in AI underscored the interconnectedness of digital systems. The 2024 ransomware attack against Change Healthcare, a major US healthcare technology provider, disrupted payment processing and prescription services nationwide. The incident halted medical billing operations for hospitals and pharmacies, demonstrating how deeply integrated private-sector intermediaries had become in the delivery of essential services. Unlike earlier ransomware attacks that primarily affected individual municipalities or corporations, the Change Healthcare disruption highlighted systemic interdependencies in the healthcare supply chain. The episode reinforced federal efforts to strengthen minimum cybersecurity requirements for critical service providers and intensified discussions about mandatory reporting and baseline security standards across high-impact sectors.

In reaction to the disturbing uptick of coordinated and targeted ransomware incidents, federal policy began to emphasize resilience, consequence management, and rapid restoration of services alongside traditional prevention and deterrence. The Department of Justice established a Ransomware and Digital Extortion Task Force (2021), while CISA, the FBI, and NSA jointly published mitigation playbooks and advisories. The Ransomware Task Force Report (2022), a multi-stakeholder initiative, called for treating ransomware as a national security crisis rather than a criminal nuisance. Subsequent operations, including international takedowns of Hive (2023) and LockBit (2024), demonstrated that law enforcement and intelligence collaboration could disrupt major ransomware networks. However, by 2025, new strains leveraging AI-assisted intrusion tools and automated lateral movement were again raising the stakes. Unfortunately, ransomware remains a constantly evolving asymmetric weapon.

7.6.1 Supply Chain and Software Assurance Policy

Perhaps no domain reveals the interdependence of global networks more starkly than the software supply chain. While the potential for adversaries to use the global supply chain as a vector for malicious cyber activity was well known and had been warned about for years, the SolarWinds compromise (2020) exposed a new weakness – the vulnerability of software update mechanisms, allowing attackers to infiltrate thousands of organizations including multiple US federal agencies through a trusted vendor's platform. Soon after, the Microsoft Exchange Server exploitation (2021) and the Log4j vulnerability (2021–2022) highlighted how dependencies buried deep within open-source libraries could threaten the entire digital economy.

In early 2021, exploitation of zero-day vulnerabilities in Microsoft Exchange Server software resulted in widespread compromise of on-premises email systems across government agencies, businesses, and critical infrastructure providers worldwide. The activity, attributed to Chinese state-affiliated actors, combined espionage objectives with indiscriminate scanning and mass exploitation. Once public disclosure occurred, criminal groups rapidly weaponized the vulnerabilities, compounding the damage. The incident demonstrated how state-sponsored discovery of software flaws could cascade into global criminal exploitation, further blurring distinctions between espionage and cybercrime. It also reinforced the urgency of rapid patching, cloud migration, and secure software development practices.

The disclosure of the Log4j vulnerability in late 2021 revealed how deeply embedded open-source components had become within global software ecosystems. Log4j, a widely used Java logging library, was present in thousands of commercial and government applications. The flaw allowed remote code execution and was rapidly exploited by both state and criminal actors. Unlike isolated vendor-specific incidents, Log4j exposed systemic dependency risk: a single vulnerable component could ripple across industries and national borders. The episode intensified federal focus on Software Bills of Materials (SBOMs), secure-by-design principles, and improved visibility into supply-chain dependencies.

While these incidents grabbed headlines, a more subtle and long-term supply-chain risk remained out of the major news cycles, the introduction of counterfeit or compromised computer and networking equipment into global markets. Investigations by US law enforcement and national security agencies show that counterfeit components remain a persistent problem in certain sectors, particularly in high-value electronics and specialized networking and defense systems.

Over time, concern has expanded beyond counterfeit goods themselves to include the integrity of hardware, firmware, and software supply chains more broadly. US policymakers and security agencies now recognize that opaque manufacturing processes, undocumented functionality, and remote update mechanisms can create strategic vulnerabilities even in legitimately manufactured products. Rather than focusing solely on deliberate "backdoors," current assessments emphasize systemic risk arising from foreign dependency, limited transparency, and concentrated control over critical technologies.

Responding to these types of attacks, Executive Order 14028 (2021) and CISA's push for SBOMs mandated detailed inventories of code components used in commercial and government systems (Executive Order 14028 2021). The order also mandated greater transparency, secure development practices, and incident reporting requirements for federal contractors. By 2023, CISA's Vulnerability Disclosure Policy Platform and VulnCheck.gov portal provided centralized mechanisms for sharing and tracking software weaknesses across sectors.

With respect to potentially compromised hardware and software being sold into American infrastructure, Congress and the executive branch began imposing restrictions on the procurement and use of equipment from Chinese manufacturers Huawei and ZTE in 2018, citing national-security concerns related to potential foreign government access and supply-chain control. The Secure and Trusted Communications Networks Act of 2019 (2020) formally prohibited the use of federal funds to purchase covered equipment and established a reimbursement program, commonly referred to as the "rip and replace" initiative, to assist smaller telecommunications providers in removing and replacing existing Huawei and ZTE infrastructure (Pallone 2019). Subsequent Federal Communications Commission actions designated the firms as national security threats, barring new authorizations and tightening restrictions on their participation in US communications systems. These measures reflected a broader shift in US cyber policy: supply-chain security was no longer confined to software integrity, but extended to strategic telecommunications hardware embedded in the nation's critical infrastructure.

The discovery of the widespread use of foreign telecommunications equipment in domestic networks resulted in Section 889 of the National Defense Authorization Act for Fiscal Year 2019, which prohibited federal agencies and contractors from procuring or using equipment produced by certain Chinese firms, including Huawei and ZTE. The provision reflected intelligence assessments that such equipment could introduce supply-chain risk into US telecommunications infrastructure. Section 889 represented a shift from reactive vulnerability management to proactive exclusion of high-risk vendors, signaling that cybersecurity policy had expanded beyond software and networks into geopolitical technology competition.

Concerns over semiconductor supply chains culminated in the CHIPS and Science Act of 2022, which authorized significant federal investment in domestic semiconductor manufacturing and research (117th US Congress 2022). Although primarily framed as economic and industrial policy, the legislation carried profound cybersecurity implications. Secure hardware supply chains are foundational to national security, and reliance on foreign manufacturing introduced both strategic vulnerability and potential compromise risk. By incentivizing domestic production and supply-chain transparency, the Act underscored the growing recognition that cyber resilience begins at the hardware level.

The broader policy lesson from these events was that cybersecurity could no longer be compartmentalized. Vulnerabilities in a single code library could cascade across finance, energy, health, and defense simultaneously. Compromised hardware could contain code embedded in firmware that would grant foreign adversaries full control over domestic communications systems. Consequently, software assurance became a national resilience priority, embedded in the 2023 National Cybersecurity Strategy's Pillar 1 ("Defend Critical Infrastructure"). The concept of "secure by design and secure by default" emerged as a guiding principle for both private developers and government procurement.

The DoD, DHS, and other federal agencies continue to view supply-chain assurance as a long-term national-security challenge, especially for critical infrastructure and defense systems. This viewpoint is driving recent efforts toward trusted suppliers, secure-by-design requirements, and diversification of manufacturing and technology

7.6.2 Cyber Incident Reporting for Critical Infrastructure Act of 2022 (CIRCIA)

The Cyber Incident Reporting for Critical Infrastructure Act of 2022 (CIRCIA 2022) marked a significant evolution in federal cyber policy by establishing mandatory reporting requirements for designated critical infrastructure entities. Under the statute, organizations experiencing substantial cyber incidents must report them to CISA within 72 hours, and ransomware payments must be reported within 24 hours. Unlike earlier information-sharing frameworks that relied largely on voluntary participation, CIRCIA signaled a shift toward regulatory expectations for transparency and situational awareness. The legislation reflected growing recognition that federal authorities lacked timely visibility into significant cyber incidents affecting essential services. By formalizing reporting requirements, Congress sought to improve national-level threat intelligence, accelerate coordinated response, and strengthen resilience across interconnected sectors.

7.6.3 Federal Cybersecurity and Infrastructure Executive Orders

In February 2020, the DoD implemented Executive Order 13905 (2020), Strengthening National Resilience through Responsible Use of Positioning, Navigation, and Timing (PNT) Services (Executive Order 13905 2020). This directive reflected growing concern over the nation's dependence on networked technologies and satellite-based timing systems. It required the development of alternative and resilient PNT capabilities to ensure continuity of operations during cyber or physical disruptions, an early example of integrating cybersecurity principles into the broader concept of national resilience.

Following several major supply-chain cyberattacks like the SolarWinds and Microsoft Exchange exploits, the federal government undertook its most ambitious modernization effort to date. On May 12, 2021, Executive Order 14028 (2021), Improving the Nation's Cybersecurity, was issued by the Biden Administration. This order fundamentally reshaped how the federal government manages, procures, and secures information technology by directing agencies to adopt Zero Trust Architecture (ZTA) principles, requiring continuous authentication, least-privilege access, and rigorous network segmentation across all federal systems (Executive Order 14028 2021). It also mandated that software vendors providing products to the government maintain secure development practices, publish a Software Bill of Materials (CISA n.d.), and report vulnerabilities transparently. The order created a Cyber Safety Review Board (CSRB) to analyze significant incidents and recommend systemic improvements, modeled after the National Transportation Safety Board (NTSB). The CSRB was sunset in 2025 as a standing body, but its reviews of major incidents informed subsequent federal guidance on software security, incident response, and coordinated disclosure.

Additionally, EO 14028 initiated a major overhaul of incident response processes, requiring standardized playbooks, accelerated logging and monitoring capabilities, and greater coordination among DHS, the FBI, and the intelligence community.

To operationalize these directives, the OMB issued Memorandum M-22-09, which provided agencies with a roadmap for achieving Zero Trust maturity by the end of Fiscal Year 2024 (OMB 2022). The memo established performance goals for identity management, device security, network segmentation, application control, and data encryption. This marked the first time that Zero Trust concepts were embedded into binding federal policy.

The combined effect of these executive orders was to shift the federal government from a compliance-driven culture to a risk-based, outcomes-oriented model. Rather than focusing solely on protecting individual systems, agencies were now required to demonstrate measurable progress in resilience, detection, and response. These policies also reinforced the growing interdependence between federal, state, and private-sector networks. This is an acknowledgment that the government cannot defend what it does not own or operate without deep collaboration.

The United States had now moved beyond fragmented cyber mandates toward an integrated federal strategy built on shared standards, modernized architectures, and continuous accountability. The next phase of policy evolution would expand this framework internationally, embedding cyber resilience and digital trust into the nation's global partnerships and strategic alliances.

7.6.4 National Cybersecurity Strategy (Biden Administration)

The culmination of more than a decade of legislative and executive action arrived in March 2023, when the Biden Administration released the National Cybersecurity Strategy (2023), the most comprehensive federal cyber policy document since the 2011 International Strategy for Cyberspace. It reflected a decisive shift in philosophy: from voluntary, market-driven approaches toward one that imposed greater accountability on technology providers, critical infrastructure operators, and federal agencies.

The strategy was organized around five strategic pillars, each representing a core national objective:

1) *Defend Critical Infrastructure:* Strengthen the resilience of key sectors such as energy, water, transportation, and healthcare through minimum security requirements and closer coordination with sector risk management agencies.
2) *Disrupt and Dismantle Threat Actors:* Expand the government's capacity to pursue cybercriminal and state-sponsored adversaries through law enforcement, intelligence sharing, and joint operations.
3) *Shape Market Forces to Drive Security and Resilience:* Realign economic incentives by placing greater responsibility on software and hardware vendors for insecure products and vulnerabilities.
4) *Invest in a Resilient Future:* Advance secure-by-design technologies, and cybersecurity workforce development.
5) *Forge International Partnerships to Pursue Shared Goals:* Integrate cyber deterrence and resilience into alliances such as NATO, the Quad, and US–EU collaborations (National Cybersecurity Strategy 2023).

A significant innovation of the 2023 Strategy was its shift in liability for insecure software and systems. Rather than relying on consumers and small organizations to bear the cost of patching vulnerabilities, the Strategy proposed reforms to hold manufacturers accountable for negligent design and implementation. This marked a turning point in national cyber policy. Security was no longer treated as a voluntary best practice, but as a fundamental expectation of doing business in the digital economy.

The Strategy also reaffirmed the federal government's commitment to ZTA, modernized identity management, and protection of the software supply chain. It directed CISA and the ONCD to lead implementation, working with agencies and the private sector to develop measurable outcomes. The ONCD's role expanded significantly, providing centralized coordination across agencies that had previously operated in silos.

In July 2023, the White House released the National Cybersecurity Strategy Implementation Plan (2023), which assigned more than 60 specific initiatives to departments and agencies, including mandatory adoption of SBOMs, modernization of industrial control system defenses, and continued collaboration through the JCDC. This plan translated the Strategy's vision into concrete milestones, timelines, and accountability mechanisms.

By emphasizing "collective defense" and "shared responsibility," the 2023 Strategy aligned national cybersecurity policy with broader trends in defense and diplomacy. It recognized that digital threats now cut across every domain – military, economic, social, and cognitive, and that effective defense requires cooperation among governments, industries, and citizens.

By 2025, the National Cybersecurity Strategy had become the umbrella under which nearly every federal cyber initiative was organized. Its implementation required alignment among CISA, ONCD, the intelligence community, the DoD, and state and local partners. This was a level of coordination previously unseen in the federal cyber enterprise. While execution remains an ongoing challenge, the Strategy's shift from voluntary compliance to regulated accountability marked the emergence of a mature, whole-of-nation approach to cybersecurity designed to endure beyond any single administration.

7.6.5 Public–Private Collaboration and Operational Integration

By the mid-2020s, public–private collaboration had evolved from ad hoc information sharing to operational integration. The JCDC became the nucleus for real-time coordination among government agencies, technology firms, and critical infrastructure operators. Its 2023–2025 initiatives such as preemptive monitoring of election systems, ransomware campaign tracking, and emergency response to the MOVEit file-transfer exploit demonstrated the feasibility of collective defense at national scale.

This new model represented a departure from the "government leads, industry follows" mindset of earlier decades. Instead, it embraced a distributed defense ecosystem, where cloud providers, ISPs, and cybersecurity vendors functioned as front-line defenders, while CISA served as the strategic integrator. The approach mirrored the "defend forward" principle used by US Cyber Command, but applied it to civilian infrastructure, a shift from static deterrence to active collaboration.

7.6.6 Offensive Cyber Operations and Deterrence Doctrine

While diplomacy sought to build stability, the United States simultaneously developed the means to deter and, if necessary, disrupt adversary cyber campaigns. This dual-track approach of cooperation and capability defined US cyber strategy through the 2010s and 2020s.

The DoD Cyber Strategy of 2018 introduced the concepts of "persistent engagement" and "defend forward," asserting that the United States must maintain continuous contact with adversaries in cyberspace to preempt attacks before they reach domestic networks (DoD 2018). This doctrine represented a strategic shift from reactive defense to proactive disruption. Under this framework, CYBERCOM was authorized to conduct operations in foreign networks to identify, monitor, and neutralize threats at their source. This approach was later codified in the 2020 National Defense Authorization Act.

These principles moved from theory to practice in several notable operations. During the 2018 US midterm elections, CYBERCOM conducted Operation

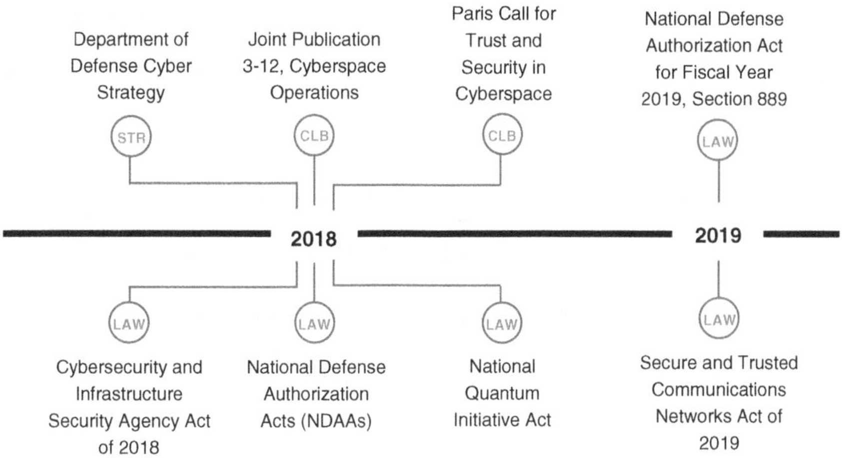

Timeline 5 2018–2019.

Synthetic Thesis, disabling Internet Research Agency infrastructure used for Russian influence operations. Similar efforts targeted Iranian and North Korean cyber units responsible for ransomware and cryptocurrency theft. In partnership with allies, US forces also engaged in coordinated counter-operations to disrupt propaganda networks supporting violent extremist groups, notably through Operation Glowing Symphony against ISIS (2016–2019).

The 2023 DoD Cyber Strategy further refined deterrence doctrine, emphasizing integration with allies and cross-domain coordination. It recognized that effective deterrence in cyberspace relies on speed, transparency, and coalition attribution. Publicly disclosing cyber operations, which were once unthinkable, became a deliberate policy tool, signaling capability and resolve without escalating to kinetic conflict (DoD 2023). The strategy also expanded focus on protecting space assets, undersea cables, and defense-industrial supply chains, acknowledging that critical military functions now depend on globally distributed digital infrastructure.

Offensive cyber operations also introduced complex policy and ethical challenges. Persistent engagement blurred the line between defense and offense, raising questions about sovereignty and escalation thresholds. To mitigate these risks, US policymakers emphasized norm-compliant conduct, ensuring that operations adhere to international law and minimize collateral impact on civilian networks. The Cyber Command Legal Framework (2024 update) formalized these commitments, outlining rules of engagement that balance operational agility with accountability.

To complicate matters, evidence of Chinese cyber espionage expanded beyond enterprise and government networks into the core infrastructure of US telecommunications providers in 2024. Public reporting by US intelligence agencies and private-sector researchers revealed that a long-running Chinese espionage campaign, often referred to in open sources as "Salt Typhoon" had compromised multiple major telephone carriers. These intrusions targeted network-management systems and lawful-intercept platforms, giving attackers the ability to access call metadata, text-message records, and, in some cases, live communications.

Unlike earlier campaigns that focused primarily on intellectual property or classified research, these operations demonstrated sustained access to the backbone of civilian communications infrastructure. US officials characterized the activity as strategic espionage rather than criminal exploitation, emphasizing the implications for national security, counterintelligence, and the privacy of government officials and private citizens alike. The incidents reinforced longstanding concerns that telecommunications networks represent a uniquely high-value target, one where cyber access can yield intelligence effects that are difficult to detect, attribute, or fully remediate.

In recent years, the United States has demonstrated how cyber tools can complement conventional military power in coordinated joint operations that extend well beyond the purely digital domain. During Operation Midnight Hammer in June 2025 (the US air campaign against Iranian nuclear facilities at Fordow, Natanz, and Isfahan) US cyber forces reportedly provided offensive and preparatory support by disrupting Iranian air defense networks, degrading command-and-control systems, and conducting indications-and-warning operations to improve targeting and force protection for kinetic strikes. Cyber effects were used both to disable enemy defensive capabilities and to gather near-real-time intelligence on Iranian force posture, illustrating how digital operations now underpin traditional air and missile campaigns.

By 2026, it became clear that implementing cyber capabilities in joint campaigns was not a novel approach, but a new modus operandi. During Operation Absolute Resolve in January 2026 (a joint operation to capture Venezuelan president Nicolás Maduro) cyber units again played a role by disrupting Venezuelan communications and facilitating rapid maneuver by US special operations forces. In February 2026, in the bombing of Iran, known as Roaring Lion in Israel and Epic Fury in the US, cyber warfare was critical in shaping intelligence, operations, and even psychological influence campaign in the American-Israeli attack (Ahronheim 2026). These cases reflect the maturation of US cyber capabilities into an integrated component of joint campaigns, where offensive and defensive cyber effects are synchronized with air, land, and naval operations to achieve strategic goals across the spectrum of conflict rather than as isolated digital campaigns.

By 2026, the integration of offensive cyber capabilities into national strategy had matured into a credible deterrent. The United States demonstrated that it could impose costs on adversaries while reinforcing a rules-based order in cyberspace. Together, these developments of diplomatic outreach, alliance strengthening, and operational assertiveness defined a new era of strategic cyber deterrence, where resilience, partnerships, and precision operations collectively sustain stability in an increasingly contested digital domain.

7.7 Emerging Policy Frontiers

By the mid-2020s, the United States had constructed a robust foundation of cybersecurity doctrine, law, and organizational capacity. Yet the very speed of technological change ensured that no framework remained stable for long. The convergence of cloud computing, operational technology, AI, and human-centric information warfare demanded new policy frontiers. These policies blurred the boundaries between technology governance, engineering design, and cognitive resilience. These emerging areas represent the next evolution of national cybersecurity policy, from compliance and control toward adaptive resilience built into the systems themselves.

7.7.1 Zero Trust, Cloud, and Identity Modernization

Among the most transformative policy shifts of the 2020s was the wholesale adoption of ZTA across the federal enterprise. Building on Executive Order 14028 (2021) and OMB Memorandum M-22-09 (2022), agencies were required to move beyond perimeter-based network models in favor of continuous verification of users, devices, and applications. This represented a philosophical change that treated every interaction as potentially compromised until proven otherwise (i.e., "Zero Trust.")

NIST's Zero Trust Architecture Standard (2020) in combination with CISA's Zero Trust Maturity Model (2021) provided the blueprints for action. CISA defined five functional pillars: identity, device, network/environment, application/workload, and data, each with maturity stages from traditional to optimized. Agencies were tasked with reaching advanced maturity levels by FY 2024 by integrating multi-factor authentication, continuous diagnostics, endpoint detection, micro-segmentation, and behavioral analytics.

At the same time, the federal cloud landscape was modernized through the FedRAMP Rev. 5 update (2023) and the Federal Cloud Computing Strategy's Cloud Smart Initiative (2024 update). These reforms emphasized security reciprocity across agencies and accelerated the authorization of commercial cloud services. They also aligned with CISA's Secure Cloud Business Applications (SCuBA) project, which standardized telemetry, logging, and configuration baselines for SaaS environments.

Identity modernization became the connective tissue of Zero Trust. The government's Identity, Credential, and Access Management (DoD 2020) modernization

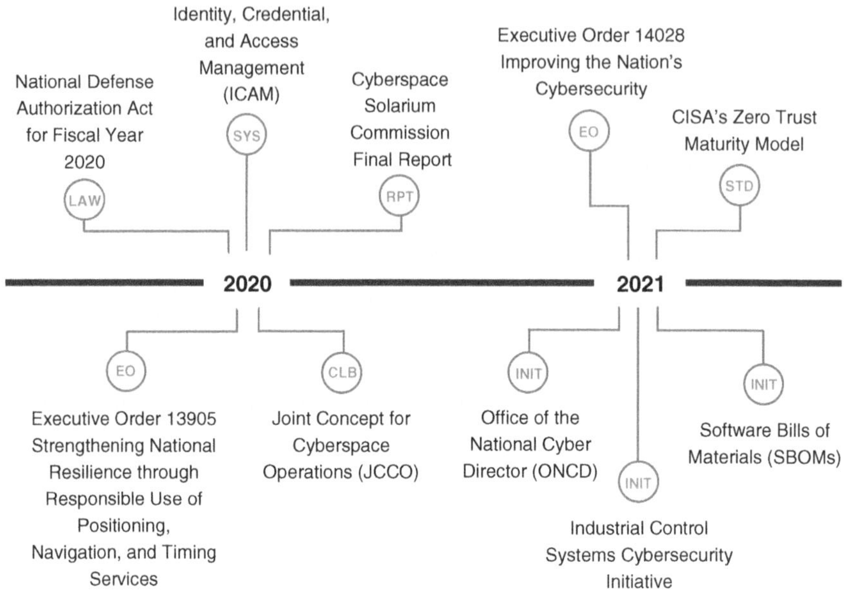

Timeline 6 2020–2021.

effort unified credential systems across civilian and defense agencies, introduced Continuous Adaptive Trust (CAT) (a method of continuously evaluating authentication in real-time, rather than just at login), and adaptive authentication and cryptographic tokens resistant to phishing. Combined, these initiatives marked a decisive break from the patchwork identity systems of the early 2000s, establishing a single trust fabric spanning cloud, edge, and endpoint environments.

By 2025, Zero Trust implementation had matured beyond compliance checklists into a living framework that guided enterprise engineering decisions. Agencies began measuring success not by the absence of incidents but by their speed of detection, containment, and recovery. This approach operationalized resilience as a measurable outcome.

7.7.2 Quantum Computing and Cryptographic Forecasts

Parallel to ZTA developments, physics research in quantum computing suggested to some policymakers that our current cryptographic methods may one day be easily cracked and therefore obsolete. In response, NIST launched a multi-year Post-Quantum Cryptography (PQC) Standardization Project, selecting four algorithms in 2024 as the first generation of quantum-resistant encryption standards. This effort was reinforced by an earlier Quantum Computing Cybersecurity Preparedness Act (2022), which mandated federal agencies to inventory vulnerable systems and plan for cryptographic migration.

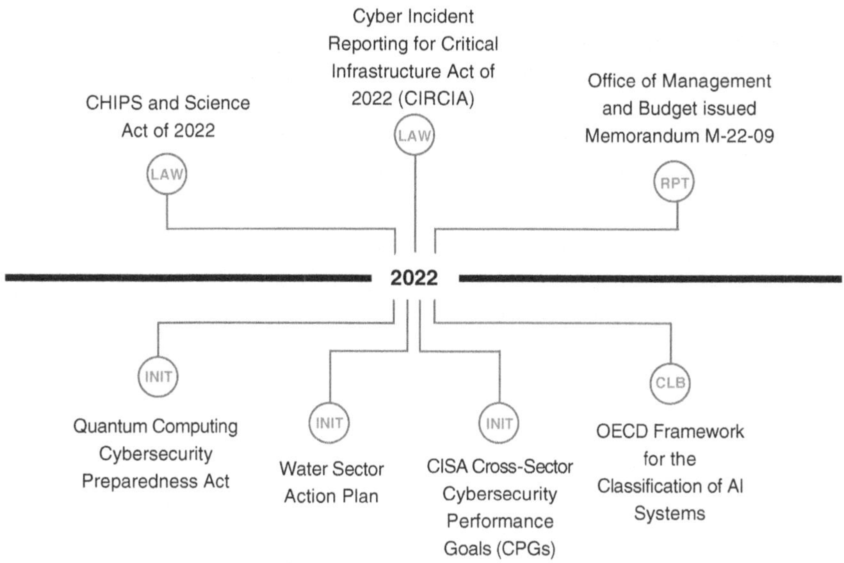

Timeline 7 2022.

By 2025, agencies were expected to begin phased adoption of PQC algorithms for both classified and unclassified systems. The OMB, in coordination with CISA and NIST, issued guidance establishing a multi-year transition roadmap that emphasized interoperability and testing before full deployment. At the same time, CISA warned that adversaries were likely conducting "harvest now, decrypt later" campaigns, collecting encrypted data today in anticipation of future decryption once quantum capabilities mature. The new cryptographic standards thus became not just a technical requirement but a strategic priority for national data protection. That said, there is an increasing level of debate over whether quantum technology itself will ever emerge, given that it has been half a century since development was started and there has been no emergence of a successful quantum computing device, not even a prototype (Gutmann 2025). A similar situation happened in physics research with respect to string theory, which no longer commands funding (Woit 2006).

7.7.3 Operational Technology (OT) and Industrial Control Systems (ICS)

As digital and physical systems became inseparable, operational technology (OT) and Industrial Control Systems (ICS) cybersecurity emerged as a central focus of national cyber policy. The ransomware attacks against Colonial Pipeline (2021) and JBS Foods (2021) demonstrated that digital intrusions could rapidly cascade into physical disruption. In response, the federal government moved to close the

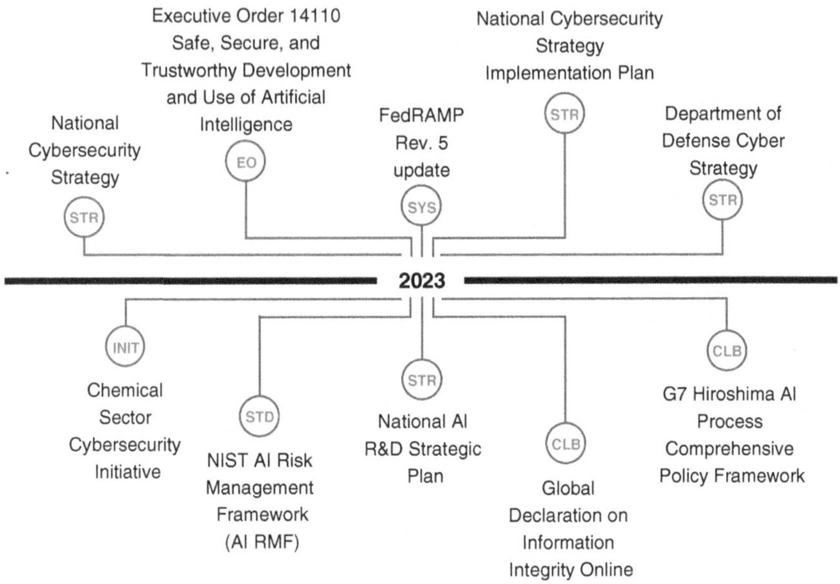

Timeline 8 2023.

longstanding divide between information technology (IT) security and engineering safety.

The Industrial Control Systems Cybersecurity Initiative (DoE 2021) launched 100-day "sprints" for the electric, natural gas, and water sectors, driving near-term improvements in visibility and threat detection. These efforts were coordinated by CISA and the DOE, leveraging partnerships with sector risk management agencies and private utilities. The initiative later evolved into the Water Sector Action Plan (2022) and Chemical Sector Cybersecurity Initiative (2023), expanding the program's scope and emphasizing measurable control-system outcomes.

Parallel efforts within DOE's Office of Cybersecurity, Energy Security, and Emergency Response (CESER) and the National Laboratories also promote engineered defenses, such as segmentation, unidirectional gateways, and consequence-focused design via a new program dubbed Cyber-Informed Engineering (CIE). CISA's Cross-Sector Cybersecurity Performance Goals (CPGs) (CISA n.d.a) incorporated similar guidance, encouraging utilities and industrial operators to engineer resilience into critical systems rather than to bolt it on.

By 2025, the integration of CIE principles into federal and industry frameworks marked a quiet revolution. Engineering disciplines were now recognized as essential partners in cybersecurity, not merely consumers of cybersecurity policy. Programs like DOE's OT Defender Fellowship and INL's Consequence-Driven Cyber-Informed Engineering (CCE) training spread this philosophy across

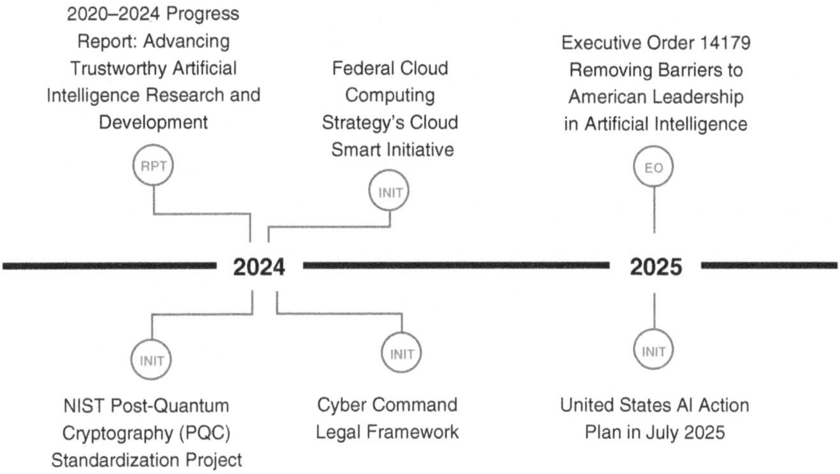

Timeline 9 2024–2025.

infrastructure sectors, helping operators understand that effective defense begins with system design, not incident response.

7.7.4 Artificial Intelligence Policy and Cognitive Security

The rapid adoption of Generative AI (GenAI) and Agentic AI tools across government, industry, and critical infrastructure led to a surge of policy activity aimed at ensuring their secure and ethical use. In October 2023, Executive Order 14110 on the Safe, Secure, and Trustworthy Development and Use of Artificial Intelligence directed federal agencies to establish comprehensive safeguards for AI models and data (Executive Order 14110 2023). It tasked NIST with developing new testing and evaluation frameworks under its AI Risk Management Framework (AI RMF) and required federal contractors to certify adherence to responsible AI development practices (NIST 2023). The DHS Science and Technology Directorate and CISA began funding research into detecting manipulated audio and video and tracing the origins of digital content.

By early 2024, the ONCD and CISA began integrating AI oversight into the broader cybersecurity ecosystem. Both agencies emphasized the concept of cognitive security, the protection of human decision-making and public perception from AI-driven manipulation, deepfakes, and misinformation. Recognizing that malicious use of AI could erode social trust as effectively as a network intrusion, policymakers began treating information reliability as an element of national cyber resilience.

These efforts also converged with international initiatives. The G7 Hiroshima AI Process, the Organisation for Economic Co-operation and Development (OECD)

Framework for the Classification of AI Systems (OECD 2022), and the EU–US Trade and Technology Council all advanced principles for transparency, watermarking, and accountability in generative-AI systems (OECD 2022). At the United Nations, member states debated measures to uphold information integrity online, including support for the Global Declaration on Information Integrity Online (2023) launched by Canada and the Netherlands in 2023 (Netherlands 2023). Collectively, these initiatives reflected growing recognition that safeguarding public trust and information reliability is inseparable from cybersecurity itself.

The 2020–2024 National AI Research and Development Strategic Plan (National Science and Technology Council 2023) further aligned AI governance with cyber policy by prioritizing secure model design, explainability, and defenses against data poisoning and model inversion attacks. The DoE and the DoD jointly expanded research into AI-enabled threat detection, while DHS initiated pilot programs using AI for infrastructure monitoring and anomaly detection in industrial control systems. At the same time, the White House convened major cloud service providers and model developers to commit to voluntary AI safety standards, a step later reinforced by legislative proposals seeking to codify minimum safeguards.

EO 14110 was rescinded on January 20, 2025, and replaced by Executive Order 14179, Removing Barriers to American Leadership in Artificial Intelligence, which declared a national priority to "sustain and enhance America's global AI dominance" and directed senior White House advisors and agency heads to develop a coordinated AI Action Plan within 180 days (Executive Order 14179 2025). The new order rescinded aspects of the earlier AI framework seen as regulatory barriers and called on agencies to review, revise, or rescind policies, directives, and regulations inconsistent with the new policy goals, emphasizing innovation, competitiveness, and national security rather than the more extensive safety reporting and oversight provisions of the 2023 directive (Trump Administration 2025).

The United States AI Action Plan delivered in July 2025 outlines a federal strategy to sustain and enhance US leadership in AI by promoting innovation, building domestic AI infrastructure, and advancing international AI diplomacy and security. The recommendations serve as a roadmap for federal agencies to align research, procurement, export strategy, and workforce development with the Administration's stated goal of global AI dominance in support of economic competitiveness and national security.

7.8 Conclusion

When the first edition of this handbook was published, the federal government's approach to cybersecurity was still emerging from its formative years. The principal focus was defining roles and responsibilities, creating basic organizational structures, and establishing the legal foundations for national cyber defense.

At that time, coordination among agencies was limited, congressional consensus was elusive, and cybersecurity policy often followed rather than anticipated technological change.

More than a decade later, the United States has entered a markedly different era. What began as a patchwork of initiatives has matured into a coherent, whole-of-nation framework that integrates law, strategy, operations, and engineering. The creation of the CISA provided a permanent home for civilian cyber defense, while the ONCD added strategic direction and accountability across government. Executive Orders 13800 and 14028, the National Cybersecurity Strategy (2023), and the modernization of FISMA and related laws have elevated cybersecurity from an IT issue to a core element of national security policy.

Equally significant has been the shift toward resilience by design. Federal policy now emphasizes measurable outcomes such as rapid detection, containment, and recovery rather than the illusion of perfect prevention. The nationwide adoption of the ZTA approach and modernization of identity and cloud systems have replaced outdated perimeter defenses with continuous verification and adaptive trust. In the nation's infrastructure sectors, the integration of Cyber-Informed Engineering (CIE) principles has begun to realign cybersecurity with the physical realities of energy, water, transportation, and manufacturing systems, bridging the long-standing divide between engineering and information assurance.

At the global level, the United States has advanced a model of strategic cyber deterrence that combines diplomacy, alliance integration, and credible operational capability. Through NATO, the G7, and the UN, cyber norms have begun to take shape around responsible state behavior, transparency, and collective defense. However, as President Trump eschews NATO and the UN and turns his attention toward a newly established Board of Peace, international partnerships in the area of cybersecurity are at risk.[1] Domestically, public–private collaboration has produced operational partnerships through entities like the JCDC, ensuring that government and industry now share both intelligence and responsibility for defense.

Looking forward, the policy frontier is rapidly expanding. Perhaps the most profound challenge lies in the protection of the cognitive domain, the integrity of human perception in an age when information itself can be manufactured at scale. Ensuring information authenticity, countering synthetic manipulation, and preserving public trust will require the same level of coordination and investment

1 Another Trump decision in was Executive Order 14347, which authorized the Department of Defense to use the historic designation "Department of War" in ceremonial and non-statutory contexts. The statutory name of the organization under Title 10 of the US Code remains the Department of Defense, as only Congress may formally rename a federal department. The executive order did not alter the department's legal authorities or organizational structure.

once reserved for network defense. Cognitive security, long an afterthought, is emerging as the defining national-security issue of the coming decade.

The story of US cybersecurity policy is thus a story of convergence. Technology, law, governance, and human behavior can no longer be treated as separate arenas. The next phase will demand engineers who understand policy, policymakers who understand systems, and a public that recognizes cybersecurity not as a specialized discipline, but as a condition of modern civilization. The United States has built the framework. What remains is to sustain it through leadership, resources, and a shared commitment to resilience in the face of constant change.

References

117th US Congress (2022). CHIPS and Science Act of 2022. https://www.congress.gov/bill/117th-congress/house-bill/4346 (accessed 24 February 2026).

2020–2024 Progress Report: Advancing Trustworthy Artificial Intelligence Research and Development (2024). https://www.nitrd.gov/pubs/AI-Research-and-Development-Progress-Report-2020-2024.pdf (accessed 24 February 2026).

Ahronheim, A. (2026). Cyber is fuel foe US, Israel's war on Iran's Islamic Regime, expert says – Interview. https://www.jpost.com/defense-and-tech/article-888820 (accessed 3 March 2026).

Center for Strategic and International Studies (CSIS) (2008). Securing Cyberspace for the 44th Presidency. https://www.nitrd.gov/documents/cybersecurity/documents/081208_securingcyberspace_44.pdf (accessed 26 February 2026).

Chairman of the Joint Chiefs of Staff (CJCS) (2018). Joint Publication 3-12, Cyberspace Operations. https://nsarchive.gwu.edu/sites/default/files/documents/4560063/Joint-Chiefs-of-Staff-Joint-Publication-3-12.pdf (accessed 27 February 2026).

Chemical Sector Cybersecurity Initiative (2023). https://www.cisa.gov/sites/default/files/2023-10/2023-summit-chemical-sector-cyber-threats-508.pdf (accessed 28 February 2026).

Cyber Command Legal Framework (2024 update). https://www.cybercom.mil/default.aspx (accessed 28 February 2026).

Cyber Incident Reporting for Critical Infrastructure Act of 2022 (CIRCIA) (2022). https://www.congress.gov/bill/117th-congress/house-bill/2471/text (accessed 24 February 2026).

Cybersecurity and Infrastructure Security Agency (CISA) (n.d.-a). Cross-Sector Cybersecurity Performance Goals (CPGs). https://www.cisa.

Cybersecurity and Infrastructure Security Agency (CISA) (2021). CISA's Zero Trust Maturity Model. https://www.cisa.gov/zero-trust-maturity-model (accessed 24 February 2026).

Cybersecurity and Infrastructure Security Agency (CISA) (n.d.-b). Software Bills of Materials (SBOMs). https://www.cisa.gov/sbom (accessed 27 February 2026).

Cybersecurity and Infrastructure Security Agency Act of 2018 (2018). https://www.congress.gov/bill/115th-congress/house-bill/3359 (accessed 24 February 2026).

Cybersecurity Information Sharing Act (2015). https://uscode.house.gov/view.xhtml?req=granuleid%3AUSC-prelim-title6-chapter6-subchapter1&saved=%7CZ3JhbnVsZWlkOlVTQy1wcmVsaW0tdGl0bGU2LWNoYXB0ZXI2LXN1YmNoYXB0ZXIxLWZyb250%7C%7C%7C0%7Cfalse%7Cprelim&edition=prelim (accessed 9 March 2026).

Cyberspace Solarium Commission (2020). Cyberspace Solarium Commission Final Report. https://www.cybersolarium.org (accessed 15 March 2026).

Department of Defense (DoD) (2020). Identity, Credential, and Access Management (ICAM) modernization effort. https://dodcio.defense.gov/Portals/0/Documents/Cyber/ICAM_Strategy.pdf (accessed 27 February 2026).

Department of Defense (DoD) (2015). Cyber Strategy. https://nsarchive.gwu.edu/document/21384-document-25 (accessed 24 February 2026).

Department of Defense (DoD) (2018). Cyber Strategy. https://dodcio.defense.gov/Portals/0/Documents/Library/CyberStrategy2018.pdf (accessed 24 March 2026).

Department of Defense (DoD) (2023). Cyber Strategy. https://media.defense.gov/2023/Sep/12/2003299076/-1/-1/1/2023_DOD_Cyber_Strategy_Summary.PDF (accessed 28 February 2026).

Department of Energy (DoE) (2021). Progress report: 100 Days of the Biden Administration's Industrial Control Systems (ICS) Cybersecurity Initiative and Electricity Subsector Action Plan. https://www.energy.gov/articles/progress-report-100-days-biden-administrations-industrial-control-systems-ics (accessed 15 March 2026).

Department of Homeland Security (DHS). (2013). Partnering for Critical Infrastructure Security and Resilience. https://www.nist.gov/system/files/documents/cybercommission/-DHS-_National_Infrastructure_Protection_Plan_-NIPP.pdf (accessed 24 February 2026).

Executive Order 13010 (1996). Critical Infrastructure Protection. https://www.federalregister.gov/documents/1996/07/17/96-18351/critical-infrastructure-protection (accessed 24 February 2026).

Executive Order 13231 (2001). Critical Infrastructure Protection in the Information Age. https://www.federalregister.gov/documents/2001/10/18/01-26509/critical-infrastructure-protection-in-the-information-age (accessed 24 February 2026).

Executive Order 13636 (2013). Improving Critical Infrastructure Cybersecurity. https://www.federalregister.gov/documents/2013/02/19/2013-03915/improving-critical-infrastructure-cybersecurity (accessed 24 February 2026).

Executive Order 13800 (2017). Strengthening the Cybersecurity of Federal Networks and Critical Infrastructure. https://www.federalregister.gov/documents/2017/05/

16/2017-10004/strengthening-the-cybersecurity-of-federal-networks-and-critical-infrastructure (accessed 24 February 2026).

Executive Order 13905 (2020). Strengthening National Resilience Through Responsible Use of Positioning, Navigation, and Timing Services. https://www.federalregister.gov/documents/2020/02/18/2020-03337/strengthening-national-resilience-through-responsible-use-of-positioning-navigation-and-timing (accessed 24 February 2026).

Executive Order 14028 (2021). Improving the Nation's Cybersecurity. https://www.federalregister.gov/documents/2021/05/17/2021-10460/improving-the-nations-cybersecurity (accessed 24 February 2026).

Executive Order 14110 (2023). Safe, Secure, and Trustworthy Development and Use of Artificial Intelligence. https://www.federalregister.gov/documents/2023/11/01/2023-24283/safe-secure-and-trustworthy-development-and-use-of-artificial-intelligence (accessed 24 February 2026).

Executive Order 14179 (2025). Removing Barriers to American Leadership in Artificial Intelligence. https://www.federalregister.gov/documents/2025/01/31/2025-02172/removing-barriers-to-american-leadership-in-artificial-intelligence (accessed 24 February 2026).

Fattahi, A. (2026). *Trump's Cyber Strategy: Offensive Ambitions, Defensive Gaps*. London: Bloomsbury Intelligence and Security Institute (BISI), https://bisi.org.uk/reports/trumps-cyber-strategy-offensive-ambitions-defensive-gaps (accessed 10 March 2026).

Federal Cloud Computing Strategy's Cloud Smart Initiative (2024 update). https://www.cio.gov/news/federal-zero-trust-data-security-guide (accessed 3 March 2026).

Federal Information Security Management Act of 2002 (FISMA) (2002). https://www.congress.gov/bill/107th-congress/house-bill/3844/text (accessed 28 February 2026).

Federal Information Security Modernization Act of 2014 (FISMA) (2014). https://www.cisa.gov/topics/cyber-threats-and-advisories/federal-information-security-modernization-act (accessed 27 February 2026).

Federal Risk and Authorization Management Program (FedRAMP) (2023 update). Rev. 5. https://www.fedramp.gov/docs/rev5/ (accessed 27 February 2026).

Feinstein, D. and Burr, R. (2015). Cybersecurity and Informaton Sharing Act of 2015. https://www.congress.gov/crs-product/IF12959 (accessed 25 July 2026).

G7 Hiroshima AI Process (2023). Hiroshima AI Process G7 Digital & Tech Ministers' Statement, Comprehensive Policy Framework. https://www.soumu.go.jp/hiroshimaaiprocess/pdf/document02_en.pdf (accessed 28 February 2026).

Government Accounting Office (GAO) (1996). Information Security: Computer Attacks at Department of Defense Pose Increasing Risks (Testimony, 05/22/96, Government Accounting Office Report T-AIMD-96-92). 22 May 1996. https://www

.govinfo.gov/content/pkg/GAOREPORTS-T-AIMD-96-92/html/GAOREPORTS-T-AIMD-96-92.htm (accessed 10 March 2026).

Gutmann, P. (2025). Why Quantum Cryptanalysis is Bollocks, Kawaiicon III video presentation (6-8 November 2025). https://www.youtube.com/watch?v=xa4Ok7WNFHY (accessed 15 March 2026).

Harmon, A. (1995). Hacking theft of $10 million from Citibank revealed. Los Angeles Times. 19 August. https://www.latimes.com/archives/la-xpm-1995-08-19-fi-36656-story.html (accessed 10 March 2026).

Healey, J. (2013). *A Fierce Domain – Documents on Key Events in Cyber History*. Vienna, VA: Cyber Conflict Studies Association.

Homeland Security Presidential Directive 12 (HSPD 12) (2004). Policy for a Common Identification Standard for Federal Employees and Contractors. https://www.dhs.gov/homeland-security-presidential-directive-12 (accessed 24 February 2026).

Homeland Security Presidential Directive 7 (HSPD 7) (2003). Critical Infrastructure Identification, Prioritization, and Protection. https://www.cisa.gov/news-events/directives/homeland-security-presidential-directive-7 (accessed 24 February 2026).

International Strategy for Cyberspace (2011). https://obamawhitehouse.archives.gov/sites/default/files/rss_viewer/international_strategy_for_cyberspace.pdf (accessed 27 February 2026).

Lieberman, J. and Collins, S. (2012). Cybersecurity Act of 2012. https://www.congress.gov/bill/112th-congress/senate-bill/2105 (accessed 24 February 2026).

Lynn, W. (2010). Defending a new domain: The Pentagon's Cyberstrategy. *Foreign Affairs*, 89(5): https://apps.dtic.mil/sti/pdfs/ADA527707.pdf (accessed 15 March 2026).

Miller, C. (2022). Throwback attack: An attack on the DoD leads to Operation Buckshot Yankee. Control Engineering. 9 December. https://www.controleng.com/throwback-attack-an-attack-on-the-dod-leads-to-operation-buckshot-yankee/ (accessed 28 March 2026).

Mylroie, L. (1995/1996). The World Trade Center Bomb: Who is Ramzi Yousef? And Why It Matters. https://irp.fas.org/world/iraq/956-tni.htm (accessed 9 March 2026).

National Cybersecurity Strategy (2023). https://bidenwhitehouse.archives.gov/wp-content/uploads/2023/03/National-Cybersecurity-Strategy-2023.pdf (accessed 24 February 2026).

National Cybersecurity Strategy Implementation Plan (2023). https://bidenwhitehouse.archives.gov/wp-content/uploads/2023/07/National-Cybersecurity-Strategy-Implementation-Plan-WH.gov_.pdf (accessed 28 February 2026).

National Defense Authorization Act for Fiscal Year 2012 (2011). https://www.govinfo.gov/content/pkg/PLAW-112publ81/pdf/PLAW-112publ81.pdf (accessed 27 February 2026).

National Defense Authorization Act for Fiscal Year 2019 (2019a). Section 889. https://www.acquisition.gov/Section-889-Policies (accessed 27 February 2026).

National Defense Authorization Act for Fiscal Year 2020 (2019b). https://www.congress.gov/bill/116th-congress/senate-bill/1790 (accessed 24 February 2026).

National Defense Authorization Acts (NDAAs) for Fiscal Year 2018 (2026 amended). https://www.govinfo.gov/app/details/COMPS-13932 (accessed 15 March 2026).

National Institute of Standards and Technology (2017). Post-Quantum Cryptography (PQC) Standardization Project. https://csrc.nist.gov/projects/post-quantum-cryptography (accessed 26 February 2026).

National Institute of Standards and Technology (NIST) (2014). Cybersecurity Framework (CSF). https://www.nist.gov/system/files/documents/cyberframework/cybersecurity-framework-021214.pdf

National Institute of Standards and Technology (NIST) (2020). Zero Trust Architecture Standard, SP800-207. https://nvlpubs.nist.gov/nistpubs/SpecialPublications/NIST.SP.800-207.pdf (accessed 15 March 2026).

National Institute of Standards and Technology (NIST) (2023). AI Risk Management Framework (AI RMF). https://www.nist.gov/itl/ai-risk-management-framework (accessed 28 February 2026).

National Quantum Initiative Act (2018). https://www.govinfo.gov/content/pkg/PLAW-115publ368/pdf/PLAW-115publ368.pdf (accessed 28 February 2026).

National Science and Technology Council (2023 update). National Artificial Intelligence Research and Development Strategic Plan. https://www.nitrd.gov/pubs/National-Artificial-Intelligence-Research-and-Development-Strategic-Plan-2023-Update.pdf (accessed 28 February 2026).

National Security Decision Directive 207 (NSDD 207) (1986). https://www.cia.gov/readingroom/docs/CIA-RDP00M00244R000500080004-4.pdf (accessed 27 February 2026).

National Security Presidential Directive 54 (NSPD-54)/Homeland Security Presidential Directive 23 (HSPD-23) (NSPD-HSPD) (2008). https://nsarchive.gwu.edu/document/17291-george-bush-national-security-presidential (accessed 24 February 2026).

National Strategy for Homeland Security (2002, 2007). https://www.dhs.gov/sites/default/files/publications/nat-strat-hls-2002.pdf (accessed 24 February 2026). https://www.dhs.gov/xlibrary/assets/nat_strat_homelandsecurity_2007.pdf (accessed 24 February 2026).

National Strategy for the Physical Protection of Critical Infrastructures and Key Assets (2003). https://www.dhs.gov/xlibrary/assets/Physical_Strategy.pdf (accessed 24 February 2026).

National Strategy for Trusted Identities in Cyberspace (NSTIC) (2010). www.dhs.gov/xlibrary/assets/ns_tic.pdf (accessed 24 February 2026).

National Strategy to Secure Cyberspace (2003). www.cisa.gov/sites/default/files/publications/cyberspace_strategy.pdf (accessed 24 February 2026).

NATO Cyber Defense Pledge (2016). https://www.nato.int/en/about-us/official-texts-and-resources/official-texts/2016/07/08/cyber-defence-pledge (accessed 24 February 2026).

NATO Standardization Office (2020). Allied Joint Concept for Cyberspace Operations (JCCO). https://assets.publishing.service.gov.uk/media/5f086ec4d3bf7f2bef137675/doctrine_nato_cyberspace_operations_ajp_3_20_1_.pdf (accessed 15 March 2026).

Netherlands (2023). Global Declaration on Information Integrity Online. https://www.government.nl/documents/diplomatic-statements/2023/09/20/global-declaration-oninformation-integrity-online (accessed 28 February 2026).

Obama Administration (2009). Assuring a Trusted and Resilient Information and Communications Infrastructure. https://nsarchive.gwu.edu/document/21424-document-28 (accessed 25 July 2026).

Obama Adminstration. (2015). US-China Cyber Agreement, https://obamawhitehouse.archives.gov/the-press-office/2015/09/25/fact-sheet-president-xi-jinpings-state-visit-united-states (accessed 28 February 2026).

Office of the National Cyber Director (ONCD) (2021). https://www.whitehouse.gov/oncd/ (accessed 26 February 2026).

OMB (2022). Memorandum M-22-09, Office of Management and Budget. https://www.whitehouse.gov/wp-content/uploads/2022/01/M-22-09.pdf (accessed 26 February 2026).

Organisation for Economic Co-operation and Development (OECD) (2022). OECD Framework for the Classification of AI Systems. https://www.oecd.org/en/publications/oecd-framework-for-the-classification-of-ai-systems_cb6d9eca-en.html (accessed 28 February 2026).

Pallone, F. (2020). Secure and Trusted Communications Networks Act of 2019. https://www.congress.gov/116/plaws/publ124/PLAW-116publ124.pdf (accessed 26 February 2026).

Paris Call for Trust and Security in Cyberspace (2018). https://www.diplomatie.gouv.fr/IMG/pdf/paris_call_cyber_cle443433-1.pdf (accessed 26 February 2026).

Payment Card Industry Security Standards Council (PCSSSC) (2024). PCI Data Security Standard (PCI DSS) v4.0.1, 11 June. https://www.pcisecuritystandards.org/standards/pci-dss/ (accessed 10 March 2026).

Presidential Commission on Critical Infrastructure Protection (PCCIP) (1997). Critical Foundations, Protecting America's Infrastructures. https://nsarchive.gwu.edu/sites/default/files/documents/2800106/Document-02-President-s-Commission-on-Critical.pdf (accessed 26 February 2026).

Presidential Decision Directive 39 (PDD 39) (1995). U.S. Policy on Counterterrorism. www.clintonlibrary.gov/sites/default/files/documents/pdd-39.pdf (accessed 24 February 2026).

Presidential Decision Directive 63 (PDD 63) (1998). Critical Infrastructure Protection. https://www.govinfo.gov/content/pkg/FR-1998-08-05/html/98-20865.htm (accessed 26 February 2026).

Presidential Decision Directive PDD 62 (PDD 63) (1998). Combating Terrorism. https://www.clintonlibrary.gov/sites/default/files/documents/pdd-62.pdf (accessed 26 February 2026).

Presidential Decision Directive PDD 67 (PDD 67) (1998). Continuity of Government Operations. https://irp.fas.org/offdocs/pdd/pdd-67.htm (accessed 26 February 2026).

Quantum Computing Cybersecurity Preparedness Act (2022). https://www.congress.gov/bill/117th-congress/house-bill/7535/text (accessed 26 February 2026).

Ransomware Task Force Report (2022). Combating ransomware, a comprehensive framework for action. Institute for Security and Technology. https://securityandtechnology.org/wp-content/uploads/2021/09/IST-Ransomware-Task-Force-Report.pdf (accessed 9 March 2026).

Ripatrazone, N. (n.d.). The Hacker Truly Adventurous. https://www.trulyadventure.us/the-hacker#:~:text=Intruder%20alert.-,Intruder%20alert.,the%20secrets%20contained%20within%20them (accessed 10 March 2026).

Sanger, D., Rutenberg, J. and Lipton, E. (2018). Racing Guccifer 2.0's Many Tentacles in the 2016 Election. The New York Times. 15 July. https://www.nytimes.com/2018/07/15/us/politics/guccifer-russia-mueller.html (accessed 15 March 2026).

Stafford (1974). Robert T. Stafford Disaster Relief and Emergency Assistance Act. https://www.govinfo.gov/content/pkg/COMPS-2977/pdf/COMPS-2977.pdf (accessed 27 February 2026).

Trump Administration (2025). United States AI Action Plan. https://www.whitehouse.gov/wp-content/uploads/2025/07/Americas-AI-Action-Plan.pdf (accessed 27 February 2026).

United States Commission on National Security /21st Century (USCNS/21) (2000). Seeking a National Strategy, The Phase II Report on a U.S. National Security Strategy for the 21st Century. https://donohueintellaw.ll.georgetown.edu/sites/default/files/assets/PhaseII.pdf, (accessed 12 March 2026).

US Senate Committee (1996). Senate Hearings on Security in Cyberspace, US Senate Permanent Subcommittee on Investigations. https://irp.fas.org/congress/1996_hr/s960605t.htm (accessed 10 March 2026).

US Senate Committee (2018). Cambridge Analytica and Other Facebook Partners: Examining Data Privacy Risks. U.S. Senate Committee on Commerce, Science, and Transportation. https://www.congress.gov/115/chrg/CHRG-115shrg58439/CHRG-115shrg58439.pdf (accessed 15 March 2026).

Water Sector Action Plan (2022). https://bidenwhitehouse.archives.gov/wp-content/uploads/2022/06/water-action-plan_final_formatted.pdf (accessed 28 February 2026).

Woit, P. (2006). *Not Even Wrong: The Failure of String Theory and the Continuing Challenge to Unify the Laws of Physics*. London: Jonathan Cape.

8

Cybersecurity Policy Catalog

This chapter uses a *catalog* of policy statements to introduce and explain the potential remediation of risk issues that frequently recur in cybersecurity policy debates. We do so with the understanding that any such collection of policy statements is constrained by the moment in time it is published. Given that the state of technology is rapidly changing, and therefore also that of cybersecurity, the list is necessarily incomplete. Nevertheless, the catalog format is useful because the large number of examples simplifies the identification of common attributes of cybersecurity policies and connections that may otherwise be hard to make. Its purpose is elucidation and awareness.

The catalog is presented in six sections, each corresponding to a domain impacted by the issues the policies therein are intended to address. Public sector organizations were introduced as Chapter 1 as a subset of organizations, but from a policy perspective the cybersecurity issues to be addressed by government are unique among organizations because it encompasses all other domains because of its enforcement power over many more people. Therefore, in the catalog, the organization section applies to government institutions, but 'Public' in the sense of 'Public Policy' is presented as its own domain.

Within each section, categories of cybersecurity risk issues most frequently encountered in the domain are listed in alphabetical order in the first column of the domain table. Policy statements germane to each domain/issue combination, if included, are listed in alphabetical order in the second column of the catalog. The issue categories are defined in Table 8.1, and all have appeared in prior chapters of this book, so a check of the index will provide additional details.

We are not the only ones to have used classification attributes to create awareness of the negative impact presented by cybersecurity risk. In a book focused on cybersecurity issues, Josephine Wolff classified cyber threats by attacker goals: money, espionage, and data exposure (Wolff 2018). She then described research

Table 8.1 Cybersecurity Issue Categories.

Issue	Criteria for Classification
Appropriate use	Related to issues that arise when user behavior deviates from explicit or tacit agreements to abide by the system owner's rules for authorized access.
Artificial intelligence	Related to the risks inherent in automated cyber advice, persuasion, and cyber decision-making without a human in the loop.
Financial services	Related to the inherent risk in the myriad of digital services, whereby individuals' and organizations' money is managed and distributed.
Custodial	Related to the responsibility and capability of organizations to secure their technology platforms and to restrict services and behavioral extraction activities to those that are unquestionably in the best interests of the customer.
Cybercrime	Related to fraud, data theft, and other misappropriation of digital assets, including malicious behavior such as bullying and stalking.
Cybersecurity principles	Related to fundamental concepts of sound cybersecurity management.
Geolocation	Related to the risks inherent in the capability of cyberspace to continuously pinpoint the physical location of an individual.
Healthcare	Related to healthcare innovations from digital access *through* concern that routine access by health professionals to patient data extends beyond what is needed for patient care.
Impersonation	Related to the ability of an individual to reliably estimate whether a persona (e.g., account name) encountered online is authorized to operate the persona, and/or a real person or some type of bot.
Industrial control	Related to the issues with industrial control processes known to be physically dangerous when tampered by cybersecurity threats.
Intellectual property	Related to policies at the organizational and national level aimed at deterring commercial espionage and/or trademark or copyright infringement.
Privacy	Related to an individual's ability to occupy cyberspace on their own terms without giving up their right to privacy (and/or be forgotten).
Research and development	Related to policies that support continuous improvement in the capability required to promote safety in cyberspace.
Risk management	Related to the capability of the organization and government to reduce cybersecurity risk to an acceptable residual level.
Supply chain	Related to the risk of dependency on technology platforms to provide services essential to the organizational mission or individual survival.
Technology platforms	Related to privacy and safety risks presented by the extraction, dispossession, surveillance, and deception policies of technology platform operators.
Warfare	Related to the potentially catastrophic use of cybersecurity weapons of mass destruction.
Workforce	Related to the demonstrably professional knowledge and skills needed to join the cybersecurity workforce.

on potential methods of creating disincentives for attackers to pursue these goals using cyberattacks. In each case, she examined the then-existing and proposed approaches to implementing these disincentives via cybersecurity policy.

Wolff classified cybersecurity policies into enforcement categories of *rules, inducements, and information* (or, more formally, *pre-emptive protection, after-an-incident liability*, and *notification*). She also classified policies by their *method* of assuring compliance. Examples are *volunteerism* (the least effective, hoping people make the right choices), *incentives* (rewards to do the right thing), or *formal requirements* (criteria to remain in business). Others, Wolff noted, classify cybersecurity policies by a wide variety of control attributes. For example, *methods of oversight* (such as audit or inspection), *low-level control listings* (such as multi-factor authentication), *specific outcomes* (for example, recovering critical business functions within 4 hours), or *reporting* (like telling regulators within 24 hours). You will see these themes echoed in the *Policy Objective* and the *Reasons for Controversy* columns of each catalog table. You will also note that each policy objective begins with the words, "This policy is intended to...." This purposeful statement is intended to drill in the fact that a crystal-clear policy objective is key to the process of creating an effective policy.

After exploring the details of how disincentives could be accomplished for policies in combinations of enforcement and control categories, Wolff lands firmly on the conclusion that public policymakers should accept the mantle of cyberattack containment. Her main argument is that the sphere of control for organizations and individuals is limited to their own activities, while dependency (or adversary) organizations have no incentive other than regulatory and legal compliance to accept responsibility for negligence with respect to cybersecurity issues. As you review the catalog with attacker goals, enforcement categories, and methods of oversight in mind, we expect you will agree. Nevertheless, in order to maintain compliance with public policy, it is essential that organizations and individuals craft their own. We hope this catalog provides them with intuitive insight into this endeavor.

The catalog herein reveals the depth and breadth of the field of cybersecurity policy. Cyberspace is a *complex* system, and cybersecurity is thus a *wicked problem*. That is, in systems engineering, the term *complicated* as applied to a system means its functions are difficult to unravel, but nevertheless, there is a deterministic method of identifying its functionality. In contrast, the behavior of a *complex* system is not predictable without analyzing its previous behavior, and even then, the forecast of future behavior is based on probability rather than systematic analysis. In systems engineering, as well as a variety of other fields with roots in sociology, the term *wicked* as applied to a problem refers to a complex and problematic situation where the solution is obviously not within reach, leaving the person(s) charged with solving the problem instead with solemn responsibility for situational improvement (Rittel and Webber 1973). Homelessness and drug addiction also fall into this category.

Nevertheless, we find the catalog approach an effective way to provide sufficient detail for users and decision-makers to recognize how the potential consequences of a given policy may affect them and/or their enterprise, whether or not it is a policy they themselves adopt or a policy that has been adopted by others. Note, we had no target for policy statement count, but for the sake of curiosity, we generated Figure 8.1 to summarize the number of policy statements per domain and issue.

Finally, we recognize that it is easy to confuse *collecting* policy statements with endorsing them. We have collected cybersecurity policy statements that, in our judgment, are realistic examples of proposals to reduce the risk of negative impact due to cybersecurity issues. They have been adopted by some and/or debated by others. Please do not read the catalog as if it is a policy document and take our normative statements as the last word. In every case, readers should balance the policy statements in this catalog and compare them to their own context and requirements. What makes sense as an excellent choice to reduce risk for some may be outweighed by cost concerns or actually present additional risk for others.

	APPROPRIATE USE	ARTIFICIAL INT	FINANCIAL SVCS	CUSTODIAL	CYBERCRIME	CYBSEC PRINCPLS	GEOLOCATION	HEALTH CARE	IMPERSONATION	INDUSTRIAL CTRL	INTEL PROPERTY	PRIVACY	RESEARCH & DEV	RISK MANAGEMENT	SUPPLY CHAIN	TECH PLATFORMS	WARFARE	WORKFORCE	TOTAL
Individual	0	0	0	0	1	0	1	0	0	0	0	4	0	0	4	4	0	0	14
Organization	10	1	0	2	0	12	4	0	0	2	1	0	9	9	17	0	0	3	70
Dependency	0	0	13	1	0	0	0	9	0	10	0	0	1	1	1	1	0	0	37
Adversary	0	0	0	0	11	0	0	0	0	0	5	0	0	0	0	1	18	0	35
Cyberspace	0	0	0	1	2	0	0	0	5	0	0	2	0	0	0	2	0	1	13
Public	0	6	1	10	3	3	0	1	1	5	0	6	2	3	1	3	0	9	54
Total:	10	7	14	14	17	15	5	10	6	17	6	12	12	13	23	11	18	13	223

Figure 8.1 Statistics on cybersecurity catalog statements.

8.1 Individual Example Policy Statements

Index	Statement	Objective	Reasons for Controversy
8.1.1 Cybercrime	Individuals who are stalked, bullied, blackmailed, and/or harassed on the internet shall be able to declare that the behavior is harassment under the law.	This policy is intended to give an individual the right to declare internet behavior as harassment, rather than leave it to subjective interpretation.	• A typical response to charges of cyber-bullying or harassment is that the perpetrator did not understand or anticipate the effect on the victim. This policy creates a situation where continued harassment after the victim's declaration is undoubtedly criminal. • This policy would let any public figure stop all internet journalism concerning his or her activities.
8.1.2 Geolocation	Purposely hiding one's physical location, or helping others hide their physical location, on the internet shall not be criminalized.	This policy is intended to allow anonymization services, as well as the installation of proxy services on bots, to mask the source of internet activities.	• Only criminals need to worry about their physical location being identified. Law enforcement should have the right to identify the source of any internet location, as it may be the source of a cyber-attack. • There are many legitimate reasons to hide one's physical location. These include eluding stalkers, spouse abuse, and political or religious persecution. Anonymization services provide needed solutions for problems faced by these individuals.
8.1.3 Privacy	Consumer devices shall not be configured with phone home features that communicate directly back to their manufacturer unless there are clear and effective instructions to the user on how to turn them off.	This policy is intended to prevent products such as cell phones, e-readers, games, and other IoT devices from gathering information and sending it back to the manufacturer or service provider with data on user interaction with the device or data on the device. This process is often without user knowledge or consent.	• This policy would allow consumers to use devices without concern that their personal information may one day be used to their detriment, even if only to avoid an onslaught of advertisements to their email address. • There are many customers of consumer devices willing to allow their service providers to monitor their behaviors in exchange for more personalized services going forward. It would make more sense simply to require software vendors to disclose the data fields that are incorporated into phone home features.

(Continued)

Index	Statement	Objective	Reasons for Controversy
8.1.4 Privacy	Each website that collects information about users shall make the fields it extracts from a user's environment collected available for user selection in order to allow them to opt out.	This policy is intended to subject all internet sites to Gramm-Leach-Bliley Act (GLBA)-like privacy rules, where the data can be used only for the purpose of providing services directly to the customer.	• Opt-out policies implemented for the GLBA were often made cumbersome and difficult to interpret. Privacy notices motivated by the Health Insurance Portability and Accountability Act (HIPAA) are generally ignored, as the alternative to signing them is to seek an alternative healthcare provider. The default in these policies should be to prevent the collection of information unless formally approved, not to require action on the part of an individual to opt out. • Any service that is offered on the internet should allow a user to opt out of personal data collection, and if companies claim that the lack of advertising revenue makes this policy unaffordable, they can instead choose to charge the users a fee for the service.
8.1.5 Privacy	Privacy policies posted on the website shall be required, and compliance shall be demonstrable.	This policy is intended to ensure there are technical safeguards in place to enforce privacy policies.	• Privacy policies are today's snake oil. In order for them to have any value as a consumer evaluation tool, they must be regulated. • Privacy policies are not contractual in nature, but statements of a company's security posture. Terms and conditions of software use are governed by end-user license agreements.
8.1.6 Privacy	Users who connect to publicly available networks, whether wired or wireless services, shall have no expectation of privacy unless the network owner explicitly makes that attestation visible.	This policy is intended to heighten user awareness that, even if there were a law against network eavesdropping on public networks, it is unenforceable. Moreover, the technology industry offers free public services solely for the purpose of collecting data on individuals, so users should never assume privacy unless there is some assurance by the service provider that the network is not vulnerable to eavesdropping.	• Even with assurance of the network owner, an individual should be aware that fraudulent assurances of privacy will exist and be wary of connecting to any public network if the operator is not known to be reputable. • Point-to-point connections from the user device to a secure web server will still be encrypted at the application level, so network operators or eavesdroppers do not necessarily have total access to user data.

8.1.7 Supply chain	Any system sold to consumers that physically monitors or results in physical changes in their homes shall be solely under their control.	This policy is intended to minimize the risk that a service provider with this capability inadvertently allows adversaries to commit privacy violations and/or cause physical harm to the homeowner.	• Advances in IoT provide features to monitor home appliances, energy systems, security systems, and other remotely accessible home automation systems, as well as automatically turn them on, off, or adjust their controls. Allowing anyone access to these features other than the homeowner or a highly controlled and transparent service provider operation could result in privacy violations and physical harm to the homeowner. • These features set the stage for network intrusions into the home environment. At best, they may be used by power companies to both spy on and adjust consumer use of electronics. At worst, they may be used by hackers to create local or regional disturbances, such as overheated appliances or neighborhood blackouts, respectively. • Smart grid features will likely be left to software and AI, which can make better overall decisions for controlling power consumption levels to ensure continuity of service for the community as a whole while minimizing the effect on each homeowner. Energy companies have vested interest in securing this software and associated infrastructure.
8.1.8 Supply chain	Individuals and organizations whose data is breached shall be notified regardless of whether the information disclosed is personally identifiable information (PII) or financial in nature.	This policy is intended to provide the basis for a national personal data breach protection law that requires notification and appropriate remediation whenever personal individual and/or proprietary organization data has been disclosed, regardless of its content.	• Most data breach notification laws single out personally identifiable and financial data when there are a wide variety of other personal and organizational data that could be used to cause harm to individuals who are exposed, for example, geolocation patterns for individuals and an organization's intellectual property.

(Continued)

Index	Statement	Objective	Reasons for Controversy
			• The state and federal jurisdictional conflict over breach notification is a recurring feature of American regulatory architecture, not unique to cybersecurity. Federal uniformity reduces compliance burden and prevents regulatory arbitrage. State variation has produced more protective standards; California's 2002 breach notification law preceded any federal equivalent by decades. Industry preference for federal preemption does not necessarily align with consumer protection interests, as federal minimums are more susceptible to downward negotiation.
8.1.9 Supply chain	Laws that require notification to customers when sensitive data is exposed shall be uniform across the relevant jurisdiction and aligned across jurisdictions where possible.	This policy is intended to provide consistency and, therefore, efficiency in data breach notification.	• Currently, every US state has its own data breach notification laws, and many non-US countries have their own laws as well. These are often inconsistent, creating inefficient and costly legal analysis that delays data breach notification. • Data breach laws should be molded by the people whose privacy is at stake. As communities can only enact laws within their own jurisdiction, these laws are properly enacted at the state level.
8.1.10 Supply chain	Multi-factor authentication shall be used to treat risks of unauthorized account access and identity theft on all publicly accessible internet sites that store user-level data of any kind.	This policy is intended to require all eCommerce sites to have strong authentication to protect user accounts from identity theft.	• A second factor of authentication that requires a person to have a personally issued single-use passcode sent to a user-controlled device, physical token-generator, or biometrics device in order to access online account in addition to a password significantly reduces the occurrence of identity theft which results in impersonation. • The infrastructure required to issue physical or biometric identity tokens and equipment could be cost-prohibitive for small business and non-for-profit institutions.

8.1.11 Technology platforms	Congress shall establish an Office of Internet Search within the Library of Congress and its mission shall be to provide trustworthy internet search results to the public that are based upon factual criteria agreed upon by experts in US nomenclature.	This policy is intended to provide the public with efficient and effective unbiased internet search results.	• Existing internet search capabilities are biased and sometimes intentionally deceptive. For example, they are often programmed to present their own products and services, sell keywords to the highest bidder, or test their AI models on which of the search results are selected or ignored by an individual user. • Searching for information has been the traditional role of librarians worldwide and there is no reason why internet search should be an exception. Librarians are currently unable to assist the public because their existing catalogs and search engines cannot compete with the speed of biased technology platform search engines. The solution is to equip librarians with a high-speed neutral search capability.
8.1.12 Technology platforms	Individuals shall be free to boycott technology platforms that do not provide strict security settings that detail exactly how their data is used and/or shared, and/or do not provide transparency on the specific functionality enabled or disabled by each security settings, to include reference to known exploits that will allow adversaries to access their data via platform loopholes or vulnerabilities, i.e., no government, eCommerce transaction, regulated entity, employer or other counterparty may compel a person or organization to become a user of such platforms.	This policy is intended to empower users to say no to instructions to become users of platforms that share or sell their data, or use it to customize experiences such as advertising and surveillance pricing.	• The practice of sharing data and customizing advertising is so ubiquitous that technology platforms business models often assume continuous income from the personal data marketplace as opposed to simply providing services to the end users who pay for them. • Organizations that have a responsibility to communicate with constituents include public utilities, municipalities and community associations, wherein members are joined by circumstances like property deeds. The practice of sharing data and customizing advertising is so ubiquitous that the boards of these organizations would be left with limited options in technology platform support. Policies like this would allow users to require alternative communication strategies, placing an undue burden on the boards.

(Continued)

Index	Statement	Objective	Reasons for Controversy
8.1.13 Technology platforms	Technology platforms shall disclose the scope and use cases for data collected on individuals sufficient for users to boycott technology platforms that do not provide strict privacy settings, and/or do not provide transparency on what data is in scope of existing security settings protection.	This policy is intended to empower users to say no to platforms that sell their data to adversaries who bombard them with advertising, fake news, and psychological manipulation.	• This policy is modeled on the lawfulness, fairness, and transparency principles contained in the European Union General Data Protection Regulation (EU GDPR) regulations, while other countries, including the United States, require no reassurance to those who opt in only to that "necessary," and users currently do not have any method of reviewing the scope of data collected about them or what is done with it.
8.1.14 Technology platforms	Technology platforms with user-controlled security and privacy settings shall transparently publish how those settings work to thwart activities performed by potential adversaries who exploit their systems to retrieve data about the user.	This policy is intended to heighten user awareness that the more data collected on them directly corresponds to the level at which they are targeted for advertising, fake news, and psychological manipulation.	• Where users are informed that the data collected on them directly corresponds to the level at which they are targeted for advertising, fake news, and psychological manipulation. they are more likely to be cognizant and therefore to avoid, cybersecurity risks presented by a platform that is known to be a frequent target of cybersecurity account hijacking, data theft, and fraud attacks.

8.2 Organization Example Policy Statements

Index	Statement	Objective	Reasons for Controversy
8.2.1 Appropriate use	All computer operating systems that allow phone home and command and control features in software running on that operating system shall give users a choice of whether to enable them.	This policy is intended to allow software companies to use such features, but only if the user can configure them.	• This policy would allow software companies to contract directly with users on how these features would be used. The ability for the user to disable them would mean that only those features that benefited users would be accepted. • Any user configurable item can also be configured by malware. This policy would not make it any safer for users to be protected from such features. They should just be entirely disabled.
8.2.2 Appropriate Use	Any software installed on computers without the express consent of the owner shall be considered trespassing.	This policy is intended to prohibit internet sites from installing software on users' machines without their knowledge.	• There is no difference from the point of view of many consumers between malware and adware. Both consume computer resources and invade privacy. • There are legitimate business purposes for running inconspicuous software on consumer desktops. For example, sometimes technology product features (e.g., printers and other peripherals) do not work as expected or are of limited utility unless there is corresponding software on the user's desktop. It is more convenient for the user for this helpful software to be installed automatically than to bother them with pop-up windows and choices they do not understand.

(Continued)

Index	Statement	Objective	Reasons for Controversy
			• When a software company is contracted to provide software support for critical software with high availability requirements, such as in industrial control systems or eCommerce payment systems, it should be up to the software support service vendor to devise the most appropriate way to provide that support. Using data from the live software installation is a frequently used option because it can assist a vendor in determining software issues that may be site-specific. • eCommerce advertisers rely on data automatically collected from consumer machines in order to identify potential customers for targeting marketing campaigns. This is an information service for the consumer as the products are ones predetermined to be of interest, given the consumer's record of internet activities. • Express consent is a concept that requires further definition. A pop-up window question is often clicked away by a user who does not even notice it, much less consent to any text that appeared in it. Yet these types of mechanisms are commonly used in place of more appropriate mechanisms for requesting user consent.
8.2.3 Appropriate use	Enterprises that allow staff to use computers for personal reasons shall set guidelines for appropriate use.	This policy is intended to acknowledge that when corporate users use corporate computers, they gain capabilities that may be inappropriate.	• Where corporate users use corporate computers in an inappropriate manner, the corporation is enabling the behavior and should be accountable. • Unless corporations encourage inappropriate behavior, they should not be held accountable for stopping it any more than they police physical behavior in the workplace.

8.2.4 Appropriate use	Individuals using computers that they do not own shall restrict their usage of those computers to the express purpose for which their access was granted.	This policy is intended to acknowledge that enterprise computers should be used in the service of the enterprise, but it places responsibility on the user to understand where lines are drawn.	• By default, the property of others should be respected, and this policy would prohibit joyriding, the practice of using computers for purposes that benefit an unauthorized user at the expense of the owner. • Computers that are accessible are assumed to be available for whatever capabilities are accessible. The burden should be on the owner to limit capabilities rather than on the user to restrict their activity. • For corporate staff to have to change computers to perform a quick personal task causes more employer expense in time wasted than the expense generated from the small diversions from work that accommodate the small tasks. • There is typically a lot of peer pressure from friends and family to contribute to social networking sites, but any disclosure of personal details may put the lives of people in positions of public trust in danger. This policy would provide such individuals with protection without admitting fear. • Doxing is a perfectly legitimate form of journalism. This policy is far too broad and restrictive of free speech. • Each individual should be in charge of their own reputation, and though it may be a good idea to provide social networking guidance to people in positions of public trust, this policy is unnecessarily paternal.

(Continued)

Index	Statement	Objective	Reasons for Controversy
8.2.5 Appropriate use	Nations shall create consistent narratives designed to explain political policy and actively propagate them on the internet.	This policy is intended to ensure nations create consistent narratives or stories on political policy to help people to understand and appreciate cultural issues.	• This is the equivalent of spending tax dollars on an ad campaign. • Other countries use public relations narratives to successfully promote commerce. Terrorist adversaries are adept at spreading false narratives, which are not currently countered. The conscious effort to develop and spread friendly narratives should be a core competency in cybersecurity policy.
8.2.6 Appropriate use	Software companies shall be prohibited from exercising command and control over consumer products.	This policy is intended to prohibit the remote access to user desktops by software vendors.	• There is no justification for sending commands to a computer that is owned by someone else, no matter what software is installed on it. • Software support processes often query the computers that run the supported software to determine status in order to plan proactive maintenance.
8.2.7 Appropriate use	Software companies shall be prohibited from implementing phone home features by default.	This policy is intended to prevent the coverage of user permission for phone home features as part of a typical End-User License Agreement (EULA).	• Computer owners have a right to control all communication to and from their computers. If software companies show a benefit to consumers from phone home features, then they should be able to sufficiently motivate consumers to actively install them instead of installing them without the owner's knowledge. • Enforcement of this policy would restrict software companies from seamlessly installing updates often needed by users to make maximum use of purchased software, which includes critical security patches. • Because software can be stolen by being copied, the phone home feature is the only way that vendors know whether their software has been pirated. It gives them control over granting licenses.

8.2.8 Appropriate use	Software installed for one product shall not install or attempt to install other products.	This policy is intended to prohibit a software product to install a package of software that includes products other than the one the user has chosen to install.	• Vendors often try to expand their presence on a user's machine by placing all of their programs in menus, and if the user tries to use ones they did not purchase, it prompts the user to purchase a license. This is an unsolicited advertisement that never goes away, creating an annoyance and a waste of computing resources. • This policy would restrict software companies from making consumers aware of the benefits of enhancing their productivity with additional products that are compatible with ones they have already selected.
8.2.9 Appropriate use	Software shall not be installed in such a way that it runs without the user's express knowledge.	This policy is intended to prohibit the installation of a software product to configure a system to start the software automatically every time the computer restarts and/or the user logs in.	• Simply because a user chooses to install a product does not mean that they wish to run it every day. Software companies who use this method of install waste computing resources and slow down other software that the user may need more. • Users often forget how to start software, and having it run all the time relieves them of the responsibility to record and remember such details. • There is no technology that would allow users to make choices about what should be running and when on all the computing devices they own. Once they install software, they expect it to be there, and would likely think it was broken if it was not always running.

(Continued)

Index	Statement	Objective	Reasons for Controversy
8.2.10 Appropriate use	The internet shall not be used to incentivize discrimination.	This policy is intended to reduce the ease with which the internet may be used to spread slander.	• This policy may have the unintended consequence of restricting many forms of criticism, and criticism is one of the most important functions of the internet. • This policy would be a deterrent to those who foment discrimination by strategically placing false rumors in social networking sites. • Everyone has their own thresholds for what is inappropriate versus playful or suggestive of discrimination. This type of policy is too broad and can only be adjudicated on a case by case basis if it can be shown that harm has occurred.
8.2.11 Artificial intelligence	Organizations shall develop Responsible, Accountable, Consulted, and Informed (RACI) matrix corresponding to every artificial intelligence (AI) program developed, supported and/or used by the organization. Minimally, the matrix shall include the CEO, BoD (Board of Directors) and all direct reports to the CEO, and shall include risk assessment and treatment for the performance of AI program itself. The operation of each business process use case for the program shall include formal approval by all assigned responsibilities in the matrix.	This policy is intended to ensure that an organization's senior management is fully aware of all AI use within the organization and are fully accountable for accepting any and all risks issue wherein the root cause may be the AI systems.	• AI is too unpredictable to allow decisions concerning its installation and operation to be tolerated without the full attention and approval of executive and senior management. • AI is too immature for senior management to become involved until the business case for its use is fully understood and approved.

8.2.12 Custodial	An organization appointed by senior management with appropriate budget and authority shall establish a program to authorize and document changes to critical digital assets, to detect changes as they occur, and to compare the detected changes to the authorization.	This policy is intended to implement change control to the extent that every detected change is verified as authorized or not authorized.	• This policy requires that a level of detail be kept for every planned change that would allow an independent observer to verify that the change was correct. As many planned changes require considerable talent just to execute, it puts too much of a burden on Operations to compare a plan to an actual change. • If plans cannot be specified to a level of detail necessary to verify change authorization, then the detail is likely not to be sufficient for informed approval either. This policy would add benefit to both processes.
8.2.13 Custodial	Lack of tested technology business recovery plan for critical services shall be considered negligence for critical consumer services.	This policy is intended to require that technology hosting providers and software services vendors maintain alternate computing facilities that may be configured to be used in the event of a main system failure, and also to test the failover from the main site to the alternate site.	• Where consumers and businesses are encouraged to rely on vendors to operate technology processes that are business or mission critical, those services shall be supported as per technology industry standards. • Unless business recovery processes are part of a service contract, customers of technology service providers should not expect them to be incorporated into services. To stay in business, a technology vendor need only offer the service, not maintain the integrity of user data. • As described by Louis Black, not having a technology recovery plan is like inventing fire, and not keeping a torch lit in case the main fire went out. Services that are completely lost would have to be reinvented.
8.2.14 Cybersecurity principles	All information shall be classified according to its content and purpose, and dissemination limited to those in roles who require it to perform designated responsibilities.	This policy is intended to ensure access controls limit information to those who need to have it to perform a given task or job function.	• This policy prevents sensitive information from being shared unnecessarily and so protects individual privacy. • This policy prevents information sharing by putting a burden of proof that they need to know information content on someone who requests information, when that person may not know the information content.

(Continued)

Index	Statement	Objective	Reasons for Controversy
8.2.15 Cybersecurity principles	All personnel shall be screened for potential security problems.	This policy is intended to ensure those who handle critical assets are trustworthy. Screening services check for indications of a poor attitude toward security, including past convictions, outstanding warrants, and substance abuse.	• Past issues with security are a good indicator of an individual's propensity to exploit a position of trust. • Any screening is a privacy violation. More emphasis should be placed on current job performance than background history. • Information used for background checks is widely available in some countries but practically non-existent in others. This puts individuals in countries who have no background records in an unfairly competitive position for jobs.
8.2.16 Cybersecurity principles	An individual who approves the disbursement of electronic assets shall never be the same as the person who distributes approved disbursements.	This policy is intended to ensure "segregation of duties" where no one individual is able to disburse electronic assets.	• Today's electronic transaction systems allow large quantities of assets to be transferred with very little effort or observation, and this policy requires that two or more people must overtly collaborate in order for electronically controlled assets to be misappropriated. It allows management to enforce accountability for asset disbursement. • The policy prevents individuals from executing transactions without the assistance of others, and so may create delays in the distribution of currency, goods, and services. • Where staff resources are scarce, this policy creates an unreasonable burden on management efforts to achieve efficiency in transaction execution.
8.2.17 Cybersecurity principles	Information shall be classified and labeled. Handling procedures for each information classification type shall be developed commensurate with the risk of misuse of information of that type.	This policy is intended to require information classification, labeling, and handling. An example is the use of the labels Top-Secret, Secret, and Unclassified. Another example is Proprietary, Confidential, and Public. In such systems, all information with the same level is protected the same way.	• Information classification requires those who originate data to analyze and make decisions as to security requirements. • Information classification systems are often abused by classifying information at a high level that does not need to be classified at a high level. This becomes a way to hide information from those who would otherwise have access to it.

8.2.18 Cybersecurity principles	Operations shall identify and report any non-business use of system resources.	This policy is intended to ensure that cyber resources that are used outside of the prescribed operations process are not authorized.	• This policy requires advance preparation of a pre-approved list of authorized uses of resources. It deprives users and their management of the needed flexibility to experiment with new uses of technology, as well as the ability to connect new devices to networks, download software, and experiment with technology services without being policed by low-level staff. • A system cannot be secured if its purpose is not well-defined. If this policy cannot be enforced, then it will not be possible to secure the system.
8.2.19 Cybersecurity principles	Operations shall monitor user activity to ensure that sharing of user access does not occur.	This policy is intended to require that each user of a system be verifiably provided with a unique login identifier, that a profile of usage behavior be associated with each login, and that anomalous behavior be investigated.	• This is a simple and effective way to detect whether users have given their passwords to others and makes it possible to pinpoint which users took what actions during investigations of system activity. • This policy would facilitate efficient and effective identification of account hijacking attempts. • Not all users should be restricted from sharing access. For example, a married couple may share the working spouse's login to their health benefits website.
8.2.20 Cybersecurity principles	Remote network access to unattended desktops shall never be allowed, even for the purposes of desktop support and maintenance.	This policy is intended to require that desktops be technically configured to allow remote support only when express permission is granted by the desktop user.	• This policy is required to maintain accountability for workstation activity. Where it is common for desktops to be commanded remotely by technology staff, the permissions assigned to the user to which the desktop is assigned may be compromised, and/or that desktop user may be able to repudiate network activity performed from the desktop. • This policy inhibits the flexibility of technology staff to provide normally intrusive services such as troubleshooting in an unobtrusive manner. For Industrial Control Systems (ICSs), shared access is sometimes an operational requirement and could be monitored by biometrics or other means.

(Continued)

Index	Statement	Objective	Reasons for Controversy
			• This policy has the unintended consequence of not being able to make use of remote desktop technology as part of operations support procedures for critical infrastructure, where it is often necessary to provide an external specialist with access normally granted only to internal staff.
8.2.21 Cybersecurity principles	Senior management shall play a hands-on role in setting enterprise security strategy, and security strategy outcomes shall be reported at the Board level.	This policy is intended to ensure senior management takes enterprise security strategy seriously. Tone at the top is an audit term used to explain that unless senior management takes a topic seriously, no one else in the organization will.	• Security management often suffers from responsibility with no authority. Moreover, too often, critical systems such as ICS are not covered under information technology (IT) security programs. • Senior management does not need to design a security strategy in order to determine what it is worth to the firm and assign appropriate resources and budget. Security management is best left to specialists.
8.2.22 Cybersecurity principles	Systems that maintain mission-critical processes, such as ICS, shall utilize some form of software application whitelisting.	This policy is intended to ensure a reference monitor is maintained to be used to identify and authorize all software on critical systems. A reference monitor is a generic term in computer security that refers to a process that intercepts requests for system resources and consults a list of authorization rules to see if the requesting subject has access to the requested object.	• Among other things, this policy would allow all systems to conform to principles of least privilege. To conforming to the "principle of least privilege" means that these systems will allow the minimum individual access required to perform a well-defined function. This would reduce overall infrastructure vulnerability due to a malicious utility employee. • This policy is reasonable only for IT systems. A typical ICS or mobile framework does not have a central point from which software is executed, much less identified, nor a list of what software a user should be able to access.

			• There is an old adage: "to a carpenter, everything looks like a nail". As systems acquire more and more software-enabled features, they are viewed as part of cyberspace. However, non-IT systems such as ICS and mobile frameworks are fundamentally different, and policies such as these assume a simplicity that does not exist and with which it would be impossible to comply.
8.2.23 Cybersecurity principles	Unencrypted data other than that required to monitor business process shall never be available to Operations.	This policy is intended to eliminate inadvertent or intentional unauthorized data disclosure to Operations staff.	• Even if all data were encrypted, there must be automated ways to decrypt it in order for it to be used, and since Operations would need a way to test those processes for integrity like any other, there is no real method of enforcing this policy. • Segregation of duties with respect to data access may be established within Operations groups so that no one individual or support group would be able to see unencrypted data without collusion.
8.2.24 Cybersecurity principles	Where the same data is used by more than one department within an organization, authoritative data sources shall be established, and each record shall be entered just once and shared with any other organization that requires it.	This policy is intended to minimize data storage and human data entry costs. This type of policy is referred to as a "data origination and reuse" or "need to share" policy. It is usually used in large organizations that process large amounts of data.	• Implementation of this policy may increase data integrity by minimizing the possibility of mistakes in cross-correlation of records between different departments in a single organization. • Organizational boundaries within which data may be freely shared can be difficult to determine when sensitive data is concerned. Data records often contain multiple fields with different security requirements, and these can be difficult to separate when designing data sharing strategies. Different departments may have different requirements to authenticate data sources, and the level of scrutiny provided by the originating department may not meet that required by a consumer department.

(Continued)

Index	Statement	Objective	Reasons for Controversy
8.2.25 Cybersecurity principles	Wherever access control has been configured to protect cyberspace assets, the identity and organizational role of each user granted access shall be tracked to ensure that the access is revoked when the purpose of granting access is no longer valid.	This policy is intended to ensure use of "identity management." It usually involves setting up a database of identity information, usually modeled on human resources and contractor data repositories, and using the database as an integral part of the user authorization workflow and automated systems audit.	• This policy should ensure that access to sensitive information is not mistakenly granted to individuals who do not need it and that it is removed from individuals who no longer need it. • Requiring users to be registered and be individually authorized may delay access to information needed to perform critical functions.
8.2.26 Geolocation	Geolocational information coordinates for any mobile device shall be available to law enforcement.	This policy is intended to require mobile devices to allow access to Geolocational information files, such as Global Positioning System (GPS) coordinates, on mobile devices upon request.	• The ability of law enforcement to track criminals would be significantly enhanced by the enforcement of this policy. • Any ability for geolocational information coordinates to be delivered from a user's device without their knowledge is an invasion of privacy and creates opportunities for misuse of the information for stalkers and other criminal or unwanted followers.
8.2.27 Geolocation	Network operators who use proxy services shall internally track user activity for immediate use in law enforcement reporting.	This policy is intended to require enterprises to quickly account for all internet activity.	• This policy would make it easy for law enforcement to quickly ascertain the identity of a cyber intruder whose source appears to be a legitimate enterprise network. • Even enterprises that have this ability today cannot execute quickly. The sheer number of internal network activity logs makes it impossible to sort through without forensic analysis.

8.2.28 Geolocation	Those who allow their networks to be used by cyber criminals shall be guilty of aiding and abetting any crime committed.	This policy is intended to require all network owners to identify all users and police their borders for unauthorized use.	• When companies or individuals allow criminals to occupy their networks, this both shelters them from investigation and equips them with cyber artillery. • The risk of unauthorized network access already presents a cost-benefit trade-off to network operators. Where unauthorized users consume network resources, their own business suffers. The decisions about how much security is good enough for their purposes belong to them. • The cost of securing all the software on one's network would put many network operators out of business. This provision should be modified to reduce the impact of negligence and instead refer to those who willfully and knowingly allow their networks to be used by criminals.
8.2.29 Geolocation	Wireless network operators shall implement geolocation technology designed to pinpoint the location of each wireless user.	This policy is intended to ensure wireless networks include signal triangulation and other technologies that could enable operators to locate users.	• This policy would make it easy for law enforcement to quickly ascertain the location of a cyber intruder whose source appears to be a wireless network. • This technology is immature and difficult to manage on large wireless networks.
8.2.30 Industrial control	Appropriate security, physical, and logical access controls shall be applied to the full range of ICS workstations and components, including control system field devices such as process sensors and actuators.	This policy is intended to require operators and technicians to have methods of verifying that all control system workstations and control system field devices are appropriately authenticated.	• Physical intruders in ICS environments may not be challenged to log in to ICS workstations or peripheral communications networks in order to operate critical infrastructure or machinery, and cyber controls are often disdained because they delay operators charged with operating and restoring systems. However, the vulnerability is real and must be remediated by research into authentication methods that are both swift and secure, and don't impact system or component operability.

(Continued)

Index	Statement	Objective	Reasons for Controversy
			• Time to operate physical access controls is reduced via biometric authentication, but do not work in a plant environment where safety glasses and gloves are mandatory. • Access controls for ICS focus on physical access to engineering workstations and control system field devices. This leaves the system vulnerable to sensor hijacking attacks that can cause the system to react with physical responses such as rising water levels, altering power distributions, and rerouting transport. • Password access concerns typically include features that lock the system screen after a specified number of attempted logins have been identified as password failures. If this occurs in an ICS, a time critical control process may not be accessible to the operator who forgot or mistyped the password. This occurrence could have impact on system ability to recover from outages or other off-normal conditions. It would be especially harmful in situations where operators are under great stress. Moreover, these features allow an attacker to deliberately send multiple wrong passwords to lock out critical workstations which can be a very dangerous situation.
8.2.31 Industrial control	Process control systems that control hazardous processes and/or materials shall be very highly restricted.	This policy is intended to restrict accidental or intentional changes in automated system control operations that could have devastating results on the health of individuals in the proximity of such systems.	• The fewer people who have access to these systems, the less likely it is that they will be controlled by anyone with malicious intent. • Process control anomalies happen for reasons other than cyber security attacks, and when they do, it is better to have open access to the process control systems in order to allow any individual capable to redirect the process.

8.2.32 Intellectual property	Organizations shall be required to take measures to reduce staff susceptibility to social engineering.	This policy is intended to require companies to consider it a fiduciary responsibility to shareholders to make sure intellectual property is protected.	• As insider access is the most common cyber weapon delivery method, fortifying this periphery would strengthen the enterprise as a whole against intellectual property theft. • Although training every company employee would present a prohibitive expense, an effective and ongoing social engineering awareness and anti-phishing program with a particular focus on senior executives and technologists who possess administrative credentials should suffice to satisfy the objective of this policy. • Any systematic corporate training program for all staff will never be able to keep up with new and innovative cybersecurity threats. Companies are better advised to concentrate on technology protection measures that do not allow users to make decisions that would jeopardize intellectual property, such as restricting user access to email and the internet.
8.2.33 Research and development	A nation's executive branch shall assemble a committee of cybersecurity experts from a variety of industries to advise on cybersecurity policy and assess cybersecurity programs.	This policy is intended to require a Nation's executive branch (e.g., the US President) to ensure that senior policymakers get the best advice from academia and industry.	• The breadth and depth of cybersecurity issues are beyond the expertise of any one individual. National leaders should have access to the most enlightened views possible. • There is no need to establish a policy at this high a level. There are already multiple paths and processes by which national leaders solicit and receive advice on critical issues like cybersecurity.
8.2.34 Research and development	Academic communities shall pursue student chapters of cybersecurity industry associations.	This policy is intended to ensure academic communities broaden student access to cybersecurity professional associations.	• Cybersecurity professional associations have experience requirements to which students should aspire, and these are freely available on websites. There is no need for a more formal awareness activity of this career path.

(Continued)

Index	Statement	Objective	Reasons for Controversy
8.2.35 Research and development	All software development shall adopt best practices for securing the software development lifecycle.	This policy is intended to require adherence to secure software coding practices and security testing.	• Secure coding practices are known to reduce vulnerabilities in deployed technology products. • Innovation requires constant change in organizational strategy and process. Secure coding practices are too static to adapt to the pace of technology growth.
8.2.36 Research and development	All systems development shall adopt best practices for securing the systems development lifecycle.	This policy is intended to require a whole-of-system approach rather than the security of a single software component.	• Best security practices require that systems security requirements be considered early in the development process and integrated into product features. • Security requirements should have no more priority than any other requirement, as a successful system will end up as a balance of qualities that are important to its stakeholders.
8.2.37 Research and development	Companies shall be given tax incentives for pursuing cybersecurity research.	This policy is intended to increase the spending in much-needed research on how to achieve cybersecurity goals.	• Investments in cybersecurity research should be judged by marketplace results, rather than simply spending which may not yield actual security benefits. • This policy would motivate the private sector to fund research in cybersecurity. It could increase their market value and also stimulate economic interest in cybersecurity products. • There is already a plethora of cybersecurity research hypotheses that were thoroughly studied, published upon, and built into products from the 1990s onward. Until there is some consensus on what constitutes progress in cybersecurity research, it would be wasteful to allow companies to benefit by self-selecting cybersecurity research goals.

8.2.38 Research and development	National competitions shall be established to reward student talent for innovation in cybersecurity. Other competitions can also reward outstanding universities and research institutions.	This policy is intended to attract talented students to the study of cybersecurity issues.	• Implementation of this policy should create a community of students interested in joining the cybersecurity workforce. • This program might reward students for studying techniques that could be used for malicious hacking, rather than defense.
8.2.39 Research and development	National governments shall help fund basic and applied research in cybersecurity risk, systems, and software, in line with priorities established by the national strategy. As much as possible, such research shall be collaborative, multi-disciplinary, and unclassified.	This policy is intended to provide funding for cybersecurity research in software, testing, computer, and network domains. It should also include multidisciplinary studies of the national security impacts (e.g., critical infrastructure safety, legal, and international affairs).	• Research and development funding not only produces new security technology that can be applied to today's threats, but motivates graduate students to study cybersecurity problems, and so contributes to the brainpower that will address future cybersecurity threats.
8.2.40 Research and development	Nations shall encourage awareness, education, and training for cyber defense starting with students in primary or middle schools and continuing through specific technical training for cyber defenders.	This policy is intended to include cyber safety, cybersecurity, and cyber ethics are moved into the mainstream curriculum.	• This policy would promote critical thinking about cybersecurity at an early age, and by so doing influence future decision-makers to incorporate ethical principles into systems of the future. Investments in training and education will drive a more sophisticated workforce and cyber specialists. • Education is a large-scale effort as many people deal with cyberspace and need varying levels of understanding. This means a potentially expensive and long-term effort. Moreover, if awareness programs are technology-specific ("practice safe faxing kids!"), they would rapidly be out of date.

(Continued)

Index	Statement	Objective	Reasons for Controversy
8.2.41 Research and development	Research and development into cybersecurity systems, technologies, and operations shall be pursued to the extent necessary to fill gaps between management objectives to secure cyberspace and current capabilities.	This policy is intended to provide management focus to secure the cyber environment with the necessary methods, tools, and procedures.	• This policy empowers managers who are accountable for controlling assets with the means by which to do so in the long term, even if their current capabilities are lacking. • Policies like this may be viewed as an open checkbook for all sorts of research related to cybersecurity without foreseeable benefit to the organization.
8.2.42 Risk management	All cyberspace systems shall undergo risk assessment.	This policy is intended to ensure that threats are considered when deciding on control procedures, and that common vulnerabilities are identified and addressed.	• This policy requires that every information system used by an organization is analyzed for security flaws. • Risk assessments follow checklist approaches to security assessment, and new and innovative technologies and threats are often missed. Moreover, the fact that a risk assessment was done does not necessarily mean that vulnerabilities were fixed. These factors combine to provide the criticism that risk assessments commonly provide a false sense of security.
8.2.43 Risk management	An organization appointed by and reporting to executive leadership shall have an appropriate budget and authority to accurately inventory mission-critical digital assets, whether in applications, devices, and/or networks.	This policy is intended to place responsibility for conducting organization-wide asset inventory with executive leadership.	• It is unfortunately all too common that the pace of technology change results in inattention to the fundamentals of sound management, and inaccurate technology asset inventory is an all-too-common audit finding. Without an inventory of cyber assets to be protected, security management is unguided and likely to be the equivalent of security theatre.

8.2.44 Risk management	An organization appointed by and reporting to executive leadership shall have appropriate budget and authority to routinely test systems for vulnerabilities and just as routinely install patches or compensating controls.	This policy is intended to place responsibility for conducting organization-wide cybersecurity vulnerability management with executive leadership.	• Though most regulatory agencies require organizations to test for vulnerabilities and patch them, it is all too common an audit finding that the patching cycles lag months or years behind the testing cycles.
8.2.45 Risk management	An organization appointed by senior management shall provide appropriate budget and authority to establish and maintain a cybersecurity program to secure digital assets throughout their corresponding systems lifecycle.	This policy is intended to place responsibility for managing an organization-wide cybersecurity program with senior management.	• Though risk assessment and vulnerability reduction processes may be in place, without an overarching security program, there is no verification or validation that security goals are achieved. • As all cybersecurity processes are supported by the IT program, the security program need not be separate, and in fact may be more effective if integrated within technology processes.
8.2.46 Risk management	An organization appointed by senior management with appropriate budget and authority shall identify how to monitor the security of these assets during the installation, maintenance, upgrade, and change-out to assure a cyber-secure system.	This policy is intended to place responsibility for managing an organization-wide cybersecurity operations and incident response with senior management.	• Where there are joint resources assigned to incident response, those responsible for supporting critical system transaction processing will always claim the lion's share of technology resources. This often leaves inadequate resources dedicated to security response. • As in the case of security program management, all cybersecurity processes are supported by the IT program, the security operations area need not be separate, and in fact may be more effective if integrated within technology processes. If resources are not adequate to provide security, technology managers should be held accountable as they are for any other system deliverable.

(Continued)

Index	Statement	Objective	Reasons for Controversy
8.2.47 Risk management	Engineers charged with architecting high-consequence systems shall be required to include designs, specifications, and operational requirements for defense, response, and cyberforensic investigation as part of their deliverables.	This policy is intended to ensure that ICS and military weapon cybersecurity requirements are not bolted on as an afterthought but integrated into the operation of the high-consequence system.	
8.2.48 Risk management	New standards shall be established to calculate return on investment in information security, and these shall acknowledge the benefits that emerge from control over assets.	This policy is intended to ensure return on security investment is calculated with a focus on the benefits from control over assets.	• Return on investment risk analysis loss probabilities are based on historical data and loss avoidance, but there is no historical data on which to base probability judgments for cybersecurity. Therefore, new types of calculations are required to accurately reflect the soundness of security investment. • Security investment is just one aspect of technology management and should be justified on the basis of the benefits it provides. No special treatment is required to ensure that benefits are considered.
8.2.49 Risk management	Operations teams shall be responsible for keeping their own inventory, and continuous audits shall verify that it is correct.	This policy is intended to ensure that the scope of device inventory is a reliable denominator for cybersecurity health check metrics.	• Some organizations have adopted a technology purchasing model wherein the people who are responsible for the safe operation of technology are prevented from controlling its inventory, largely due to legacy instances of technology staff selling a portion of the equipment, creating shadow inventory. Unfortunately, low-level clerks in purchasing departments assigned to asset inventory do not take the onboarding and offboarding processes as seriously as needed for administrators to maintain security, with the consequence that security on new devices may not be enabled in a timely fashion, and unnecessary deprecated devices may not be disabled in a timely fashion.

8.2.50 Risk management	Senior management shall appoint a Chief Information Security Officer to bear the responsibility of cybersecurity management.	This policy is intended to ensure high-level leadership and coordination for the organization's information security strategy, policy, and operations.	• If security advocates are placed high enough in management to be peers of Chiefs in other areas such as the Chief Legal Officer and Chief Financial Officer, the need for security in organizational process and procedure should get sufficient management attention to be successful. • A culture of security is not created by the appointment of an individual. Where upper management appreciates the need for security, it can be done in a variety of matrix management structures. Where they do not, such an appointment will place the individual in a position of responsibility without authority.
8.2.51 Supply chain	All cybersecurity regulations applicable to Department of Defense (DoD) networks shall be applicable to defense industrial base networks used to provide services to the DoD.	This policy is intended to require cybersecurity standards set for government agencies to extend to companies that provide them with the products and services they use to carry out their missions.	• This policy would eliminate a weak link in protection requirements around defense-related information and make it harder for espionage agents to learn about Department of Defense activities. • This policy is too inclusive as it extends to all defense contractors, not just those that provide critical services or are in possession of classified information. Moreover, not all DoD security requirements are publicly announced, and this policy would require widespread sharing of these requirements.

(Continued)

Index	Statement	Objective	Reasons for Controversy
8.2.52 Supply chain	All cyberspace components destined for military use shall be made in the country.	This policy is intended to reduce the risk of embedded malicious code in devices destined for use in military applications.	• Most cyber hardware and software are produced overseas, potentially creating a security risk while also impacting the US job market. • This policy is entirely impractical and would run up Department of Defense (DoD) IT budgets drastically. Moreover, it may not even buy much protection if the designs are made outside the country, by foreign corporations or by foreign nationals working for US companies. • All countries are subject to the "not made here" problem when it comes to hardware and software. The US enjoyed a unique position for decades when manufacturing was largely done domestically. However, globalized supply systems have changed the economics of production, moving manufacturing to locations where labor and materials are cheaper.
8.2.53 Supply chain	All personnel at all suppliers of cyberspace components destined for military or industrial control system use shall be screened for potential security problems.	This policy is intended to require those who handle products destined for military or industrial environments, such as the nation's critical infrastructure, to be rated trustworthy.	• Screening for security problems is a minimum requirement. A full background check or a Department of Defense (DoD) security clearance might also be required for more sensitive programs. • Since component makers of software, personal computers (PCs), and networking gear usually do not know the end user of their systems, this policy would mean every maker would have to comply, which would be overly broad. • Screening should only be necessary when a risk assessment dictates. Blanket policies such as these are unnecessarily expensive. • Screening may expose employees to violations of privacy expectations, or could reveal historical information that could harm the employee's future employment potential in non-critical environments.

8.2.54 Supply chain	Automated inventory systems in critical infrastructure, such as health care shall be subject to regulatory audit.	This policy is intended to require regulatory oversight for critical automated inventory management systems.	• Automated supply chain management systems often rely on highly vulnerable technologies such as radio frequency identification (RFID) chips embedded into labels of packages. Overreliance on these technologies as a replacement for actual inspection of inventory items could blind management to actual shortages. • Inventory is a critical business asset and companies have considerable vested interest in the integrity of these systems. External auditors are unlikely to add value to business process oversight for their own critical assets. • Although external auditors are unlikely to add value to business process oversight for their own critical assets, where not-for-profit companies or municipalities perform needed community services, consciousness of potential loss via theft is minimal. Inventories are not as closely watched. Regulatory oversight may be beneficial in these cases.
8.2.55 Supply chain	Cybersecurity access control mechanisms shall be rated for effectiveness, and this rating shall be required to be included in all cybersecurity sales literature.	This policy is intended to require an authoritative agency to develop criteria to evaluate the strength of access controls such as logins and passwords.	• Every system is different, so an access control that works for one may not work for another, which would render the rating meaningless. • In physical security, as secure specifications are developed, they are adopted in the form of local codes and ordinances, which, if demonstrably effective, may be raised to state and federal standards. The same practice should be followed for systems security.

(Continued)

Index	Statement	Objective	Reasons for Controversy
8.2.56 Supply chain	Cybersecurity suppliers shall be prohibited from sharing security intellectual property with hostile nation-states.	This policy is intended to add security products to the list of munitions prohibited from export to hostile nation-states (State 2010).	• This policy would make it easier to pinpoint cybersecurity intellectual property leaks by restricting information flow between sets of security companies and hostile nation-states. • This policy would prevent US companies from protecting their global infrastructure in places where the need is greatest.
8.2.57 Supply chain	Diagnostic laboratories used to record and correlate food sample measurements and customer complaints shall be owned and operated by domestic entities.	This policy is intended to require all the information used to make decisions about food safety within the jurisdiction of national borders.	• As cyber-attack patterns grow more sophisticated, all information that contributes to consumer safety should be considered a potential cyberwar or cyber terrorist target. • Many food sources originate outside of the national cyber space infrastructure and it is not feasible to transfer control of laboratory networks to firms for protectionist reasons because competing services are readily available in the country of origin.
8.2.58 Supply chain	Nations shall use their acquisition policies to create incentives for IT companies to improve the security of their products.	This policy is intended to give nations leverage to negotiate improved security for IT equipment: hardware and software, networking equipment, desktops, automated control systems, and more.	• If national governments, often the consumers purchasing in the largest quantities, negotiate for improved security, it will bring benefits not only to those national governments (in the form of improved security) but to companies in that nation and indeed to all consumers worldwide. If systems are more secure out-of-the-box, then costs will be cheaper over their life cycle. • It is difficult for national bureaucracies to change procurement practices and improved security can often make systems marginally more expensive at the onset (though cheaper over the whole life cycle).

8.2.59 Supply chain	Onboarding and other administrative processes shall be designed to facilitate rather than delay business functions.	This policy is intended to ensure efficient security procedures in order to quickly complete onboarding and other administrative procedures.	• Many security procedures in large organizations are so burdensome that they inhibit productivity for authorized users. • Security procedures are required to ensure security, and that businesses should incorporate time delays into their onboarding processes rather than pressure security personnel to make quick decisions. Information security should rather benefit from the equivalent of a just-say-no campaign.
8.2.60 Supply chain	Software security standards shall be required to legally operate eCommerce internet sites.	This policy is intended to establish minimum security controls on all eCommerce services.	• Given the risk to consumers of potential malware, impersonation, and asset theft resulting from insecure websites, no website should be able to offer consumer services without abiding by established security standards. • There are no established security standards that will guarantee safety from attack, and no enforcement mechanism that would provide assurance that any given website abides by them.
8.2.61 Supply chain	Software security standards shall be required to legally operate eCommerce internet sites.	This policy is intended to establish minimum security controls on all eCommerce services.	• Given the risk to consumers of potential malware, impersonation, and asset theft resulting from insecure websites, no website should be able to offer consumer services without abiding by established security standards. • There are no established security standards that will guarantee safety from attack, and no enforcement mechanism that would provide assurance that any given website abides by them.

(Continued)

Index	Statement	Objective	Reasons for Controversy
8.2.62 Supply chain	Software support shall not be fully automated.	This policy is intended to require software support processes to always allow a customer to contact an individual to resolve support issues.	• Software flaws are expected not just in delivered process, but also in automated support system. Any technology vendor that provides support must give customers a way to talk to a person in order at least to report support issues. For example, there are often flaws in automated support mechanisms, such as loops in customer support trouble-reporting systems that do not allow customers to submit details of their problems, or choices constrained to a list of technical problems that do not include the one experienced by the customer. • Software companies price software according to the level of effort it will take to support. Where the level of effort is expected to be minimal, the price is cheaper, and customers get what they pay for.
8.2.63 Supply chain	Software vendors shall allow third parties to review code for security flaws.	This policy is intended to allow third parties to inspect software vendor code for security flaws.	• Software vendors would have to expose their Intellectual Property to third parties, as access to their code would be required to comply with this policy. • Third-party code review or penetration testing cannot be done without access to the code. The benefits of code review to users outweigh the threats to intellectual property from a small set of security testers, who could easily be screened and/or bonded.

8.2.64 Supply chain	Software vendors shall be liable for damage resulting from code malfunctions.	This policy is intended to allow software vendors to be liable for production malfunctions.	• End User License Agreements are currently contrived to deprive end users of any rights to liability for production malfunctions. Software vendors should be subject to the same standards of product liability as any other industry. • Software may malfunction for a variety of reasons, and many of these have nothing to do with the code. A user may install the software on a platform without the necessary resources for it to operate. Malfunction in these cases would not be the fault of the software vendor.
8.2.65 Supply chain	The Department of Defense (DoD) shall specify the organizational management structure that defense suppliers shall use to manage cybersecurity programs.	This policy is intended to require Defense Industrial Base (DIB) companies to adhere to management structures specified by the DoD.	• Specification of security management structures in DIB companies and organizations will reduce the risk of management mistakes. • Business leaders may feel that they should not be told how to organize their management structures, that what is important is to produce goods and services conforming to what is specified in a performance contract.
8.2.66 Supply chain	The Federal Trade Commission shall require all organizations to assess and document technology service provider concentration risk, and shall implement continuity measures where a single provider failure would impair the ability of the organization to conduct essential operations.	This policy is intended to require organizations to treat single-provider dependency as a risk requiring active management – through contractual continuity requirements, technical redundancy, or documented manual backup procedures rather than an implicit condition of technology procurement.	• Adopting this policy will strengthen technology platforms that exhibit significant concentration serving critical sectors. The point is easily demonstrated by incidents and outages that created simultaneous operational disruption across the provider's entire client population in critical industries. For example, Change Healthcare, CrowdStrike, Cloudflare, and Amazon Web Services. • Existing third-party risk management guidance, regulators, and NIST already address concentration risk within broader vendor management frameworks. A standalone policy requirement may create confusion about the relationship between concentration risk assessment and existing third-party risk management obligations.

(Continued)

Index	Statement	Objective	Reasons for Controversy
8.2.67 Supply chain	Where a third-party information systems service is utilized to achieve business objectives, security requirements commensurate with the risk to business process of systemic failure of that service shall be contractually imposed and compliance monitored.	This policy is intended to require computing services used to perform critical business functions to have and monitor internal security programs aligned with the risk of business failure.	• Though a business may not, by virtue of outsourcing, transfer its regulatory requirements via contractual relationships, service contracts that include security requirements and audit clauses allow it to provide appropriate due diligence while reaping the benefits of economies of scale and specialized expertise in service delivery that are available from specialized service providers. • The major reason why a business contracts for information services is that it has no internal competency to perform them. Therefore, even oversight functions that seek evidence that contractual requirements are met are typically performed by staff with minimal understanding of the outsourced service, who are satisfied with a checklist rather than an investigative approach.
8.2.68 Workforce	An organization appointed by senior management with appropriate budget and authority shall ensure that appropriate cybersecurity awareness and training have been provided to all appropriate personnel at an accepted time interval.	This policy is intended to ensure organizational cybersecurity programs are executed by staff appropriately trained for their role in the program.	• It may not be obvious to a staff member how their behavior enhances or detracts from the cybersecurity program. Security training makes their responsibilities with respect to security clear and makes them accountable for their role in the security program. For businesses with ICS, appropriate ICS awareness and training should be required. • Many individuals have no ability to adversely affect information security and such widespread training programs are thus a waste of resources.

8.2.69 Workforce	Individuals in positions of responsibility with respect to cybersecurity shall be certified to be competent in the field.	This policy is intended to require cybersecurity professionals to join cybersecurity professional associations (sometimes even a specific one), pass a certification test, and remain a member.	• It is critically important that individuals who have responsibility for security measures fully understand how their job functions contribute to the overall cybersecurity landscape. Certifications provide the broad security background necessary to provide this view. • There is no consensus among cybersecurity experts that people who have achieved any of the available certifications are more competent to do a cybersecurity job than someone with equivalent experience who is not certified. This type of policy favors individuals who can afford to pay for certification tests and annual certification fees. • Whether or not there is any existing professional body of knowledge agreed upon to be necessary for cybersecurity professionals to understand, it is irrelevant to the fact that a certification process acknowledges the need for one and that cybersecurity professionals have to undergo some preliminary version of the desired test in the meantime while it is being developed. This allows the process to be established to receive the body of knowledge when it becomes available.
8.2.70 Workforce	Management shall collect data on cybersecurity professional hiring and use it to determine cybersecurity hiring effectiveness.	This policy is intended to require management due diligence to ensure that plans for cybersecurity hiring have been successful.	• This policy forces managers who recruit and hire cybersecurity personnel to assess the effectiveness of their efforts. These assessments should lead to continuous improvement in cybersecurity staffing effectiveness. • This type of policy should be a routine function of human resource management endeavors and should not be specific to cybersecurity. Creating special functions for cybersecurity that overlap with routine management unnecessarily overburdens cybersecurity managers with extra paperwork.

8.3 Dependency Example Policy Statements

Index	Statement	Objective	Reasons for Controversy
8.3.1 Custodial	Regulations such as privacy of personal data, GLBA, and due diligence in detection of and response to threats, Fair and Accurate Credit Transaction Act (FACTA), to customer accounts shall apply uniformly to all institutions that handle consumer information.	This policy is intended to require all companies that handle sensitive information on consumers to comply with these regulations, not just Financial Services.	• The unequal application of regulatory standards to financial and non-financial firms conducting similar lines of business is an ongoing concern, both in terms of competition and with respect to the notion that a break in the weakest link of a chain wreaks havoc upon the chain as a whole. • Financial institutions are the only type of organization where actual consumer assets are at risk, and hence there is no need to extend security requirements to other industries. • When these laws were first established, technology platforms holding personal financial data were largely B2B services. Now there are few barriers to entry for any type of internet-enabled consumer transaction platforms.
8.3.2 Financial services	A financial services cybersecurity policy framework shall be developed to allocate security responsibility and financial liability for critical payment infrastructure compromise through the endpoint failure of a member institution.	This policy is intended to require infrastructure operators and member institutions to establish liability frameworks as a condition of network participation.	• Absence of pre-established liability allocation frameworks forces affected parties into costly post-incident dispute resolution, delays recovery of fraudulently transferred funds, and creates moral hazard by obscuring the relationship between cybersecurity investment and financial consequence.

	This framework shall establish that the allocation of security responsibility and financial liability among the infrastructure operator, the compromised institution, and recipient institutions shall be governed by the pre-established policy framework rather than determined through post-incident litigation.		• Pre-established liability frameworks may be difficult to negotiate among network participants operating under different legal jurisdictions, may conflict with established commercial arrangements, and may not anticipate the specific circumstances of novel attack methodologies.
8.3.3 Financial services	Bank regulatory authorities shall increase minimum regulatory capital requirements where the cybersecurity risk profile of a financial institution indicates systemic security issues.	This policy is intended to require banks to maintain loss-absorbing capacity where cybersecurity risk exposures indicate potential for significant financial harm.	• Capital requirements are an institution-level instrument protecting depositors and counterparties of the holding institution. They do not interrupt technical or confidence contagion propagating to other institutions before financial losses are realized at the source. An institution with adequate capital can still serve as a vector for malware propagation or operational disruption independent of its solvency. • Internal loss data can inform capital for firm-specific cyber risk, but cross-institutional propagation losses are not observable by the source institution. No established methodology aggregates downstream losses imposed on others through contagion and feeds them back into the source institution's capital requirement. • Cyber risk is not primarily a risk-taking choice in the way credit or market risk is. Institutions already face strong incentives to prevent incidents through reputational, regulatory, and operational consequences. The marginal incentive effect of additional capital requirements may be limited.

(Continued)

Index	Statement	Objective	Reasons for Controversy
8.3.4 Financial services	Critical technology providers whose services support essential functions at multiple financial institutions, including payment infrastructure operators, core banking platform vendors, and cloud service providers, shall be subject to systemic risk designation and oversight commensurate with their concentration and critical functions in the financial system, independent of whether they hold a financial institution charter.	This policy is intended to close the regulatory gap in which essential financial infrastructure providers are examined only through microprudential extension of client oversight under 12 U.S.C. § 1867(c) rather than on the basis of their own systemic importance. Designation should use a multi-factor assessment incorporating aggregate client institution assets, criticality of specific functions, substitutability, and portability, not client count alone.	• The EU's Digital Operational Resilience Act (DORA), Critical Third-Party Provider designation offers a comparable international model. The US Financial Stability Oversight Council (FSOC) authority covers designated financial market utilities but has not been extended to core banking vendors or hyperscale cloud providers despite equivalent functional concentration. • 12 U.S.C. § 1867(c) is a microprudential authority, an extension of client institution supervision, not an independent macroprudential designation tool, though regulators apply macroprudential models to prioritize examinations under it. Oversight commensurate with systemic importance may require new statutory authority. • Three regulatory attempts spanning a decade, Regulation Identifier Number (RIN) 7100-AE61 (2016 Enhanced Cyber Risk Management Standards), RIN 3064-AG09 (Operational Resilience Rule), and RIN 3064-AF97 (Third-Party Service Relationship Reporting), did not produce final rules. That pattern suggests the obstacles to Core Technology Provider (CTP) oversight are structural rather than incidental, whether rooted in political resistance, unresolved methodological gaps in measuring systemic importance, or both.

8.3.5 Financial services	Cyber incident reporting requirements shall be grounded in a clear and defensible regulatory purpose, with the scope, timeline, and recipient of required reports calibrated to the specific supervisory or public protection function the requirement is intended to serve, and the regulatory purpose, intended beneficiaries, and operational mechanism shall be specified at the time of promulgation.	This policy is intended to establish a coherent standard for incident reporting regulation. Existing requirements are based on regulatory purposes, but the basic information they require is similar enough to streamline all cybersecurity-related regulatory reporting into an umbrella system, on the model the Bureau of Cyber Statistics recommended by the Solarium Commission.	• Different reporting processes serve legitimately distinct functions. The banking agencies' 36-hour Computer Security Incident Notification Rule serves a supervisory early warning function, enabling regulators to assess institutional viability, coordinate resolution planning, and determine whether incidents are propagating across supervised endpoints, with direct operational authority to act on the information received. The US Cyber Incident Reporting for Critical Infrastructure Act (CIRCIA) framework serves a threat intelligence aggregation function, enabling the identification of attack campaigns targeting multiple sectors, sharing indicators of compromise with potential victims, and develop a national picture of adversary tactics that no single sector regulator could assemble.
8.3.6 Financial services	Cybersecurity programs at financial institutions shall explicitly address operational resilience and continuity of critical functions as distinct objectives, with separate governance, investment, and testing requirements from controls addressing confidentiality and integrity.	This policy is intended to require financial institutions to maintain or rapidly restore critical functions when preventive and/or detective controls fail.	• In financial services, the unavailability of critical payment and settlement functions propagates to counterparty institutions through operational contagion within hours, making recovery speed a systemic concern beyond the affected institution. Current regulatory requirements focus on transaction confidentiality and integrity. The control architectures fundamentally differ from those needed for resiliency. • Prescribing resilience as an explicit objective raises the principles-versus-prescriptive tension: recovery architectures are institution-specific, and mandating separate governance and testing requirements constrains flexibility.

(Continued)

Index	Statement	Objective	Reasons for Controversy
			• Resilience requirements scale with the criticality and complexity of protected functions, creating compliance cost asymmetries between large and small institutions. • Existing frameworks, financial service regulator business continuity management guidance, and DORA already address resilience. Separate explicit treatment may be redundant where institutions have implemented established frameworks.
8.3.7 Financial services	Financial institution crime pattern analysis data shall be made available to all consumers in aggregate or non-attributed form, without identifying specific institutions, to avoid amplifying confidence contagion through public attribution of security failures to named institutions.	This policy is intended to require that banks report crimes such as security breaches and identity theft, and that this data be shared with the general public in a form that informs consumer awareness without triggering institution-specific confidence contagion. Public attribution of significant breach or fraud patterns to a named institution may produce rational but destabilizing consumer responses, including deposit withdrawal or account migration, disproportionate to the underlying cyber event.	• Financial institutions voluntarily share identity theft and fraud pattern information through industry associations such as the Financial Services Information Sharing and Analysis Center (FS-ISAC). Financial Crimes Enforcement Network's (FinCEN) Suspicious Activity Report (SAR) program under the Bank Secrecy Act (BSA) provides regulators with system-wide crime pattern intelligence across the banking sector, though BSA confidentiality provisions prohibit institutions from disclosing SAR filings or their existence, creating a structural barrier between regulatory intelligence and public awareness. • While financial institutions may experience large-scale fraud and data breaches without informing the general public, there will be no incentive to make security a marketplace differentiator. Aggregate reporting without attribution may reduce that market incentive further by insulating institutions from reputational consequences of poor security.

8.3.8 Financial services	Financial institution regulatory authorities shall not define how security controls shall work, and instead emphasize that financial institutions shall accomplish goals for security for every consumer.	This policy is intended to hold financial institutions responsible for safeguarding customers' data and assets against outcome-based standards rather than prescriptive control requirements. Principles-based regulation allows institutions to implement controls suited to their specific technology architecture, risk profile, and business model. Financial institutions vary sufficiently in size, infrastructure, and operational characteristics that prescriptive controls calibrated to one institution type will be ill-fitted to others.	• The principles-based versus prescriptive distinction has different implications depending on whether risk is contained within the institution or propagates to others. For risks that propagate through shared infrastructure, where one institution's failure harms others who had no control over its compliance choices, the externality problem creates a case for prescriptive minimum floors that endpoints cannot opt below. • Distributed trust architectures cannot rely solely on endpoint self-assessment. Where any single endpoint's failure imposes costs on all participants, some minimum prescriptive floor may be necessary. This controversy also appears in emerging blockchain governance literature.
8.3.9 Financial services	Financial institutions processing real-time payment transactions shall implement fraud detection controls capable of evaluating transaction risk within the transaction processing window, without relying on post-transaction review mechanisms that cannot interrupt completed transfers.	This policy is intended to require institutions operating real-time payment to satisfy security obligations prior to the time the payment is complete.	• The Electronic Funds Transfer Act (EFTA) requires reimbursement for unauthorized transactions. The Truth in Lending Act (TILA) limits consumer liability for unauthorized credit card use; Uniform Commercial Code (UCC) Article 4A imposes liability on banks executing payment orders from compromised accounts absent commercially reasonable security procedures. Though when these laws were first past, manual in person transaction processing made pre-payment enforcement difficult, today virtually all payment activity is automated. Once funds transfer internationally, recovery proves difficult or impossible.

(Continued)

Index	Statement	Objective	Reasons for Controversy
			• Real-time fraud detection requirements impose architectural constraints that disadvantage smaller institutions lacking investment capacity for machine-learning-based transaction monitoring • Outcome-based fraud liability already creates market incentives to invest in real-time detection without prescribing technical means. A prescriptive architectural requirement risks constraining innovation in detection methodology.
8.3.10 Financial services	Financial institutions shall implement cybersecurity controls that protect transaction data integrity against unauthorized modification with equal rigor to controls protecting customer data confidentiality against unauthorized disclosure.	This policy is intended to provide financial services customers protection again threat actors who find loopholes in transaction processes that allow them to modify account balances, alter transaction records, or corrupt regulatory filings to cause direct financial harm and regulatory non-compliance ensure that integrity controls receive architectural priority commensurate with the financial and systemic consequences of data modification attacks.	• Attacks on transaction integrity currently do not trigger intrusion detection systems configured to detect anomalous behaviors because those systems are tuned to detect data breaches, not analyze data content. • Existing regulatory frameworks such as the Federal Financial Institutions Examination Council (FFIEC) Information Security Booklet and NIST SP 800-53 already address integrity as a core security objective alongside confidentiality and availability. A policy requiring equal rigor may be redundant where institutions have implemented established frameworks. • Defining equivalence between confidentiality and integrity controls is technically complex, as the two objectives require different control architectures. A policy requiring equal rigor without defining measurement criteria may produce inconsistent compliance interpretations across examination jurisdictions.

8.3.11 Financial services	Real-time peer-to-peer payment platforms shall provide consumers with pre-configurable transaction controls, including payee whitelisting, velocity limits, and amount thresholds, and shall implement a reversal window for transactions exceeding those parameters or flagged by recipient account risk scoring.	This policy is intended to address the structural gap between the irrevocability of real-time payment systems and the consumer protection framework of the EFTA, which protects consumers from unauthorized transfers but does not protect consumers who are deceived into authorizing transfers they would not otherwise make. This authorized-but-deceived category, in which a consumer initiates a transfer based on fraudulent instructions received outside the payment channel, falls outside both EFTA's unauthorized transfer protections and the traditional positive-pay model designed for commercial check fraud. Pre-configurable controls provide a technical mechanism by which consumers can constrain permitted transfers in advance, converting out-of-parameter transactions into unauthorized transfers subject to EFTA protection.	• Payment platform operators and their owner banks argue that a consumer who authenticates, initiates, and directs a transfer within the platform has authorized the transaction as a matter of law and fact, and that requiring reimbursement removes consumer incentives for caution while shifting the burden of criminal activity to institutions. • The Consumer Financial Protection Bureau (CFPB) filed suit in December 2024 against Early Warning Services and three major banks alleging failures in fraud prevention safeguards, but dropped the lawsuit in March 2025 following changes in agency leadership, leaving the authorized-but-deceived gap unresolved. • Mandating pre-configurable controls and reversal windows imposes architectural requirements that may increase transaction latency and operating cost, disadvantaging smaller institutions. • The United Kingdom (UK) addressed the equivalent problem through mandatory reimbursement rules requiring sending and receiving payment service providers to split authorized push payment fraud losses, a model the United States has not adopted.

(Continued)

Index	Statement	Objective	Reasons for Controversy
8.3.12 Financial services	Regulators shall establish multilateral cross-border coordination frameworks for systemically important critical technology providers operating across jurisdictions, analogous to the supervisory college model applied to globally systemically important banks (G-SIBs), enabling coordinated incident response, examination information sharing, and pre-incident continuity planning.	This policy is intended to extend the supervisory college model, established under Financial Stability Board (FSB) principles to coordinate home and host regulators for G-SIBs, to CTPs whose operations span multiple regulatory environments. Cloud providers, core banking vendors, and financial messaging infrastructure operators serving institutions across jurisdictions are currently examined only through each jurisdiction's microprudential authority over local clients, with no body aggregating the cross-border picture.	• Financial regulators lack direct jurisdictional authority over CTPs that are not chartered financial institutions, making the legal basis for cross-border CTP coordination less established than for G-SIB supervisory colleges. • DORA's Lead Overseer model establishes CTP oversight within the EU but has no formal coordination mechanism with non-EU regulators overseeing the same provider's global operations. • The FSB has published work on operational resilience and third-party risk, but has not produced a binding multilateral CTP coordination framework. • National regulators are reluctant to share supervisory intelligence across borders even for G-SIBs. That reluctance is likely more pronounced for CTPs where the supervisory relationship is indirect, and the legal basis for coordination is nascent.
8.3.13 Financial services	The systemic importance of a core technology provider (CTP) to the financial sector shall be assessed using a multi-factor framework incorporating the aggregate assets of client financial institutions, the criticality of specific functions provided, substitutability, and portability of client data, and oversight intensity shall be calibrated to that assessed importance.	This policy is intended to apply the same regulatory scrutiny to CTPs as is applied to the financial institutions that incorporate them into their own operations because "core" provider supporting general ledger and settlement operations presents a materially different systemic profile than one providing non-critical functions. Compromise can propagate to client institutions through technical contagion	• Measuring systemic importance for technology providers lacks an established quantitative methodology. Unlike credit or market risk, systemic cyber risk at the CTP level relies on qualitative assessments of interconnectedness and substitutability for which no standardized framework exists. • 12 U.S.C. § 1867(c) is a microprudential authority. Oversight calibrated to systemic importance may require new statutory authority rather than reliance on existing examination powers extended through client institution relationships.

		via software updates or administrative access, operational contagion through service unavailability, financial contagion through settlement disruption, or confidence contagion through uncertainty about data integrity and service continuity	• Existing FFIEC enterprise risk assessment requirements scale to institution size, leaving smaller institutions with lighter CTP assessment obligations, a limitation in the existing framework rather than evidence that the gap this policy addresses does not exist. • Three regulatory attempts to establish heightened CTP standards, RIN 7100-AE61, RIN 3064-AG09, and RIN 3064-AF97, did not produce final rules, suggesting structural rather than incidental obstacles to implementation.
8.3.14 Financial services	Where financial harm may occur through the failure of shared financial infrastructure, including payment networks, core technology providers, and fintech intermediaries, the allocation of security accountability and financial liability among all contributing parties shall be governed by pre-established frameworks rather than determined through post-incident litigation.	This policy is intended to close accountability gaps resulting from failures at nonbank fintech transaction intermediaries by distinguishing accountability (prospective governance obligations defining who ensures adequate controls exist) from liability (retrospective allocation of losses after harm occurs).	• The authorized-but-deceived liability gap in peer-to-peer payment platforms is one instance of the broader problem: multilateral architectures distribute harm across parties whose respective contributions resist apportionment under frameworks designed for bilateral relationships. • Distributed ledger architectures present a distinct accountability challenge: the absence of a central operator removes the primary accountability anchor that existing frameworks assume. The Guiding and Establishing National Innovation for U.S. Stablecoins Act (GENIUS P.L. 119-27) establishes stablecoin issuer liability but leaves protocol-level accountability unaddressed. • Existing instruments, UCC Article 4A, correspondent agreements, and payment network rules, provide partial mechanisms that additional frameworks may conflict with or duplicate.

(Continued)

Index	Statement	Objective	Reasons for Controversy
			• The UK Priority Services Register's mandatory 50/50 loss-splitting for authorized push payment fraud offers an alternative allocation model that the United States has not adopted. • In the absence of such frameworks s, the Bangladesh Bank SWIFT breach produced years of contested loss allocation. Pre-established frameworks connected to network participation or service agreements provide clarity that reactive litigation cannot.
8.3.15 Healthcare	Access to healthcare data shall be contingent upon evidence that such access is required to diagnose or treat a specific case.	This policy is intended to limit health information data sharing only for a specific purpose.	• Qualified healthcare providers should not be worried about justification for data access. It is enough that they be subject to audit. • Qualified healthcare providers should not be required to provide justification for data access in advance of treatment because it would slow down the healthcare delivery. It is enough that they be subject to audit. • All access to personal healthcare data must be justified with reference to a specific patient and condition requiring healthcare provider attention. • Access to healthcare data is often justified by the needs of law enforcement to develop a criminal case against victims of violence, who may not be able or willing to prosecute their attackers. Criminal investigations may also require healthcare providers to provide records of patient care in the course of developing cases that are not focused on the patient as a victim, but as a potential suspect, witness, or other relevant relationship to the crime. Hence, all such records shall be made available to law enforcement with proper oversight and approval.

8.3.16 Healthcare	Access to healthcare data shall be granted at the institutional level.	This policy is intended to accept the premise that institutional participation in a network such as the Homeland Security Information Network (HSIN) should be justification for data download from other institutions, and that access to individual health records need not be justified on a case-by-case basis.	• Where an institution may provide data from multiple sources via a single interface, time is saved in searching for records, and decisions based on the data may be made more quickly. Combining database from multiple sources allows this. • Access granted at the individual level would preserve accountability for individual possession of information and provide traceability in the event of data leakage or misuse. • The ability to combine health data from multiple sources into a data mart within any HSIN participant will result in a complete loss of control over data and synchronization issues with data history. Without a national plan for healthcare data integrity, this is likely to lead to poor decisions due to incomplete data.
8.3.17 Healthcare	All systems used by a healthcare company shall be operated in compliance with the Health Insurance Portability and Accountability Act (HIPAA) Privacy and Security Rules.	This policy is intended to require all healthcare companies to use HIPAA-specific administrative, physical, and technical safeguards to assure the confidentiality, integrity, and availability of electronic protected health information.	• Information may be transferred internally within the organization via unexpected methods. Making the scope of the company's HIPAA program the entire systems environment ensures that such unanticipated transfers do not result in unintentional exposure of electronic protected health information. Many companies' office systems maintain information that is just as sensitive as electronic health information, for example, PII about their own employees. • The HIPAA compliance program is very expensive to operate, and the scope of the regulation is very clear. Narrowing the implementation strategy to administrative, physical, and technical safeguards for only the systems that store and transmit electronic protected health information allows adequate protection without unnecessary cost, which would be passed to consumers.

(Continued)

Index	Statement	Objective	Reasons for Controversy
8.3.18 Healthcare	Cybersecurity regulation with respect to healthcare shall impose technology requirements for data protection based on information classification.	This policy is intended to provide least privilege access to sensitive healthcare data in every format in which it is currently used in all logistics and provider systems.	• Organizations are not currently motivated to secure data. Even HIPAA regulations allow data sharing beyond patient needs, given patient consent. Patients in need of healthcare are too preoccupied to make informed decisions on long-term use of their health data, and so should be able to rely on privacy without being asked to sign it away. • Any technology requirement may increase the cost of service delivery or delay access to much-needed data to support emergency healthcare decisions, so unless there is a specific return on investment in terms of either overall healthcare effectiveness or cost reduction in logistics or provider systems, it does not make sense to further legislate cybersecurity for healthcare data.
8.3.19 Healthcare	Health information shall be required to be digitized so that historical health information can follow the consumer.	This policy is intended to require the healthcare industry to take advantage of the tools and techniques available in the information age to allow patients to receive the benefit of records from former healthcare providers when consulting new ones. It is an essential requirement for service portability.	• The availability of digitized health information for every patient will increase the overall accuracy of diagnostics that require knowledge of past history to be accurate, especially in cases where patients are unconscious or otherwise unable to communicate their history in the time of medical crisis.

8.3.20 Healthcare	Medical standards promoting plug-and-play interoperability standards shall be enforced.	This policy is intended to require standards for medical device interoperability data sharing capability.	• The interoperability standard would facilitate security requirements, such as not allowing public access to sensitive data, as security protocols are currently criticized as potential hindrances to timely care. • The interoperability requirements facilitate economies of scale and minimize data portability problems at healthcare service providers. • Interoperability standards, if not combined with security requirements, may make the problem worse, as they would make healthcare data more widely available. They should not be adopted without companion security models and guidance for appropriate and authorized use of sensitive data. • The interoperability requirements are justified not only by economies of scale and data portability issues, but also by continued development of healthcare data standards and a significant increase in the technical and material support provided by the federal government for public–private partnerships in this area.
8.3.21 Health care	Non-repudiation and accuracy of data shall be addressed by the healthcare provider policy prior to confidentiality.	This policy is intended to require that the ability to identify who modified data and whether it is correct should be the primary goal of a healthcare security program.	• Healthcare resources are scarce and privacy should not be the overarching priority on how to spend security dollars. No one ever died of embarrassment, but they have died by getting the wrong prescription. • This policy assumes that security dollars are static. The same security control measures that protect integrity may be leveraged to ensure some measure of privacy.

(Continued)

Index	Statement	Objective	Reasons for Controversy
8.3.22 Healthcare	Software for automated healthcare provider systems, such as radiation and medicine delivery shall be designed using safety and security models.	This policy is intended to require design safety and security principles, such as failure in safe mode and allocation of least resources.	• Software for specialized equipment should not be burdened with unnecessary subroutines. The best way to control it is to minimize functionality and train operators. • Failure to observe known safety and security principles in such potentially dangerous devices amounts to negligence and technology malpractice. The lack of attention to security in the design process of these systems has the effect that they have many of the same security vulnerabilities as industrial control systems.
8.3.23 Healthcare	Systems such as the Nationwide Health Information Network (NHIN) shall maintain a Data Use and Reciprocal Support Agreement (DURSA) with companies with whom it shares health information.	This policy is intended to require that companies that release data assure the data protection capability of third parties to whom they release it.	• Patient data must be immediately available in order to be useful for emergency patient treatment. Any security due diligence requirement for data sharing may restrict a healthcare provider's ability to save a life. • Though ubiquitous information sharing of healthcare information without pre-vetting of a purpose may not be appropriate for normal operating procedure, all healthcare information should be shared without question in situations of widespread crisis, such as fires and hurricanes. • Nationally recognized data sharing with only DURSA-like agreements amounts to a handshake, and so trusting parties are at the mercy of those who break the rules. As audit-based evidence is not required to join these NHIN-like networks, there is no deterrent for anyone within the medical profession to create a market in sensitive healthcare data.

8.3.24 Industrial control	Control system protocols used in automated communication between ICS components shall be reliably authenticated and secured, where possible.	This policy is intended to establish a standards body dedicated to the development, implementation, testing, and distribution of new secure protocols designed for use in high-reliability, deterministic systems.	• The protocols used to communicate between ICS devices use control system unique protocols, such as Modbus (derived from Modular Bus), Distributed Network Protocol 3 (DNP-3), and Inter-Control Center Communications Protocol (ICCP) were developed without cybersecurity or authentication. Although there may not be confidentiality requirements for the data itself, the lack of encryption makes them easy to spoof, and the lack of authentication ensures the success of hijacking attacks. • Some IT groups have suggested that ICS "wrap" these protocols in TCP/IP to facilitate security and interoperability between IT systems and ICS systems. Wrapping them in TCP/IP can make them even more vulnerable. TCP/IP is not deterministic, and consequently, TCP/IP should only be used for non-process or non-safety-critical communications. • Copying internet protocols rather than developing secure and efficient security for ICS communication may be used to justify increased accessibility for ICS controls, such as internet connectivity, and the loss of isolation could lead to worse vulnerabilities than those that currently exist. It will also subject ICS to the same threats that IT systems face, like phishing and ransomware.

(Continued)

Index	Statement	Objective	Reasons for Controversy
8.3.25 Industrial control	Energy industry regulatory standards shall be strengthened to address the increasing risk of reliance on cyberspace.	This policy is intended to ensure that the energy industry is held to the highest standards of cybersecurity protection.	• Current energy industry security standards have been demonstrated to be less than adequate. For example, applying the North American Electric Reliability Corporation Critical Infrastructure Protections (NERC CIP) would not have prevented many actual cybersecurity incidents, including several major cyber-related electric outages. • NERC CIPs have exclusions, such as addressing only routable protocols, that exclude incidents such as Stuxnet and Aurora from even being considered. • It has been observed in other industries that regulatory oversight does not increase security controls. If the industry does not self-identify the controls that are important to their operations, then they will not be adequately addressed.
8.3.26 Industrial control	ICS communication shall be on isolated networks.	This policy is intended to prevent connecting ICSs to the internet and is intended to prevent adversaries from attacking critical infrastructure through publicly available portals.	• Internet connectivity to cyber-physical infrastructure should be minimized. • Wireless protocols used by cyber-physical systems should be configured to restrict access to authorized physical devices, thus eliminating the possibility of rogue and potentially malicious access. • Whether critical infrastructure or not, connecting cyber-physical system devices directly to the internet should be avoided. In the May-June U.S. Department of Homeland Security (DHS) Monitor 2015 on Page 4, DHS stated, "If you're connected, you're likely infected." DHS emphasizes that connecting ICS systems to the internet leads to cyber intrusions and attacks, such as the injection of the malicious surveillance software, BlackEnergy, into power grids and the December 2015 cyberattack on the Ukrainian grid.

8.3.27 Industrial control	ICS design criteria shall include requirements for cybersecurity.	This policy is intended to ensure that cybersecurity requirements are incorporated into designs and would prompt research into cybersecurity specifications for upgrading chips in legacy control systems and field devices.	• ICS designs are primarily based on performance and safety of physical processes. It is common for ICS to utilize designers to specify microprocessors with limited memory and performance that preclude the use of cybersecurity technology such as encryption, authentication, and robust signal monitoring. • The ability to use electronics in unintended ways is commensurate with the functionality and data storage capacity of the circuitry. The ability to use ICS in unexpected ways is at least partially dependent on the capability in these circuits. Awareness that malfunctions or intentional manipulation of the data content of ICS cyber-enabled functionality should inspire overall system designs that protect it from intentional or accidental corruption. • Awareness that ICS malfunctions or intentional manipulation should motivate cyber malfunction detection measures that are currently missing and need to be developed to identify intentional or unintentional cyber incidents. • Electronically controlled physical devices may be controlled physically as well as logically. Malfunction detection measures currently prevalent in ICS should be able to compensate for intentional or unintentional cyber functionality failures.

(Continued)

Index	Statement	Objective	Reasons for Controversy
8.3.28 Industrial control	ICS design shall include the capability for cyber forensics.	This policy is intended to remediate the situation that many programmable logic controllers (PLCs), distributed control systems (DCSs), supervisory control and data acquisition (SCADA), and control system field devices systems do not identify or adequately store the digital evidence that would be useful in cybersecurity investigations.	• Industrial accidents happen frequently, and investigations inspect cyberspace logs and configurations if they are available, but most ICS have been designed to minimize data storage in order to maximize performance. This area is ripe for research and development to determine what specific types of cyber forensics are needed and how they would be utilized in the least invasive manner possible. • The ICS community has the knowledge base to understand what physical parameters are required to perform a root-cause analysis of an incident. Consequently, the ICS community has developed the detailed forensics for physical parameters: temperature, pressure, level, flow, motor speed, current, voltage, etc. However, many legacy/field device components of an ICS have minimal to limited capability of storing such data for later review and do not log cybersecurity forensics.
8.3.29 Industrial control	ICS operation shall require clock synchronization.	This policy is intended to ensure that various atomic clocks and satellite services provide robust and reliable time synchronization for electronic systems.	• ICSs are deterministic systems and are programmed to observe real-time requirements for process sensor activity and /or information flow. Hence, communications must occur within a prescribed period of time prior to automated action changing the system state. This policy would minimize the risk of ICS malfunction due to time synchronization issues. • Reliable and timely communications are critical for maintaining the operations of ICSs.

			• The introduction of some signal validation, minimal authentication, and adequate speed (that is, some latency is acceptable). • A major recommendation from the 2003 Northeast Outage was the need for time synchronization. Phasor measurement units for the electric grid will require very precise time measurements.
8.3.30 Industrial control	Security certification and testing programs for verifying adequate security in ICSs shall be established.	This policy is intended to produce and maintain verification strategies to ensure that ICSs address security in their design and implementation, as well as to develop new ICS systems that are inherently secure by design.	• ICSs are systems of systems. It has been demonstrated that ostensibly secure systems can be compromised, and it is obvious that insecure systems can be compromised. As security depends on how the systems are installed and maintained, any system certification is a snapshot in time. When part(s) of the system that can change the cyber environment change (hardware, software, communications, possibly even people), the system needs to be recertified. • ICS covers such a wide range of systems and industries that it is not clear how requirements for ICS cybersecurity testing could be validated and by whom.
8.3.31 Industrial control	Security certification programs for ICS security personnel shall be established and include lessons on how to manage and test cybersecurity features (or lack thereof) in level 0 devices such as sensors, drives, actuators, and robots.	This policy is intended to augment professional engineering licenses with cybersecurity competency requirements.	• Similar to the lack of ICS security curricula, there is a gap in personnel certifications specifically addressing ICS cybersecurity field devices (process sensors and actuators). Consequently, there is a need to assess the competency of individuals working in this field who address the union of IT and ICS field device applications.

(Continued)

Index	Statement	Objective	Reasons for Controversy
			• ICS security is an emerging, highly specialized field of engineering. It combines the disciplines of control system engineering, the specific engineering domain, IT security, industrial networking, risk management, and safety system engineering. It also requires an understanding of commercial platforms (e.g., Windows, UNIX, LINUX, SQL, etc.). • IT certifications such as CISSP and CISM are focused on traditional IT and do not address the unique issues of ICS. Even the SANS ICS certification does not acknowledge the difference in cybersecurity capabilities, or lack thereof, between level 0 and level 1 PLCs.
8.3.32 Industrial control	Systems that monitor and control flammable, explosive, chemical, or nuclear facilities shall be designed so that cyber incidents are monitored and mitigated before they can cause facilities to fail in an unsafe manner.	This policy is intended to ensure that systems that monitor and control flammable, explosive, chemical, or nuclear facilities shall be designed so that cyber incidents are monitored and mitigated before they can cause facilities to fail in an unsafe manner.	• This policy would ensure that appropriate cybersecurity controls are implemented in facilities to prevent catastrophic failures, potentially affecting the health and safety of the public. Typical facilities include power plants, refineries and chemical plants, water treatment facilities, pipeline facilities, and certain manufacturing facilities. • The electronic infrastructure that controls and monitors flammable, explosive, chemical, or nuclear facilities can be cyber vulnerable. In case of failures, whether unintentional or malicious, alarms should be activated and safety systems initiated. • Mechanical devices that have electronic components are often not classified as software, and so logical functions are not tested beyond the current use cases for the device.

8.3.33 Industrial control	The ICS community shall actively and formally apply software assurance principles to all development of ICS software.	This policy is intended to establish a requirement that all software supporting ICS is supported by a management process designed to maximize adherence to requirements and minimize the introduction of accidental or intentional vulnerabilities.	• Certain security tests that are widely utilized to test IT can adversely affect the operation of ICSs or result in operator confusion. Examples include using port scanning tools that result in ICS components freezing up or worse. Rather than require the same tests, the requirement should be to identify a set of security tests more suited for ICS software testing.
8.3.34 Research and development	Cybersecurity research and development needs additional focus on cybersecurity technologies specific to ICSs. Interdisciplinary programs on cybersecurity of industrial control systems shall be developed and incorporated into university computer science, engineering, and public policy programs.	This policy is intended to fill a gap in university-level interdisciplinary programs on cybersecurity in industrial control systems.	• There is little understanding of the actual ICS needs or the ICS technical limitations. ICS cybersecurity R&D is needed to address appropriate ICS needs. Little ICS cybersecurity research is devoted to the non-Windows-based field devices, which are not IT-type systems. • Separating research into different types of cybersecurity systems may fragment what little money is available. Rather than create a new field, ICS should be brought into mainstream security curriculum. • ICS security is much less understood, has little expertise, and is often not considered critical. Focused research in this area would be useful in educating both the public and owner/operators on potential risks.
8.3.35 Risk management	Organizations engaged in public relations responses to cyberattacks shall take into account both outrage (such as perceived negligence) and hazard (actual damage).	This policy is intended to hold organizations accountable for poor cybersecurity practices that put others' information at risk.	• Cybersecurity professionals often observe that media reporting on cybercrime sometimes unnecessarily feeds outrage even for low hazard events. This is particularly apparent in the daily news cycle on otherwise low-news days. In order to reduce the unnecessary stress among potential victims, if any, organizations faced with these unnecessary cybersecurity alarms should be prepared with strategies to manage them.

(Continued)

Index	Statement	Objective	Reasons for Controversy
8.3.36 Supply chain	Any commercial enterprise that monitors physical or cybersecurity or is authorized to make changes to security settings or to monitor within the customer's physical locations or systems via remote access shall be subject to the same stringent background checks and security standards targeted at military contractors.	This policy is intended to minimize the risk that a service provider with this capability inadvertently allows adversaries to cause widespread physical harm to life and property.	• Advances in smart grid technology provide features to monitor and change the configuration of hardware and software for both cyber and cyber-physical systems, as well as automatically turn them on, off, or adjust their controls. If a service provider with this capability were to succumb to insider threat attacks, the results could be widespread physical harm to life and property. • These features set the stage for network intrusions into the customer environment. They may be used for widespread surveillance or to create cyber and/or physical disturbances at the individual, local, or regional level.
8.3.37 Technology platforms	Technology platforms that provide software as a service (SaaS) and publish Application Programming Interfaces (APIs) for use by its customers shall posthaste provide patches or workarounds for security vulnerabilities identified by customers or otherwise known to be exploited in a manner that leaves customer data confidentiality, integrity, or availability negatively impacted.	This policy is intended to provide criteria for vendor patches to security vulnerabilities that impact customers, without customers having to	• Given the plethora of vulnerable online services, there is complacency within the technology platform industry on which vulnerabilities need to be addressed as well as the timeframe it takes to mitigate vulnerabilities. This policy would allow recourse for users whose data is breached in platforms that did not immediately take action when the negative impact due to an exploited vulnerability was identified.

8.4 Adversary Example Policy Statements

Index	Statement	Objective	Reasons for Controversy
8.4.1 Cybercrime	Existing international organizations, such as North Atlantic Treaty Organization (NATO), Association of Southeast Asian Nations (ASEAN), Organization of American States (OAS), EU, and African Union (AU), shall include cybercrime as part of all their deliberations and treaties.	This policy is intended to encourage international organizations to embrace solutions to cybercrime, just as they would for any problem that requires international cooperation to resolve.	• International organizations sometimes work at the level of least-common denominator (the blandest statement that all nations can agree to), which may end up leaving the status quo and respect for each other's laws. Such an agreement would be a step backward, as some investigations have already seen field-office-level cooperation between nations. • These organizations should play a key role in eliminating the sanctuaries for malicious actors as well as to improve the understanding of politicians and bureaucrats of the implications of cybercrime.
8.4.2 Cybercrime	Financial institutions that are convicted of allowing online criminal money-laundering shall be barred from offering the exploited financial services online.	This policy is intended to prevent financial institutions from repeating transactions known to be used by criminals to hide profits and move them into legitimate investments.	• As financial institutions make more money from deposits of criminal profits, and expensive financial transactions that are used by criminals to hide these profits which they may be expected to lose if caught, they have little incentive to discontinue these practices when simply fined. • Money-laundering can never be actually stopped. Financial institutions are already audited against money laundering regulations and as long as good faith efforts exist to prevent it, they should not be held liable for the crimes of others.

(Continued)

Index	Statement	Objective	Reasons for Controversy
8.4.3 Cybercrime	Individuals who use false identities or anonymous access to commit cyber-bullying shall receive mandatory jail terms.	This policy is intended to add penalties to convicted cyber bullies who do not identify themselves to their victims.	• Those who cloak their identity to harass others have obviously premeditated their crime and are aware that their behavior is inappropriate. • Not all instances of cyber bullying, even premeditated ones, are commensurate with punishment of jail time.
8.4.4 Cybercrime	Individuals who use false identities or anonymous access to report false crimes or emergencies, as well as those who witness such events without reporting them, shall receive mandatory jail terms.	This policy is intended to deter anonymous internet or phone access which is often used to divert emergency response teams to false emergencies, leading to false arrests and diluted resources available for real emergencies.	• This type of inappropriate use of the internet disregards the need for response to genuine human tragedy, and individuals who commit such offenses are likely to exhibit other sociopathic tendencies, so should not be allowed to remain in society. • This type of inappropriate use of the internet is typically done by juveniles, and mandatory jail time may be an inappropriately harsh punishment.
8.4.5 Cybercrime	Nations shall be prepared to treat cyberattacks from a technical, criminal, or national security perspective, depending on the specifics of the attack.	This policy is intended to improve readiness of cyberattacks in these areas. Nations need the mindset and capability to see and respond appropriately.	• This will give nations greater flexibility in their response, while including all cyber law enforcement in the potential for national defense measures. • Nations lacking resources will need to divide their limited personnel, technology, and funding between each of these three perspectives to deal with attacks.

8.4.6 Cybercrime	Nations shall become signatories to the Convention on Cybercrime or the more recent UN Convention Against Cybercrime and encourage other nations to do the same. Nations shall then implement the Convention by passing additional required laws to criminalize cyberattacks.	This policy is intended to increase the criminal consequences of cyberattacks. The Convention on Cybercrime, originally from the Council of Europe, is an international treaty to harmonize laws that nations should pass to criminalize malicious activity on the internet and set reasonable minimum internal standards for nations. More recently, members of the United Nations have ratified a Convention Against Cybercrime (the Hanoi Convention).	• As more nations join the Convention, there are fewer sanctuaries for malicious actors to hide.
8.4.7 Cybercrime	Nations shall create a national computer emergency response team to provide a 24/7 point of contact, assist companies in that nation by sharing best practices and other means, respond to significant incidents and vulnerabilities, and provide situational awareness for cyberspace.	This policy is intended to give a focus for security, allowing fast recognition of events, coordination within the country and with other countries, and faster response to incidents.	• Not only it is now an international expectation that nations will have the capability to conduct these standard functions, but each of these will significantly improve security and response. • Though an important function, a national Computer Emergency Response Team (CERT) needs personnel, training, funding, and other resources. To be effective, nations will need to ensure other such teams exist for key areas, such as industrial control systems, the domain name system, or other key technologies.
8.4.8 Cybercrime	Nations shall ensure their law enforcement, prosecutors, and judges have sufficient expertise and tools to be able to investigate and respond adequately to reported cyberattacks and prosecute cybercrime.	This policy is intended to ensure the qualifications of the many organizations involved in enforcing cybercrime, from local police (at the metropolitan, county, or state level), national police, prosecutors at all levels, and judges at all levels.	• Passing laws to criminalize malicious cyber activity is not enough. For them to be effective, all parts of the law enforcement system must have the training and tools to ensure the laws are enforced and effective. • If done well, this is a long-term (and potentially expensive) effort to help local and national police, judges, and prosecutors understand this new area of crime.

(Continued)

Index	Statement	Objective	Reasons for Controversy
8.4.9 Cybercrime	The Department of Education shall set standards for the cybersecurity of children's websites that include safe content, parental monitoring features, and comprehensive user screening to ensure they are uninhabited by adult predators.	This policy is intended to require websites aimed at children to meet standards for safe content, oversight, and identification of all participants.	• Current open ability for adults to reach out to children on any website, whether under false identities or not, enables unmonitored cybercrime. This policy would provide parents with a way to allow uninhibited communication between children online. • The technology to enforce this policy is prohibitively expensive, and unless funded by communities or government, would likely be limited to an elite few who could afford participation.
8.4.10 Cybercrime	The internet shall not be used to incentivize violence against persons or property.	This policy is intended to deter people from using the internet to direct violent behavior.	• The use of internet messaging to quickly gather large groups of people to a certain location for criminal purposes, known as flash mobs, is a violation of the personal liberty of those who are the intended victims of the gathering, and the rights of these individuals should outweigh the rights of free speech among criminals. • This policy will allow the use of tech platforms like Facebook to plan large-scale attacks for political purposes to be treated similarly to hate crimes.
8.4.11 Cybercrime	The use of steganography to hide pornographic pictures shall be prohibited.	This policy is intended to prohibit the use of steganography with pornographic pictures. Steganography is software that combines the content of two pictures in such a way that only one can be seen by typical picture viewing software, while the other may be extracted easily with steganography software.	• Hiding pornographic pictures with technology may actually have a benefit in that it will shield them from the view of those who may be offended by them. • Even when cyber criminals are identified, it is often difficult to prosecute because many nations provide a safe harbor for their citizens. These are political and diplomatic issues and should be solved by politicians and diplomats.

8.4.12 Intellectual property	Business intelligence services shall be regulated and their activities monitored to ensure that they can produce legal claim to the information they provide to clients.	This policy is intended to limit information shared by business intelligence companies to that which is demonstrably legitimate obtained available and deter them from cyber espionage.	• As hostile nations will not adopt regulations that prevent them from Advanced Persistent Threat (APT), this type of policy puts friendly nations at a competitive disadvantage. • There is a fine line between business intelligence and intellectual property theft. Both activities have the overt objective of finding out as much as possible about a competitor's plans and products.
8.4.13 Intellectual property	Existing international organizations, such as NATO, ASEAN, OAS, EU, and AU, shall play a key role in coordinated response to major national cybersecurity incidents.	This policy is intended to encourage international organizations to create frameworks that will help resolve to national cybersecurity incidents.	• Many of the problems of cyber conflict are not technical. They are political and diplomatic and should be solved by politicians and diplomats. • After a major cyberattack, these groups may be able to help prevent escalation and assist politicians to find key answers to difficult technical questions (such as attribution of the attack). • International organizations sometimes work at the level of least-common denominator (the blandest statement that all nations can agree to), which may not be helpful during a cyber conflict.
8.4.14 Intellectual property	Preservation of national intellectual property shall be a key diplomatic objective.	This policy is intended to require intellectual property issues to be at the forefront of international diplomatic relations efforts.	• Lack of a formal diplomatic response to get to the bottom of the numerous confirmed intellectual property thefts committed in cyber space amounts to tacit acknowledgement that the only solution is economic or physical conflict. Diplomatic efforts in this area are in their infancy and innovative approaches are required to bring about peaceful resolution. • As most intellectual property theft is profit-motivated, it is performed by individual companies and their governments have very little control over their activities.

(Continued)

Index	Statement	Objective	Reasons for Controversy
8.4.15 Intellectual property	Scanning systems and networks belonging to others for vulnerabilities without their express permission shall be forbidden.	This policy is intended to prohibit the scanning of networks beyond one's own perimeter which is a critical capability in planning a cyberattack.	• Network scanning is normally performed in order to find vulnerabilities in the target systems. Those vulnerabilities are then exploited during an attack. Similar to intelligence gathering, unauthorized scanning of company or organization networks should be treated as a criminal plan. • Because of the internet's lack of attribution and the difficulty in performing tracebacks, apparent source internet addresses of scanning computers must not be assumed to be the actual IP address of an adversary's computer. This policy would be difficult to enforce. • Network scanning is a form of research that is a valuable source of information on the cyberspace landscape. It would destroy some company's business models.
8.4.16 Intellectual property	Those who commit intellectual property theft shall be barred from selling those products internationally.	This policy is intended to deter intellectual property theft by imposing financial penalties in confirmed cases.	• Such deterrence is irrelevant. It is currently beyond forensic capability to make a non-reputable claim that any given company has benefited from intellectual property theft, and even if they do, they have already been rewarded in the marketplace by their customers. • Such coordinated effort against a competitor would amount to anti-trust, which is a worse problem for consumers than intellectual property theft.

8.4.17 Technology platforms	Technology platforms that provide free services to criminals organizing cyberattacks or physical crimes shall be subject to state, federal, and international charges of aiding and abetting criminal and/or martial activity.	This policy is intended to incentivize technology platforms to sustain efficient and effective monitoring, evaluation, and cessation of user activity that participates in criminal or martial activity such as the organization of the January 6 attack on the US Capitol and the Rohingya genocide by the armed forces of Myanmar.	• This policy would close a purposeful loophole in the Communications Decency Act (CDA) that protects technology platforms from liability for user-generated content, labeling them as distributors as opposed to publishers. At the time, this was supposed to encourage the growth of technology platforms. However, now the tech platforms are so big that they can provide free enterprise-level computing to organized groups of thousands of users that conspire for free to commit crimes and atrocities. This level of support for criminal activity is equivalent to handing them money to support their operations and should be legally treated as such.
8.4.18 Warfare	Cyber offense shall be treated as a valid, sometimes even preferred, military capability.	This policy is intended to prioritize cyberattacks over more traditional physical attacks as a first consideration for all military operations.	• Cyberattacks on large-scale critical infrastructure may indeed have disproportionate effects. • While cyberattacks may have unintended or substantial consequences, cyber offensives have generally been used by states as non-kinetic attacks that neither kill nor cause permanent damage. They have tended to be de-escalatory. • A cyberattack that disables an air defense site rather than the site being targeted with a kinetic bomb, probably will save the lives of site operators. Likewise, a cyberattack against an electrical power system could be configured to cause damage that is much more transient and reversible than a similar impact caused by a kinetic attack. Where commanders have access to non-kinetic and non-lethal capabilities, it is more humane to use these attacks.

(Continued)

Index	Statement	Objective	Reasons for Controversy
8.4.19 Warfare	International arms control efforts shall include a focus on requirements to report zero-day vulnerabilities to the party responsible for fixing them and restricting the sale of cybersecurity vulnerabilities and the operation of corresponding exploit kits.	This policy is intended to increase awareness that cybersecurity weapons hold the same, if not more, destructive capability as other weapons of mass destruction.	• The proliferation of offensive cyber capabilities would be extremely difficult, if not impossible, to stop. They are difficult to define, relatively inexpensive, and can be developed in any basement or computer lab. Any treaty to stop proliferation would be nearly impossible to verify or enforce. • International arms control efforts could also be focused on limiting the scope of permissible targets and use of cyberattacks and not generally the weapons themselves. Possible frameworks to do that include existing restrictions of the laws of armed conflict, or new constructs seeking to limit the use of cyber technology. • The definition of the term "munition" or "weapon" in cybersecurity may not be well enough understood for this policy to be effectively enforced. • Cyberattacks can be conducted covertly, with difficult attribution, so if there is a prohibited attack, it might be difficult to determine whom to hold responsible.
8.4.20 Warfare	International humanitarian law shall apply to conflicts in cyberspace.	This policy is intended to categorize conflict in cyberspace as International humanitarian law (also known as the law of armed conflict). It is the traditional law used by nations to determine when it is legal to engage in armed conflict and what methods are considered ethical and legal. As cyber subversion and sabotage have potentially harmful consequences for humans, especially when directed at critical infrastructure, humanitarian ethical rules apply.	• Because international humanitarian law is widely accepted (though of course with disagreement on specific cases), having it as a root of laws pertaining to cyber conflict makes sense. However, problems with attribution for cyber espionage, subversion, and sabotage present new ethical dilemmas for consideration for inclusion in humanitarian law. Other avenues for deterring covert cyberwar should be considered.

8.4.21 Warfare	Militaries shall conduct realistic exercises of their cyber defense plans, including the public sector and other nations.	This policy is intended to ensure the execution of Cybersecurity exercises, which allow participants to walk through or enact simple scenarios to give participants practice in decision-making, test themselves against a given response standard, or familiarize participants with response plans. Exercises are also used to explore new concepts to determine what appropriate responses might be.	• To be done well, exercises can require extensive planning beforehand. In general, the better quality of training and lessons requires higher levels of planning and resources. Hence the cost-benefit of exercises may not outweigh the alternative, which is to study current cyber-espionage cases. • Tabletop exercises are heralded as ideal learning tools, but if not designed well, can entrench assumptions and existing dogma. Moreover, the most critical decision makers are typically absent from the exercises, and they are reduced to methods to generate data to fill reports with warnings of things the exercise developers already know about.
8.4.22 Warfare	Militaries shall ensure their workforce that "faces the adversary" most gets additional training on the extent to which technology controls their physical equipment, vehicles, and weapons.	This policy is intended to ensure all who have a primary role of attacking or defending against the adversary have a similar combat mindset as their cybersecurity-specific peers.	• Because of the prevalence of cyberattacks originating from inside, it may not be possible to determine which section of the military cyber workforce will be most adversary-facing. All staff should have equal ability to recognize and deal with adversarial cyber threats.
8.4.23 Warfare	Militaries shall widely coordinate between offensive and defensive cyber operations, between kinetic and cyber, between attack and exploitation, and with civilian counterparts.	This policy is intended to ensure coordination with both its own supply chain and targeted asset owners as a critical factor for any military operations. These are cyber-command's civilian counterparts.	• Each of these actions is needed because of the unique nature of cyberspace. Not only is it new and generally untested, but effects can cascade and impact unintended civilian systems. Any counterattacks may be seen as proportional by an adversary but be targeted directly at the host nation's critical infrastructure. • Coordination with potentially numerous individuals from multiple organizations will necessarily slow down the tempo of cyber operations. • Many skilled cyber-defense operations centers are owned and operated by highly skilled private sector cybersecurity analysts. Where the military chooses not to coordinate with them, they will lose access to desperately needed talent.

(Continued)

Index	Statement	Objective	Reasons for Controversy
8.4.24 Warfare	Military leadership of a nation shall ensure there are programs to safely share information with and between companies in their Defense Industrial Base.	This policy is intended to ensure safe data sharing in the Defense Industrial Base (DIB).	• This policy is in line with best practices in other sectors, such as finance, and helps coordinate to find and prevent intrusions into companies that maintain information on traditional weapons manufacturers, as well as service providers and others who have access to military information. • Military encouragement of providing safe communications conduits between DIBs must be careful to ensure that companies do not take advantage of the opportunities to collaborate against the government on prices or programs.
8.4.25 Warfare	Military leadership shall be cautious about certain targets and capabilities: active defense, cyber operational preparation of the environment, and targeting foreign critical infrastructures.	This policy is intended to provide guidance to military leadership on cyber plans. Active defense usually means a capability to "hack back" at systems involved in attacks. Cyber elements are intruding into foreign systems prior to an offensive attack. Foreign infrastructures will be depended on by foreign militaries and, as such, are usually legal targets.	• In each of these areas, it is usually entirely legal for militaries to pursue these targets and capabilities; however, it should be done very cautiously.
8.4.26 Warfare	Military leadership shall consider cyberspace as a new domain in which warfare can occur, just like the traditional domains of air, land, space, and maritime.	This policy is intended to provide guidance to military leadership on cyberspace. Like the other domains, it is a place with international, personal, and commercial interests, with its own geography. Unlike space and the air, it has very low barriers to entry.	• Considering cyberspace as a domain helps not only to raise the importance of cyberspace but also makes it easier for non-specialists to understand. • An unintended consequence of military classification of cyberspace as a domain is that military operations may treat it as a warfighting domain, forgetting it is dominated by the private sector. • Cyber space is no more a domain than artillery is a domain. It is a tool to be used in operations for air, sea, space, and land.

8.4.27 Warfare	Military leadership shall coordinate planning for cybersecurity response and retaliation efforts with potentially impacted private sector organizations.	This policy is intended to provide guidance to military leadership on cyber planning for retaliation that will minimize negative impact on critical infrastructure. Cyberspace is dominated by the private sector as it is not in other domains. In space, air, and even in the open ocean, those domains are dominated by emptiness. Even on land, people will flee a conflict if they can. There are no such options in cyberspace where the "space" itself was created and owned by the private sector.	• The military has a propensity to classify its operations as secret, so any mandate to work with the private sector is likely to end up with arguments on classification efforts that will compete with the private-sector's ability to benefit from cyber military operations.
8.4.28 Warfare	Military leadership shall over time integrate their capability and forces for cyber conflict into their traditional war-fighting doctrines and structures.	This policy is intended to establish the integration of cybersecurity in military operations. Historically, military cyber capabilities have been linked to intelligence, to special offensive programs, or to information technology reinforcement programs. This puts cybersecurity outside the normal understanding of missions operated by military organizations.	• It may be difficult for many diverse cybersecurity operations to become integrated because the capability itself is exceptionally sensitive. • Where a military organization is relatively immature at integrating cyber capabilities, forced consolidation will detract from the missions and defense programs for which the small cyber conflict units were originally developed, and leave those programs with a critical lack of cybersecurity support. • Cyber operations are often more similar to intelligence operations than traditional destructive military effects. Combining them with the latter may detract from their true nature.

(Continued)

Index	Statement	Objective	Reasons for Controversy
8.4.29 Warfare	Military leadership shall prioritize cyber defense over offense.	This policy is intended to establish military priorities for cyber operations. Cyber defense is the ability to stop adversaries from effectively using cyber offensive capabilities. Cyber offense (using non-kinetic cyber capabilities to attack adversaries in cyberspace) is also considered an important military capability.	• Without a functioning cyberspace, nations may be unable to run their economy, make political decisions during conflict, or generate military force. Any or all of these might be disrupted by an adversary if defense is not considered the highest priority. • Defense can be complex and expensive, while offenses can be a deterrent, and thus also contribute to defense. Theoretically, some adversaries are deterred by a sufficiently advanced offense.
8.4.30 Warfare	Military leadership shall prioritize developing rules of engagement for cyberspace that mirror those for other domains, but applied to the stark differential realities of cyberspace.	This policy is intended to prioritize the development of cyberspace rules of engagement, which specify when and how a friendly force may use force against others. In kinetic warfare, these can be relatively straightforward or (such as during irregular warfare) very difficult. In cyber conflict, they will be difficult not only because it is a new domain of warfare, but because of the technical nature of cyberspace.	• This policy should make rules of engagement very restrictive compared to the current state of no rules, until, over time, political leaders, commanders, operators, and lawyers become more familiar and knowledgeable with cyber conflicts and capabilities and understand the boundaries between adversaries, that, if agreed upon, may keep both sides safe. • Restrictive rules of engagement will limit commanders from properly employing cyber capabilities, which reduce their ability to thwart impending cyberattacks. • Where rules of engagement do not exist, militaries may be conducting hostile and damaging cyber space operations without the oversight or knowledge of their own government. • Rules of engagement are what keep militaries on the legal side of international humanitarian law.

8.4.31 Warfare	Military leadership shall promulgate a declaratory policy to help set international norms and help set defense expectations.	This policy is intended to set norms and expectations of cyber military operations. A declaratory policy could include elements like no-first-use against broad societal targets, no use of polymorphic viruses or worms, not having attacks appear to come from protected entities (like hospitals), and similar items.	• A declaratory policy improves transparency and helps guide the development of capabilities and doctrine. If well-worded, they do not necessarily take away options. Rather, they rightfully restrict options that should never be considered. • Declaratory policies allow adversaries to anticipate actions.
8.4.32 Warfare	The military shall enhance the skill sets of its cyber workforce, to include the traditional cyber workforce of IT specialists, in combination and coordination with staff needed for missions related to the "contested domain" of cyberspace.	This policy is intended to ensure military staff proficiency in cyber military operations, including the day-to-day operation of IT systems used in places like headquarters. Often, the term "cyber workforce" is conflated with the "IT workforce." Militaries require cyber skills in both day-to-day and mission operations that are unrelated to typical IT support, such as operational technology (OT) specialists, industrial control system specialists, cyber defenders, military planners, Judge Advocate Generals, and intelligence support.	• There should be no division between IT support of the military and staff required to conduct cyber space missions. Running military technology should be considered a mission on equal footing with other defense missions. Any other approach would leave IT staff not responsible for cyber defense. • A focus on cyber assignments delegated to non-IT staff can overweigh the importance of those who conduct attacks, who are typically a small percentage of the total cyber workforce. This may create the false impression that their services are more important than cyber defense assignments.
8.4.33 Warfare	The United Nations and National Governments shall consider cyber-enabled subversive undermining of the power, authority, or stability of a government, organization, or individual, or criminal activity.	This policy is intended to criminalize subversive undermining of the power, authority, or stability of a government or organization, using cyber misinformation, espionage, sabotage, and infiltration.	• Worldwide adoption of this policy would put an end to the Zero-Day vulnerability market, making the objective of cyberspace return to international communication as opposed to dominion over people and property. • A shift in leadership to endorse this approach would provide the moral high ground missing in today's nation-states' cavalier abuse of cyberspace in their relentless quest for power.

(Continued)

Index	Statement	Objective	Reasons for Controversy
8.4.34 Warfare	The United Nations shall consider nation-state cyber espionage and/or sabotage intrusions "threat or use of force."	This policy is intended to discourage cyber espionage and sabotage intrusions in seeming preparation for war in the absence of a declaration of war.	• The fact that spying is considered a privilege of nation-states is at the root of the cyber-espionage problem as well as the issues concerning theft of international property. UN Charters should focus on facilitating open communication and mutual respect to a level that makes spying moot, as well as support innovation to deter spying on all fronts. • The difficulty in attribution for cyber intrusions makes it very difficult to hold a nation-state accountable for cyberattacks, even when it is obvious that their own citizens participated in them.
8.4.35 Warfare	Where there is a market failure to secure and defend against attacks, nations shall document those failures and create targeted regulation to close these gaps.	This policy is intended to ensure a targeted response to cyberattacks impacting markets. Such regulations could be just for specific common carriers, like Tier-1 telecommunication companies, or for all Internet Service Providers, or indeed even for all organizations using the internet.	• Regulations are the ways societies deal with common problems that are not met by the markets. As such, these would be continuous with the traditional behavior of nations, and not new or radical. • While this policy may be advisable in the event of market failure, regulations must come with conditions, such as to be specific to identified gaps; be minimally invasive; be technology neutral; and allow the regulated organization latitude on how best to meet their obligation. Such measures could include auditable cybersecurity risk assessment detailing functional specifications for systems and networks. • As cyberspace can be considered a commons, any regulations would best be coordinated between nations (at least those that have the most cyber space infrastructure) and be in the interest of all nations. Also, of course, poorly designed or implemented regulations could restrict communication between people and be far worse than the security problems the regulations were meant to remedy.

8.5 Cyberspace Example Policy Statements

Index	Statement	Objective	Reasons for Controversy
8.5.1 Custodial	The International Telecommunications Union (ITU) shall focus efforts in cybersecurity on capacity building for nations. These shall include developing computer emergency response teams, advising on security (especially for backbone networks), training and education, assistance on national strategies, and similar efforts.	This policy is intended to raise recognition that the ITU organization is well-positioned to play a key role in setting international goals and priorities for cybersecurity.	• The ITU has a long history and tradition of being involved in global telecommunications efforts and can be a significant global force to improve cybersecurity. Not only will this help the developing world to use cyberspace to improve their economy, it will help other nations by policing new malicious actors and threats from these rapidly connecting nations.
8.5.2 Cybercrime	It shall be illegal to install and run software on machines owned by someone else without their express consent. All legitimate software execution shall be recognizable to the average computer user.	This policy is intended to prohibit running software on a machine without the knowledge of the computer user. Websites frequented by consumers frequently require software to be running on the user desktop in order for the site to display properly. These sites often will run the software on the user's machine with minimal or no notice to the user that new software is being introduced to their system.	• This type of policy would enlist the eCommerce software industry into helping the consumer manage his or her own desktop, and lay the framework for consumer awareness of the difference between legitimate and illegitimate software installs. This policy is aimed at helping the user recognize which programs they intended to install and which are malicious. • Although advertisers may claim this software is executed to enhance their ability to tailor ads to consumer preferences, organized crime uses these same mechanisms to trick users into installing malicious code. • This behavior is already prohibited by law in the Computer Fraud and Abuse Act, the fact that the Act goes unenforced is indicative of the immaturity of cybercrime enforcement mechanisms

(Continued)

Index	Statement	Objective	Reasons for Controversy
8.5.3 Cybercrime	The IETF shall establish security protocols that make it easy to spot and stop malvertising.	This policy is intended to require the internet advertising community to work together to stop malvertising, just as critical infrastructure industries such as banking or energy work together to stop cybercrime.	• Criminal advertising and coupon fraud are enabled by current advertising industry practices. This policy puts the burden of a solution to these problems on the community that enables criminals to exploit their users.
8.5.4 Impersonation	Assuming a false identity on the internet shall be prohibited.	This policy is intended to prohibit signing up for a service or on a website with a name that does not correspond to a real person. This differs from anonymous access in that there is a trail of activity associated with the false name itself while anonymous access does not have the label of a name with which to correlate the activity.	• Misrepresentation of identity is deceptive and manipulative. There is no justification for such communication. • Fear of consequence for publishing one's views is adequate justification for assuming false identity. It allows otherwise repressed individuals freedom to communicate on subjects of interest, which may be necessary for their own mental or physical health. • If this policy were enforced, individuals who are persecuted or stalked, whether their persecutors be political or personal, would have to reveal their internet identity and personal contacts in order to use the internet, so it would in effect prevent them from doing so at a time when they need it most.
8.5.5 Impersonation	Generic IDs required for software operation shall be accessible solely by the purchaser/owner of the software.	This policy is intended to prevent vendors from delivering software provisioned with predefined passwords for generic IDs.	• Delivering software with access passwords that are known to the entire community of software users is equivalent to delivering it with a known security vulnerability that allows outsiders to impersonate internal administrators. • Predefined passwords make products initially easy to use. Customers who wish to increase their cybersecurity posture have the option of changing these passwords.

8.5.6 Impersonation	International and national standards organizations shall issue standards for identity assurance ratings and these shall be required labels on eCommerce websites.	This policy is intended to publish identity assurance standards in a consumer-readable format. International and national standards organizations currently publish security standards for a wide variety of authentication technologies, but not currently in the format of consumer-readable ratings. Rather, they are implementation guides for system owners.	• This policy would establish a standard that would help eCommerce businesses determine the veracity of various security software vendor claims for utility in securely identifying users. • Like food labeling, requiring publication of the content of security technology would help educated consumers distinguish between secure and unsecure sites. The intended side effect could be a market preference for secure eCommerce. • Many websites publish security seals, which generally mean that they have purchased a given security software product or service, but there is no standard that would give such seals any independent validation of security utility. This policy would provide guidelines for interpreting website security claims. • Websites may present security claims without implementing them properly. Without an enforcement provision, this policy would be meaningless, and the effort to enforce security standards on all websites is beyond the scope of any government.
8.5.7 Impersonation	It shall be illegal in all jurisdictions for a person to use the PII of another individual to sign up for an internet service or website.	This policy is intended to prevent Impersonation of another human user. This differs from using a person's digital identity in that the real person corresponding to the information entered did not sign up for the service or website themselves at all.	• Though this policy may already be in effect when it comes to financial services such as taking out loans in someone else's name, there are other situations where malicious users will sign up using someone else's information to create a complete identity in order to anchor it to another real person, such as when criminals use children's social security numbers and create complete internet identities in order to travel internationally.

(Continued)

Index	Statement	Objective	Reasons for Controversy
			• This policy is needed to prevent people from social engineering an individual's social and political connections by signing up as them on social networking sites. These social engineering techniques are often used to gather information with which to launch cyberattacks, and so enforcement of this policy would prevent cybercrime. • Individuals often delegate internet access on purpose, as when a celebrity delegates internet presence to an agent. As long as this practice is prevalent, it may be used as justification for violating policies like these.
8.5.8 Impersonation	Use of email addresses for sending credential information or PII shall be prohibited.	This policy is intended to prevent sending sensitive information over insecure methods of communication.	• Email is often transmitted in cleartext and may pass through several relay machines prior to reaching its destination. It is typically stored unencrypted. Sending personal authentication information via email is equivalent to public exposure of PII. • The issue is not the use of email but the unsecure nature of email. Rather than adopt this policy, policies for securing email should be investigated. • Decisions concerning the risk of information theft should be left to individual or corporate discretion. • Use of an unsecure protocol for resetting passwords reduces the security of the authentication itself to the easiest way to eavesdrop on email.

8.5.9 Privacy	A suitable not-for-profit Internet Administration Entity shall provide a platform for individuals to sell prespecified data about themselves to regulated data exchanges, and no other personally identifiable data market shall be permitted.	This policy is intended to provide an effective method for users to opt out of all user-related data extraction online, as well as negotiate the amount of data they are willing to share in return for some benefit.	• A plethora of platforms profit by collecting and selling user data, and this would provide a method for users to profit by participation or fully opt out. • There are a wide variety of ways that individuals can be profiled on the internet, and none should be allowed without considering recommendations from a privacy advocacy group such as the Electronic Frontier Foundation (EFF). • Information on the internet site usage is collected by eCommerce vendors, and rightfully belongs to them. As long as individual attribution is not made using names or (email) addresses, such information is a valuable asset and owners should be allowed to sell it.
8.5.10 Privacy	All internet communication shall be attributable to an individual.	This policy is intended to require identification and authentication as a condition for internet connectivity. No anonymous access would be allowed.	• Cyberspace anonymity is critical to protect the identities of whistleblowers, crime reporting, consumer surveys, journalists doing sensitive research, and victims of harassment. • As cyberattacks may be launched from any internet location, this policy would allow immediate identification of the source of any attack. • Internet sites are currently places where groups of similar interest allow anonymous membership to promote free speech and uninhibited discussion without fear of retribution. This policy would destroy those freedoms. • Anonymous access allows personal, commercial, and political rivals to commit slander without attribution.

(Continued)

Index	Statement	Objective	Reasons for Controversy
			• There are many situations where an individual needs to access the internet only for a few minutes, such as to print out a boarding pass at a hotel or to check a reference in a library. Prohibiting anonymous access would have the unintended consequences of prohibiting all such conveniences. • This policy requires a global identification system which does not currently exist, so there would be no way to implement it.
8.5.11 Technology Platforms	Technology platforms serving more than 10% of cyberspace users shall be prevented from acquiring other technology companies.	This policy is intended to significantly lower the probability that any one technology platform becomes a monopoly.	• It has been established that the technology industry has a century-long history of purchasing small businesses with similar services in order to prevent them from becoming significant competitors. This has significantly narrowed the scope of commercial services available in cyberspace. • Cyberspace is too immature to place trust in any one or two technology platforms to determine the features available to worldwide users as most have seen little respect for user privacy. The threat of monopolies is more than economic but existential to individual and organizational self-determination.

8.5.12 Technology platforms	Technology platforms that sell user data must enter into a contract with users before data extraction and provide each user with 25% of the revenue generated from data about them.	This policy is intended to significantly lower the probability that users involuntarily give up their rights to privacy simply by visiting a technology platform.	• It has been established that the technology industry routinely harvests and sells data about users without their informed consent.
8.5.13 Workforce	All consumers shall be trained on cybersecurity measures.	This policy is intended to advocate teaching consumers how to make choices that will decrease the probability that they will be cybercrime victims. Consumers affect their own security when they choose passwords and click on links.	• Simple cyber-attacks can be thwarted by training users. For example, password-guessing attacks can be thwarted by training users on how to choose a hard password. • Organized cybercrime uses highly sophisticated techniques to which even security experts fall victim. Training consumers is a waste of money and provides them with a false sense of security. • It is unfair to expect a consumer to have to be technical enough to pass training to use the internet. This blames the victim for the crime about to occur; energy is better spent in deterrence and prosecution measures.

8.6 Public Example Policy Statements

Index	Statement	Objective	Reasons for Controversy
8.6.1 Artificial intelligence	All AI model providers must provide technical documentation, instructions for use, gain legal permission to use any copyrighted materials, and publish a summary about the content used for training the model. AI model providers who violate this policy shall compensate the legal data owners, and the ownership of the illegal AI model codebase and associated OT shall be transferred to the set of impacted data owners.	This policy is intended to follow the lead of the EU AI Act in requiring those who train AI models to obtain legal permission from data owners prior to ingesting data, even if the data was publicly available.	• Not all AI models rely on external training data. Those who do not use it may be hesitant to publish details of what processes they use to train their models. • Where AI model owners illegally ingest copyrighted and privately held information, the rightful data owners are currently left with no avenue for compensation except lengthy and expensive civil court cases. This policy would make such misuse a federal crime, thereby allowing law enforcement to impose the ownership transfer penalty based on the outcome of criminal prosecution for data theft and misuse.
8.6.2 Artificial intelligence	Artificially intelligent programs that are not deterministic shall not be used to control physical objects.	This policy is intended to prevent programs from using probabilities to direct physical activity.	• It has been established that AI algorithms that rely on probabilistic reasoning are prone to error, and a fault in physical space may have a devastating negative impact on human safety.
8.6.3 Artificial intelligence	Developers of AI models shall write, implement, comply with, and clearly and conspicuously publish on their website a risk management strategy and corresponding assessment for each model that is designed and developed.	This policy is intended to establish AI risk management strategies for the purpose of regulating associated controls in the interests of public safety and privacy, following the model of California Senate Bill 53.	• Although the California Senate Bill 53 is a major step in the right direction, leaving the risk management strategy solely in the hands of AI companies in this age of AI immaturity itself may present unacceptable risk.

8.6.4 Artificial intelligence	Government shall enact regulations that require AI organizations to classify AI models into levels that include, but are not limited to, unacceptable risk, high risk, high impact with respect to critical infrastructure support systems, systemic risk, maturity risk, and low risk. In addition, they shall establish a Cyber Security Regulatory organization to maintain and enforce corresponding cybersecurity and safety requirements to which developers and service providers of AI models shall be subject to compliance.	This policy is intended to establish AI risk levels for the purpose of regulating associated controls in the interests of public safety and privacy, following the model of the EU AI Act.	• Although the EU AI act is growing in specificity, the relative immaturity of the AI field makes it hard to fully classify all intended use cases for AI models. Even the unacceptable risk category, meant to ban ubiquitous facial recognition and manipulative AI, has exceptions for law enforcement, and law enforcement exceptions have been known to be abused by those in political power.
8.6.5 Artificial intelligence	It shall be illegal to create artificially intelligent programs that imitate the behavior of a human individual.	This policy is intended to prevent technology companies from trafficking in human likenesses.	• Laws exist that establish that people cannot be deep-faked without their consent, but unexpected or unauthorized use of deepfakes for which the creators obtain consent for a given purpose is very difficult to control, and many people regret their decisions to provide consent.
8.6.6 Artificial intelligence	Sector Risk Management Agencies (SRMAs) and Consumer regulatory agencies shall publish and enforce requirements for AI risk management aimed at preventing immature and/or reckless use of AI in critical infrastructure and technology platforms used by the general public.	This policy is intended to hold AI operators liable for the potential negative impact of operational use of AI, whether or not they developed the models.	• Not all SRMAs are currently empowered to impose requirements on the critical infrastructure industries for which they provide oversight. This policy change would authorize them to require and conduct model evaluations and impose cybersecurity controls, such as adversarial testing, and track and report cybersecurity and safety incidents stemming from AI usage.

(Continued)

Index	Statement	Objective	Reasons for Controversy
8.6.7 Custodial	Any and all cybersecurity mechanisms that are required regulatory controls shall be freely available to all industry owners and operators.	This policy is intended to disrupt private antitrust collaborations such as the Certification Authority Browser Forum (CABF) from setting self-serving rules that allow them to exclusively control cybersecurity components of technology infrastructure.	• The technology platform industry positions forums such as CABF as neutral standards-setting bodies rather than anti-competitive collaborations. • If essential cybersecurity services were run by independent experts like those at NIST or MITRE, they would be more likely to serve public rather than private interests.
8.6.8 Custodial	Internet service providers (ISPs) shall filter at their client connections to ensure that the source address of incoming traffic is within some legitimate network prefix range allocated to the corresponding customer.	This policy is intended to require that customers own the address space that they request their ISP to route.	• This policy would prevent hosting services from offering internet gateway services and thus create a barrier to entry in the ISP marketplace. • This policy would require the establishment of a trusted repository of allocated IP address space (commonly called "prefixes") that includes the owning organization and the ISP that connects that organization to the internet. • This policy would ensure that any entity that routes to the internet is accountable for identifying the origination of the traffic they actually route.
8.6.9 Custodial	ISPs shall offer connectivity services equally to all individuals for any lawful use without discrimination.	This policy is intended to require companies to offer the same services to all equally, referred to as "net neutrality."	• This policy should make it difficult, if not impossible, for internet communication to be partitioned according to any political, social, or commercial agenda. • This policy will protect eCommerce services from being cut off from customers due to their choice of ISP. • There is no evidence that ISPs intend to segregate traffic. This policy does not allow ISPs to control over the marketing of their own resources.

			• This policy has the potentially unintended consequence that ISPs will be limited in their ability to inspect network traffic, and thus be restricted from providing potentially valuable security services. • This policy is typically recommended to be enforced only at the carrier level, when in fact it is the local and peer connectivity service providers who currently have limited sets of service offerings. • The internet of today is no longer an experiment, but is a business operated by profit-seeking firms. It should be allowed to function in a manner that generates profits for those companies that operate and maintain it, while providing goods and services at a level that customers are willing to pay for. Economic supply and demand should drive internet operations, not mandatory access to all locations with no regard for cost or consumer demand. • If enforced at all, the policy would result in regulatory oversight that would present significant costs to ISPs and so create a barrier to entry for small businesses.
8.6.10 Custodial	ISPs shall offer security services to filter malware and other criminal activities.	This policy is intended to require all ISPs to make methods of detecting and preventing the transmission of malicious software available to their clients upon request. These services are often referred to as "Clean Pipe" and/or "Deep Packet Inspection."	• This requirement would give ISPs the right to inspect all content sent or received by their clients. • This requirement would slow all internet transmission as all content would be required to be inspected. It would not catch all malicious software, as zero-day threats and social engineering attacks would not be part of the filters. • This requirement may end up in filtering out unusual protocols which may be necessary to operate unusual systems such as industrial control systems, which could have devastating consequences if it interfered with the command and control features of those systems.

(Continued)

Index	Statement	Objective	Reasons for Controversy
			• This requirement could be abused by including non-malicious software or communications in the list of malicious software to be filtered. Political or commercial competitors could effectively be removed from the internet. • This requirement would save all internet customers from expensive and time-consuming malware and antivirus activities. • Liability would be unclear in terms of how much responsibility ISPs would have for missing malware or criminal behavior. • This requirement could lead to general filtering of any content deemed "unsafe" by a governing body, including political speech, music, or video downloads, photographs, and other censored content.
8.6.11 Custodial	ISPs shall require substantial proof of identification from all customers, and log all internet connectivity from each customer so it can be available for potential law enforcement measures.	This policy is intended to require ISPs to strongly identify all users, similar to a bank's requirements to Know Your Customer.	• Anonymous access to the internet facilitates cybercrime by allowing individuals to remain anonymous or hide behind false identities. • The internet has long been accepted as a place where anonymous free speech can be conducted. Requiring positive identification of all users will severely impact the ability for citizens of all countries to express themselves in a manner that has no attribution. • Any systematic identification and log requirements would undoubtedly be abused by law enforcement, especially in countries that restrict free speech and other personal liberties. Anonymous internet communications played a significant role in the Middle Eastern revolutions of 2011.

8.6.12 Custodial	The national government shall consider providing government assistance to victims of widespread cyberattacks, as it does for damage caused by natural disasters.	This policy is intended to put massive cyberattacks on the same footing as hurricanes and floods for the purposes of Federal response and remediation assistance.	• Victims of cyberattacks are no less impacted by damage than by physical damage to the same computers. This policy would allow the government to assist impacted businesses and individuals with emergency support, such as loans to restore business environments. • This policy has far-reaching and unknown economic impact on government and may be misused to pursue claims for every new malware. This should be reserved for only catastrophes and where there is a gap between existing insurance policies. Such assistance should not be for malware (even if very significant and damaging) unless the damage becomes equivalent to that from a physical natural disaster.
8.6.13 Custodial	National governments shall identify and cooperate with sectoral, regional, and local cybersecurity-related organizations in cybersecurity threat intelligence activity. Where needed, governments can support the best-of-breed groups with funding or other direct support.	This policy is intended to ensure that both threat and defense information is solicited from communities of cybersecurity expertise and freely shared among public and private institutions to expand cybersecurity expertise.	• There are many cybersecurity-related organizations, many of which are voluntary. These include a wide range of expertise found in places like FIRST (Forum of Incident Response and Security Teams), Information Systems Audit and Control Association (ISACA), ShadowServer Foundation, and System Administrators, Auditors, and Network Administrators (SANS), with common goals for internet security. Their combined expertise should be leveraged for the public good. • Without easy access to information on threats and corresponding vulnerabilities, it is impossible to adequately assess cybersecurity risk. Well-defined procedures to share threat and vulnerability information will benefit the community as a whole.

(Continued)

Index	Statement	Objective	Reasons for Controversy
8.6.14 Custodial	National governments shall publish unclassified, regular periodic threat assessments to national cybersecurity.	This policy is intended to require national agencies to combine the findings of their investigations of threat actor activity periodically into a consolidated report at an appropriate classification level. It should especially cover threats to the critical infrastructure sectors, ISPs and telecommunication networks, and industrial control systems, including satellites.	• Planning and protection require information. Such a report will be invaluable to establish a baseline of threats to help companies convince their management of the threat and secure resources appropriate to the threat. • If poorly written, without a commitment to protect the private sector, much information in such a report would be either too high-level ("Watch out for Chinese hackers") or too low ("patch your system with the x, y, and z patches"). • Many worthwhile groups might (or already have) foundered for lack of short-term funding or other government cooperation. There are not enough organizations at the local level to provide cybersecurity expertise to those who need it. This policy will provide expert assistance to local efforts to secure information assets and fight cybercrime.
8.6.15 Custodial	The National Institute of Standards and Technology shall set regulatory standards for critical infrastructure system cybersecurity that include all system components, cyber and physical.	This policy is intended to support the Social Security Administrations (SSAs) and regulators in all aspects of critical infrastructure so they can apply best practices rather than have them all devise their own.	• The National Institute of Standards and Technology (NIST) either has or can easily recruit the expertise to maintain standards on the reliability and interoperability of any type of cyber-enabled devices and should be exploited to address cybersecurity-sensor interoperability issues, especially in the non-technology-related critical infrastructure, where domain expertise may be lacking (e.g., healthcare).

8.6.16 Custodial	The National Vulnerability Database (NVD) shall host a process wherein cybersecurity threat and vulnerability information shall be systematically collected and shared in a manner that maximizes privacy and minimizes liability.	This policy is intended to require that vulnerabilities be reported despite obvious disincentives for companies to share information on poor cybersecurity. This policy is meant to remove those impediments to information sharing.	• This policy will provide an easy way for companies to avoid blame for negligence in software product development as well as in information handling procedures. It will discourage liability avoidance using secure practice, as companies will instead participate fully in information disclosure only after security vulnerabilities have been exploited. Existing national vulnerability reporting sites adequately cover current information-sharing requirements. • As soon as vulnerability information is shared, the malicious community devises exploits for them that further erode victims' security. Vulnerability information should be kept confidential.
8.6.17 Cybercrime	eCommerce advertising that includes redirection of individual computers to sites via links that they did not intentionally follow shall be illegal.	This policy is intended to prohibit redirection to unintentional sites due to malvertising. Organized cyber criminals often purchase online advertising in order to direct user traffic to sites that infect their computers with malware.	• This policy would significantly reduce the ease with which malicious attackers can reach unsuspecting individuals.
8.6.18 Cybercrime	Media stories on cybercrime shall be based on authoritative sources, and any requests to the public to contribute evidence shall be channeled through law enforcement skilled in assessing its relevance before being announced to the media.	This policy is intended to deter the media from using "low news cycle" days to hype cybercrimes that are not verified to come from an accountable source.	• This policy could be interpreted as a requirement to divulge the sources of reports of cybercrime, though it is not a stated intention, it would be required for enforcement.

(Continued)

Index	Statement	Objective	Reasons for Controversy
8.6.19 Cybercrime	Public institutions collecting crime data that includes cybercrime shall use the Phillips Taxonomy as a classification system so law enforcement and others investigating similar cases have the maximum amount of precision in matches for a minimal amount of search.	This policy is intended to make it easier to quickly identify and analyze historical cybercrimes similar to one in progress, so law enforcement and prosecutors may benefit from the experience of other investigations of similar incidents.	• Existing databases of historical crime available to law enforcement do not have the granularity to easily pinpoint commonalities in cyberattacks. Although a cyber-specific database was recommended by the Solarium report, because the Phillips taxonomy is already a training tool for law enforcement, adding these fields to existing databases would provide the quickest way of closing the gap.
8.6.20 Cybersecurity principles	Government shall create a security metrics, or "dashboard," reporting system whose scope is the systems and networks operated by the government.	This policy is intended to require that systems and networks supported by the standards-setting arm of the government be monitored and measured according to established standards.	• An alarming number of government agencies routinely fail cybersecurity audits. Such a dashboard would make it very obvious to the leadership of these agencies that they are personally responsible for maintaining an effective cybersecurity program. • This activity is already supported by the standards-setting arm of the government (in the US, the Department of Commerce, which includes NIST), and government systems are already uniformly subject to security management requirements (e.g., Federal Information Security Modernization Act [FISMA]), which require management monitoring, and a "dashboard" policy is redundant. • This policy would require first an inventory of systems supporting the government as a whole, and so would create transparency for its dependency on system security.

8.6.21 Cybersecurity principles	Identity management and authentication for individuals who operate government and/or critical infrastructure systems shall be centrally controlled.	This policy is intended to require a system that includes a database of individuals who have access to critical infrastructure, a method to authenticate those people, and a way to provide them with access to government and/or critical infrastructure systems for which they are authorized.	• A central function that tracks individual access to critical infrastructure would allow functions such as personnel background checks and strong access control to increase in standardization, as well as take advantage of economies of scale. • Any large-scale government project designed to provide access to private infrastructure deprives the private property owner of the ability to manage their own assets. Such actions are evidence of totalitarian regimes, not peaceful efforts to solve community security problems. • The level of control provided by such a centralized authentication system would potentially itself introduce a large threat, as it may be exploited to gain widespread administrative access to critical infrastructure. • This policy is reasonable only for IT systems. A typical ICS or mobile framework does not have a central point at which users are identified, nor a system-wide list of functions a user should have access to. It tends to rely on IDs delivered with machines and so does not typically integrate with enterprise identity management systems.
8.6.22 Cybersecurity principles	Political leadership shall develop and declare a national cyber strategy for offense and defense, supporting policies, and coordinate these with allies and other key stakeholders.	This policy is intended to require a national security strategy for cyberspace that will highlight key decisions and how they support agreed-upon goals. Issues to be addressed would be the balance between offense and defense, the role of key organizations, coordination of operations, and interaction with civilian authorities and the private sector.	• Strategies are effective ways for top leadership to give transparency to their intent and provide guidance to their bureaucracy. • National strategies for cyberspace can often be overclassified–causing unneeded concern from outsiders—and overmilitarize cyber conflict, seeing it as a problem that militaries are best equipped to solve.

(Continued)

Index	Statement	Objective	Reasons for Controversy
8.6.23 Financial services	Financial institutions designated as systemically important shall report cybersecurity incidents with potential systemic contagion effects to financial stability authorities within timeframes sufficient to permit coordinated response before contagion propagates through payment networks.	This policy is intended to ensure that institutions whose failures could threaten financial stability report to macroprudential supervisors within windows permitting pre-emptive coordination.	• Existing incident reporting frameworks, including those established by CIRCIA and Securities and Exchange Commission (SEC) cybersecurity disclosure rules, address reporting to cybersecurity authorities and investors but do not specifically require reporting to financial stability authorities such as the Financial Stability Oversight Council at speeds calibrated to contagion propagation timelines. • Defining which incidents carry systemic contagion potential requires real-time judgment under conditions of uncertainty, and overly broad definitions may generate notification floods that obscure genuinely systemic events.
8.6.24 Healthcare	Healthcare regulators shall establish requirements for wireless devices implanted in patients to have strong authentication prior to the operation of command and control features.	This policy is intended to prevent systematic abuses or perhaps even a criminal marketplace in exploiting implant vulnerabilities to murder or extort potential victims.	• While there is no known threat to patient health due to wireless cybersecurity attacks, research into the security of these devices introduces an unnecessary cost. • There is a wide variety of medical devices with electronic circuits that accept commands that change electronic signals and medicine doses. There are no current security standards with which they are controlled. • As these devices allow remote command and control capabilities, any malicious individual who understands how they work may commit murder without any trace of evidence (and may have already).

8.6.25 Impersonation	Possession and/or use of credentials that correspond to another person's digital identity shall be subject to criminal and civil penalties.	This policy is intended to prevent a form of impersonation, called account hijacking, which differs from false identity in that the credentials used correspond to a real individual, but not the one who signed up for the service that issued the credentials.	• This policy would prohibit markets in internet logins and provide law enforcement with means for prosecution before such logins were used to commit crimes like identity theft. • Credentials are often shared on purpose for economic reasons, as when people share access to download sites they use infrequently so that each can download their share allocated to one account. This policy would have the unintended consequence of making each user purchase their own account to such eCommerce sites. Though it would benefit vendors, it would limit the rights of consumers. • Credentials are often shared on purpose, as when an executive delegates tasks to an executive assistant. Unless and until technology evolves to allow this use case, such policies will generally be ignored for the sake of convenience.
8.6.26 Industrial control	Cybersecurity literature whose scope includes cyber-physical systems shall observe IT, OT, and ICS distinctions and consider in scope the impact of cyber on all components of ICS systems, whether or not they themselves have cyber capabilities.	This policy is intended to address the threat of undetected physical and cyber sabotage to ICS via modifications and interruptions of vulnerable physical components that are not within the scope of OT, such as signal transmissions and sensor configurations.	• Although the National Critical Infrastructure Protect Plan has always included cybersecurity within its scope of requirements, the application of technology capabilities to protect and detect malicious or unintentional physical process disruption represents a failure of that approach disguised as a vocabulary issue. This policy addresses that issue by specifically calling out ICS components that currently are not addressed by OT controls to be in the scope of a broader cybersecurity review focused on safety and reliability.

(Continued)

Index	Statement	Objective	Reasons for Controversy
8.6.27 Industrial control	ICS regulators shall ensure that cybersecurity incidents in ICSs are shared in a systematic and reliable fashion that includes enough information for similar ICS owner/operators to secure their systems against similar cyberattacks.	This policy is intended to establish training to identify control system incidents as being cyber-related. The control system cyber incidents should then be analyzed to determine scope and impact, and as input to develop appropriate control system cyber security mitigation systems.	• The fact that the Purdue Model prescribes no cybersecurity control features for its "level 0" foundation of sensors, actuators, drives, and robots, highlights an urgent need for training engineers and network security personnel to learn how to recognize whether a control system incident is cyber-related.
8.6.28 Industrial control	International treaties shall be established to ensure that connections between critical infrastructures shall meet engineered to withstand cybersecurity attacks.	This policy is intended to give the government jurisdiction to protect the critical infrastructures from cyberattacks.	• Policy does not need to establish a national border in cyberspace in order to give government jurisdiction to protect critical infrastructures. A more reasonable policy would be for critical infrastructures to be declared a national asset and set appropriate international cybersecurity standards for shared critical infrastructures. • This policy would give the government jurisdiction to monitor and block access to internet connectivity points connecting critical infrastructures.
8.6.29 Industrial control	Nations shall mandate the strength of encryption used for identification, authentication, and monitoring ICS data commensurate with the potential impact of misuse of ICS in the critical infrastructure sectors for data storage.	This policy is intended to establish a requirement for cybersecurity data control requirements for the ICS to be extended to those in possession of ICS data (this is for data at rest).	• As in all industries, companies operating critical infrastructure often share data with government, industry participants, service providers, and contractors. • This policy will match the high criticality of information in these sectors with concomitant protection. This information should not rely on the insecure data storage and communications protocols on the internet.

8.6.30 Industrial control	Publication of current cybersecurity threats and corresponding statutory and legal frameworks that address cybersecurity for critical ICSs shall be reported by the corresponding regulator annually, and drafts of the document shall be shared with industry control system cybersecurity and safety experts for public comment.	This policy is intended to fill a knowledge gap wherein national agencies promulgating regulations and other publicly funded organizations that perform cybersecurity threat intelligence are generally not intimately familiar with ICS cybersecurity issues. The outcome should be the publication of cybersecurity and information security standards that include control system issues vetted by control system experts and combine their findings annually into a consolidated report that includes laws related to ICS cybersecurity and safety, as well as create a community of expert reviewers in the spirit of NIST, which solicits public comment prior to the publication.	• The findings, conclusions, and recommendations resulting from such a review will be invaluable to inform future legislation. • Though examination of existing legislation in comparison with a changing environment is a good idea, the way this policy is worded, there is no strategic objective. Such an open-ended review may result in a waste of taxpayer dollars. • Annual publication of such a report is meaningless; this should not be a report process, but an expectation for government security services that the comparison should be constantly updated and available in order to ensure that controls continuously improve in the face of changing threats.
8.6.31 Privacy	Consumer protection agencies shall prohibit unsolicited personalization.	This policy is intended to require that personalization be treated as personally identifiable data, which currently focuses mostly on financial data.	• Where website visitors do not pay for the service, they are not customers of the website and so are not considered website consumers. • Setting priorities for consumer protection agencies with respect to privacy regarding personalization would require greater transparency, user-settable controls, enhanced security, limit data retention, and methods for user consent and/or disclosure.

(Continued)

Index	Statement	Objective	Reasons for Controversy
8.6.32 Privacy	Government shall enact law that requires NIST to create a new set of individual identifiers and associated, strictly enforced data sharing limitations and technical privacy control standards. These identifiers shall replace the existing social security numbers and email addresses, and it shall be illegal to have this set of identifiers in a database for any purpose other than one clearly identified in the standard. The standard shall also specify a secure method of collecting information on individuals at the data field level, and associated data privacy controls that shall be implemented by any person or organization maintaining those data fields. Organizations wishing to store and use these data fields must provide proof of express consent and allow individuals to withdraw that consent at any time, and the withdrawal request process must automatically purge that user's data.	This policy is intended to establish privacy standards at the federal level that are enforceable by federal law, and in addition render existing personally identifiable data fields that are known to have been widely compromised, such as Social Security Numbers, to be replaced with identifiers that have legally binding privacy standards. It is also intended to provide internet identifiers and associated anonymity features such as centralized email aliases, to protect individuals from being targeted based on technology platform surveillance data sharing.	• It is currently possible to purchase the social security number and associated contact and family information of almost any individual on the black market and the only way to protect citizens from the existing degree of rampant fraud and identify theft is to build cybersecurity into a new end-to-end acceptable use model of a national identifier going forward. • This policy will allow different personal identifiers to be established for different purposes and create a set and/or hierarchy of identifiers that allow, for example, a person to have one identifier for social media, another for eCommerce, and another for tax purposes. This type of identifier segregation and associated acceptable use law will limit the capability of technology platforms to exercise surveillance pricing and other personally invasive person tracking systems.

8.6.33 Privacy	The government shall pass a national data security and privacy protection law establishing and standardizing requirements for the collection, retention, and sharing of user data, including affording users the right to be forgotten.	This policy is intended to do for the United States what the GDPR did for EU citizens: hold technology service providers liable for safeguarding data that may be used to identify, stalk, or steal from a person.	• As observed in the Solarium report, the loss or exposure of personally sensitive information is becoming more common and more severe, and each instance provides malign actors with additional opportunities for exploitation, espionage, or attack. Moreover, other countries are using such laws to protect their citizens, making it more likely that technology services providers that openly sell or share users' personal data will focus on US citizens because there is no law against it.
8.6.34 Privacy	International not-for-profit organizations focused on human rights issues shall help nations to harmonize information classification efforts to better tackle differences in privacy laws between nations.	This policy is intended to support consistency of privacy law definitions globally.	• Global standards might allow improved understanding of privacy requirements, improve privacy for citizens, and allow economies of scale in information handling procedures for multinational organizations. • Such harmonization may be impossible as the differences regarding the economic impact on their eCommerce businesses may make even harmonization among allies unbridgeable without significant effort. A single, global privacy standard is likely both impossible and unwanted, however, international organizations might be able to help agree on basic principles or classifications that can smooth harmonization.

(Continued)

Index	Statement	Objective	Reasons for Controversy
8.6.35 Privacy	It shall be illegal to change prices based on user profiling, including but not limited to historical user profiles and automated detection of user attributes, including behavior.	This policy is intended to significantly lower the probability that the same product would be offered on the same technology platform at different prices based on an Automated Decision Making (ADM) expectation that a user should be treated unfairly.	• Tech platforms have automated pricing strategies using surplus user behavioral data to determine the price a user is shown for any given transaction, though the same person can use a different browser that has stored different attributes and see a higher or lower price for the exact same product on the exact same platform. Because a user cannot control the personal data collection, surveillance pricing is a privacy violation. • Surveillance pricing has been frequently challenged by the FTC (Federal Trade Commission) as an unfair trade practice enabled by the inappropriate use of user data.
8.6.36 Privacy	Nations shall include significant privacy protections in all of their cyber initiatives.	This policy is intended to require initiatives focused on identifying and tracking activity to adhere to privacy policies.	• Well-designed security initiatives can enhance privacy as well, as hackers and other malicious actors are no longer able to gain access to private information. • Privacy is a more pressing concern for some people than security, depending on the situation. Occasionally, there will be tradeoffs between security and privacy, and societies will have to make the best possible tradeoffs between these two laudable goals on a case-by-case basis.
8.6.37 Research and development	The government shall establish a Bureau of Cyber Statistics charged with collecting and providing statistical data on cybersecurity and the cyber ecosystem to inform policymaking and government programs.	This policy is intended to ensure that governments have access to, and provide, structured information about cybersecurity incidents and have trained statisticians, in a politically independent agency, to analyze the data, as they do with other important issues.	• The current lack of specificity with respect to Cybersecurity in crime incident reporting hampers the efforts of law enforcement and insurance agencies to observe and predict trends.

8.6.38 Research and development	NIST shall annually analyze and classify all cybersecurity tools with significant market share, and assess and report on use cases and a method of measuring effectiveness for each category.	This policy is intended to provide much-needed guidance for individuals and companies facing a very confusing array of choices in cybersecurity technology, some of which are completely ineffective and others that actually lower the state of cybersecurity within an organization.	• Currently, cybersecurity tools and techniques have no effectiveness criteria, and vendors routinely create products that boast security claims that are totally unfounded. • Such an assessment could easily result in a subjective exercise as opposed to an informative report. At worst, it could be a witch hunt targeted at the subjective evaluation of waste.
8.6.39 Risk management	Government shall codify responsibilities and ensure sufficient resources for the Cybersecurity and Infrastructure Security Agency (CISA) and sector risk management agencies (SRMAs) in the identification, assessment, and management of national and sector-specific risk.	This policy is intended to produce a RACI matrix to make clear who is responsible, accountable, informed, and consulted in public-private collaboration to protect critical infrastructure from cybersecurity threats.	• The purpose in pairing critical infrastructure operators with government partners (the SRMAs) was that they would work together to reduce cybersecurity risk, but these efforts have made little progress in the two decades since the relationship was established.
8.6.40 Risk management	The government shall create the House Permanent Select and Senate Select Committees on Cybersecurity to consolidate budgetary and legislative jurisdiction over cybersecurity issues, as well as traditional oversight authority.	This policy is intended to focus congress on a strategic approach to holistic cybersecurity legislation with a permanent committee and expert staff, as recommended by the Solarium Commission.	• Currently, cybersecurity issues are addressed by Congress one issue at a time, and no single Congressperson has developed enough expertise to holistically approach the dangers of cyberspace. As described in the Solarium report, there should be permanent congressional committees dedicated to cybersecurity risk issues.

(Continued)

Index	Statement	Objective	Reasons for Controversy
8.6.41 Risk management	Government shall strengthen the Cybersecurity and Infrastructure Security Agency (CISA) in its mission to ensure national resilience of critical infrastructure, to promote a more secure cyber ecosystem, and to serve as the central civilian cybersecurity authority to support federal, state, local, and private-sector cybersecurity efforts.	This policy is intended to restore the CISA organization from a passive reporting agency to an effective cyberspace risk management agency with capabilities in alignment with the recommendations of the Solarium report.	• CISA's mission is to protect critical infrastructure from cybersecurity threats, but it has not been adequately resourced or empowered to do so. The agency's convening power is not widely understood or consistently recognized. In addition, the agency lacks the analytic capacity and resources to lead efforts to mitigate national systemic cybersecurity risk. • CISA's capability has been sharply curtailed due to recent funding cuts, and critical national security initiatives have been negatively impacted (e.g., Elections Infrastructure Information Sharing and Analysis Center [EI-ISAC] and Multi-State Information Sharing and Analysis Center [MS-ISAC]).
8.6.42 Supply chain	National governments shall ensure that sensitive information held by vendors is given the same protection it would be given by the government agency contracting with that vendor.	This policy is intended to set a common standard for commercial organizations that cannot pass along responsibility for regulatory compliance simply because technology services are outsourced.	• This policy would hold government agencies responsible for safeguarding information, regardless of whether it has been handed to vendors or not. • Governments must ensure that service providers they enlist protect information at government-established standards. This could include PII (such as names or personal identification numbers, e.g., US Social Security Numbers) or intellectual property on government programs or projects (such as weapons development or acquisition). This policy would require not only sufficient protection of this information but also notification to the government if there were a security breach in the environment containing this information.

8.6.43 Technology platforms	A regulatory agency shall be charged with setting rules on valid versus biased search results and rating Internet Search Providers on their performance in meeting accuracy targets.	This policy is intended to provide users with accurate search results.	• Current search engines sell search terms entered by the user as "words" and display links provided by the buyer. This renders search results inaccurate for most users. • Search terms, or "words" sold by search engines, often are sold to companies that are competitive and contain names, intellectual property, or trademarks of competitors, with the result that users searching for specific companies are intentionally diverted from their objective. • Political campaigns often buy search terms.
8.6.44 Technology platforms	The government shall pass a law establishing that final goods assemblers of software, hardware, and firmware are liable for damages from incidents that exploit known and unpatched vulnerabilities.	This policy is intended to provide recourse for users of software where a vulnerability is found. Currently, they have to mitigate their inherited vulnerability, creating costs that should be unnecessary, or take the vulnerable system offline, creating the potential for business interruption.	• The Solarium report observes there has not been a clearly defined duty of care for technology vendors to take responsibility for developing and issuing patches for known vulnerabilities in their products and services, the timeliness of those patches, and maintaining a vulnerability disclosure policy. This is still the case today.
8.6.45 Technology platforms	It shall be illegal for Technology Platforms to use data from other technology platforms in their own business interests without legally contracting for a business relationship.	This policy is intended to prevent large technology platforms from cannibalizing small business catalogs without their permission, as Amazon Web Services (AWS) did to thousands of artisan sites in December 2025.	• Large technology platforms are continually pushing the boundaries of antitrust by cannibalizing or minimizing the contributions of their competitors. • Thousands of site owners, many of whom purposely avoided presenting their products for sale on impersonal sites like Amazon, received unexpected and often incorrect orders because Amazon copied their catalogs and made assumptions about their sales process that were unfounded.

(Continued)

Index	Statement	Objective	Reasons for Controversy
8.6.46 Workforce	Accreditation, training, and certification programs shall be established for all personnel working in cyber-physical systems.	This policy is intended to fill a gap as there is currently no standard curriculum for cyber-physical security and few certifications or interdisciplinary academic programs for cybersecurity of cyber-physical systems.	• There is a large body of knowledge in cybersecurity, and requirements for accreditation would ensure that working professionals are accountable for applying it. However, the same cannot be said for cyber-physical systems. • As there is no agreed-upon standard cyber-physical system security curriculum, widespread adoption of a specific training program and guaranteed subsequent hiring programs may have the unexpected consequence of reducing the variety of cybersecurity expertise within government agencies. These concerns are even more exacerbated for industrial control systems.
8.6.47 Workforce	Government shall charge NIST with creating a software engineering professional license program wherein those calling themselves software engineers would have to complete a curriculum, pass tests, and service apprenticeships to demonstrate that they are qualified to produce safe and secure software.	This policy is intended to increase the level of professionalism software engineers have with respect to safety and security to a level similar to civil and mechanical engineers, electricians, and other professions, wherein inattention to confidentiality, integrity, and availability can directly lead to losses of life and property.	• While this professional license would provide some assurance that there is a body of knowledge that software developers can use to produce safe software, the ease with which software developers can produce code would make it very difficult to enforce en mass. Though it would still make distinguishing resume material and, like other engineering professions, at least allow employers a method of verifying the license is active.

8.6.48 Workforce	Government shall charge NIST, in concert with Office of Management and Budget (OMB) and DHS, with creating a technology infrastructure professional license program required to operate SaaS, PaaS and IaaS infrastructure.	This policy is intended to hold the accountability technology platform operators have with respect to safety and security to a level similar to civil and mechanical engineers, electricians, and other professions wherein inattention to confidentiality, integrity, and availability can directly lead to losses of life and property.	• Though control systems cyberattacks generally have high severity impact than information technology cybersecurity incidents, critical physical system components such as sensors rarely have built-in control system authentication capabilities.
8.6.49 Workforce	National governments shall ensure all staff (not just those involved in IT or cybersecurity) are trained on the cybersecurity knowledge and skills required to comply with classified and unclassified data handling requirements and approved information sharing protocols.	This policy is intended to require every government job function to have cybersecurity responsibilities defined in a manner that is not repudiable.	• All government employees handle sensitive information and so all play a role in protecting it. This policy would make the level of compliance with existing national security policy visible to policy-makers, and so inform future legislation.
8.6.50 Workforce	National governments shall make university scholarships available to students wishing to pursue studies in cybersecurity, in return for a period of government service.	This policy is intended to motivate students to study cybersecurity at the college level. Undergraduate college curriculums typically do not include cybersecurity specialization.	• There are not enough knowledgeable cybersecurity professionals in the nation to fill the jobs expected to be required to safeguard national interests. A national scholarship program would provide a pipeline of qualified professionals. • Graduates of undergraduate programs will not have much cybersecurity expertise. Cybersecurity focus usually starts at the Masters level because the amount of foundational knowledge required to practice cybersecurity in any given domain requires undergraduate concentration in the domain itself.

(Continued)

Index	Statement	Objective	Reasons for Controversy
			• This policy would motivate the creation of cybersecurity curriculum and also motivate students to pursue cybersecurity work in government. It may also encourage universities to develop programs where none currently exist, such as cybersecurity of industrial control systems.
8.6.51 Workforce	National governments shall pass laws to ensure companies do not use customer data in ways other than those required to execute the transactions or provide services, unless the customer has opted-in to such sharing.	This policy is intended to prohibit companies to sell data about their customer base to marketing companies and/or to tailor the user experience based on collected or purchased data on personal attributes, unless specifically agreed to be the customer.	• This policy would not only enforce privacy but also help prevent the spread of data to additional entities where it may be compromised by attackers. Since the customer never did business with the compromised entity, their information should not be exposed to such risk. • Sharing information provides benefits to many customers as it allow specially targeted offers in the customer's interest and customized navigation.
8.6.52 Workforce	National governments shall review existing laws to determine how they apply to cybersecurity and determine if there are any gaps and if any need to be updated (such as to be more technology-neutral).	This policy is intended to require laws related to cybersecurity to be reviewed at the national level. Some laws may need to be updated; others may be found to offer novel solutions to problems of cybersecurity.	• This policy would allow security rules to protect privacy to be set by social scientists rather than technologists. • A good example of a law that should be critically examined in a cybersecurity context is the U.S. Defense Production Act and Telecommunications Act of 1934. The findings, conclusions, and recommendations resulting from such a review should inform legislative staff to introduce new laws or amend old ones. Often, reviews of old laws have led to conflicts between privacy advocates and security practitioners.

8.6.53 Workforce	The US government shall promote digital literacy, civics education, and public awareness to build societal resilience to foreign malign cyber-enabled information operations.	This policy is intended to directly combat cyber-enabled disinformation warfare operations conducted by hostile nation-states seeking to persuade US citizens that their country is doomed and their only option is to give up on democracy.	• As recommended in the Solarium report, by promoting modern civics education and digital literacy programs, the US government can assist in enhancing the average American's ability to discern the trustworthiness of online content, and thereby reduce the impact of malicious foreign cyber-enabled information campaigns, without running afoul of concerns about regulating speech.
8.6.54 Workforce	There shall be national criteria for evaluating cybersecurity academic, accreditation, and training programs, all cybersecurity training used by government and critical infrastructure shall be verified to meet those criteria, and a list of all those meeting those criteria shall be published.	This policy is intended to create a guide for the average citizen or organization to easily find a credible cybersecurity training firm.	• It is very hard to know which vendors are capable of meeting claims that they provide adequate cybersecurity training. This policy would provide much needed guidance to government agencies and critical infrastructure operators who are individually evaluating training programs. • Currently, all organizations fend for themselves in evaluating cybersecurity training. The multiple simultaneous evaluations of the same training programs are not cost-effective, especially for industrial control systems because there are no effective industry standards. • Publication of an "authorized" list of cybersecurity training programs would be a disincentive for entrepreneurs poised to enter the cybersecurity training market, and eventually lower both the availability and the quality of available training options.

References

Rittel, H. W. J. and Webber, M. M. (1973). Dilemmas in a general theory of planning. *Policy Sciences*, 4(2): 155–169.

State (2010). ITAR & Export Controls. https://www.pmddtc.state.gov/ddtc_public?id=ddtc_public_portal_itar_landing, US Department of State. (accessed 25 July 2026).

Wolff, J. (2018). *You'll See This Message When It Is Too Late: The Legal and Economic Aftermath of Cybersecurity Breaches*. Cambridge, MA: The MIT Press.

9

Conclusion

Technology is always advancing, constantly changing, and testing the bounds of what is *possible*. The law moves much more slowly, defining within that vast universe of the possible and arriving during rare moments of consensus on what is *permissible*. Those of us dealing with cybersecurity policy must work within those constraints to determine what is actually *preferable*.

Different people and organizations will have different ideas about what is actually preferable. To inform those choices, each chapter in this book introduced a different perspective on cybersecurity policy. Chapter 1 provided basic definitions and ways to think about policy, such as the five domains of Users, Organizations, Dependencies, Adversaries, and Cyberspace and their relationship to Public Policy. Chapter 2 showed the development of technology and policy over time. Chapter 3 reflected on the governance, metrics, risk management, and other key topics related to managing cybersecurity risk. Chapter 4 examined a range of topics on cybersecurity communication strategies. Chapter 5 provided sound guidance for policymakers facing a wide range of cybersecurity risk issues. Chapter 6 explored the state of the practice in cybersecurity education, certification, and related workforce issues. Chapter 7 detailed how the US government has tackled cybersecurity policies over the past three decades. Chapter 8 shared a plethora of cybersecurity issues and related policy statements that have been swimming around the five domains for years, though many of the most critical issues to address have not made it to the policy level for remediation.

The chapters were purposely fitted with building blocks that allowed later chapters to leverage concepts and examples introduced earlier in our dialog, culminating in the catalog of cybersecurity issues that would otherwise have been incomprehensible to newcomers in the field. These layers offer different perspectives on the same basic ground truth: the evolving complexity of security issues presented by an ever-expanding and developing cyberspace. Combined, the chapters illustrate the complexity of cybersecurity policy and the corresponding difficulties faced by policymakers. Even longtime cybersecurity risk experts and organizations with strong governance and mature cybersecurity policies are hesitant to push cybersecurity mandates and are constantly checking to manage the risk of unintended consequences. Moreover, we have no doubt that as cyberspace and cybersecurity continue to change, so will any taxonomy of policy issues, making future decisions that much more difficult.

The authors have accordingly summarized enough background information to ensure that the reader is prepared to face, understand, and reason analytically about any cybersecurity policy issue, whether legacy or new. To that end, it has been necessary to encourage a thorough understanding of the past in order for our readers not to repeat it. Nevertheless, the pace of change in cyberspace is accelerating so much that those immersed in cybersecurity policy issues may find omissions in the range of possibilities for topics that might potentially have been included. Certainly, there have been a substantial amount of updates needed since the first edition came out over a decade ago. To those whose favorite issue has been unintentionally omitted, we leave it for you to publicize and just hope that this book will bring more informed participants to your cybersecurity policy debates. And please contact us so we can include it in the next edition of this guidebook!

We hope that at least one message is clear: that there is no blueprint available to produce cybersecurity, no standards that provide a magic bullet, and no course of action that is clear of potential obstruction. One message from the history covered in this book is that cybersecurity concerns are usually not a priority for technologists and entrepreneurs, nor are they likely to be in the future. Indeed, if we could push for one single policy, it would be to change that dynamic, which would cascade cybersecurity to all of us, everywhere. Rather, every stakeholder, whether an individual internet user, an organization, a service provider, or a government, should be aware of its own policies and maintain its own security, in line with its own risk appetite and strategy. Unless and until cyberspace itself achieves some level of consistent behavior, every person and organization must unfortunately, seek their own best interests.

As science fiction has often depicted the situation of space colonists stranded in a remote corner of the universe, what governance exists in cyberspace is remote and has little power without the consent of the governed. Like the Wild West upon which many science fiction stories were based, lawlessness and vigilantism operate in parallel while helpless victims and bystanders frequently succumb to attacks. Even the most enlightened and benevolent nation-states have their hands full trying to address the myriad of cybersecurity policy issues and at the same time keeping a lid on cyber conflict.

Unfortunately, cyberattacks are this century's *assassin's mace*, a legendary club-like weapon that can be hidden up a sleeve and, with skill, could be used to break an adversary's sword in combat (Hambling 2009). The analogy is that, like the mace compared to the sword, cyberwarfare is cheaper than physical warfare and can be used to defeat a more powerful adversary, depending on the skill of its operator. Moreover, successful cyber espionage and sabotage often allow cyberwarfare to remain either undetected or deniable. This strange new world requires new paradigms in cybersecurity policy beyond the governance structures that exist today.

Cybersecurity policy development is not an easy task, nor is it confined to the boundaries of technology, law, and policy. This new digital age requires innovative, blended thinking that crosses such boundaries, and just as urgently as it was in the dawn of the industrial revolution. We hope that this reference will contribute to the cybersecurity novice's ability to properly interpret cybersecurity directives and to assist today's cybersecurity policymakers in creating effective and lasting policy. We also hope that, armed with this foundation to rally others, the cybersecurity expert readers of this book will launch efforts to improve human experience within the ever-altering cyber landscape of the future.

Reference

Hambling, D. (2009). China looks to undermine U.S. power, with 'Assassin's Mace'. Wired. 2 July. https://www.wired.com/2009/07/china-looks-to-undermine-us-power-with-assassins-mace/ (accessed 12 March 2026).

Glossary

Access control lists list of permissions with respect to files and programs allocated to computer users, e.g., read, write, execute; may be listed for individual users or groups of users, where groups are designated by membership lists or attributes of a user record designated as a role

Account hijacking using persistent or preauthenticated session access credentials for an online account that belongs to someone else to execute transactions without their knowledge

Account takeover using credentials for an online account that belong to someone else to impersonate them online; may include changing authentication methods like passwords to prevent access by the real account owner

Advanced persistent threat an adversary who is continually actively engaged in reconnaissance on a specific victim, collecting information for purposes of cyber espionage and/or destructive cyber attack

Agentic AI An AI model outfitted with a harness engineered to leverage AI models autonomously take iterative steps toward a stated goal

Algorithmic bias occurs when systematic errors in machine learning algorithms produce unfair or discriminatory outcomes. The bias can reflect or reinforce existing socioeconomic, racial, and gender biases

Anthropomorphism the interpretation of nonhuman things or events in terms of human characteristics, as when one senses malice in a computer or hears human voices in the wind

Anti-malware software designed to detect and minimize the damaging impact of malicious software

Anti-virus software designed to detect and minimize the damaging impact of malicious, self-replicating, and/or polymorphic software

Attack Surface generally, the boundary of a system and its external environment; specifically the set of system interfaces that allow interaction with its external environment

Authentication confirming identity, the process to ensure that people or things are who they say they are

Availability the timely delivery of functional capability

Badness-ometer a scale on which every reading indicates security is bad

Bandwidth a measure of the amount of data that can simultaneously traverse through a telecommunications line

Binary a numbering system that uses only 1s and 0s

Bit an electronic representation of a 1 or a 0, typically combined with other bits to represent information in binary message formats

Bluetooth a network protocol for close-range wireless communication

Bogon short for bogus networks, this term refers to a packet on the internet that identifies its source as unallocated address space

Border Gateway Protocol a network communications protocol used to send data between internet sites

Bot short for robot, it refers to software

Botnet multiple bots answering to the same command and control operator

Bug a coding error in software

Business logic in the context of security, rules for handling information that are programmed in software

Byte a set of 8 bits typically used to represent a single character in a binary numbering system

Carrier a telecommunications company that transports data between physical locations, may be satellite, cellular, and/or land-based

Certificates cryptographic keys, which may be verified to be associated with organizations or individuals

Chief Information Security Officer a title associated with the highest-ranking individual whose sole function within an organization is to manage an organization-wide security program

CIA triad confidentiality, integrity, and availability

Click fraud the act of charging an internet site for a user selecting a link to it, when no real person clicked on the link, often accomplished with automated software

Collection a cyberattack stage wherein the attacker gathers data of interest to their goal

Command and control a cyberattack stage wherein the attacker remotely communicates with compromised systems to execute processes

Computer Emergency Response Team an organization whose mission is to receive reports of cyber incidents and gather a team qualified and motivated to resolve them

Confidence contagion mechanism by which a cyber incident at one institution triggers precautionary behavioral responses at unaffected institutions, propagating systemic stress through perception rather than through code, operational dysfunction, or financial loss; the confidence channel that can propagate negative effects throughout a system without any underlying technical failure at the receiving institution

Confidentiality a system capability to limit dissemination of information to authorized individuals or agents

Contagion accelerators system structural characteristics that amplify or accelerate systemic transmission of cyber events; three primary accelerators identified in the cybersecurity policy literature are: dependency (functional criticality of a service, modified by substitutability and portability), concentration (breadth of common exposure across institutions), and trust (reliance on authenticated connections and presumed legitimacy of credentialed instructions)

Content in the context of cyberspace, refers to information represented by data

Content filters strings of text that may be compared to data to determine whether it contains specific information, e.g., NNN-NN-NNNN, where N translates to any number, is often used as a content filter for a US social security number

Control activity any combination of people, process, and technology whose purpose is to achieve a control objective

Control objectives statement of management intention on security posture

Correspondent banking a relationship in which an organization's bank (the correspondent) provides payment, clearing, settlement, or other services to another bank (the respondent), typically to facilitate cross-border or intermarket transactions that the respondent cannot conduct independently. Correspondent relationships create network dependencies through which operational or financial contagion can propagate, with the potential for negative impact on the originating organization's bank balance.

Credential access a cyberattack stage wherein the attacker steals account names and passwords

Credentials information used to identify a user and authenticate that user to a computer, also referred to as login credentials

Crime as a service a business model for cybercrime in which vendors sell packaged tools and services used to commit cybercrimes such as phishing, ransomware, malware, and botnets

Crimeware software created for the purpose of executing Crime as a Service

Cryptography a method of hiding data in binary format by using complex calculations to combine it with sequences of other data referred to as keys

Cybersecurity the prevention of damage to, protection of, and restoration of computers, electronic communications systems, electronic communications services, wire communication, and electronic communication, including information contained therein, to ensure its availability, integrity, authentication, confidentiality, and nonrepudiation

Cybersecurity frameworks a set of cybersecurity controls such as policies, processes, standards, and procedures documented at a generic level and applicable across multiple organizations. Written by regulators, professional associations, and standards organizations, frameworks attempt to provide a roadmap to cybersecurity competency

Cybersecurity policy directives designed to maintain cybersecurity, whether for an individual, an organization, or cyberspace as a whole

Defense evasion a cyberattack stage wherein attacker takes steps to avoid being detected

Defense Industrial Base companies whose primary customer is the US government

Denial of service an intentional shut down of system communications

Denial of view deprivation of the ability to view systems status, or otherwise corrupt the data normally viewed by a system operator

Dial-back a mechanism that records a phone number calling, disconnects the incoming call, and initiates an outbound call to the same number only if it has been previously authorized to connect to that number

Digital signature an analogy with identification via signing a name with cursive handwriting; not specific to any one of the plethora of technologies that have been adopted for that purpose

Discovery a cyberattack stage wherein the attacker scans and learns the target system environment

Distributed control systems systems that allow multiple avenues of administration

Distributed denial of service an intentional shutdown of system communications cause by multiple, independently operating computers whose activities are purposefully coordinated to fully consume available network bandwidth of a victim's system

Distributed Network Protocol a set of industrial control system communications protocols that segment messages into three components (physical, data, and application)

Domain a generic term that refers to territory controlled by a given ruler that, in this book, refers to a classification of perspectives by the constituents of any given cybersecurity policy

Domain Name Services a way to identify at which internet address the computer corresponds to an internet Uniform Resource Locator

Domain squatting using a trademark, copyright, or identifier similar to a well-known site to register a domain name on the internet that appears with probability to belong to the trademark or brand owner

Doxxing The misuse of theoretically private information, often obtained by cyber intrusions. Disclosing embarrassing or otherwise damaging personal information about someone on the internet

E-commerce "e" is short for electronic, and e-commerce refers to business conducted over the internet

Email originally, email as in e-commerce, where "e" stood for "electronic," now in mainstream vocabulary as email, or messages sent or received using internet mail protocols

Encryption the process of using cryptography to hide data content

End user a person who uses a computer or mobile device, typically used to refer to those without the advantage of administrative privileges

End User License Agreements software industry verbiage created to form a legal compact between software providers and software users, typically one-sided, with benefit to providers for rendering user data into products

Endpoint Detection and Response software designed to detect and minimize damage (see Anti-Virus) and also to alert SecOps to its presence

Execution a cyberattack stage wherein the attacker runs malicious code

Exfiltration a cyberattack stage wherein the attacker steals data

Field instrumentation Physical sensors and mechanisms with electronic circuits that integrate with industrial control systems

Financial contagion a mechanism by which cybersecurity-related losses at one institution transmit financial stress to counterparties through interbank exposures, credit line reductions, collateral demands, and balance-sheet linkages, without requiring technical compromise at the affected counterparties

Firewalls electronic devices deployed to intercept all traffic sent and received between two networks for the purpose of restricting the type of data destinations and protocols allowed between them

Flaw in the context of software, a flaw is a design that is unable to meet all requirements for the intended functionality simultaneously. "Flaw" may also refer specifically to the portion of software code that, if and when replaced, would allow for a design that met specifications

Footprint slang for data that an automated software scan could pattern match to identify that malicious code or vulnerabilities are present in a system

Freeware software that anyone is authorized to use without purchasing it

Global Positioning System protocols used in a system of systems context that allows software on an electronic device to communicate with multiple satellites in order to determine its location on earth

Graphical user interface software representation of information used to view information on and/or operate computers

Hactivism political protest conducted in cyberspace

Harness Software designed to leverage AI models to achieve goals in a manner that requires minimal to no human interaction; may interact with operating systems, databases, software, and/or other agents to achieve assigned tasks.

Host intrusion detection systems a file integrity detection and alerting systems, such as tripwire

Identify the date an anomaly or problem was observed by the SecOps team or identified by a customer, user, or administrator and referred to the organization via any channel, such as a customer service ticket, a phone call, or a website designed for anonymous whistleblowers

Identity theft impersonation of an individual using data that is associated with computerized records that identify the individual

Impact an ordinal scale of cyberattack loss estimates with a verifiable set of measures such as time spent in investigation, cost of incident remediation, business opportunity lost due to outage, monetary loss, and/or estimated value of data breached

Impersonation a method by which a user may manipulate data within an authentication session or order to appear to the authenticating system as a different individual who is an authorized system user

Industrial control system cyber-enabled automation within systems that control physical processes

Infostealer malware that steals information out of a user's browser and potentially other desktop content

Initial access a cyberattack stage wherein the attacker accesses the target network

Integrity refers to the ability to maintain the authenticity, accuracy, and provenance of recorded and reported information within digital technology

Intelligent electronic devices a device that include software control, monitoring, and communications functions within a Supervisory Control and Data Acquisition system

Inter-Control Center Communications Protocol international protocol for industrial control system communication that conforms to the seven-layer OSI model

Internet Assigned Numbers Authority the organization that authorizes internet users to claim ownership to address space

Internet Corporation for Assigned Names and Numbers the organization that sets the rules for determining how internet users may claim ownership to address space and name space

Internet Engineering Task Force an organization that allows technologists to propose and collaborate on internet standards

Internet Protocol Security a set of encryption algorithms designed for internet traffic published by the Internet Engineering Task Force

Internet service provider organization that provides its customers with physical or wireless connectivity to the internet

Internet-facing systems that are available to users on the internet for access to services and data. Users can access these systems outside of an organization's internal network

Intrusion detection system refers to network monitoring for malware and/or damage impact to cyber space resources, and corresponding alerting to SecOps when threats are identified

Intrusion prevention system an Intrusion Detection System service enhancement that includes anti-malware software that terminates the network connection of any network activity identified to be a threat based on Intrusion Detection System monitoring

Job control technicians professionals who manage large quantities of computer processes, ensuring that the required dependencies of each are available at the time they are executed, and the output of each is available when required

Joyriding using computers in an unauthorized fashion to play online games or other peaceful purposes

Jump server a server whose primary use is to allow a process to jump from one network into an isolated one

Key management people, process, and technology coordinated to keep track of encryption keys to ensure the availability of encrypted data

Lateral movement a cyberattack stage wherein the attacker moves from one device to another in the target environment

Least privilege dictates that users should have the minimum access they need to perform a technology task and no more

Login information used by a user to present evidence of authorized access; the system uses the evidence to identify and authenticate the user to a computer and to automate availability of functions the user is allowed to access within the system, also referred to as "credentials"

Loss of control deprivation of the ability to enter system commands

Loss of view deprivation of the ability to monitor system logs, alerts, dashboards, and video of system operation in real time

Macroprudential supervision financial cybersecurity, regulatory oversight approach focused on system-wide financial stability rather than the soundness of individual institutions; complements microprudential supervision by assessing whether the failure of a particular entity or infrastructure node poses disproportionate systemic threats based on interconnectedness, substitutability, and concentration of critical services

Malvertising advertisements that contain links to websites that download malware onto to unsuspecting user computers

Malware software designed with malicious intent to spy on user activities, steal data, or damage the integrity or service availability of targeted computers

Mash-up website that incorporates links from many other websites in order to maintain its full set of features, such as linking to calendar applications and shopping cart applications running on a different web service provider, and displaying status from those applications continually throughout the user experience on its primary site

Memory the place where a computer keeps its pipeline of code instructions

Messaging a generic term to refer to any process by which messages are sent electronically, via server protocols such as email, chat, or peer-to-peer protocols

Microprudential supervision financial cybersecurity, regulatory oversight approach focused on assessing the safety, soundness, and compliance of individual institutions in isolation; operates on the premise that ensuring each institution's soundness produces system-wide resilience (an assumption demonstrated to be insufficient for highly interconnected systems by systemic risk research and the 2008 financial crisis)

Modbus messaging structure used to communicate commands within industrial control systems.

Multifactor authentication authentication factors are what you have, what you know, and what you are; any authentication process that uses more than one of these techniques to authenticate a user is multifactor authentication

Mutual identification any process by which two devices connected over a network can identify the other simultaneously prior to creating a communications channel between them

Name space in the context of the internet, the convention of names that end in Domain Name Services divisions of domains, as in the examples of Top Level Domains such as ".com."

National Infrastructure Protection Plan US Department of Homeland Security publication that describes multi-agency and public-private coordination plans to protect critical industry sectors from cyberattack

Negative Externality a situation in which an economic transaction between two parties has an unintended negative impact on an uninvolved third party

Net neutrality unrestricted ability of content to move freely over the internet

Network Address Translation a communications protocol that allows a network routing device to label the same computer with different network addresses depending on which network interface is communicating with the computer

Network listening copying network traffic to a device for which it was not addressed, for the purpose of eavesdropping on network communications

Network zone a set of network addresses for which communications security is managed by surrounding them with common traffic chokepoints and similar traffic filters

Neural network computational model influenced by the human brain, designed to recognize patterns, make predictions, and learn from data

Node any network-connected electronic device that has communication capabilities

Nonpublic personal information information that is classified by any law as not to be shared for any purpose other than to deliver an agreed upon service (e.g., the US Gramm-Leach-Bliley Act classifies nonpublic personal information related to online banking)

Non-repudiation where confidentiality dictates that only authorized people can view specific information, non-repudiation specifies that information received from someone, it is provably from them, meaning the recipient or a third party can verify and validate the sender or creator

Open source software whose source code is freely available on the internet and whose owners encourage others to add features; participation in such software projects may require the participant to observe license agreements

Open Systems Interconnection a model for communicating information that specifies segmenting messages into layers corresponding to the communications technology that will deliver the information

Operating system a computer program that allows hardware to be controlled using a standard set of utilities that are the same no matter what hardware is being accessed

Operational contagion mechanism by which disruption at a shared infrastructure provider propagates dysfunction to dependent institutions without necessarily spreading malicious code. For example, in Financial Services, disruption of a payment clearing system prevents all dependent institutions from processing transactions regardless of their individual security posture, producing simultaneous operational failure across institutions rather than sequential

Operational resilience capacity of an operation to restore online services in a manner consistent with their customer service agreements (e.g., to be operating effectively within business hours, or for example, in financial services, to execute transactions and make records available within defined timeframes following a disruption). Distinct from availability (whether systems remain accessible) in that resilience addresses recovery speed and its systemic implications (for example, having alternative suppliers to be resilient to prolonged outages within dependencies may have cascading effects)

Packet in the context of the TCP protocol, a packet is a variable-length string of bits representing data fields that are processed by internet communications systems in order to relay information

Patch a portion of software code contrived to replace portions of code that are operating incorrectly, without replacing the entire code base for the affected application or product

Penetrating test a software security quality assurance technique that checks for known vulnerabilities by engaging a cyberdefense human to imitate the behavior of a human threat actor, a form of badness-ometer

People, process, and technology a reference to the fact that systemic operational processes require a coordinated trial of people, process, and technology to ensure continuous functionality

Persistence a cyberattack stage wherein the attacker maintains a foothold within the target systems environment

Personally identifiable information information that can be used to create negatively impacting individual liability for humans via activities performed by threat actors who hijack or take over their online accounts

Pharming act of a threat actor dropping malicious links on websites known to be frequented by targeted victims

Phishing act of a threat actor sending an unsolicited email or other message that appears to be from a friendly source, but instead lures a user into accepting malware onto their computer and/or disclosing sensitive information such as login credentials

Phone home a software or malware feature that initiates communication back to the software vendor who supports it or the crimeware operator who operates it, respectively

Policy servers computers that store security software configuration setting standard specifications, not to be confused with governance policy

Polymorphic malware category of malware that constantly changes its identifiable features, such as file names, encryption keys, or signatures, to better evade detection by traditional end-point detection (e.g., antivirus) software

Port an addressable place in memory on a computer that sends and receives network communications

Privilege escalation a cyberattack stage wherein the attacker gains higher-level permissions, such as systems administrator login credentials

Privileged access management governance controls limiting, monitoring, and auditing the activities of users with elevated system privileges, e.g., administrative accounts, vendor remote access, and service accounts

Programmable logic controllers any device that allows automated command entry in an industrial control system

Proxy servers a computer that is designed to intercept network communications bounds for a given destination, such as the internet, and check it against a set of rules for acceptable use prior to allowing it to continue to its destination

Public key cryptography a cryptographic algorithm that uses split keys to allow a user to keep the private component while allowing others to identify the user using a public component

Quad nations United States, Japan, India, and Australia

Ransomware malware that encrypts all reachable data on the victim environment and communicates a demand to the victim for ransom to be paid to get the data back

Reconnaissance a cyberattack stage wherein the attacker gathers information of use in creating an attack plan

Reference monitor software that allows an operating system to allocate its resources to only authorized users by interrupting all resource requests and comparing them to access control lists before allowing them to be answered

Remote access the ability to use the resources of a computer without being collocated with it, usually via a phone line or internet connection, but may be wireless or satellite enabled

Requests for comment the standard name for a proposed internet technology standard (see the internet Engineering Task Force archives at www.ietf.org)

Resource development a cyberattack stage wherein the attacker creates resources they can use to support operations, such as malware

Reverse engineer a process of examining systems and/or software to determine how it works

Risk and control self-assessment an internal process through which an organization maps its cybersecurity and operational risk controls against a selected framework's requirements, typically producing a gap analysis visualization identifying where recommended controls are absent, partial, or not yet documented

Salami technique a way to shave off a slither of a transaction in a way that would not be caught by those auditing around the computer

SecOps Security Operations

Secure Socket Layer a generic term to refer to all secure communications protocols that allow traffic between end users and web servers to be encrypted, technically replaced by Transport Layer Security

Security information management refers to a system that collects logs from a variety of sources to allow SecOps to use a single portal to investigate user activity

Security operations a department within an enterprise whose mission includes detecting and responding to security incidents

Security theatre attempts at providing information protection that fail for reasons that are obvious to cybersecurity professionals

Social engineering threat actor tactic of using friendly persuasion to gain information that may be used to commit account hijacking, identity theft, and theft of intellectual property, including espionage

Spam the term originated as a canned meat product, but now refers to undesirable online messages, most frequently email

Spear-phishing targeted phishing attack directed at specific individuals, crafted to appear credible to the recipient, often referencing real relationships, titles, or institutional context, and is commonly used to deliver malware or capture credentials as an initial access technique

Spoof a method by which one system may manipulate data within a communication protocol in order to display the technical attributes of another system through a network interface; spoofing is the system equivalent of impersonation

Spyware malware designed to capture user keystrokes and other activities in order to complete profile information on them, to sell to advertisers or crimeware operators, or to conduct espionage or APT activities

Substitutability the degree to which viable alternatives to organizational dependencies exist and can be activated within operationally relevant timeframes if a primary provider fails or is compromised

Supervisory Control and Data Acquisition a system of systems that is used both to monitor and enter commands to a set of devices that collectively control a physical process

Surveillance capitalism gathering information about an individual's behavior on the internet in order to provide customized advertising to be displayed to that specific individual with statistical guarantees to advertisers that the ads will influence that individual's behavior

System of systems a system that has a specific mission or purpose only in combination with other independently operating systems that have missions or purposes separate from their use in combination

Technical contagion mechanism by which cyber compromise propagates across organizational boundaries through trusted technical connections, such as shared networks, software update channels, or vendor-managed access; distinguished from operational, financial, and confidence contagion in that technical contagion spreads the compromise itself, i.e., malicious code or unauthorized access, rather than its operational or financial consequences

Technology malpractice negligence in management techniques to meet information security requirements

Timesharing services services that allowed people to rent time on computers, encompass computing infrastructure, multipurpose platforms, and single-purpose software applications

Top level domains the last component of internet domain names approved by Internet Corporation for Assigned Names and Numbers, and therefore the root of internet domain name verification for domain names registered under that component (e.g., .com, .org, and .net)

Traffic filters specification of the network traffic protocols to be allowed into a network zone, and may also include the source or destination internet address, which is also the basis of firewall rules

Traffic Light Protocol an ordinal measure that specifies the classification level of potentially sensitive information

Transmission Control Protocol a specification for data sent between network devices, specifies, among other things, how many bits are reserved in what order for the network address to which the data should be sent, the protocol under which it should be interpreted, and the application that should be used to process the data upon receipt

Transport Layer Security an internet communication encryption specification update to Secure Socket Layer, that is, the current generic reference for most secure communications methods that allow traffic between end users and web servers to be encrypted in transit

Tripwire software that monitors file attributes to detect and alert when files are modified or deleted

Unallocated address space internet addresses that are purposely not assigned to any entity in order for all entities to use them internally, as defined in the Internet Engineering Task Force

Uniform resource locator a combination of internet Domain Name Services host name and file system location that facilitates internet information posting and retrieval

Universal serial bus protocol for data communications between an operating system and peripheral storage devices

Virtual private network a cryptography-enabled method of confidential communication between multiple computers over a public network, typically using Internet Protocol Security

Wheel of pain a reference to ancient and medieval servility, where slaves labor on turnstiles or prisoners are attached to torture mechanisms

Worm a program that automatically replicates itself, identifies new targets, and traversed a network to attack each target

Zero trust architecture technology architecture that observes the cybersecurity tenet that all network traffic is untrusted, and therefore security must be architected to verify and secure all resources, authorize only based on least privilege, strictly enforce access control, and inspect and log all user activity including network traffic

Acronyms

3LoD	Three Lines of Defense
ACH	Automated Clearing House
ADM	Automated Decision Making
AHA	American Hospital Association
AI	Artificial Intelligence
AI RMF	AI Risk Management Framework
AICPA	American Institute of Certified Public Accountants
AIOs	Activities, Interests, Opinions
AIS	Automated Indicator Sharing
AoC	Affirmation of Commitments
AP	Associated Press
API	Application Programming Interface
APK	Android Package Kit
APT	Advanced Persistent Threat
ARCYBER	Army Cyber Command
ARPANET	Advanced Research Projects Agency Network
ASEAN	Association of Southeast Asian Nations
ATF	Bureau of Alcohol, Tobacco, and Firearms
ATMs	Automated Teller Machine
AU	African Union
AWS	Amazon Web Services
B2B	Business to Business
BBS	Bulletin Board Systems
BCBS	Basel Committee on Banking Supervision
BJS	Bureau of Justice Statistics
BSA	Bank Secrecy Act
C&C	Command and Control
CASB	Cyber Safety Review Board (a function of CISA)
CaaS	Crime as a Service, or: Crimeware as a Service

CABF	Certification Authority Browser Forum
CAE	Centers of Academic Excellence
CAPEC	Common Attack Pattern Enumeration and Classification
CSRB	Cyber Safety Review Board
CAT	Continuous Adaptive Trust
CCDCOE	Cooperative Cyber Defence Centre of Excellence
CCE	Consequence-Driven Cyber-Informed Engineering
CCM	Cloud Controls Matrix
CCSP	Certified Cloud Security Professional
CCTI	Center on Cyber and Technology Innovation
CDA	Communications Decency Act
CEO	Chief Executive Officer
CERT	Computer Emergency Response Team
CERT	Computer Emergency Response Team
CESER	Office of Cybersecurity, Energy Security, and Emergency Response
CFAA	Computer Fraud and Abuse Act
CFPB	Consumer Financial Protection Bureau
CGEIT	Certified in the Governance of Enterprise IT
CHIPS	Clearing House Interbank Payments System
CIA	Central Intelligence Agency
CIAO	Critical Infrastructure Assurance Office
CIE	Cyber-Informed Engineering
CIO	Chief Information Officer
CIP	Critical Infrastructure Protection
CIPAC	Critical Infrastructure Partnership Advisory Council
CIRCIA	Cyber Incident Reporting for Critical Infrastructure Act
CIRT	Computer Incident Response Team
CIS	Center for Internet Security
CISA	Cybersecurity and Infrastructure Security Agency, or: Certified Information Security Auditor
CISM	Certified Information Security Manager
CISO	Chief Information Security Officer
CISSP	Certified Information Systems Security Professional
CITAC	Computer Investigations and Infrastructure Threat Assessment Center
CKD Global	Cobalt Digital Marketing, Dealer Services and Kerridge Computer Company Global
CMF	Cyber Mission Force
CMTs	Combat Mission Teams
CNCI	Comprehensive National Cybersecurity Initiative

CNO	Computer Network Operations
COBIT	Control Objectives for Information Technology
COO	Chief Operations Officer
COSO	Committee of Sponsoring Organizations (of the Treadway Commission)
COVID	Coronavirus Disease
CPE	Common Platform Enumeration
CPG	Cybersecurity Performance Goals
CPT	Cyber Protection Team
CRISC	Certified in Risk and Information Systems Control
CRO	Chief Risk Officer
CS&C	Office of Cybersecurity and Communications
CSA	Cloud Security Alliance
CSCF	Customer Security Controls Framework
CSIRT	Computer Security Incident Response Team
CSIS	Center for Strategic and International Studies
CSO	Chief Security Officer
CSRB	Cyber Safety Review Board
CST	Cyber Support Team
CTI	Cyber Threat Intelligence
CTO	Chief Technology Officer
CTP	Core Technology Provider
CVE	Common Vulnerability Enumeration
CVSS	Common Vulnerability Scoring System
CWE	Common Weakness Enumeration
CYBERCOM	Cyber Command
DAMA	Data Management Association
DARPA	DoD Advanced Research Projects Agency
DAST	Dynamic Application Security Testing
DBIR	Data Breach Investigations Report
DBT	Design Basis Threat
DCCC	Democratic Congressional Campaign Committee
DCIS	Defense Criminal Investigative Service
DCS	Distributed Control Systems
DDoS	Distributed Denial of Service
DEA	Drug Enforcement Agency
DHS	Department of Homeland Security
DIB	Defense Industrial Base
DISA	Defense Information Systems Agency
DMZ	Demilitarized Zone
DNA	Deoxyribonucleic Acid

DNC	Democratic National Committee
DNP	Distributed Network Protocol
DoC	Department of Commerce
DoD	Department of Defense
DoDIG	DoD Office of Inspector General's
DoE	Department of Energy
DoJ	Department of Justice
DORA	Digital Operational Resilience Act
DoT	Department of Treasury
DURSA	Data Use and Reciprocal Support Agreement
DVD	Digital Versatile Disc
EDPAA	Electronic Data Processing Audit Association
EEGs	Electroencephalograms
EEOB	Eisenhower Executive Office Building
EFF	Electronic Frontier Foundation
EFTA	Electronic Fund Transfer Act
EI-ISAC	Election Infrastructure Information Sharing and Analysis Center
EPSS	Exploit Prediction Scoring System
ERM	Enterprise Risk Management
EU	European Union
EuLAs	End-User License Agreements
FACA	Federal Advisory Committee Act of 1972
FACTA	Fair and Accurate Credit Transaction Act
FBI	Federal Bureau of Investigation
FCC	Federal Communications Commission
FDD	Foundation for Defense of Democracies
FDIC	Federal Deposit Insurance Corporation
FedRAMP	Federal Risk and Authorization Management Program
Fedwire	Federal Reserve Wire Network
FEMA	Federal Emergency Management Agency
FFIEC	Federal Financial Institutions Examination Council
FFRDC	Federally Funded Research and Development Center
FinCEN	Financial Crimes Enforcement Network
FISMA	Federal Information Security Modernization Act
FLTCYBERCOM	Fleet Cyber Command
FMECA	Failure Modes, Effects, and Criticality Analysis
FSB	Financial Stability Board
FSCO	Financial Stability Oversight Council
FS-ISAC	Financial Services Information Sharing and Analysis Center
FSR	Financial Services Roundtable

GCCs	Government Coordinating Councils
GDPR	General Data Protection Regulation
GenAI	Generative AI
GENIUS	Guiding and Establishing National Innovation for U.S. Stablecoins
GIG	Global Information Grid
GLBA	Grahm-Leach-Bliley Act
GNC	Global NetOps Center
GNOSC	Global Network Operations and Security Center
GPS	Global Positioning System
GQM	Goal Question Metric
GRC	Governance Risk and Compliance, or: Governance Risk and Control
GSD	General Staff Department
HCISPP	HealthCare Information Security and Privacy Practitioner
HHS	Health and Human Services
HIDS	Host Intrusion Detection System
HIPAA	Health Insurance Portability and Accountability Act
HMI	Human Machine Interface
HSC	Homeland Security Council
HSIN	Homeland Security Information Network
HSMS	Homeland Security Management System
HSPD	Homeland Security Presidential Directive
HTML	HyperText Markup Language
HUD	Housing and Urban Development
I2P	The Invisible Internet Project
IaaS	Infrastructure as a Service
IAM	Identity and Access Management Systems
IANA	Internet Assigned Numbers Authority
IC3	Internet Crime Complaint Center
ICANN	Internet Corporation for Assigned Names and Numbers
ICAT	Internet Categorization of Attacks Toolkit
ICCP	Inter-Control Center Communications Protocol
ICS	Industrial Control System
ICT	Information and Communications Technology
ID	Identifier
IDS	Intrusion Detection System
IED	Intelligent Electronic Device
IEEE	Institute of Electrical and Electronics Engineers
IETF	Internet Engineering Task Force
IFCC	Internet Fraud Complaint Center

IIA	Institute for Internal Auditors
IO	Input-Output
IoT	Internet of Things
IP	Internet Protocol
IPS	Intrusion Prevention System
IPSec	Internet Protocol Security
IPTF	Infrastructure Protection Task Force
IRC	Internet Relay Chat
ISA	International Society for Automation
ISACA	Information Systems Audit and Control Association
ISAC	Information Sharing and Analysis Center
ISI	Information Security Institute
ISMS	Information Security Management System
ISO/IEC	International Organization for Standardization and the International Electrotechnical Commission
ISPs	Internet Service Providers
ISR	Intelligence, Surveillance, and Reconnaissance
ISRG	Internet Security Research Group
IT	Information Technologies
IT/OT	Information Technology Operational Technology
ITU	International Telecommunications Union
JCCO	Joint Concept for Cyberspace Operations
JCDC	Joint Cyber Defense Collaborative
JFCC-NW	Joint Functional Component Command-Network Warfare
JOC	Joint Operations Center
JTF	Joint Task Force
JTF-CND	Joint Task Force-Computer Network Defense
JTF-CNO	Joint Task Force-Computer Network Operations
JTF-GNO	Joint Task Force-Global Network Operations
KEV	Known Exploited Vulnerability
LAN	Local Area Network
LLM	Large Language Model
MAGTF	Marine Air-Ground Task Force
MARFORCYBER	Marine Forces Cyber Command
MDO	Multi-Domain Operations
Modbus	Modular Bus
MS-ISAC	Multi-State Information Sharing and Analysis Center
MSSP	Managed Security Service Providers
MUCD	Military Unit Cover Designator
NAICS	North American Industry Classification System
NASA	National Aeronautics and Space Administration

NATO	North Atlantic Treaty Organization
NCCIC	National Cybersecurity and Communications Integration Center
NCF	National Critical Functions
NCIRP	National Cyber Incident Response Plan
NCSD	National Cyberspace Security Division
NCVS	National Crime Victimization Survey
NDAAs	National Defense Authorization Acts
NERC CIP	North American Electric Reliability Corporation Critical Infrastructure Protections
NFS	National Science Foundation
NHIN	Nationwide Health Information Network
NHSA	National Homeland Security Agency
NIAC	National Infrastructure Advisory Council
NIBRS	National Incident-Based Reporting System
NICE	National Initiative for Cybersecurity Education
NIMS	National Incident Management System
NIPC	National Infrastructure Protection Center
NIPP	National Infrastructure Protection Plan
NIST	National Institute of Standards and Technology
NIST-CSF	NIST Cyber Security Framework
NMT	National Mission Team
NPISP	National Plan for Information Systems Protection
NPPD	National Protection and Programs Directorate
NSA	National Security Agency
NSC	National Security Council
NSDD	National Security Decision Directive
NSF	National Science Foundation
NSFNET	National Science Foundation Network
NSPD	National Security Presidential Directive
NSS	National Security Staff
NSTIC	National Strategy for Trusted Identities in Cyberspace
NTIA	National Telecommunications and Information Administration
NTSB	National Transportation Safety Board
NVD	National Vulnerability Database
OAS	Organization of American States
OCC	Office of the Comptroller of the Currency
OCEAN	Openness, Conscientiousness, Extraversion, Agreeableness, and Neuroticism
ODNI	Office of the Director of National Intelligence

OECD	Organisation for Economic Co-operation and Development
OHS	Office of Homeland Security
OIG	Office of the Inspector General
OMB	Office of Management and Budget
ONCD	Office of the National Cyber Director
OPM	Office of Personnel Management
OSI	Open Systems Interconnection
OT	Operational Technology
OWASP	Open Worldwide Application Security Project
PaaS	Platform as a Service
PC	Personal Computer
PCCIP	Presidential Commission on Critical Infrastructure Protection
PCI DSS	Payment Card Industry Data Security Standard
PCI SSC	Payment Card Industry Security Standards Council
PCIPB	President's Critical Infrastructure Protection Board
PDD	Presidential Decision Directive
PE	Professional Engineer
PERA	Purdue Enterprise Reference Architecture
PI	Private Investigator
PII	Personally Identifiable Information
PLA	People's Liberation Army
PLC	Programmable Logic Controller
PNT	Positioning, Navigation, and Timing
PPE	Principles and Practice of Engineering Exam
PPSP	Policies, Processes, Standards, Procedures
PPT	People, Process, and Technology
PQC	Post-Quantum Cryptography
PSR	Priority Services Register
QSA	Qualified Security Assessor
R&D	Research and Development
RaaS	Ransomware as a Service
RACI	Responsible, Accountable, Consulted, and Informed
RCSA	Risk and Control Self-Assessment
RDP	Remote Desktop Protocol
RFC	Requests for Comment
RFID	Radio Frequency Identification
RIN	Regulation Identifier Number
ROC	Report on Compliance
SaaS	Software as a Service

SANS	System Administrators, Auditors, and Network Administrators
SAR	Suspicious Activity Report
SAST	Static Application Security Testing
SATCOM	Satellite Communications
SBOMs	Software Bills of Materials
SCADA	Supervisory Control and Data Acquisition
SCC	Sector Specific Council
SCuBA	Secure Cloud Business Applications
SEC	Securities and Exchange Commission
SECDEF	Secretary of Defense
SecOps	Security Operations
SIEM	Security Information and Event Management
SIM	Security Information Management
SLTT	State, Local, Tribal, and Territorial
SOC	System and Organization Controls
SQL	Structured Query Language
SRI	Stanford Research Institute
SRMA	Sector Risk Management Agency
SSA	Social Security Administration
SSE	Systems Security Engineering
SSG	Sector-Specific Goal
SSID	Service Set Identifier
SSL	Secure Socket Layer
SSO	Single Sign On
STAR	Security, Trust, Assurance, and Risk
STEM	Science, Technology, Engineering, and Mathematics
STRATCOM	Strategic Command
SWIFT	Society for Worldwide Interbank Financial Telecommunication
TCB	Trusted Computing Base
TCP/IP	Transmission Control Protocol/Internet Protocol
TILA	Truth in Lending Act
TLP	Traffic Light Protocol
TLS	Transport Layer Security
TNT	Trinitrotoluene
TPO	Technology Platform Operator
TTC	Trade and Technology Council
TTPs	Tactics, Techniques, and Procedures
U.S.C.	United States Code
UCC	Uniform Commercial Code

UCG	Unified Coordination Group
UDP	User Datagram Protocol
UHG	UnitedHealth Group
UK	United Kingdom
UN	United Nations
UN GGE	United Nations Group of Governmental Experts
UPI	User Profile Information
URL	Uniform Resource Locator
USAF	United States Air Force
USB	Universal Serial Bus
USCC	United States China Economic and Security Review Commission
US-CERT	United States Computer Emergency Response Team
USCNS/21	United States Commission on National Security in the 21st Century
USCYBERCOM	United States Cyber Command
USSPACECOM	United States Space Command
USSS	United States Secret Service
USSTRATCOM	United States Strategic Command
VA	Veterans Administration
VERIS	Vocabulary for Event Recording and Incident Sharing
VNC	Virtual Network Computing
VPN	Virtual Private Network
WAF	Web Access Firewall
WEP	Wired Equivalent Privacy
WHOCSS	White House Office of Cyber Space Security
WNCRY	WannaCry
WTC	World Trade Center
ZTA	Zero Trust Architecture

Index

d

r

s

Wiley The manufacturer's authorized representative according to the EU General Product Safety Regulation is Wiley-VCH GmbH, Boschstr. 12, 69469 Weinheim, Germany, e-mail: Product_Safety@wiley.com.

Printed and bound by CPI Group (UK) Ltd, Croydon, CR0 4YY
07/09/2026
02211644-0002